Beginner's Ukrainian

WITH INTERACTIVE ONLINE WORKBOOK

SECOND EDITION

The publication of this textbook was made possible, in part, with:
a grant from the Harriman Institute at Columbia University,
a grant from the Heritage Foundation of the First Securities Savings Bank of Chicago,
the financial support of the Ukrainian Studies Fund, Inc.,
the financial support of the Shevchenko Scientific Society, USA from the John and Elisabeth Chlopecky Fund.

Beginner's Ukrainian

WITH INTERACTIVE ONLINE WORKBOOK

SECOND EDITION

YURI SHEVCHUK

Hippocrene Books, Inc

New York

Design and layout: Natasha Mikhalchuk
Cover design: Natasha Mikhalchuk
Cover illustration: Lev Sloujitel

Previous edition ISBN: 978-0-7818-1268-9

For information, address:
HIPPOCRENE BOOKS, INC.
171 Madison Avenue
New York, NY 10016
www.hippocrenebooks.com

Cataloging-in-Publication Data available from the Library of Congress.

ISBN-13: 978-0-7818-1324-2
ISBN-10: 0-7818-1324-7

Printed in the United States of America.

MIX
Paper from
responsible sources
FSC® C011935

This is the first textbook of the elementary Ukrainian level to be accompanied by an interactive website.

It offers a wealth of material to maximize quick and effective acquisition of modern Ukrainian pronunciation, reading, speaking, and comprehension skills for both independent and instructor-guided learners. The website includes data that both replicate and amplify the contents of the textbook:

✓ audio files with recordings of all introductory dialogues, conversational, grammar, and pronunciation drills

✓ the most important vocabulary for everyday use such as numerals, frequently used adjectives, etiquette formulas

✓ additional dialogues and text

A great majority of the audio exercises are designed to be interactive. The users therefore will be able to download the files they need and monitor their progress independently and confidently by using the exercise keys and audio recordings by speakers from various regions, age and gender groups of contemporary Ukraine.

The interactive Beginner's Ukrainian website can be accessed at:

www.hippocrenebooks.com/beginnersukrainian

Зміст | Contents

+--+
| **INTERACTIVE BEGINNER'S UKRAINIAN WEBSITE:** |
| www.hippocrenebooks.com/beginnersukrainian |
+--+

Introduction

This self-teaching manual is designed to help a wide variety of learners, both independent and instructor-assisted, to develop the ability to communicate in Ukrainian in typical every-day life situations. The material is offered in small and manageable portions following the principle that *less is more*. The focus is on the basics that reflect the logic of the language while some of the exceptions are ignored for the sake of simplicity. Technical terminology is avoided as much as possible in favor of terms that are easily accessible to individuals without special linguistic training. For those who have no experience of language learning a glossary of basic linguistic terminology is provided at the end of the book. The textbook consists of fifteen lessons. The first three teach the learner how to read and write in Ukrainian. Each of the following lessons 4-15 has the same structure:

1) Brief contents of the lesson, including its general conversational topic, related grammar, and competencies or expressions and phrases used to perform more specific communicative functions, such as, for example, asking a question, introducing oneself, offering an explanation, and the like.

2) A dialogue that introduces a given conversational topic like "Family," "Leisure," "Traveling," "Shopping" and others that are most likely to be of use in a real-life setting. In addition each dialogue serves as an illustration of grammar explained in the respective lesson. The dialogue is limited only to the material presented in the lesson or which has already been learned earlier. The learner can use each dialogue as a basis to create with language. For example, the phrase **Моє́ ім'я́ – Ю́рій.** *My name is Yuri.* from Dialogue 4 can be taken as a model to produce a new phrase by substituting in turn each of its components:

a) **Твоє́ ім'я́ – Ю́рій.** *Your name is Yuri.*; **Його́ ім'я́ – Ю́рій.** *His name is Yuri.* **Ва́ше ім'я́ – Ю́рій.** *Your name is Yuri.*

b) **Моє́ прі́звище etc. ...** *My family name is ...*

c) **Моє́ ім'я́ – Іва́н (Рома́н, Марі́я, О́льга)** *My name is Ivan (Roman, Maria, Olha).*
Having mastered these simple building blocks, the learner can create their own new combinations, i.e, **Моє́ ім'я́ – Ю́рій, а її́ ім'я́ – Марі́я.** *My name is Yuri and her name is Maria.* Thus each dialogue becomes a point of departure for the learner's linguistic creativity which can be virtually unlimited.

3) English translation of the dialogue closely follows the Ukrainian original. Sometimes, when called for, it includes verbatim rendition of the structures that are not found in English in order to familiarize the learner with specifically Ukrainian expressions. For example, **Рома́нові подоба́ється диви́тися фі́льми.** will be translated both in literary English as *Roman likes to watch films* and verbatim *lit. To watch films pleases Roman**. An asterisk (*) is used to mark such verbatim renditions or other artificial constructs whose goal is to facilitate learning by revealing the peculiarities of the Ukrainian language that are not found in English.

4) Notes on the dialogue briefly explain any grammar and vocabulary that are not covered in the respective lesson that would otherwise complicate understanding of the dialogue. They can always be amplified by consulting the Dictionary at the end of the textbook.

5) Additional vocabulary and expressions pertaining to the respective communicative roles introduced in the lesson.

6) Grammar is presented in its immediate connection to the needs of everyday communication. That is why first the learner will find out what can be said by a particular form (function) and then how this form is constructed (formation). The rules are laid out in a simple manner with the principal ending given a visual prominence and its variants indented.

7) Exercises aim at helping the learner understand how the introduced material functions in real communication. The exercises are mostly interactive and consist of a cue **C** or question **Q** and answer **A** to it. Each has a model to be followed by the learner. In their totality, they are designed to help the learner develop the communicative skills which approach the fluency of a native Ukrainian. Repetition and recycling of the previously learned material is gradually amplified by a new one. Each exercise has *Keys* that can be both read and listened to from the interactive website that largely mirrors and amplifies the textbook. The learner should aim at developing the capacity to react correctly to the cues in the exercises by hearing and without reading. An important part of the exercises are those assignments that require the learner's use of the quickly expanding Ukrainian language Internet resources.

8) Questions on dialogue that revisit the main topic of the lesson, encourage the learner to bring their personal experience in, and discuss it relying on the already acquired grammar and vocabulary.

9) A scripted skit concludes every lesson and is a scenario that the learner is asked to enact with a partner using the conversational and grammar material learned in the lesson. The skit is not to be treated as a translation assignment but as general guidance for a conversation. Therefore, every time it is inacted, the students will use a different language, just like one notion, for example, a greeting, surprise, agreement, delight, etc., can be expressed in a number of different ways. To move on to the next lesson the learner needs to master the material of all previous lessons.

The fifteen lessons are followed by the glossary *Basic Linguistic Terms Used in the Textbook* that will help those without the experience of foreign language learning to make sense of the grammar explanations and the indispensible terminology used in this, and in fact, in the great majority of other foreign language textbooks. The glossary will be particularly helpfull for self-learners.

The core grammar of the *Beginner's Ukrainian* is distilled in the easily usable Grammar Tables (pp. 316-331). They should be consulted both as a quick reference source, and a handy way to compare specific grammatical forms, for example, the dative case endings with those of locative case, for differences and similarities.

An especially valuable and unique feature of this textbook is its extensive dictionary (pp. 341-429). In a departure from Ukrainian textbooks published in the past, it not only gives an immediate English equivalent of a word but explains how to use it and provides all its essential forms. The learner should immediately "befriend" the dictionary and consult it as much as possible while learning the new material and reviewing the old one, preparing assignments, including essay-writing, translation, etc., and, most importantly, while creating with language and producing their own Ukrainian speech. In order to make the dictionary, as well as the entire textbook, maximally effective and fun, the learners should carefully familiarize themselves with the list of abbreviations used throughout the textbook (next page) and with the introduction *How to Use the Dictionary* (pp. 342-343).

Developing the learner's **listening comprehension** and pronunciation is a strategic goal of this textbook. All the dialogues and lists of thematic words are vocalized by native speakers who represent the modern Ukrainian literary standard pronunciation. In addition, a great majority of the exercises are constructed in a way as to allow the user to interact with the speaker as if in a real life exchange. Each such recorded exercise is marked by an icon of earphones and can be accessed on a special Internet web site at: **http://www.hippocrenebooks.com/beginnersukrainian**

Every lesson has a set of exercises meant to help the learner to effectively master a correct Ukrainian pronunciation.

Acknowledgments

My thanks to Dr. Alla Parkhomenko of the National Academy of Sciences of Ukraine in Kyiv who painstakingly read the manuscript and offered useful comments, corrections, and recommendations. I am grateful to Professor Frank Miller of Columbia University for his encouragement to write this textbook, and his advice and support as I worked on the manuscript.

I should like to thank my enthusiastic students of Ukrainian at Columbia University and Harvard Summer School, particularly, though not exclusively, Olivia Hall, Ali Kinsela, Jason Stout, Sarah Diaz, Brendan Nieubuurt and others, who worked with the first edition of *Beginner's Ukrainian* and offered useful feedback that greatly helped to improve its second edition.

I should like to acknowledge with much appreciation Natasha Mikhalchuk who designed and typeset the textbook in a way that makes it easy and fun to use.

The photographic illustrations have been generously offered by friends, acquaintances, and, remarkably, often complete strangers from all parts of Ukraine, including Kyiv, Odesa, Donetsk, Rivne, the Carpathians, Lviv and other locations, who responded with wonderful enthusiasm to my call for help. Many photos were taken by Americans and Canadians who traveled to Ukraine. In their totality the illustrations represent both the way Ukrainians see themselves and are seen by others. My thanks are to the following photographers:

Larysa Artiuhina, Viktoria Bondar, Serhiy Bukovsky, Maksym Haiduchenko, Adriana Helbig, Oles Hardzhuk, Olha Hodovanets, Tetiana Illina, Anastasia Kekutia, Ali Kinsela, Yelyzaveta Kliuzko, Natalka Kononchuk, Arina Kostina, Bohdana Kostiuk, Andrew Kotliar, Ivan Kozlenko, Svitlana Kravs, Hanya Krill, Mykola Kulchynsky, Alla Likhachova, Lidia Lykhach, Roman Malko, Valentyn Marchenko, Dmytro Moiseiev, Marko Moudrak, Oleh Nechydiuk, Alla Parkhomenko, Roman Pechyzhak, Tetiana Pechonchyk, Lidia Poliak, Yevhen Ravsky, Tetiana Savchuk, Natalka Shama, Serhii Shama, Natalia Shevchuk, Ihor Strembytsky, Victoria Susak, Roman Tashleetsky, Anna Tchergueiko, Halyna Tymoshchuk, Olena Tymoshenko, Valentyn Vasianovych, Olha Vesnianka, Yevhenia Viatachaninova, Olena Voitenko, Volodymyr Voitenko, Viacheslav and Denys Volynshchykov, Ksenia Yachmetz, Tetiana Yahysh, Hanna Yarovenko, and Andriy Zvynnyk.

**This book is dedicated in loving memory to my teachers
Yuri Zhluktenko and Tamara Yavorska.**

Скоро́чення | Abbreviations

A	answer (in interactive exercises)	*ord.*	ordinal numeral
A.	accusative case	*pa.*	past tense
adj.	adjective	*part.*	particle
adv.	adverb	*pf.*	perfective aspect
affirm.	affirmative	*pers.*	person, personal
anim.	animate	*phr.*	phrase, phraseologism
C	cue (in interactive exercises)	*pl.*	plural number
card.	cardinal numeral	*posn.*	position as opposed to direction of motion
cf.	compare for example		
coll.	collective numeral or noun	*poss.*	possessive
colloq.	colloquial	*pr.*	pronoun
comp.	comparative degree of adjectives or adverbs	*pred.*	predicative word, structure
		prep.	preposition
conj.	conjunction	*pres.*	present tense
count.	countable nouns	**Q**	question (in interactive exercises)
D.	dative case	*refl.*	reflexive verb
dem.	demonstrative pronoun	*sb*	somebody
dim.	diminutive	*sg.*	singular number
dir.	direction of motion as opposed to static position	*sth*	something
		tran.	transitive (of verbs taking direct objects)
emph.	emphatic		
Eng.	English	*uncount.*	uncountable nouns
f.	feminine	*uni.*	uni-directional verb
fam.	familiar, informal style	*v.*	verb
fig.	figurative (sense)	*var.*	variant
form.	formal, polite style	*V.*	vocative case
fut.	future tense		
Gal.	Galician, variant used in the provinces of Lviv, Ternopil, and Ivano-Frankivsk		
G.	genitive case		
im.	imperative form of the verb		
impf.	imperfective aspect		
inan.	inanimate		
indecl.	indeclinable		
indef.	indefinite		
inf.	infinitive of verb		
I.	instrumental case		
inter.	interjection		
interr.	interrogative		
intr.	intransitive (of verbs that have no direct objects)		
lit.	literally, verbatim		
L.	locative case		
m.	masculine		
mod.	modal word		
multi.	multi-directional verb		
n.	noun		
N.	nominative case		
nt.	neuter		
num.	numeral		
neg.	negative particle, negated sentence or form		
old	old Soviet usage		

Лéкція | Lesson 1

In this chapter you will learn:

Seventeen letters of the Ukrainian alphabet
To read and write words composed of them
To point out to and ask about things around you
To give simple affirmative and negative statements
To make a simple contrast between things

Essentials of Ukrainian Spelling

There is a more or less direct correspondence between the sound and the letter that denotes it in writing. Each letter is attached to only one sound. Therefore, to spell a word in Ukrainian simply means to pronounce it. The Ukrainian equivalent of *"Spell your name!"* **Назві́ть своє́ ім'я́.** literally means "Say your name."

Compared to the English alphabet Ukrainian letters can be organized into three groups:

1. True friends are those denoting the same sounds in both languages: **А, Е, І, О, З** (handwritten), **К, М,** and **Т**.

2. False friends are those that look the same or very similar but denote different sounds:
В /v/, **И** /i/, **Н** /n/, **Р** /r/, **С** /s/, **Х** /kh/, and **ь** (*soft sign* has no sound of its own, learners often liken it to the number *6*).

3. Strangers are those that are not found in the English alphabet at all:
Б /b/, **Г** /h/, **Ґ** /g/, **Є** /je/, **Ж** /zh/, **Ї** /ji/, **Й** /j/, **Л** /l/, **Ф** /f/, **Ц** /ts/, **Ш** /sh/, **Щ** /shch/, **Ю** /ju/, and **Я** /ja/.

Українська Абе́тка | Ukrainian Alphabet

Ukrainian has a Cyrillic-based alphabet of 33 letters, each signifying a respective sound. Ukrainians write in a cursive script, therefore it is important to learn writing and reading in cursive from the start.

Printed	Cursive	Name in ABC	Pronounced as	Phonetic symbol
А, а	А, а	/a/	/a:/ in *palm*	/a/
Б, б	Б, б	/be/	/b/ in *best*	/b/
В, в	В, в	/ve/	/v/ in *van* or /w/ in *win*	/v/ or /w/
Г, г	Г, г	/he/	/h/ in *inhale*	/h/
Ґ, ґ	Ґ, ґ	/ge/	/g/ in *get*	/g/
Д, д	D, д	/de/	/d/ in *dad*	/d/ or /d'/
Е, е	Е, е	/e/	/e/ in *bed*	/e/
Є, є	Є, є	/je/	/je/ in *yet*	/je/ or /e/
Ж, ж	Ж, ж	/zhe/	/zh/ in *measure*	/zh/ or /zh'/
З, з	З, з	/ze/	/z/ in *zoo*	/z/ or /z'/
И, и	И, и	/y/	/y/ in *livid*	/y/
І, і	І, і	/i/	/i:/ in *feet*	/i/
Ї, ї	Ї, ї	/ji/	/ji/ in *yield*	/ji/
Й, й	Й, й	/jot/	/j/ in *yes*	/j/
К, к	К, к	/ka/	/k/ in *sky*	/k/
Л, л	Л, л	/el/	/l/ in *ball*	/l/ or /l'/
М, м	М, м	/em/	/m/ in *most*	/m/
Н, н	Н, н	/en/	/n/ in *not*	/n/ or /n'/
О, о	О, о	/o/	/o:/ *law*	/o/
П, п	П, п	/pe/	/p/ in *spade*	/p/
Р, р	Р, р	/er/	/r/ in *red*	/r/ or /r'/
С, с	С, с	/es/	/s/ in *grass*	/s/ or /s'/
Т, т	Т, т	/te/	/t/ in *stop*	/t/ or /t'/
У, у	У, у	/u:/	/u:/ in *ruse*	/u/
Ф, ф	Ф, ф	/ef/	/f/ in *fix*	/f/
Х, х	Х, х	/kha:/	/kh/ in Scottish *loch*	/kh/
Ц, ц	Ц, ц	/tse/	/ts/ in *lots*	/ts/ or /ts'/
Ч, ч	Ч, ч	/che/	/ch/ in *chess*	/ch/
Ш, ш	Ш, ш	/sha/	/sh/ in *shed*	/sh/
Щ, щ	Щ, щ	/shcha/	/shch/ in *fresh cheese*	/shch/
..., ь	..., ь	znak mjakshennia	softens previous consonant	/...'/
Ю, ю	Ю, ю	/ju/	/ju/ in *pure*	/ju/ or /u/
Я, я	Я, я	/ja/	/ja/ in *yard*	/ja/ or /a/

Украї́нські лі́тери. Гру́па 1 | Ukrainian Letters. Group 1.

Vowels			
Printed	Cursive	Pronounced	Phonetic & Comments
А, а	*А, а*	/a/ as in p**a**lm	/a/
Е, е	*Е, е*	/e/ as in b**e**d	/e/
І, і	*І, і*	/i/ as in f**ee**t	/i/, softens previous consonant
О, о	*О, о*	/o/ as in l**a**w	/o/

Consonants			
Printed	Cursive	Pronounced	Phonetic & Comments
К, к	*К, к*	/k/ as in s**k**y	/k/, never soft
М, м	*М, м*	/m/ as in **m**y	/m/, never soft
Т, т	*Т, т*	/t/ as in s**t**ay	/t/ and /t'/
Ц, ц	*Ц, ц*	/ts/ as in ca**ts**	/ts/ and /ts'/

Note 1.1. Pronunciation of vowels

Ukrainian vowels are pronounced without noticeable reduction both under the stress and unstressed,

те́ма /téma/ *a theme*, **ко́ма** /kóma/ *a comma*

When not under the stress, the vowels /e/ and /o/ "parrot" other vowels.

The unstressed /e/ is pronounced with a shade of /y/. This is reflected in transcription by /e^y/,

мета́ /me^{y}tá/ *a goal*

The unstressed /o/ is pronounced with a shade of /u/. This is reflected in transcription by /o^u/,

коме́та /ko^{u}méta/ *a comet*

Take note. An unstressed /o/ is never pronounced as /a:/ in Ukrainian.

Впра́ви Exercises

∩ 1.1. Listen and repeat after the speaker. Copy these letter combinations in cursive.

ка	ке	кі	ко	ак	ек	ік	ок	**кіт** *a cat*
ка	*ке*	*кі*	*ко*	*ак*	*ек*	*ік*	*ок*	*кіт*
/ka/	/ke/	/ki/	/ko/	/ak/	/ek/	/ik/	/ok/	/kit/

ма	ме	мі	мо	ам	ем	ім	ом	**ма́ма** *a mom*
ма	*ме*	*мі*	*мо*	*ам*	*ем*	*ім*	*ом*	*мама*
/ma/	/me/	/mi/	/mo/	/am/	/em/	/im/	/om/	/máma/

та	те	ті	то	ат	ет	іт	от	**та́то** *a dad*
та	*те*	*ті*	*то*	*ат*	*ет*	*іт*	*от*	*тато*
/ta/	/te/	/ti/	/to/	/at/	/et/	/it/	/ot/	/táto/

ца	це	ці	цо	ац	ец	іц	оц	**це** *this is (these are)*
ца	*це*	*ці*	*цо*	*ац*	*ец*	*іц*	*оц*	*це*
/tsa/	/tse/	/tsi/	/tso/	/ats/	/ets/	/its/	/ots/	/tse/

∩ 1.2. Repeat after the speaker. Copy these words in cursive and mark stresses.

ма́ма /máma/ *a mommy* — *ма́ма*
ті́тка /títka/ *an aunt* — *ті́тка*
тома́т /to^{u}mát/ *a tomato* — *тома́т*
мака́ка /makáka/ *a macaque monkey* — *мака́ка*
о́ко /óko^u/ *an eye* — *о́ко*

Note 1.2. Word Stress

Ukrainian word stress has no fixed place. A stressed vowel is somewhat longer than an unstressed one. The stress is marked by an acute accent placed over the stressed vowel,

така́ /taká/ *such*, **те́ма** /téma/ *a theme*

Treat the stress as if it were a letter. Do mark it while writing a word and always memorize it.

Note 1.3. Pronunciation of consonants /k/ and /t/

In contradistinction to their English counterparts the Ukrainian consonants /k/ and /t/ lack aspiration. The consonant /t/ is pronounced by putting the tip of the tongue to the upper teeth, not the gums of the upper teeth as in English. It is never pronounced like /ts/ when followed by /i/,

тіка́ти /tikáty^e/ *to run away*

Note 1.4. Pointing to things near and far

To point out somebody or something the words **це** /tse/ *this* and **то** /to/ *that* are used. **Це** is contrasted with **то** as are the English *this* and *that*,

Це ма́ма, а то та́то. /tse ма́ma a to та́toᵘ/ *This is mommy, and that is dad.*

The Ukrainian present tense form of the verb *to be* is normally omitted from the statements of such a type. Its presence is implied,

Це ті́тка То́ма. /tse ті́tka То́ma/ *This is Aunt Toma.*

Це ма́ма і та́то. /tse ма́ma i та́toᵘ/ *These are mommy and dad.*

Take note. A rising tone is signified by ↗. It is similar to that in *Do you?*

A falling tone is signified by ↘. It is similar to that in *I do.*

Note 1.5 Yes/no questions

Like in English, Ukrainian general questions, i.e. questions that ask for a yes/no answer, can be posed simply by pronouncing a given affirmative statement with a rising tone. Compare the statement with the general question:

Це ↘ ма́ма. *This is ↘ mom.*

Це ↗ ма́ма? *This is ↗ mom?*

та́то /та́toᵘ/ *a dad* — *та́то*
те́ма /те́ma/ *a theme* — *те́ма*
ко́мік /kо́mik/ *a comedian* — *ко́мік*
мі́тка /mі́tka/ *a mark* — *мі́тка*
ко́ма /kо́ma/ *a comma* — *ко́ма*
мета́ /meᵘtá/ *a goal* — *мета́*
ацте́к /atsté́k/ *an Aztec* — *ацте́к*

🎧 **1.3.** Say in Ukrainian who/what these people/things are.

1. Це кіт. 2. Це мак. 3. Це та́то. 4. Це ма́ма.

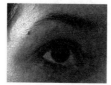

5. Це о́ко. 6. Це тома́т. 7. Це мака́ка. 8. Це ті́тка.

9. Це То́ма. 10. Це о́цет. 11. Це мета́. 12. Це като́к

🎧 **1.4.** Pose a general question based on the given word. Give a full affirmative answer.

Model. ко́ма *a comma* **Q** Це ↗ко́ма? *Is this a comma?*
A ↘Так, це ↘ко́ма. *Yes, this is a comma.*

1. ті́тка 2. ма́ма 3. кіт 4. мака́ка 5. То́ма 6. тома́т 7. мак 8. о́ко

1.5. Pair each printed word with its cursive equivalent. Copy all the words in cursive.

мак /mak/	_____	1. *То́ма*
та́то /та́toᵘ/	_____	2. *тома́т*
мака́ка /makáka/	_____	3. *мі́тка*
ма́ма /ма́ma/	_____	4. *ті́тка*
ті́тка /tі́tka/	_____	5. *ко́ма*
тома́т /toᵘма́t/	_____	6. *та́то*
То́ма /tо́ma/	_____	7. *мака́ка*
ко́ма /kо́ma/	_____	8. *ма́ма*
мі́тка /mі́tka/	_____	9. *мак*

1.6. Point to two things at the same time. Use the word **і** or **та**, both meaning *and*.

Model. **C** Це *this*, то *that*
A Це і то *this and that* or Це та то *this and that*

1. Ма́ма, ті́тка
2. Та́то, ма́ма
3. То́ма, ма́ма
4. Ті́тка, та́то
5. Кіт, мака́ка
6. То́ма, та́то

🎧 **1.7.** State that something is in your immediate proximity and that something else is removed from you. Use the opposition Це ... , а то ... . *This is … and that is …*

Model. **C** ко́ма *a comma*, мі́тка *a mark*
A Це ↗ко́ма, а то ↘мі́тка. *This is a comma, and that's a mark.*

1. Та́то, ма́ма
2. Ма́ма, ті́тка
3. Тома́т, мак
4. То́мка, ко́мік
5. Ті́тка, та́то
6. Кіт, мака́ка

🎧 **1.8.** Listen carefully and mark the words you hear.

ма́ма ✓   *мі́тка* ✓   *та́то* ✓   *мак* ✓
це ✓   *тома́т* ✓   *мо́ка* ✓   *то* ✓
о́цет   *ті́тка* ✓   *То́мка* ✓   *мака́ка* ✓

🎧 **1.9.** Engage a partner in an exchange. Follow the model. Then write down in cursive each of these exchanges. Mark stresses everywhere.

Model. Ма́ма *a mom*   **Q** Це – ↗ма́ма? *Is this mom?*
A О ↘так, це – ↘ма́ма. *Oh yes, this is mom.*

1. та́то
2. ко́ма
3. о́цет
4. ті́тка
5. То́мка
6. мак
7. мака́ка
8. кіт
9. ацте́к

1.10. Unscramble the words. Mark the stresses.

1. ткаті _____
2. мате _____
3. акамак _____
4. отат _____
5. амам _____
6. ікт _____
7. кма _____

Note 1.6. Likening things

The joining words **і** /i/ and **та** /ta/ both correspond to the English *and*. Both have the same meaning and are used to present two things as similar in one way or another,

ма́ма та та́то *mommy and dad*
кіт і мака́ка *a cat and a macaque*
Take note. Ta is used after vowels, whereas **i** after consonants.

Note 1.7. Contrasting things
The word **а** /a/ *and, but, while* is used to contrast things in Ukrainian,
Це ↗ма́ма, а то ↘та́то. *This is mom and (while) that is dad.*

Це ті́тка, а це кіт.

Note 1.8. Affirmative word так *yes*
Agreement is expressed in Ukrainian by the word **так** /tak/ *yes*. For added emphasis the expression
О ↘так /o tak/ *Oh yes* is used. It is pronounced with a falling tone.

Молодий театр. Київ
Molodyi Theater. Kyiv

баба a grandma

 1.11. Dictation. Listen carefully and fill in the blanks with what you hear. Mark the stresses.

1. Ц___ тітк___ Том___ .
2. Т___ мака___ т___ кі___.
3. Ц___ ма___, а т___ тат___.

1.12. Complete the crossword puzzle.

Across
1. Tomato ✓
3. Cat ✓
4. Dad ✓
7. Goal
8. Eye

Down
1. Aunt ✓
2. Mom ✓
5. Yes ✓

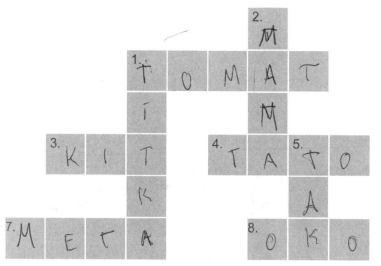

 1.13. Fill in the blanks with missing letters. Pronounce, then write each word in cursive. Mark the stresses.

ма__а	о__о	т__тка	ма__ака
м__та	то__ат	ко__ета	т__то
мі__ка	__ома	т__ма	__іт

Українські лíтери. Грýпа 2 | Ukrainian Letters. Group 2.

Vowels			
Printed	*Cursive*	Pronounced	Phonetic
Я, я	*Я, я*	/ja/ in **yard**	/ja/ and /'a/
Ю, ю	*Ю, ю*	/ju/ in **view**	/ju/ and /'u/
И, и	*И, и*	/y/ in **livid**	/y/
У, у	*У, у*	/u:/ in **ruse**	/u/

Consonants			
Printed	*Cursive*	Pronounced	Phonetic
Б, б	*Б, б*	/b/ as in **best**	/b/, always hard
Д, д	*D, д*	/d/ as in **dad**	/d/ and /d'/
З, з	*З, з*	/z/ as in **zoo**	/z/ and /z'/
Й, й	*Й, й*	/j/ as in **yes**	/j/ always soft, never occurs before **а**, **е**, **і**, **и**, and **у**
Н, н	*Н, н*	/n/ as in **not**	/n/ and /n'/

∩ 1.14. Listen and repeat after the speaker. Copy these letter combinations in cursive.

ба	бе	би	бі	бо	бу	аб
ба	*бе*	*би*	*бі*	*бо*	*бу*	*аб*
/ba/	/be/	/by/	/bi/	/bo/	/bu/	/ab/

еб	иб	іб	об	уб	ба́ба *a grandma*	
еб	*иб*	*іб*	*об*	*уб*	*ба́ба*	
/eb/	/yb/	/ib/	/ob/	/ub/	/bába/	

- - - - - - - - - -

да	де	ди	ді	до	ду	ад
да	*де*	*ди*	*ді*	*до*	*ду*	*ад*
/da/	/de/	/dy/	/di/	/do/	/du/	/ad/

ед	ид	ід	од	уд	дід *a grandad*	
ед	*ид*	*ід*	*од*	*уд*	*дід*	
/ed/	/yd/	/id/	/od/	/ud/	/did/	

- - - - - - - - - -

за	зе	зи	зі	зо	зу	аз
за	*зе*	*зи*	*зі*	*зо*	*зу*	*аз*
/za/	/ze/	/zy/	/zi/	/zo/	/zu/	/az/

ез	из	із	оз	уз	зуб *a tooth*	
ез	*из*	*із*	*оз*	*уз*	*зуб*	
/ez/	/yz/	/iz/	/oz/	/uz/	/zub/	

- - - - - - - - - -

на	не	ни	ні	но	ну	ан
на	*не*	*ни*	*ні*	*но*	*ну*	*ан*
/na/	/ne/	/ny/	/ni/	/no/	/nu/	/an/

ен	ин	ін	он	ун	монуме́нт *a monument*	
ен	*ин*	*ін*	*он*	*ун*	*монуме́нт*	
/en/	/yn/	/in/	/on/	/un/	/moᵘnumént/	

∩ 1.15. Listen and repeat after the speaker. Copy these letter combinations in cursive.

дай	бий	зей	май	мий	зой	бій
дай	*бий*	*зей*	*май*	*мий*	*зой*	*бій*
/daj/	/byj/	/zej/	/maj/	/myj/	/zoj/	/bij/

знайо́мий an acquaintance

✏ Note 1.9. Picky letter Й, й

The letter **Й, й** /j/ appears after all vowels. It rarely appears before consonants. **Й, й** never appears before the vowels **а**, **е**, **і**, **и** or **у** because the Ukrainian alphabet has special letters denoting the combinations of /j/ with these vowels:

/j + a/ = **я**
/j + e/ = **є**
/j + i (и)/ = **ї**
/j + y/ = **ю**

That is why instead of the letter combinations **йа**, **йе**, **йі (йи)**, and **йу** the letters **я**, **є**, **ї**, and **ю** are used respectively. There is no special letter for the sound combination /j+o/. The consonant /j/ should not be pronounced as a short vowel /i/.

й appears only before the vowel **о**,

знайо́мий /znajómyᵉj/ *an acquaintance*

той	дуй	цей	йой	музе́й *a museum*
той	*дуй*	*цей*	*йой*	*музе́й*
/toj/	/duj/	/tsej/	/joj/	/muzéj/

Note 1.10. The vowel И, и /y/

In unstressed syllables, the vowel /y/ tends to be pronounced with a shade of /e/, hence its transcription symbol /yᵉ/, **Тимко́** /tyᵉmkó/ *Tim*, **бу́ти** /bútyᵉ/ *to be*, **дити́на** /dyᵉtýna/ *a child*.

Take note. The vowel /y/ is never pronounced as /i/. Convergence of the vowels /y/ and /e/ when they are not under the stress is typical of Ukrainian.

монуме́нт

Note 1.11. How to ask WHERE?

The Ukrainian word for *where?* is **де?**
Де ↘ма́ти? /de mátyᵉ/ *Де ма́ти?* *Where is the mother?*
Де ↘Зі́на? /de zína/ *Де Зі́на? Where's Zena?*
Like in English this type of question uses a falling tone.

Note 1.12. How to say NO

The word **ні** /ni/ *no* is used to give a short negative answer to a yes/no question,

Q Це ↗ Зі́на? /tse zína/ *Це Зі́на? Is this Zena?*

A ↘Ні, це ↘Да́на. /ni tse Dána/ *Ні, це Да́на. No, this is Dana.*

∩ 1.16. Repeat after the speaker. Copy these words in cursive and mark the stresses.

ба́нка /bánka/ *a jar*	*ба́нка*
банкома́т /bankoᵘmát/ *an ATM*	*банкома́т*
буди́нок /budýnoᵘk/ *a building*	*буди́нок*
знайо́мий /znajómyᵉj/ *an acquaintance*	*знайо́мий*
музе́й /muzéj/ *a museum*	*музе́й*
дити́на /dyᵉtýna/ *a child*	*дити́на*
дуб /dub/ *an oak*	*дуб*
зима́ /zyᵉmá/ *winter*	*зима́*
зуб /zub/ *a tooth*	*зуб*
ма́ти /mátyᵉ/ *a mother*	*ма́ти*
монуме́нт /moᵘnumént/ *a monument*	*монуме́нт*
ціна́ /tsiná/ *a price*	*ціна́*
о́ко /ókoᵘ/ *an eye*	*о́ко*
обі́д /oᵘbíd/ *a lunch*	*обі́д*

∩ 1.17. Ask where these people or things are.

дити́на дуб зуб ціна́ ба́нка банкома́т

обі́д бана́н буди́нок монуме́нт коме́та

∩ 1.18. Engage in a Q-and-A exchange. Note the rising tone in the question and the falling one in the negative answer.

Model. Зі́на /zína/ *Zena* vs Да́на /dána/ *Dana*.
Q Це ↗ Зі́на? /tse zína/ *Is this Zena?*
A ↘Ні, це ↘ Да́на. /ni tse dána/ *No, this is Dana.*

1. та́то /tátoᵘ/ *a dad*   vs   дід /did/ *a grandad*
2. ма́ма /máma/ *a mommy*   vs   ба́ба /bába/ *a grandma*
3. кіт /kit/ *a cat*   vs   мака́ка /makáka/ *a macaque*
4. музе́й /muzéj/ *a museum*   vs   буди́нок /budýnoᵘk/ *a building*
5. мак /mak/ *a poppy flower*   vs   бана́н /banán/ *a banana*

∩ 1.19. Respond to the question. Use **ні** *no* to give a negative answer and **не** *not* to negate a particular word.

Model. та́то /tа́toᵘ/ *a dad*, дід /did/ *a grandad*
Q Це ↗ та́то? /tse tа́toᵘ/ *Is this a dad?*
A ↘Ні, це не ↗та́то, а ↘ дід. /ni tse ne tа́toᵘ a did/
No, this isn't dad, but grandad.

1. Зі́на *Zena*, Да́на *Dana*
2. ті́тка *an aunt*, ма́ти *a mother*
3. Тимко́ *Tim*, Зе́нон *Zenobius*
4. То́ма *Toma*, Ні́на *Nina*

∩ 1.20. Read these words. Pair each with its equivalent written in cursive. Copy all the words in cursive.

обі́д /oᵘbíd/ *a lunch*	_____	1. *дити́на*
ціна́ /ts'iná/ *a price*	_____	2. *знайо́мий*
дити́на /dyᵉtýna/ *a child*	_____	3. *банкома́т*
ба́нка /bа́nka/ *a jar*	_____	4. *кандида́т*
дикта́нт /dyᵉktа́nt/ *a dictation*	_____	5. *ба́нка*
до́ма /dóma/ *at home*	_____	6. *буди́нок*
буди́нок /budýnoᵘk/ *a building*	_____	7. *дикта́нт*
банкома́т /bankoᵘmа́t/ *an ATM*	_____	8. *ціна́*
знайо́мий /znajómyᵉj/ *an acquaintance*	_____	9. *до́ма*
кандида́т /kandyᵉdа́t/ *a candidate*	_____	10. *обі́д*

∩ 1.21. Practice the pronunciation of the soft consonants /d'/ /z'/ /n'/, /t'/, and /ts'/ in opposition to their hard counterparts /d/, /z/, /n/, /t/, and /ts/.

ди	ді	зи	зі	ни	ні	ти	ті	ци	ці	ді́ти *children*
ди	*ді*	*зи*	*зі*	*ни*	*ні*	*ти*	*ті*	*ци*	*ці*	*ді́ти*
/dy/	/d'i/	/zy/	/z'i/	/ny/	/n'i/	/ty/	/t'i/	/tsy/	/ts'i/	/dítyᵉ/

да	дя	за	зя	на	ня	та	тя	ца	ця	та́ця *a tray*
да	*дя*	*за*	*зя*	*на*	*ня*	*та*	*тя*	*ца*	*ця*	*та́ця*
/da/	/d'a/	/za/	/z'a/	/na/	/n'a/	/ta/	/t'a/	/tsa/	/ts'a/	/tа́ts'a/

ду	дю	зу	зю	ну	ню
ду	*дю*	*зу*	*зю*	*ну*	*ню*
/du/	/d'u/	/zu/	/z'u/	/nu/	/n'u/

ту	тю	цу	цю	коцюба́ *a poker*
ту	*тю*	*цу*	*цю*	*коцюба́*
/tu/	/t'u/	/tsu/	/ts'u/	/koᵘts'ubа́/

∩ 1.22. Repeat after the speaker. Copy these words in cursive and mark the stresses.

цятка /ts'а́tka/ *a spot*   *ця́тка*
обіця́нка /oᵘbíts'а́nka/ *a promise*   *обіця́нка*

Note 1.13. Ukrainian for NOT

The word **не** /ne/ is the Ukrainian equivalent of the English *not*, used to negate a particular word or a whole sentence,

Q Це ↗ та́то? /tse tа́toᵘ/ *Це та́то?*
Is this dad?

A Це не ↘ та́то. /tse neᵘ tа́toᵘ/ *Це не та́то.* *This is not dad.*

Note 1.14. Hard and soft consonants

Many Ukrainian consonants can be hard or soft depending on the letter following it.

Consonants **б**, **м**, and **к** are always hard. The consonant **й** is always soft.

The **д**, **з**, **н**, **т**, and **ц** can be both hard and soft. To make a hard consonant soft the body of the tongue is lifted towards the roof of the mouth. In transcription, the softness is marked by an apostrophe put after the soft consonant. Compare the first hard /n/ and second soft /n'/ in *El Niño* /el nín'o/.

There are several ways of marking a soft consonant. One is by the letters **і**, **я**, and **ю** which make the preceding consonant soft:
ціна́ /ts'iná/ *a price*
дю́на /d'úna/ *a dune*
Тетя́на /teᵘt'а́na/ *Tetiana*

After consonants, the letter **я** /ja/ is pronounced as /a/,
ня́ня /n'а́n'a/ *a babysitter*
маля́ /mal'а́/ *a kid*

The letter **ю** /ju/ is pronounced as /u/,
тютю́н /t'ut'ún/ *tobacco*

Це діти.

Юнона

ди́ня /dýn'a/ *a melon*   *диня*
ня́ня /n'án'a/ *a babysitter*   *няня*
дитя́ /dyᵉt'á/ *a baby*   *дитя*
котеня́ /koᵘteᵞn'á/ *a kitten*   *котеня*
цуценя́ /tsutseᵞn'á/ *a puppy*   *цуценя*
Мики́та /myᵉkýta/ *Mykyta (masculine name)*   *Микита*
тума́н /tumán/ *a fog*   *туман*
ді́ти /d'ítyᵉ/ *children*   *діти*
коцюба́ /koᵘts'ubá/ *a poker*   *коцюба*

∩ **1.23.** Practice the pronunciation of the vowels **я** and **ю** at the beginning of words.

яб	яд	яз	як	ям	ян	ят	яц	язи́к *a tongue*
яб	*яд*	*яз*	*як*	*ям*	*ян*	*ят*	*яц*	*язик*
/jab/	/jad/	/jaz/	/jak/	/jam/	/jan/	/jat/	/jats/	/jazýk/

я́ба	я́да	я́за	я́тка	я́ма	я́на	я́та	я́ца	як? *how?*
яба	*яда*	*яза*	*ятка*	*яма*	*яна*	*ята*	*яца*	*як*
/jába/	/jáda/	/jáza/	/játka/	/jáma/	/jána/	/játa/	/játsa/	/jak/

я́дя	я́зя	я́ня	я́тя	я́ся	яки́й	яйце́ *an egg*
ядя	*язя*	*яня*	*ятя*	*яся*	*який*	*яйце*
/jád'a/	/jáz'a/	/ján'a/	/ját'a/	/jás'a/	/jakýj/	/jajtsé/

юб	юд	юз	юк	юм	юн	ют	юц	Ю́та *Utah*
юб	*юд*	*юз*	*юк*	*юм*	*юн*	*ют*	*юц*	*Юта*
/jub/	/jud/	/juz/	/juk/	/jum/	/jun/	/jut/	/juts/	/júta/

ю́бу	ю́зу	ю́ку	ю́му	ю́ну	ю́ту	ю́цу	юна́к *a youth*
юбу	*юзу*	*юку*	*юму*	*юну*	*юту*	*юцу*	*юнак*
/júbu/	/júzu/	/júku/	/júmu/	/júnu/	/jútu/	/jútsu/	/junák/

ю́дю	ю́зю	ю́ню	ю́тю	ю́цю	Юно́на *Juno*
юдю	*юзю*	*юню*	*ютю*	*юцю*	*Юнона*
/júd'u/	/júz'u/	/jún'u/	/jút'u/	/júts'u/	/junóna/

∩ **1.24.** Practice the pronunciation of the **я** and **ю** after another vowel.

кая́к	мая́к	бая́н	Ма́я	бе́я	ту́я	моя́ *my (mine)*
каяк	*маяк*	*баян*	*Мая*	*бея*	*туя*	*моя*
/kaják/	/maják/	/baján/	/mája/	/béja/	/túja/	/moᵘjá/

Дія́на	нія́к	а́кція	дота́ція	му́мія	ака́ція *an acacia*
Діяна	*ніяк*	*акція*	*дотація*	*мумія*	*акація*
/dijána/	/niják/	/ákts'ija/	/doᵘtáts'ija/	/múmija/	/akáts'ija/

бо́ю	ми́ю	зна́ю	ті́каю	даю́	танцю́ю	дя́кую *thank you*
бою	*мию*	*знаю*	*тікаю*	*даю*	*танцюю*	*дякую*
/bóju/	/mýju/	/znaju/	/tikáju/	/dajú/	/tants'úju/	/d'ákuju/

1.25. Repeat after the speaker. Copy these words in cursive and mark the stresses.

юна́к /junák/ a youth		*юна́к*
Юката́н /jukatán/ Yukatan		*Юката́н*
Яки́м /jakým/ Joachim		*Яки́м*
дя́кую /d'ákuju/ thank you		*дя́кую*
мая́к /maják/ a lighthouse		*мая́к*
кая́к /kaják/ a kayak		*кая́к*
ма́ю /máju/ I have		*ма́ю*
я́ма /jáma/ a pit		*я́ма*
Ю́та /júta/ Utah		*Ю́та*

юна́к

1.26. Pair each printed word with its equivalent written in cursive. Copy all the words in cursive.

ди́ня /dýn'a/ a melon	_____	1. *Яки́м*
Тетя́на /teᵞt'ána/ Tetiana (name)	_____	2. *ня́ня*
ця́тка /ts'átka/ a spot	_____	3. *дитя́*
ня́ня /n'án'a/ a babysitter	_____	4. *дя́кую*
котеня́ /koᵘteᵞn'á/ a kitty	_____	5. *ди́ня*
юна́к /junák/ a youth	_____	6. *обіця́нка*
цуценя́ /tsutseᵞn'á/ a puppy	_____	7. *цуценя́*
обіця́нка /oᵘbíts'ánka/ a promise	_____	8. *котеня́*
дя́кую /d'ákuju/ thank you	_____	9. *ця́тка*
Яки́м /jakým/ Joachim	_____	10. *Тетя́на*
дитя́ /dyᵉt'á/ a baby	_____	11. *юна́к*

1.27. Underline feminine and neuter nouns in Exercises 1.25 and 1.26.

1.28. Listen carefully and mark the words you hear.

1. *дити́на ✓ обід Тетя́на ✓ ня́ня ✓ банкома́т знайо́мий зуб тютю́н ✓ обіця́нка дя́кую ✓*
2. *цуценя́ юна́к ✓ Зі́на ✓ буди́нок кандида́т музе́й ціна́ коцюба́ котеня́ ді́ти ацте́к*

1.29. Unscramble the words. Read them aloud. Mark the stresses.

1. кудяю	*дя́кую*	
2. нятеко	*котеня́*	
3. индя	*ди́ня*	
4. ютнтю		
5. яння	*ця́тка*	
6. кацят	*ця́тка*	
7. акню	*юнка*	
8. цобіянка	*обі́цянка*	
9. тияд	*дитя*	
10. цняецу	*цуценя́*	

Note 1.16. Gender of nouns

All Ukrainian nouns have a gender, either masculine, feminine, or neuter. For instance all baby animal names are neuter:

дитя́ /dyᵉt'á/ a baby
цуценя́ /tsutseᵞn'á/ a puppy

A useful indicator of noun gender is the ending. Nouns ending in ~a (~я) with the exception of baby animal names are feminine:

мета́ /meᵞtá/ a goal
та́ця /táts'a/ a tray

Це котеня́?

Що тут є?

1.30. Dictation. Listen carefully and fill in the blanks with what you hear. Mark the stresses.

1. Ту_ буди́н__.
2. А д_ ті́тк_ Тетя́__? Та_.
3. Наді́_ і Зо́_ ту_.
4. Це котен_?
5. Д_ банком__? Та_.
6. Це Яки_? Н_, це н_ Яки_, а Тим__.
7. Це не дити́__, а юна́_.
8. Та_ не Дія́__, а Наді́_.

1.31. Complete the crossword puzzle.

Across
1. ATM ✓
4. Where ✓
5. Lighthouse ✓
7. Babysitter ✓
8. Kitten ✓

Down
1. Building ✓
2. Cat ✓
3. Acacia ✓
6. Kayak ✓
9. How ✓

1.Б	а	н	к	о	м	3.А	Т
У		і				К	
4.Д	е	т		5.М	А	Я	6.К
И				У			А
7.Н	я	н	я	і			Я
О				я			К
8.К	о	т	е	н	9.Я		
					А		

1.32. Circle each soft consonant. Explain why it is soft. Mind the consonants that are incapable of being soft. Refer to Note 1.14.

музе́й	Яки́м	цуценя́	дити́на	мій	коня́ка
ті́тка	ко́ма	кая́к	тютю́н	ця́тка	о́цет
Юно́на	тома́т	дя́кую	ди́ня	Тетя́на	котеня́
коме́та	мі́тка	ака́ція	та́ця	мета́	монуме́нт

1.33. Fill in the blanks with the missing letters. Rewrite words in cursive. Mark the stresses.

д я́ кую	дити́ н а	Зі н а	Я а́нкомат
обі ц янка	котеня́	Я ким	Ю нак
ди́н я	ма я́ к	Юн а́ на	__кація
я__це	ня н я	__ятка	

Це То́ма та ма́ма.

1.34. Say the sentences in Ukrainian. Write them down in cursive.

1. Is this mom? No, this is not mom. This is Aunt Tetiana.
2. Is this dad? Yes, this is dad.
3. Where is the bank? The bank is here.
4. The child is at home.
5. This is a kitten and that is a puppy.
6. This is a tray. Thank you.
7. This is not Mykyta but Diana.
8. Where's an ATM here?

1.35. Translate these sentences into Ukrainian.

1. There is a museum there.
2. And where is Aunt Toma? At home.
3. Nadia and Zoia are there.
4. Is this a poppy?
5. Where is the price? Here.
6. Is this a comma? This is no comma, but a mark.
7. Mykyta is an acquaintance.
8. There is a spot here.
9. This is not a baby, but a youth.
10. Where is the dictation?

1.36. Match the Ukrainian names with their English equivalents. Write each Ukrainian name in cursive.

1. Mykyta	2. Zoia	3. Tymko	4. Toma	5. Yakym	6. Diana
1. Яки́м	2. Тимко́	3. Мики́та	4. Зо́я	5. Дія́на	6. То́ма

Note 1.17. Challenge of Ukrainian stress

With the exception of Ukrainian dictionaries and language textbooks, the word stress in Ukrainian is not normally marked either in handwriting or in print. To meet this added challenge, Ukrainian language learners of all levels will be well-advised always to mark the word stress when writing. If unsure, they should verify its position by the dictionary or easily available Internet language resources. One of them is introduced in Exercise 1.37.

Завда́ння для Міжнаро́дної мере́жі
Internet assignment

1.37. Visit the website Dictionaries of Ukraine *Словники Украї́ни*, **http://lcorp.ulif.org.ua/dictua/**
Type into the search window on the left each of the words below. Click on the button **пошук** *search* to do the search. Verify the stress by the website (center of page). Re-write each word in cursive and mark the stresses.

1. мотоцикл		7. байка	
2. дудка		8. дотація	
3. ботаніка		9. задум	
4. цукат		10. кімната	
5. одеколон		11. ідея	
6. наука		12. музикант	

нау́ка:
У Ри́мському університе́ті «Ля Сап'є́нца» вивча́ють. украї́нську.

Л́екція | Lesson 2

In this chapter you will learn:

Nine more letters of the Ukrainian alphabet
Personal pronouns
To say to whom something belongs
To inquire about general qualities of an object and give its simple description
To introduce yourself

Note 2.1. Two-Faced Letter В, в

The letter **В, в** can be pronounced /v/ as in *van* and /w/ as in *win*.

1. It is pronounced as /v/ before vowels: **вода́** /voᵘdá/ *water*, **мо́ва** /móva/ *a language*, **ка́ва** /káva/ *coffee*.

2. It is pronounced as a short /u/, identical to the second element of the English diphthong /ou/ in *go, row, slow*, after vowels or before consonants. Its transcription sign is /w/,

а́вто /áwtoᵘ/ *a car*, **за́втра** /záwtra/ *tomorrow*, **ко́вдра** /kówdra/ *a blanket*. Because in the latter position, /w/ sounds like a short /u/, the letter **в** often alternates with the letter **у** in spelling variants of the same words,

вдо́ма /wdóma/ and **удо́ма** /udóma/ *at home*, **вра́нці** /wránts'i/ and **ура́нці** /uránts'i/ *in the morning*, **вро́да** /wróda/ and **уро́да** /uróda/ *beauty*.

Take note. In Ukrainian, the letter **В, в** is never pronounced as /f/.

Украї́нські лі́тери. Гру́па 3. Ukrainian Letters. Group 3.

Vowels			
Printed	*Cursive*	Pronounced	Phonetic & Comment
Є, є	*Є, є*	/je/ in **yet**	/je/ or /e/
Ї, ї	*Ї, ї*	/ji/ in **yield**	/ji/, never occurs after consonants

Consonants			
Printed	*Cursive*	Pronounced	Phonetic
В, в	*В, в*	/v/ in **van** or /w/ in **win**	/v/ or /w/, always hard
Г, г	*Г, г*	/h/ in **inhale**	/h/, always hard
Л, л	*Л, л*	/l/ in **ball**	/l/ or /l'/
Р, р	*Р, р*	/r/ in **red**	/r/ or /r'/
Х, х	*Х, х*	/kh/ in Scottish **loch**	/kh/, always hard
Ш, ш	*Ш, ш*	/sh/ in **shed**	/sh/, always hard, soft only when lengthened
..., ь	*..., ь*	softens previous consonant	/...'/

 Впра́ви Exercises

Львів. Пло́ща Ри́нок.
Lviv. Market Square

∩ **2.1.** Listen and repeat after the speaker. Copy these letter combinations in cursive.

ва	ве	ви	ві	во	ву	ав
ва	*ве*	*ви*	*ві*	*во*	*ву*	*ав*
/va/	/ve/	/vy/	/vi/	/vo/	/vu/	/aw/

ев	ив	ів	ов	ув	він *he*	
ев	*ив*	*ів*	*ов*	*ув*	*він*	
/ew/	/yw/	/iw/	/ow/	/uw/	/він/	

га	ге	ги	гі	го	гу	аг	ег	иг	іг	ог	уг	ого́! *whoa!*
га	*ге*	*ги*	*гі*	*го*	*гу*	*аг*	*ег*	*иг*	*іг*	*ог*	*уг*	*ого́!*
/ha/	/he/	/hy/	/hi/	/ho/	/hu/	/ah/	/eh/	/yh/	/ih/	/oh/	/uh/	/oᵘhó/

ла	ле	ли	лі	ло	лу	лю	ля
ла	*ле*	*ли*	*лі*	*ло*	*лу*	*лю*	*ля*
/la/	/le/	/ly/	/li/	/lo/	/lu/	/l'u/	/l'a/

ал	ел	ил	іл	ол	ул	юл	ял	ліле́я *a lily*
ал	*ел*	*ил*	*іл*	*ол*	*ул*	*юл*	*ял*	*ліле́я*
/al/	/el/	/yl/	/il/	/ol/	/ul/	/jul/	/jal/	/l'iléja/

∩ **2.2.** Repeat after the speaker. Copy these words in cursive and mark stresses.

а́вто /áwto/ *a car* — *а́вто*
голова́ /hoᵘloᵘvá/ *a head* — *голова́*
валіза /valíza/ *a suitcase* — *валіза*
го́луб /hólub/ *a pigeon* — *го́луб*
вода́ /voᵘdá/ *water* — *вода́*
вино́ /vyᵉnó/ *wine* — *вино́*
вони́ /voᵘný/ *they* — *вони́*
Гали́на /halýna/ *Halyna* — *Гали́на*
нога́ /noᵘhá/ *a leg* or *foot* — *нога́*
газе́та /hazéta/ *a newspaper* — *газе́та*
літа́к /liták/ *an airplane* — *літа́к*
мо́ва /móva/ *a language* — *мо́ва*
люди́на /l'udýna/ *a person* — *люди́на*

Гали́на *Halyna*

∩ **2.3.** Listen and repeat after the speaker. Copy these letter combinations in cursive.

ра	ре	ри	рі	ро	ру	рю	ря
ра	*ре*	*ри*	*рі*	*ро*	*ру*	*рю*	*ря*
/ra/	/re/	/ry/	/ri/	/ro/	/ru/	/r'u/	/r'a/

ар	ер	ир	ір	ор	ур	юр	яр	брат *a brother*
ар	*ер*	*ир*	*ір*	*ор*	*ур*	*юр*	*яр*	*брат*
/ar/	/er/	/yr/	/ir/	/or/	/ur/	/jur/	/jar/	/brat/

ха	хе	хи	хі	хо	ху	ах
ха	*хе*	*хи*	*хі*	*хо*	*ху*	*ах*
/kha/	/khe/	/khy/	/khi/	/kho/	/khu/	/akh/

ех	их	іх	ох	ух	юх	ях	хто *who*
ех	*их*	*іх*	*ох*	*ух*	*юх*	*ях*	*хто*
/ekh/	/ykh/	/ikh/	/okh/	/ukh/	/jukh/	/jakh/	/khto/

ша	ше	ши	ші	шо	шу	аш
ша	*ше*	*ши*	*ші*	*шо*	*шу*	*аш*
/sha/	/she/	/shy/	/shi/	/sho/	/shu/	/ash/

еш	иш	іш	ош	уш	юш	яш	рушни́к *a towel*
еш	*иш*	*іш*	*ош*	*уш*	*юш*	*яш*	*рушни́к*
/esh/	/ysh/	/ish/	/osh/	/ush/	/jush/	/jash/	/rushnýk/

∩ **2.4.** Repeat after the speaker. Copy these words in cursive and mark the stresses.

шко́ла /shkóla/ *a school* — *шко́ла*
Хома́ /khoᵘmá/ *Thomas* — *Хома́*
хто /khto/ *who* — *хто*
рушни́к /rushnýk/ *a towel* — *рушни́к*

✎ **Note 2.2. Letter И, и vs Ш, ш**

To avoid mixing up the letters *и* **и** for /y/ and *ш* **ш** for /sh/ when they follow one another in handwritten text, the letter *ш* is often underlined *ш̲*;

~ши~ *ши̲* as in маши́на *маши̲на* /mashýna/ *a machine*, ши́нка *ши̲нка* /shýnka/ *ham* and
~иш~ *иш̲* as in ти́ша *ти̲ша* /týsha/ *silence*, лише́ *лише̲* /lyshé/ *only*

метро́ metro

ха́та	/kháta/	a home	ха́та
крамни́ця	/kramnýts'a/	a store	крамни́ця
метро́	/meᵘtró/	subway	метро́
ву́хо	/vúkho/	an ear	ву́хо
рука́	/ruká/	an arm or hand	рука́
моро́зиво	/moᵘrózyᵉvo/	ice cream	моро́зиво
хліб	/khlib/	bread	хліб
шва́гер	/shváher/	a brother-in-law	шва́гер
гора́	/hoᵘrá/	a mountain	гора́

🎧 **2.5.** Listen and repeat after the speaker. Copy these letter combinations in cursive.

де	зє	лє	нє	тє	цє	єв	єг
де	зє	лє	нє	тє	цє	єв	єг
/d'e/	/z'e/	/l'e/	/n'e/	/t'e/	/ts'e/	/jew/	/jeh/

єд	єз	єк	єн	єр	є́вро a euro
єд	єз	єк	єн	єр	є́вро
/jed/	/jez/	/jek/	/jen/	/jer/	/jéwroᵘ/

дає́	має́	діє́	зяє́	лає́	ниє́	тєе́	рoє́
дає́	має́	діє́	зяє́	лає́	ниє́	тєе́	рoє́
/dajé/	/majé/	/díje/	/z'áje/	/láje/	/nýje/	/téje/	/róje/

буяє́	цеє́	крає́	цює́	моє́	твоє́	єно́т a raccoon
буяє́	цеє́	крає́	цює́	моє́	твоє́	єно́т
/bujáje/	/tséje/	/kráje/	/ts'úje/	/moᵘjé/	/tvoᵘjé/	/jeᵘnót/

✏️ **Note 2.3. Letter Є, є**

Є, є can be pronounced as /e/ and /je/.
1. It is pronounced as /e/ only after consonants. The consonant followed by the є is always soft,
да́вне /dáwn'e/ *ancient*, **тре́тє** /trét'e/ *third*, **горі́шнє** /hoᵘríshn'e/ *upper.*

2. It is pronounced /je/ as in *yet* at the beginning of a word or after a vowel,
єно́т /jeᵘnót/ *a raccoon*, **Євге́н** /jeᵘwhén/ *Eugene*, **є́вро** /jéwroᵘ/ *a euro*, **зна́є** /znáje/ *he knows.*

🎧 **2.6.** Listen and repeat after the speaker. Copy these letter combinations in cursive.

мої́	гаї́	твої́	неї́	рої́	хвої́	тіє́ї
мої́	гаї́	твої́	неї́	рої́	хвої́	тіє́ї
/moᵘjí/	/hají/	/tvoᵘjí/	/néji/	/roᵘjí/	/khvóji/	/tijéji/

цiє́ї	їв	ї́хав	їг	їз	їк	їм	водії́ drivers
цiє́ї	їв	ї́хав	їг	їз	їк	їм	водії́
/ts'ijéji/	/jiw/	/jíkhaw/	/jih/	/jiz/	/jik/	/jim/	/voᵘdijí/

Note 2.4. Letter Ї, ї

The letter Ї, ї is pronounced /ji/ as in *yield*. It appears only at the beginning of a word or after a vowel,

ї́хні /jíkhn'i/ *their*
ї́хати /jíkhatyᵉ/ *to drive*
Ї́вга /jíwha/ *Eugenia*
лі́нії /l'ín'iji/ *lines*
музе́ї /muzéji/ *museums*

The letter Ї, ї can never follow a consonant. In the rare cases it does, there is always an apostrophe inserted in between. The consonant it follows is always a part of the prefix,
з'ї́зд /zjizd/ *a congress*

🎧 **2.7.** Engage in a Q-and-A exchange. Use the pictures. Practice sentences both with and without the є.

Model. 🇶 ↘Хто це? /khto tse/ *Who is this?* (та́то *dad*) or
Хто це ↘є? /khto tse je/ *Who is this?*
🇦 Це ↘та́то. /tse táto ᵘ/ *This is dad.* or
Це є ↘та́то. /tse je táto ᵘ/ *This is dad.*

ма́ма   *єно́т*   *люди́на*

Тимко́   *ті́тка Ната́лка*   *лев*

⌒ 2.8. Ask where somebody or something is. Answer replacing the noun with the corresponding personal pronoun.

Model. люди́на *a person*, тут *here*
  Q Де ↘ люди́на? /de l'udýna/ *Where is the person?*
  A Вона́ ↘ тут. /voᵘná tut/ *She is here.*

1. музе́й *a museum*, там *there*
2. валі́за *a suitcase*, тут *here*
3. ті́тка *an aunt*, до́ма *at home*
4. а́вто *a car*, там *there*
5. буди́нок *a building*, тут *here*
6. шко́ла *a school*, там *there*
7. вікно́ *a window*, тут *here*
8. банкома́т *an ATM*, там *there*
9. ціна́ *a price*, тут *here*
10. метро́ *a subway (station)*, там *there*
11. хлі́б *bread*, тут *here*
12. вино́ *wine*, там *there*

⌒ 2.9. Engage in a short Q-and-A exchange. Replace the nouns with the 3ʳᵈ person pronouns of corresponding gender. Use the same gender indicators as in the previous exercise.

Model. люди́на **Q** Це ↗ люди́на? /tse l'udýna/ *Is it a person?*
  A Ні, це не ↘вона́. /ni tse neʸ voᵘná/ *No, it's not her.*

1. літа́к *an airplane*
2. єно́т *a raccoon*
3. рушни́к *a towel*
4. вода́ *water*

✎ Note 2.5. To be or not to be?

The Ukrainian for *to be* is **бу́ти**. In the present tense, it has only one form **є** which corresponds to the English *am, is,* and *are,*

  Ма́ти є до́ма. *Mother is home.*
  Ма́ти та ті́тка То́ма є до́ма. *Mother and Aunt Toma are at home.*
  Я є тут. *I am here.*

In everyday speech, the verb *to be* in the present tense is completely omitted,

  Дід до́ма. *The granddad is home.*
  Ціна́ тут. *The price is here.*
  Молоко́ тут. *The milk is here.*
  Дити́на там. *The child is there.*

✎ Note 2.6. Personal pronouns

Ukrainian personal pronouns are:
я /ja/ *I*, **ти** /ty/ *you*, **він** /vin/ *he*, **вона́** /voᵘná/ *she*, **воно́** /voᵘnó/ *it*, **ми** /my/ *we*, **ви** /vy/ *you*, **вони́** /voᵘný/ *they*.

Unlike English, Ukrainian has two 2ⁿᵈ person pronouns, the singular **ти** and the plural **ви**. Both are translated as *you*. To address a person in a familiar manner the singular form **ти** *you* is used, while the plural **ви** *you* serves for a formal address.
The three 3ʳᵈ person singular pronouns correlate with three genders,

  m. **він** *he* with masculine
  f. **вона́** *she* with feminine
  nt. **воно́** *it* with neuter

All Ukrainian nouns, whether names of living beings or of inanimate things, have a gender. Depending on its gender a noun can be replaced by a respective 3ʳᵈ person pronoun,

  Де (*m.*) **банк?** *Where is the bank?*
  Він тут. *It's here.*
  Де (*f.*) **ка́ва?** *Where is the coffee?*
  Вона́ там. *It's there.*
  Де (*nt.*) **а́вто?** *Where is the car?*
  Воно́ там. *It's there.*

Note 2.7. Gender indicators of nouns

Nouns ending in the vowels **~a** (**~я**) are mostly feminine,

ціна́ *a price,* **ба́нка** *a jar,* **та́ця** *a tray,* **ди́ня** *a melon.*

Nouns ending in a consonant are mostly masculine,

язи́к *a tongue,* **буди́нок** *a building,* **музе́й** *a museum,* **день** *a day,* **готе́ль** *a hotel*

Nouns ending in the vowels **~o** or **~e** are mostly neuter,

є́вро *a euro,* **вино́** *wine,* **вікно́** *a window,* **мо́ре** *a sea,* **го́ре** *misfortune.*

Це Ївга?

Note 2.8. Soft sign ь: Letter without sound

The soft sign **ь** is the only letter in the alphabet that represents no sound of its own. Its sole function is to indicate that the preceding consonant is soft. Its transcription symbol is …',

день /den'/ *a day,* **ні́готь** /n'íhoᵘt'/ *a finger (toe) nail,* **корабе́ль** /koᵘrabel'/ *a ship.*

In this function, it is similar to such softening vowels as **я, є, ю,** and **i.** The soft sign never follows a vowel or occurs at the beginning of a word. It never follows the consonants that cannot be soft, namely: **б, в, м, к, г, х, ш,** and some others.

5. о́ко *an eye*
6. газе́та *a newspaper*
7. Ївга *Eugenia*
8. метро́ *a subway*
9. знайо́мий *an acquaintance*
10. Євге́н *Eugene*
11. Гали́на *Halyna*
12. моро́зиво *an ice cream*
13. Я́ків *Jacob*
14. лі́кар *a doctor*
15. молоко́ *milk*
16. гора́ *a mountain*

🎧 **2.10.** Listen and repeat after the speaker. Copy these letter combinations in cursive.

бадь	**бузь**	**заль**	**гать**	**таць**	**кінь**	**лінь**
бадь	*бузь*	*заль*	*гать*	*таць*	*кінь*	*лінь*
/bad'/	/buz'/	/zal'/	/hat'/	/tats'/	/kin'/	/l'in'/

лізь	**миль**	**раць**	**мідь**	**хвать**	**мить**	**день** *a day*
лізь	*миль*	*раць*	*мідь*	*хвать*	*мить*	*день*
/l'iz'/	/myl'/	/rats'/	/mid'/	/khvat'/	/myt'/	/den'/

🎧 **2.11.** Repeat after the speaker. Copy these words in cursive and mark the stresses.

біль /bil'/ *a pain*	*біль*
день /den'/ *a day*	*день*
корабе́ль /koᵘrabel'/ *a ship*	*корабель*
кві́тень /kvíten'/ *April*	*квітень*
тра́вень /tráven'/ *May*	*травень*
кана́дець /kanádeᵘts'/ *a Canadian*	*канадець*
гро́ші /hróshi/ *money*	*гроші*
добри́день /doᵘbrýdeᵘn'/ *hello*	*добридень*
італі́єць /ital'íjets'/ *an Italian*	*італієць*
готе́ль /hoᵘtel'/ *a hotel*	*готель*
гамане́ць /hamanéts'/ *a wallet*	*гаманець*
дя́дько /d'ád'koᵘ/ *uncle*	*дядько*
Ївга /jíwha/ *Eugenia*	*Ївга*

🎧 **2.12.** Pair each printed word with its equivalent written in cursive. Copy all the words in cursive.

готе́ль /hoᵘtel'/ *a hotel*	___	1. *людина*
ні́готь /níhoᵘt'/ *a finger (toe) nail*	___	2. *Ївга*
газе́та /hazéta/ *a newspaper*	___	3. *добридень*
єно́т /jeᵘnót/ *a raccoon*	___	4. *хліб*
літа́к /l'iták/ *an airplane*	___	5. *готель*
добри́день /doᵘbrýdeᵘn'/ *hello*	___	6. *газета*

Ї́вга /jíwha/ *Eugenia*   ___   7. *літа́к*
дя́дько /d'ád'ko*ᵘ*/ *uncle*   ___   8. *шко́ла*
шко́ла /shkóla/ *a school*   ___   9. *дя́дько*
є́вро /jéwro*ᵘ*/ *a euro*   ___ 10. *валі́за*
вино́ /vy*ᵉ*nó/ *wine*   ___ 11. *музе́й*
хліб /khl'ib/ *bread*   ___ 12. *ні́готь*
музе́й /muzéj/ *a museum*   ___ 13. *вино́*
валі́за /val'íza/ *a suitcase*   ___ 14. *єно́т*
люди́на /l'udýna/ *a person*   ___ 15. *є́вро*

 2.13. Identify the words that have soft consonants. Circle each such soft consonant. Explain why it is soft. Mind the consonants that are incapable of being soft. Refer to Notes 2.8 and 2.9

валі́за	Євге́н	люди́на	газе́та	ні́готь
добри́день	готе́ль	ка́ва	ву́хо	Тимі́ш
кві́тень	вікно́	гамане́ць	гора́	є́вро
лі́кар	італі́єць	Хома́	го́луб	тра́вень
гро́ші	хліб	єно́т	дя́дько	ля́лька

 2.14 Listen carefully and mark the words you hear.

1. а́вто ✓   Я́ків   вино́ ✓   о́ко ✓   ні́готь ✓
   є́вро ✓   готе́ль ✓   ка́ва   ха́та ✓   шко́ла ✓

2. єно́т ✓   моро́зиво   брат   біль ✓   кана́дець ✓
   гро́ші ✓   Хома́ ✓   Я́на ✓   літа́к ✓   Євге́н ✓

3. музе́й   Ї́вга ✓   тра́вень   вино́ ✓   корабе́ль ✓
   ву́хо ✓   го́луб   люди́на ✓   Гали́на ✓   гамане́ць ✓

2.15. Determine the gender of these nouns. Cross out in each row the noun that does not belong there by gender.

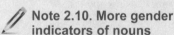

1. ~~ба́тько~~   а́вто   вікно́ *window*   є́вро   о́ко   ву́хо *ear*   молоко́ *milk*   , neutral?
2. люди́на   ті́тка   нога́   ха́та *none*   Ї́вга   ~~Мико́ла~~   гора́
3. ~~Гали́на~~   вода́   ка́ва   голова́   Ві́тя   газе́та   те́ма
4. ~~ціна́~~   музе́й   ~~дя́дько~~   єно́т   брат   корабе́ль   лі́кар
5. готе́ль   ні́готь   Я́ків   літа́к   ~~валі́за~~   гамане́ць   банкома́т

 2.16. Say who these things belong to. Use the respective gender form of the possessive pronoun *my* **мій, моя́, моє́.**

Model. *m.* ба́тько *a father*
Q Це ба́тько? *Is this a father?*
A Так, це мій ба́тько. Він мій. *Yes, this is my father. He is mine.*
   f. ма́ти *a mother*
Q Це ма́ти? *Is this a mother?*
A Так, це моя́ ма́ти. Вона́ моя́. *Yes, this is my mother. She is mine.*

Note 2.9. Softening letters

To determine whether or not a consonant is soft one needs to look at the letter following it. Consonants followed by the letters **я, є, ю,** and **ь** are soft. Consonants followed by the letter **і** are also soft, but not always.

The consonants **б, в, м, г, к, х, ш** are never soft, even if followed by **є, ю,** or **я.** They are never followed by **ь.**

Note 2.10. More gender indicators of nouns

Nouns ending in **~а, ~я,** and **~о,** which refer to men are of masculine gender:
   та́то *a dad*
   ба́тько *a father*
   ді́до *a grandad*
   дя́дько *an uncle*

proper names of men:
   Мико́ла /my*ᵉ*кóla/ *Mykola (Nicholas)*
   Хома́ /kho*ᵘ*má/ *Thomas*
   Оле́кса /o*ᵘ*léksa/ *Alexis*
   Ві́тя /vít'a/ *Vitia (Victor)*
   Мишко́ /my*ᵉ*shkó/ *Mike*
   Дмитро́ /dmy*ᵉ*tró/ *Dmytro*
   Ро́мко /rómko*ᵘ*/ *Roman*
   Юрко́ /jurkó/ *Yurko (George)*

Note that the noun **люди́на** /l'udýna/ *a human being* is of the feminine gender,
   Іва́н – це на́ша люди́на. *Ivan is our kind of man.*

Note 2.11. Possessive pronouns

The Ukrainian equivalents of the English pronoun *my (mine)* are
мій /mij/ for masculine nouns
моя́ /moʰjá/ of feminine nouns, and
моє́ /moʰjé/ of neuter nouns,

m. **мій ба́тько** *my father*
f. **моя́ ма́ти** *my mother*
nt. **моє́ а́вто** *my car*

Note 2.12. Possessive pronouns for singular *your(s)*

The Ukrainian equivalents of the English pronouns *your* and *yours* pertaining to the informal 2nd person singular are:

твій /tvij/ for masculine nouns
твоя́ /tvoʰjá/ for feminine nouns
твоє́ /tvoʰjé/ for neuter nouns,

m. **твій ба́тько** *your father*
f. **твоя́ ма́ти** *your mother*
nt. **твоє́ а́вто** *your car*

твоє́ вікно́

---

nt. а́вто *a car*
Q Це а́вто? *Is this a car?*
A Так, це моє́ а́вто. Воно́ моє́. *Yes, this is my car. It is mine.*

1. ка́ва *coffee*
2. вікно́ *a window*
3. дя́дько *an uncle*
4. буди́нок *a building*
5. цуценя́ *a puppy*
6. ті́тка *an aunt*
7. брат *a brother*
8. ха́та *a house*
9. люди́на *a person, man*
10. шко́ла *a school*
11. валі́за *a suitcase*
12. гамане́ць *a wallet*
13. вино́ *wine*

2.17. Unscramble these words. Mark the stresses.

1. тельог _____
2. кваа _____
3. талік _____
4. нотігь _____
5. рогіш _____
6. надкаець _____
7. тазгае _____
8. орльабек _____
9. ікнов _____
10. шлока _____
11. одав _____
12. ліавза _____

∩ 2.18. Ask whether or not something belongs to your partner. Use the respective gender form of the possessive pronoun *your (yours)* **твій, твоя́, твоє́.**

Model. *m.* кіт *a cat*
Q Тут ↘ кіт. /tut kit/ Він ↗твій? /vin tvij/
There is a cat here. Is it yours?
A ↘ Ні, він зо́всім не ↘ мій. /ni vin zówsim ne mij/
No, it's not mine at all.

1. рушни́к /rushnýk/ *a towel*
2. хліб /khlib/ *bread*
3. кни́га /knýha/ *a book*
4. моро́зиво /moʰrózyᵉvo/ *ice cream*
5. вода́ /voʰdá/ *water*
6. гри́вня /hrývn'a/ *a hryvnia*
7. тютю́н /t'ut'ún/ *tobacco*
8. вино́ /vyᵉnó/ *wine*

9. дити́на /dyᵉtýna/ *a child*
10. бана́н /banán/ *a banana*
11. ди́ня /dýn'a/ *a melon*
12. котеня́ /koᵘteᵞn'á/ *a kitten*
13. ба́нка /bánka/ *a jar*
14. квито́к /kvyᵉtók/ *a ticket*
15. лі́кар /l'íkar/ *a doctor*

∩ **2.19.** Say whose things these are. Choose the appropriate possessive pronoun. Follow the model.

Model. Він *he*, ба́тько *a father*
  Q Хто це? *Who is it?*
  A Це його́ ба́тько. *This is his father.*

1. Я *I*, брат *a brother*
2. Вона́ *she*, знайо́мий *an acquaintance*
3. Ти *you*, є́вро *a euro*
4. Він *he*, цуценя́ *a puppy*
5. Я *I*, шко́ла *a school*
6. Гали́на *Halyna*, вікно́ *a window*
7. Ї́вга *Eugenia*, ха́та *a house*
8. Я́ків *Jacob*, друг *a friend*
9. Мико́ла *Nicholas*, ма́ти *a mother*
10. Ти *you*, моро́зиво *ice cream*
11. Вона́ *she*, обі́д *lunch*
12. Я *I*, я́блуко *an apple*
13. Хома́ *Thomas*, дя́дько *an uncle*
14. Євге́н *Eugene*, кімна́та *a room*

∩ **2.20.** Dictation. Listen carefully and fill in the blanks with what you hear. Mark stresses.

1. Д_ є канаде__?
2. Ві_, я і бра_ Дмитр_ дом_.
3. Ту_ є тіт__ Їв__ та дядь_ Хом_.
4. Ц_ бра_ Тимі_?
5. Н_, ц_ не ві_, це дядь__ Мико__.
6. Та_ є ма__, бать__ і ді__.
7. Хт_ це та_ є?
8. Ц_ люди__, а та_ кі_ і єно_.

∩ **2.21.** Fill in the blanks with the missing letters. Pronounce and write down the words in cursive. Mark the stresses.

_аліза, голо_а, л_дина, _алина, ру_ник, т_то, _азета, к_амниця, _ома, мо_озиво, _нот, _ука, М_кола, доб_идень, італі_ць, гаманец_, є_ро, му_ей, _ата, гро_і, квітен_, канадец_, ліка_, Єв_ен, Ї_га, а_то

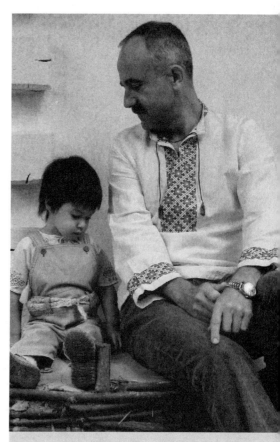

ба́тько та його́ до́нька

✏ **Note 2.13. Possessive pronouns його́** *his* **and її** *her(s)*

The Ukrainian equivalent of the English pronoun *his* is **його́** /joᵘhó/ for all genders,
  m. **його́ ба́тько** *his father*
  f. **його́ ма́ти** *his mother*
  nt. **його́ а́вто** *his car*

The Ukrainian possessive pronoun **її** /jiji/ is the equivalent of the English *her (hers)* for all genders,
  m. **її банк** *her bank*
  f. **її ву́лиця** *her street*
  nt. **її а́вто** *her car*

на́ша коле́га О́льга та її
автомобі́ль

Note 2.14. Possessive pronouns for *our(s)*

The Ukrainian equivalents of the English pronouns *our* or *ours* are:

наш /nash/ for masculine nouns
на́ша /násha/ for feminine nouns
на́ше /náshe/ for neuter nouns:

    m. **наш рушни́к** *our towel*
    f. **на́ша шко́ла** *our school*
    nt. **на́ше вино́** *our wine*

2.22. Complete the crossword puzzle.

Across
1. He
4. Bread
5. Ship
8. Racoon
10. Aunt
14. April
15. Eye
16. Leg

Down
1. Ear
2. Foot
3. Pain
6. Father
7. Airplane
9. Fingernail
11. Kitten
12. Book

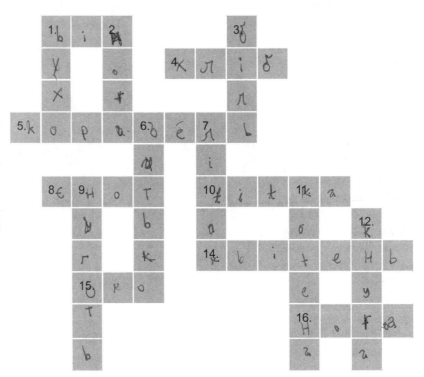

2.23. Combine the right gender form of the possessive pronoun *наш* with each of these nouns.

Model. шко́ла *a school*
    Q Де на́ша шко́ла? /de násha shkóla/ *Where's our school?*
    A Вона́ тут. /voᵘná tut/ *It is here.*

1. ба́тько
2. а́вто
3. ті́тка
4. кіт
5. мета́
6. та́то
7. ба́ба

8. буди́нок
9. вікно́
10. знайо́мий
11. обі́д
12. дити́на
13. ба́нка
14. дід

2.24. Ask whether or not something belongs to your partner. Use the respective gender form of the possessive pronouns ваш, ваша, ваше́ *pl. your(s)*.

Model. *m.* олівець *a pencil*
> **Q** Тут ↘олівець. /tut ol'ivéts'/ Він ↗ваш? /vin vash/
> *There is a pencil here. Is it yours?*
> **A** ↘Ні, він зо́всім не ↘наш. /ni vin zówsim ne nash/
> *No, it's not ours at all.*

1. цуценя́
2. хліб
3. ди́ня
4. кни́га
5. моро́зиво
6. музе́й
7. гри́вня

8. а́вто
9. валі́за
10. літа́к
11. котеня́
12. ба́нка
13. газе́та
14. молоко́

2.25. Ask where something that belongs to them is. Use the required form of the possessive pronoun for *their(s)* and a personal pronoun instead of the noun.

Model. *m.* ми́ло *soap*
> **Q** Де їхнє ↘ми́ло? /de jíkhn'e mýloᵘ/ *Where is their soap?*
> **A** Воно́ он ↘там. /voᵘnó oᵘn tam/ *It's over there.*

1. зо́шит *a notebook*
2. вода́
3. музе́й
4. кни́га
5. лі́кар
6. а́вто
7. гамане́ць

8. дя́дько
9. квито́к
10. котеня́
11. кімна́та *a room*
12. банк
13. ка́ва
14. вікно́

2.26. Cross out the nouns that do not agree in gender with the possessive pronoun in each of the groups.

1. мій — ба́тько, брат, тютю́н, Хома́, ~~Гали́на~~, Я́ків
2. моя́ — ~~ву́хо~~, ті́тка, рука́, шко́ла, люди́на, Івга́
3. твоє́ — а́вто, вікно́, вино́, цуценя́, ~~кни́га~~, котеня́
4. наш — буди́нок, ~~ка́ва~~, о́цет, Євге́н, музе́й, літа́к
5. ва́ша — валі́за, ~~хліб~~, ціна́, голова́, мо́ва, ліле́я
6. їхнє — ~~дя́дько~~, є́вро, моро́зиво, вікно́, цуценя́

2.27. Say that something or somebody is here. Follow the model and match personal and possessive pronouns. Make sure to use the correct gender form of possessive pronouns.

Model. **C** Це він, а то кни́га. *This is him, and that is a book.*
> **A** Це його́ кни́га. *This is his book.*

Це моє́ моро́зиво.

1. Це я, а то олівце́ць.
2. Це він, а то мо́ва.
3. Це ми, а то шко́ла.
4. Це я, а то ма́ти.
5. Це вони́, а то гамане́ць.
6. Це ти, а то ка́ва.
7. Це ми, а то кіт.
8. Це вони́, а то газе́та.
9. Це вона́, а то хло́пець. *a boyfriend*
10. Це я, а то я́блуко.
11. Це ти, а то зо́шит.
12. Це ми, а то о́зеро. *a lake*
13. Це він, а то ті́тка.
14. Це ви, а то кімна́та.
15. Це вони́, а то дитя́.
16. Це ви, а то літа́к.

Note 2.17. The selective softener ~i.

In actual speech, certain consonants, that are capable of being both hard and soft, are often pronounced hard before the ~i. This is especially true of the consonants д, т, з, с, л, н, and ц,

ді́вчина *a girl*, ті́тка *an aunt*, зір *vision*, сіль *salt*, полі́т *flight*, ніс *a nose*.

Such hard pronunciation before the ~i is entirely within the Ukrainian literary standard.

Завда́ння для Міжнаро́дної мере́жі
Internet assignment

2.28. Visit the website Dictionaries of Ukraine *Словники України*, url: **http://lcorp.ulif.org.ua/dictua/**
a) Type into its search window on the left, marked by the word **пошук** *search*, each of the words below, verify the stress by the website (see center of page) and mark it. Click on the button пошук to do the search.

Ukrainian	English	Ukrainian	English
дороговказ		кохання	
магазин		машина	
переходити		бородатий	
квітка		контактувати	
кватирка		холодно	
кінокартина		березень	
допомога		запалювати	

b) Find a Ukrainian translation tool on the Internet and determine the meaning of each word above.

Лéкція | Lesson 3

In this chapter you will learn:

The remaining seven letters of the Ukrainian alphabet
To inquire about qualities of an object and give its simple description
To count to ten, to add and subtract
To introduce yourself and ask about somebody else's name and family name

Note 3.1. Consonant ґ /g/

The consonant **ґ** /g/ is mostly limited to sound-imitating words:

ґедзь /gedz'/ *a gadfly*

and unassimilated foreign borrowings:

ґрунт /grunt/ *soil*

йоґу́рт /jógurt/ *yogurt*

In assimilated foreign words **ґ** is eventually replaced by **г**:

газе́та /hazéta/ *a newspaper* instead of **ґазе́та** /gazéta/,

генера́ція /heⁿneⁿráts'ija/ *a generation* instead of **ґенера́ція** /geⁿneⁿráts'ija/

Украї́нські лі́тери. Гру́па 4. | Ukrainian Letters. Group 4.

Consonants			
Printed	*Cursive*	Pronounced	Phonetic
Ґ, ґ	*Ґ, ґ*	/g/ in **g**et	/g/, always hard
Ж, ж	*Ж, ж*	/zh/ in mea**s**ure	/zh/, always hard; soft only when lengthened /zh'zh'/
П, п	*П, п*	/p/ in **sp**ade	/p/, always hard
С, с	*С, с*	/s/ in gra**ss**	/s/ or /s'/
Ф, ф	*Ф, ф*	/f/ in **f**ix	/f/, always hard
Ч, ч	*Ч, ч*	/ch/ in **ch**ess	/ch/, always hard; soft only when lengthened /ch'ch'/
Щ, щ	*Щ, щ*	/shch/ in fre**sh ch**eese	/shch/, always hard

 Впра́ви Exercises

Note 3.2. Pronunciation of П, п /p/

Ukrainian consonant **П, п** /p/ in contrast to its English counterpart is pronounced without an aspiration.

3.1. Listen and repeat after the speaker. Copy these letter combinations in cursive.

ґа	ґе	ґи	ґі	ґо	ґу	аґ	еґ
ґа	*ґе*	*ґи*	*ґі*	*ґо*	*ґу*	*аґ*	*еґ*
/ga/	/ge/	/gy/	/gi/	/go/	/gu/	/ag/	/eg/

иґ	іґ	оґ	уґ	юґ	яґ	ґа́нок *a doorstep*
иґ	*іґ*	*оґ*	*уґ*	*юґ*	*яґ*	*ґа́нок*
/yg/	/ig/	/og/	/ug/	/jug/	/jag/	/gáno^{u}k/

жа	же	жи	жі	жо	жу	аж
жа	*же*	*жи*	*жі*	*жо*	*жу*	*аж*
/zha/	/zhe/	/zhy/	/zhi/	/zho/	/zhu/	/azh/

еж	иж	іж	ож	уж	яж	жі́нка *a woman, wife*
еж	*иж*	*іж*	*ож*	*уж*	*яж*	*жі́нка*
/ezh/	/yzh/	/izh/	/ozh/	/uzh/	/jazh/	/zhínka/

па	пе	пи	пі	по	пу	ап	еп
па	*пе*	*пи*	*пі*	*по*	*пу*	*ап*	*еп*
/pa/	/pe/	/py/	/pi/	/po/	/pu/	/ap/	/ep/

ип	іп	оп	уп	юп	яп	папі́р *paper*
ип	*іп*	*оп*	*уп*	*юп*	*яп*	*папі́р*
/yp/	/ip/	/op/	/up/	/jup/	/jap/	/papír/

фа	фе	фи	фі	фо	фу	аф	еф
фа	*фе*	*фи*	*фі*	*фо*	*фу*	*аф*	*еф*
/fa/	/fe/	/fy/	/fi/	/fo/	/fu/	/af/	/ef/

Це — *жі́нка*. This is a woman.

иф	іф	їф	оф	уф	юф	яф	**фах** *a profession*
иф	*іф*	*їф*	*оф*	*уф*	*юф*	*яф*	*фах*
/yf/	/if/	/jif/	/of/	/uf/	/juf/	/jaf/	/fakh/

3.2. Repeat after the speaker. Copy these words in cursive and mark the stresses.

ґу́дзик /gúdzyᵉk/ *a button*   *ґу́дзик*
па́лець /páleᵘts'/ *a finger, toe*   *па́лець*
фа́рба /fárba/ *paint*   *фа́рба*
пан /pan/ *mister, gentleman*   *пан*
їжа /jízha/ *food*   *їжа*
па́спорт /pásport/ *a passport*   *па́спорт*
футбо́л /futból/ *football (soccer)*   *футбо́л*
план /plan/ *a plan*   *план*
журна́л /zhurnál/ *a magazine*   *журна́л*
фільм /fil'm/ *a film*   *фільм*
пі́вдень /píwdeᵘn'/ *the south, midday*   *пі́вдень*
телефо́н /teᵘleᵘfón/ *a telephone*   *телефо́н*
ти́ждень /týzhdeᵘn'/ *a week*   *ти́ждень*

3.3. Listen and repeat after the speaker. Copy these letter combinations in cursive.

са	се	сє	си	сі	со	су	сю	ся	ас
са	*се*	*сє*	*си*	*сі*	*со*	*су*	*сю*	*ся*	*ас*
/sa/	/se/	/s'e/	/sy/	/s'i/	/so/	/su/	/s'u/	/s'a/	/as/

ес	ис	іс	ос	ус	юс	яс	**сусі́д** *a neighbor*
ес	*ис*	*іс*	*ос*	*ус*	*юс*	*яс*	*сусі́д*
/es/	/ys/	/is/	/os/	/us/	/jus/	/jas/	/sus'íd/

ча	че	чи	чі	чо	чу	ач	еч	ич
ча	*че*	*чи*	*чі*	*чо*	*чу*	*ач*	*еч*	*ич*
/cha/	/che/	/chy/	/chi/	/cho/	/chu/	/ach/	/ech/	/ych/

іч	оч	уч	юч	яч	**чолові́к** *a man, husband*
іч	*оч*	*уч*	*юч*	*яч*	*чолові́к*
/ich/	/och/	/uch/	/juch/	/jach/	/choᵘloᵘvík/

ща	ще	щи	щі	що	щу
ща	*ще*	*щи*	*щі*	*що*	*щу*
/shcha/	/shche/	/shchy/	/shchi/	/shcho/	/shchu/

ащ	ещ	єщ	ищ	іщ	їщ	**що** *what*
ащ	*ещ*	*єщ*	*ищ*	*іщ*	*їщ*	*що*
/ashch/	/eshch/	/jeshch/	/yshch/	/ishch/	/jishch/	/shcho/

ощ	ущ	ющ	ящ	**щока́** *a cheek*
ощ	*ущ*	*ющ*	*ящ*	*щока́*
/oshch/	/ushch/	/jushch/	/jashch/	/shchoᵘká/

 Це – чоловік. *This is a man.*

Note 3.3. Pronunciation of Щ, щ /shch/

This consonant is a unity of two sounds: /sh/ as in *shut* and /ch/ as in *chess*, pronounced together as one consonant. To practice щ /shch/, pronounce the combinations *push chairs*, *Irish child*, or *fish chowder* as one word. Make sure that you fully articulate the second component of this consonant as /ch/ and not /t/.

Note 3.4. Lengthened consonants

A beautiful feature of the Ukrainian sound system is consonant lengthening. It occurs when a consonant doubles in the position between two vowels, the second vowel often being я or ю. Lengthened consonants before these vowels are therefore always soft. Lengthening commonly occurs at the end of a word,

пита́ння /pyᵉtán'n'a/ *a question*
зі́лля /z'íl'l'a/ *weeds*
збі́жжя /zbizh'zh'a/ *grain*

It can also occur in other positions,
щоде́нник /shchoᵘdénnyᵉk/ *a diary*
сса́ти /ssátyᵉ/ *to suck*
відда́ти /viddátyᵉ/ *to give away*

Consonant lengthening gives a special staccato quality to the flow of Ukrainian speech. Most importantly, it changes the meaning of what is said, cf.,
Ві́тя /vít'a/ *Victor*
ві́ття /vít't'a/ *branches*

Not all consonants are capable of lengthening. Lengthening most commonly affects н, т, л, ц, д, з, and с. The consonants г, ґ, й, к, м, п, р, ф, х, and щ do not get lengthened.

дозвілля leisure

3.4. Repeat after the speaker. Copy these words in cursive and mark the stresses.

сестра́ /seᵘstrá/ *a sister*	*сестра́*
борщ /borshch/ *borshch*	*борщ*
чо́вен /chóveᵘn/ *a boat*	*чо́вен*
стіл /s't'il/ *a table*	*стіл*
пі́сня /pís'n'a/ *a song*	*пі́сня*
ща́стя /shchás't'a/ *happiness*	*ща́стя*
ді́вчина /díwchyᵉna/ *a girl*	*ді́вчина*
те́ща /téshcha/ *a mother-in-law*	*те́ща*
стіле́ць /s't'iléts'/ *a chair*	*стіле́ць*
щі́тка /shchitka/ *a brush*	*щі́тка*
час /chas/ *time*	*час*
текст /tekst/ *a text*	*текст*
таксі́вка /taks'iwka/ *a taxi*	*таксі́вка*
чек /chek/ *a check*	*чек*
хло́пець /khlópeᵘts'/ *a boy*	*хло́пець*

3.5. Listen and repeat after the speaker. Practice the opposition of single and lengthened consonants. Copy these letter combinations in cursive.

та́ня	та́ння	га́ня	га́ння	ка́ня	ка́ння
та́ня	*та́ння*	*га́ня*	*га́ння*	*ка́ня*	*ка́ння*
/tán'a/	/tán'n'a/	/hán'a/	/hán'n'a/	/kán'a/	/kán'n'a/

да́ня	да́ння	за́ня	за́ння	пита́ння *a question*
да́ня	*да́ння*	*за́ня*	*за́ння*	*пита́ння*
/dán'a/	/dán'n'a/	/zán'a/	/zán'n'a/	/pyᵉtán'n'a/

литя́	лиття́	та́тя	та́ття
литя́	*лиття́*	*та́тя*	*та́ття*
/lyᵉt'a/	/lyᵉt't'a/	/tát'a/	/tát't'a/

га́тя	га́ття	ро́тя	ро́ття	життя́ *a life*
га́тя	*га́ття*	*ро́тя*	*ро́ття*	*життя́*
/hát'a/	/hát't'a/	/rót'a/	/rót't'a/	/zhyᵉt't'á/

кі́ля	кі́лля	рі́ля	рілля́	би́ля	би́лля
кі́ля	*кі́лля*	*рі́ля*	*рілля́*	*би́ля*	*би́лля*
/kíl'a/	/kíl'l'a/	/ril'á/	/ril'l'á/	/býl'a/	/býl'l'a/

зі́ля	зі́лля	ті́ля	ті́лля	дозві́лля *leisure*
зі́ля	*зі́лля*	*ті́ля*	*ті́лля*	*дозві́лля*
/z'íl'a/	/z'íl'l'a/	/tíl'a/	/tíl'l'a/	/doᵘzvíl'l'a/

ви́ся	ви́сся	ло́ся	ло́сся	є́ся	є́сся
ви́ся	*ви́сся*	*ло́ся*	*ло́сся*	*є́ся*	*є́сся*
/výs'a/	/výs's'a/	/lós'a/	/lós's'a/	/jés'a/	/jés's'a/

и́ся	**и́сся**	**ну́ся**	**ну́сся**	**воло́сся** *hair*
и́ся	*и́сся*	*ну́ся*	*ну́сся*	*воло́сся*
/ýs'a/	/ýs's'a/	/nus'a/	/nus's'a/	/voᵘlós's'a/

⌒ 3.6. Repeat after the speaker. Copy these words in cursive and mark the stresses.

пла́ття /plát't'a/ *a dress* — *пла́ття*
письме́нник /pyᵉs'ménnyᵉk/ *a writer* — *письме́нник*
дозві́лля /doᵘzvíl'l'a/ *leisure* — *дозві́лля*
Га́нна /hánna/ *Hannah* — *Га́нна*
сміття́ /smit't'a/ *trash* — *сміття́*
бажа́ння /bazhán'n'a/ *a will, desire* — *бажа́ння*
життя́ /zhyᵉt't'a/ *a life* — *життя́*
страхі́ття /strakhít't'a/ *horror* — *страхі́ття*
пита́ння /pyᵉtán'n'a/ *a question* — *пита́ння*
па́нна /pánna/ *miss, an unmarried woman* — *па́нна*
ві́дділ /víd'd'il/ *a department* — *ві́дділ*
взуття́ /wzut't'a/ *footware* — *взуття́*
пони́зззя /poᵘnýz'z'a/ *lower lands* — *пони́зззя*
годи́нник /hoᵘdýnnyᵉk/ *a watch, clock* — *годи́нник*

мала́ музи́ка a little musician

⌒ 3.7. Animate versus inanimate objects. Ask what each of the pictures represents. Use either **хто?** *who?* or **що?** *what?*

Model. **Q** Хто це? *Who is it?* **A** Я ду́маю, це Петро́.
/ja dúmaju tse peᵘtró/ *I think this is Peter.*
 Q Що це? *What is it?* **A** Я ду́маю, це фотогра́фія.
/ja dúmaju tse foᵘtoᵘhráfija/ *I think this is a photo.*

1. чай	2. щеня́	3. су́мка	4. журна́л
5. па́спорт	6. годи́нник	7. пла́ття	8. па́нна

| 9. таксі́вка | 10. Га́нна | 11. взуття́ | 12. щі́тка |

✎ Note 3.5. Interrogative word що?

The interrogative word **що?** /shcho/ *what?* is used in reference to inanimate objects in questions like **Що це?** *What is it?* **Що тут (є)?** *What is here?* **Що там (є)?** *What is there?* As reference to inanimate objects **що?** is opposed to **хто?** *who?* that refers to living beings. Note that in answers to such questions **що** is replaced by a noun,

Що це? - Це пла́ття. *It's a dress.*

Note 3.6. Gender indicators of nouns

Nouns ending in ~ння, ~ття, and ~лля are more often than not of neuter gender, and therefore correlate with the personal pronoun воно́ *it,*

Це ↗завда́ння? /tse zawdán'n'a/ *Is this the assignment?*

↘Так, це ↘воно́. /tak, tse voⁿnó/ *Yes, this is it.*

Це ↗пла́ття? /tse plát't'a/ *Is this the dress?*

   ↘Так, це ↘воно́. /tak, tse voⁿnó/ *Yes, this is it.*

Це ↗дозві́лля? /tse doⁿzvil'l'a/ *Is this leisure?*

   ↘Так, це ↘воно́. /tak, tse voⁿnó/ *Yes, this is it.*

Names of baby animals end in ~a or ~я and are of the neuter gender,

цуценя́ /tsutseⁿn'á/ *a puppy*

котеня́ /koⁿteⁿn'á/ *a kitten*

порося́ /poⁿroⁿs'á/ *a piglet*

щеня́ /shcheⁿn'á/ *a puppy*

курча́ /kurchá/ *a chicken*

теля́ /teⁿl'á/ *a calf*

3.8. Determine the grammatical gender of these nouns by their endings. Pronounce and write each of them in cursive. Refer to Notes 1.16, 2.10 and 3.6. Use the dictionary to check your answers.

Noun	Transcription	Meaning	Gender: *m, f, nt.*
хло́пець	/khlópeⁿts'/	*a boy*	
жі́нка	/zhínka/	*a woman*	
щеня́	/shcheⁿn'á/	*a puppy*	
о́ко	/ókoⁿ/	*an eye*	
письме́нник	/pyⁿs'ménnyk/	*a writer*	
пло́ща	/plóshcha/	*a square*	
ву́лиця	/vúlyⁿts'a/	*a street*	
нога́	/noⁿhá/	*a foot, leg*	
ву́хо	/vúkhoⁿ/	*an ear*	
котеня́	/koⁿten'á/	*a kitten*	
завда́ння	/zawdán'n'a/	*an assignment*	
ді́вчина	/díwchyⁿna/	*a girl*	
дя́дько	/d'ád'koⁿ/	*an uncle*	
журналі́ст	/zhurnalíst/	*a journalist*	
пан	/pan/	*a gentleman*	
люди́на	/l'udýⁿna/	*a person*	
студе́нт	/studént/	*a student*	
пита́ння	/pyⁿtán'n'a/	*a question*	
дощ	/doshch/	*rain*	

3.9. Listen and repeat after the speaker. Practice the pronunciation of **р** and the labials **б, п, в, ф,** and **м** before **я, є, ю,** and **ї.** Copy these letter combinations in cursive.

ба	б'я	па	п'я	ва	в'я	фа	ф'я
ба	*б'я*	*па*	*п'я*	*ва*	*в'я*	*фа*	*ф'я*
/ba/	/bja/	/pa/	/pja/	/va/	/vja/	/fa/	/fja/

ма	м'я	ра	р'я	об'я́ва	*an announcement*
ма	*м'я*	*ра*	*р'я*	*об'я́ва*	
/ma/	/mja/	/ra/	/rja/	/oⁿbjáva/	

бе	б'є	пе	п'є	ве	в'є	фе	ф'є
бе	*б'є*	*пе*	*п'є*	*ве*	*в'є*	*фе*	*ф'є*
/be/	/bje/	/pe/	/pje/	/ve/	/vje/	/fe/	/fje/

ме	м'є	ре	р'є	кар'є́ра	*a career*
ме	*м'є*	*ре*	*р'є*	*кар'є́ра*	
/me/	/mje/	/re/	/rje/	/karjéra/	

бу	б'ю	пу	п'ю	ву	в'ю	фу	ф'ю
бу	*б'ю*	*пу*	*п'ю*	*ву*	*в'ю*	*фу*	*ф'ю*
/bu/	/bju/	/pu/	/pju/	/vu/	/vju/	/fu/	/fju/

му	м'ю	ру	р'ю	комп'ю́тер	*a computer*
му	*м'ю*	*ру*	*р'ю*	*комп'ю́тер*	
/mu/	/mju/	/ru/	/rju/	/koⁿmpjúteⁿr/	

бі	б'ї	пі	п'ї	ві	в'ї	фі	ф'ї
бі	*б'ї*	*пі*	*п'ї*	*ві*	*в'ї*	*фі*	*ф'ї*
/bi/	/bji/	/pi/	/pji/	/vi/	/vji/	/fi/	/fji/

мі	м'ї	рі	р'ї	об'їзд *a detour*
мі	*м'ї*	*рі*	*р'ї*	*об'їзд*
/mi/	/mji/	/ri/	/rji/	/oᵘbjízd/

∩ 3.10. Repeat after the speaker. Copy these words in cursive and mark stresses.

п'ять /pjáť/ *five* — *п'ять*
суб'є́кт /subjékt/ *a person* — *суб'єкт*
об'їзд /oᵘbjízd/ *a detour* — *об'їзд*
м'яч /mjach/ *a ball* — *м'яч*
кар'є́ра /karjéra/ *a career* — *кар'єра*
де́в'ять /dévjať/ *nine* — *дев'ять*
комп'ю́тер /koᵘmpjúteʸr/ *a computer* — *комп'ютер*
м'я́со /mjásoᵘ/ *meat* — *м'ясо*
об'є́м /oᵘbjém/ *volume* — *об'єм*
п'я́тниця /pjátnyᵉts'a/ *Friday* — *п'ятниця*
подві́р'я /poᵘdvírja/ *a courtyard* — *подвір'я*
в'юн /vjun/ *an eel* — *в'юн*

∩ 3.11. Pair each printed word with its equivalent written in cursive. Copy all the words in cursive.

па́нна	1. *воло́сся*
фільм	2. *ти́ждень*
журна́л	3. *таксі́вка*
ти́ждень	4. *ді́вчина*
ґу́дзик	5. *фільм*
дощ	6. *ґу́дзик*
ді́вчина	7. *дощ*
воло́сся	8. *м'яч*
м'яч	9. *телефо́н*
хло́пець	10. *сестра́*
телефо́н	11. *па́нна*
ща́стя	12. *журна́л*
таксі́вка	13. *ща́стя*
сестра́	14. *їжа*
життя́	15. *стіле́ць*
їжа	16. *хло́пець*
стіле́ць	17. *життя́*

∩ 3.12. Listen carefully and mark the words you hear.

1. *па́лець   хло́пе́ць   чо́вен   котеня́   пі́сня*
ві́ття   щеня́   м'яч   бажа́ння   кар'є́ра/

хло́пець і ді́вчина

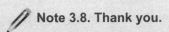

Note 3.8. Thank you.

Memorize these expressions:

Дя́кую. /d'ákuju/ *Thank you.*

Будь ла́ска. /bud' láska/ *Please.*
You are welcome. Here you are.

Про́шу. /próshu/ *Here your are.*
You are welcome.

Ду́же дя́кую. /dúzheᵘ d'ákuju/
Thank you very much.

Ду́же про́шу. /dúzheᵘ próshu/
You are very welcome.

The expression **будь ла́ска** is used both in response to expressions of gratitude and also as an equivalent of the English *please*:

Скажі́ть, будь ла́ска, де мій бра́т Васи́ль? *Tell me please where is my brother Vasyl?*

Ось, будь ла́ска, ва́ша ка́ва.
Here's your coffee, please.

 Note 3.9. Numerals from 1 to 10

Memorize these numerals:

0. **нуль** /nul'/ *zero*

1. **оди́н** /oᵘdýn/ *one*

2. **два** /dva/ *two*

3. **три** /try/ *three*

4. **чоти́ри** /choᵘtýryᵉ/ *four*

5. **п'ять** /pjat/ *five*

6. **шість** /shis't'/ *six*

7. **сім** /s'im/ *seven*

8. **ві́сім** /vís'im/ *eight*

9. **де́в'ять** /dévjat'/ *nine*

10. **де́сять** /dés'at'/ *ten*

2. *фільм Вітя завдання пан п'ятниця телефон щастя вулиця питання сестра*

3. *життя стілець годинник м'ясо об'їзд Ганна вухо дівчина щока панна*

⌒ 3.13. Unscramble the words. Mark the stresses.

1. чинівад _____
2. хуво _____
3. елтеонф _____
4. лцьопех _____
5. улцвия _____
6. палощ _____
7. льміф _____
8. занавдня _____
9. жтяит _____
10. страсе _____

3.14. Review exercises and notes of Lesson 3 and write out in cursive nouns, sorting them by the following categories:

1. family members
2. parts of human body
3. professions
4. proper names
5. animals
6. inanimate objects
7. other persons

⌒ 3.15. Read out loud and write in cursive each of these numerals. Mark stresses.

2	9	10	4	1	0	3	8	5
7	6	1	3	9	4	10	5	8

⌒ 3.16. Engage in a brief Q-and-A exchange. Be mindful of the gender forms of possessive and interrogative pronouns you use.

Model. **C** ба́тько /bá't'koᵘ/ *a father;* мій *mine*
Q Скажі́ть, будь ла́ска, чий це ба́тько?
Tell me please, whose father is it?
A Він мій. *He is mine.*

1. ка́ва *coffee;* ваш *pl. yours*
2. пла́ття *a dress;* її *hers*
3. чолові́к *a husband;* її *hers*
4. щі́тка *a brush;* твій *sg. yours*
5. годи́нник *a watch;* їхній *theirs*

6. жі́нка *a wife*; його́ *his*
7. бажа́ння *a desire*; мій *mine*
8. котеня́ *a kitten*; ваш *pl. yours*
9. журна́л *a magazine*; наш *ours*
10. комп'ю́тер *a computer*; його́ *his*
11. газе́та *a newspaper*; їхній *theirs*
12. чек *a check*; ваш *pl. yours*

3.17. Complete the crossword puzzle.

Across
3. Taxi
5. Zero
6. Check
7. Boy
11. Car
12. Two
13. Puppy
14. Day

Down
1. Happiness
2. Gentleman
4. Window
7. Boyfriend
8. Square
9. House
10. Time
12. Thank you

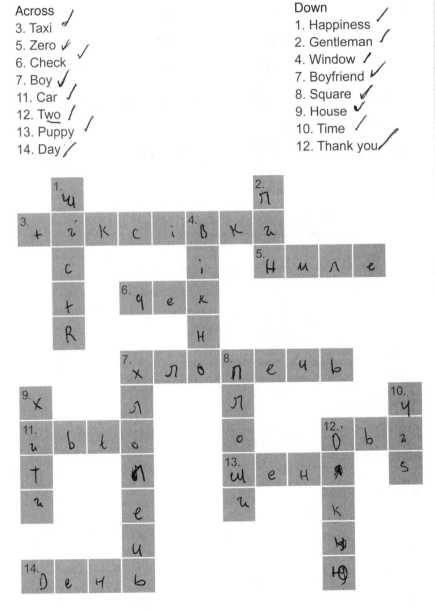

3.18. Fill in the missing gender forms of these adjectives. Memorize the adjectives.

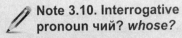

Note 3.10. Interrogative pronoun чий? *whose?*

The Ukrainian equivalents of the English *whose?* are:

чий? /chyj/ for masculine nouns,
чий ба́тько? *whose father?*

чия́? /chyᵉjá/ for feminine nouns,
чия́ ма́ти? *whose mother?*

чиє́? /chyᵉjé/ for neuter nouns,
чиє́ а́вто? *whose car?*

Це їхній леле́ка.

Note 3.11. Tell me please

To ask politely for information the expression **скажі́ть, будь ла́ска** *tell me please* is customarily used. This expression is addressed to **ви** *you* (2nd *pers. pl.*) and implies that the person addressed is a stranger or in some sense socially removed,

Скажі́ть, будь ла́ска, де тут банк? *Tell me please, where is a bank here?*

An informal variant of the same phrase is **скажи́, будь ла́ска**, addressed to **ти** *you* (2nd *pers. sg.*),

Скажи́, будь ла́ска, як її ім'я́? *Tell me please, what's her name?*

Note 3.12. Gender of adjectives

Each Ukrainian adjective has three gender forms. The masculine form ends in ~ий (~ій), the feminine form in ~а (~я), and the neuter form in ~е (~є).

There is a direct correlation of these forms, for if the masculine adjective has the ~ий ending then its feminine ending will be ~а and the neuter one will be ~е,

m. вели́кий *big, f.* вели́ка, *nt.* вели́ке

The masculine ending ~ій necessarily corresponds to the feminine ~я and the neuter ~є,

m. си́ній *blue, f.* си́ня, *nt.* си́нє.

Most of Ukrainian adjectives belong to the ий-type. ll dictionaries give only the masculine form of adjectives.

masculine	feminine	neuter	translation
га́рний	га́рни	гарне	*beautiful, nice*
малий	мала́	мале	*small*
Великих	Вели́ка	вели́ке	*big*
оста́нній	оста́ння	оста́нне	*last*
старій	стара́	старе́	*ancient, old*
цікавий	ціка́ва	ціка́ве	*interesting*
Дорогий	дорога́	Дороге́	*expensive*
нови́й	Нова́	Нове	*new*
молоди́й	молода́	молоде́	*young*
Ве́рхній	ве́рхня	ве́рхнє	*upper*
нудний	Нудна́	нудне́	*boring*
Деше́вий	дешева	Дешеве	*cheap*

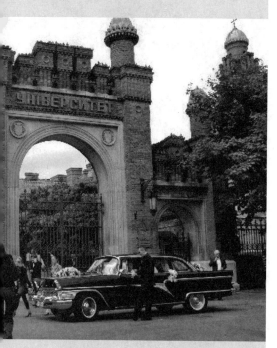

Це старе́ авто. *This is an old car.*

Note 3.13. Adjective-noun agreement

Adjectives always agree in gender with the nouns they describe,

m. вели́кий банк *a big bank*
f. вели́ка кімна́та *a big room*
nt. вели́ке мі́сто *a big city*

3.19. Combine adjectives with nouns. Make sure to use the correct gender form of the adjective. Use the expression Ось... *Here is...*

Model. **C** деше́вий *cheap,* пла́ття *a dress*
A Ось деше́ве пла́ття. *Here is a cheap dress.*

1. га́рний *beautiful,* ді́вчина *a girl*
2. мали́й *small,* буди́нок *a building*
3. вели́кий *big,* мі́сто *a city*
4. оста́нній *last,* по́тяг *a train*
5. ціка́вий *interesting,* люди́на *a person*
6. молоди́й *young,* жі́нка *a woman*
7. дороги́й *expensive,* а́вто *a car*
8. нудни́й *boring,* програ́ма *a program*
9. до́вгий *long,* ву́лиця *a street*
10. нови́й *new,* студе́нт *a student*
11. важки́й *difficult,* завда́ння *an assignment*
12. украї́нський *Ukrainian,* пі́сня *a song*

3.20. Use the adjective+noun collocations from the previous exercise to engage in a short informal exchange and ask about an object in question.

Model. **C** деше́вий *cheap,* пла́ття *a dress.*
Q Скажи́, будь ла́ска, яке́ це́ пла́ття?
Tell me please what (kind of) dress is this?
A Воно́ деше́ве. *It's cheap.*

3.21. Fill in the blanks with missing letters. Treat the apostrophe like a letter. Write down the words in cursive. Mark the stresses.

_апір, _рунт, _інка, жи_тя, філ_м, м_ясо, тижден_, _удзик, па_на, ї_а, се_тра, _анок, п_ятниця, воло_ся, бор_, хло_ець, завдан_я, десят_, _ітка, ком_'ютер, годин_ик, пло_а, _урналіст, _лаття, дев'_ть, ві_ім

 3.22. Cross out the nouns that do not agree in gender with the interrogative pronoun in each of the groups.

1. яки́й   ти́ждень, фільм, брат, папі́р, ~~ву́лиця~~, борщ, друг
2. чия́   ня́ня, ті́тка, ді́вчина, сестра́, по́друга, люди́на, ~~Хома́~~
3. чиє́   пита́ння, вікно́, пла́ття, п'я́тниця, завда́ння, ~~щеня́~~
4. яка́   їжа, ка́ва, ба́нка, Ї́вга, таксі́вка, ~~бажа́ння~~
5. яке́   воло́сся, вино́, ~~дя́дько~~, м'я́со, а́вто, мі́сто
6. чий   пан, письме́нник, папі́р, борщ, дя́дько, стіле́ць, ~~життя́~~

 3.23. Read these equations out loud in Ukrainian. For models consult Note 3.16.

дода́ти *to add:*

1. 2+3=	7. 8+2=
2. 7+2=	8. 4+3=
3. 5+1=	9. 4+4=
4. 2+6=	10. 6+4=
5. 0+10=	11. 3+3=
6. 3+5=	12. 5+5=

відня́ти *to subtract:*

1. 10-1=	7. 5-2=
2. 9-9=	8. 10-4=
3. 4-3=	9. 4-2=
4. 8-1=	10. 7-5=
5. 6-3=	11. 3-2=
6. 7-2=	12. 8-4=

3.24. Engage in a formal Q-and-A with a partner. Use the required gender form of the numeral **оди́н** *one* (See Note 3.17). Use the suggested numeral in your answer. Note that **лише́** means *only*.

Model. пита́ння /py^eta̋n'n'a/ *a question*; 3
Q Скажі́ть, будь ла́ска, тут лише́ одне́ пита́ння?
/ksazhít' bud' láska tut ly^eshé o^udné py^eta̋n'n'a/
Is there only one question here?
A Ні, тут їх три. /n'i, tut jikh try/ *No, there are three of them here.*

1. музе́й /muzéj/ *a museum*; 3
2. мі́сто /místo^u/ *a city*; 10
3. по́тяг /pót'ah/ *a train*; 2
4. газе́та /hazéta/ *a newspaper*; 8
5. котеня́ /ko^ute^un'a̋/ *a kitten*; 4
6. люди́на /l'udýna/ *a person*; 7
7. готе́ль /ho^utel'/ *a hotel*; 6
8. м'яч /mjach/ *a ball*; 8
9. таксі́вка /taks'íwka/ *a taxi cab*; 3
10. комп'ю́тер /ko^umpjúter/ *a computer*; 7
11. завда́ння /zawda̋n'n'a/ *an assignment*; 10

Note 3.14. Demonstrative expression Ось ...

Another common way of pointing to something or somebody is the expression **Ось (є) ...** *Here is ...,*
Ось (є) мій нови́й друг Рома́н.
Here's my new friend Roman.
Ось (є) моя́ стара́ по́друга Яри́на.
Here's my old (female) friend Yaryna.
The present tense form of the verb **бу́ти** *to be*, **є** is normally omitted in such expressions.

Note 3.15. Interrogative word яки́й? *what?*
To inquire about the qualities of an object the interrogative word **яки́й** /jakýj/ *what, what kind of*, is used. It has three gender forms: *m.* **яки́й**, *f.* **яка́** /jaka̋/, *nt.* **яке́** /jake̋/.

Note 3.16. Mathematic equations in Ukrainian
To read the mathematic equations for addition, the verb **дода́ти** /do^udáty^e/ *to add* is used. For subtraction, the verb **відня́ти** /vidn'áty^e/ *to take away* is used. The Ukrainian for *equals* is **дорі́внює** /do^urí̋wn'uje/, *lit. makes.*
   1+1=2 is read as:
Оди́н дода́ти оди́н дорі́внює два.
lit. One to add to one equals two.
   2-1=1 is read as:
Два відня́ти оди́н дорі́внює оди́н.
lit. Two minus one equals one.

These statements correlate with the questions
Скі́льки бу́де оди́н дода́ти оди́н?
How much is one plus one? and
Скі́льки бу́де два відня́ти оди́н?
How much is two minus one?

Note 3.17. Numeral оди́н *one*

The numeral **оди́н** *one*, stands out from the rest of the numerals by the fact that, similar to adjectives, it has three gender forms:

m. **оди́н** /oᵘdýn/, *f.* **одна́** /oᵘdna/, and *nt.* **одне́** /oᵘdne/.

Also like adjectives, this numeral agrees in gender with the noun it describes,

m. **по́верх** /póveᵘrkh/ *a floor* – **оди́н по́верх** *one floor*

f. **кімна́та** /kimnata/ *a room* – **одна́ кімна́та** *one room*

nt. **лі́жко** /l'ízhkoᵘ/ *a bed* – **одне́ лі́жко** *one bed*

Note 3.18. Consonants incapable of softening

Memorize the following consonants that are never soft and hence never followed by a soft sign ~ь:

- the labials б /b/, п /p/, в /v/, ф /f/, м /m/, as well as the non-labial р /r/;

- the hissing consonants ж /zh/, ч /ch/, ш /sh/, щ /shch/. The hissing consonants can soften only in the case when they are lengthened,

збі́жжя /zbízh'zh'a/ *grain*, **узбі́ччя** /uzbích'ch'a/ *side of the road*, **узви́шшя** /uzvýsh'sh'a/ *an elevated place.*

Ось мій університе́т.
Here is my university.

12. щеня́ /shcheᵘn'a/ *a puppy*; 7
13. годи́нник /hoᵘdýnnyᵉk/ *a watch*; 6
14. жі́нка /zhínka/ *a woman*; 3
15. пла́ття /plat't'a/ *a dress*; 2
16. фотогра́фія /foᵘtoᵘhrafija/ *a photograph*;

∩ 3.25. Dictation. Listen carefully, fill in the blanks. Mark the stresses.

1. Ос_ мій батьк_ Іва_. Ві_ ліка_.
2. А ос_ мо_ мат_ Гали__. Вон_ економі__.
3. Ту_ ваш_ завданн_. Вон_ довг_.
4. Ц_ їхні_ будино_. Ві_ велики_.
5. Ту_ лиш_ одн_ ав__. Вон_ нов_ і дорог_.

∩ 3.26. Exchange comments with a partner about the following topics. Use the vocabulary that you learned so far. Make sure that the adjectives are in gender agreement with their nouns.

Model. long day
C Яки́й до́вгий де́нь! *What a long day!*
A Так, ду́же до́вгий! *Yes, very long!*

1. nice song
2. big building
3. interesting film
4. boring assignment
5. beautiful city
6. young mother
7. expensive wine
8. small puppy
9. difficult life
10. cheap room

∩ 3.27. Ask about a given object. Make sure that the interrogative words and adjectives agree in gender with the nouns.

Model. Кни́жка *a book,* мій *my,* ціка́вий *interesting.*

Q Скажі́ть будь ла́ска, що це? *Tell me please, what is this?*
A Це кни́жка. *This is a book.*
Q А чия́ це кни́жка? *And whose book is it?*
A Моя́. *Mine.*
Q Яка́ вона́? *What kind (of book) is it?*
A Я зна́ю, що вона́ ціка́ва. *I know that it is interesting.*

1. університе́т *a university*, наш, вели́кий *big*
2. ву́лиця *a street*, її, до́вгий *long*
3. завда́ння *an assignment*, наш, легки́й *easy*
4. впра́ва *an exercise*, твій, важки́й *difficult*
5. підру́чник *a textbook*, його́, до́брий *good*
6. мі́сто *a city*, мій, стари́й *old*
7. валі́за *a suitcase*, наш, вели́кий *big*
8. комп'ю́тер *a computer*, їхній, дороги́й *expensive*
9. крамни́ця *a store*, їхній, мали́й *small*
10. молоко́ *milk*, ва́ш, холо́дний *cold*
11. село́ *a village*, їхній, га́рний *beautiful*

Іва́н та Іва́нна. Неформа́льна розмо́ва.

Note 3.19. Украї́нські імена́ Ukrainian names

Memorize these expressions used to find out a person's name:

fam., for **ти**
Як твоє́ ім'я́? /jak tvoᵘjé imjá/ *What's your name?*
Як твоє́ прі́звище? /jak tvoᵘjé prizvyᵉshcheʸ/ *What's your surname?*

form., for **ви**
Як ва́ше ім'я́? /jak vásheʸ imjá/
Як ва́ше прі́звище? /jak vásheʸ prizvyᵉshcheʸ/

 1. Неформа́льна розмо́ва | Informal Conversation

А. Приві́т. *Hello.*
Б. Приві́т. *Hello.*
А. Скажи́, будь ла́ска, як твоє́ ім'я́? *Tell me please what's your name?*
Б. Моє́ ім'я́ – Іва́н. А як твоє́ ім'я́? *My name is Ivan. And what's your name?*
А. А моє́ ім'я́ – Іва́нна. *And my name is Ivanna.*
Б. Ду́же приє́мно. *Very glad to meet you.*
А. Теж ду́же приє́мно. *Very glad to meet you too.*

 2. Форма́льна розмо́ва | Formal Conversation

А. До́брий день. *Good afternoon.*
Б. До́брий день. *Good afternoon.*
А. Скажі́ть, будь ла́ска, як ва́ше ім'я́ та прі́звище? *Tell me please what are your name and surname?*
Б. Моє́ ім'я́ – Тара́с, прі́звище – Дми́трик. А ва́ше ім'я́ та прі́звище? *My name is Taras, my surname is Dmytryk. And what are your name and surname?*
А. Моє́ ім'я́ – Оле́кса, прі́звище – Козаче́нко. *My name is Oleksa, my surname is Kozachenko.*
Б. О́тже ви – пан Оле́кса Козаче́нко. *So you are Mr. Oleksa Kozachenko.*
А. Так. А ви пан Тара́с Дми́трик. *Yes. And you are Mr. Taras Dmytryk.*
Б. Ду́же приє́мно. *Very glad to meet you.*
А. Теж ду́же приє́мно. *Very glad to meet you too.*

Note 3.20. Being Casual About It

fam. **Приві́т!** /pryᵉvít/ *Hello! Hi!*
fam. **Се́рвус!** /sérvus/ *Hello! Hi!* or *Take care! So long!* Used both as a casual greeting and farewell, similar to the Italian *Ciao!*, especially popular in Western Ukraine.
Ду́же приє́мно /dúzheʸ pryᵉjémnoᵘ/ *I'm very glad (to meet you).*
fam. **Тим ча́сом** /tyᵉm chásoᵘm/ *Take care. So long.*

Моя́ по́друга Яри́на лю́бить со́няшники.

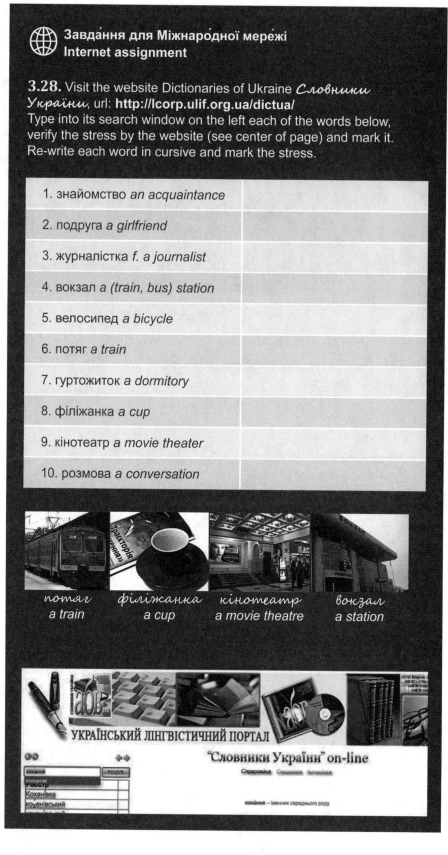

Завда́ння для Міжнаро́дної мере́жі
Internet assignment

3.28. Visit the website Dictionaries of Ukraine *Словники*
Украї́ни, url: **http://lcorp.ulif.org.ua/dictua/**
Type into its search window on the left each of the words below,
verify the stress by the website (see center of page) and mark it.
Re-write each word in cursive and mark the stress.

1. знайомство *an acquaintance*	
2. подруга *a girlfriend*	
3. журналістка f. *a journalist*	
4. вокзал *a (train, bus) station*	
5. велосипед *a bicycle*	
6. потяг *a train*	
7. гуртожиток *a dormitory*	
8. філіжанка *a cup*	
9. кінотеатр *a movie theater*	
10. розмова *a conversation*	

потяг   філіжанка   кінотеатр   вокзал
a train   a cup   a movie theatre   a station

Лéкція | Lesson 4

Dialogue:
Приéмно познайóмитися
Glad to Meet You

Grammar:
Case. Nominative case singular
Nominal declension
Commonly used adjectives
Numerals 11-19

Competencies:
To introduce oneself, greet, and say goodbye
To indicate a person's profession
Informal ways of address
Ask who somebody is and what a word means
To divide and multiply

Приві́т, я – Ю́рій.
А як твоє́ ім'я́?

4. Діяло́г. Приє́мно познайо́митися.

Лари́са: Приві́т. Моє́ ім'я́ Лари́са. Як твоє́ ім'я́?

Ю́рій: Моє́ ім'я́ – Ю́рій. Добри́день. Лари́са – це га́рне ім'я́.

Лари́са: Дя́кую. А як твоє́ прі́звище?

Ю́рій: Моє́ прі́звище – Петре́нко.

Лари́са: Зна́чить, ти – Ю́рій Петре́нко.

Ю́рій: Так, Ю́рій Петре́нко, або́ про́сто Юрко́. А ти? Лари́са ..?

Лари́са: Лари́са Бойчу́к, або́ про́сто Ле́ся.

Ю́рій: Я – нови́й студе́нт.

Лари́са: Я – теж студе́нтка, але́ не нова́. Я тут уже́ рік.

Ю́рій: Ра́дий познайо́митися.

Лари́са: Я теж ра́да познайо́митися. До побачення!

Ю́рій: На все до́бре.

4. Dialogue. Glad to meet you.

Larysa: Hello. My name is Larysa. What is your name?

Yuri: Hi. My name is Yuri. Larysa is a nice name.

Larysa: Thank you. And what's your family name?

Yuri: My family name is Petrenko.

Larysa: So you are Yuri Petrenko.

Yuri: Yes, Yuri Petrenko, or simply Yurko. And you are Larysa ..?

Larysa: Larysa Boichuk, or simply Lesia.

Yuri: I am a new student.

Larysa: I am also a student, but not a new one. I have been here for one year already.

Yuri: Glad to meet you.

Larysa: I am also glad to meet you. Goodbye!

Yuri: All the best.

🎧 Знайо́мство | Making an Acquaintance

Familiar mode	Formal mode	*English*
Приві́т!	**До́брий день**	*Hello.*
Як тебе́ зва́ти?	**Як вас зва́ти?**	*What's your name?*
Знайо́мся, будь ла́ска ...	**Знайо́мтеся, будь ла́ска ...**	*Please meet ...*
Скажи́, будь ла́ска ...	**Скажі́ть, будь ла́ска ...**	*Tell me please ...*
Ви́бач	**Ви́бачте**	*Excuse me*
Бува́й!	**До побачення!**	*Good-bye!*
Приє́мно познайо́митися.		*It's a pleasure to meet you.*

✏️ Нота́тки до діяло́гу
Notes on the Dialogue

До побачення! Goodbye!

the dash (–)

The dash is used when the verb є *am (is, are)* is omitted in the present tense before a noun, that it links to the subject,

Він – тури́ст. *He is a tourist.*

The dash is not used when an adjective is linked to the subject,

Окса́на молода́. *Oksana is young.*

На все до́бре! Take care! (*lit.* For all the good!)

Ко́рисні ви́рази на щоде́нь | Useful Everyday Expressions

звича́йно	of course, certainly
пе́вна річ	of course, certainly
спаси́бі, *var.* дя́кую	thank you
нема́ за́ що	don't mention it

📖 Грама́тика | Grammar

Ukrainian is a language with a highly developed system of word endings. Endings serve to denote the role of the word in speech and its relations with other words. In this respect, all words fall into two groups:
1) those that change their endings
2) those that stay unchanged irrespective of the role they play in a sentence.

Nouns (**ба́тько** *a father*, **ма́ти** *a mother*, **мі́сто** *a city*), adjectives (**вели́кий** *big*, **га́рний** *nice*, **ціка́вий** *interesting*), pronouns (**я, ти; мій, твій**), verbs (**бу́ти** *to be*, **ма́ти** *to have*, **зна́ти** *to know*), and some other words belong to the first group. Adverbs (**ду́же** *very*, **бага́то** *much*), conjunctions (**і, та** *and*, **а** *but, and*), prepositions (**у** *in*, **на** *on*, **до** *to*), and some others belong to the words that always stay unchanged.

Відмі́нок *Case*

In sentences, nouns can perform different roles, e.g., the doer of the action, its addressee, etc. Each role corresponds to a specific ending. In English, such roles are expressed by the word order or by prepositions. The change of the word order changes the meaning of the sentence. Compare *Peter knows Maria* and *Maria knows Peter*. In Ukrainian, such roles are expressed by word endings rather than the word order. The Ukrainian equivalent of these two sentences are respectively: **Петро́ зна́є Марі́ю. Марі́я зна́є Петра́.** Unlike in English, their meaning does not change with the change of the word order, **Марі́ю зна́є Петро́. Петра́ зна́є Марі́я.**

To put the noun into a sentence one needs to know the ending it has in each of the roles it plays. These roles are otherwise called *functions*. The relation between a specific ending and the sentence function is called **відмі́нок** *case*. Ukrainian nouns have seven cases: **називни́й** *nominative*, **родови́й** *genitive*, **дава́льний** *dative*, **знахі́дний** *accusative*, **ору́дний** *instrumental*, **місце́вий** *locative*, **кли́чний** *vocative*. Adjectives agree with nouns in gender, number, and case. Therefore they also have all seven cases.

Називни́й відмі́нок одни́ни Nominative Case Singular

Іме́нники *Nouns*
Nominative case correlates with the questions
хто? *who?* **що?** *what?*

*Це наш студе́нт
Петро́ Дороше́нко.*

Що це за стари́й до́брий пан?

Фу́нкція *Function*

Often the function of a particular case is manifest in its very name. Nominative as in Latin *nomen* 'name' is used to name things, as in **Це університе́т.** *This is a university.* **То мій друг Тара́с.** *That's my friend Taras.* The nominative is the case in which the subject of the sentence always appears,

Моя́ сестра́ – до́бра студе́нтка. *My sister is a good student.* Nominative case singular is the form in which nouns and adjectives appear in dictionaries.

Закі́нчення *Ending*

Nominative singular endings, or the dictionary form of the word:
~а (~я), ~о, ~е, consonant, and **double consonant** *plus* ~я

∩ Ча́сто вжи́вані прикме́тники
Frequently Used Adjectives

	adjective		its opposite
до́брий	good, kind, tasty (of food)	пога́ний	bad
вели́кий	big, great	мали́й	small, little
ціка́вий	interesting	нудни́й	boring
га́рний	nice, pretty, beautiful	потво́рний	ugly, repulsive
молоди́й	young	стари́й	old
нови́й	new	да́вній	ancient
до́вгий	long	коро́ткий	short
гаря́чий	hot	холо́дний	cold
широ́кий	wide, broad	вузьки́й	narrow
близьки́й	near, close	дале́кий	distant, far
дороги́й	dear, expensive	деше́вий	cheap
важки́й	heavy, hard, complicated	легки́й	light, easy
си́льний	strong, powerful	слабки́й	weak, feeble
здоро́вий	healthy	хво́рий	sick, ill
швидки́й	fast, quick, rapid	повільний	slow
бага́тий	rich, wealthy	бі́дний	poor

📖 Впра́ви *Exercises*

∩ **4.1.** Engage in a Q-and-A about the following subjects. Use interrogative words **хто?** or **що?** depending on whether the noun is a living being or thing.

Model.
C 1) нови́й *new,* 2) студе́нтка *a female student,* or а́вто *a car*
Q 1) Хто це? *Who is this?* 2) Що це? *What is it?*
A 1) Це нова́ студе́нтка. *This is a new female student.*
   2) Це нове́ а́вто. *This is a new car.*

	Adjectives	Nouns
1.	знайо́мий *familiar*	*m.,* чолові́к *man*
2.	вели́кий *big*	*f.,* ха́та *house*
3.	мали́й *little*	*m.,* хло́пець *boy*
4.	стари́й *old*	*nt.,* мі́сто *city*
5.	нови́й *new*	*m.,* студе́нт *student*
6.	зеле́ний *green*	*nt.,* де́рево *tree*
7.	молоди́й *young*	*f.,* ма́ма *mom*
8.	важли́вий *important*	*m.,* університе́т *university*
9.	щасли́вий *happy*	*m.,* та́то *dad*
10.	те́плий *warm*	*nt.,* лі́то *summer*
11.	ціка́вий *interesting*	*f.,* кни́жка *book*
12.	тяжки́й *hard*	*nt.,* пита́ння *question*
13.	до́вгий *long*	*f.,* ву́лиця *street*
14.	смачни́й *delicious*	*m.,* борщ *borshch*
15.	до́брий *good*	*m.,* вчи́тель *teacher*

га́рний пан

4.2. Engage in a Q-and-A exchange. The pronoun **чий? (чия́?, чиє́?)** should agree with the noun it modifies.

Model.

C я́блуко, *nt., apple* / я, *I*
Q Скажі́ть, будь ла́ска, чиє́ це я́блуко?
   (form.) Tell me please, whose apple is it?
A Воно́ моє́. *It's mine.*

1. ім'я́, *nt., name* / він *he*
2. університе́т, *m., university* / ми *we*
3. мі́сто, *nt., city* / вони́ *they*
4. студе́нтка, *f. female student* / вона́, *she*
5. прі́звище, *nt., surname* / ви, *pl. you*
6. ба́тько, *m., father* / я, *I*
7. сестра́, *f., sister* / ти, *sg. you*

4.3. Make up a dialogue. Use the nouns and adjectives on the next page.

Model.

Q Що це? — What's this?
A Це я́блуко. — It's an apple.
Q Яке́ воно́? — What kind is it?
A Воно́ ду́же смачне́. — It's very tasty.
Q А, чиє́ це я́блуко? — And whose apple is it?
A Це моє́ (твоє́, її́, на́ше, etc.) я́блуко. — This is my (your, her, our, etc.) apple.

Оде́са. Яка́ чудо́ва о́пера!

	Nouns	Adjectives	Possessive pronouns
1.	*f.,* кни́жка *book*	ціка́вий *interesting*	мій *my*
2.	*nt.,* мі́сто *city*	га́рний *beautiful*	її *her*
3.	*m.,* університе́т *university*	стари́й *old*	наш *our*
4.	*f.,* ка́ва *coffee*	соло́дкий *sweet*	його́ *his*
5.	*nt.,* а́вто *car*	нови́й *new*	твій, *sg. your*
6.	*m.,* по́їзд *train*	швидки́й *fast*	їхній *their*
7.	*f.,* сім'я́ *family*	вели́кий *big*	їхній *their*

гуцу́льська сім'я́
a Hutsul family

Віта́ння та проща́ння *Greetings and Goodbyes*

До́брого ра́нку!	*Good morning!*
До́брий день!	*Good afternoon!*
До́брий ве́чір!	*Good evening!*
Приві́т!	*Hello!*
Як спра́ви?	*How are you?*
До́бре.	*Well.*
Непога́но.	*Not bad.*
До поба́чення!	*Goodbye!*
На все до́бре!	*All the best!*
Нара́зі	*So long!*
Хай щасти́ть!	*Good luck!*

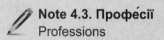 **4.4.** React to the following. Use the material of this lesson. Try to be creative.

1. Приві́т!
2. Як спра́ви?
3. Моє́ ім'я́ Сашко́.
4. Ми не знайо́мі.
5. Хто це таки́й?
6. Я нови́й студе́нт Іва́н Тарасю́к.
7. Де ваш університе́т?
8. Скажі́ть, будь ла́ска, як вас зва́ти?
9. Ду́же дя́кую.

4.5. Choose the correct etiquette mode. Make a clear distinction between the forms meant for 2nd person singular **ти** and 2nd person plural **ви.**

1. Say hello to your friend.
2. Ask the name of a fellow-traveler of the same age.
3. Greet a cashier at a railway station at 2:00 PM.
4. Greet an unfamiliar lady in her forties at 11:00 AM.
5. Ask a young person for information.
6. Say goodbye to your Ukrainian friend.
7. Ask a stranger in the street for information.

Note 4.2.
Коли́ та як віта́тися
When to say what greeting

Ukrainians greet each other in the following ways:

До́брого ра́нку! *Good morning!*

from 6:00 AM to 12:00 PM

До́брий день! or **До́брого дня!**
Good afternoon!
from 12:00 PM to 6:00 PM

До́брий ве́чір! *Good evening!*
from 6:00 PM to 12:00 AM.

The more familiar and casual

Добри́день! *Hello!* is often used at

any time of day.

The expression **Добра́ніч!** or **На добра́ніч!** is used to bid goodbye in the evening.

Note 4.3. Профе́сії
Professions

To refer to a person's profession in a statement or question, the expression **за фа́хом** *by profession* is used,

За фа́хом пан Васи́лько – воді́й. *By profession Mr. Vasylko is a driver.*
Хто Марі́я за фа́хом? *What is Maria? (lit. Who is Maria by profession?)*
Хто ви за фа́хом? *What are you? (lit. Who are you by profession?)*

8. Greet your professor at 5:00 PM.
9. Say goodnight.
10. Ask for the name and family name of a stranger.

∩ 4.6. Read the names of the professions and try to guess their meaning. Compare against the exercise keys.

акто́р	фото́граф	архіте́ктор
банкі́р	істо́рик	капіта́н
журналі́ст	інжене́р	ме́неджер
фі́зик	секрета́р	економі́ст
піяні́ст	диплома́т	консульта́нт
архео́лог	біо́лог	диза́йнер

∩ 4.7. Make up a dialogue. Use the one below as a model and the names of professions from the previous exercise.

Model. ти / економі́ст / він / фі́зик
Q Хто ти за фа́хом? *What are you by profession?*
A Я – економі́ст. А він? *I'm an economist. And he?*
Q А він – фі́зик. *And he is a physicist.*
A Як ціка́во! *How interesting!*

1. ти / акто́р / вона́ / банкі́р
2. він / журналі́ст / ти / піяні́ст
3. вона́ / ме́неджер / він / фото́граф
4. Рома́н / архіте́ктор / Ю́рій / інжене́р
5. Окса́на / фото́граф / Яри́на / консульта́нт
6. Íгор / економі́ст / Васи́ль / архео́лог

∩ 4.8. Answer the questions. Negate the adjective in the statement. Give an alternative from the list of Frequently Used Adjectives.

Model. **Q** Ця ву́лиця до́вга? *Is this street long?*
A Ні, вона́ не до́вга, а ду́же коро́тка.
No, it is not long, but very short.

1. Ця кни́жка ціка́ва?
2. Це завда́ння важке́?
3. Цей борщ гаря́чий?
4. Ця ма́ма молода́?
5. Цей чолові́к си́льний?
6. Цей університе́т вели́кий?
7. Ця студе́нтка хво́ра?
8. Це лі́то холо́дне?
9. Цей хло́пець пога́ний?
10. Ця дівчина потво́рна?
11. Цей по́їзд швидки́й?
12. Це мі́сто бага́те?

Воли́нський університе́т
Volyn University

Га́нна за фа́хом –
фото́граф
Hanna is a photographer by profession

✏ Note 4.4. How to Point to Things
The demonstrative pronoun **цей** is equivalent to the English *this* and points to an object that is relatively close to the speaker. It has three gender forms:
m. **цей**, *f.* **ця**, *nt.* **це**,
m. **цей інжене́р** *this engineer*
f. **ця студе́нтка** *this female student*
nt. **це перо́** *this pen*

Знайомтеся – пані
Марічка та панна Ярка.

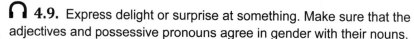 **4.9.** Express delight or surprise at something. Make sure that the adjectives and possessive pronouns agree in gender with their nouns.

Model. Гарний, картина, наш
C Яка гарна картина! *What a beautiful picture!*
A Так, дуже гарна, і вона наша. *Yes, very beautiful, and it's ours.*

1. швидкий, авто, мій
2. смішний *funny*, пес *a dog*, його
3. дорогий, ресторан, її
4. старий, школа, ваш
5. зелений, вулиця, твій
6. нудний, лист *a letter*, їхній
7. цікавий, питання, їхній
8. смачний *tasty*, борщ, твій
9. високий, дерево, ваш
10. важкий, завдання, твій
11. великий, кімната, мій
12. дешевий, комп'ютер, ваш

4.10. Write each diminutive next to its formal variant. Determine the gender of each name. Use the appendices (Table 17) to check your answers.

Formal name		Diminutive
1. Лариса		а. Лана
2. Юрій		б. Максимко
3. Микола		в. Галя
4. Ярина		г. Сашко
5. Ярема		ґ. Леся
6. Галина		д. Юрко
7. Ігор		е. Мартуся
8. Надія		є. Дана
9. Максим		ж. Таня
10. Богдана		з. Сергійко
11. Олександ(е)р		и. Миколка
12. Світлана		і. Яремко
13. Сергій		ї. Надійка
14. Марта		й. Ярка
15. Тетяна		к. Ігорко

Це Сашко Гончаренко,
мій старий друг.

4.11. Introduce a new friend to an old one. Use the matches you made in the previous exercise.

Model.
Q Хто ця приємна дівчина? *Who is this nice girl?*
A Це моя нова подруга Марія, або просто Марічка.
This is my new friend Maria or simply Marichka.

Q Хто цей приємний хлопець? *Who is this nice boy?*
A Це мій новий друг Олександ(е)р або просто Сашко.
This is my new friend Oleksander or simply Sashko.

∩ **4.12.** Practice asking for a person's name or surname. Chose the correct form of the possessive pronoun.

Model.
C Я *I*, ім'я́ *name*
A Як моє́ ім'я́? *What's my name?*

1. Він, прі́звище	4. Ти, прі́звище	7. Вона́, ім'я́
2. Вони́, ім'я́	5. Ви, прі́звище	8. Я, прі́звище
3. Ти, ім'я́	6. Вони́, прі́звище	9. Ви, ім'я́

∩ **4.13.** Describe each person or thing listed in Exercise 4.1. Use the required gender of the demonstrative pronoun **цей** (*f.* ця, *nt.* це).

Model.
C Нови́й *new*, студе́нтка *a female student*
A Ця студе́нтка нова́. *This female student is new.*

∩ **4.14.** Put the demonstrative pronoun **той** and the accompanying adjective in the required gender.

Model.
C Чолові́к *a man*, нудни́й *boring*
A Той чолові́к нудни́й. *That man is boring.*

1. Жі́нка, бага́тий	8. Мі́сто, зеле́ний
2. Друг, близьки́й *close*	9. Завда́ння, ціка́вий
3. По́тяг, оста́нній	10. Ті́тка, висо́кий
4. Дитя́, мали́й	11. Прі́звище, украї́нський
5. Юна́к, си́льний	12. Ді́вчина, розу́мний *wise*
6. Кімна́та, дороги́й	13. Пита́ння, прости́й
7. Італі́єць, знайо́мий	14. Лист, до́вгий

∩ **4.15.** Listen to this conversation. Read it with a partner, then adapt the words to your situation.

Розмо́ва *Conversation*

Мико́ла: Добри́день, Оле́но!
Оле́на: Приві́т, Мико́ло!
Мико́ла: Як спра́ви?
Оле́на: До́бре, дя́кую. А як твої́?
Мико́ла: Спаси́бі, теж непога́но.
Оле́на: Я ду́же ра́да.
Мико́ла: І я теж ду́же ра́дий.
Оле́на: Бува́й.
Мико́ла: Хай щасти́ть.

Note 4.5. Diminutive names

Almost any Ukrainian proper name, whether feminine or masculine, has at least one, and often more, short forms, or diminutives. They are used by friends, colleagues, and people who know each other well enough to be on familiar terms as informal, more intimate, or affectionate way of calling a friend,

form. **Марі́я** *Maria* – *dim.* **Марі́чка, Мару́ся, Мару́сенька**
form. **Яри́на** – *dim.* **Я́рка, Я́рочка, Яру́ся, Яру́ня**
form. **Іва́н** *Ivan* – *dim.* **Іва́сь, Іва́сик, Іва́нко, Ванько́**
form. **Олекса́ндер** *Oleksander* – *dim.* **Сашко́, Оле́сь, Лесь, Ле́сик.**

In Table 17 of the appendices you can find the diminutive variants of many common Ukrainian proper names.

Note 4.6. Demonstrative pronoun той *that*

The demonstrative pronoun **той** *that* refers to an object relatively removed from the speaker. Its gender forms are:

m. **той**, *f.* **та**, and *nt.* **те**,
  m., **той борщ** *that borshch*
  f., **та ді́вчина** *that girl*
  nt., **те мі́сто** *that city*

Ці дівча́та — студе́нтки.
These girls are students.

∩ **4.16.** Say and write the sentences in Ukrainian. Use the vocabulary and grammar of the lesson. Consult the dictionary if necessary.

1. Tell me please, what is her name and surname.
2. Please meet, this is my old friend Ivan Kozachenko.
3. Ivan is a good student.
4. Lviv is their favorite Ukrainian city.
5. This young man is not a banker, but an economist.
6. That book is very interesting, but this one is boring.
7. She is a beautiful and kind girl.
8. Our house is new and big.
9. What is his brother by profession?
10. This is a hard question and that is an easy answer.
11. This old man is an interesting photographer.
12. That young woman is a happy mother.
13. What a boring film!
14. This car is not expensive, it's very cheap.

∩ **4.17.** Listen carefully to these questions. Use the dialogue at the beginning of this lesson to answer the questions.

1. Як його́ ім'я́?
2. Як її́ ім'я́?
3. Яке́ ім'я́ Лари́са?
4. Як його́ прі́звище?
5. Як її́ прі́звище?
6. Ю́рій, або́ про́сто як?
7. Лари́са, або́ про́сто як?
8. Хто є нови́й студе́нт?
9. Хто є стари́й студе́нт?
10. Скі́льки ча́су Лари́са вже є тут?

 Note. 4.7. Відмі́на іме́нників
Nominal Declension

All Ukrainian nouns fall into four groups or *declensions* based on the types of endings taken in various cases. Each declension is determined by two features:

1) grammatical gender and 2) ending.

1. *The first declension* is comprised of feminine and masculine nouns that end in ~**a** or ~**я**,

    f. **шко́ла** *a school*, *f.* **земля́** *a land*; *m.* **невда́ха** *a loser*,
    m. **сирота́** *an orphan*, *m.* **суддя́** *a judge*.

A great majority of Ukrainian nouns ending in ~**a** (~**я**) are of feminine gender. For this reason the first declension is often called the *feminine declension* in grammar books.

2. *The second declension* is comprised of masculine nouns that end in a consonant (**ø**) or in the vowel **~о** for names of men, and neuter nouns that end in **~о**, **~е**, and **~я**,

　m. **рік** *a year, m.* **ба́тько** *a father, m.* **дя́дько** *an uncle,*
　nt. **мі́сто** *a city, nt.* **по́ле** *a field, nt.* **пита́ння** *a question.*

The **я**-ended neuter nouns have a lengthened consonant before the ending,

　nt. **пита́ння** *a question,* **життя́** *life,* **узбі́ччя** *roadside,*
　коха́ння *love,* **роздорі́жжя** *crossroads.*

That is an easy way of telling them apart from feminine and the very few masculine nouns ending in **-я** like

　f. **пі́сня** *a song, f.* **ви́шня** *a cherry, f.* **ня́ня** *a babysitter,*
　m. **Пе́тя** *Petia (diminutive of the name Petro).*

Because a great majority of the second declension nouns are masculine, it is often called the masculine declension.

3. *The third declension* is comprised of feminine nouns ending in one consonant, or in the consonant cluster **~сть**,

　річ *a thing,* **ніч** *a night,* **любо́в** *love,* **ра́дість** *joy.*

The noun **ма́ти** *a mother* also belongs to the third declension.

4. *The fourth declension* is comprised of neuter nouns, that are the names of baby animals ending in **~а** or **~я**,

　курча́ *a chicken,* **порося́** *a piglet,* **дитя́** *a baby,*
　цуценя́ *a puppy,* **котеня́** *a kitten.*

Note that the noun **ім'я́** *a name* also belongs to the fourth declension. Nominal declension endings can be found in Tables 1-3 of the appendices, pp. 316-317.

∩ **4.18.** Determine the declension of these nouns. Be sure to take into account their gender, ending, and meaning.

котеня́	фотогра́фія	кіт	ті́тка	тома́т	люди́на
олівце́ь	ву́лиця	ра́дість	мі́сто	завда́ння	Тимко́
ніч	бажа́ння	ка́ва	Ві́тя	зуб	річ
музе́й	вікно́	па́нна	дя́дько	ди́ня	стіле́ць
життя́	ді́вчина	ма́ти	пан	взуття́	любо́в
а́вто	Гали́на	лі́кар	їжа́	ву́хо	журна́л
жі́нка	таксі́вка	вино́	пло́ща	хло́пець	ім'я́

Listening comprehension

∩ **4.19.** Read the questions first, then listen to the text "Знайо́мтеся, це – Окса́на Миките́нко" and answer the questions.

1. Хто така́ Окса́на?
2. Яка́ її́ спеція́льність?

Note 4.8. Consonants without letters

There are two consonants in Ukrainian that have no single letter of their own. Therefore each uses a combination of two letters. They are /dzh/ signified in writing by **дж** and /dz/ signified in writing by **дз**. Each of them is an indivisible sound and their two elements are pronounced together.

The consonant **дж** /dzh/ is identical to the English /d☐/ in *John* or *job*,

　ходжу́ /kho^{u}dzhu/ *I walk,* **джаз** /dzhaz/ *jazz,* **джерело́** /dzhe^{y}re^{y}lo/ *a spring, source.*

The consonant **дз** /dz/ has no direct English counterpart and sounds like two final consonants pronounced together in *He rea**ds**. She lea**ds**. It nee**ds**.

　дзе́ркало /dzérkalo/ *a mirror*
　дзвін /dzvin/ *a bell*
　дзьоб /dz'ob/ *a beak*
　родзи́нка /ro^{u}dzýnka/ *a raisin*

Exception. When the first element of these consonants, the **д** /d/, is part of a prefix and the second is a part of the root then the two elements **д** /d/, **ж** /zh/ and **д** /d/, **з** /z/ are pronounced as separate sounds,

підживи́ти /pid.zhy^{e}vы́ty^e/ a synonym of **живи́ти** /zhy^{e}vы́ty^e/ *to nourish*

надзвукови́й /nad.zvuko^{u}výj/ *supersonic* from **звукови́й** /zvuko^{u}výj/ *acoustic.*

Яки́й га́рний зеле́ний парк!

Окса́на Миките́нко, студе́нтка

3. Яке́ її захо́плення?
4. Де живе́ її сім'я́?
5. Хто таки́й Яросла́в Миките́нко?
6. Хто він за фа́хом?
7. Яки́й чоловік її та́то?
8. Хто за фа́хом Олекса́ндра Миките́нко?
9. Яка́ вона́ жі́нка?
10. Хто таки́й Сірко́?
11. Чому́ його́ ім'я́ Сірко́?

∩ **4.20.** Translate the following text into English. If necessary, use the dictionary. Then summarize the text in a few Ukrainian sentences.

Знайо́мтеся: це Окса́на Миките́нко

Добри́день. Моє́ ім'я́ Окса́на, а прі́звище Миките́нко. Я живу́ в Ки́єві. За́раз студе́нтка в Ки́ївському націона́льному університе́ті. Моя́ спеція́льність — украї́нська мо́ва та літерату́ра, а моє́ вели́ке захо́плення — старе́ європе́йське кіно́ та теа́тр. Моя́ сім'я́ теж тут живе́. Знайо́мтеся: ось мій та́то. Його́ ім'я́ — Яросла́в. Він є інжене́р-меха́нік. Яросла́в Миките́нко висо́кий та симпати́чний чоловік. А це моя́ ма́ма. Її ім'я́ — Олекса́ндра. Вона́ — економі́стка. Моя́ ма́ма га́рна та весе́ла жі́нка. А це моє́ улю́блене цуценя́. Воно́ сі́ре, тому́ його́ ім'я́ є Сірко́. Моє́ цуценя́ мале́ньке і коха́не. Сірко́ і я ма́йже за́вжди ра́зом.

4.21. Describe each of these pictures based on the text above about the Mykytenko family.

Це я, Юрко́

Ната́лка, моя́ жі́нка

Марі́чка, на́ша кі́шка

∩ **4.22.** Listen carefully and mark the numerals you hear.

сімна́дцять	трина́дцять	де́сять	шістна́дцять	дев'ятна́дцять
п'ятна́дцять	нуль	одина́дцять	п'ять	чоти́ри
сім	шість	вісімна́дцять	два	чотирна́дцять
двана́дцять	три	ві́сім	де́в'ять	оди́н

Note 4.9. Numerals *eleven to nineteen*.

Memorize the cardinal numerals from *eleven to nineteen*. The consonant **д** /d/ in the cluster ~**дц**~ /dts'/ is assimilated to the soft **ц** /ts'/ after it and therefore, instead of being fully pronounced, the /d/ becomes a stop /¬/ while the following soft /ts'/ is fully pronounced.

English	Ukrainian and transcription
eleven	**одина́дцять** /oᵘdyᵉná¬ts'at'/
twelve	**двана́дцять** /dvaná¬ts'at'/
thirteen	**трина́дцять** /tryᵉná¬ts'at'/
fourteen	**чотирна́дцять** /choᵘtyᵉrná¬ts'at'/
fifteen	**п'ятна́дцять** /pjatná¬ts'at'/
sixteen	**шістна́дцять** /shisná¬ts'at'/
seventeen	**сімна́дцять** /s'mná¬ts'at'/
eighteen	**вісімна́дцять** /vis'imná¬ts'at'/
nineteen	**дев'ятна́дцять** /deᵛvjatná¬ts'at'/

The stress in the numerals from 11 to 19 is invariably on the syllable ~**на́**~.

4.23. Read these equations out loud in Ukrainian.

помно́жити на *to multiply by*

1. 1 x 10 =	4. 5 x 3 =	7. 2 x 3 =	10. 4 x 2 =	13. 15 x 0 =
2. 3 x 4 =	5. 2 x 8 =	8. 3 x 3 =	11. 7 x 2 =	14. 19 x 1 =
3. 4 x 4 =	6. 6 x 2 =	9. 5 x 2 =	12. 2 x 2 =	15. 8 x 2 =

поділи́ти на *to divide by*

1. 2 ÷ 2 =	4. 15 ÷ 5 =	7. 10 ÷ 5 =	10. 17 ÷ 1 =	13. 11 ÷ 1 =
2. 12 ÷ 4 =	5. 6 ÷ 2 =	8. 0 ÷ 19 =	11. 15 ÷ 3 =	14. 12 ÷ 2 =
3. 9 ÷ 3 =	6. 8 ÷ 4 =	9. 14 ÷ 2 =	12. 16 ÷ 8 =	15. 10 ÷ 2 =

4.24. Numeric dictation. Listen carefully to the speaker and write down in words the cardinal numerals. Read each of the numerals aloud.

4.25. Read the addresses of these people. Spell out all numerals and abbreviations. Follow the model.

Model.

C Ігор Дмитру́к, вул. Собо́рна, 7, кв. 2
Ihor Dmytruk, 7 Soborna St., Apt. 2

A Ігор Дмитру́к. Його́ адре́са: ву́лиця Собо́рна, буди́нок но́мер сім, кварти́ра но́мер два.
Ihor Dmytruk. His address is: number 7 Soborna Street, apartment number 2.

1. Рома́н Новачу́к, вул. Зеле́на, 11, кв. 7
2. Мела́нія Олі́йник, вул. Садова́, 3, кв. 19
3. Марко́ Пінчу́к, вул. Європе́йська, 10, кв. 5
4. Яре́ма Хмельни́цький, вул. Катедра́льна, 18, кв. 12
5. Світла́на та Любоми́р Павлюки́, вул. Шкільна́, 9, кв. 15
6. Лука́ш Петрунча́к, вул. За́мкова, 16, кв. 1
7. Ната́ля Ти́ха, вул. Пека́рська, 4, кв. 17
8. Андрі́й Павли́шин, вул. Ки́ївська, 6, кв. 20
9. Кири́ло Васи́льченко, вул. Пошто́ва, 5, кв. 2
10. Богда́на Пилипе́нко, вул. Вокза́льна, 13, кв. 16

4.26. Ask who these people are. Use the required gender form of the adjective **таки́й** *such*.

Model.

C Пан Чуга́й *Mr. Chuhai*, нови́й лі́кар *a new physician*

Q Хто таки́й пан Чуга́й? *Who is Mr. Chuhai?*

A Здає́ться, він – нови́й лі́кар. *He seems to be a new physician.*

Note 4.10. Multiplication and division

To read a mathematic equation of multiplication the expression **помно́жити** /po^{u}mnózhy^{e}ty^e/ **на** *to multiply by* is used. For the equation of division **поділи́ти на** /po^{u}dilýty^e/ *to divide by* is used.

6 x 3 = 18 is read as **Шість помно́жити на три дорі́внює вісімна́дцять.** *Six times three equals eighteen. (lit. Six to multiply by three equals eighteen.)*

14 ÷ 2 = 7 is read as **Чотирна́дцять поділи́ти на два дорі́внює сім.** *Fourteen divided by two equals seven. (lit. Fourteen to divide by two equals seven.)*

Note 4.11. Хто таки́й ..?
Who is ...? **Що таке́ ..?**
What is...?

To inquire about an unknown person, **Хто таки́й ..?** *Who is ..?* is used. The adjective **таки́й** *such* agrees in gender with the noun it refers to:

Хто таки́й Тара́с? *Who is Taras?* or **Хто він таки́й?** *Who is he?*
Хто така́ Богда́на? *Who is Bohdana?* or **Хто вона́ така́?** *Who is she?*

The answer to such questions usually is like, **Тара́с – це наш нови́й працівни́к.** *Taras is our new worker.* **Богда́на – це їхня журналі́стка.** *Bohdana is their journalist.*

To solicit information about an unknown word, the cliché **Що таке́ ...?** *lit. What is ...?* is used. It actually means *What does the "..." mean?* This cliché stays the same irrespective of the gender of the noun whose meaning it asks to explain because the neuter adjective **таке́** *such* agrees with the interrogative word **що?** which refers to an entity of the neuter gender. This question can be posed to any noun, whether animate or inanimate, whose meaning needs to be explained,

Олі́вець? Що таке́ олі́вець? *A pencil? What is a pencil?*
Архіте́ктор? Що таке́ архіте́ктор? *An architect? What is an architect?*
Я не розумі́ю, що таке́ офіція́нтка. *I don't understand what* офіція́нтка *is.*

The expression **Що тут (там) таке́?** means *What's going on here (there)?*

Ната́лія На́ум

Іва́н Миколайчу́к

Олекса́ндр Довже́нко

Лі́на Косте́нко

Тара́с Проха́сько

Дани́ло Садови́й

1. Олекса́ндер Довже́нко, украї́нський кінорежисе́р *a Ukrainian director*
2. Лі́на Косте́нко, відо́ма пое́тка *f. a known poet*
3. Ната́лія На́ум, чудо́ва акто́рка *a wonderful actress*
4. Тара́с Проха́сько, їхній улю́блений письме́нник *their favorite writer*
5. Іва́н Миколайчу́к, славе́тний кіноакто́р *a famous film actor*
6. Я́ків Васи́льченко, ду́же до́брий водı́й *a very good driver*
7. Па́нна Мела́нія, його́ знайо́ма украї́нка *a Ukrainian woman he knows*
8. Дани́ло Садови́й, її хло́пець *her boyfriend*
9. Па́ні Садова́, моя́ ті́тка *my aunt*
10. Софı́я Миките́нко, його́ моло́дша сестра́ *his younger sister*

🎧 **4.27.** Ask someone to explain the meaning of the unknown word.

Model.
🅒 «Украї́нський ти́ждень» *The Ukrainian Week*, популя́рний журна́л *a popular magazine*
🆀 Ви́бачте, що таке́ «Украї́нський ти́ждень»? *Excuse me, what does The Ukrainian Week mean?*
🅐 Це популя́рний журна́л. *It's a popular magazine.*

Володи́мирець

Кере́лівка

Десна́   кінокарти́на

1. Володи́мирець, моє́ рі́дне мі́сто *my hometown*
2. Десна́, вели́ка і га́рна рі́чка *a large and beautiful river*
3. Михальчу́к, типо́ве украї́нське прі́звище *a typical Ukrainian family name*
4. Роксоля́на, старе́ жіно́че ім'я́ *an old feminine name*
5. Світли́на, те саме́, що фотогра́фія *the same thing as a photograph*
6. Кінокарти́на, те саме́, що фільм *the same thing as a film.*
7. Прорізна́, одна́ стара́ ву́лиця *an old street*
8. Борщ, традиці́йний украї́нський суп *the traditional Ukrainian soup.*
9. Кере́лівка, ду́же відо́ме село́ *a very well-known village*
10. Сві́тязь, ду́же га́рне і вели́ке о́зеро *a very nice and big lake*

🌐 **Мо́вні ресу́рси на мере́жі.**
Language resources on the web.

4.28. Go to google images search engine and type into the search window the Ukrainian word **знайомство**. Report in writing on at least four instances of **Хто знайо́миться?** *Who is getting acquainted?*

1. Describe these people using the adjectives you learned.
2. Give them Ukrainian names and family names (Table 17, p. 327-329).
3. Mention their professions.
4. Be ready to tell everything in your own words.

Юрко́ Кульчи́нський за фа́хом музика́нт.

 4.29. Enact a conversation with a partner. Use the material you learned in this and previous lessons. Where necessary consult the dictionary.

Сце́нка за сцена́рієм «Знайо́мство»
Scripted Skit: *Getting Acquainted*

Enact the skit with a partner. Closely follow the script. Use the material of the lesson and the English-Ukrainian dictionary. Be creative.

Bohdana (Богда́на): Greets Oleksander.
Oleksander (Олекса́ндер): Greets Bohdana in return.

річка Смо́трич, мі́сто
Кам'яне́ць-Поді́льський

Bohdana: Politely asks Oleksander's name.
Oleksander: Introduces himself only by name. Asks Bohdana's name.

Bohdana: Introduces herself only by name.
Oleksander: Indicates that he likes her name.

Bohdana: Thanks for the compliment. Asks how Oleksander is.
Oleksander: Says he is fine and returns the question.

Bohdana: Says she is not bad. Apologizes and asks for Oleksander's family name.
Oleksander: Gives his family name. (Choose a family name in Table 18 «Some Common Ukrainian Family Names», appendices, p. 329). Asks for Bohdana's family name.

Bohdana: Gives her family name.
Oleksander: Concludes by repeating her name and surname.

Bohdana: Agrees and offers the informal variant of her name (Consult Table 17 «Some Common Ukrainian Names», appendices, p. 327).
Oleksander: Introduces himself by name and family name and asks her to call him simply by the diminutive of his name.

Bohdana: Expresses pleasure at meeting him.
Oleksander: Says he is also pleased and bids goodbye.

Bohdana: Bids goodbye wishing him all the best.

Лéкція | Lesson 5

Dialogue:
Канíкули: цікáво і недóрого
Vacations: Interesting and Inexpensive

Grammar:
Aspect of the verb
Past imperfective and perfective tenses
Nominative case plural
Numerals 20-99

Competencies:
Vacations
Nationalities
Present and past possibility

Крим — це ду́же га́рні місця́.

💬 5. Діяло́г. Каніку́ли: ціка́во і недо́рого.

Мико́ла: Ле́се, це ти? Як приє́мно! Старі́ дру́зі! Приві́т!
Ле́ся: Приві́т, Мико́ло. Як спра́ви?
Мико́ла: До́бре, дя́кую. Ми не ба́чилися ці́ле лі́то!
Ле́ся: Що ти роби́в? Сиді́в удо́ма чи мо́же, куди́сь ї́здив?
Мико́ла: Я та мої́ дру́зі Тара́с і Рома́н ра́зом ї́здили на мо́ре.
Ле́ся: Ну і як було́?
Мико́ла: Ду́же до́бре, ве́село – про́сто чудо́во!
Ле́ся: Де са́ме ви відпочива́ли?
Мико́ла: Ти чу́ла про Коктебе́ль? Це Крим, це ду́же га́рні місця́.
Ле́ся: Чому́ Коктебе́ль, а не Я́лта чи Євпато́рія?
Мико́ла: Тому́ що там мо́жна до́бре відпочи́ти: те́пле мо́ре, го́ри, га́рна приро́да.
Ле́ся: Так, і ду́же дорогі́ готе́лі та рестора́ни.
Мико́ла: Ні, там мо́жна знайти́ деше́ві кварти́ри. Ми купува́ли проду́кти і готува́ли все самі́.
Ле́ся: Я за́вжди хоті́ла так провести́ каніку́ли: ціка́во і недо́рого.

✏️ Нота́тки до діяло́гу
Notes on the Dialogue

Ле́се, Мико́ло These are special forms of the names **Ле́ся** and **Мико́ла**, i.e., the vocative case, which are used when the person is directly addressed. More on the vocative case in Lesson 6.

до́ма, *adv.,* *var.* **удо́ма, вдо́ма** home, at home; Unlike the *Eng.* equivalent it denotes only static location of people in their home, but not a homebound motion.

куди́сь, *adv.* some place, to some place; indicates direction of motion, not location. The particle **~сь** added to an interrogative pronoun turns it into an indefinite pronoun, **що** *what* - **щось** something, **хто** *who* - **хтось** *someone,* **де** *where* - **десь** somewhere, **коли** *when* - **коли́сь** *some day, once,* **чому́** *why* - **чому́сь** *for some reason.*

💬 5. Dialogue. Vacation: Interesting and Inexpensive.

Mykola: Lesia, is that you? How nice! Old friends! Hello!
Lesia: Hello, Mykola. How are you?
Mykola: Fine, thank you. We haven't seen each other the entire summer!
Lesia: What have you been doing? Sat around at home or maybe traveled someplace?
Mykola: I traveled with my friends Taras and Roman to the sea.
Lesia: Well, and how was it?
Mykola: Very well, entertaining – simply great!
Lesia: Where exactly did you vacation?
Mykola: Have you heard of Koktebel? It's the Crimea, very beautiful places.
Lesia: Why Koktebel and not Yalta or Yevpatoria?
Mykola: Because there one can have a good rest – a warm sea, mountains, beautiful nature.
Lesia: Yes, and very expensive hotels and restaurants.
Mykola: No, there one can find cheap apartments. We bought groceries and cooked everything ourselves.
Lesia: I have always wanted to spend my vacations that way: interesting and inexpensive.

Грама́тика | Grammar

Інфініти́в дієсло́ва　Infinitive of the Verb

The infinitive is the form under which verbs are registered in all dictionaries. It simply names the action without specifying its relation to the moment of speaking, i.e., the infinitive has no specific tense. All infinitives can be easily identified by the ending **~ти**,

бу́ти *to be,* **зна́ти** *to know,* **ба́чити** *to see,* **жи́ти** *to live,* **каза́ти** *to say,* **ї́сти** *to eat,* **спа́ти** *to sleep,* **ми́ти** *to wash,* **чита́ти** *to read.*

Some verbs in addition to **~ти**, have a second ending **~ся** or its variant **~сь**. It stays in all the forms of the verb (more on p. 248),

диви́тися or **диви́тись** *to look (at),* **смія́тися** or **смія́тись** *to laugh,* **вага́тися** or **вага́тись** *to hesitate,* **сумніва́тися** or **сумніва́тись** *to doubt.*

Вид дієсло́ва　Verbal Aspect

Фу́нкція | Function
Each Ukrainian verb can describe an action either as a process or a result and has two respective forms called aspects – imperfective and perfective. For example the Ukrainian for *to read* is **чита́ти** *to be reading* and **прочита́ти** *to have read.*

The **imperfective** aspect of the verb presents its action as a process, or something habitual that repeats over time,

Я писа́в до не́ї щоти́жня. *I wrote to her every week (repeatedly).*

The perfective aspect depicts a one-time action as something already completed or restricted in some manner and often focuses on its result, **Я написа́в до не́ї вчо́ра.** *I wrote to her yesterday (one time, started and finished).*

A verb normally has two infinitives – imperfective and perfective, as well as two aspects in the past and future.

The present tense has only the imperfective aspect. The opposition ongoing vs completed action can be expressed in the present by the combination of modal verbs + infinitive (imperfective or perfective), **Зараз Микола ма́є писа́ти лист.** *Now Mykola has to write a letter.* (imperfective simply naming the action, meaning to write and not to edit or send the letter) vs **Зараз Микола ма́є написа́ти лист.** *Now Mykola has to write a letter.* (perfective meaning – he needs to start and finish writing, so he can send it).

From now on, both aspectual forms of the infinitive for each verb will be listed here and both should be memorized. Some verbs are defective and have only one aspect: *impf.* **бу́ти** *to be,* **ма́ти** *to have.*

ї́здити на мо́ре	to go (travel) to the sea-shore (*lit.* to the sea)
са́ме, *adv.*	exactly, precisely, namely; used for emphasis usually after the interrogative pronoun to be emphasized, **хто са́ме?** *exactly who?* **де са́ме?** *exactly where?*
так, *adv.*	so, that way, in such a manner; so well
наприклад, *adv.*	for example, for instance
обов'язко́во, *adv.*	by all means (in *affirm.*), **Тре́ба обов'язко́во подиви́тися цей фільм.** *One needs to see this film by all means.*
мо́жна, *pred., impers.* to + *inf.*	one can, we can, it's possible; used to express a possibility or permission to do something, **Тут мо́жна чита́ти.** *One can (is allowed to) read here.* Also in impersonal statements, **Тут мо́жна знайти́ деше́ві готе́лі.** *Here one can find cheap hotels.* When negated, it expresses impossibility or prohibition, **Тут не мо́жна кури́ти.** *No smoking here.*
ве́село чудо́во ціка́во недо́рого *adv.*	entertainingly wonderfully interestingly inexpensively

(For more on adverbs see Lesson 7, p. 113-114.)

Note 5.1. Typical past time expressions

вчо́ра /wchóra/ *yesterday*
коли́сь /koᵘlýs'/ *once*
неда́вно /neᵘdávnoᵘ/ *recently, lately*
позавчо́ра /poᵘzawchóra/ *the day before yesterday*
тоді́ /toᵘd'i/ *then*
торі́к /toᵘrík/ *last year*
мину́лого ти́жня (мі́сяця, ро́ку) /myᵉnúloho týzhn'a /mís'ats'a, róku/ *last week (month, year)*
мину́лої о́сени (зими́, весни́) /myᵉnúloᵘji óseᵘnyᵉ /zyᵉmý, veᵘsný/ *last fall (winter, spring)*
мину́лого лі́та /myᵉnúloᵘhoᵘ l'íta/ *last summer*
ти́ждень (мі́сяць, рік) то́му /týzhdeᵘn' (m'is'ats', rik) tómu/ *a week (month, year) ago*

Note 5.2. Typical expressions of habitual action

ча́сом /cháso"m/ *at times, sometimes*
ча́сто /chástoᵘ/ *often*
час від ча́су /chas vid chásu/ *from time to time*
за́вжди /záwzhdyᵉ/ *always*
і́ноді /ínoᵘdi/ *sometimes*
рі́дко /rídkoᵘ/ *seldom*
ніко́ли /n'ikólyᵉ/ *never*
як пра́вило /jak právyᵉlo/ *as a rule*
звича́йно /zvyᵉchájno/ *usually,*
  var. зазви́чай /zazvýchaj/

Мину́лий недоко́наний час Past Imperfective Tense

Фу́нкція | *Function*

The past imperfective denotes an action that was in progress or occurred at some moment in the past, **Тоді́ моя́ сестра́ чита́ла.** *My sister was reading then.* It presents the action as:

1) repetitive or habitually occurring. It is used with such words as **ча́сто** *often,* **рі́дко** *rarely,* **і́ноді / і́нколи / ча́сом** *sometimes,* **час від ча́су** *from time to time,* **ніко́ли** *never,* **за́вжди** *always,* **звичайно** *usually,* **як пра́вило** *as a rule.*

  Рома́н ча́сто (рі́дко) писа́в листи. *Roman often (rarely) wrote letters.*

2) an open-ended process without regard for whether or not it was ever completed. The verb may be accompanied by **тоді́** *then,* **до́вго** *for long,* **трива́лий час** *for a long time,* **вчо́ра** *yesterday,* **позавчо́ра** *the day before yesterday,* **мину́лого ти́жня (мі́сяця, ро́ку)** *last week (month, year),* **від + G. … до + G.** *… from … to.*

Украї́нські пластуни́ у Нью-Йо́рку
Ukrainian girl and boy scouts in New York

3) a one-time specific action in the past, a statement of fact with the implication that there is no need to repeat the action again. In this meaning it is often accompanied by the adverb **вже (уже́)** *already.* In this usage, the imperfective past is synonymous with the perfective past.

Ми вже ба́чили цей фільм. *We already saw this film.* (We do not need to see it the second time.)

Утво́рення | *Formation*

Past (im)perfective endings
~в, ~ла, ~ло, and ~ли

The dictionary form of the verb, or infinitive, is used to make the past tense, both imperfective and perfective. The past imperfective (as well as perfective) tense has four forms: three singular and one plural. All four are derived by replacing the ending ~ти in the imperfective infinitive with a respective past tense ending:

~в for masculine singular,
   жи́ти *to live* - **Він (я, ти) жив.** *He (m. I, m. You) lived.*
~ла for feminine singular,
   жи́ти *to live* - **Вона́ (я, ти) жила́.** *She (f. I, f. You) lived.*
~ло for neuter singular,
   жи́ти *to live* - **Воно́ жило́.** *It lived.*
~ли for plural of all genders,
   жи́ти *to live* - **Вони́ жили́.** *They lived.*

If the **~ти** of the infinitive is preceded by a consonant, the masculine form is derived simply by dropping the **~ти**,

бі́гти *to run* – **Він (я, ти) біг.** *He (I, You) ran.* but *f.* **Вона́ бі́гла.** *She ran.* *nt.* **Воно́ бі́гло.** *It ran.* *pl.* **Вони́ бі́гли.** *They ran.* Other such cases are:

кла́сти *to put* - **він клав, вона́ кла́ла,** нести́ *to carry* - **він ніс, вона́ несла́,** везти́ *to transport* - **він віз, вона́ везла́,** вести́ *to lead* - **він вів, вона́ вела́,** плести́ *to spin* - **він плів, вона́ плела́,** рости́ *to grow* - **він ріс, вона́ росла́.**

Verbs that end in **~ся** (**~сь**) form their past tense the same way as those without and keep the **~ся** or *var.* **~сь**,
ми́тися *to wash oneself* – *m.* **він ми́вся,** *f.* **вона́ ми́лася,** *nt.* **воно́ ми́лося,** *pl.* **вони́ ми́лися**
боя́тися *to be afraid* – *m.* **він боя́вся,** *f.* **вона́ боя́лася,** *nt.* **воно́ боя́лося,** *pl.* **вони́ боя́лися**

Мину́лий доко́наний час Past Perfective Tense

Фу́нкція | *Function*

The past perfective tense depicts a past action as completed and focuses on its result. It also presents the action as happening only once – not a repeated occurrence. It is often accompanied by such words as
вже (уже́) *already,* **ще не** *not yet,* **наре́шті** *finally,* **одра́зу** *immediately, at once:* **Рома́н уже́ звари́в вече́рю.** *Roman has already cooked dinner.*
Оле́на ще не закі́нчила пере́клад. *Olena has not yet finished the translation.*
Ми наре́шті подиви́лися нови́й фільм. *We have finally watched a new film.*

Утво́рення | *Formation*
The past perfective is formed the same way as the past imperfective with the only difference that it uses perfective infinitive instead of the imperfective one, *pf.* **запита́ти** ask –
   Він запита́в. *He asked.*
   Вона́ запита́ла. *She asked.*
   Воно́ запита́ло. *It asked.*
   Вони́ запита́ли. *They asked.*

Подру́ги Ксе́ня та Ре́йчел купи́ли каву́н.

Note 5.3. Irregular past tense forms

Memorize the past imperfective forms of these irregular verbs:
іти́ (йти́) *to go* –
   m. **він ішо́в** *he went*
   f. **вона́ йшла** *she went*
   nt. **воно́ йшло** *it went*
   pl. **вони́ йшли** *they went*
йти *to go* is an identical in meaning variant of **іти́.** It is used after the words ending in a vowel, **Мико́ла йшов.** *Mykola went.*
   і́сти *to eat* –
   m. **він їв** *he ate*
   f. **вона́ ї́ла** *she ate*
   nt. **воно́ ї́ло** *it ate*
   pl. **вони́ ї́ли** *they ate*
могти́ *to be able* –
   m. **він міг** *he could*
   f. **вона́ могла́** *she could*
   nt. **воно́ могло́** *it could*
   pl. **вони́ могли́** *they could*

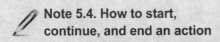

Note 5.4. How to start, continue, and end an action

The verbs that express the beginning, continuation, and completion of an action can be followed only by an imperfective infinitive. This rule has no exceptions. The verbs are:

impf. **почина́ти**

   pf. **поча́ти** *to begin*

impf. **закі́нчувати**

   pf. **закі́нчити** *to finish*

impf. **продо́вжувати**

   pf. **продо́вжити** *to continue,*

Сергі́й поча́в чита́ти.
Serhiy began to read.
Ма́рта закі́нчувала працюва́ти.
Marta was finishing working.
Ми продо́вжували танцюва́ти.
We continued dancing.

The stress in the past imperfective and perfective is mostly the same as in their respective infinitives. Some frequently used verbs however do not follow this rule,

бу́ти *to be* but **Вона́ була́. Вони́ були́.**
пи́ти *to drink* but **Вона́ пила́. Вони́ пили́.**
ли́ти *to pour* but **Вона́ лила́. Вони́ лили́.**
жи́ти *to live* but **Вона́ жила́. Вони́ жили́.**

Note 5.5. Memorize these aspectual pairs of verbs

(The dictionary offers the perfective form in the entry for every imperfective verb after the semicolon, **ста|ва́ти ~ють; ста́ти** to become)

impf.	pf.	Eng.
будува́ти	збудува́ти	to build
вари́ти	звари́ти	to cook
відпочива́ти	відпочи́ти	to rest
вчи́ти	ви́вчити	to study, learn sth
дивити́ся	подиви́тися	to watch, look
дзвони́ти	подзвони́ти	to call, telephone
йти	прийти́	to go; pf. to come
ї́сти	з'ї́сти	to eat
купува́ти	купи́ти	to buy
ми́ти	поми́ти	to wash, clean
переклада́ти	перекла́сти	to translate
писа́ти	написа́ти	to write
пита́ти	запита́ти	to ask (a question)
поя́снювати	поясни́ти	to explain
роби́ти	зроби́ти	to do, make
розумі́ти	зрозумі́ти	to understand
слу́хати	послу́хати	to listen
чита́ти	прочита́ти	to read
шука́ти	знайти́	to search, look for; to find (in pf.)

Називни́й відмі́нок множини́   Nominative Case Plural

Іме́нники   Nouns

Фу́нкція **|** *Function*

Nominative plural is used in **two situations**:

1) when the plural noun is the subject of the sentence,
Ці кана́дці – на́ші дру́зі. *These Canadians are our friends.*

2) when the noun follows the numerals of quantity **два** *two*, **три** *three*, **чоти́ри** *four*, which appear either on their own,
два бра́ти *two brothers*, **три кни́жки** *three books*, **чоти́ри сестри́** *four sisters* or as part of a composite numeral like **два́дцять два**

студе́нти *twenty-two students*, три́дцять чоти́ри ро́ки *thirty-four years*, п'ятдеся́т три хвили́ни *fifty-three minutes*. (For more on nouns after 2, 3, and 4 see Lesson 11, pp. 202-203.)

Утво́рення | *Formation*

Nominative plural endings:
~и (~і, ~ї), ~а (~я)

~и for all masculine and feminine nouns with hard stems, i.e., that end in a hard consonant,

m. студе́нт *a student* - студе́нти *students*
ба́тько *a father* - батьки́ *fathers*
брат *a brother* - брати́ *brothers*
f. копі́йка *a kopek* - копі́йки *kopeks*
кни́жка *a book* - книжки́ *books*
сестра́ *a sister* - се́стри *sisters*

~і for all masculine and feminine nouns with soft and mixed stems,

m. вчи́тель *a teacher* - вчителі́ *teachers*
m. това́риш *a friend* - товариші́ *friends*
f. гри́вня *a hryvnia* - гри́вні *hryvnias*
f. ву́лиця *a street* - ву́лиці *streets*
m. and f. суддя́ *a judge* - су́дді *judges*
f. миш *a mouse* - ми́ші *mice*
f. по́дорож *a trip* - по́дорожі *trips*
f. ві́дповідь *an answer* - ві́дповіді *answers*

~ї for nouns ending in ~й, '~я, and ~ія,

m. музе́й *a museum* - музе́ї *museums*
m. геро́й *a hero* - геро́ї *heroes*
f. сім'я́ *a family* - сі́м'ї *families*
f. істо́рія *a story* - істо́рії *stories*

~а for all neuter nouns of hard stems,

мі́сто *a city* - міста́ *cities*
село́ *a village* - се́ла *villages*
вікно́ *a window* - ві́кна *windows*
сло́во *a word* - слова́ *words*
прі́звище *a last name* - прі́звища *last names*

~я for all neuter nouns with soft stems,

по́ле *a field* - поля́ *fields*
мо́ре *a sea* - моря́ *seas*
пита́ння *a question* - пита́ння *questions*
бажа́ння *a desire* - бажа́ння *desires*
пла́ття *a dress* - пла́ття *dresses*
(Thus neuter nouns ending in double consonant + я have the same nominative singular and plural.)

✎ Note 5.6. Types of word stems

A great majority of words in Ukrainian have a stem or the unchanging part, and an ending or the part that changes. The stem is the word minus its ending,

ба́тько *a father* has the stem батьк~, likewise мат~ is the stem of ма́ти *a mother*, авт~ is the stem of а́вто *a car*.

In the nouns that end in a consonant, the stem is the same as the entire word,

по́тяг *a train*, ніж *a knife*, лі́кар *a doctor*.

There are three types of stems. Each is determined by its final consonant:

1. **Hard stems** end in a hard consonant,

ха́та *a house*, брат *a brother*, Мико́ла *Mykola (a masculine name)*.

2. **Soft stems** end in a soft consonant, вчи́тель *a teacher*, сіль *salt*, обли́ччя *a face*.

3. **Mixed stems** end in the consonants ж, ч, ш, щ, and р,

ніж *a knife*, плече́ *a shoulder*, пло́ща *a square*, лі́кар *a doctor*.

Ці весе́лі ді́ти що́йно почали́ навча́тися.

малий український селянин

◀)) SOUND CHANGES ◀)▶
in the nominative plural of nouns

Dropping of ~o~ (~e~)

~o~ and ~e~ in the last syllable of second declension masculine nouns are dropped in the nominative plural,

куто́к *a corner* - **кутки́** *corners*
сон *a dream* - **сни** *dreams*
украї́нець *a Ukrainian* - **украї́нці** *Ukrainians*
кіне́ць *an end* - **кінці́** *ends*
день *a day* - **дні** *days*

Change of ~i~ to ~o~ (~e~)

~i~ changes to ~o~ (~e~) in the final syllable in second declension masculine and third declension feminine nouns,

m. **кіт** *a cat* - **коти́** *cats*
m. **папі́р** *paper* - **папе́ри** *papers*
f. **річ** *a thing* - **ре́чі** *things*
f. **ніч** *a night* - **но́чі** *nights*

Masculine nouns with suffixes ~а́нин (~я́нин) loose the final ~н in *N. pl.*:

кия́нин *a citizen of Kyiv* - **кия́ни** *citizens of Kyiv*
росія́нин *a Russian* - **росія́ни** *Russians*
селяни́н *a peasant* - **селя́ни** *peasants*
християни́н *a Christian* - **християни** *Christians*

Note the irregular *N. pl.* forms of other frequently used nouns:

друг *a friend* - **дру́зі** *friends*
люди́на *a person* - **лю́ди** *people*
ді́вчина *a girl* - **дівча́та** *girls*
дити́на *a child* - **ді́ти** *children*
ма́ти *a mother* - **матері́** *mothers*
ім'я́ *a name* - **імена́** *names*

Names of baby animals, i.e. nouns of fourth declension, acquire the ending ~та in *N. pl.*:

курча́ *a chicken* - **курча́та** *chickens*
щеня́ *a puppy* - **щеня́та** *puppies*
котеня́ *a kitten* - **котеня́та** *kittens*

щеня́

теля́

котеня́

порося́

 The stress in the nominative plural highly varies and has three principal patterns:

1) the stress stays on the same syllable as in *N. sg.*,
студе́нт *a student* - **студе́нти** *students*, **магази́н** *a store* - **магази́ни** *stores*

2) the stress falls on the stem in *N. sg.* and shifts onto the ending in *N. pl.*,
ба́тько *a father* - **батьки́** *fathers*, **брат** *a brother* - **брати́** *brothers*, **дя́дько** *an uncle* - **дядьки́** *uncles*

3) the stress falls on the ending in *N. sg.* and shifts onto the stem in *N. pl.*,
сестра́ *a sister* - **се́стри** *sisters*, **рука́** *a hand* - **ру́ки** *hands*, **нога́** *a leg* - **но́ги** *legs*, **голова́** *a head* - **го́лови** *heads*.

At this stage, it is best to memorize the nominative plural stress.

Прикме́тники   Adjectives

Adjectival nominative plural endings:
~i (~ï)

All the adjectives, possessive pronouns, and ordinal numerals have the nominative plural ending ~i and therefore lose the gender distinction,
вели́кий *big* – **вели́кі, си́ній** *blue* – **си́ні, цей** *this* – **ці, той** *that* – **ті, наш** *our* – **на́ші**.
The pronouns ending in ~**ій** take the ending ~**ï** and undergo the **i – о** vowel change in their stems,
мій *my* – **мої́, твій** *your* – **твої́, свій** *one's own* – **свої́**.

Note 5.7. Consonant В, в /v/ in word final position

The Ukrainian /v/ is a voiced consonant, i.e., when it is pronounced the vocal chords vibrate. Its voiceless counterpart /f/ is pronounced without the participation of the voice. At the end of the word, the voiced /v/ does not ever become a /f/. On the contrary, it resembles a short labialized vowel /u/, signified in transcription by /w/. In the past tense masculine forms, the result is a number of diphthongs:
роби́ти *to do* -
    Він роби́в. /ro^ubýw/ *He did.*
чита́ти *to read* -
    Він чита́в. /chy^etáw/ *He read.*
іти́ *to walk* -
    Він ішо́в. /ishów/ *He walked.*
бу́ти *to be* -
    Він був. /buw/ *He was.*
сиді́ти *to sit* -
    Він сиді́в. /sy^edíw/ *He sat.*

📖 Впра́ви   Exercises

🎧 **5.1.** Listen and repeat after the speaker. Practice the voiced /w/ in the masculine past tense forms.

Model.
C *inf.* ма́ти *to have*
A Він мав. *He had.*

будува́ти *to build*
відпочива́ти *to rest*
диви́тися *to look*
йти *to go, walk*
купува́ти *to buy*
переклада́ти *to translate*
поя́снювати *to explain*
слу́хати *to listen*

вари́ти *to cook*
вчи́ти *to study, learn*
дзвони́ти *to call, telephone*
ї́сти *to eat*
ми́ти *to wash, clean*
писа́ти *to write*
роби́ти *to do, make*
шука́ти *to look for, to find*

∩ 5.2. Form the past imperfective from these infinitives.

Model.
C він, співа́ти *to sing*
A Він коли́сь так співа́в. *He once sang so (that way).*

ми, писа́ти
вони́, роби́ти
воно́, ду́мати
він, чита́ти
воно́, спа́ти
він, переклада́ти

ви, працюва́ти
він, говори́ти
вона́, жи́ти
вони́, хоті́ти
вона́, відпочива́ти
вона́, ї́сти

Ми коли́сь ве́село подорожува́ли.

∩ 5.3. Form sentences in the past imperfective. Replace the subject by the respective personal pronoun.

Model.
C мій брат *my brother*, завжди́ *always*, бага́то чита́ти *to read a lot*
A Він завжди́ бага́то чита́в. *He always read a lot.*

1. твоя́ ма́ма, ча́сто, співа́ти
2. мала́ ді́вчина, час від ча́су, ї́сти
3. мої́ батьки́ *parents*, завжди́, бага́то працюва́ти *to work a lot*
4. всі ді́ти *all children*, як пра́вило, люби́ти цуке́рки *to like candies*
5. Мико́ла та Іри́на, ча́сто, ї́здити на мо́ре *to travel to the seaside*
6. мій друг, завжди́, слу́хати ра́діо *to listen to the radio*
7. ї́хнє дитя́, ча́сто, диви́тися на це де́рево *to look at the tree*
8. мої́ батьки́, і́ноді, купува́ти вино́ *to buy wine*
9. Іва́н Ханє́нко, ча́сом, дзвони́ти додо́му *to call home*
10. на́ші студе́нти, ча́сто, ду́мати про Украї́ну *to think about Ukraine*

∩ 5.4. Transform the past imperfective into the past perfective. Use the table in the grammar section.

Model. C Вчо́ра Мирosла́в до́вго роби́в завда́ння. *Yesterday Myroslav was doing the assignment for a long time.*
A Мирosла́в вже зроби́в завда́ння. *Myroslav has already done the assignment.*

1. Вчо́ра Соломі́я до́вго писа́ла впра́ви.
2. Позавчо́ра Яри́на до́вго диви́лася фільм.

На вака́ціях дівча́та ча́сто роби́ли впра́ви.

3. Вчо́ра Марко́ до́вго вари́в ї́сти.
4. Позавчо́ра Стефа́нія до́вго вчи́ла нові́ слова́.
5. Мину́лого мі́сяця Рома́н і Ната́лка до́вго відпочива́ли на мо́рі.
6. Вчо́ра ми до́вго йшли додо́му.
7. Вчо́ра Мико́ла до́вго мив по́суд.
8. Позавчо́ра О́льга до́вго купува́ла проду́кти.
9. Вчо́ра ба́тько до́вго слуха́в ра́діо.
10. Мину́лого ти́жня вони́ до́вго шука́ли готе́ль.
11. Окса́на до́вго чита́ла журна́л.
12. Мину́лого ро́ку робітники́ до́вго будува́ли нови́й теа́тр.

5.5. Say and write each sentence in Ukrainian. Note that the English verb + *inf.* or verb + ~*ing* form correspond to the Ukrainian verb + *impf. inf.*

1. We began to understand.
2. He finished listening.
3. She began to read.
4. They started to study.
5. They finished speaking.
6. It (the baby) finished eating.
7. We began to watch.
8. The child started to ask.
9. The boy started to work.

Га́ня продо́вжувала роби́ти фільм.

5.6. Rewrite each sentence to transform a past action in process into a completed past action.

Model.
C Марко́ до́вго роби́в завда́ння. *Marko was doing the assignment for a long time.*
A Марко́ **наре́шті** зроби́в завда́ння. *Marko finally did the assignment.*

1. Мій брат до́вго писа́в лист.
2. Яросла́в до́вго переклада́в текст.
3. Яри́на до́вго вари́ла борщ.
4. Васи́ль до́вго вчив нові́ імена́.
5. Мико́ла до́вго мив по́суд.
6. Оле́на до́вго роби́ла завда́ння.
7. Тимі́ш до́вго чита́в газе́ти.
8. Володи́мир до́вго поя́снював це пра́вило.
9. Робітники́ до́вго будува́ли нови́й суперма́ркет.
10. Ми до́вго шука́ли його́ улю́блений музе́й.

5.7. Express the idea of a failed effort. Combine an imperfective past for an effort undertaken with a perfective past of the same word for a result that never materialized. Use the previous exercise and follow the model.

Оле́кса до́вго диви́вся альбо́м.

Note 5.8. Masculine names of nationalities

Many nouns that name nationalities of the masculine gender are subject to e-dropping. The *N. pl.* stress is on the same syllable as in *N. sg.*:

Model. алба́нець *an Albanian –* **алба́нці** *Albanians*

1. украї́нець *a Ukrainian*
2. америка́нець *an American*
3. іспа́нець *a Spaniard*
4. кана́дець *a Canadian*
5. мексика́нець *a Mexican*
6. палести́нець *a Palestinian*
7. кита́єць *a Chinese*
8. ні́мець *a German*
9. австрі́єць *an Austrian*
10. япо́нець *a Japanese*
11. аргенти́нець *an Argentinian*

With the e-dropping, the finale **~єць** in the singular becomes **~йці** in the plural.

Model. австралі́єць *an Australian –* **австралі́йці** *Australians*

1. англі́єць *an Englishman*
2. канаді́єць *var. a Canadian*
3. італі́єць *an Italian*
4. колумбі́єць *a Colombian*
5. бельгі́єць *a Belgian*
6. нігері́єць *a Nigerian*
7. чилі́єць *a Chilean*
8. сирі́єць *a Syrian*

Take note. In Ukrainian, names of nationalities are written in lower case.

Model
C Марко́ до́вго роби́в завда́ння. *Marko was doing the assignment for a long time.*
A Марко́ до́вго роби́в завда́ння, але́ так і не зроби́в. *Marko was doing the assignment for a long time and never finished (did it).*

Phonetics. Drill dropping the ~o~

🎧 **5.8.** Listen carefully and repeat. Practice dropping the vowel /o/ in the final syllable of the consonant-ended masculine nouns when forming the nominative plural. Take note of the *N. pl.* stress.

Model.
Stress Pattern A. Stress remains on the same vowel.
C я́рмаро́к *a fair*
A я́рмарки *fairs*

буди́нок *a building*	поча́ток *a beginning*
ґа́нок *a doorstep*	прову́лок *a lane*
понеді́лок *Monday*	ра́нок *a morning*
вівто́рок *Tuesday*	ви́няток *an exception*
гурто́житок *a dormitory*	ри́нок *a market*
ко́рок *a cork*	сніда́нок *a breakfast*
подару́нок *a gift*	спи́сок *a list*

Stress Pattern B. Stress is on the last syllable.
C місто́к *a little bridge*
A містки́ *little bridges*

квито́к *a ticket*	куто́к *a corner*
сон *a dream*	листо́к *a sheet; leaf*
огіро́к *a cucumber*	па́рубок *a bachelor*
лісо́к *a grove*	тано́к *a dance*
замо́к *a lock*	като́к *a skating rink*

Phonetics. Drill dropping the ~e~

🎧 **5.9.** Listen carefully to the speaker and repeat. Practice dropping the vowel /e/ in the final syllable of the consonant-ended masculine nouns when forming the nominative plural. Take note of the *N. pl.* stress.

Model.
Stress Pattern A. Stress remains on the same vowel.
C ні́мець *a German man*
A ні́мці *German men*

та́нець *a dance*	науко́вець *a scientist*
хло́пець *a boy*	у́чень *a pupil*

украї́нець *a Ukrainian man*	ду́рень *a dumbhead*
рі́вень *a level*	бу́день *a weekday*
пі́вень *a rooster*	пе́рстень *a ring* (пе́рсні)

Stress Pattern B. Stress is on the last syllable.
C речене́ць *a deadline*
A реченці́ *deadlines.*

день *a day*	кіне́ць *an end*
голубе́ць *a cabbage roll*	гамане́ць *a wallet*
млине́ць *a pancake*	фахіве́ць *a specialist*
олівець *a pencil*	горобе́ць *a sparrow*
покупе́ць *a buyer*	продаве́ць *a salesperson*

Ці хло́пці ходи́ли на конце́рт.

🎧 **5.10.** Make inquiries about a group of people. Form nominative plural of the nouns designating nationalities.

Model. хло́пець *a guy,* украї́нець *a Ukrainian man*
Q Що це за хло́пці? *Who are these guys?*
A Це на́ші знайо́мі украї́нці. *These are the Ukrainians we know.*

Тара́с - украї́нець.

Гіша́м - норве́жець.

Фа́біо - італі́єць.

Рейна́льдо - куби́нець.

1. люди́на *a person,* португа́лець
2. студе́нт *a student,* італі́єць
3. лі́кар *a physician,* япо́нець
4. чолові́к *a man,* англі́єць
5. тури́ст *a tourist,* іспа́нець

6. гість *a guest,* кана́дець
7. юна́к *a male youth,* америка́нець
8. профе́сор *a professor,* аргенти́нець
9. футболі́ст *a soccer player,* брази́лець
10. спортсме́н *an athlete,* колумбі́єць

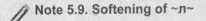

✏️ **Note 5.9. Softening of ~л~**

The consonant ~л~ before the dropping ~е~ becomes soft in the nominative plural form,
па́лець *a finger (toe)* -
  па́льці *fingers (toes)*
стіле́ць *a chair* -
  стільці́ *chairs*
брази́лець *a Brazilian* -
  брази́льці *Brazilians*
португа́лець *a Portuguese* -
  португа́льці *pl. Portuguese*
Memorize the special case of
ти́ждень *a week* - *pl.* **ти́жні** *weeks*

Note 5.10. Expression of Possibility

To indicate a possibility of action, the word **мо́жна** *one can* is used in impersonal expressions that refer to nobody specifically: *Where can one buy tickets? When can one call? How can one find information?*

When the result is important, **мо́жна** is followed by a perfective infinitive, **Де мо́жна відпочи́ти?** *Where can one rest?*

Коли́ мо́жна пообі́дати? *When can one have lunch?*

When negated, **не мо́жна** can be followed by both imperfective and perfective infinitive,

impf. **Тут не мо́жна відпочива́ти.** *One may not rest here. (never)*

pf. **Тут не мо́жна відпочи́ти.** *One may not rest here. (at this moment, under these specific circumstances)*

To describe past tense situations one uses **було́** (which is past tense neuter singular form of the verb **бу́ти** *to be*) + **мо́жна**,

Тут було́ мо́жна відпочи́ти. *One could rest here.*

Тоді́ було́ мо́жна пообі́дати. *Then one could have lunch.*

These two words can trade places without changing the meaning of the utterance,

Тут мо́жна було́ відпочи́ти.

Тоді́ мо́жна було́ пообі́дати.

When negated, the past tense of this expression can have two variants:

1) usually the negative particle **не** *not* is put before **мо́жна** which is followed by **було́**,

Там не мо́жна було́ до́бре відпочи́ти. *One could not have a good rest there.*

2) less commonly **не** is put before **було́** which is followed by **мо́жна**,

Вчо́ра не було́ мо́жна спа́ти. *One could not sleep yesterday.*

5.11. React to the cue. Put the entire phrase in the nominative plural.

Model.
C Це ціка́ва кни́жка. *This is an interesting book.*
A Тут усі́ книжки́ ціка́ві. *Here, all books are interesting.*

гарна ді́вчина

мала́ дити́на

1. Це смачна́ стра́ва.
2. Це нови́й студе́нт.
3. Це неціка́ва газе́та.
4. Це мала́ дити́на.
5. Це стара́ істо́рія.
6. Це твій америка́нець.
7. Це висо́ке де́рево.
8. Це на́ша ма́ти.
9. Це близьки́й друг.
10. Це украї́нське ім'я́.
11. Це га́рна ді́вчина.
12. Це вели́ке мі́сто.
13. Це висо́ка люди́на.
14. Це моя́ улю́блена стра́ва.

5.12. Transform the sentences into plural.

Model.
C Мій брат міг чита́ти. *My brother could read.*
A Тоді́ мої́ брати́ могли́ чита́ти. *Then my brothers could read.*

1. Наш друг міг пла́вати.
2. Ця ді́вчина могла́ співа́ти.
3. Їхня ма́ти могла́ працюва́ти.
4. Її ба́тько міг чита́ти.
5. Ва́ша жі́нка могла́ вари́ти.
6. Ця люди́на могла́ розповіда́ти.
7. Цей учи́тель міг поя́снювати.
8. Та украї́нка могла́ слу́хати.

5.13. Say each phrase in Ukrainian.

1. all great people
2. all small children
3. these pretty women
4. those Ukrainian words
5. delicious apples
6. all old chairs
7. all hryvnias
8. these kopeks
9. these new cities
10. those happy girls
11. all names and family names
12. all my favorite friends

⌒ **5.14.** Make an inquiry. Use **мо́жна** + *pf. inf.* If necessary consult the dictionary for the perfective infinitive.

Model.
C Де? *Where?* дивитися фі́льми *to watch films*
A Де мо́жна подиви́тися фі́льми? *Where can one watch films?*

1. Як? вари́ти ї́сти
2. Коли́? слу́хати ра́діо
3. Де? купува́ти проду́кти
4. Як? шука́ти готе́ль
5. Коли́? чита́ти всі ці книжки́
6. Як? закі́нчувати ці впра́ви
7. Коли́? продо́вжувати працюва́ти
8. Як? будува́ти нови́й готе́ль так шви́дко
9. Де? га́рно прово́дити кані́кули
10. Коли́? дзвони́ти додо́му
11. Що? писа́ти
12. Що? поя́снювати

У Криму́ мо́жна ду́же ціка́во провести́ вака́ції.

Listening comprehension

⌒ **5.15.** Read the questions and make sure you understand them. Listen to the text "Ідеа́льні вака́ції" online and answer the questions.

1. Куди́ ї́здив Михайло?
2. Коли́ він ї́здив відпочива́ти?
3. Як назива́ється мі́сто, де відпочива́в Михайло?
4. Хто ще ї́здив туди́?
5. Що роби́ли дру́зі на мо́рі?

⌒ **5.16.** Listen to the text "Ідеа́льні вака́ції" once again and render in English as much of the content as you can.

⌒ **5.17.** Translate this text into English. Summarize the contents in Ukrainian in three or four sentences.

Ідеа́льні вака́ції
Торік Михайло Бойчу́к ї́здив відпочива́ти на мо́ре. Коли́сь він чув ціка́ві ре́чі про мі́сто Бердя́нськ і за́вжди хоті́в поба́чити його́. Він та його́ близькі́ дру́зі Окса́на та Бори́с ї́здили ра́зом. Всі вони́ ду́же до́бре провели́ кані́кули.
Мо́ре було́ те́пле, пого́да га́рна, кварти́ра недорога́, а ї́жа смачна́. Ча́сто дру́зі купува́ли проду́кти та готува́ли ї́сти са́мі. Вони́ бага́то купа́лися, гра́ли у футбо́л, чита́ли ціка́ві книжки́ чи диви́лися рі́зні фі́льми у кінотеа́трі. Це були́ ї́хні про́сто ідеа́льні вака́ції — ціка́ві, весе́лі та недорогі́.

Михайло Бойчу́к торік відпочива́в на мо́рі.

Note 5.11. Украї́нські свята́
Ukrainian holidays

Нови́й рік *New Year*, January 1
Різдво́ (*colloq.* **Ко́ляди**) *Christmas*,
January 7
Василя́ (**стари́й Нови́й рік**) *St. Basil's
Day*, January 14
Водо́хреще (*also* **Йорда́н**) *Epiphany*,
January 19
Вели́кдень *Easter*
День ма́тері *Mother's Day*, second
Sunday of May
Трі́йця (*colloq.* **Зеле́ні свята́**)
Pentecost
День Незале́жности *Independence
Day*, August 24

Па́м'ятник Св.
Володи́мирові у Ки́єві
St. Volodymyr's monument in Kyiv

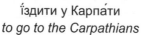 **5.18.** Memorize these expressions and use them when speaking about your recent vacation.

Що мо́жна роби́ти на вака́ціях? What can one do during vacation?

сиді́ти вдо́ма *to sit at home*　　ї́здити на о́зеро *to go to a lake*

ї́здити у Карпа́ти　　　　ї́здити на мо́ре
to go to the Carpathians　　*to go to the seaside*

сиді́ти вдо́ма	to sit around at home
ї́здити у по́дорож	to go on a trip
ї́здити у го́ри, у Карпа́ти, на мо́ре, на о́зеро	to travel to the mountains, to the Carpathians, to the seaside, to a lake
на мо́рі мо́жна купа́тися, пла́вати, засма́гати, гра́ти у м'яч	by the sea one can bathe, swim, get suntanned, play ball
у го́рах (Карпа́тах) мо́жна гуля́ти, збира́ти тра́ви, я́годи, гриби́	in the (Carpathian) mountains one can go for a hike, gather herbs, berries, mushrooms

Да́ти відпові́ді на ці пита́ння. Provide answers to these questions.
1. Що ви роби́ли в оста́нні вака́ції?
2. Куди́ ви ї́здили?
3. Що ви роби́ли на мо́рі чи у го́рах?
4. Як ви прове́ли час?

 **5.19.** Engage a partner in an exchange. Use the building blocks given below. Follow the model. Note the word order of the answer.

Model.

C Іва́н *Ivan,* де? *where?* вчо́ра подиви́тися фі́льми
to watch films yesterday

Q Що хоті́в зна́ти Іва́н? *What did Ivan want to know?*

A Він хоті́в зна́ти, де мо́жна було́ вчо́ра подиви́тися фі́льми.
Ivan wanted to know where one could watch films yesterday.

1. Воло́дя, як? вчо́ра звари́ти ї́сти
2. Ната́ля, коли? послу́хати ці пісні́ мину́лого ти́жня
3. ва́ші се́стри, де? купи́ти сві́жі о́вочі мину́лої зими́
4. Марко́, як? позавчо́ра знайти́ деше́ві квитки́
5. ви, коли? вчо́ра прочита́ти всі оста́нні нови́ни
6. Ле́ся, як? тоді́ закі́нчити писа́ти дома́шні завда́ння
7. Павло́, коли? продо́вжити працюва́ти
8. Марі́я та Васи́ль, як? до́бре відпочи́ти мину́лої о́сени
9. твої́ дру́зі, де? га́рно провести́ кані́кули то́рік
10. Мико́ла, коли? вчо́ра подзвони́ти додо́му

Phonetics. Drill shifting ~i~ to ~o~ (~e~)

5.20. Listen carefully to the speaker and react to the cue changing the ~i~ to ~o~ (~e~) when forming the nominative plural of these nouns. Check yourself against the speaker.

Model.
Stress Pattern A. *N. pl.* stress remains on the same vowel.
C *f.* ніч *a night*
A но́чі *nights*

m. гість *a guest*   *m.* порі́г *a doorstep*
m. вхід *an entrance*   *m.* ви́хід *an exit*
m. сік *juice*   *m.* твір *a work*
m. при́від *an excuse*   *m.* ріг *a street corner*
m. полі́т *a flight* (польо́ти)   *m.* дзвін *a bell*
m. ви́бір *a choice*   *f.* сіль *salt*

Stress Pattern B. *N. pl.* stress shifts to the last syllable.
C *m.* кіт *a cat*
A коти́ *cats*

m. ко́лір *a color* (кольори́)   *m.* о́стрів *an island*
m. ніс *a nose*   *m.* бати́г *a whip*
m. бік *a side*   *m.* стіл *a table*
m. рік *a year*   *m.* двір *a courtyard*
m. плід *a fruit*   *m.* живі́т *a stomach*
m. пиро́г *a pie*   *m.* ве́чір *an evening*
m. віз *a wagon*   *m.* рід *a gender*

i/e change
f. річ *a thing* - ре́чі *things*   *m.* ко́рінь *a root* - ко́рені *roots*
f. піч *an oven* - пе́чі *ovens*   *m.* папі́р *a paper* - папе́ри *papers*

Note 5.12. Числі́вники від двадцяти́ до дев'ятдесяти́
Numerals from twenty to ninety-nine

Memorize the cardinal numerals from *twenty* to *ninety*. Note that in the middle of numerals **два́дцять** and **три́дцять**, the consonant д /d/ in the cluster -дц- /dts/ is assimilated to the following soft ц /ts'/ and therefore instead of being fully pronounced it becomes a stop /¬/. Listen carefully to and imitate the speaker.

Listen and repeat after the speaker the numerals from twenty to ninety:

twenty	два́дцять	/dvá¬ts'at'/
thirty	три́дцять	/try¬ts'at'/
forty	со́рок	/sóroᵘk/
fifty	п'ятдеся́т	/pja¬deʸs'át/
sixty	шістдеся́т	/shizdeʸs'át/
seventy	сімдеся́т	/s'imdeʸs'át/
eighty	вісімдеся́т	/vis'imdeʸs'át/
ninety	дев'ятдеся́т	/devja¬deʸs'át/
	or дев'яно́сто	/devjanóstoᵘ/

Коля́дники (carol-singers) га́рно співа́ли на Рі́здво.

Вели́кдень – це його́ улю́блене свя́то

Note 5.13. Composite numerals

Numerals denoting tens and units, like twenty-two, thirty-four, seventy-nine, are composed of two words: a numeral for tens + a numeral for units. There is no hyphen between the two,

два́дцять оди́н *twenty-one*
три́дцять два *thirty-two*
со́рок чоти́ри *forty-four*
шістдеся́т п'ять *sixty-five*
сімдеся́т оди́н *seventy-one*
вісімдеся́т сім *eighty-seven*
дев'ятдеся́т де́в'ять *ninety-nine*
or дев'яно́сто де́в'ять

⋒ **5.21.** Say and write these sentences down in Ukrainian. Use the vocabulary and grammar of the lesson. Consult the dictionary.

1. The friends have not seen each other the entire week.
2. Mykola and Lesia went to the sea together.
3. There, one can find cheap hotels and good restaurants.
4. These Americans have always wanted to see the Carpathians and the Crimea.
5. How did those happy girls spend their holidays?
6. This isn't only one book. These are all my books.
7. Their brothers often traveled to the sea.
8. She already wrote all exercises and translated the English texts.
9. These Ukrainians spent a whole week here.
10. How can one find interesting new films?
11. Where can one have a good rest?
12. Their guests heard strange things about this distant and old city.
13. I finally found his university.
14. The students had been doing the assignment for a long time and finally finished.

⋒ **5.22.** Listen carefully and mark the numerals you hear.

два́дцять	три́дцять	трина́дцять
шістна́дцять	п'ятдеся́т	три́дцять два
сімдеся́т чоти́ри	шістдеся́т вісім	два́дцять де́в'ять
дев'ятдеся́т сім	со́рок чоти́ри	дев'ятдеся́т вісім
одина́дцять	де́сять	п'ятдеся́т чоти́ри
шістдеся́т	двана́дцять	дев'ятдеся́т
п'ятна́дцять	вісімдеся́т шість	чотирна́дцять
вісімдеся́т	два́дцять оди́н	п'ятдеся́т сім

⋒ **5.23.** Numeric dictation. Listen carefully to the speaker and write down the Ukrainian numerals that you hear as Arabic numbers. Read out loud what you have written.

⋒ **5.24.** Listen carefully to these questions and answer each of them based on Dialogue 5.

1. Скі́льки не ба́чилися Мико́ла та Ле́ся?
2. Що роби́в Мико́ла на каніку́ли?
3. Хто такі́ Тара́с і Рома́н?
4. Куди́ ра́зом ї́здили дру́зі?
5. Де са́ме відпочива́ли Мико́ла, Тара́с і Рома́н?
6. Що таке́ Коктебе́ль?
7. Чому́ хло́пці ви́брали са́ме Коктебе́ль?
8. Які́ кварти́ри мо́жна знайти́ там?
9. Що купува́ли дру́зі ї́сти?
10. Хто готува́в ї́сти?

11. Як Ле́ся завжди́ хоті́ла провести́ кані́кули?
12. Як ви провели́ оста́нні лі́тні кані́кули?

🌐 Завда́ння для Міжнаро́дної мере́жі
Internet assignment

5.25. Find the Ukrainian equivalents of these words and expressions using the Google Translator: http://www.google.com/ig Write them down. Mark all stresses with the help of **http://lcorp.ulif.org.ua/dictua/**

You can use these words in the description of your last vacation.

mushroom		berry	
to photograph		bush	
fish		animal	
to fish		bird	
tent		postcard	
put up a tent		forest	

Скажі́ть, будь ла́ска, що роби́ли на вака́ціях Рома́н і Яри́на?

5.26. Enact a conversation with a partner. Use the material you learned in this and previous lessons. Where necessary, consult the dictionary.

Сце́нка за сцена́рієм «Кані́кули»
Scripted Skit «Holidays»

Roman (Рома́н): Greets Yaryna and expresses pleasure at seeing her.
Yaryna (Яри́на): Greets Roman. Notes that they have not seen each other for a long time. Asks how he is.

Roman: He is OK. Asks how she spent summer holidays. Did she stay home or go somewhere?
Yaryna: She did not stay home. She and her sisters Natalia and Maria traveled to the Carpathian Mountains together.

Roman: Expresses excitement. Asks what they did there.
Yaryna: They rested, saw interesting places, villages, and cities.

Roman: Which places, villages, and cities for example.
Yaryna: They saw such big cities as Ivano-Frankivsk and Uzhorod, and also such small towns as Kolomyia, Yaremche, and Kosiv. People there were very hospitable. Asks Roman how he spent his summer vacation.

Андрі́й за́вжди люби́в лови́ти
ри́бу взи́мку, а не влі́тку.

Roman: A year ago he went to the seashore and this year he decided to stay (лиши́тися) home.
Yaryna: Says it's not a big problem, because Kyiv is a wonderful and very interesting city.

Roman: Adds that it is particularly so in the summer. There are excellent museums, good and inexpensive restaurants, green parks, movie houses, and theaters.
Yaryna: Agrees saying that Kyiv is nice not only in the summer but also in spring and fall.

Roman: Kyiv is not a very pleasant city in winter.
Yaryna: Disagrees saying that even in winter Kyiv can be interesting.

Лёкція | Lesson 6

Dialogue:
Моя сім'я. *My Family*

Grammar:
Present tense
Locative singular
How to pose questions
Vocative
Numerals 100-1,000

Competencies:
Saying where somebody or something is
Describing a family
Addressing a person
Feminine names of nationalities
Phone numbers

Молода́ сім'я́: та́то, ма́ма, син і дочка́

💬 6. Діяло́г. Моя́ сім'я́.

Юрко́: Яри́но, я ма́ю щось ціка́ве. Хо́чеш подиви́тися?

Яри́на: Так, хо́чу. Що це? Фотогра́фія? Як ціка́во!

Юрко́: На цій фотогра́фії моя́ сім'я́ на Хреща́тику. Ліво́руч – мій та́то Мико́ла Васи́льович.

Яри́на: Де він працю́є?

Юрко́: Він – інжене́р в електро́нній компа́нії.

Яри́на: А право́руч, напе́вно, твоя́ ма́ма?

Юрко́: Так, її ім'я́ Марі́я, по ба́тькові - Петрі́вна.

Яри́на: Де працю́є твоя́ ма́ма?

Юрко́: Вона́ – журналі́стка у вечі́рній газе́ті «Експре́с».

Яри́на: Ця га́рна ді́вчина у це́нтрі – це твоя́ сестра́?

Юрко́: Так, це – Оле́на, моя́ моло́дша сестра́. Вона́ ще вчи́ться у сере́дній шко́лі.

Яри́на: Де живе́ твоя́ сім'я́?

Юрко́: Вони́ живу́ть в моє́му рі́дному мі́сті Оде́сі.

Яри́на: Ка́жуть, Оде́са га́рне мі́сто. Я за́вжди хоті́ла побува́ти там.

💬 6. Dialogue. My family.

Yurko: Yaryna, I've got something interesting. Would you like to see?

Yaryna: Yes, I would. What is it? A photograph? How interesting!

Yurko: This picture is of my family on Khreshchatyk Street. On the left is my dad Mykola Vasyliovych.

Yaryna: Where does he work?

Yurko: He's an engineer at an electronic company.

Yaryna: And on the right is probably your mom?

Yurko: Yes, her name is Maria, her patronymic is Petrivna.

Yaryna: Where does your mom work?

Yurko: She is a journalist at the evening newspaper *Express*.

Yaryna: This nice girl in the center is your sister?

Yurko: Yes, this is Olena, my younger sister. She is still in high school.

Yaryna: Where does your family live?

Yurko: They live in my hometown Odesa.

Yaryna: They say Odesa is a beautiful city. I have always wanted to visit there.

✏️ **Нота́тки до діяло́гу**
Notes on the Dialogue

на фотогра́фії, *phr.*	in the picture (*lit.* on the picture), the same preposition **на** + *L.* is used in similar expressions **на сві́тлині** *in a photograph*, **на карти́ні** *in a picture*, **на ка́рті** *on a map*.
журналі́стка, *f.*	female journalist. Names of professions in Ukrainian often have masculine and feminine forms, *cf. m.* **журналі́ст** and *f.* **журналі́стка**, *m.* **лі́кар** *a male physician* and *f.* **лі́карка** *a female physician*. (More in Lesson 10, Note 10.13, p.189.)

Хреща́тик, *m. or* **ву́лиця Хреща́тик** *L. sg.* **на Хреща́тику** *or* **на ву́лиці Хреща́тик**	Khreshchatyk, the main and most popular street of Kyiv, takes its name from **Хреща́тий Яр** *Khreshchaty Yar, lit. Ravine of the Crossing Roads.* This wide street, lined with chestnut trees, is about a mile long. Running from Besarabska Square (**Бесара́бська пло́ща**) to Independence Square (**Майда́н Незале́жности**) and on to European Square (**Європе́йська пло́ща**), it is the most popular place to hang out for residents and guests alike. Closed for traffic on weekends it becomes a pedestrian zone and venue for all kinds of festivals and concerts. (For more on important streets of Kyiv see Lesson 11, Note 11.2, pp. 198-199.)
по ба́тькові	patronymic, *lit.* after father, i.e., a middle name derived from the first name of the person's father and is used as official form of address or reference, Микола **Васи́льович** Бойчу́к *Mykola Vasyliovych Boichuk,* Марія **Петрі́вна** Козаче́нко *Maria Petrivna Kozachenko.* Since independence it has been increasingly omitted, **Мико́ла Бойчу́к, Марі́я Козаче́нко**. (More in Lesson 13, p. 250.)
ще, *adv.*	yet (in *neg.* sentences), **Марія ще не чита́є.** *Maria does not read yet.*; still (in *interr.* sentences) **Ти ще тут?** *Are you still here?*
бува́ти; *pf.* **по~** **у** + *L.*	to frequent, visit or make a trip to a city, a place (museum, restaurant, street, etc); requires locative with prepositions **в/у** or **на**, **Він ча́сто бува́є у цьому теа́трі.** *He often visits this theater.* **Я хо́чу побува́ти у Льво́ві.** *I want to visit Lviv.* **Ви вже побува́ли на Хреща́тику?** *Have you already been to Khreshchatyk?* When such sentences are negated, the *impf.* **бува́ти** is used instead of **побува́ти**, **Ми ніко́ли не бува́ли в Оде́сі.** *We have never been to Odesa.* **Я ніко́ли не бува́в у цьому музе́ї.** *I have never visited this museum.*

 Note 6.1. Ви́рази про сім'ю́
Expressions about family, *sg. and pl.*

чоловіки́	**men**
ба́тьк|о, ~и	*father*
та́т|о, ~и	*dad*
чолові́к, ~и	*husband*
син, ~и	*son*
брат, ~и	*brother*
дід, ~и	*grandfather*
ону́к, ~и	*grandson*
дя́дьк|о, ~и	*uncle*
небі́ж, ~ожі *or*	*nephew*
племі́нник, ~и	
ро́дич, ~і	*relative*
моло́дший	*younger*
близьки́й	*close*
жі́нки	**women**
ма́т|и, ~ері́	*mother*
ма́м|а, ~и	*mom, mommy*
жі́нк|а, ~и *or*	*wife*
form. дружи́н|а, ~и	
дочк|а́, ~и	*daughter*
colloq. до́ньк|а, ~и	
сестр|а́, ~и	*sister*
ба́б|а, ~и	*grandmother*
ону́к|а, ~и	*granddaughter*
ті́тк|а, ~и	*aunt*
небо́г|а, ~и	*niece*
племі́нниц|я, ~і	
ро́дичк|а, ~и	*relative*
ста́рший	*elder*
дале́кий	*distant*

 Грама́тика | Grammar

Тепе́рішній час Present Tense

Фу́нкція *Function*

The present tense denotes an action that coincides in time with the moment of speaking, **Тепе́р Петро́ живе́ тут.** *Now Petro lives here.* Typical indicators of present tense are:

тепе́р, за́раз *now,* **сього́дні** *today,* **цього́ ти́жня** *this week* **цього́ мі́сяця (ро́ку, лі́та)** *this month (year, summer),* **ціє́ї зими́ (о́сени, весни́)** *this winter (fall, spring)*

Утво́рення *Formation*

Ukrainian verbs have six forms of the present, each corresponding to one of the six personal pronouns. There are two patterns of present tense formation. Each uses its own distinct set of six endings. They are called *conjugations.* The difference between the two conjugations

Хто є на цій світлині?

Óля лю́бить фотографува́ти все, що ба́чить.

is not in meaning but only in form. The dictionary form of the verb (infinitive) is not helpful here and the ***present tense stem*** should be memorized as the basis to which respective endings are added. This stem is provided in the dictionary of this textbook, it is separated from the ending by (|), **ба́ч|ити, ~ать; по~**, *tran.* to see.

The first conjugation has a hard and a soft variety. The hard variety (A) is when the present tense stem of the verb ends in a hard consonant. The soft variety (B) is when the stem ends in the consonant /j/, which, as you already know, is always soft.

First conjugation, or the ***уть-conjugation***, has the following set of endings:

(A)

1st pers.	sg.	я	~у	pl.	ми	~емо
2nd pers.	sg.	ти	~еш	pl.	ви	~ете
3rd pers.	sg.	вона́	~е	pl.	вони́	~уть

Here are the present tense forms of the verb **жи́ти** *to live*.

The present tense stem is **жив~**:

1st pers.	sg.	я живу́ *I live*	pl.	ми живемо́ *we live*
2nd pers.	sg.	ти живе́ш *you live*	pl.	ви живете́ *you live*
3rd pers.	sg	вона́ живе́ *she lives*	pl.	вони́ живу́ть *they live*

The same pattern is followed by the verbs **іти́ (йти)** *to go, walk*. Its present tense stem is **ід~ (йд~)**:

1st pers.	sg.	я йду́ *I go*	pl.	ми йдемо́ *we go*
2nd pers.	sg.	ти йде́ш *you go*	pl.	ви йдете́ *you go*
3rd pers.	sg.	вона́ йде́ *she goes*	pl.	вони́ йду́ть *they go*

Other verbs of this conjugation are: **писа́ти (пиш~)** *to write*, **могти́ (мо́ж~)** *to be able (can)*. (The present tense stem is given in parentheses immediately following the infinitive. The stress-marked vowel shows the place of stress in present tense set of forms when it is not mobile.)

When the ***present tense stem*** ends in /j/ it produces the soft variants of first conjugation endings since the combination of sounds /j/+/e/ is signified by the letter **є** and that of /j/+/u/ - by **ю**:

(B)

1st pers. sg.	я	~ю		pl. ми	~ємо
2nd pers. sg.	ти	~єш		pl. ви	~єте
3rd pers. sg.	вона́	~є		pl. вони́	~ють

A case of the soft first conjugation is the verb **ма́ти (май~)** *to have*:

1ˢᵗ pers.	*sg.*	**я ма́ю** *I have*	*pl.*	**ми ма́ємо** *we have*	
2ⁿᵈ pers.	*sg.*	**ти ма́єш** *you have*	*pl.*	**ви ма́єте** *you have*	
3ʳᵈ pers.	*sg.*	**вона́ ма́є** *she has*	*pl.*	**вони́ ма́ють** *they have*	

Other such verbs are: **зна́ти (знай~)** *to know*, **працюва́ти (працю́й~)** *to work*, **чита́ти (чита́й~)** *to read*, **розка́зувати (розка́зуй~)** *to tell*, **дя́кувати (дя́куй~)** *to thank*, **розумі́ти (розумі́й~)** *to understand*.

Second conjugation, or the **ать-conjugation**, has the following set of endings:

1ˢᵗ pers. sg.	**я**	**~у**	*pl.* **ми**	**~имо**	
2ⁿᵈ pers. sg.	**ти**	**~иш**	*pl.* **ви**	**~ите**	
3ʳᵈ pers. sg.	**вона́**	**~ить**	*pl.* **вони́**	**~ать**	

Here are the present tense forms of the second conjugation verb **ба́чити (бач~)** *to see*:

1ˢᵗ pers. sg.	**я ба́чу** *I see*	*pl.* **ми ба́чимо** *we see*
2ⁿᵈ pers. sg.	**ти ба́чиш** *you see*	*pl.* **ви ба́чите** *you see*
3ʳᵈ pers. sg.	**вона́ ба́чить** *she sees*	*pl.* **вони́ ба́чать** *they see*

Second conjugation is further complicated by the stem final consonant shift which affects only one or two personal endings. At this point it is best to memorize the conjugation of each verb.

The differences in the endings of the two conjugations can be reduced to the so-called link-vowel, i.e, the initial vowel of every ending. With the exception of the 1ˢᵗ person singular and the 3ʳᵈ person plural the link-vowel of the *first conjugation* is **~е~** or its soft variety **~є~**,

> **я іду́, ти іде́ш, вона́ іде́, ми ідемо́, ви ідете́, вони́ іду́ть**
> **я ма́ю, ти ма́єш, вона́ ма́є, ми ма́ємо, ви ма́єте, вони́ ма́ють**

The link-vowel of the second conjugation is **~и~**,

> **я ба́чу, ти ба́чиш, він ба́чить, ми ба́чимо, ви ба́чите, вони́ ба́чать.**

Since in Ukrainian the vowels **е** /e/ and **и** /y/ resemble one another in an unstressed position, it is good to keep in mind that the link **~е~** (**~є~**) corresponds to the 3ʳᵈ person plural ending **~уть** (**~ють**) while the **~и~** corresponds to the **~ать** (**~ять**). This rule is helpful when you hesitate whether to write **е** or **и** in other personal forms of the verb.

The stress in the present tense can be stable or mobile. It is stable when the final syllable of the 3ʳᵈ *pers. pl.* is stressed. In that case, the final syllable in all other personal forms is also stressed,

дава́ти *to give* – я даю́, ти дає́ш, він дає́, ми даємо́, ви дає́те, вони́ **даю́ть**

сиді́ти *to sit* – я сиджу́, ти сиди́ш, він сиди́ть, ми сидимо́, ви сидите́, вони́ **сидя́ть**

бі́гти *to run* – я біжу́, ти біжи́ш, він біжи́ть, ми біжимо́, ви біжите́, вони́ **біжа́ть**

Note 6.2. Some irregular 2ⁿᵈ conjugation verbs:

вози́ти *to carry (by vehicle)* – вожу́, во́зиш, во́зить, во́зимо, во́зите, во́зять
ї́здити *to drive* – ї́жджу, ї́здиш, ї́здить, ї́здимо, ї́здите, ї́здять
ходи́ти *to go* - ходжу́, хо́диш, хо́дить, хо́димо, хо́дите, хо́дять
сиді́ти *to sit* - сиджу́, сиди́ш, сиди́ть, сидимо́, сидите́, сидя́ть

плати́ти *to pay* – плачу́, пла́тиш, пла́тить, пла́тимо, пла́тите, пла́тять
леті́ти *to fly* - лечу́, лети́ш, лети́ть, летимо́, летите́, летя́ть

люби́ти *to like* – люблю́, лю́биш, лю́бить, лю́бимо, лю́бите, лю́блять
роби́ти *to do* – роблю́, ро́биш, ро́бить, ро́бимо, ро́бите, ро́блять
спа́ти *to sleep* – сплю, спиш, спить, спимо́, спите́, сплять
диви́тися *to look* – дивлю́ся, ди́вишся, ди́виться, ди́вимося, ди́витеся, ди́вляться

ї́сти *to eat* – їм, їси́, їсть, їмо́, їсте́, їдя́ть

Вони грають у новому художньому фільмі.

Щодня Богдана ходила на заняття по вулиці Друкарській.

Stress can be stable in other positions,

хотíти *to want* – я хочу, ти хочеш, він хоче, ми хочемо, ви хочете, вони **хочуть**

бачити *to see* – я бачу, ти бачиш, він бачить, ми бачимо, ви бачите, вони **бачать**.

Mobile stress patterns vary. One is with the final syllable stressed in *1st pers. sg.* and initial one stressed in all other personal forms,

робити *to do* – я роблю, ти робиш, він робить, ми робимо, ви робите, вони **роблять**

казáти *to say* – я кажу, ти кажеш, він каже, ми кажемо, ви кажете, вони **кажуть**.

Місцевий відмінок однини Locative Case Singular

The locative case correlates with the questions
на кому? *on whom?* **на чому?** *on what?*

Функція *Function*

The locative case signifies a position in place or time. Hence there are the locative of place and the locative of time. It is the only case that is always used with a preposition.

Locative of place is used with the prepositions:

1) **у (в)** *in, inside* to signify location inside a space,
кімната *a room* - **у кімнаті** *in a room*, **готель** *a hotel* - **у готелі** *in a hotel*, **парк** *a park* - **у парку** *in a park*;

2) **на** *on, upon* to signify location on a surface or on top of some object,
стіл *a table* - **на столі** *on a table*, **полиця** a shelf - **на полиці** *on a shelf*, **студент** *a student* - **на студентові** *on a student*;

3) **по** *along, around, through* means a space through or within which a movement occurs,
місто *a city* - **по місту** *around a city*, **площа** *a square* - **по площі** *through a square*, **вулиця** *a street* - **по вулиці** *along a street*.

Locative of time is used with the prepositions:

1) **у (в)** + *name of month or a year in L.*,
березень *March* - **у березні** *in March*, **цей рік** *this year* - **у цьому році** *this year* (More in Lesson 10, p. 180);

2) **о (об)** + ordinal numeral in *L.* + **годині**, to indicate the hour of an event,
перша година *the first hour* - **о першій годині** *at one o'clock*, **одинадцята година** *the eleventh hour* - **об одинадцятій годині** *at eleven o'clock* (More in Lesson 9, pp. 158-159);

Утво́рення | *Formation*

Іме́нники   Nouns

The nominal locative endings:
~і (~ї), ~у (~ю), ~ові (~еві, ~єві)

These endings are used depending on the gender, stem type, and whether or not the noun signifies a living being or an inanimate object. Of the three endings, ~і is by far the most frequently used.

~ові is taken by animate masculine nouns with a hard consonant at the end of stem or the ~о ending,
брат *a brother* - **на бра́тові** *on a brother*, **Петро́** *Petro* - **на Петро́ві** *on Petro*.

~еві is taken by animate masculine nouns with a soft stem final consonant or ~ж~, ~ч~, ~ш~, ~щ~, and ~р~, **прия́тель** *a friend* - **на прия́телеві** *on a friend*, **вчи́тель** *a teacher* - **на вчи́телеві** *on a teacher*, **лі́кар** *a physician* - **на лі́каревi** *on a physician*.

~єві is taken by animate masculine nouns with ~й as their stem final consonant, **Андрі́й** - **на Андрі́єві** *on Andriy*; **водій** *a driver* - **на водієві** *on a driver*.

~у is taken by:

1) inanimate masculine and neuter nouns whose stems end in ~к, **рівча́к** *a ditch* - **у рівчаку́** *in a ditch*, **парк** *a park* - **у па́рку** *in a park*, **Нью-Йо́рк** *New York* - **у Нью-Йо́рку** *in New York*; for a notable exception see Note 6.5;

2) some monosyllabic 2nd declension masculine nouns, with no suffix ~к, **сад** *a garden* - **у саду́** *in a garden*, **сніг** *snow* - **у снігу́** *in snow*, **Крим** *the Crimea* - **у Криму́** *in the Crimea*;

3) animate masculine nouns that would normally take the **~ові** (~еві, ~єві) so as to avoid heavy sounding sequences made of several such nouns. One noun should then take the **~ові** while the rest take the ~у (~ю) ending,
Павло́ Полі́щу́к *Pavlo Polishchuk* - **на Павло́ві Полі́щуку́** or **на Павлу́ Полі́щуко́ві** *on Pavlo Polishchuk*; **письме́нник Іва́н Франко́** *the writer Ivan Franko* - **на письме́нникові Іва́ну Франко́ві** or **на письме́нику Іва́ну Франко́ві** *on the writer Ivan Franko*.

~ю is taken by the soft stem variety of the second and third group of nouns,
гай *a grove* - **у гаю́** *in a grove*, **край** *an edge* - **на краю́** *on the edge*, **водій Григо́рій** *driver Hryhoriy* - **на водієві Григо́рію** *on driver Hryhoriy*.

Note 6.3. Preposition на *at* in set expressions

Memorize these set expressions with the preposition **на** *on, at, in*:

вокза́л *a (big) station* - **на вокза́лі** *at a (big) station*

головпошта́мт *a central post-office* - **на головпошта́мті** *at the central post-office*

заво́д *a plant* - **на заво́ді** *at a plant*

заня́ття *a class* - **на заня́тті** *in a class*

інтерне́т *the Internet* - **на** or **в інтерне́ті** *on the Internet*

ле́кція *a lecture* - **на ле́кції** *at a lecture*

по́шта *a post-office* - **на по́шті** *at a post-office*

сві́тлина *a photo* - **на сві́тлині** *in a photo*

ста́нція *a station* - **на ста́нції** *at a station*

фа́брика *a factory* - **на фа́бриці** *at a factory*

факульте́т *a (university) department* - **на факульте́ті** *in a department*

фотогра́фія *a photo* - **на фотогра́фії** *in a photo*

Миха́йло Бондаре́нко працю́є на Півде́нному вокза́лі.

Note 6.4. Preposition по and ending ~у (~ю)

When used with the preposition **по** *on, around, through*, the inanimate masculine and neuter nouns that would normally take the ~i ending in the *L. sg.*, take the ~у (~ю) ending, cf.,

на вокза́лі *in a station* - **ходи́ти по вокза́лу** *to walk around a station*

у теа́трі *at a theater* - **ходи́ти по теа́тру** *to walk around a theater*

у мі́сті *in a city* - **ходи́ти по мі́сту** *to walk through a city*

у селі́ *in a village* - **бі́гати по селу́** *to run around a village*

у не́бі *in the sky* - **літа́ти по не́бу** *to fly through the sky*

у по́лі *in a field* - **бі́гати по по́лю** *to run through a field*

на мо́рі *on the sea* - **пла́вати по мо́рю** *to sail the sea*

Чому́ на цій жі́нці украї́нська вишива́на соро́чка?

 Note 6.5. Special case of рік

Locative singular of the noun **рік** *year* is **у ро́ці** *in a year*,

Я працю́ю тут у цьо́му ро́ці. *I work here this year.*

~i is the most frequently used *L. sg.* ending and is taken by all other nouns, namely (1) all feminine, (2) all neuter, (3) all masculine nouns ending in ~а (~я), and (4) inanimate masculines ending in a consonant,

(1) **ка́рта** *a map* - **на ка́рті** *on a map*, **пло́ща** *a square* - **на пло́щі** *on a square*, **ву́лиця** *a street* - **на ву́лиці** *on a street*, **любо́в** *love* - **у любо́ві** *in love*;

(2) **мо́ре** *a sea* - **у мо́рі** *in a sea*, **село́** *a village* - **у селі́** *in a village*, **пита́ння** *a question* - **у пита́нні** *in a question*;

(3) **Мико́ла** *Mykola* - **на Мико́лі** *on Mykola*, **суддя́** *a judge* - **на судді́** *on a judge*;

(4) **ліс** *a forest* - **у лі́сі** *in a forest*, **університе́т** *a university* - **в університе́ті** *in a university*, **по́їзд** *a train* - **у по́їзді** *in a train*;

~ï is taken by 1st declension nouns ending in ~ія, **істо́рія** *a story* - **в істо́рії** *in a story*, **фотогра́фія** *a photo* - **на фотогра́фії** *in a photo*, **Фра́нція** *France* - **у Фра́нції** *in France*.

A number of nouns undergo sound changes in their stems as they form the locative singular. There are three such changes.

🔊 SOUND CHANGES 🔊
in the locative singular of nouns

Velar consonant shift before ~i

The velar consonants are **г** /h/, **х** /kh/, **ґ** /g/, and **к** /k/. They are called so because they are pronounced in the velum, the soft palate of the mouth cavity.
First and second declension nouns whose stems end in the consonants ~г, ~к, ~х undergo the consonant shift before ~i, whereby

~г becomes ~з: **но|га́** *a leg* - **на нозі́** *on a leg*
~к becomes ~ц: **Аме́ри|ка** *America* - **в Аме́риці** *in America*
~х becomes ~с: **по́вер|х** *a floor* - **на по́версі** *on a floor*

Dropping of ~o~ (~e~)

~о~ and ~е~ in the last syllable of 2nd declension masculine nouns are dropped,

кут|о́к *a corner* - **у кутку́** *in a corner*
сон *a dream* - **у́ві сні** *in a dream*
украї́н|ець *a Ukrainian* - **на украї́нцеві** *on a Ukrainian*
кін|е́ць *an end* - **у кінці́** *in the end*
д|ень *a day* - **у дні** *in a day*

Change of ~і~ to ~o~ (~e~)

~і~ changes to ~o~ (~e~) in the final syllable in 2nd declension masculine and 3rd declension feminine nouns,

> *m.* кіт *a cat* - **на кото́ві** *on a cat*
> *m.* папі́р *paper* - **на папе́рі** *on paper*
> *f.* річ *a thing* - **у ре́чі** *in a thing*

The stress in the locative singular is mostly the same as in *N. sg.* In monosyllabic nouns, it often moves to the final syllable,

> стіл *a table* - **на столі́** *on a table*, лист *a letter* - **у листі́** *in a letter*, борщ *borshch* - **у борщі́** *in borshch*, сніг *snow* - **на снігу́** *on snow*.

In other monosyllabic nouns the stress is immobile,

> світ *the world* - **у сві́ті** *in the world*, дім *a house* - **у до́мі** *in a house*, ніс *a nose* - **у но́сі** *in a nose*.

У "Вели́кій ло́жці" мо́жна сма́чно та недо́рого пої́сти.

Особо́ві займе́нники Personal Pronouns

For locative singular case forms of personal pronouns see p. 322 in the appendices.

Прикме́тники та поря́дкові числі́вники
Adjectives and Ordinal Numerals

The adjectival locative endings:
~ому (~ьому), ~ій

The adjectival endings depend on the stem type of the adjective and gender of the noun they modify:

~ому for hard stems of masculine and neuter gender,
вели́ке мі́сто *a big city* - **у вели́кому мі́сті** *in a big city*, дру́гий стіл *the second table* - **на дру́гому столі́** *on the second table*;

~ьому for soft stems of masculine gender,
оста́нній по́їзд *the last train* - **на оста́нньому по́їзді** *on the last train*, си́нє мо́ре *a blue sea* - **у си́ньому мо́рі** *in a blue sea*;

~ій for all feminine gender adjectives,
ціка́ва кни́жка *an interesting book* – **у ціка́вій кни́жці** *in an interesting book*, тре́тя годи́на *the third hour* – **о тре́тій годи́ні** *at three o'clock*.

– Чи Оре́ст студе́нт?
– Так, звича́йно. Він студе́нт у Черніве́цькому університе́ті.

Як ста́вити пита́ння   How to Ask Questions

There are **four types** of questions:
1) **general or yes/no-questions**, *Do you read?*
2) **special questions** beginning with question words *who, what, how, where, etc., How old are you?*
3) **alternative questions** offering a choice with conjunction *or, What do you like more – to read or to write?*
4) **disjunctive questions**, which are really statements of fact ending in a tag to solicit listener's confirmation, *She is twenty, isn't she?*

1. Зага́льні пита́ння   *General questions*

General questions are structurally the same as affirmative sentences but uttered with a rising intonation, such as:
Ти ⟍ чита́єш. *You read.* and **Ти ⟋ чита́єш?** *Do you read? (lit. You read?)*
They also can be formed by using a special interrogative particle **чи** put at the beginning of the affirmative sentence which is uttered with a rising intonation,

Ти ⟍ студе́нт. *You are a student.* – **Чи ти ⟋ студе́нт?** *Are you a student?*
Це ⟍ стіл. *This is a table.* – **Чи це ⟋ стіл?** *Is this a table?*
Це їхня ⟍ кни́жка. *This is their book.* – **Чи це ⟋ їхня кни́жка?** *Is this their book?*

2. Спеція́льні пита́ння   *Special questions*

Special questions are posed to a particular component of a statement, usually a word. The word addressed is thus the answer to the special question. For example, the sentence **Їхня кни́жка тут.** *Their book is here.* allows posing such special questions as

Чия́ кни́жка тут? *Whose book is here?* – the answer is **Їхня.** *Theirs.*
Де їхня кни́жка? *Where is their book?* – the answer is **Тут.** *Here.*
Що є тут? *What is here?* – the answer is **Кни́жка.** *A book.*

Special questions are always formed using question words. They are pronounced with a falling intonation,

Де він ⟍ жив тоді́? *Where did he live then?*
Скі́льки вам ⟍ ро́ків? *How old are you?*
Які́ жінки це ⟍ каза́ли? *What women said it?*
Чо́му ви хоті́ли ⟍ прийти́? *Why did you want to come?*
Де вона́ ⟍ спа́ла? *Where did she sleep?*

🖋 **Note 6.6. Пита́льні слова́** Question words

who?	**хто?**	Хто це таки́й?	*Who is it?*
what? *(used alone)*	**що?**	Що це таке́?	*What is it?*
where?	**де?**	Де твій університе́т?	*Where is your university?*

where from?	зві́дки?	Зві́дки ти?	Where from are you?
where to?	куди́?	Куди́ ти йдеш?	Where are you going to?
when?	коли́?	Коли́ твій по́їзд?	When is your train?
why?	чому́?	Чому́ вона́ ра́да?	Why is she happy?
how?	як?	Як спра́ви?	How are things?
what? (what kind of?)	яки́й? *m.*	Яки́й це профе́сор?	What professor is he?
	яка́? *f.*	Яка́ це ву́лиця?	What street is it?
	яке́? *nt.*	Яке́ це пита́ння?	What question is it?
	які́? *pl.*	Які́ це ву́лиці?	What streets are these?
whose?	чий? *m.*	Чий це брат?	Whose brother is it?
	чия́? *f.*	Чия́ це сестра́?	Whose sister is it?
	чиє́? *nt.*	Чиє́ це а́вто?	Whose car is it?
	чиї́? *pl.*	Чиї́ це брати́?	Whose brothers are these?
how many (much)?	скі́льки?	Скі́льки це кошту́є?	How much does it cost?

The English *what?* can refer both to a thing and a quality. In Ukrainian, two different words are used for these two occasions:

що? for a thing, **Що ти чита́єш?** *What do you read?*

яки́й? for a quality, **Яки́й журна́л ти чита́єш?** *What magazine do you read?*

In the case of the first question, **що?** correlates with a noun or personal pronoun,

Що це тут? *What is here?* - **Це журна́л.** *It's a magazine.* - **Він ціка́вий.** *It is interesting.*

In the case of the second question, **яки́й?** corresponds to an adjective,

Яки́й він студе́нт? *What kind of student is he?* - **До́брий.** *A good one.*

To learn how to make the correct choice between **що?** and **яки́й?** see Note 6.12.

The Ukrainian **скі́льки?** is equivalent to the English *how many?* and *how much?* It is used both with countable nouns:

скі́льки днів (до́ларів, годи́н)? *how many days (dollars, hours)?*

and uncountable nouns:

скі́льки ча́су (води́, робо́ти)? *how much time (water, work)?*

(More in Lesson 12)

The interrogative pronouns **хто?** *who?* and **що?** *what?* require the predicate in the 3rd pers. sg. even if the answer to the question is anticipated to be in the plural,

Хто живе́ у Херсо́ні? *Who lives in Kherson?* - **Мої́ батьки́.** *My parents do.*

Що було́ на столі́? *What was on the table?* - **Її́ книжки́.** *Her books.*

When posing questions in the past tense, **хто?** is treated as if it were a masculine noun,

Хто тут був? *Who was here?* - **Тут була́ Оле́на.** *Olena was here.*

For the same purpose, the pronoun **що?** is treated as if it were a neuter noun,

Що було́ вчо́ра в шко́лі? *What was (took place) at school yesterday?* - **Вчо́ра в шко́лі був чудо́вий конце́рт.** *Yesterday, there was a great concert at school.*

 Note 6.7. Word order in special questions

When the subject is a noun, it swaps places with the predicate in a special question. This subject-predicate inversion does not occur when the subject is a pronoun, cf.,

Де живе́ Іва́н? *Where does Ivan live?* but **Де він живе́?** *Where does he live?*

Чому́ дзвони́в нови́й студе́нт? *Why did the new student call?* but **Чому́ він дзвони́в?** *Why did he call?*

Скі́льки ча́су ма́ють ці дівча́та? *How much time do these girls have?* but **Скі́льки ча́су вони́ ма́ють?** *How much time do they have?*

Чому́ це мала́ Окса́нка така́ ду́же серйо́зна?

3. Альтернати́вні пита́ння Alternative questions

Alternative questions are structurally similar to general questions, but unlike the general questions, they all offer a choice between two options,

Ти студе́нт чи виклада́ч? *Are you a student or an instructor?*
Ці фі́льми ціка́ві чи нудні́? *Are these films interesting or boring?*

Two conjunctions **або́** and **чи** are equivalent to the English *or*. The alternative questions use only **чи**,
Це ↗ їхня чи ва́ша ↘ кни́жка? *This is their book or yours?*
In alternative questions, the first member of the option is pronounced with a rising tone while the second member with a falling one,
Ти ↗ жив чи ті́льки ↘ працюва́в там? Did you live or only work there?*

4. Розділо́ві пита́ння *Disjunctive questions*

Disjunctive questions structurally are statements of fact which always end with a tag asking for the listener's confirmation. In this case, Ukrainian is much simpler than English and uses the same tag **чи не так?** (*lit.* isn't it so?) for all occasions,

Ти ↘ студе́нт, чи не ↗ так? *You are a student, aren't you?*
Ви хоті́ли ↘ прийти́, чи не ↗ так? *You wanted to come, didn't you?*
Це ↘ва́ша кни́жка, чи не ↗ так? *This is your book, isn't it?*
The affirmative part of such a question is pronounced with a falling intonation and the tag with a rising one.

Кли́чний відмі́нок The Vocative Case

Ukrainian has a special form of nouns that is used only to address a person. It is called the *vocative case*. In this textbook, the vocative is limited to only human proper names in the dialogues opening each lesson,
N. sg. **Мико́ла** *m. Mykola* - *V. sg.* **Мико́ло!**
N. sg. **Ка́тря** *f. Katria* - *V. sg.* **Ка́тре!**

In real life though, animals and personalized inanimate objects can also be addressed in the vocative,
N. sg. **ко́тик** *dim. a cat* - *V. sg.* **мій коха́ний ко́тику!** *my beloved cat!*
N. sg. **край** *a country* - *V. sg.* **мій кра́ю!** *my country!*

In addresses consisting of the noun **пан** *mister* plus the family name, only the word **пан** is in the vocative while the family name stays in the nominative case,
N. sg. **пан Са́вченко** *Mr. Savchenko* - **па́не Са́вченко!**
N. sg. **пан Васи́льченко** *Mr. Vasylchenko* - **па́не Васи́льченко!**

When the noun **пан** is used with the first name, name of profession or position, both words assume the form of the vocative,

N. sg. **пан Іва́н** *Mr. Ivan** - *V. sg.* **па́не Іва́не!**
N. sg. **пан до́ктор** *Mr. Doctor** - *V. sg.* **па́не до́кторе!**
N. sg. **пан водій** *Mr. driver** - *V. sg.* **па́не воді́ю!**

Note 6.8. Familiar forms of address

When a person is directly called by name, the person's name takes the vocative case form,

Це Петро́ *This is Petro.*
Пе́тре, як спра́ви? *Petro, how are you?*
Це О́льга. *This is Olha.*
О́льго, де ти була́? *Olha, where have you been?*

A familiar way of reference is by the first name, **Ю́рій** *Yuri*, **Марі́я** *Maria*. An even more familiar way are diminutive forms of the first name (Refer to Note 4.5.)

Another way to reference an individual is by *first name + patronymic*:
Ю́рій Ві́кторович, Марі́я Васи́лівна.

By the degree of formality this is more or less equivalent to **пан/па́ні** + first name. Since 1991, there has been a tendency to replace the formula *first name + patronymic* as allegedly transplanted from Russian for the more indigenous formula **пан/па́ні** + first name. For formation of patronymics see Lesson 13, p. 250. At present, both forms are acceptable. When addressing a person, the form of address is in the vocative case **па́не Ю́рію, па́ні Марі́є, Ю́рію Ві́кторовичу, Марі́є Васи́лівно.**

(For more on the formation and use of vocative see the grammar section opposite.)

When the noun **па́ні** *mistress* is used with the first name, only the name takes the form of the vocative,

N. sg. **па́ні Окса́на** *Mrs. Oksana** - *V. sg.* **па́ні Окса́но!**
N. sg. **па́ні Ната́ля** *Mrs. Natalia** - *V. sg.* **па́ні Ната́ле!**

When **па́ні** is used with the surname, name of profession or title, both words stay the same as the nominative,

N. sg. **па́ні до́ктор** *Mrs. Doctor** - *V. sg.* **па́ні до́ктор!**
N. sg. **па́ні доце́нт** *Mrs. Assistant Professor* - *V. sg.* **па́ні доце́нт!**
N. sg. **па́ні Івче́нко** *Mrs. Ivchenko* - *V. sg.* **па́ні Івче́нко!**
N. sg. **па́ні Світли́чна** *Mrs. Svitlychna* - *V. sg.* **па́ні Світли́чна!**

Утво́рення *Formation*

The vocative plural of nouns is the same as the nominative plural. Vocative of adjectives and possessive pronouns is the same as their nominative,

N. pl. **Мико́ла та Оле́на – мої́ дороги́ дру́зі.** *Mykola and Olena are my dear friends.*
V. pl. **Дороги́ дру́зі, ми ра́ді віта́ти вас.** *Dear friends, we are glad to have you.*
N. pl. **Ці пані́ та пано́ве приї́хали із Торо́нта.** *These ladies and gentlemen came from Toronto.* **Шано́вні пані́ та пано́ве! Прошу́ захо́дити.** *Respected Ladies and Gentlemen, please come in.*

The vocative singular endings:
~о, ~е (~є), ~у (~ю)

~о is taken by feminine and masculine nouns ending in ~**а**, **ма́ма** *mama* - **ма́мо!** **сестра́** *sister* - **се́стро!** **па́нна** *young lady* - **па́нно!** **Мико́ла** *Mykola* - **Мико́ло!**

~е is taken by:
1) feminine and masculine nouns ending in ~**я**, **О́ля** *Olia* - **О́ле!**, **Га́ля** *Halia* - **Га́ле!** **бабу́ся** *grandma* - **бабу́се!** **суддя́** *a judge* - **су́дде!**
2) masculine nouns ending in a hard consonant, as well as in ~**ж**, ~**ч**, ~**ш**, ~**щ**, and ~**р**, **брат** *a brother* - **бра́те!** **Тара́с** *Taras* - **Тара́се!** **сусі́д** *a neighbor* - **сусі́де!** **пан** *mister* - **па́не!** **лі́кар** *a doctor* - **лі́каре!** **профе́сор** *a professor* - **профе́соре!**
3) feminine nouns ending in a consonant, both hard and soft, **ніч** *a night* - **но́че!** **любо́в** *love* - **любо́ве!** **ю́ність** *youth* - **ю́носте!** **ста́рість** *old age* - **ста́росте!**

~є is taken by feminine and masculine nouns ending in ~**ія**, **Марі́я** *Maria* - **Марі́є**, **Наді́я** *Nadia* - **Наді́є**, **месі́я** *a messiah* - **месі́є!**

 Note 6.9. Vocative in messages

The vocative case is obligatorily used to address recipients of letters and e-mail messages. Here are some of the common forms of address opening a letter:
Дороги́й дру́же! *Dear friend!*
Дорога́ по́друго! *Dear (f.) friend!*
Коха́на по́друго! *Beloved (f.) friend!*
Шано́вні пані́ та пано́ве! *Esteemed Ladies and Gentlemen!*
Вельмишано́вний па́не Петре́нко! *Highly esteemed Mr. Petrenko!*
Лю́бий бра́те! *Beloved brother!*
Лю́ба Наді́йко! *Beloved Nadiika!*

Надійка Світлична

~y is taken by the masculine nouns ending in ~г, ~ґ, ~к, ~х, and some others,

ба́тько *a father* - ба́тьку! дя́дько *an uncle* - дя́дьку! as well as та́то *dad* - та́ту! син *a son* - си́ну! дід *a grandad* - ді́ду! (For some notable exceptions see Note 6.10.)

~ю is taken by the masculine nouns ending in a soft consonant, вчи́тель *a teacher* - вчи́телю! водій *a driver* - водію! украї́нець *a Ukrainian* - украї́нцю! Андрі́й *Andriy* - Андрі́ю! Ю́рій *Yuriy* - Ю́рію!

The stress in the vocative case is usually the same as in the nominative. In the nouns with the final syllable stressed, the vocative stress usually moves to the preceding syllable,

N. sg. **сестра́** *a sister* - *V.* **се́стро!**
N. sg. **Юрко́** *Yurko* - *V.* **Ю́рку!**
N. sg. **Сашко́** *Sashko* - *V.* **Са́шку!**
N. sg. **Петро́** *Petro* - *V.* **Пе́тре!**
N. sg. **Павло́** *Pavlo* - *V.* **Па́вле!**
but
N. sg. **водій** *a driver* - *V.* **водію!**
N. sg. **Васи́ль** *Vasyl* – *V.* **Васи́лю!**
N. sg. **Іва́н** *Ivan* - *V.* **Іва́не!**
N. sg. **Степа́н** *Stepan* – *V.* **Степа́не!**
N. sg. **Рома́н** *Roman* - *V.* **Рома́не!**

Note 6.10. Common vocative forms

Memorize these vocative forms:
Бог *God* - Бо́же!
друг *a friend* - дру́же!
хло́пець *a boy* - хло́пче!
чолові́к *a man* - чолові́че!
ма́ти *a mother* - ма́ти!
па́ні *madam* - па́ні!
ону́к *grandson* - ону́че!

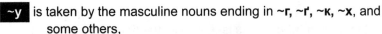

Впра́ви Exercises

6.1. Conjugate the verbs in the present tense. The numbers in parentheses indicate the respective verb conjugation.

1. **Жи́ти (жив~)** *to live* (1). Ви жив_____ тут? Так, звича́йно, я жив_____ тут. А ваш друг де жив_____? Теж тут? Ні, він і його́ батьки́ не жив_____ тут.

2. **Люби́ти (люб~)** *to like, love* (2). Ти люб_____ чита́ти? Так, я ду́же люб_____. А ви люб_____? Ми теж люб_____, а вони́ не люб_____.

3. **Працюва́ти (працюй~)** *to work* (1) Де вона́ працю_____? У Ки́єві. А ти де працю_____? Я теж там працю_____. Ми всі працю_____ у Ки́єві.

4. **Чита́ти (читай~)** *to read* (1) Що ти чита_____? Я чита_____ книжки́. А ви? А ми чита_____ газе́ти.

5. **Писа́ти (пиш~)** *to write* (1). Що вона́ пиш _____? Лист. А ти що пиш _____? Я нічо́го не пиш _____. Зате́ вони́ пиш _____ есе́й.

Богда́на працю́є на ра́діо.
Вона́ чудо́вий журналі́ст.

6. **Хотíти (хоч~)** *to want* (1). Ви хо́ч ____ додо́му? Так, ми ду́же хо́ч ____. І не тíльки ми, вони́ теж хо́ч ____. А ти хіба́ не хо́ч ____?

7. **Зна́ти (знай~)** *to know* (1) Ви не зна́ ____ , де Мико́ла? Ні, ми не зна́ ____. Мо́же, Окса́на зна́ ____? Ні, але́ вони́ напе́вно зна́ ____.

8. **Ба́чити (ба́ч~)** *to see* (2) Я тут ба́ч ___ щось ціка́ве. А ти ба́ч ___? Ні. Зате́ він ба́ч ___, всі вони́ ба́ч ___.

9. **Ду́мати (ду́май~)** *to think* (1) Як ти ду́ма____, це до́бре? Я ду́ма____, що ні. Але́ вона́ ду́ма____, що так. А ви що ду́ма____?

10. **Говори́ти (говор~)** *to speak* (2) Я говор ___ по-украї́нському. Ти гово́р____ по-украї́нському? Ні, але́ мій друг гово́р____. Всі на́ші студе́нти гово́р____. А ви гово́р____ чи ні?

Чи ви зна́єте, що за́раз ро́бить його́ син Андрі́йко?

🎧 **6.2.** Say and write the sentences in Ukrainian. You can find prompts in the dialogue or use the dictionary.

1. I like to read.
2. Where do your parents live?
3. Who is an engineer?
4. I know Oksana is a student.
5. We like to think.
6. Ivan lives in Kherson.
7. We very much want to visit this village.
8. What is your home town?
9. They want to see our photos.
10. Their elder brother studies at a high school.
11. She has interesting films.
12. Pavlo often works and rarely rests.

🎧 **6.3.** Form general questions from these statements. Use both intonation-only and *чи*-types.

Model. На цій фотогра́фії є моя́ сім'я́. *In this picture is my family.*
   1. На цій фотогра́фії ↗є моя́ сім'я́? *Is my family in this picture?*
   2. Чи на цій фотогра́фії ↗є моя́ сім'я́? *Is my family in this picture?*

1. Його́ сім'я́ живе́ у Микола́єві.
2. Твоє́ ім'я́ Рома́н.
3. Вони́ говоря́ть украї́нською.
4. Марі́я зна́є, де Іва́н.
5. Його́ сестра́ вже пи́ше.
6. Студе́нти хо́чуть додо́му.
7. Ти ди́вишся нови́й фільм.
8. Вони́ лю́блять украї́нські стра́ви.
9. Мо́жна запита́ти.
10. Яри́на ціка́ва дівчина.

Їхня моло́дша дочка́ Соломі́я

Note 6.11. Voiced and voiceless consonants

Each consonant can be classified as voiced or voiceless. Voiced consonants are pronounced with the participation of the voice, when the speaker's vocal chords are vibrating,
з /z/, л /l/, м /m/, р /r/, н /n/, й /j/.

Voiceless consonants involve no voice participation and the vocal chords are resting,
к /k/, п /p/, с /s/, ф /f/, х /kh/, щ /shch/

A voiced consonant usually has one voiceless counterpart, pronounced in the same manner, the only difference being that the vocal chords are resting. Here are nine such pairs. The first member is a voiced consonant and the second is its voiceless counterpart:

б /b/ - п /p/	в /v/ - ф /f/
д /d/ - т /t/	з /z/ - с /s/
ж /zh/ - ш /sh/	дж /dzh/ - ч /ch/
дз /dz/ - ц /ts/	г /h/ - х /kh/
ґ /g/ - к /k/	

In many languages, voiced consonants become voiceless at the end of a word or before other voiceless consonant,
б /b/ becomes п /p/, в /v/ becomes ф /f/, д /d/ becomes т /t/, and so on. Ukrainian differs from its Slavic neighbors Russian and Polish by that its voiced consonants regularly stay voiced in such positions:
хліб *bread* is pronounced as /khli'ib/ and not /khli'ip/
бе́рег *a shore* is pronounced as /bére^{u}h/ and not /bére^{u}kh/

6.4. Form as many special questions to these statements as you can. Use appropriate interrogative pronouns. Answer your questions with just one word.

На цій світли́ні я та мій та́то Юрко́.

Model.

C Ліво́руч мій та́то. *On the left is my dad.*
Q 1: Де мій та́то? *Where is my dad?*
Q 2: Хто є ліво́руч? *Who is on the left?*
Q 3: Чий та́то ліво́руч? *Whose dad is on the left?*
A Ліво́руч. *On the left.*
A Мій та́то. *My dad.*
A Мій. *Mine.*

1. Її ім'я́ – Марі́я.
2. Їхня сім'я́ живе́ в Украї́ні.
3. На цій світли́ні моя́ сім'я́.
4. Юрко́ лю́бить америка́нські пісні́.
5. Іва́н зна́є ці ціка́ві книжки́.
6. Сього́дні моя́ сестра́ працю́є.
7. На́ші сусі́ди ма́ють вели́кий буди́нок.
8. Ці воді́ї завжди́ слу́хають прогно́з пого́ди *(weather forecast)*.

6.5. Form alternative questions from these statements. Use the prompted alternatives. Put the verbs in parentheses in the present tense form.

Model:

C На цій фотогра́фії (бу́ти) ва́ша / їхня сім'я́.
In this picture (to be) your / their family.
A На цій фотогра́фії є ↗ ва́ша чи ↘ їхня сім'я?
In this picture, is there your or their family?

1. Його́ сім'я́ (жи́ти) у Микола́єві / Оде́сі.
2. Ти (сні́дати / обі́дати) у цьому́ рестора́ні.
3. Вони́ (говори́ти) украї́нською / росі́йською.
4. Марі́я (хоті́ти / могти́) допомогти́.
5. Його́ / її сестра́ вже (писа́ти).
6. Їхні дру́зі (жи́ти / працюва́ти) у Ки́єві.

7. Ти (диви́тися) нови́й / стари́й фільм.
8. Вони́ (люби́ти) украї́нські / францу́зькі стра́ви.
9. Рома́н й Оле́г до́бре (зна́ти) Ки́їв / Львів.
10. Ви (переклада́ти) ціка́вий / нудни́й текст.

Phonetics. Drill shifting the velar r /h/ before ~i

 6.6. Listen to the speaker for the cue and form locative singular shifting the velar **r** /h/ to **з** /z/ before the ending **~i**. Check against the speaker.

Model.
C доро́га *a road*
A на доро́зі *on the road*

1st declension, f.:

пова́га *respect*   ува́га *attention*
спра́га *thirst*   відли́га *thaw*
кни́га *a book*   кри́га *ice*
небо́га *a niece*   триво́га *an alarm*
підло́га *a floor*   воло́га *humidity*
перемо́га *a victory*   вимо́га *a demand*
допомо́га *help*   нога́ *a leg*
ска́рга *a complaint*   че́рга *a queue, line*
по́слуга *a service*   подру́га *female friend*
окру́га *a district*   поту́га *might*
прися́га *an oath*   вага́ *weight*

2nd declension, m.:

о́круг *a district*   плуг *a plow*
архіпела́г *an archipelago*   епіло́г *an epilogue*
бе́рег *a shore*   круг *a circle*
луг *a meadow*   о́дяг *clothes*

На бе́резі мо́ря росте́ па́льма.

 6.7. Form disjunctive questions from these statements. Put the verbs in parentheses in the required present tense form.

Model.
C Ва́ша жі́нка (працюва́ти) у бібліоте́ці. *Your wife (to work) in the library.*
A Ва́ша жі́нка працю́є у ↘ бібліоте́ці, чи не ↗ так? *Your wife works in the library, doesn't she?*

1. Твої́ брати́ за́раз (вчи́тися) в університе́ті.
2. Сього́дні ми (вече́ряти) у на́шому улю́бленому рестора́ні.
3. Ті америка́нці тепе́р (відпочива́ти) в Алу́шті.
4. Улі́тку її́ ті́тка (спа́ти) на балко́ні.
5. Уве́чері їхні знайо́мі завжди́ (сиді́ти) у кав'я́рні.
6. Ва́ші дівча́та ча́сто (зупиня́тися) у цьо́му гурто́житку.
7. Ви (жарту́вати).

📝 **Note 6.12. Що *vs* яки́й**

To make sure that you use the correct Ukrainian equivalent of the English *what?* follow a simple rule:
If *what?* can be substituted for *what kind of?* use **яки́й? (яка́? яке́? які́?)**. When this substitution is not possible, use **що?**

У цій львівській аптéці продають не тільки ліки.

6.8. Translate the questions into Ukrainian. Choose a correct interrogative word **що?** *what?* or **який? (яка? яке? які?)** *what kind of?* Consult the dictionary if necessary.

1. What do you do in the morning?
2. What assignment did you have last week?
3. What is in that room?
4. What tickets did the students buy?
5. What are these boys buying?
6. What's in the picture?
7. What people are on this list?
8. What questions did Roman have?
9. What does Maria want to know?
10. What credit cards does this restaurant accept?

Phonetics. Drill shifting the velar к /k/ before ~i

🎧 **6.9.** Listen to the speaker for the cue and form locative singular shifting the velar **к** /k/ to **ц** /ts/, before the ending **~i**.

Model. 🅒 аптéка *a pharmacy*
🅐 в аптéці *in a pharmacy*

1st declension, f.:

рука́ *a hand*	бібліотéка *a library*
скля́нка *a glass*	поми́лка *a mistake*
слу́хавка *a phone receiver*	ка́зка *a fairy tale*
мандрíвка *a trip*	підготóвка *preparation*
за́гадка *a riddle*	сусíд|ка *f. a neighbor* (на ~ці)
ло́жка *a spoon*	жін|ка *a woman* (на ~ці)
му́зика *music*	запра́в|ка *a gas station* (на ~ці)
полíтика *politics*	рíч|ка *a river* (на ~ці)
клíніка *a clinic*	фа́бри|ка *a factory* (на ~ці)
су́мка *a handbag*	плів|ка *a film* (на ~ці)

🎧 **6.10.** Say what these people think. Conjugate the given verbs in the present. If needed, consult the dictionary.

Model.
🅒 він, Марíя, за́раз, працюва́ти, компáнія *he, Maria, to work, company*
🅐 Він ду́має, що за́раз Марíя працю́є в компа́нії. *He thinks that now Maria works for the company.*

1. я, вони, за́раз, вчи́тися, університéт
2. ти, я, звича́йно, вечéряти, рестора́н
3. ми, ва́ші дру́зі, за́вжди, відпочива́ти, Одéса
4. вони, їхня сестра́, ча́сом, снíдати, лíжко
5. вона́, твій брат, інóді, зупиня́тися, готéль
6. я, на́ші хло́пці, сидíти, кав'я́рня

На цій кубинці оригінáльна су́кня.

7. ми, цей америка́нець, тепе́р, жи́ти, Я́лта.
8. ти, мій дя́дько, завжди́, спа́ти, балко́н

∩ **6.11.** Answer the questions. Use the required present tense form of the verb (imperfective aspect).

Model.

Q Ти вже ↗ написа́в лист? *Have you already written the letter?*

A Ні, я все ще ↘ пишу́. *No, I'm still writing.*

1. Твій брат вже відпочи́в?
2. Ти вже перекла́в текст?
3. Ви вже звари́ли борщ?
4. Васи́ль вже ви́вчив нові́ слова́?
5. Ми вже поми́ли таріл́ки?
6. Оле́на вже зроби́ла завда́ння?
7. Вони́ вже прочита́ли газе́ти?
8. Володи́мир вже знайшо́в готе́ль?
9. Робітники́ вже збудува́ли суперма́ркет?
10. Ми вже подиви́лися музе́й?
11. Ти вже послу́хала ра́діо?
12. Ви вже купи́ли проду́кти?
13. Сім'я́ вже повече́ряла?
14. Пархо́менко вже перекла́в цей текст?

Phonetics. Drill shifting the velar к /k/ before ~i.

∩ **6.12.** Answer the question. Drill the к /k/ - ц /ts/ velar shift with feminine names of nationalities.

Model. це мо́дне пальто́ *this fashionable coat,*
украї́нка *a Ukrainian woman.*

Q На ко́му ви ба́чили це мо́дне пальто́?
On whom did you see this fashionable coat?

A На цій украї́нці. *On this Ukrainian woman.*

1. цей га́рний капелю́х *this nice hat,* есто́нка *an Estonian woman*
2. цей легки́й годи́нник *this light watch,* мароќа́нка *a Moroccan woman*
3. цей ділови́й костю́м *this business suit,* іра́нка *an Iranian woman*
4. такі́ золоті́ сере́жки *such gold earrings,* швейца́рка *a Swiss woman*
5. ці елега́нтні шо́рти *these elegant shorts,* австралі́йка *an Australian woman*
6. таки́й шкіряни́й жаке́т *such a leather jacket,* італі́йка *an Italian woman*
7. такі́ дороги́ ту́флі *such expensive shoes,* іспа́нка *a Spanish woman*
8. таке́ мо́дне взуття́ *such fashionable footwear,* че́шка *a Czech woman*

 Note 6.13. Feminine names of nationalities

Masculine names of nationalities ending in ~нець, украї́нець *a Ukrainian,* each have a feminine counterpart ending in ~нка, украї́нка *a Ukrainian woman,*

есто́нець *an Estonian* -
    есто́нка *an Estonian woman*
мароќа́нець *a Moroccan* -
    мароќа́нка *a Moroccan woman*
алба́нець *an Albanian* -
    алба́нка *an Albanian woman*
іра́нець *an Iranian* -
    іра́нка *an Iranian woman.*

The masculine ending ~ець correlates with the feminine ending ~ка,

лито́вець *a Lithuanian* -
    лито́вка *a Lithuanian woman*
швейца́рець *a Swiss* -
    швейца́рка *a Swiss woman.*

The masculine ending ~єць correlates with the feminine ending ~йка,

австралі́єць *an Australian* –
    австралі́йка *Australian woman*
кита́єць *a Chinaman* -
    кита́йка *a Chinese woman*
лівіє́ць *a Libyan* -
    ліві́йка *a Libyan woman*
кені́єць *a Kenyan* -
    кені́йка *a Kenyan woman.*

The stress in the feminine noun is the same as in the masculine one.

Note 6.14. Velar shift in feminine names of nationalities

Feminine names of nationalities undergo the к /k/ - ц /ts/ velar shift when forming the locative singular,

украї́нка *a Ukrainian woman* -
    на украї́нці
лито́вка *a Lithuanian woman* -
    на лито́вці
кита́йка *a Chinese woman* -
    на кита́йці

as well as other such feminine names with the stem ending in ~к~,

по́лька *a Polish woman* -
    на по́льці
че́шка *a Czech woman* -
    на че́шці
францу́зка *a French woman* -
    на францу́зці

Оленка часто читає книжки про мистецтво і театр.

∩ **6.13.** Answer the questions using prompts. Pay attention to the choice of prepositions **в** vs **на**.

Model.
Q Де був Оста́п? *Where was Ostap?* університе́т *university*
A Оста́п був в університе́ті. *Ostap was at the University*.

1. Де була́ Окса́на? кімна́та
2. Де було́ це дитя́? їда́льня
3. Де були́ ва́ші дру́зі? теа́тр
4. Де був цей водій? зупи́нка
5. Де була́ ва́ша сестра́? крамни́ця
6. Де було́ це я́блуко? стіл
7. Де є інтерне́т-по́слуги? по́шта
8. Де були́ його́ батьки́? украї́нський музе́й
9. Де працю́є твоя́ ма́ма? цей заво́д
10. Де був Мико́ла? наш парк
11. Де була́ Оле́на? нови́й банк
12. Де вони́ зустріча́ються? центра́льний вокза́л
13. Де був ваш квито́к? моя́ рука́
14. Де мо́жна купи́ти квитки́ на по́їзд? залізни́чна ста́нція

Phonetics. Drill shifting the velar x /kh/ before ~i

∩ **6.14.** Listen to the speaker for the cue and form locative singular shifting the velar **x** /kh/ to **c** /s/ before the ending **~i**. Check against the speaker.

Model. **C** по́верх *a floor*
A на по́версі *on a floor*

1st declension, f.:

невда́ха *a loser*	кома́ха *an insect*
мура́ха *an ant*	пта́ха *a bird*
стрі́ха a *thatch roof*	блоха́ *a flea*
панчо́ха *a stocking*	му́ха *a fly*
свекру́ха *mother-in-law*	ма́чуха *a stepmother*
бреху́ха *a liar*	бля́ха *tin*
пи́ха *arrogance*	епо́ха *an epoch*
втíха *consolation*	при́мха *a whim*
розру́ха *a ruin*	по́суха *a drought*
завірю́ха *blizzard*	заду́ха *stuffy air*

2nd declension, m.:

ву́хо *an ear*	пух *down*
дух *spirit*	рух *movement*
капелю́х *a hat*	по́рох *powder*
льох *a cellar*	горо́х *beans*
по́верх *a floor*	кожу́х *a sheepskin coat*

🎧 **6.15.** Enact an exchange. Ask and say where somebody was born. Use city prompts.

Model.
🅒 Марі́я *Maria*, Оде́са *Odesa*
🅠 У яко́му мі́сті народи́лася Марі́я? *In what city was Maria born?*
🅐 Вона́ народи́лася в Оде́сі. *She was born in Odesa.*

1. Петро́, Жито́мир
2. Ната́лка, Херсо́н
3. Яри́на, Доне́цьк
4. Макси́м і Ма́рта, Ки́їв
5. Тама́ра, Луцьк
6. Íгор, Мадри́д

7. Богда́н і Тара́с, Я́лта
8. Її́ сестра́, Ві́нниця
9. Їхні брати́, Запорі́жжя
10. Моя́ ді́вчина, Маріу́поль
11. Його́ ба́тько, Ха́рків
12. Іва́н, Нью-Йо́рк

🎧 **6.16.** Answer the questions. Put the adjectives and pronouns in the locative singular masculine (neuter) or feminine.

Model.
🅒 *m. or nt.* У яко́му мі́сті живе́ Марі́я?
    In what (kind of) city does Maria live? стари́й *old*
🅐 У старо́му мі́сті. *In an old city.*
🅒 *f.:* У які́й кни́жці ви це знайшли́?
    In what (kind of) book did you find it? їхній *their*
🅐 У їхній кни́жці. *In their book.*

1. На які́й по́шті мо́жна купи́ти ма́рки? центра́льний
2. У яко́му рестора́ні ви вече́ряєте? їхній кита́йський
3. У які́й кімна́ті вона́ живе́? його́ сві́тлий і вели́кий
4. На які́й фа́бриці вона́ працю́є? цей моде́рний
5. На яко́му вокза́лі ви зустріча́єтеся? той залізни́чний
6. По які́й ву́лиці ти хо́диш? мій зеле́ний і чи́стий
7. У яко́му мі́сці ви відпочива́єте? наш улю́блений
8. У яко́му університе́ті вони́ вча́ться? Ки́ївський
9. У які́й кіношко́лі ти працю́єш? Нью-Йо́ркський
10. У яко́му гурто́житку ти зупини́вся? оста́нній на цій ву́лиці
11. У які́й бібліоте́ці ви познайо́милися? твій університе́тський
12. У чиє́му до́мі він живе́? мій стари́й

🎧 **6.17.** Answer the questions. Make sure you choose the right preposition, **в (у)** *in* or **на** *on*, to go with the locative.

Model. 🅠 Де ви були́? *Where were you?* той бе́рег *that shore.*
          🅐 На то́му бе́резі. *On that shore.*

1. Де живе́ Рома́н? тре́тій по́верх
2. Де працю́є Окса́на? університе́тська бібліоте́ка
3. Де народи́вся твій друг? моє́ рі́дне мі́сто
4. Де був профе́сор Козаче́нко? Півні́чна Аме́рика
5. Де ви ба́чили це га́рне пла́ття? моло́дша сестра́ О́льга

Іри́на народи́лася у Ха́ркові

*Як ви ду́маєте,
хто ці мо́дні па́нни ?*

6. Де стоя́ть кві́ти? вели́кий стіл
7. Де вели́кий стіл? той куто́к
8. Де їхня сім'я́? ця кольоро́ва світли́на
9. Де висить карти́на? поро́жня бі́ла стіна́
10. Де ти знайшо́в цей готе́ль? їхній нови́й путівни́к
11. Де він купи́в квитки́? залізни́чна ста́нція
12. Де працю́ють ва́ші ста́рші брати́? комп'ю́терна фа́брика

∩ **6.18.** Say and write the sentences in Ukrainian. Use the vocabulary and grammar of the lesson, consult the dictionary.

1. Who is in this interesting picture?
2. Who are his parents?
3. My friends have always wanted to see Kyiv and take a walk along Khreshchatyk Street.
4. Where do they vacation this year?
5. Whose sister is to the left, his or theirs?
6. We always eat very late.
7. They like to watch old films, don't they?
8. Where to are they writing so often?
9. By profession Kateryna is a journalist, but now she works at a factory.
10. At the railroad station, one can buy newspapers, tickets and even flowers.
11. In this picture in the middle, is my boyfriend Roman. To the left, is his younger brother Vasylko and to the right, his elder sister Olia.
12. At what post office can one find Internet services?

∩ **6.19.** Address these persons using the vocative case.

Model.
C Світла́на *Svitlana*, Павло́ *Pavlo*
A. Добри́день, Па́вле, як спра́ви? *Hello, Pavlo, how are you?*
B. Ду́же до́бре. Дя́кую, Світла́но. *Very well. Thank you, Svitlana.*

1. О́льга, Григо́рій
2. Лари́са, Ната́ля
3. сусі́д, сусі́дка
4. ба́тько, дочка́
5. ба́бця, О́ленка
6. друг, Андрі́й
7. жі́нка, чолові́к

8. Анато́лій, ма́ма
9. та́то, син
10. при́ятель, при́ятелька
11. діду́сь, ону́к
12. сестра́, Мико́ла
13. коле́га, Рома́н
14. Іва́н, Яри́на

∩ **6.20.** Start a letter by addressing the person you are writing it to. Use the vocative.

Model.
C по́друга *(female) friend*
A Дорога́ по́друго! *Dear (female) friend!*

1. лю́бий друг
2. дорога́ сестра́
3. хоха́ний приятель
4. пан Тара́с
5. пан лі́кар
6. па́ні Михайле́нко
7. профе́сор Васи́льченко
8. шано́вний студе́нт
9. дороги́й лі́кар
10. лю́ба ті́тка
11. па́нна Світла́на
12. пан Миколайчу́к
13. пан Са́вченко
14. коха́на по́друга

🎧 **6.21.** Read the questions and make sure you understand each of them. Listen to the text **"Гончаре́нки у Льво́ві"** and answer the questions.

1. Хто є на світли́ні?
2. Де провели́ великодні кані́кули Гончаре́нки?
3. Де са́ме у Льво́ві є Гончаре́нки на світли́ні?
4. Хто такий Яросла́в Гончаре́нко?
5. Хто така́ Ори́ся Гончаре́нко?
6. Де вчи́ться Іва́сь?
7. На які́й спеція́льності навча́ється Іва́сь?
8. У яко́му кла́сі навча́ється Марі́чка?

🎧 **6.22.** Translate the text into English. Summarize the contents in Ukrainian in three or four sentences.

Гончаре́нки у Льво́ві

Добри́день. Я Юрко́. А ось світли́на. Хо́чете подиви́тися? На ній чоти́ри осо́би, всі ма́ють прі́звище Гончаре́нко. Це на́ша сім'я́.

Мину́лого ро́ку ми вирішили ра́зом провести́ великодні вака́ції у Льво́ві. На світли́ні на́ша сім'я́ у само́му середмі́сті Льво́ва, на Пло́щі Ри́нок. У це́нтрі – мої́ батьки́. Про́шу познайо́митися. Мій та́то – Яросла́в Гончаре́нко. Він економі́ст і працю́є в одно́му вели́кому комерці́йному ба́нку у мі́сті Ха́ркові. Моя́ ма́ма, Ори́ся Гончаре́нко, виклада́є у Ха́рківському націона́льному університе́ті. Її спеція́лізація – украї́нське моде́рне мисте́цтво.

Ліво́руч на світли́ні мій ста́рший брат Іва́сь. Він студе́нт і навча́ється у Ки́ївській націона́льній консервато́рії, на дру́гому ку́рсі, на спеція́льності «джа́зова му́зика».

Право́руч – моя́ моло́дша сестра́ Марі́чка. Вона́ – школя́рка і навча́ється у пе́ршому кла́сі у тій са́мій сере́дній шко́лі, в які́й коли́сь учи́вся я.

Те́пер я диза́йнер і вже два ро́ки працю́ю в архітекту́рній компа́нії «Фаса́д». Ми всі живемо́ у Ха́ркові. Лише́ Іва́сь живе́ у Ки́єві. Ми ду́же га́рно провели́ тоді́ вака́ції у Льво́ві.

Львів, Лати́нський собо́р у старо́му середмі́сті

Гончаре́нки на пло́щі Ри́нок у Льво́ві

Note 6.15. Dropping ~e~ in final syllable

Drill on your own dropping the vowel ~e~ in the final syllable of the 2nd declension masculine nouns when forming the locative singular. Use the material in Exercise 5.9 as well as in Notes 5.8 and 5.9. Bear in mind that the ~e~ is dropped both before the ~i and ~ові types of locative singular endings,

па́лець *a finger* -
  на па́льці *on a finger*

украї́нець *a Ukrainian man* -
  на украї́нцеві *on a Ukrainian man*

Phonetics. Drill dropping the ~о~

🎧 **6.23.** Listen carefully to the speaker and repeat. Practice dropping the vowel ~о~ in the final syllable of the consonant-ended masculine nouns when forming the locative singular.

Model 1. Locative with the preposition в (у) *in*,

Stress Pattern A. Stress remains on the same vowel.
C буди́нок *a building* **A** у буди́нку *in a building*

буди́нок *a building*	ви́няток *an exception*
за́мок *a castle*	сніда́нок *breakfast*
гурто́житок *a dormitory*	спи́сок *a list*
за́тінок *a cool place*	поря́док *order*
подару́нок *a gift*	мо́зок *brain*
прову́лок *a lane*	промі́жок *a time period*
паку́нок *a package*	прила́вок *a counter*

Stress Pattern B. Stress is on the last syllable.
C куто́к *a corner* **A** у кутку́ *in a corner*

ставо́к *a pond*	квито́к *a ticket*
рядо́к *a line (of words)*	сачо́к *a landing-net*
пиріжо́к *a pie*	огіро́к *a cucumber*
візо́к *a cart*	віно́к *a wreath*
замо́к *a lock*	лісо́к *a grove*
садо́к *a garden*	мішо́к *a bag*

Model 2. Locative with the preposition на *on*

Stress Pattern A. Stress remains on the same vowel.
C раху́нок *an account* **A** на раху́нку *on the account*

поча́ток *a beginning*	я́рмарок *a fair*
ри́нок *a market*	ма́єток *household*
ґа́нок *a doorstep*	па́сок *a belt*
світа́нок *sunrise*	па́рубок *a bachelor*
полу́денок *lunch*	підлі́ток *a teenager*
цвя́шок *a nail*	ту́рок *a Turk*

Stress Pattern B. Stress is on the last syllable.
C квито́к *a ticket* **A** на квитку́ *on a ticket*

листо́к *a sheet*	волосо́к *a hair*
гвіздо́к *a nail*	місто́к *a small bridge*
ланцюжо́к *a chain*	молото́к *a hammer*
шнуро́к *a lace, string*	пеньо́к *a stump*
поясо́к *a belt*	значо́к *a badge*
шмато́к *a piece*	свисто́к *a whistle*

6.24. Describe this family picture. Use the text above as a template and the vocabulary of this lesson. If need be, consult the dictionary.

 6.25. Listen carefully and mark the numerals you hear.

сто дéсять	трúста двана́дцять	тúсяча сто	шістсо́т два́дцять	чотúриста п'ять
сімсо́т дéв'ять	п'ятсо́т чотúри	двíсті сімдеся́т	сто п'ятна́дцять	дев'ятсо́т сім
вісімсо́т трúдцять	тúсяча вíсім	двí тúсячі	сімсо́т п'ятдеся́т	со́рок тúсяч
дев'ятсо́т п'ятдеся́т	чотúриста дéсять	шістдеся́т вíсім	двана́дцять	п'ятдеся́т сім
трúста одина́дцять	двíсті тúсяч	п'ятдеся́т	вісімдеся́т шість	двí тúсячі вíсім

 6.26. Numeric dictation. Listen carefully to the speaker and write down in words the cardinal numerals. Read out loud each of the numerals.

📞 Note 6.17. How to read a phone number

Phone numbers are read as they are written, i.e., grouped into larger numerals instead of by each separate digit as is the case in English. The logical stress falls on the last number in each group. After each group there is a small pause,

276-40-18   is read as **двíсті сімдеся́т ↗шість, ↗со́рок, ↘вісімна́дцять**

70-21-99   **↗сімдеся́т, два́дцять ↗одúн, дев'яно́сто ↘дéв'ять,**

2-16-33   **↗два, ↗шістна́дцять, трúдцять ↘трú**

A zero at the beginning of a numeric group is read separately, without a pause after it,

067-234-56-67 нуль шістдеся́т ↗сім, двíсті трúдцять чотúри, п'ятдеся́т ↗шість, шістдеся́т ↘сім

096-28-30-200 нуль дев'яно́сто ↗шість, два́дцять ↗вíсім, ↗трúдцять, ↘двíсті

🔢 Note 6.16. Numerals one hundred - one thousand

Memorize the cardinal numerals from one hundred to nine hundred:

one hundred	**сто**	/sto/
two hundred	**двíсті**	/dvísti/
three hundred	**трúста**	/trýsta/
four hundred	**чотúриста**	/choᵘtýryᵉsta/
five hundred	**п'ятсо́т**	/pjatsót/
six hundred	**шістсо́т**	/shissót/
seven hundred	**сімсо́т**	/s'imsót/
eight hundred	**вісімсо́т**	/vis'imsót/
nine hundred	**дев'ятсо́т**	/deᵛvjatsót/
one thousand	**(одна́) тúсяча**	/oᵘdná týs'acha/

Скажú, будь ла́ска, якúй твíй но́вий но́мер телефо́ну?

If the number is not broken down into groups by dashes, it is up to the individual speaker to break it into numerals of tens and hundreds, but never thousands,

1567 інформаці́йна слу́жба *information service* - **п'ятна́дцять, шістдеся́т сім, 204360 готе́ль «Роксола́на»** *the Roksolana Hotel* - **два́дцять, со́рок три, шістдеся́т** or **дві́сті чоти́ри, три́ста шістдеся́т.**

But this number is never read as **дві́сті чоти́ри ти́сячі три́ста шістдеся́т.**

 **6.27.** Read these telephone numbers in Ukrainian. Follow the rules described in Note 6.17.

Телефо́нний дові́дник Telephone directory

таксі́ *taxi* 223-17
довідко́ва слу́жба *information service* 211-57
мілі́ція *police* 630-20-41
швидка́ допомо́га *ambulance* 273-92-15
а́втовокза́л *bus station* 750-830
залізни́чний вокза́л *railway station* 809-11-11
банк *bank* 444-555

Прива́тні телефо́ни Private telephone numbers

Авра́менко, Світла́на	095-240-76-60
Адамчу́к, Левко́	066-410-51-02
Банду́ра, Тама́ра	096-333-20-11
Василе́нко, Марі́я	234-15-50
Гордійчу́к, Семе́н	067-249-19-91
Ле́вченко, Ві́ра	97-68-43
Москале́нко, Васи́ль	050-988-18-22
Юхи́менко, Іва́н	089-540-88-90

6.28. Listen carefully to the questions and answer each of them using Dialogue 6.

1. Що ма́є Юрко́?
2. Хто є на фотогра́фії?
3. У яко́му мі́сті є сім'я́ Юрка́ на фотогра́фії?
4. Хто на фотогра́фії стої́ть ліво́руч?
5. У які́й компа́нії працю́є ба́тько?
6. Хто на фотогра́фії стої́ть право́руч?
7. Хто за фа́хом його́ ма́ма?
8. Як назива́ється газе́та, у які́й працю́є ма́ма?
9. Хто така́ Оле́на?
10. У які́й шко́лі вчи́ться Оле́на?
11. Де живе́ його́ сім'я́?
12. Що за́вжди хоті́ла зроби́ти Яри́на?

∩ **6.29.** Study the map of Ukraine and answer the questions. In each answer, use as much as possible the grammatical forms found in the question. If need be, refer to Table 19 in the appendices, pp. 330-331.

Model.

Q У якій части́ні Украї́ни розташо́вується мі́сто Луцьк? *In what part of Ukraine is the city of Lutsk located?*

A Воно́ (розташо́вується) на за́ході Украї́ни. *It is (located) in the west of Ukraine.*

1. Де розташо́вується мі́сто Су́ми?
2. У якій части́ні Украї́ни розташо́вується мі́сто У́жгород?
3. На яко́му мо́рі стої́ть Севасто́поль?
4. Яка́ краї́на лежи́ть на схо́ді від Украї́ни *(from Ukraine)*?
5. На якій рі́чці стої́ть мі́сто Черні́гів?
6. У якій части́ні Украї́ни розташо́вується Херсо́н?
7. На якій рі́чці стої́ть мі́сто Чернівці́?
8. Які́ краї́ни лежа́ть на за́ході від Украї́ни *(from Ukraine)*?
9. Які́ міста́ стоя́ть на Дніпрі́?
10. У якій части́ні Украї́ни розташо́вується Ві́нниця?
11. Які́ вели́кі рі́чки є в Украї́ні?
12. Які́ моря́ є на цій ма́пі?
13. Які́ міста́ лежа́ть на схо́ді Украї́ни?
14. Які́ краї́ни є на цій ма́пі?

Note 6.18. Ма́па Украї́ни
Map of Ukraine

Among the verbs used to indicate the location of an object on the map are:

розташо́ву|ватися, ~ються *to be located*
сто|я́ти, ~я́ть *to stand*, and
лежа́ти, ~а́ть *to lie* and simply
бу́ти *to be* are used.

Оде́са розташо́вується на пі́вдні.
Odesa is located in the south.
Ки́їв стої́ть на Дніпрі́.
Kyiv stands on the Dnipro.
Ця краї́на лежи́ть у це́нтрі Євро́пи.
This country lies in the center of Europe.
Чо́рне мо́ре є на пі́вдні. *The Black Sea is in the south.*

Memorize these expressions and use them to describe a city's geographic position:

пі́вніч *north* - на пі́вночі *in the north*
пі́вдень *south* - на пі́вдні *in the south*
за́хід *west* - на за́ході *in the west*
схід *east* - на схо́ді *in the east*
це́нт(е)р *center* - у це́нтрі *in the center*

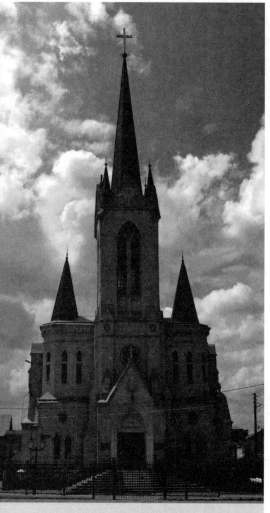

німе́цька це́рква в місті Луцьку, що на рі́чці Стир

Мо́вні ресу́рси на мере́жі. Украї́нська Вікіпе́дія.
Language resources on the web. Ukrainian Wikipedia.

6.29. Using the Ukrainian language Wikipedia find out:
1) what body of water (водо́йма) each of these cities is situated on;
2) which province of Ukraine (о́бласть) each of the cities is in.

Міста́: Бі́ла Це́рква, Богоду́хів, Го́рлівка, Жме́ринка, Криви́й Ріг, Ми́ргород, Ні́жин, Олександрі́я, Са́рни.

6.30. Enact a conversation with a partner. Use the material you learned in this and previous lessons. If necessary, consult the dictionary.

Сце́нка за сцена́рієм «Моя́ сім'я́»
Scripted Skit *My Family*

[Oleh is showing his girlfriend Nadia a picture of his family.]

Oleh (Оле́г): Says his family is in this picture. Offers Nadia to take a look.
Nadia (Наді́я): Expresses her keen interest in the picture.

Oleh: Introduces his father by name and last name.
Nadia: Says such a last name is very common in Ukraine.

Oleh: Introduces his mother also by name and last name (she has a last name different from his father's).
Nadia: Asks why his mother has a different (і́нше) last name.

Oleh: It is a long story. But this is not a problem in his family.
Nadia: Says she understands. Asks where his parents work.

Oleh: His father is an engineer and works at a post office. His mother is a doctor and works in a hospital.
Nadia: Guesses that a little boy in the picture on the left is Oleh's brother.

Oleh: Affirmative. It is his younger brother Yarema. He is a pupil in a secondary school in Zhytomyr. He likes to study.
Nadia: Assumes that the young lady on the right is Oleh's sister.

Oleh: Affirmative. It is his elder sister Lesia. She is a student at a university in Lviv.
Nadia: Assumes that Lesia therefore does not live in Zhytomyr but in Lviv. Asks if it is difficult to live in a different city.

Oleh: At first it was not easy. Now hard times are in the past. Lesia likes Lviv very much. She says it's a beautiful and very special city.
Nadia: Expresses hope that maybe one day (коли́сь) she and Oleh can travel there together.

Ле́кція | Lesson 7

Dialogue:
Що я люблю́ роби́ти
What I like to do

Grammar:
Accusative singular
Expression of intention **ду́мати** + *inf.*
Imperfective future tense
Verb **бу́ти** *to be*, in the future tense
Adverbs

Competencies:
Favorite pastimes
What's in the movies
Days of the week
Expressing future possibility
Designating temperatures
Describing the weather
Names of people and institutions

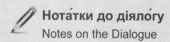

Як ти ду́маєш, що вони́ роблять на дозві́ллі?

🗩 7. Діяло́г. Що я люблю́ роби́ти.

Яри́на: Рома́не, що ти ду́маєш роби́ти на вихідні́?
Рома́н: Я бу́ду відпочива́ти, як за́вжди.
Яри́на: Що ти звича́йно ро́биш на дозві́ллі?
Рома́н: Чита́ю якусь ціка́ву кни́жку.
Яри́на: А за́раз яку́ кни́жку ти чита́єш?
Рома́н: За́раз я чита́ю Ле́ся Подерв'я́нського, його́ нову́ п'є́су «Вимо́глива Га́ля». Чита́ла?
Яри́на: Ні, не ті́льки не чита́ла, але́ на́віть не чу́ла. Я теж люблю́ чита́ти. Особли́во про полі́тику та про спорт.
Рома́н: Ча́сом я та́кож дивлю́ся телеві́зор чи слу́хаю му́зику. Яку́ му́зику лю́биш ти?
Яри́на: О́перу, джаз та украї́нську поп-му́зику.
Рома́н: А я люблю́ кіно́ і теа́тр.
Яри́на: Сього́дні вве́чері я ду́маю подиви́тися нови́й фільм. Він назива́ється «Мама́й».
Рома́н: Так-так, я чув про ньо́го. Він іде́ у кінотеа́трі «Украї́на».
Яри́на: Якщо́ хо́чеш, мо́жемо піти́ ра́зом.
Рома́н: Добре. Сього́дні вве́чері бу́демо диви́тися «Мама́я».

🗩 7. Dialogue. What I like to do.

Yaryna: Roman, what are you going to do on the weekend?
Roman: I will be resting as always.
Yaryna: What do you usually do at leisure?
Roman: I read an interesting book.
Yaryna: And now what book are you reading?
Roman: Now I am reading Les Poderviansky, his new play *Demanding Halia*. Have you read it?
Yaryna: No, not only have I not read it, I never heard of it. I also like to read. Especially about politics and sports.
Roman: Sometimes I also watch TV or listen to music. What music do you like?
Yaryna: Opera, jazz, and Ukrainian pop.
Roman: And I like movies and theater.
Yaryna: Tonight I am going to watch a new film. It's entitled *Mamay*.
Roman: Yes, yes. I heard about it. It's on at the Ukraina Movie Theater.
Yaryna: If you like we can go together.
Roman: Alright. Tonight we'll be watching "Mamay."

✎ Нота́тки до діяло́гу
Notes on the Dialogue

ду́мати (ду́май~), ~ють + *inf., colloq.*	*to be going to do sth, to plan to do sth* (*lit.* to think). Is used only in *impf.* as expression of intention to do sth, **Я ду́маю поба́чити Ха́рків.** *I intend to see Kharkiv.*

вихідні́, *pl.* of *adj.* вихідни́й	a day-off. Shortened of **вихідни́й день**, *lit.* going-out day, hence **вихідні́** *weekend*, **на вихідні́** *A. pl. on the weekend.*
яки́йсь, *m.*, яка́сь, *f.*, яке́сь, *nt.*, які́сь, *pl.*	some, some kind of. Is declined as an adjective with the particle ~**сь** attached to the ending, **яку́сь** is *A. sg.* of **яка́сь.**
люби́ти (люб~), ~ять, *tran.*	to like, love. When followed by *inf.* means to like (to do sth); with noun as direct object can mean both *to like*, **Я люблю́ цю програ́му.** *I like this program.* and *to love*, **Мико́ла лю́бить Марі́ю.** *Mykola loves Maria.*;
	люби́ти + *inf.* is often used when speaking of one's favorite pastimes.
слу́хати (слу́хай~), ~ють; послу́хати, *tran.*	to listen to. Unlike in English, this verb takes a direct *A.* object without any preposition, **слу́хати ра́діо (програ́му, му́зику, сестру́, бра́та)** to listen to the radio (a program, music, one's sister, brother).
назива́|тися, ~ються, *intr.*	to be called, to have the title of, **Як ~є́ться ця карти́на?** *What's the title of this picture?* (more rarely of a person) to have the name of + *I.* **Він ~є́ться Петро́м.** *His name is Petro.*
іти́ (ід~), іду́ть; пройти́, *var.* йти, *intr.*	(about a film, theater play) to be on, **Де йде цей фільм?** *Where is this film being shown?* **Цей фільм ско́ро бу́де йти у на́шому кінотеа́трі.** *This film will soon be on at our movie theater.*
"Мама́й"	the title of a feature film by director Oles Sanin, which was Ukraine's official entry for the Oscars in 2004. Mamay is a legendary Cossack, symbolizing the Ukrainian spirit of freedom.

📖 Грама́тика | Grammar

Знахі́дний відмі́нок однини́ Accusative Case Singular

Accusative correlates with the questions
про ко́го? *about whom?* **про що?** *about what?*

Фу́нкція *Function*

A simple way of understanding the function of the accusative is by taking note of the situations in which it is used. Two types of such situations are common:
1) verbs that require a noun or noun phrase (attribute + noun) in the accusative;
2) prepositions which require the accusative.

1. Here are some verbs which require the accusative:
ма́ти *to have*, **роби́ти** *to do*, **ї́сти** *to eat*, **пи́ти** *to drink*, **чу́ти** *to hear*, **слу́хати** *to listen to*, **ба́чити** *to see*, **люби́ти** *to like, love*, **каза́ти** *to say*, **чека́ти** *to wait*, **купува́ти** *to buy*, **писа́ти** *to write*, **чита́ти** *to read*, **розумі́ти** *to understand*, **пам'ята́ти** *to remember*.
All these verbs are called transitive *(tran.)*. Each expresses an action directed to the object without the mediation of a preposition.

2. Prepositions requiring the accusative include:
про *about*, as in **Я чув про цьо́го чолові́ка.** *I heard about this man.*
каза́ти про ко́го? / **про** що? *to tell about sb/sth*; **розповіда́ти про** *to narrate about sb/ sth*; **пита́ти про** *to ask about sb/ sth*; **ду́мати про** *to think about sb/ sth.*

У ві́льний час вони́ ча́сто гра́ють на ко́бзі.

Piano Cafe на Подолі
вул. Ярославська, 56-б, Київ

Вхід 70 грн.

Дрес-код: ретро-стиль

Украı̈нське танго
вечı́рка у стилı̈ 1930-х

16 грудня, в недı̇лю, о 17:30

Ярина й Рома́н хо́дять танцюва́ти та́нго.

In colloquial speech, the preposition **за** *about* is used with the same meaning:
Ти вже каза́в за ньо́го. *You already told (me) about him.*

на 1) *for*, as in **на понедı̇лок** *for (by) Monday*, **на насту́пний ти́ждень** *for next week* or
2) *at*, as in **диви́тися на ко́го? / на що?** *to look at sb/ sth*
3) *on*, as in **ста́вити на що?** *to put (sth) on sth*; **Він поста́вив ва́зу на стı̇л.** *He put the vase on a table.*

у/в *on (a day of the week)*, as in **Я відпочива́ю у субо́ту.** *I rest on Saturday.* **У се́реду було́ ду́же хо́лодно.** *It was very cold on Wednesday*

Знахı̇дний у пита́ннях *Accusative in Questions*

Accusative correlates with interrogative pronouns **кого́?** *who(m)?* relating to living beings and **що?** *what?*, relating to inanimate objects. Thus **Кого́ ти ба́чиш?** *Whom do you see?* and **Що ти ба́чиш?** *What do you see?* The same accusative structure is used with other verbs requiring the accusative,

ма́ти *to have* - **Кого́ (що) ти ма́єш?** *Whom (what) do you have?*
зна́ти *to know* - **Кого́ (що) ти зна́єш?** *Whom (what) do you know?*
чу́ти *to hear* - **Кого́ (що) ти чу́єш?** *Whom (what) do you hear?*
люби́ти *to love, like* - **Кого́ (що) ти лю́биш?** *Whom (what) do you like?*

Утво́рення *Formation*

Іме́нники *Nouns*

Nominal accusative singular endings:
~у (~ю), ~а (~я).

The endings of the accusative depend on the declension type of noun and, for masculine nouns with zero ending, also on whether they are animate or inanimate.

~у is taken by feminine and masculine nouns ending in **~а (~я)**, **Це** *f.* **кни́жка.** *This is a book.* - **Я ба́чу кни́жку.** *I see a book.* **Це** *m.* **Мико́ла.** *This is Mykola* - **Я люблю́ Мико́лу.** *I like Mykola.*

~ю is taken by feminine and masculine nouns ending in **~я**, **Це** *f.* **Марı́я.** *This is Maria.* - **Я ду́маю про Марı́ю.** *I think about Maria.* **Ось** *m.* **Ілля́.** *Here is Illia.* - **Він ди́виться на Іллю́.** *He is looking at Illia.*

~а is taken by animate masculine nouns with a zero ending and hard stem, **Це брат.** *This is my brother.* - **Я ба́чу бра́та.** *I see my brother.* **Там ı̈хнı̇й журналı̇ст.** *There's their journalist there.* - **Вона́ зна́є ı̈хнього журналı̇ста.** *She knows their journalist.*

~я is taken by animate masculine nouns with a zero ending and soft stem, **Це вчи́тель.** *This is a teacher.* - **Я зна́ю вчи́теля.** *I know a teacher.*

same as N. The following groups of nouns in the accusative are identical to the nominative:

1) inanimate masculine nouns with a zero ending, **Це університе́т.** *This is a university.* - **Я ба́чу університе́т.** *I see a university.* **Ось теа́тр.** *Here's the theater.* - **Я люблю́ теа́тр.** *I like the theater.*

2) all feminine nouns ending in a consonant, **Це любо́в.** *This is love.* - **Я зна́ю любо́в.** *I know love.*

3) all neuter nouns, **Це мі́сто.** *This is a city.* - **Я ба́чу мі́сто.** *I see a city.* **Ось завда́ння.** *Here's an assignment.* - **Я роблю́ завда́ння.** *I am doing an assignment.*

Accusative singular of **ма́ти** *a mother* is **ма́тір**, **Це його́ ма́ти.** *This is his mother.* - **Я зна́ю його́ ма́тір.** *I know his mother.*

 The stress in the accusative singular is identical to the nominative singular, **ону́ка Га́нна** *grandaughter Hanna* - **Він лю́бить ону́ку Га́нну.** *He loves his granddaughter Hanna.* In some cases, the stress is mobile, **Васи́ль Ма́рченко** *Vasyl Marchenko* - **Я ба́чу Василя́ Ма́рченка.** *I see Vasyl Marchenko.*

🔊 SOUND CHANGES 🔊
in the accusative singular of noun

Dropping of ~o~ (~e~)

~o~ and ~e~ in the last syllable of 2nd declension animate masculine nouns are dropped in the accusative singular,

па́рубок *a youth, bachelor* - **про па́рубка** *about a youth, bachelor*
украї́нець *a Ukrainian* - **про украї́нця** *about a Ukrainian*
у́чень *a pupil* - *colloq.* **за у́чня** *about a pupil*

Change of ~i~ to ~o~ (~e~)

~i~ often changes to ~o~ (~e~) in the final syllable of 2nd declension animate masculine nouns,

кіт *a cat* - **про кота́** *about a cat*
кінь *a horse* - **про коня́** *about a horse*
   but **дід** *a grandfather* - **про ді́да** *about a grandfather*

Що ви зна́єте за Сашка́ та Сла́вку?

Всі зна́ють їхнього ді́да.

Це міліціонéри. Всі водії
їх дýже люблять.

Особóві займéнники Personal Pronouns

Personal pronouns have two forms of the accusative depending on whether or not they are used with a preposition. Without a preposition their accusative forms are:
я *I* - **менé** *me*, ти *you* - **тебé** *you*, він *he* - **йогó** *him*, вонá *she* - **її** *her*, воно *it* - **йогó** *it*, ми *we* - **нас** *us*, ви *you* - **вас** *you*, вони *they* - **їх** *them*.

When personal pronouns in the accusative follow prepositions like **про** *about* and **на** *at* or other, they all, with the exception of **ми/нас** *we/us* and **ви/вас** *you*, undergo the following changes:

1) stress shift to the front, **менé** - **про мéне**, **тебé** - **про тéбе**,
Ти бáчиш менé. *You see me.* - **Ти дýмаєш про мéне.** *You think about me.*

2) initial consonant change for **їх** - **про них**,
Ти бáчиш їх. *You see them.* - **Ти дýмаєш про них.** *You think about them.*

3) both stress shift to the front and initial consonant change for **йогó** - **про ньóго**, **її** - **про нéї**,
Ти бáчиш її. *You see her.* - **Ти дýмаєш про нéї.** *You think about her.*

For the accusative of possessive, demonstrative, and interrogative pronouns see the appendices, Tables 6-10, pp. 322-324.

When these pronouns refer to an animate masculine noun, their accusative is the same as genitive,
Якóго америкáнця ти знáєш? *What American man do you know?* - **Тогó.** *That one.*

When they refer to an inanimate masculine noun, their accusative is the same as nominative,
Який журнáл ви хóчете? *What magazine do you want?* - **Той.** *That one.*
Cf. **Це мій друг.** *This is my friend.* - **Я бáчу мого дрýга.** *I see my friend.*
Це мій університéт. *This is my university.* - **Я бáчу мій університéт.** *I see my university.*

Прикмéтники Adjectives

Adjectival accusative singular endings:
~ого (~ього), **~ий** (~ій); **~у** (~ю); **~е** (~є)

~ого is taken by masculine hard-stem adjectives accompanying animate nouns in the accusative,
Це новий студéнт. *This is a new student.* - **Я бáчу новóго студéнта.** *I see a new student.*

Олéнка знáє цю істóрію
й чáсто про нéї дýмає.

~ього is taken by masculine soft-stem adjectives accompanying animate nouns in the accusative,
Ось тре́тій тури́ст. *Here's the third tourist.* - **Він зна́є тре́тього тури́ста.** *He knows the third tourist.*

The accusative form of the masculine adjectives modifying inanimate nouns is the same as their nominative,
Це нови́й фільм. *This is a new film.* - **Я дивлю́ся нови́й фільм.** *I am watching a new film.* **Ось тре́тій ваго́н.** *Here's the third (train) car.* - **Я шука́ю тре́тій ваго́н.** *I'm looking for the third (train) car.*

~у is taken by hard-stem feminine adjectives,
Це стара́ ха́та. *This is an old house.* - **Я ба́чу стару́ ха́ту.** *I see an old house.*

~ю is taken by soft-stem feminine adjectives,
Це оста́ння ха́та. *This is the last house.* - **Я ба́чу оста́нню ха́ту.** *I see the last house.*

The accusative of neuter adjectives is the same as their nominative form,
Це вели́ке мі́сто. *This is a big city.* - **Він лю́бить це вели́ке мі́сто.** *He likes this big city.*

У насту́пну се́реду вони́ ї́дуть відпочива́ти на рі́чку.

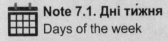 **Note 7.1. Дні ти́жня**
Days of the week

The Ukrainian week starts on Monday and ends on Sunday. The names of weekdays are spelled in lower case. The expressions *on Monday, this Monday, last Monday, next Monday* are equivalent to the Ukrainian:

у (в) + day of week in *A. sg.*

- Яки́й сього́дні день?
What day is it today?
- Сього́дні понеді́лок.
Today is Monday.

№	Day of week	on Monday, etc.	this Monday, etc.	last Monday, etc.	next Monday, etc.
1.	**понеді́лок** *Monday*	у понеді́лок	у цей понеді́лок	у мину́лий понеді́лок	у насту́пний понеді́лок
2.	**вівто́рок** *Tuesday*	у вівто́рок	у цей вівто́рок	у мину́лий вівто́рок	у насту́пний вівто́рок
3.	**середа́** *Wednesday*	у се́реду	у цю се́реду	у мину́лу се́реду	у насту́пну се́реду
4.	**четве́р** *Thursday*	у четве́р	у цей четве́р	у мину́лий четве́р	у насту́пний четве́р
5.	**п'я́тниця** *Friday*	у п'я́тницю	у цю п'я́тницю	у мину́лу п'я́тницю	у насту́пну п'я́тницю
6.	**субо́та** *Saturday*	у субо́ту	у цю субо́ту	у мину́лу субо́ту	у насту́пну субо́ту
7.	**неді́ля** *Sunday*	у неді́лю	у цю неді́лю	у мину́лу неді́лю	у насту́пну неді́лю

Note the stress shift in **середа́** *Wednesday* - **у се́реду** *on Wednesday.*

Насту́пного ти́жня у Рі́вному бу́дуть пока́зувати нови́й фільм Валенти́на Вася́но́вича.

Майбу́тній недоко́наний час   Imperfective Future Tense

Фу́нкція   *Function*

The imperfective future tense presents a future action as an open-ended process, without regard to its completion or result or as such that will repeatedly occur over a period of future time,
У готе́лі Яри́на бу́де жи́ти оди́н ти́ждень. *In the hotel, Yaryna will be staying for one week.* **Насту́пного ро́ку Іго́р бу́де вивча́ти англі́йську мо́ву.** *Next year, Ihor will be studying the English language.*

It is also used to express two parallel future actions in process,
Насту́пного ро́ку Іго́р бу́де подорожува́ти, а ми бу́демо працюва́ти. *Next year Ihor will be traveling and we will be working.*

Adverbial modifiers used with the imperfective future indicate:

1) a future moment or a future period,
ско́ро *soon*, **незаба́ром** *soon*, **за́втра** *tomorrow*, **післяза́втра** *the day after tomorrow*, **насту́пного ти́жня (мі́сяця, ро́ку, понеді́лка, etc.)** *next week (month, year, Monday, etc.);*

2) repetitive occurrence in the future,
ча́сто *often*, **за́вжди** *always*, **звича́йно** *usually*, **як пра́вило** *as a rule*, or non-occurrence as with **ніко́ли** *never;*

3) a delimited time period, **про́тягом** + *G.* *for (duration),* **про́тягом годи́ни (дня, но́чі, мі́сяця)** *for an hour (a day, night, month);* **від** + *G.* ... **до** + *G.* ... *from ... to ...* , **від понеді́лка до субо́ти** *from Monday to Saturday,* **від тре́тьої годи́ни до п'я́тої** *from five o'clock to six.* (For the genitive of time expressions see Lesson 8, pp. 132-133.)

A period of time within which a future action takes place can be indicated by a noun or a noun phrase in the accusative. No preposition is used,
A. sg. **Я бу́ду працюва́ти одну́ годи́ну.** *I'll work for an hour.*

Other such expressions are: **ти́ждень** *a week,* **мі́сяць** *a month,* **три дні** *three days,* **п'ять мі́сяців** *five months,* **доба́** *twenty-four hours,* etc. all used in the accusative without preposition.

Утво́рення   *Formation*

There are two forms of the imperfective future in Ukrainian:
1) the analytic or a two-word future;
2) the synthetic, or a one-word future.

We shall first learn the analytic imperfective future formation.
It consists of the verb **бу́ти** *to be* in future + *imperfective infinitive* of the notional verb. The verb **бу́ти** is conjugated in the imperfective future by number and person while the imperfective infinitive of the notional verb remains unchanged.

The verb **бу́ти** *to be*, conjugated in the future:

я **бу́ду**	*I'll be*	ми **бу́демо**	*we'll be*
ти **бу́деш**	*sg. you'll be*	ви **бу́дете**	*pl. you'll be*
він **бу́де**	*he'll be*	вони́ **бу́дуть**	*they'll be*

Here is the conjugation of the verb **жи́ти** *to live*, in the analytic imperfective future:

я **бу́ду жи́ти**	*I'll live*	ми **бу́демо жи́ти**	*we'll live*
ти **бу́деш жи́ти**	*you'll live*	ви **бу́дете жи́ти**	*you'll live*
він **бу́де жи́ти**	*he'll live*	вони́ **бу́дуть жи́ти**	*they'll live*

Take note. Be sure to use only the imperfective infinitive to form the imperfective future. This rule has no exceptions.

General questions are formed either by giving an interrogative (rising) intonation to the affirmative sentence,
Я там ↗бу́ду жи́ти? *Will I live there?*
or by the particle **чи** put at the beginning of the affirmative statement which is pronounced as a question:
Чи я там ↗бу́ду жи́ти? *Will I live there?*
The particle **чи** does not get any logical stress.

Negative statements are formed by inserting the particle **не** before the verb **бу́ти** in the affirmative statement. **Бу́ти** also gets the logical stress.
Я там не ↘бу́ду жи́ти. *I will not live there.*
The negative statement is pronounced with a falling intonation.

Прислі́вник   Adverb

Фу́нкція *Function*

An adverb is a word that modifies an adjective, verb, or other adverb, expressing relations of manner, time, place, circumstance, cause, degree, probability and so on:
до́бре *well*, **до́вго** *for long*, **можли́во** *possibly*, **про́сто** *simply, straight*, **рі́вно** *exactly*, **незаба́ром** *soon*, **ра́зом** *together*.

An adverb can describe:
1) a verb,
Мико́ла чита́в шви́дко. *Mykola read quickly.* **Я ходжу́ пові́льно.** *I walk slowly.*
2) an adjective,
Це ду́же ціка́ва істо́рія. *This is a very interesting story.*
3) another adverb,
Надво́рі було́ ду́же хо́лодно. *It was very cold outside.*

Adverbs can be accompanied by such intensifiers as **ду́же** *very*, **на́дто**, *var.* **зана́дто** *too, excessively*.

У насту́пну неді́лю ми всі бу́демо святкува́ти Вели́кдень.

Note 7.3. Parallel forms of adverbs

Some adverbs can take both the endings ~o and ~e, without any change of their meaning,

(на)пе́вно and (на)пе́вне *perhaps*
даре́мно and даре́мне *in vain*
(на)вми́сно and (на)вми́сне *on purpose.*

Утво́рення *Formation*

In terms of formation adverbs fall into two groups:

1) those formed from respective adjectives, like the English *adv. nicely* from *adj. nice,*
га́рний *nice* - **га́рно** *nicely,* **холо́дний** *cold* - **хо́лодно** *coldly,* **ціка́вий** *interesting* - **ціка́во** *interestingly,* **смішни́й** *funny* - **смішно́** *in a funny way.*
Such de-adjectival adverbs usually precede the word they describe,
бага́то працюва́ти *to work hard,* **ма́ло спа́ти** *to sleep little;*

2) adverbs that have no relation to an adjective, like the English *together, well,* usually follow the word they describe,
поверну́ти право́руч *to turn right,* **прийти́ ра́зом** *to come together,* **подиви́тися вго́ру** *to look upward.*

Adverbial endings: ~o and ~e

Adverbs are formed by replacing the adjectival ending **~ий** (**~ій**) with the suffix **~о** (**~ьо**),

ско́рий *rapid* - **ско́ро** *rapidly,* **доста́тній** *sufficient* - **доста́тньо** *sufficiently,* **ні́жний** *tender* - **ні́жно** *tenderly,* **гру́бий** *rude* - **гру́бо** *rudely,* **постíйний** *constant* - **постíйно** *constantly,* **яскра́вий** *bright* - **яскра́во** *brightly.*

A small group of adverbs derived from adjectives with a mixed stem type (ending in **~ж, ~ч, ~ш, ~щ,** and **~р**) have the ending **~е,**
ду́жий *big* - **ду́же** *very,* **до́брий** *good* - **до́бре** *well,* **хоро́ший** *good* - **хоро́ше** *well,* **байду́жий** *indifferent* - **ба́йдуже** *all the same, indifferently,* **гаря́чий** *hot* - **гаря́че** *passionately, hotly.*

Unlike adjectives or pronouns, adverbs do not decline.

The stress in adverbs more often than not is on the same syllable as in the corresponding adjective (see above).
The stress falls on the first syllable in adverbs that are derived from adjectives with the stress on the final syllable,

швидки́й *quick* - **шви́дко** *quickly*
легки́й *easy* - **ле́гко** *easily*
важки́й *heavy* - **ва́жко** *heavily*
тонки́й *thin* - **то́нко** *thinly*
смачни́й *delicious* - **сма́чно** *deliciously*
гидки́й *ugly* - **ги́дко** *in a disgusting manner*

Ма́рта га́рно малю́є про́сто на ву́лиці Хреща́тику у Ки́єві.

📖 Впра́ви Exercises

🎧 **7.1.** Answer the questions. Practice the accusative singular. Use one noun at a time from the prompts in parentheses.

1. Що ти сього́дні ро́биш? (завда́ння, впра́ва, пере́клад)
2. Що п'є Іва́н на сніда́нок? (ка́ва, чай, молоко́)
3. Що вони́ купу́ють тут? (хліб, вино́, газе́та)
4. Що ти вже зна́єш? (текст, мі́сто, Оде́са)
5. Що ви за́раз їсте́? (борщ, ковбаса́, я́блуко)
6. Що вони́ чита́ють уве́чері? (журна́л, кни́жка, істо́рія)
7. Що ти пи́шешура́нці? (лист, запи́ска)
8. Що ви лю́бите? (архітекту́ра, кіно́, бале́т)
9. Кого́ ми ба́чимо? (вчи́тель, студе́нт, Ната́лія, Андрі́й, Катери́на)
10. Кого́ слу́хає Окса́на? (ба́тько, ма́ма, Ю́ля, по́друга)

🎧 **7.2.** Answer the questions. Put the nouns in parentheses in the accusative required by prepositions **про** *about* and **на** *at*. Use one noun at a time.

1. Про що вона́ розповіда́є? (університе́т, шко́ла, істо́рія)
2. Про ко́го ти ду́маєш? (студе́нт, дід, ба́ба, ті́тка)
3. Про що ти пам'ята́єш? (фотогра́фія, Ки́їв, Украї́на)
4. Про ко́го вони́ розповіда́ють? (студе́нтка, ба́тько, Матві́й)
5. Про що ви ду́маєте? (завда́ння, стаття́, Оде́са)
6. Про ко́го ти пам'ята́єш? (ма́ти, брат, сім'я́, Софі́я)
7. На що ти ди́вишся? (карти́на, мі́сто, ву́лиця)
8. На ко́го вони́ ди́вляться? (Ла́ра, друг, по́друга, Іва́н)

🎧 **7.3.** Provide a full answer to each question. Put the expressions in parentheses into the accusative.

1. Що вона́ ро́бить? (ціка́ве завда́ння)
2. Що ми їмо́? (до́бра ковбаса́)
3. Що я чита́ю? (улю́блена газе́та)
4. Що він зна́є? (ди́вна істо́рія)
5. Що ти пи́шеш? (до́вгий лист)
6. Що вони́ лю́блять? (украї́нська літерату́ра)
7. Що ви слу́хаєте? (нова́ програ́ма)

Phonetics. Drill dropping the ~o~ in animate masculine nouns (2nd declension) in the accusative singular.

🎧 **7.4.** Listen carefully to the cue and react.

🄲 Ось новачо́к. *Here is a novice.*
🄰 Я ду́маю про новачка́. *I think about the novice.*

Хри́стя слу́хає свою́ стару́ по́другу.

Тимі́ш пока́зує одну́ ціка́ву світли́ну, яку́ він зроби́в неда́вно.

Ви їх напе́вно зна́єте, бо я вже коли́сь розка́зував про них.

Stress Pattern A. The stress remains on the same vowel.

ту́рок a *Turk*	па́рубок a *bachelor*
підлі́ток a *teenager*	чоловічо́к *dim. a little man*
наща́док a *descendant*	сві́док a *witness*
саморо́док *fig. a gifted person*	жа́йворонок a *lark*
одноліток a *person of same age*	пото́мок an *offspring*

Stress Pattern B. Stress is on the last syllable.

ватажо́к a *commander*	дружо́к *dim. a friend*
землячо́к *dim. a compatriot*	дідо́к *dim. an old man*
синок *dim. a son*	пастушо́к *dim. a shepherd*
новачо́к a *novice*	бичо́к a *calf*

7.5. Answer the questions. Use the words in parentheses.

1. Яку́ мо́ву ти зна́єш? (украї́нська)
2. Яко́го викладача́ ти лю́биш? (наш нови́й)
3. Яку́ ле́кцію вони́ слу́хають? (до́вга і нудна́)
4. Яки́й університе́т ви ба́чите? (ваш стари́й)
5. Яке́ мі́сто вона́ зна́є? (це америка́нське)
6. Яку́ кни́жку вони́ чита́ють? (ціка́ва)
7. Яку́ ка́ву ви п'єте́? (соло́дка і гаря́ча)
8. Яки́й фільм ми ди́вимося? (смішни́й)

Phonetics. Drill dropping the ~e~ in animate masculine nouns (2ⁿᵈ declension) in the accusative singular.

7.6. Listen carefully to the cue and react.

C Ось продаве́ць. *Here is a salesperson.*
A Ми вже ба́чили цього́ продавця́. *We have already seen this salesperson.*

Stress Pattern A. Stress remains on the same vowel.

хло́пець a *boy*	мовозна́вець a *linguist*
мисли́вець a *hunter*	за́єць a *hare*
урядо́вець an *official*	службо́вець a *white-collar worker*
промо́вець a *speaker*	незнайо́мець a *stranger*
коха́нець a *lover*	чужи́нець a *foreigner*

Stress Pattern B. Stress is on the last syllable.

покупе́ць a *buyer*	горобе́ць a *sparrow*
плаве́ць a *swimmer*	краве́ць a *tailor*
боре́ць a *fighter*	творе́ць a *creator*
мите́ць an *artist*	співе́ць a *singer*

7.7. Answer the questions. Put names of weekdays in the accusative.

1. Коли́ Ма́рта працю́є? (середа́)
2. Коли́ ви лю́бите ходи́ти в кіно́? (субо́та або́ четве́р)
3. Коли́ ти ба́чиш його́ сестру́? (вівто́рок)
4. Коли́ ви ма́єте ле́кцію? (п'я́тниця)
5. Коли́ він запро́шує тебе́ на ка́ву? (понеді́лок)
6. Коли́ вони́ слу́хають о́перу? (неді́ля)

 7.8. React to the statement.

Model. **C** Це Іва́н, а це ти. *This is Ivan, and this is you.*
A Іва́н тебе́ зна́є. Він ча́сто про те́бе ду́має.
Ivan knows you. He often thinks about you.

1. Це Петро́, а це ми.
2. Це Макси́м, а це вона́.
3. Це Окса́на й О́льга, а це вони́.
4. Це ти, а це він.
5. Це ми, а це ви.
6. Це моя́ сестра́, а це ти.
7. Це ви, а це ми.
8. Це Оле́г і Васи́ль, а це я.
9. Це я, а це воно́.

A bit more: Do the same exercise. Replace the pair зна́ти / ду́мати with:
a) ба́чити *to see* / пита́ти про *to ask about*;
b) люби́ти *to like* / розка́зувати про *to tell (stories) about*
Use the dictionary if need be. Translate each of your sentences.

✏ **Note 7.4. Улю́блені заня́ття**
    Favorite pastimes

Що ти лю́биш роби́ти (чита́ти, слу́хати, вари́ти)?	What do you like to do (read, listen to, cook)?
У що ви лю́бите гра́ти?	What (games) do *pl.* you like to play?
На чо́му ви лю́бите гра́ти?	What (instrument) do you like to play?
Про що вони́ лю́блять говори́ти?	What do they like to talk about?
На дозві́ллі мо́жна:	At leisure one can:
диви́тися + *A.* **телеві́зор (фільм, програ́му, конце́рт)**	to watch TV (a film, program, concert)
слу́хати + *A.* **му́зику (о́перу, ра́діо, програ́му)**	to listen to music (opera, radio, a broadcast)
чита́ти + *A.* **ціка́ву кни́жку (газе́ту, журна́л)**	to read an interesting book (newspaper, magazine)
готува́ти їжу	to cook food
гуля́ти у па́рку (по мі́сту)	to walk in the park (around town)
бі́гати	to jog
ходи́ти до + *G.* **музе́ю (теа́тру, кіна́)**	to go to a museum (theater, movies)

Оре́ст Налива́йко лю́бить співа́ти та гра́ти на гіта́рі.

ходи́ти в го́сті	to visit (friends, acquaintances)
ходи́ти на + *A.* конце́рт (виста́ву, ви́ставку)	to go to a concert (performance, exhibition)
гра́ти у + *A.* футбо́л (баскетбо́л, те́ніс, волейбо́л)	to play soccer (basketball, tennis, volleyball)
гра́ти на + *L.* фортепія́ні (гіта́рі, скри́пці, банду́рі)	to play the piano (guitar, violin, bandura)
відпочива́ти	to rest, relax; to vacation

Note 7.5. How to express intention

In colloquial Ukrainian speech, the intention to do something is expressed by the imperfective aspect of the verb **ду́мати** *to think*, followed by an infinitive. The construction **ду́мати** + *inf.* corresponds to the English *to be going to (to be planning to)* + *inf.*, **Оле́на ду́має подиви́тися цей фільм за́втра.** *Olena is going to watch this film tomorrow.*

The choice of the aspect of the infinitive depends on how the intended action is described. If it is an open-ended process, without regard to its completion then the imperfective infinitive is used, **Що ви ду́маєте роби́ти у вихідні́?** *What are you going to do on the weekend?*

The imperfective infinitive may also mean that the speaker is hesitant about his intention, **Миха́йло ду́має купува́ти нове́ а́вто.** *Mykhailo is going to buy a new car. (He is not a hundred percent sure).*

If it is important to present the intended action as completed, then the perfective infinitive is used, **Вони́ ду́мають повече́ряти ра́зом.** *They are planning to have dinner together.*

When a past intention is expressed, the verb **ду́мати** takes the form of the past imperfective tense, **Мину́лого мі́сяця ми ду́мали побува́ти у Пари́жі.** *Last month we were going to visit Paris.*

Note that the verb **ду́мати** expresses past intention only when it is used in the imperfective past tense form.

7.9. Respond to the question. Put the verb into the analytic imperfective future.

Model.
a) Ти вже сні́дав? *Did you have breakfast yet?* – Ні, але́ я ско́ро бу́ду сні́дати. *No, but I will soon be having breakfast.*
b) А Ма́рта? *And Marta?* – Ма́рта теж ско́ро бу́де сні́дати. *Marta will also be having breakfast soon.*
c) А вони́? *And they?* – Вони́ теж ско́ро бу́дуть сні́дати. *They will also soon be having breakfast.*

1. a) Ви вже обі́дали? b) А я? c) А вона́?
2. a) Іва́н уже́ дзвони́в? b) А твої́ дру́зі? c) А ви?
3. a) Ти вже спав? b) А Миха́йло? c) А його́ брати́?
4. a) Марі́я і Ната́ля вже ї́ли? b) А ви? c) А батьки́?
5. a) Петро́ вже диви́вся фільм? b) А та ді́вчина? c) А ці кия́ни?

7.10. Transform the sentences into the analytic imperfective future. Use suggested adverbial modifiers of future.

Model.
C Мико́ла вмі́є пла́вати. *Mykola can swim.* насту́пного мі́сяця *next month*
A Насту́пного мі́сяця Мико́ла бу́де вмі́ти пла́вати. *Next month, Mykola will be able to swim.*

1. Петро́ пи́ше лист. уве́чері.
2. Яри́на ди́виться переда́чу. че́рез пів годи́ни.
3. Рома́н і Ната́лка відпочива́ють на мо́рі. насту́пного ти́жня.
4. Ми йдемо́ додо́му. че́рез годи́ну.
5. О́льга купу́є проду́кти. за́втра вра́нці.
6. Окса́на переклада́є цей текст. насту́пної п'я́тниці.
7. Вони́ замовля́ють квитки́. післяза́втра.

7.11. Transform the sentences into the analytic imperfective future.

Model.
C Я ще не зна́ю про це. *I do not yet know about it.* за́втра *tomorrow*
A Я бу́ду зна́ти про це за́втра *I will know about it tomorrow.*

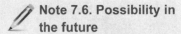

1. Оре́ст ще не працю́є на цій фа́бриці. насту́пного мі́сяця.
2. Ле́ся ще не живе́ у цьо́му гурто́житку. ско́ро.
3. Ці ді́ти ще не чита́ють. незаба́ром.
4. Ви ще не пи́шете про це. за́втра.
5. Ти ще не гово́риш про свій план. у понеді́лок.
6. Ми ще не розмовля́ємо по́льською. насту́пного ро́ку.
7. Ці хло́пці ще не вча́ться в Ки́ївському університе́ті.
   че́рез два мі́сяці (in two months).
8. Ми ще не ї́демо по поку́пки (going shopping). за́втра.
9. Го́сті ще не обі́дають. че́рез годи́ну.
10. Петро́ ще не вмі́є пла́вати. насту́пного мі́сяця.
11. Ми ще не відпочива́ємо на мо́рі. насту́пного ти́жня.

∩ 7.12. Express an intention. Use **ду́мати** + *pf. inf.* Consult the dictionary for perfective infinitives. Replace nouns for pronouns.

Model. **Q** Чи ти коли́-не́будь бува́в в Украї́нському музе́ї?
Have you ever visited the Ukrainian Museum?
A Ні, але́ я ду́маю незаба́ром побува́ти в ньо́му.
No, but I intend to visit it soon.

1. Чи ви коли́-не́будь слу́хали цю ра́діо програ́му?
2. Чи О́льга коли́-не́будь розка́зувала про на́шу по́дорож?
3. Чи ва́ші ро́дичі коли́-не́будь ба́чили її́ нову́ кварти́ру?
4. Чи вона́ коли́-не́будь вари́ла украї́нський борщ?
5. Чи Мико́ла коли́-не́будь диви́вся цей фільм?
6. Чи ї́хні студе́нти коли́-не́будь слу́хали о́перу «Запоро́жець за Дуна́єм» *Cossack beyond the Danube (classical Ukrainian opera)*?
7. Чи ти коли́-не́будь чита́ла рома́н «Московія́да»?
8. Чи ваш профе́сор коли́-не́будь поя́снював цей текст?
9. Чи вони́ коли́-не́будь зупиня́лися у цьо́му готе́лі?
10. Чи Марі́я та Оле́г коли́-не́будь вече́ряли у цьо́му рестора́ні?
11. Чи ці кана́дці коли́-не́будь відпочива́ли в Я́лті?
12. Чи ви коли́-не́будь дзвони́ли по комп'ю́теру?

∩ 7.13. Ask about the possibility of doing something in the future.

Model. Іва́н; де за́втра подиви́тися цей фільм
Ivan; where to watch this film tomorrow
Q Про що пи́ше Іва́н? *What is Ivan writing about?*
A Він пи́ше про те, де мо́жна бу́де за́втра подиви́тися цей фільм.
He is writing about where it will be possible to watch this film tomorrow.

1. Яросла́в; як у ві́льний час піти́ на конце́рт чи на виста́ву
2. Оле́на; коли́ насту́пного ти́жня послу́хати о́перу «Карме́н»
3. ва́ші сусі́ди; де за́втра поба́чити ї́хнього росі́йського го́стя
4. на́ші студе́нти; де у Льво́ві зустрі́тися післяза́втра
5. Петро́; як у Ки́єві подиви́тися нову́ виста́ву у теа́трі
6. Оле́кса і Софі́я; коли́ насту́пного лі́та пої́хати на мо́ре
7. Тара́с і Бори́с; як знайти́ гро́ші на нови́й комп'ю́тер
8. Га́нна і Дани́ло; коли́ ле́гко перекла́сти цей англі́йський текст

✎ Note 7.6. Possibility in the future

The expression (**бу́ти**) **мо́жна**, which indicates a possibility of action becomes **бу́де мо́жна** to express such a possibility in the future,
Тут бу́де мо́жна поговори́ти. *Here one will be able to have a conversation.*
Коли́ бу́де мо́жна пої́сти? *When will one be able to eat?*

Like in the past tense (see Lesson 5, p. 70), these two words can trade places without changing the meaning of the utterance,
Тут мо́жна бу́де поговори́ти. Коли́ мо́жна бу́де пої́сти?

When negated, this expression can have two variants:
1) usually the negative particle **не** is put before **мо́жна** which is followed by **бу́де**,
Там не мо́жна бу́де до́бре відпочи́ти. *One will not be able to have a good rest there.*
2) less commonly the negative particle **не** is put before **бу́де** which is followed by **мо́жна**,
За́втра не бу́де мо́жна подзвони́ти. *One will not be able to make a call tomorrow.*

У цій кав'я́рні мо́жна бу́де зустрі́тися й поговори́ти.

9. Мари́на; як побува́ти у Льво́ві, У́жгороді та Терно́полі насту́пної о́сени
10. Твої по́льські по́други; де насту́пного ро́ку провести́ лі́тні кані́кули ра́зом.
11. Ти; як у майбу́тньому подзвони́ти додо́му безкошто́вно

 Note 7.7. Adverbs in weather descriptions

Adverbs are customarily used to describe weather conditions,

Надво́рі хо́лодно (те́пло, га́ряче, прохоло́дно). *It's cold (warm, hot, cool) outside.*

Note 7.8. Температу́ра
Temperature

Ukrainians, like other Europeans, use the Centigrade temperature scale with zero (0ºC) as the freezing point.

The normal human body temperature is +36.6ºC. The boiling point is +100º C.

The noun **гра́дус** *degree*, takes three forms depending on the numeral it follows:

1) **гра́дус** after the numeral **оди́н** *one* and the composite numerals ending in **оди́н**, **оди́н гра́дус** *one degree* (1ºC), **со́рок оди́н гра́дус** *forty-one degrees* (41ºC), **сто оди́н гра́дус** *a hundred and one degrees* (101ºC)

2) **гра́дуси** after the numerals **два** *two*, **три** *three*, and **чоти́ри** *four*, and the composite numerals ending in **два**, **три**, and **чоти́ри**, **два гра́дуси** *two degrees* (2ºC), **три́дцять чоти́ри гра́дуси** *thirty-four degrees* (34ºC), **со́рок три гра́дуси** *forty-three degrees* (43ºC)

3) **гра́дусів** after the numerals **нуль** *zero*, **п'ять** *five,* and more, **п'ять гра́дусів** *five degrees* (5ºC), **одина́дцять гра́дусів** *eleven degrees* (11ºC), **двана́дцять гра́дусів** *twelve degrees* (12ºC), **трина́дцять гра́дусів** *thirteen degrees* (13ºC), **чотирна́дцять гра́дусів** *fourteen degrees* (14ºC), **шістдеся́т гра́дусів** *sixty degrees* (60ºC)

 The temperature values below zero are read with the sign **мі́нус** *minus,*

За́раз мі́нус три гра́дуси. *It's minus three degrees* (-3ºC) *now.*
У вівто́рок ма́є бу́ти мі́нус де́сять гра́дусів. *It is expected to be minus ten* (-10ºC) *on Tuesday.*

7.14. Form adverbs from these adjectives. Check your adverbs using the dictionary.

Model. холо́дний *cold* - хо́лодно *coldly*

adjective	adverb
холо́дний *cold*	
те́плий *warm*	
прохоло́дний *cool*	
гаря́чий *hot*	
со́нячний *sunny*	
ясни́й *clear (of sky)*	
хма́рний *cloudy*	
похму́рий *gloomy, cloudy (of sky)*	
ві́тряний *windy*	
мо́крий *wet*	
слизьки́й *slippery*	

Пого́да в Украї́ні *Weather in Ukraine*

7.15. Describe the weather in Ukraine. Use the adverbs from the previous exercise. Note general conditions and the air temperature.

Model.
У Яре́мчі сього́дні хо́лодно. Температу́ра мі́нус три гра́дуси. *It's cold in Yaremche today. The temperature is -3ºC.*

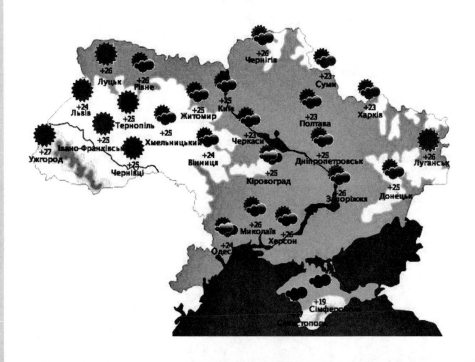

7.16. Read the questions and make sure you understand each of them. Listen to the text "Захо́плення" and answer the questions.

1. Яке́ прі́звище ма́є дівчина, що розка́зує про се́бе?
2. Мару́ся - це пестли́ве ім'я́. Як її офіці́йне ім'я́?
3. Як са́ме прово́дить Мару́ся своє́ дозві́лля?
4. Що вона́ лю́бить диви́тися?
5. Що прочита́ла Мару́ся нещода́вно?
6. Хто її улю́блений письме́нник?
7. Як пи́шуть Євге́нія Кононе́нко та Лю́бко Де́реш?
8. Хто написа́в рома́н «На зга́дку про майбу́тнє»?
9. Що ви мо́жете сказа́ти про письме́нника Дмитра́ Ві́тра?
10. У яко́му мі́сті живе́ пан Ві́тер?
11. Про що нови́й рома́н цього́ письме́нника?
12. Що таке́ «Звича́йна спра́ва»?
13. Хто таки́й Валенти́н Вася́нович?
14. Про що фільм «Звича́йна спра́ва»?
15. Що ду́має Мару́ся про цю кінокарти́ну?
16. Як Мару́ся прово́дить дозві́лля надво́рі?

 7.17. Translate this text into English. Summarize in Ukrainian in three or four sentences.

Захо́плення

Приві́т! Мене́ зва́ти Мару́ся Лю́бченко. Я - студе́нтка у Воли́нському націона́льному університе́ті, що в мі́сті Лу́цьку. Я за́вжди стара́юся ціка́во та приє́мно прово́дити своє́ дозві́лля. Найбі́льше я люблю́ чита́ти книжки́, а тако́ж диви́тися нові́ та старі́ кінофі́льми. Тя́жко сказа́ти, хто са́ме мій улю́блений письме́нник. Але́ я особли́во люблю́ Євге́нію Кононе́нко та Лю́бка Де́реша. Вони́ ду́же рі́зні, а пи́шуть одна́ково ціка́во й оригіна́льно.

Нещода́вно я прочита́ла нови́й рома́н, що назива́ється «На зга́дку про майбу́тнє». Його́ написа́в молоди́й таланови́тий письме́нник Дмитро́ Ві́тер. Він живе́ у мі́сті Полта́ві. Це розпо́відь про одного́ до́сить ди́вного юнака́, яки́й мо́же ба́чити майбу́тнє.

Учо́ра я подиви́лася нову́ худо́жню кінокарти́ну «Звича́йна спра́ва». Її зафільмува́в у 2012 ро́ці таланови́тий украї́нський кінорежисе́р Валенти́н Вася́нович. Це трагікоме́дія про одного́ ки́ївського інтелектуа́ла, яки́й гу́бить робо́ту, по́тім жі́нку, сім'ю́ і наре́шті вла́сну го́лову. Я ду́маю, що це ду́же ціка́вий і провокати́вний фільм. Книжки́ та фі́льми, літерату́ра та кінемато́граф — це дале́ко не всі мої́ захо́плення.

Я тако́ж ду́же люблю́ прово́дити час надво́рі — гра́ти у футбо́л, те́ніс, баскетбо́л і на́віть про́сто до́вго гуля́ти па́рком чи стари́м мі́стом, звича́йно, коли́ на ву́лиці га́рна пого́да.

Note 7.8. Температу́ра
Temperature. Cont'd.

The temperature values above zero are read with the sign **плюс** *plus* or no sign at all, **Він ма́є температу́ру плюс три́дцять ві́сім гра́дусів** (or **три́дцять ві́сім гра́дусів**) (+38°C). *He has a temperature of thirty-eight degrees.*

Day and night air temperatures can be designated by the expressions:

1) **де́нна температу́ра** *day temperature* and **нічна́ температу́ра** *night temperature,*

Сього́дні у Я́лті де́нна температу́ра два́дцять сім гра́дусів, а нічна́ – шістна́дцять. *Today the day temperature in Yalta is twenty-seven degrees and the night temperature is sixteen.*

2) **уде́нь** *during the day* and **уночі́** *at night,*

Сього́дні уде́нь у Я́лті температу́ра два́дцять сім гра́дусів, а вночі́ – шістна́дцять. *Today the temperature in Yalta during the day is twenty-seven degrees and at night sixteen*

Яка́ сього́дні температу́ра
у Льво́ві?

∩ **7.18.** Form adverbs from the adjectives given and introduce the adverbs into these sentences. Translate the sentences.

Model. **C** ра́дий, *happy.* Я мо́жу допомогти́ вам. *I can help you.*
A Я мо́жу ра́до допомогти́ вам. *I can gladly help you.*

1. бага́тий. Марко́ люби́в спа́ти.
2. смачни́й. На свя́то ми лю́бимо ї́сти.
3. зручни́й. Я зна́ю, як мо́жна подорожува́ти.
4. ціка́вий. Тара́с мо́же писа́ти про це.
5. коро́ткий. Цей виклада́ч не вмі́є говори́ти.
6. до́вгий. Всі хо́чуть жи́ти.
7. недале́кий. Це пра́вда, що ви працю́єте?
8. си́льний. Мене́ боли́ть голова́.
9. пога́ний. Мину́лої но́чі вона́ спа́ла.
10. нудни́й. Як мо́жна так розпові́да́ти цю істо́рію!
11. деше́вий. Катери́на зна́є, де мо́жна купи́ти мо́дні ре́чі.
12. дороги́й. Петро́ не хо́че продава́ти цей квито́к.
13. легки́й. Ура́нці я люблю́ посні́дати.
14. швидки́й. Ми прийшли́ додо́му.

∩ **7.19.** Say and write the sentences in Ukrainian. Use the vocabulary and grammar of this and previous lessons. Where required, consult the dictionary.

1. Ternopil is my home town because I was born there.
2. At what station are you planning to meet?
3. On the weekend my close relatives will be at our place.
4. In his free time, Pavlo always listens to the opera, but next Saturday he will be walking around the old town.
5. I know that a new Ukrainian film will soon be on in the local movie house.
6. This beautiful street is called Volodymyrska.
7. This is some very strange but interesting story.
8. Next Friday, we are going to play soccer at the university.
9. One day somebody will be speaking about it somewhere.
10. Yaryna likes music very much. She especially likes to play the piano.
11. Usually my working days are Monday, Tuesday, and Wednesday but next Monday I'll have a day off. Instead I'll work on Thursday.

∩ **7.20.** Answer the question about day and night temperatures in various cities of Ukraine. Use the required form of the noun **гра́дус** *degree.*

Model. Ки́їв, +10ºC / +2ºC

| День | Слабка хмарність, невеликий дощ | **+10°** |
| Вечір | Слабка хмарність, невеликий сніг | **+2°** |

Q Яка́ сього́дні температу́ра у Ки́єві?
What is the temperature in Kyiv today?
A Сього́дні у Ки́єві де́нна
температу́ра – плюс де́сять гра́дусів, а нічна́ – плюс два гра́дуси.
The day temperature in Kyiv today is plus ten degrees and the night temperature is plus two degrees.

1. Полта́ва, +6°С / - 2°С
2. Ха́рків, -3°С / -12°С
3. Терно́піль, -5°С / -10°С
4. Кременчу́к, +14°С / +5°С
5. Ні́жин, +13°С / +10°С
6. Черні́гів, +22°С / +12°С
7. Севасто́поль, -4°С / -10°С

8. Льві́в, +21°С / +14°С
9. Херсо́н, +33°С / +25°С
10. Луцьк, +24°С / +11°С
11. Жито́мир, 0°С / -9°С
12. Оде́са, -1°С / -8°С
13. Ми́ргород, +18°С / +9°С
14. Ві́нниця, +7°С / 0°С

🎧 **7.21.** Enact a short dialogue with a partner. Make a clear distinction between the names of humans and those of non-humans.

Model 1, *for humans*: чолові́к *a man,* Марко́ Стрі́ха *Marko Strikha*

A. Диві́ться, ось чолові́к, про яко́го я говори́в. *Look, here's the man I spoke about.*
B. Як зва́ти цього́ чолові́ка? Я забу́в його́ ім'я́. *What's he called? I forgot his name.*
A. Його́ зва́ти Марко́ Стрі́ха. *He's called Marko Strikha*
B. Дя́кую. Бу́ду зна́ти. *Thank you. It's good to know.*

Model 2, *for all others*: кни́жка *a book,* «Ціка́ві істо́рії» *"Interesting Stories"*

A. Диві́ться, ось кни́жка, про яку́ я писа́ла. *Look, here's the book I wrote about.*
B. Я забу́в її на́зву. Як назива́ється ця кни́жка? *I forgot its title. What's this book called?*
A. Вона́ назива́ється «Ціка́ві істо́рії». *It's called Interesting Stories.*
B. Дя́кую. Бу́ду зна́ти. *Thank you. It's good to know.*

1. молоди́й інжене́р *a young engineer,* Ігор Сергійчу́к *Ihor Serhiichuk*
2. її університе́т *her university,* Украї́нський католи́цький університе́т *Ukrainian Catholic University*
3. їхня по́льська по́друга *their Polish girlfriend,* Ма́ґда Зелі́нська *Magda Zielinska*
4. та америка́нська журналі́стка *that American (female) journalist,* Ме́лані Франко́ *Melanie Franco*
5. ціка́ва кінорежисе́рка *an interesting (female) film director,* Га́нна Ярове́нко *Hanna Yarovenko*
6. стари́й журна́л *an old magazine,* «Кіно́» *"Kino"*
7. Га́рна кав'я́рня *a nice café,* «Дзиґа» *Dzyga*
8. моя́ нова́ стаття́ *my new article,* «Украї́нське кіно́ сього́дні» *"Ukrainian Cinema Today"*
9. кіноакто́р *a film actor,* Богда́н Беню́к *Bohdan Beniuk*
10. ки́ївська ву́лиця *a street in Kyiv,* Володи́мирська *Volodymyrska*
11. та галере́я *that gallery,* «Мисте́цький Арсена́л» *Art Arsenal*
12. недороги́й готе́ль *an inexpensive hotel,* «Еней» *Aeneus*
13. худо́жній фільм *a feature film,* «Складна́ ді́вчина Га́ля» *Complicated Girl Halia*
14. ди́вна карти́на *a strange picture,* «Їхні молоді́ роки́» *"Their Young Years"*

Note 7.9. Імена́ vs на́зви
Names vs titles

Ukrainian differentiates between two types of proper nouns: names of people and names of things. To ask about a person's name, one uses
Як ва́ше (його́, її, etc.) ім'я́ (прі́звище)? (Refer to Note 3.19) or
Як зва́ти + *A., What is sb called.,*
Як зва́ти ва́шого ста́ршого бра́та?
What's your elder brother called?
Як зва́ти її ті́тку? *What's her aunt called?*

The second type of question correlates with the answer ***A. of person* + зва́ти + name** *(first and second name),*
Мого́ бра́та зва́ти Яре́ма Ковальчу́к.
My brother is called Yarema Kovalchuk.
Її ті́тку зва́ти Катери́на Максимчу́к.
Her aunt is called Kateryna Maksymchuk.

To ask about the title of a novel, film, newspaper, company, hotel, etc. one uses
Як назива́ється + *N. of the thing What is the title of ...*
Як назива́ється це мі́сто (село́)?
What's the name of this city (village)?
Як назива́ється той готе́ль? *What's the name of that hotel?*
Як назива́ється їхня компа́нія?
What's their company called?

In Ukrainian, a person has **ім'я́** *a name.* A subject, other than a human being, has **на́зва**, translated as *name* or *title.*

Що мо́же ма́ти на́зву "Світли́на"?

Note 7.10. Що йде в кінотеа́трі? *What's on in the movie theater?*

To ask about a film title one typically says, **Як назива́ється цей фільм?** *What's the title of this film?*

The answer to it is **Цей фільм назива́ється «По́дорож».** *This film is entitled The Journey.*

 Note 7.11. На́зви фі́льмів, книжо́к та устано́в Names of Films, Books, and Institutions

When the name of an institution or a work of letters, film, etc. includes a generic name like **кінотеа́тр** *a movie theater* and a proper name like **«Панора́ма»** *Panorama*, the generic name is written in lower case while the proper name is capitalized and put in quotation marks. Other such examples are:
кінокарти́на «Земля́» *the motion picture* Earth
рома́н «Марі́я» *the novel* Maria
готе́ль «Десна́» *the Desna Hotel*
журна́л «Украї́нський ти́ждень» *the Ukrainian Week magazine*
книга́рня «Є» *the YE bookstore*

When such composite names and titles are used in a sentence, only the generic name is declined while the proper name stays the same as if protected by quotation marks,
Ми ба́чили цю сце́ну у кінокарти́ні «Земля́». *We saw this scene in the motion picture Earth.*
Богда́н живе́ у готе́лі «Десна́». *Bohdan lives in the Desna Hotel.*
Це всі мої́ журна́ли «Украї́нський ти́ждень». *These are all my Ukrainian Week magazines.*
Ми ду́же лю́бимо книга́рню «Є». *We very much like the YE Bookstore.*

15. украї́нський худо́жник-модерні́ст *Ukrainian modernist artist*, Все́волод Макси́мович *Vsevolod Maksymovych*

7.22. Engage a partner in this Q-and-A exchange. Use prompts of film titles below. Note that х/ф stands for a feature film (худо́жній фільм) and д/ф for a documentary (документа́льний фільм).

1. Як назива́ється цей документа́льний фільм?
2. Як назива́ється цей худо́жній фільм?
3. Як назива́ється ваш улю́блений худо́жній фільм?
4. Як назива́ється ваш улю́блений документа́льний фільм?
5. Яки́й фільм ви ба́чили оста́нній раз?
6. Яки́й фільм ви хо́чете поба́чити насту́пного ра́зу?
7. Яки́й фільм ви хо́чете подиви́тися зно́ву?
8. Як назива́ється фільм, у яко́му гра́є Іва́н Миколайчу́к?

Підка́зки Prompts
«Мама́й», х/ф.
«Чолові́к, жі́нка», х/ф.
«Кінома́нія», д/ф.
«Механі́чний помара́нч», х/ф.
«Ті́ні забу́тих пре́дків» (Shadows of Forgotten Ancestors), х/ф.
«Бо́ні та Клайд», х/ф.
«Живі́», д/ф.
«За двома́ зайця́ми», х/ф.

7.23. Engage a partner in a short exchange. Find out what is on in these Lviv movie theaters. Each number in the chart refers to a film in the list below it.

Q Що йде в кінотеа́трі «Львів» у понеді́лок? *What's on in the Lviv Movie Theater on Monday?*

A У понеді́лок у цьо́му кінотеа́трі йде худо́жній фільм «Мама́й» *On Monday, the feature film "Mamay" is on in this movie theater.*

Кінотеа́тр	вівто́рок		середа́		четве́р		п'я́тниця		субо́та		неді́ля	
«Львів»	2;	9	8;	5	9;	10	9;	10	5;	9	9;	2
«Украї́на»	1;	10	7;	3	9;	7	3;	10	7;	1	9;	10
«Кінопанора́ма"	3;	2	2;	1	2;	4	1;	3	4;	3	4;	1
«Батькі́вщина»	4;	9	1;	9	10;	4	4;	9	1;	4	1;	10
«Копе́рнік»	7;	2	1;	2	3;	7	8;	2	3;	2	3;	8
«Со́кіл»	9;	10	1;	6	3;	4	4;	7	9;	2	3;	4

1. «Мама́й», украї́нський худо́жній фільм; режисе́р Оле́сь Са́нін

2. «Звича́йна спра́ва» *Business as Usual*, украї́нський худо́жній фільм; режисе́р Валенти́н Вася́нович

3. «Чолові́к, жі́нка», францу́зький худо́жній фільм; режисе́р Жан-Люк Ґода́р

4. «Живі́» *The Living*, украї́нський документа́льний фільм; режисе́р Сергі́й Буко́вський

5. «Украї́на. Наро́дження на́ції» *Ukraine. Birth of a Nation*, по́льський документа́льний фільм; режисе́р Є́жи Го́фман

6. «Механі́чний помара́нч» *Clockwork Orange*, англі́йський худо́жній фільм; режисе́р Сте́нлі К'ю́брик

7. «Незнайо́мка» *The Unknown Woman*, італі́йський худо́жній фільм; режисе́р Джузе́ппе Торнато́ре

8. «Бо́ні та Клайд», америка́нський худо́жній фільм; режисе́р А́ртур Пен

9. «Типо́ве льві́вське вби́вство» *A Typical Lviv Murder*, росі́йський документа́льний фільм; режисе́р Є́ґор Лімо́нов

10. «Едва́рд Дми́трик. Життя́ у Голіву́ді», украї́нський документа́льний фільм; режисе́р Дани́ло Прихо́дько

Режисе́р Оле́сь Са́нін й опера́тор Сергі́й Михальчук фільму́ють нову́ кінокарти́ну.

🎧 **7.24.** Study the chart from the previous exercise and answer these questions.

1. Як зва́ти режисе́ра, яки́й зафільмува́в кінокарти́ну «Бо́ні та Клайд»?

2. Хто таки́й Сергі́й Буко́вський?

3. Яки́й фільм розповіда́є про украї́нсько-америка́нського режисе́ра Е́дварда Дми́трика?

4. Які́ фі́льми не йдуть у кінотеа́трі «Копе́рнік»?

5. Які́ украї́нські фі́льми йдуть у мі́сті Льво́ві?

6. Які́ фі́льми йдуть у кінотеа́трі «Со́кіл»?

7. Які́ худо́жні фі́льми йдуть у Льво́ві цього́ ти́жня?

8. Які́ документа́льні фі́льми йдуть у Льво́ві цього́ ти́жня?

9. Хто зафільмува́в кінокарти́ну «Звича́йна спра́ва»?

10. Яки́й фільм «Механі́чний помара́нч» - францу́зький чи англі́йський?

11. Яки́й фільм ви бу́дете диви́тися у субо́ту і в яко́му кінотеа́трі?

12. У яко́му кінотеа́трі мо́жна бу́де подиви́тися кінокарти́ну «Чолові́к, жі́нка» в цю п'я́тницю?

13. Які́ америка́нські кінокарти́ни йдуть у Льво́ві?

14. Що таке́ «Незнайо́мка»?

15. Яку́ на́зву ма́є кінокарти́на, яку́ зафільмува́в режисе́р Є́жи Го́фман?

Мо́вні ресу́рси на мере́жі.
Language resources on the web.

7.25. Use an Internet search engine or the Ukrainian Wikipedia and find answers to three-four questions at a time.

1. Хто таки́й Ю́рій Ілле́нко? Поясни́ти.
2. Хто таки́й Іва́н Миколайчу́к? Поясни́ти.
3. Які́ фі́льми зроби́в Олекса́ндер Довже́нко?
4. У яко́му фі́льмі грав Тара́с Денисе́нко?
5. У яко́му фі́льмі гра́ла Ната́ля На́ум?
6. Які́ фі́льми зроби́в Валенти́н Васяно́вич?
7. Хто така́ Мари́на Вро́да?
8. Що таке́ «Украї́на в огні́»?
9. Які́ кінокарти́ни зафільмува́в Андрі́й До́нчик?
10. Хто гра́є у фі́льмі «Бі́лий птах з чо́рною озна́кою»?
11. Які́ фі́льми зроби́в Леоні́д Оси́ка?
12. Хто гра́є у фі́льмі «Камі́нний хрест»?

7.26. Listen carefully to the questions and answer them using Dialogue 7.

1. Що ду́має роби́ти Рома́н на вихідні́?
2. Що звича́йно ро́бить Рома́н на дозві́ллі?
3. Яку́ кни́жку за́раз чита́є Рома́н?
4. Як зва́ти а́втора п'є́си, яку́ чита́є тепе́р Рома́н?
5. Як назива́ється ця п'є́са?
6. Що зна́є Яри́на про цю п'є́су та її́ а́втора?
7. Про що лю́бить чита́ти Яри́на?
8. Що ча́сом ди́виться Рома́н?
9. Що слу́хає Рома́н?
10. Яку́ му́зику лю́бить Яри́на?
11. Що ду́має зроби́ти Яри́на сього́дні?
12. Яки́й фільм ду́мають подиви́тися ра́зом Яри́на та Рома́н?
13. В яко́му кінотеа́трі йде цей фільм?
14. Коли́ са́ме сього́дні бу́дуть диви́тися дру́зі фільм "Мама́й"?
15. Яки́й фільм ви диви́лися оста́нній раз? Коли́ та де?

 7.27. Engage a partner in a conversation about her /his pastime.

1) Find out each detail noted in the chart below.
2) Write them all down in Ukrainian.
3) Write a short report in Ukrainian about what you learned.

Васи́ль звари́в украї́нський обі́д і запроси́в на ньо́го Га́лю.

Про що пита́ти партне́ра	партне́р-1	партне́р-2	партне́р-3
Що ви лю́бите роби́ти на дозві́ллі?			
Яку́ му́зику ви лю́бите?			

Яку книжку ви чита́ли неда́вно (на́зва, а́втор, про що вона́)?			
Як ча́сто ви хо́дите до кінотеа́тру та музе́ю?			
Хто ва́ша улю́блена акто́рка чи акто́р?			
Яку́ кінокарти́ну ви диви́лися оста́нній раз (на́зва, режи́сер, акто́ри, про що вона́)?			
Про які́ украї́нські фі́льми ви чу́ли?			
Хто ваш улю́блений письме́нник чи письме́нниця?			
В які́ спорти́вні і́гри ви лю́бите гра́ти?			
Як ви прово́дите ві́льний час у селі́?			

7.28. Enact a conversation with a partner. Use the material you have learned by now. Where necessary consult the dictionary.

Сце́нка за сцена́рієм «Вихідні́»
Scripted Skit: *Weekend*

Vasyl (Васи́ль): Greets Halia casually.
Halia (Га́ля): Responds to his greeting and asks how he is doing.

Vasyl: Says that he had a very difficult week at work. Expresses that it is finally Friday.
Halia: She worked hard all week as well she is ready to rest a little.

Vasyl: Asks what Halia intends to do on the weekend.
Halia: She is not sure yet. Last weekend she sat all day long at home, read an interesting novel, watched TV. Expresses intention to do something new this weekend.

Vasyl: Asks what exactly "something new" means.
Halia: Things she rarely does. For example, she rarely goes to a concert or an opera. Asks what Vasyl intends to do on the weekend.

Vasyl: He always tries to spend time outdoors. He likes to play soccer, basketball, and tennis or simply to walk in the park.
Halia: Asks Vasyl what he likes to do in the evening when he has some free time.

Vasyl: Most of all he likes to watch a good film at home or in a movie theater. But this time, he also intends to do something entirely new.
Halia: Asks exactly what "entirely new" is.

Vasyl: He wants to cook a nice Ukrainian dinner and ... invite Halia.
Halia: Repeats in disbelieve his last phrase. Says that it is a great idea. Vasyl's invitation is such a pleasant surprise.

Vasyl: Adds that then (after dinner), they can watch a new French film. He bought it last week. (Think of a possible film title.)
Halia: Says that she likes French films. It is a great plan.

Мі́сто Володи́мирець, що на воли́нському Полі́ссі, зеле́не і приємне.

Лéкція | Lesson 8

Dialogue:
Запрóшення на вечéрю
Invitation to dinner

Grammar:
Genitive singular
Double negation

Competencies:
Inviting people
Whose is it?
How to be negative
Ukrainian restaurants on the Internet

8. Діяло́г. Запро́шення на вече́рю.

Íгор: Макси́ме, я хо́тів би запроси́ти тебе́ і Тетя́ну на вече́рю.

Макси́м: Ду́же дя́кую. Коли́ і де бу́де вече́ря?

Íгор: Ціє́ї п'я́тниці, у ме́не вдо́ма. Пропону́ю піти́ ра́зом пі́сля ле́кції профе́сора Пилипе́нка.

Макси́м: Ле́кція профе́сора Пилипе́нка? Я не зна́ю про не́ї.

Íгор: Він відо́мий істо́рик, а його́ ле́кції завжди́ ду́же ціка́ві.

Макси́м: Тоді́ я теж і́ду. Не зна́ю, що ду́має роби́ти Тетя́на.

Íгор: Мо́жеш подзвони́ти до не́ї за́раз і запита́ти?

Макси́м: Тетя́ни нема́є вдо́ма. Ко́жної середи́ вона́ хо́дить пла́вати.

Íгор: А мобі́лка, чи вона́ ма́є мобі́лку?

Макси́м: Звича́йно. Хто сього́дні без мобі́лки?

Íгор: Чудо́во! Мо́жемо домо́витися про вече́рю вже за́раз.

Макси́м: На жаль, ні, бо Тетя́на не бере́ телефо́ну до басе́йну.

Íгор: Гара́зд. Тоді́ кра́ще почека́ти до ве́чора.

Макси́м: До́бре, Íгоре. До ве́чора.

8. Dialogue. Invitation to dinner.

Ihor: Maksym, I'd like to invite you and Tetiana for dinner.

Maksym: Thank you very much. When and where will the dinner be?

Ihor: This Friday, at my place. I suggest we go together after Prof. Pylypenko's lecture.

Maksym: Prof. Pylypenko's lecture? I don't know about it.

Ihor: He is a well-known historian, and his lectures are always very interesting.

Maksym: Then I am coming too. I don't know what Tetiana is going to do.

Ihor: Can you call her now and ask?

Maksym: Tetiana is not home. Every Wednesday she goes swimming.

Ihor: And a cell phone, does she have a cell phone?

Maksym: Of course. Who is without a cell phone today?

Ihor: Great! We can decide on a suitable time for the dinner now.

Maksym: Unfortunately not so, because Tetiana does not take her mobile phone to the swimming pool.

Ihor: Alright. Then it's better to wait till the evening.

Maksym: Fine, Ihor. Till the evening.

Ко́жної середи́ Тетя́на хо́дить до басе́йну пла́вати.

✎ Нота́тки до діало́гу   Notes on the Dialogue

запро́шу|вати, ~ють; запроси́ти, + A. (sb) + на + A. (for an event) or до + G. (to a place or institution)	to invite sb, take sb out for dinner, breakfast, lunch, opera, **запроси́ти дру́га на обі́д, на о́перу** *to invite a friend for lunch, the opera,* **запроси́ти до музе́ю (університе́ту, теа́тру)** *to invite to a museum (university, theater).* For more on destination of action see Lesson 13, p. 259.
пропону́|вати, ~ють; за~, + A. or pf. inf.	to suggest sth or doing sth; to offer; to propose, **Що ти пропону́єш зроби́ти?** *What do you suggest doing?* **Він одра́зу запропонува́в допомо́гу.** *He immediately offered help.*
іти́, ід|у́ть; піти́, під|у́ть + на + A. (for an event) or до + G. (to a place or institution)	to go to, attend (**конце́рт** *concert,* **фільм** *film,* **ви́ставку** *exhibition,* **побаче́ння** *meeting*), **Він хо́че піти́ на ле́кцію.** *He wants to go to a lecture.;* **Студе́нти іду́ть до музе́ю.** *The students are going to a museum.*
фахіве́ць з + G.	expert, specialist in sth (name of the field in G.), **ф. з (із) істо́рії (літерату́ри, мисте́цтва)** *expert in history (literature, art)*
мобі́л|ка, *f. colloq.*	a mobile phone, *short for* **мобі́льний телефо́н, по ~ці** on mobile
ніко́го, *G. of* ніхто́	nobody, **Ніко́го нема́є вдо́ма.** *There is nobody home.;* **Ми тут ніко́го не зна́ємо.** *We do not know anybody here (lit. We don't know nobody here).* Note that there is a double negation in the Ukrainian sentence - **ніко́го** *nobody* and **нема́є** *there isn't.*
ніко́го, *G. of* ніщо́	nothing, **Я ніко́го не розумі́ю.** *I don't understand anything.;* **Миха́йло ніко́го не пам'ята́є.** *Mykhailo does not remember anything. (lit. I don't know nothing.*)*

📖 Грама́тика | Grammar

Родови́й відмі́нок однини́   Genitive Case Singular

Genitive correlates with the questions
кого́? *of who?* **чого́?** *of what?*

Фу́нкція *Function*

1. Genitive case expresses the relationship of possession, **кни́жка вчи́теля** *a teacher's book (lit. a book of the teacher),* **ба́тько Катери́ни** *Kateryna's father (lit. the father of Kateryna),* **вікно́ ма́тері** *mother's window (lit. the window of a mother).* The second noun in such expressions denotes the owner and takes the form of the genitive.

2. Genitive case indicates that one noun relates to or otherwise describes the other. The first noun is in the nominative and the second is in the genitive, **план мі́ста** *a plan of the city,* **пробле́ма життя́** *the problem of life,* **майда́н Незале́жности** *Independence Square (lit. Square of Independence).*

3. When affirmative sentences with a direct object in the accusative are negated, the direct object takes the form of the genitive, **Марі́я ма́є кни́жку.** *Maria has a book.* - *neg.* **Марі́я не ма́є**

Ось портре́т їхньої ста́ршої до́ньки Катери́ни.

Ці соло́дкі я́блука для мало́ї Катру́сі.

Note 8.1. Compact expression of frequency

The collocation **кожни́й** + noun that expresses the idea of frequency has a more compact, one-word synonym. In it, instead of the adjective **ко́жний** *every*, the prefix **що~** is added to the respective noun in the genitive singular case, cf.

ко́жного ра́зу = щора́зу *every time*
ко́жного дня = щодня́ *every day*
ко́жного ве́чора = щове́чора *every evening*
ко́жної годи́ни = щогоди́ни *every hour*
ко́жної но́чі = щоно́чі *every night*

кни́жки. *Maria doesn't have a book.* **Рома́н пи́ше лист.** *Roman is writing a letter.* - neg. **Рома́н не пи́ше листа́.** *Roman is not writing a letter.* **Сестра́ їсть я́блуко.** *The sister is eating an apple.* - neg. **Сестра́ не їсть я́блука.** *The sister is not eating an apple.*

4. The construction **у** + *G. of animate noun* + **бу́ти** + *object in N.* indicates:

a) possession of something by somebody and is synonymous with the expressions using the verb **ма́ти** *to have* + object in *A.*,

У не́ї є а́вто. *She has a car.*, cf. **Вона́ ма́є а́вто.**
У ме́не була́ ві́за. *I had a visa.*, cf. **Я ма́ла ві́зу.**
В Оле́ни бу́де до́вга подоро́ж. *Olena will have a long trip.*, cf., **Оле́на бу́де ма́ти до́вгу подоро́ж.**

b) location of somebody or something at somebody's home,

Я жив у сестри́ Ната́лії мі́сяць. *I lived at my sister Natalia's (place) for a month.*
Сього́дні ва́ші дру́зі вече́ряють у нас. *Today your friends have dinner at our place.*

When a given person does not have sth, **бу́ти** in the above structure expressing possession is replaced by
нема́(є) for the present tense,

У не́ї нема́(є) а́вта. *She has no car.* same as **Вона́ не ма́є а́вта.**
не було́ for the past,

У ме́не не було́ ві́зи. *I had no visa.* same as **Я не ма́ла ві́зи.**
не бу́де for the future,

В Оле́ни не бу́де до́вгої подоро́жі. *Olena won't have a long trip.* same as **Оле́на не бу́де ма́ти до́вгої подоро́жі.**

The noun that indicates the absent object is in the genitive.

When an expression like **Мико́ла (є) тут.** *Mykola is here.* **Ка́рта (є) там.** *The map is there.* are negated, the subject takes the genitive, while the verb **є** is replaced by
a) **нема́(є)** in the present,

Мико́ли нема́є тут. *Mykola isn't here.* **Ка́рти нема́є там.** *The map isn't there.*
b) **не було́** in the past,

Мико́ли не було́ тут. *Mykola wasn't here.* **Ка́рти не було́ там.** *The map wasn't there.*
c) **не бу́де** in the future,

Мико́ли не бу́де тут. *Mykola won't be here.* **Ка́рти не бу́де там.** *The map won't be there.*

5. The genitive is frequently used to express a point in the past, present, or future with nouns described by the adjectives:
цей *this*, **той** *last (lit. that)*, **мину́лий** *last*, **насту́пний** *next*, **ко́жний** *every*.
Such adjective+noun expressions of time are simply put in the genitive singular. Memorize these typical expressions of time in the genitive:

цьо́го ти́жня	this week	ціє́ї п'я́тниці	this Friday
того́ ро́ку *or* (торі́к)	last year	тіє́ї весни́	last spring
мину́лого понеді́лка	last Monday	насту́пного четверга́	next Thursday
мину́лої середи́	last Wednesday	насту́пної суботи	next Saturday
ко́жної суботи	every Saturday	ко́жного четверга́	every Thursday
насту́пного ра́зу	next time	ко́жного ра́зу	every time

Утво́рення *Formation*

Іме́нники Nouns

The nominal genitive endings:
~и (~і, ~ї), ~а (~я), ~у (~ю)

~и is taken by:
(a) feminine and masculine nouns ending in **~а**,
(b) feminine nouns ending in two consonants,
(c) the group of baby animal nouns with suffixes **~ат, ~ят, ~ен**,

кни́жка *a book* - **без кни́жки** *without a book*
мо́лодість *youth* - **після мо́лодости** *after youth*
курча́ *a chicken* - **без курча́ти** *without a chicken*, and also
ім'я́ *a name* - **без і́мени** *without a name*;

~і is taken by the same nouns ending in **~я** or of mixed stem, and consonant-ended feminine nouns,
земля́ *land* - **без землі́** *without land*, **річ** *a thing* - **без ре́чі** *without a thing*, **ніч** *a night* - **до но́чі** *till the night*;

~ї is taken by feminine and masculine nouns ending in **~ія**, and the noun **сім'я́** *a family*,
фотогра́фія *a photo* - **без фотогра́фії** *without a photo*,
сім'я́ *a family* - **без сім'ї́** *without a family*;

~а is taken by:
1) all consonant and **о**-ended animate masculine and all neuter nouns of hard stem, *m.* **брат** *a brother* - **без бра́та** *without a brother*, *m.* **ба́тько** *a father* - **без ба́тька** *without a father*, *nt.* **а́вто** *a car* - **без а́вта** *without a car*;

2) a smaller group of frequently used inanimate masculine nouns ending in a hard consonant,
словни́к *a dictionary* - **без словника́** *without a dictionary*, **лист** *a letter* - **для листа́** *for a letter*, **по́їзд** *a train* - **до по́їзда** *to a train*, **авто́бус** *a bus* - **без авто́буса** *without a bus*.

Note 8.2. Prepositions followed by genitive case

The genitive is required after prepositions such as:
    від *from*
    з (*var.* **із, зі**) *from (origin)*
    до *to, till*
    після *after*
    без *without*
    крім *except for, besides*
    для *for*
    біля *near, next to*
від середи́ до суботи *from Wednesday to Saturday*
з Украї́ни *from Ukraine*
після дощу́ *after the rain*
без су́мніву *without a doubt*
крім ме́не *except for me*
для ма́тері *for the mother*
для вчи́теля *for the teacher*
біля мо́ря *near the sea.*

Note 8.3. Five special nouns favoring the ending ~и

The ending **~и** is also taken by these five feminine nouns:
любо́в *love* - **без любо́ви** *without love*
кров *blood* - **без кро́ви** *without blood*
сіль *salt* - **без со́ли** *without salt*
о́сінь *autumn* - **до о́сени** *till autumn*
Русь *Rus (historical name of Ukraine)* - **столи́ця Руси́ Ки́їв** *the capital of Rus Kyiv.*

Note 8.4. The special case of ма́ти *mother*

Genitive singular of **ма́ти** *a mother* is **ма́тері, Вона́ подзвони́ла до ма́тері.** *She called her mother.*

Від вівто́рка до п'я́тниці Га́нна займа́ється в університе́ті.

 Note 8.5. Mixed stem nouns

Masculine and neuter nouns with stems ending in the consonants ~ж, ~ч, ~ш, ~щ also take the genitive ending ~**а**,
ро́дич *a relative* - **для ро́дича** *for a relative*
прі́звище *a last name* - **без прі́звища** *without a last name*

~**я** is taken by the animate and inanimate masculine and neuter nouns ending in a soft consonant, *m.* **вчи́тель** *a teacher* - **без вчи́теля** *without a teacher*; **олі́ве́ць** *a pencil* - **без олівця́** *without a pencil*; *nt.* **завда́ння** *a task* - **без завда́ння** *without a task*; *nt.* **мо́ре** *a sea* - **бі́ля мо́ря** *near a sea.*

The inanimate masculine nouns that take the ~**а** (~**я**) ending include:

1) days of the week,
понеді́лок *Monday* - **до понеді́лка** *till Monday*, **вівто́рок** *Tuesday* - **пі́сля вівто́рка** *after* Tuesday, and the special case of **четве́р** *Thursday* - **до четверга́** *till Thursday,* with the ~**г**~ in G. case;

2) names of months,
ве́ресень *September*, **сі́чень** *January* - **від ве́ресня до сі́чня** *from September to January,* **мі́сяць гру́день** *the month of December* - **про́тягом мі́сяця гру́дня** *for the duration of the month of December* The exception is the word **лю́тий** *February. Derived from an adjective, it takes the ending* ~**ого, пі́сля лю́того** *after February;*

3) names of flowers and trees,
тюльпа́н *a tulip* - **без тюльпа́на** *without a tulip*, **со́няшник** *a sunflower* - **без со́няшника** *without a sunflower*, **ґладуіо́лус** *a gladiolus* - **без ґладуіо́луса** *without a gladiolus*, **нарци́с** *a daffodil* - **без нарци́са** *without a daffodil*, **горі́х** *a walnut tree* - **бі́ля горі́ха** *near a walnut tree*, **дуб** *an oak tree* - **бі́ля ду́ба** *near an oak tree*, **клен** *a maple tree* - **бі́ля кле́на** *near a maple tree*, **в'яз** *an elm tree* - **бі́ля в'я́за** *near an elm tree;*

4) names of cities,
Ки́їв - **до Ки́єва** *to Kyiv*, **Льві́в** - **до Льво́ва** *to Lviv*, **Ха́рків** - **до Ха́ркова** *to Kharkiv*, **Черні́гів** *Chernihiv* - **до Черні́гова** *to Chernihiv.*

The dictionary at the end of the textbook furnishes the G. sg. ending for each consonant-ended inanimate masculine noun. It is given after the grammatical gender, right before the description of its meaning, **олі́в|е́ць,** *m.,* ~**ця** *a pencil.*

~**у** is taken by most inanimate consonant-ended masculine nouns of hard stems, **університе́т** *a university* - **бі́ля університе́ту** *near a university*, **текст** *a text* - **без те́ксту** *without a text*, **дощ** *rain* - **без дощу́** *without rain;*

~**ю** is taken by the same of soft stems, **музе́й** *a museum* - **бі́ля музе́ю** *near a museum*, **біль** *a pain* - **без бо́лю** *without pain*, **не́жить** *a cold* - **без не́житю** *without a cold.*

This group includes nouns denoting:

1) buildings and institutional premises,
дім *a house* - **до́му**, **буди́нок** *a building* - **буди́нку**, **магази́н** *a store* - **магази́ну**, **інститу́т** *an institute* - **інститу́ту;**

2) most foreign borrowings,
проє́кт *a project* - **проє́кту**, **пара́граф** *a paragraph* - **пара́графу**,
сенс *sense* - **се́нсу**, **текст** *a text* - **те́ксту**;

3) natural phenomena,
буреві́й *a hurricane* - **буреві́ю**, **град** *hail* - **гра́ду**, **дощ** *rain* - **дощу́**,
моро́з *frost* - **моро́зу**, **сніг** *snow* - **сні́гу**.

◀)) SOUND CHANGES ◀)|
in the genitive singular of nouns

Dropping of ~o~ (~e~)
Vowels ~o~ and ~e~ in the final syllable of the masculine nouns
ending in a consonant are dropped in the genitive singular:

> **куто́к** *a corner* - **без кутка́** *without a corner*
> **листо́к** *a leaf* - **без листка́** *without a leaf*
> **украї́нець** *a Ukrainian* - **без украї́нця** *without a Ukrainian*
> **олівець** *a pencil* - **без олівця́** *without a pencil*
> **стіле́ць** *a chair* - **без стільця́** *without a chair*

Change of ~i~ to ~o~ (~e~)
Vowel ~i~ in the final syllable of the masculine and feminine nouns
ending in a consonant becomes ~o~ or, less often, ~e~ in the
genitive singular,

> **ніс** *a nose* - **без но́са** *without a nose*
> **стіл** *a table* - **без стола́** *without a table*
> **ко́лір** *a color* - **без ко́льору** *without a color*
> **ра́дість** *joy* - **без ра́дости** *without joy*
> **злість** *anger* - **без зло́сти** *without anger*
> and ~o~ to ~e~,
> **папі́р** *paper* - **без папе́ру** *without paper*
> **річ** *a thing* - **без ре́чі** *without a thing*

Мину́лого бе́резня мої́ дру́зі з
Ки́єва ї́здили у по́дорож до Ри́ма.

🖉 **Note 8.6. Міста́ та краї́ни**
Cities vs countries

Follow a simple rule, whereby in the
G. sg., masculine nouns that are city
names take the ending **~a** (~я) while
those that are country names take the
ending **~у** (~ю),

**Торі́к Людми́ла Куц ї́здила до
Стамбу́ла.** *Last year Liudmyla Kuts
went to Istanbul.*

Чи ви ма́єте нови́ни з Єги́пту? *Do
you have news from Egypt?*

The stress in the genitive singular is mostly identical with that
in the nominative singular and is relative to the order of
syllables, i.e., if the last syllable is stressed in the nominative
singular, the last syllable stays stressed in the genitive singular, even if
in absolute terms it is not the same vowel,
N. sg. **Васи́ль** *Vasyl* - *G. sg.* **без Василя́** *without Vasyl*

The stress stays on the same syllable even if the specific vowel
stressed in *N. sg.* vanishes in *G. sg.* as in
листо́к *a leaf* - **без листка́** *without a leaf*
кіне́ць *an end* - **без кінця́** *without end*
This occurs in words with a stressed final syllable.

Павли́на – ста́рша сестра́ мало́го Наза́ра.

Займе́нники Pronouns

The genitive of personal and other pronouns can be found on pp. 322-324 in the appendices. Note that, like with the accusative case, some personal pronouns change their form and stress in the genitive depending on whether or not they follow a preposition, *G.* of **вона́** *she* is **її** and **до не́ї** *to her*, *G.* of **він** *he*, is **його́** and **до ньо́го** *to him*. These changes are reflected in the appendices.

Прикме́тники Adjectives

Adjectival genitive endings:
~ого (~ього), ~ої (~ьої)

~ого is taken by the masculine and neuter adjectives of hard stems, *m.* **нови́й студе́нт** *a new student* - **для ново́го студе́нта** *for a new student*; *nt.* **вели́ке мі́сто** *a big city* - **бі́ля вели́кого мі́ста** *near a big city*;

~ього is taken by the masculine and neuter adjectives of soft stems, *m.* **оста́нній по́їзд** *the last train* - **пі́сля оста́ннього по́їзда** *after the last train*; *nt.* **тре́тє вікно́** *the third window* - **бі́ля тре́тього вікна́** *near the third window*;

~ої is taken by feminine adjectives of hard stems, **нова́ студе́нтка** *a new (female) student* - **для ново́ї студе́нтки** *for a new (female) student*, **стара́ ха́та** *an old house* - **бі́ля старо́ї ха́ти** *near an old house*;

~ьої is taken by feminine adjectives of soft stems, **оста́ння ніч** *the last night* - **до оста́нньої но́чі** *till the last night*, **тре́тя ха́та** *the third house* - **бі́ля тре́тьої ха́ти** *near the third house*.

📖 Впра́ви Exercises

🎧 **8.1.** Pose a question using the words given and then answer it. Note that the expresssion **це (є)** *this is* stays unchanged for all genders.

Model. кни́жка *a book,* брат *a brother*

Q Чия́ це кни́жка? *Whose book is it?*
A Це кни́жка бра́та. *This is my brother's book. (lit. This is a book of my brother.)*

1. газе́та, профе́сор
2. університе́т, друг
3. по́друга, Васи́ль Дмитру́к
4. па́спорт, тури́стка
5. фі́льми, бібліоте́ка
6. валі́за, О́ля

7. кварти́ра, Мико́ла
8. а́вто, дя́дько
9. фо́то, америка́нець
10. ре́чі, виклада́ч
11. пое́зія, Тара́с Шевче́нко
12. гро́ші, Андрі́й Бондаре́нко

МУЗЕЙ
ОДНІЄЇ ВУЛИЦІ

⌒ **8.2.** Use the genitive to express a relationship between the two notions.

Model. пробле́ма *a problem,* стрес *stress*
Q Як ви ду́маєте, що це таке́? *What do you think this is?*
A Здає́ться, це пробле́ма стре́су. *It seems to be a problem of stress.*

1. пита́ння, час
2. спра́ва, смак
3. кіне́ць, мі́сяць
4. поча́ток, навча́ння
5. сере́дина, о́сінь
6. пере́клад, текст
7. план, ле́кція
8. це́нт(е)р, мі́сто
9. час, відпочи́нок
10. значе́ння, сло́во
11. день, ма́ти
12. ро́зклад, робо́та

⌒ **8.3.** React to the statement. Follow the word order in the model.
Note that the prepositions **до** *to* and **без** *without* require the genitive.

Model.
C Це Га́нна, а це ти. *This is Hanna, and this is you.*
A Га́нна тебе́ не зна́є, тому́ вона́ до те́бе не пи́ше.
Hanna doesn't know you, that's why she doesn't write to you.

1. Це Богда́на, а це ви.
2. Це Яросла́в, а це воно́.
3. Це Дмитро́ й Софі́я, а це вони́.
4. Це я, а це він.
5. Це ми, а це вона́.
6. Це моя́ ті́тка, а це ти.
7. Це ви, а це ми.
8. Це Кири́ло й Оле́кса, а це я.
9. Це я, а це вона́.
10. Це ти, а це він.

Ось світли́на старо́ї гуцу́льської це́ркви в Карпа́тах.

Ще тро́хи   A bit more
Do the same exercise. Replace the pair **не зна́ти** + *G.* / **писа́ти до** + *G.* for:
a) **не потребува́ти** + *G. not to need* / **роби́ти завда́ння без** + *G. to do the assignment without ...*

C Це Га́нна, а це ти. *This is Hanna, and this is you.*
A Га́нна тебе́ не потребу́є, тому́ вона́ ро́бить завда́ння без те́бе. *Hanna doesn't need you, that's why she does the assignment without you.*

b) **не люби́ти** + *G. to not like* / **зверта́тися до** + *G.* **по допомо́гу** *to turn to sb for help.* Use the dictionary if need be. Translate each of your sentences.

C Це Га́нна, а це ти. *This is Hanna, and this is you.*
A Га́нна тебе́ не лю́бить, тому́ вона́ не зверта́ється до те́бе по допомо́гу.
Hanna doesn't like you that's why she does not turn to you for help.

Мину́лого четверга́ вони́ всі ходи́ли до зоопа́рку в Я́лті.

Ця доро́га йде́ до старо́го за́мку.

∩ **8.4.** Give a negative answer to each question. Change the accusative object into the genitive.

Model.
Q Чи Марі́я ма́є **нову́ кни́жку**? *Does Maria have a new book?*
A Ні, Марі́я не ма́є **ново́ї кни́жки**. *No, Maria doesn't have a new book.*

1. Чи О́ля ро́бить ціка́ве завда́ння?
2. Чи ви їсте́ до́бру ковбасу́?
3. Чи ти чита́єш нови́й рома́н?
4. Чи він зна́є украї́нську істо́рію?
5. Чи Яри́на пи́ше до́вгий лист?
6. Чи вони́ лю́блять моде́рну архітекту́ру?
7. Чи ми слу́хаємо улю́блену програ́му?
8. Чи я зна́ю росі́йську мо́ву?
9. Чи ми лю́бимо цього́ викладача́?
10. Чи ми шука́ємо ва́шу стару́ шко́лу?
11. Чи вона́ зна́є це америка́нське мі́сто?
12. Чи вони́ чита́ють неціка́вий текст?

Phonetics. Drill dropping the ~o~ in the genitive singular of the masculine nouns of the 2ⁿᵈ declension.

∩ **8.5.** Drop the ~o~ in the final syllable of the inanimate masculine nouns taking the *G. sg.* ending ~**y**.

Stress Pattern A. The stress remains on the same vowel.

N буди́нок *a building*
A без буди́нку *without a building*

ґа́нок *a doorstep*	за́мок *a castle*
гурто́житок *a dormitory*	полу́денок *lunch*
ви́няток *an exception*	поря́док *an order*
сніда́нок *breakfast*	спи́сок *a list*
мо́зок *a brain*	промі́жок *a time period*
поча́ток *a beginning*	ри́нок *a market*
за́тінок *a cool place*	світа́нок *a sunrise*
маєто́к *a household*	я́рмарок *a fair*

∩ **8.6.** Answer the questions. Use the expression **нема́є**. Note the word order.

Model.
Q Рома́н Тарасю́к у Га́нни? *Is Roman Tarasiuk at Hanna's place?*
A Ні, Рома́на Тарасюка́ у не́ї нема́є. *No, Roman Tarasiuk isn't at hers.*

1. Його́ друг у те́бе?
2. Америка́нська газе́та у Ма́рка?

3. Ваш нови́й сусі́д в Оле́га Петрунчака́?
4. Моя́ су́мка в па́на Козаче́нка?
5. Твоя́ по́друга в Севери́на Куце́нка?
6. На́ша ті́тка в них?
7. Оле́на в Сашка́ Яре́менка?
8. Профе́сор Пилипе́нко у вас?
9. Той нудни́й кия́нин у те́бе?
10. Та симпати́чна кана́дка в Ірине́я Ковальця́?

Phonetics. Drill dropping the ~o~
in the genitive singular of the masculine nouns of 2nd declension.

🎧 **8.7.** Drop the vowel **~o~** in the final syllable of the inanimate masculine nouns taking the ending **~a**.

Stress Pattern A. The stress remains on the same vowel.

C шлу́нок *a stomach*
A для шлу́нка *for the stomach*

подару́нок *a gift*	пі́дмурок *a foundation*
зні́мок *a photo*	заголо́вок *a headline*
прову́лок *a lane*	ко́рок *a cork*
прила́вок *a counter*	недо́палок *a cigarette but*

Stress Pattern B. The stress is on the last syllable.

C куто́к *a corner*
A без кутка́ *without a corner*

ставо́к *a pond*	рядо́к *a line (of words)*
пиріжо́к *a pie*	візо́к *a cart*
замо́к *a lock*	садо́к *a garden*
квито́к *a ticket*	огіро́к *a cucumber*
тано́к *a dance*	каро́к *a neck*
мішо́к *a bag*	лісо́к *a grove*

🎧 **8.8.** Say and write the English phrase in Ukrainian. Use the genitive of time.

1. last week	8. this month
2. last year	9. next Sunday
3. this year	10. every Friday
4. last Saturday	11. this week
5. next Thursday	12. this autumn
6. every day	13. last summer
7. last time	14. every time

Дру́зі домо́вилися зустрі́тися біля Місько́го буди́нку вчи́теля.

Зі Льво́ва до Сидне́я в Австра́лії не завжди́ тре́ба до́вго їхати.

Note 8.7. Dropping the ~e~ in final syllable

Drill on your own. Drop the vowel ~e~ in the final syllable of the 2nd declension masculine animate nouns. Use the material of Note 5.8 Masculine Names of Nationalities, p. 68,

C украї́нець *a Ukrainian man*
A для украї́нця *for a Ukrainian man*

голубе́ць - без голубця́

8.9. State which city these people are traveling to and from. Use **з (із)** *from* and **до** *to*.

Model.
C Ма́рта *Marta*, Ки́їв *Kyiv*, Оде́са *Odesa*
A Ма́рта їде з Ки́єва до Оде́си. *Marta is traveling from Kyiv to Odesa.*

1. Андрі́й та Михайло, Херсо́н, Ялта
2. ми, Нью-Йо́рк, Пари́ж
3. ти, Варша́ва, Ха́рків
4. моя́ по́друга, Микола́їв, Доне́цьк
5. Ле́ся, Москва́, Черні́гів
6. я, Рим, Барсело́на
7. ви, Бо́стон, Монреа́ль
8. його́ дру́зі, У́жгород, Ві́нниця

Phonetics. Drill dropping the ~e~
in the genitive singular of the inanimate masculine nouns of 2nd declension.

8.10. Listen carefully and repeat. Practice dropping the ~e~ in the final syllable of the inanimate masculine nouns taking the ending ~**a** (~я). Check yourself against the speaker.

Stress Pattern A. The stress remains on the same vowel.
C ра́нець *a backpack*
A без ра́нця *without a backpack*

рі́вень *a level*	сі́чень *January*
ку́сень *a piece*	бе́резень *March*
па́лець *a finger, toe*	кві́тень *April*
гучномо́вець *a loudspeaker*	тра́вень *May*
оселе́дець *a herring*	че́рвень *June*
пе́рець *pepper*	ве́ресень *September*

Stress Pattern B. The stress is on the last syllable.
C чо́вен *a boat*
A без човна́ *without a boat*

день *a day*	олівце́ць *a pencil*
млине́ць *a pancake*	прапоре́ць *dim. a flag*
кіне́ць *an end*	гамане́ць *a wallet*
хлібе́ць *dim. bread*	взіре́ць *a model*
стіле́ць *a chair*	голубе́ць *a cabbage roll*
бухане́ць *a loaf*	кагане́ць *a night-lamp*
синце́ць *a bruise*	проміне́ць *dim. ray*

⌒ **8.11.** Express the destination of action. Use **до** + *G.*

Model.
Ⓒ Ма́рта *Marta,* писа́ти *to write,* наш вчи́тель *our teacher,*
ко́жний ти́ждень *every week*
Ⓐ Ма́рта пи́ше до на́шого вчи́теля ко́жного ти́жня (щоти́жня).
Marta writes to our teacher every week.

1. вони́, дзвони́ти, їхній ба́тько, ко́жна п'я́тниця
2. я, зверта́тися (*turn to*), цей експе́рт, ко́жний рік
3. Олекса́ндер і Ні́на, ходи́ти в го́сті (*pay a visit to*), Марі́я та
Степа́н, ко́жна субо́та
4. ти, прихо́дити (*come to our place*), ми, ко́жний ве́чір
5. ви, писа́ти, ма́ти, ко́жна середа́

Як ці молоді́ лю́ди ї́дуть
з Берди́чева до Полта́ви.

Phonetics. Change ~i~ to ~o~ in Ukrainian city names.

⌒ **8.12.** Answer the question, state the origin of the person.
The stress remains on the same vowel.

Model. Ⓒ Яросла́в *Yaroslav,* Ко́сів *Kosiv.*
Ⓠ Зві́дки Ярослав? *Where's Yaroslav from?*
Ⓐ Він із Ко́сова. *He is from Kosiv.*

1. Мари́на *Maryna,* Черні́гів *Chernihiv*
2. Па́ні Ковале́нко *Mrs. Kovalenko,* Су́ботів *Subotiv*
3. Степа́н Тарасю́к *Stepan Tarasiuk,* Ха́рків *Kharkiv*
4. Ори́ся Гале́та *Orysia Haleta,* Боле́хів *Bolekhiv*
5. Окса́на Франко́ *Oksana Franko,* Си́хів *Sykhiv*
6. Пан Миколайчу́к *Mr. Mykolaichuk,* Терно́піль *Ternopil*
7. Па́нна Тютю́нник *Ms. Tiutiunnyk,* Крижо́піль *Kryzhopil*
8. Па́ні Марі́я Москале́нко *Mrs. Maria Moskalenko,* Косто́піль
Kostopil
9. О́льга й І́гор Петруки́ *Olha and Ihor Petruks,* Горо́хів *Horokhiv*
10. Бори́с Каламе́р *Borys Kalamar,* Поді́л *Podil (old part of Kyiv)*
11. Се́стри Кова́лів *the Kovaliv sisters,* Раде́хів *Radekhiv*
12. Лари́са Ду́ма *Larysa Duma,* Львів *Lviv*
13. Оле́кса Степане́нко *Oleksa Stepanenko,* Фа́стів *Fastiv*

Phonetics. Drill changing the ~i~ to ~o~
in the consonant-ended masculine nouns which take the genitive
singular ending ~**a** (~я).

⌒ **8.13** Listen to the cue and react. Check yourself against the
speaker.
Model.
Ⓒ Стіл *a table*
Ⓐ Я не пам'ята́ю нія́кого стола́. *I don't remember any table.*

Васи́лько Москале́ць із
Луга́нської о́бласти.

Note 8.8. How to be negative. Double negation

Unlike English, Ukrainian sentences such as *Roman doesn't know anything.* require a double negation:

1) of the predicate by putting in front of it the negative particle **не** *not*;

2) of what is actually negated (nothing, nobody, nowhere, no way, never, etc.),

Pavlo did not understand anything. **Павло́ нічо́го не зрозумі́в.** *lit. Pavlo didn't understand nothing*.*

Yaryna did not go anywhere. **Яри́на ніку́ди не ходи́ла.** *lit. Yaryna didn't go nowhere.**

We did not buy any milk. **Ми не купи́ли нія́кого молока́.** *lit. We did not buy no milk.**

Take note of these correlates used for a double negation:

хто? *who?* - **ніхто́** *nobody* (*G. sg.* кого́ - ніко́го, до ко́го - ні до ко́го): **Ніхто́ не зна́є.** *Nobody knows.*

що? *what?* - **ніщо́** *nothing* (*G. sg.* чого́ - нічо́го, до чо́го - ні до чо́го): **Він нічо́го не ба́чив.** *He didn't see anything.*

m. **яки́й?** *what kind of?* - **нія́кий?** *no +* *n.* (*G. sg.* яко́го - нія́кого? до яко́го - ні до яко́го?): **Вони́ не їдя́ть нія́кого м'я́са.** *They don't eat any meat.*

f. **яка́?** *what kind of?* - **нія́ка** *no + n.* (*G. sg.* яко́ї? - нія́кої, до яко́ї? - ні до яко́ї): **Ми не ма́ємо нія́кої інформа́ції.** *We don't have any information.*

коли́? *when?* - **ніко́ли** *never.* **Я ніко́ли тут не був.** *I have never been here.*

posn. **де?** *where?* - *posn.* **ніде́** *nowhere:* **Васи́ль ніде́ не працю́є.** *Vasyl doesn't work anywhere.*

dir. **куди́?** *where to?* - *dir.* **ніку́ди** *to nowhere:* **Я ніку́ди не йду.** *I am not going anywhere.*

Stress Pattern A. The stress remains on the same vowel.

ніс *a nose*	па́гін *an offshoot*
ослі́н *a stool*	о́стрів *an island*
віз *a wagon*	дзвін *bell*

Stress Pattern B. The stress is on the last syllable.

баті́г *a whip*	Острі́г *Ostrih (city)*
барлі́г *a lair*	стіг *a haystack*
пирі́г *a pie*	

Phonetics. Drill changing the ~і~ to ~о~ in the consonant-ended inanimate masculine nouns which take the genitive singular ending **~у (~ю)**.

🎧 **8.14.** Listen to the cue and react.

Model.
C Ріг *a street corner*
A Я не пам'ята́ю нія́кого ро́гу. *I don't remember any street corner.*

Stress Pattern A. The stress remains on the same vowel.

грім *a thunder*	поді́л *lower city*
піт *sweat*	порі́г *a doorstep*
плід *a fruit*	поті́к *a flow*
сік *juice*	біль *a pain*
рід *gender, family*	заги́н *a platoon*
брід *a ford*	окрі́п *boiling water*
зріст *height*	рік *a year*

But **лід** *ice* - **льо́ду**, **ко́лір** *a color* - **ко́льору**, **полі́т** *a flight* - **польо́ту**.

🎧 **8.15.** Explain why. Follow the model.

Model. Миха́йло *Mykhailo,* Ло́ндон *London,* Варша́ва *Warsaw*
Q Чому́ Миха́йло не зайшо́в до нас? *Why didn't Mykhailo call on us?*
A Бо він поверну́вся з Ло́ндона й одра́зу пої́хав до Варша́ви. *Because he returned from London and immediately went to Warsaw.*

1. ти, Ки́їв, Оде́са
2. ви, Пари́ж, Ха́рків
3. Окса́на, Москва́, Рим
4. Роксоля́на та Бори́с, Херсо́н, Я́лта
5. Олекса́ндер, Луга́нськ, Терно́піль
6. ва́ші знайо́мі поля́ки, Маріу́поль, У́жгород

Phonetics. Drill changing the ~i~ to ~o~

in the consonant-ended feminine nouns which take the genitive singular ending ~и.

Ці молоді́ лю́ди з географі́чного це́нтру Євро́пи.

🎧 **8.16.** Listen to the cue and react.

C можли́вість *a possibility, opportunity*
A для тако́ї можли́вости *for such a possibility*

ра́дість *joy*
мо́лодість *youth*
злість *anger*
ми́лість *mercy*
ду́рість *stupidity*
свідо́мість *consciousness*
бі́дність *poverty*
посере́дність *mediocrity*
ні́жність *tenderness*
ме́ншість *a minority*

ві́рність *fidelity*
го́рдість *pride*
че́сність *honesty*
є́дність *unity*
складні́сть *complexity*
рі́вність *equality*
гі́дність *dignity*
му́жність *courage*
ці́нність *value*
бі́льшість *a majority*

🎧 **8.17.** Express the idea of proximity to a place. Use **бі́ля** *near* + G.

Model. **C** Мій дім *my house*
 A бі́ля мо́го до́му *near my house*

1. залізни́чний вокза́л
2. авто́бусна ста́нція
3. вели́кий буди́нок
4. оста́ннє вікно́
5. старе́ мі́сто
6. худо́жній музе́й
7. украї́нський рестора́н
8. чо́рний телефо́н
9. твій о́фіс
10. ї́хній кінотеа́тр

🎧 **8.18.** Give negative answers to the questions. Be sure to use a double negation. Replace nouns with personal pronouns.

Model. **Q** Що ро́бить Андрі́й? *What does Andrii do?*
 A Він нічо́го не ро́бить. *He doesn't do anything.*

1. Що ти пита́єш?
2. Що зна́ють ці студе́нти?
3. Що розка́зували ї́хні ро́дичі про Оде́су?
4. Що ціка́вого ба́чив Рома́н на ви́ставці?
5. Що вони́ хо́чуть принести́ на вечі́рку?
6. Що ду́має про це економі́ст ва́шої компа́нії?
7. Що бу́дуть купува́ти ці америка́нці у продукто́вій крамни́ці?

Авто́бусна ста́нція

8. Що ви замовля́єте на вече́рю?
9. Що вона́ пита́ла профе́сора?
10. Що ви чу́ли про цю поді́ю?

🎧 **8.19.** Give a negative answer to each question. Practice the double negation. Change the accusative object into the genitive and use *m.* **нія́кого**, *f.* **нія́кої**.

Model. Q Чи вона́ ма́є нову́ кни́жку? *Does she have a new book?*
A Ні, вона́ не ма́є нія́кої кни́жки взагалі́. *No, she doesn't have any book at all.*

1. Чи Степа́н ро́бить дома́шнє завда́ння?
2. Чи вони́ їдя́ть свиня́че м'я́со (pork meat)?
3. Чи ти чита́єш її́ нову́ статтю́?
4. Чи вони́ зна́ють украї́нську му́зику?
5. Чи Світла́на пи́ше есе́й про цьо́го пое́та?
6. Чи вони́ лю́блять моде́рну літерату́ру?
7. Чи ми ди́вимося улю́блену програ́му?
8. Чи цей англі́єць переклада́є вірш Оле́га Лише́ги?
9. Чи школярі́ слу́хають цьо́го вчи́теля?
10. Чи мандрівники́ знайшли́ зру́чний готе́ль?
11. Чи Петро́ ба́чив це італі́йське мі́сто?
12. Чи та журналі́стка розумі́є украї́нську мо́ву?

Phonetics. Drill changing the ~i~ to ~e~ in the final syllable of the consonant-ended masculine nouns, which take the genitive singular ~a (~я).

🎧 **8.20.** Write a statement with a double-negation. The stress remains on the same vowel.

C Це ко́рінь. *This is the root.*
A Я не зна́ю нія́кого ко́реня. *I don't know any root.*

Ки́їв *Kyiv*	кури́інь *a hut*
про́мінь *a ray*	ле́гінь *a young man*
ка́мінь *a stone*	Зо́лочів *Zolochiv (a city)*
ре́мінь *a belt*	Жида́чів *Zhydachiv (a city)*
кре́мінь *a flint*	Ка́нів *Kaniv (a city)*

🎧 **8.21.** Say and write each sentence in Ukrainian. If necessary consult the dictionary.

1. She invited my friend first for coffee and then to the theater.
2. Their colleagues decided to go to a Chinese restaurant for lunch.
3. Mr. Pylypenko is a well-known specialist in Ukrainian culture.
4. Olena has a mobile phone, therefore, I can always call her.
5. They agreed to meet next Friday near the main post-office.

Книга́рня розташо́вується на ро́зі ву́лиці Ру́ської та Се́рбської.

Вони́ провели́ три годи́ни на букіністи́чному ри́нку і не купи́ли жо́дної кни́жки.

6. I suggest waiting for our friend Natalia. We cannot go to the university without her, can we?

7. The guys will watch the TV program at my place.

8. Miss Tarasenko will be working in Kharkiv from this Monday to next Thursday.

9. I think that a trip to New York is only a matter of time.

10. We haven't yet seen this new play. We haven't seen any play.

11. Do you have an excursion to the zoo or to the botanical garden after the class?

12. The students did not say anything about the exam.

8.22. Listen carefully to the questions and answer each of them based on Dialogue 8.

1. Куди́ хо́че Ігор запроси́ти Макси́ма та Тетя́ну?

2. Де і коли́ бу́де вече́ря?

3. Пі́сля чиє́ї ле́кції бу́де вече́ря?

4. Хто таки́й профе́сор Пилипе́нко?

5. Коли́ хо́дить Тетя́на до басе́йну?

6. Чому́ Ігор попроси́в Макси́ма подзвони́ти до Тетя́ни?

7. Чому́ хло́пці не змогли́ домо́витися про вече́рю одра́зу?

8. Про що домо́вилися Ігор та Макси́м?

9. Куди́ ви оста́нній раз запро́шували дру́га чи по́другу?

8.23. Read the questions and make sure you understand each of them. Listen to the text "Святко́ва вече́ря для Макси́ма" and answer the questions.

1. Коли́ у Макси́ма Задоро́жного день наро́дження?

2. Як зва́ти ді́вчину Макси́ма?

3. Як назива́ють Макси́ма та Людми́лу їхні близькі́ дру́зі?

4. У яко́му університе́ті вча́ться ці молоді́ лю́ди?

5. Чому́ типо́ві студе́нти не їдя́ть у рестора́ні?

6. Хто така́ Ната́лка?

7. Чому́ Ната́лка зна́є всі рестора́ни мі́ста?

8. Коли́ виріша́є Лю́да, до яко́го рестора́ну запроси́ти Макси́ма?

8.24. Translate the text into English. Use the dictionary.

Святко́ва вече́ря для Макси́ма.

Насту́пного ти́жня у Макси́ма Задоро́жного уроди́ни. Людми́ла Ма́рченко, його́ ді́вчина, ду́має зроби́ти для коха́ного хло́пця приє́мну несподі́ванку. Вона́ виріша́є запроси́ти Ма́кса на вече́рю до яко́гось га́рного рестора́ну. До яко́го са́ме Лю́да ще не зна́є.

Макс і Лю́да – студе́нти Ха́рківського університе́ту. Вони́ вча́ться на факульте́ті украї́нської літерату́ри, живу́ть у гурто́житку і, як типо́ві студе́нти, звича́йно не їдя́ть у рестора́ні, бо це до́сить до́рого. Але́ це не пробле́ма, бо вони́ ду́же лю́блять готува́ти. Не ди́вно, що Лю́да ма́ло зна́є про рестора́ни мі́ста. Вона́ дзво́нить до ста́ршої сестри́ Ната́лки, теж Ма́рченко, пора́дитися.

Сього́дні у Лю́ди для Ма́кса приє́мна несподі́ванка.

На уроди́ни ма́тері вони́ всі ходи́ли до ресторáну "Корóна Ві́товта".

Натáлка - економі́ст, непогáно заробля́є, геть не лю́бить готувáти і знáє, напéвно, кóжний дóбрий чи погáний ресторáн мі́ста. Вонá кáже, що мі́сяць тому́ недалéко від худóжньої галерéї відкри́вся нови́й італі́йський ресторáн «Каравáджо». Коли́ Людми́ла чýє «італі́йський ресторáн», вонá дýмає, що крім пі́ци там нічóго не даю́ть, а вонá не лю́бить пі́ци. Людми́ла їсть пі́цу лише́ тоді́ та там, коли́ та де немáє жóдної і́ншої стрáви.

Натáлка самá не лю́бить пі́ци, алé у цьóму ресторáні вонá булá вже три рáзи і кóжного рáзу смáчно і теж зóвсім недóрого вечéряла. Особли́во дóбре там рóблять стрáви із ри́би, салáти та десéрт. Це ще не все, бо крім дóброї кýхні там приє́мна атмосфéра, симпати́чні офіція́нти та жи́ва джаз-мýзика. Лю́да чýє ці словá сестри́ і нарéшті виріша́є, що «Каравáджо» - ідеáльне мі́сце для святкóвої вечéрі. Це бýде спрáвді приє́мна несподі́ванка для її́ Макси́ма на уроди́ни.

8.25. Describe Liudmyla, Maksym, and Natalka in three-four sentences.

 Завда́ння для Міжнарóдної мерéжі
Internet Assignment

8.26. Use an Internet search engine and find four restaurants in Lviv. Write answers to the following questions.

1. Як назива́ється кóжний ресторáн?
2. Якá адрéса кóжного ресторáну?
3. Яку́ кýхню пропону́ють у кóжному ресторáні?

8.27. Use the Kyiv restaurant portal http://lasoon.com.ua/ukr or any other related Ukrainian language portal you can find. Identify the restaurants in Ukraine where you can have dishes of these cuisines:

украї́нська кýхня *Ukrainian cuisine*
італі́йська кýхня *Italian cuisine*
францýзька кýхня *French cuisine*
япóнська кýхня *Japanese cuisine*
європéйська кýхня *European cuisine*

8.28. Using the Ukrainian language Internet resources and the key words **украї́нське меню́** put together a Ukrainian menu. It should include:

1. Закýски.
2. Пéрші стрáви.
3. Дрýгі стрáви (головні́ стрáви абó гаря́чі стрáви).
4. Десéрт (солóдке).
5. Напої́.

See if you can explain what is every dish in your menu.

Як запро́шувати кого́сь куди́сь.
How to invite somebody somewhere.

8.29. Answer the questions. Choose the correct preposition with the verb **запро́шувати кого́сь** *на + A.* or *до + G. to invite somebody to.* Consult Notes on the Dialogue, p. 131.

1. Куди́ запро́сив Марко́ свого́ коле́гу Павла́ Левчука́? (ціка́ва ле́кція)
2. Куди́ ду́має Ната́ля запроси́ти тітку Ори́сю з Ха́ркова? (ка́ва, популя́рна місце́ва кав'я́рня)
3. Куди́ запро́шує Лі́дію Оле́кса Поля́к? (істори́чний музе́й, нова́ ви́ставка)
4. Куди́ ти хо́чеш запроси́ти Наза́ра Яво́рського? (конце́рт джа́зової му́зики, філармо́нія)
5. Куди́ Окса́на запроси́ла Ві́ктора на його́ уроди́ни? (рестора́н "Барсело́на", га́рна вече́ря)
6. Куди́ запро́шує вас профе́сор Хмельни́цький? (важли́ва науко́ва конфере́нція)
7. Куди́ вони́ запроси́ли го́стя з Херсо́на? (сенсаці́йна виста́ва, драмати́чний теа́тр)
8. Куди́ мо́жна влі́тку запроси́ти па́ні Ма́рту? (ліс, приє́мний відпочи́нок)
9. Куди́ запроси́ла Кали́на Коза́к дя́дька Са́шка? (серйо́зна розмо́ва)
10. Куди́ тре́ба було́ запроси́ти їх, коли́ була́ га́рна пого́да (ботані́чний сад, до́вга прогу́лянка)

8.30. Enact a conversation with a partner. Use the material you have learned so far. Where necessary consult the dictionary.

Сце́нка за сцена́рієм «Дру́зі домовля́ються про зу́стріч»
Scripted Skit: *Friends Arranging for Meeting*

Victor (Ві́ктор): Casually greets Andriy by name.
Andriy (Андрі́й): Greets Victor back and asks what is new.

Victor: He is glad that Andriy is asking because he has some very interesting news.
Andriy: What kind of news – of his personal life or from the University?

Victor: Of personal life. Asks whether or not Andriy remembers what hobby Victor has.
Andriy: Affirmative. Everybody knows that Victor is a great collector of contemporary and classical Ukrainian cinema.

Victor: Exactly so. Tells how last year, he started looking for the Ukrainian classical film by Leonid Osyka entitled *Zakhar Berkut*. Now he finally found it!
Andriy: Expresses his disbelief. Asks what he means "finally found it." Found at somebody's place, in a library or in a store..? Where?

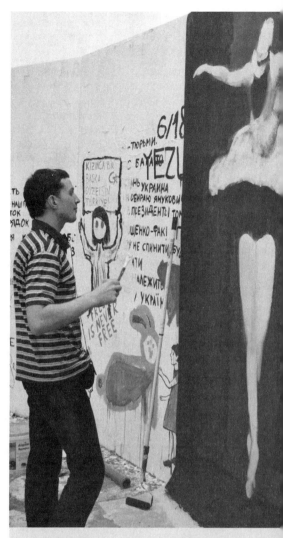

Матві́й Авра́менко запро́шує всіх нас до своє́ї сту́дії на ма́йстер-клас з маля́рства.

Режисе́р Леоні́д Оси́ка – кла́сик
украї́нського поети́чного кіна́.
(1944-2001)

Victor: He found a DVD of the film by accident on the Internet and immediately bought it for his collection.
Andriy: Congratulates Victor. Expresses a desire to watch the film. He has not yet seen it.

Victor: Says that was exactly why he started talking about it. Asks whether Andriy can invite him to his place.
Andriy: Does not understand what is going on. Victor knows he does not need a special invitation from Andriy.

Victor: Admits he knows that. But today he has a problem. His DVD-player broke last week and so now he cannot watch the new film.
Andriy: Says that it is no problem. He will be glad to invite Victor to his place and watch *Zakhar Berkut* together.

Victor: Thanks him and asks when this can be done.
Andriy: Tomorrow and the day after tomorrow he won't be home in the evening. Proposes to do it this Saturday.

Victor: Saturday suits him fine.
Andriy: Expresses satisfaction and says he will see Victor on Saturday evening at his place.

Лéкція | Lesson 9

Dialogue:
Що нам трéба до стóлу
What we need for the table

Grammar:
Dative singular
Ordinal numerals

Competencies:
Buying groceries
Age
Fondness, need, uncertainty, necessity, and desire
Time by the clock
Ukrainian national cuisine
Ordering food in restaurant

Холоди́льник зно́ву поро́жній?
Не мо́же цього́ бу́ти!

9. Діяло́г. Що нам тре́ба до сто́лу.

Ма́рта: Мико́ло, нам тре́ба купи́ти проду́кти до сто́лу. Холоди́льник зно́ву поро́жній.

Мико́ла: Бо́же, як шви́дко лети́ть час! Здає́ться, що лише́ вчо́ра була́ п'я́тниця, і ми роби́ли поку́пки.

Ма́рта: З того́ ча́су вже пройшо́в ти́ждень. Сього́дні зно́ву п'я́тниця. Нам зно́ву пора́ йти до суперма́ркету.

Мико́ла: А це не мо́же почека́ти оди́н день? За́втра вихідни́й і у нас бу́де бі́льше ві́льного ча́су.

Ма́рта: Так, мо́же. Тоді́ сього́дні нам тре́ба бу́де йти на обі́д та вече́рю до рестора́ну.

Мико́ла: Ма́рто, сказа́ти пра́вду, я геть не про́ти вече́рі у до́брому рестора́ні.

Ма́рта: Я сама́ не пам'ята́ю, коли́ ми там були́ оста́нній раз.

Мико́ла: З і́ншого бо́ку, кра́ще ї́сти в рестора́ні, коли́ нам хо́четься, а не коли́ закі́нчилися проду́кти у холоди́льнику.

Ма́рта: Я теж так ду́маю. Крім то́го я ма́ю охо́ту звари́ти сього́дні щось особли́ве. Але́ що са́ме, я не впе́внена.

Мико́ла: Я зна́ю! На пе́ршу стра́ву пропону́ю щавле́вий борщ, а на дру́гу – інди́чку у грибо́вій підли́ві.

Ма́рта: Су́пер! Але́ ти ма́єш допомогти́ мені́.

Мико́ла: Звича́йно. Мені́ за́вжди подо́балося допомага́ти тобі́ на ку́хні.

Ма́рта: Домо́вилися. А тепе́р до суперма́ркету.

Мико́ла: Чека́й хвили́нку. Споча́тку нам тре́ба написа́ти спи́сок.

Ма́рта: До́бре. Пишу́: інди́чка, бі́лі гриби́, вершки́, молоко́, сир, ма́сло, я́йця, олі́я, ши́нка. Що ще?

Мико́ла: Помідо́ри, огірки́ та цибу́ля на сала́т. До ре́чі, яки́й бу́де гарні́р до інди́чки - карто́пля, рис чи горо́дина?

Ма́рта: Ні, ні. Для по́вної гармо́нії на гарні́р ма́є бу́ти ті́льки гре́чка.

Мико́ла: О́тже - гре́чка. Мені́ здає́ться, що ми забу́ли ще щось ду́же важли́ве.

Ма́рта: Звича́йно, у нас нема́є хлі́ба!

Мико́ла: Пишу́: хліб і рога́лики на сніда́нок. Наш спи́сок гото́вий. Тепе́р нам мо́жна йти купува́ти проду́кти.

9. Dialogue. What we need for the table.

Marta: Mykola, we need to buy some groceries for the table. The refrigerator is empty again.

Mykola: Oh God. How quickly the time flies! It seems Friday was only yesterday and we were buying groceries.

Marta: A week has passed since then. Today is Friday again. Again it's time for us to go to the supermarket.

Mykola: Can't it wait a day? Tomorrow is our day off and we'll have more free time.

Marta: Yes, it can. Then today we'll have to go to a restaurant for lunch and dinner.

Mykola: Marta, to tell the truth I am not at all against a dinner in a good restaurant.

Marta:	I myself do not remember the last time we were there.
Mykola:	On the other hand, it's better to eat in a restaurant when we want to, rather than when we have no food left in the refrigerator.
Marta:	I think so too. Besides I am in the mood to cook something special. Exactly what, I am not yet sure.
Mykola:	I know. For the first course I propose a sorrel soup, and for the second turkey in a porcini mushroom sauce.
Marta:	Super! But you need to help me.
Mykola:	Of course. I have always liked to help you around the kitchen.
Marta:	It's a deal. And now to the supermarket.
Mykola:	Wait a while. First we need to write a list.
Marta:	Okay. I am writing: a turkey, porcini mushrooms, cream, milk, cheese, butter, eggs, oil, ham. What else?
Mykola:	Tomatoes, cucumbers, and onion for salad. By the way, what side dish will there be for the turkey: potatoes, rice or vegetables?
Marta:	No, no. For a complete harmony the side dish can be only buckwheat.
Mykola:	So buckwheat. It seems to me we forgot something very important.
Marta:	Of course, we don't have bread.
Mykola:	I am writing down: bread and croissants for breakfast. Our list is ready. Now we can go to buy the groceries.

Мико́лі Кривоно́сові подо́бається допомага́ти свої́й жі́нці Ма́рті на ку́хні.

 Нота́тки до діяло́гу   Notes on the Dialogue

проду́кти, *pl.*	produce, groceries; **купува́ти проду́кти** *to buy groceries*; **моло́чні проду́кти** *dairy products*
до сто́лу, *G.*	for the table, to eat; **Що вам купи́ти до сто́лу?** *What food should I buy for you?*
пора́ + *inf.*	it's time, also used with *D.* logical subject; **Нам пора́ йти додо́му.** *It's time for us to go home.* **Йому́ вже пора́ зна́ти це.** *It's time he knew this.*
щавле́вий борщ	sorrel soup, also known as **зеле́ний борщ** green borshch, the second most popular type of borshch after **черво́ний борщ** red (or beetroot and cabbage) borshch
phr. **домо́вилися**	*It's a deal.* Expression used to express agreement.

Поку́пки до сто́лу   Shopping for groceries

Які́ проду́кти мо́жна купува́ти?	What groceries can one buy?
Купува́ти мо́жна: молоко́, сир, я́йця, городину, фру́кти, м'я́со, напо́ї, со́ки.	One can buy: milk, cheese, eggs, vegetables, fruits, meat, drinks and juices.
Де мо́жна купува́ти проду́кти?	Where can one buy groceries?

Купува́ти проду́кти мо́жна: у суперма́ркеті, у магази́ні, у продукто́вій крамни́ці, на ри́нку, на база́рі.	One can buy groceries: in a supermarket, in a store, in a food store, on a market, in a market (bazaar).
Де мо́жна заплати́ти за проду́кти?	Where can one pay for groceries?
За проду́кти мо́жна заплати́ти у ка́сі.	One can pay for groceries at a cash register.
Скі́льки молока́ нам (вам) тре́ба купи́ти?	How much milk do we (you) need to buy?
Нам тре́ба одна́ пля́шка молока́.	We need one bottle of milk.
Скі́льки це ко́штує?	How much does it cost?
Це ко́штує рі́вно чоти́ри гри́вні.	It is exactly four hryvnias (*lit*. It costs exactly four hryvnias).

📕 Грама́тика | Grammar

Дава́льний відмі́нок однини́ Dative Case Singular

Dative correlates with the questions
кому́? *to whom?* **чому́?** *to what?*

Фу́нкція *Function*

The dative case can indicate:

1. To whom or for whom something is being done, given, written, bought, etc. The noun in the dative is the animate addressee or recipient of the action, expressed by such verbs as **дава́ти** *to give*, **писа́ти** *to write*, **співа́ти** *to sing*, **каза́ти** *to say*, **посила́ти** *to send*, **бажа́ти** *to wish*, **поя́снювати** *to explain*, **дя́кувати** *to thank*, in such sentences as:
   Петро́ дає́ кни́жку Гали́ні. *Petro gives a book to Halyna.*
   Гали́на пи́ше лист Петро́ві. *Halyna writes a letter to Petro.*
   Іва́н розка́зує істо́рію Марі́ї. *Ivan tells a story to Maria.*
The second noun following these verbs after direct accusative object takes the dative.

2. The logical subject in the expressions of such a type as:
   Гали́ні здає́ться, (що) ... *It seems to Halyna that ...*
   Петро́ві подо́бається чита́ти. *Petro likes to read.*

3. The age of a living being or inanimate object:
   Іва́нові оди́н рік. *Ivan is a year old.*
   Цьому́ буди́нку три́ста ро́ків. *This house is three hundred years old.*

Па́нові Са́вченку ціка́во зна́ти, чи гото́ва вече́ря.

4. Necessity, obligation, advice, permission, and prohibition with such words as **тре́ба** and *var.* **потрі́бно** *to need, to be necessary,* **слід** *should,* **мо́жна** *to be possible (allowed),* **не мо́жна** *not to be allowed:*

Марі́ї тре́ба (потрі́бно) купи́ти хлі́ба.
Maria needs to buy bread. (necessity)
Тури́стові потрі́бно знайти́ готе́ль.
The tourist needs to find a hotel. (necessity)
Оле́гові слід про це поду́мати.
Oleh should think about it. (advice)
Чи нам мо́жна тут переночува́ти?
May we stay for the night here? (permission)
Ніко́му не мо́жна кури́ти тут.
Nobody is allowed to smoke here. (prohibition)

Note that **тре́ба** and **потрі́бно** both mean *to need, to be necessary.* The difference between the two is that **тре́ба** is more colloquial and **потрі́бно** is more formal.

5. The relationship of cause and effect with the preposition **завдяки́** *thanks to, due to:*

Ми це ма́ємо завдяки́ Миха́йлові. *We have this thanks to Mykhailo.*
Завдяки́ со́нячній пого́ді ми провели́ ці́лий день надво́рі.
Thanks to sunny weather we spent all day outdoors.

Завдяки́ is one of the very few prepositions in Ukrainian that requires the dative.

Цьо́му юнако́ві тре́ба поба́чити Ки́єво-Пече́рську Ла́вру.

Утво́рення   *Formation*

Іме́нники   **Nouns**

The nominal dative singular endings:
~і (~ї), ~ові (~еві, ~єві), ~у (~ю)

~і is taken by all the feminine nouns and masculine nouns ending in ~а (~я), and neuter nouns with the suffixes ~ан~/~ян~ and ~ен~:

f. **О́ля** *Olia* - **Ми купу́ємо кни́жку О́лі.** *We buy the book for Olia.*
f. **ніч** *a night* - **завдяки́ но́чі** *thanks to the night*
f. **сіль** *salt* - **завдяки́ со́лі** *thanks to salt*
m. **Мико́ла** *Mykola* - **Він пи́ше Мико́лі.** *He writes to Mykola.*
nt. **дитя́** *a child* - **Він дає́ цуке́рку дитя́ті.** *He gives candy to a child.*

~ї is taken by feminine and masculine nouns ending in ~ія, so that the dative form of the noun will have the letter cluster ~ії at the end,
Марі́я *Maria* - **Я подзвони́в Марі́ї.** *I rang up Maria.*
істо́рія *history* - **завдяки́ істо́рії** *thanks to history*

Оле́нці подо́бається гімна́стика.

✎ Note 9.1. The special case of ма́ти a *mother*

Dative singular of **ма́ти** a *mother*, is **ма́тері**,
Я пишу́ лист ма́тері. *I write a letter to my mother.*

Завдяки́ ново́му велосипе́дові, Стефа́н мо́же щосубо́ти ї́здити до лі́су по гриби́.

~ові is taken by animate masculine nouns with a hard consonant or ~о ending,
студе́нт a *student* - **Вона́ пи́ше студе́нтові.** *She writes to a student.*
ба́тько a *father* - **завдяки́ ба́тькові** *thanks to the father;*

~еві is taken by the animate masculine nouns whose stem ends in a soft consonant or in the ~ж~, ~ч~, ~ш~, ~щ~, and ~р~,
учи́тель a *teacher* - **Я сказа́в учи́телеві.** *I told the teacher.*
лі́кар a *physician* - **завдяки́ лі́кареві** *thanks to a physician;*

~єві is taken by the animate masculine nouns whose stem ends in ~й,
Андрі́й *Andriy* - **Він допомага́є Андрі́єві.** *He helps Andriy.*
водій a *driver* - **завдяки́ водіє́ві** *thanks to the driver,*

~у is taken by inanimate masculine and neuter nouns with hard stems,
університе́т a *university* - **завдяки́ університе́ту** *thanks to the university,* **куто́к** a *corner* - **завдяки́ кутку́** *thanks to the corner*
я́блуко an *apple* - **завдяки́ я́блуку** *thanks to the apple*

~ю is taken by inanimate masculine and neuter nouns with soft stem,
музе́й a *museum* - **завдяки́ музе́ю** *thanks to a museum*
кіне́ць an *end* - **завдяки́ кінцю́** *thanks to the end*
пита́ння a *question* - **завдяки́ пита́нню** *thanks to the question.*

The endings ~**ові** (~**еві**/ ~**єві**) and ~**у** (~**ю**) are often used interchangeably for animate and inanimate masculine nouns with a consonant ending specifically so as to avoid a heavy sounding sequence in proper names that include a given name, patronymic, and family name. In such instances it is enough to use the ~**ові** (~**еві**/ ~**єві**) just once,
Петро́ Васи́льович Пилипе́нко
  a) **Вона́ пи́ше Петро́ві Васи́льовичу Пилипе́нку.** *or*
  b) **Вона́ пи́ше Петру́ Васи́льовичеві Пилипе́нку.** *or*
  c) **Вона́ пи́ше Петру́ Васи́льовичу Пилипе́нкові.** *She writes to Petro Vasyliovych Pylypenko.*
It is quite common to use the endings ~**ові** (~**еві**/ ~**єві**) also for inanimate masuline nouns, **завдяки́ її́ листо́ві** *thanks to her letter.*

◀)) SOUND CHANGES ((▶
in the dative singular of nouns

Velar shift before ~i
First and second declension nouns, whose stems end in the velars ~г, ~к, and ~х undergo, the consonant shift before ~i, whereby:
  ~г becomes ~з, **нога́** a *leg* - **нозі́**
  ~к becomes ~ц, **дочка́** a *daughter* - **дочці́**
  ~х becomes ~с, **му́ха** a *fly* - **му́сі**

Dropping of ~o~ (~e~)
~o~ and ~e~ in the last syllable of 2ⁿᵈ declension masculine
nouns are dropped in the dative singular,

куто́к *a corner* - кутку́
сон *a dream* - сну
украї́нець *a Ukrainian* - украї́нцеві
кіне́ць *the end* - кінцю́ *or* кінце́ві
день *a day* - дню

In the dative singular of nouns
~і~ changes to ~о~ (~е~) in the final syllable in 2ⁿᵈ declension
masculine and 3ʳᵈ declension feminine nouns,

m. кіт *a cat* - ко́тові
m. міст *a bridge* - мосту́ *or* мосто́ві
m. папі́р *paper* - папе́ру
f. ніч *a night* - но́чі
f. річ *a thing* - ре́чі

but not in:

m. дід *a grandfather* - ді́дові

Поет Сергій Жада́н подарува́в
Юрко́ві свою́ оста́нню книжку.

Займе́нники Pronouns

The dative forms of personal, possessive, and demonstrative
pronouns can be found in the appendices.

Прикме́тники Adjectives

The adjectival dative singular endings:
~ому (~ьому) and ~ій.

~ому is taken by masculine adjectives with a hard stem:
нови́й комп'ю́тер *a new computer* - завдяки́ ново́му комп'ю́теру
thanks to a new computer; до́брий друг *a good friend* - Мико́ла
пи́ше до́брому дру́гові. *Mykola writes to a good friend.*

~ьому is taken by masculine adjectives of a soft stem:
літній день *a summer day* - завдяки́ лі́тньому дню *thanks
to a summer day,* оста́нній студе́нт *the last student* - Він
ка́же це оста́нньому студе́нтові. *He says it to the last
student.*

~ій is taken by all feminine adjectives:
ціка́ва ді́вчина *an interesting girl* - Він пи́ше ціка́вій ді́вчині. *He's
writing to an interesting girl.* оста́ння студе́нтка *the last f. student* -
завдяки́ оста́нній студе́нтці *thanks to the last f. student.*

Take note. All adjectives have identical endings in the dative and
locative cases.

Note 9.2. Dative in Questions

Кому́ два́дцять ро́ків?
Who is twenty years old?
Скі́льки ро́ків Тара́сові?
How old is Taras?
Кому́ ти пи́шеш?
To whom do you write?
Які́й ді́вчині тре́ба квито́к?
What girl needs a ticket?

Note 9.3. Скі́льки тобі́ (*form.* вам) ро́ків? How Old Are You?

How old are you? in Ukrainian is
Скі́льки тобі́ (*form.* вам) ро́ків?
The logical subject (you) is in the dative.
How old were you? **Скі́льки тобі́ (*form.* вам) було́ ро́ків?** and
How old will you be? **Скі́льки тобі́ (*form.* вам) бу́де ро́ків?**

Take note. In Ukraine, it is considered impolite to ask a woman about her age.

Ніхто́ не мо́же сказа́ти, скі́льки ро́ків цій ха́ті.

Пита́ння про вік та відповіді на них
Questions about age and answers to them

Скі́льки мені́ ро́ків?	*How old am I?*
Мені́ два́дцять ро́ків.	*I am twenty.*
Скі́льки тобі́ ро́ків?	*How old are you? (fam.)*
Тобі́ двана́дцять ро́ків.	*(fam.) You are twelve.*
Скі́льки йому́ ро́ків?	*How old is he?*
Йому́ п'ять ро́ків.	*He is five.*
Скі́льки їй ро́ків?	*How old is she?*
Їй шість ро́ків.	*She is six.*
Скі́льки нам ро́ків?	*How old are we?*
Нам со́рок ро́ків.	*We are forty.*
Скі́льки вам ро́ків?	*How old are you? (form.)*
Вам п'ятде́сят ро́ків.	*(form.) You are fifty.*
Скі́льки їм ро́ків?	*How old are they?*
Їм вісімна́дцять ро́ків.	*They are eighteen.*

In such indications of age, the Ukrainian word **рік** *year* is obligatory, not optional as in English.
The same structure with the logical subject in the dative is used for many other common expressions. *What do you like to do (to eat, to drink, to see,* etc.) corresponds to the Ukrainian **Що тобі́ (вам) подо́бається роби́ти?**

Поря́дкові числі́вники   Ordinal Numerals

Ordinal numerals signify an object's position in a sequence and correlate with the questions **яки́й?** *what (kind of)?* **котри́й?** *which?*

Фу́нкція   Function

Ordinal numerals are used to indicate:
1) dates: **Сього́дні п'я́те кві́тня.** *Today is the fifth of April.* (For more on dates see Lesson 10, p. 180.)

2) time by the clock: **За́раз п'я́та годи́на.** *It is five o'clock now.* or **Конце́рт почина́ється о сьо́мій годи́ні.** *The concert starts at seven o'clock.* (For more see pp. 158-159.)

Утво́рення   Formation

Ordinal numeral endings:
sg. ~**ий** (~ій), ~**а** (~я), ~**е** (~є), and *pl.* ~**і**

Ordinal numerals are formed by adding the ending **~ий** to the respective cardinal numeral: **двана́дцять** *twelve* – **двана́дцятий** *twelfth*

Ordinal numerals "behave" like adjectives, i.e., they take the same case endings, and agree with the nouns they modify in gender, case, and number,

> *m.* **одина́дцятий день** *the eleventh day*
> *f.* **одина́дцята ніч** *the eleventh night*
> *nt.* **одина́дцяте се́ло** *the eleventh village*
> *pl.* **одина́дцяті две́рі** *the eleventh door*

All ordinal numerals with the exception of **тре́тій** *third*, have a hard stem:
> *f.* **тре́тя середа́ мі́сяця** *the third Wednesday of the month*
> *nt.* **со́рок тре́тє число́ журна́лу** *the forty-third issue of a magazine*, *pl.* **тре́ті лі́ки** *the third medicine*

На тре́тій день відпочи́нку дівча́та ви́рішили піти́ на пляж.

∩ **Поря́дкові числі́вники від пе́ршого до деся́того**
Ordinal numerals from first to tenth

cardinal	Eng.	ordinal m.	ordinal f.	ordinal nt.	ordinal pl.	Eng.
оди́н	one	пе́рший	пе́рша	пе́рше	пе́рші	first
два	two	дру́гий	дру́га	дру́ге	дру́гі	second
три	three	тре́тій	тре́тя	тре́тє	тре́ті	third
чоти́ри	four	четве́ртий	четве́рта	четве́рте	четве́рті	fourth
п'ять	five	п'я́тий	п'я́та	п'я́те	п'я́ті	fifth
шість	six	шо́стий	шо́ста	шо́сте	шо́сті	sixth
сім	seven	сьо́мий	сьо́ма	сьо́ме	сьо́мі	seventh
ві́сім	eight	во́сьмий	во́сьма	во́сьме	во́сьмі	eighth
де́в'ять	nine	дев'я́тий	дев'я́та	дев'я́те	дев'я́ті	ninth
де́сять	ten	деся́тий	деся́та	деся́те	деся́ті	tenth

Ordinal numerals from eleventh to nineteenth are formed in a regular way:
> *m.* **двана́дцятий**, *f.* **двана́дцята**, *nt.* **двана́дцяте**,
> *pl.* **двана́дцяті** *twelfth*

Take note. In composite numerals consisting of more than one word, such as **сто два́дцять де́в'ять** *one hundred and twenty-nine*, only the last word takes the form of the ordinal while the rest stays cardinal,

> **сто два́дцять дев'я́тий** *one hundred and twenty-ninth*
> **дві ти́сячі чотирна́дцятий рік** *the year twenty fourteen*

Likewise when such a composite ordinal numeral is declined, only its last word takes a respective case ending whereas the rest stays in the nominative singular:
> **Це для сто два́дцять дев'я́тої студе́нтки.** *This is for the one hundred and twenty-ninth female student.* (For more on the declension of composite ordinal numerals see Lesson 10, p. 180.)

У на́шому рестора́ні вам пропону́ють гаря́чі пе́рші та дру́гі стра́ви.

Украї́нський музе́й у Нью-Йо́рку розташо́ваний на Шо́стій ву́лиці, що на Мангете́ні.

Пе́рший авто́бус на Рафа́лівку відхо́дить об одина́дцятій ра́нку.

Поря́дкові числівники від одина́дцятого до дев'ятна́дцятого
Ordinal numerals from eleventh to nineteenth

cardinal	card. Eng.	ordinal m.	ordinal Eng.
одина́дцять	eleven	одина́дцятий	eleventh
двана́дцять	twelve	двана́дцятий	twelfth
трина́дцять	thirteen	трина́дцятий	thirteenth
чотирна́дцять	fourteen	чотирна́дцятий	fourteenth
п'ятна́дцять	fifteen	п'ятна́дцятий	fifteenth
шістна́дцять	sixteen	шістна́дцятий	sixteenth
сімна́дцять	seventeen	сімна́дцятий	seventeenth
вісімна́дцять	eighteen	вісімна́дцятий	eighteenth
дев'ятна́дцять	nineteen	дев'ятна́дцятий	nineteenth

Поря́дкові числівники від двадця́того до со́того
Ordinal numerals from twentieth to one hundredth

cardinal	card. Eng.	ordinal m.	ordinal Eng.
два́дцять	twenty	двадця́тий	twentieth
три́дцять	thirty	тридця́тий	thirtieth
со́рок	forty	сороко́вий	fortieth
п'ятдеся́т	fifty	п'ятдеся́тий	fiftieth
шістдеся́т	sixty	шістдеся́тий	sixtieth
сімдеся́т	seventy	сімдеся́тий	seventieth
вісімдеся́т	eighty	вісімдеся́тий	eightieth
дев'ятдеся́т	ninety	дев'ятдеся́тий	ninetieth
дев'яно́сто	ninety	дев'яно́стий	ninetieth
сто	one hundred	со́тий	one hundredth

The stress in the first ten ordinal numerals and those from *twentieth* to *ninetieth* is mobile. In ordinal numerals from *eleventh* to *nineteenth*, it is the same as in the respective cardinal numerals,

чотирна́дцять fourteen - **чотирна́дцятий** fourteenth.

Час за годи́нником   Time by the clock

The Ukrainian equivalent of *What time is it (now)?* is **Котра́ (за́раз) годи́на?** To indicate the exact hour of the day the construction with the feminine form of ordinal numeral is used:

> **За́раз** + **(є)** + *f. of ordinal numeral* + **годи́на.**

За́раз (є) пе́рша годи́на. *It's one o'clock now.*

The same construction in the past tense is: **Тоді́ була́ пе́рша годи́на.** *It was one o'clock then.* **Коли́ він дзвони́в, була́ тре́тя годи́на.** *When he called it was three o'clock.*

In the future tense, these sentences are: **Тоді́ бу́де пе́рша годи́на.** *It will be one o'clock then.* **Коли́ він бу́де дзвони́ти, бу́де тре́тя годи́на.** *When he will be calling it will be three o'clock.*

 Like all continental Europeans, Ukrainians use the 24-hour time frame. 1:00 AM in Ukrainian is **пе́рша годи́на** (*lit.* the first hour), 1:00 PM is **трина́дцята годи́на** (*lit.* the thirteenth hour) or, *colloq.* **пе́рша (годи́на) дня.** The adverb **рі́вно** is equivalent to the English *exactly* or *sharp*, and can either precede or follow the hour, **За́раз рі́вно пе́рша годи́на.** or **За́раз пе́рша годи́на рі́вно.** *It's exactly 1:00 AM now.*

To indicate the hour, the respective feminine ordinal numeral is used while the minutes are indicated by a cardinal numeral,

> **За́раз + (є) +** *f. of ordinal numeral* **+ годи́на +** *cardinal numeral* **+ хвили́н (хвили́ни** *or* **хвили́на)**

За́раз (є) пе́рша годи́на де́сять хвилин. *It's 1:10 AM now.*

Whereas the noun **годи́на** stays in the same case form in the statements of the type **За́раз пе́рша годи́на п'ять хвили́н.**, the case form of **хвили́на** *a minute* changes depending on the cardinal numeral it follows. Memorize these three forms:

N. sg. **хвили́на** is used after the numeral *f.* **одна́** *one*, and the composite cardinal numerals ending in **одна́:**
Була́ двадця́та годи́на два́дцять одна́ хвили́на. *It was 8:21 PM.*

N. pl. **хвили́ни** is used after the numerals *f.* **дві** *two*, **три** *three*, **чоти́ри** *four*, and the composite cardinal numerals ending in **дві**, **три**, and **чоти́ри**,
Була́ сьо́ма годи́на три́дцять чоти́ри хвили́ни. *It was 7:34 AM.*

G. pl. **хвили́н** is used after the rest of the cardinal numerals,
Коли́ він приї́хав, була́ дру́га годи́на оди́надцять хвили́н. *When he arrived it was 2:11 AM.*

The question *At what time ..?* is equivalent to the Ukrainian **О котрі́й годи́ні ...?** or its more colloquial variant **О котрі́й ...?:**
О котрі́й годи́ні прихо́дить по́тяг? *At what time does the train arrive?*
colloq. **О котрі́й поча́вся конце́рт?** *At what time did the concert begin?*

To indicate the time of an event, Ukrainians use the construction with the locative of time

> **о (об) +** *f. of ordinal numeral in L. sg.* **+ годи́ні +** *cardinal in N. sg.* **+ хвили́на (хвили́ни, хвили́ни)**

Літа́к прибува́є о пе́ршій годи́ні де́сять хвили́н. *The airplane arrives at 1:10 AM.*

О котрі́й годи́ні прихо́дить наш по́їзд?

 Note 9.4. Preposition об *at*

The preposition **об** *at* is used only before the numeral **одина́дцята** *eleventh*, **об одина́дцятій годи́ні** *at 11:00 AM.*

Note 9.5. Shorthand time indications

In casual speech, the nouns **годи́на** *an hour*, and **хвили́на** *a minute*, are omitted,
о пе́ршій три́дцять *at one thirty*, instead of a more formal **о пе́ршій годи́ні три́дцять хвили́н** *lit.* *at one hour thirty minutes.* When the number of minutes is fewer than ten and the noun **хвили́на** is omitted, the word **нуль** *zero* is used before the minute,
Ле́кція почала́ся о пе́ршій нуль п'ять. *The lecture started at 1:05 cf.*
Ле́кція почала́ся о пе́ршій годи́ні п'ять хвили́н.

Лука́ш подарува́в моло́дшому
брато́ві Яре́мі цуценя́ Оріо́на.

📖 Впра́ви Exercises

🎧 **9.1.** Answer the questions. Use the dative. Pay attention to the word order.

Model.
Q Кому́ дзво́нить Мико́ла? *Who does Mykola call?* ба́тько *father.*
A Мико́ла дзво́нить ба́тькові. *Mykola calls his father.*

1. Кому́ пи́ше лист О́льга? по́друга
2. Кому́ купу́є штани́ Марі́я? Мико́ла Прихо́дько
3. Кому́ замовля́є готе́ль Степа́н? ба́тько
4. Кому́ вони́ допомага́ють? Ната́лка та Тара́с
5. Кому́ вона́ посила́є гро́ші? ма́ти
6. Кому́ ви дає́те хліб? Іва́н Пінчу́к
7. Кому́ вони́ дару́ють кві́ти? О́льга
8. Кому́ ми пока́зуємо мі́сто? гість
9. Кому́ ти розказа́в істо́рію? друг
10. Кому́ пла́тить тури́ст? каси́р

🎧 **9.2.** Revisit the previous exercise and replace all nouns with pronouns.

Model.
Q Мико́ла дзво́нить ба́тькові? *Does Mykola call his father?*
A Так, він дзво́нить йому́. *Yes, he calls him.*

🎧 **9.3.** Give short answers to the questions. Put the adjectives or pronouns in the dative.

Model.
Q Яко́му дру́гові дзво́нить Мико́ла? *What friend does Mykola call?* близьки́й. *close*
A Близько́му. *A close one.*

1. Яко́му студе́нтові профе́сор ка́же це? оста́нній
2. Які́й ді́вчині ти подо́баєшся? та га́рна
3. Які́й дити́ні лише́ оди́н рік? ця мала́
4. Чиє́му брато́ві тре́ба працюва́ти? їхній
5. Чиї́й ті́тці ми допомага́ємо? ва́ша
6. Яко́му чолові́кові ти не ві́риш? незнайо́мий
7. Які́й тури́стці тре́ба поясни́ти це? америка́нська
8. Яко́му робітнико́ві він дає́ інформа́цію? тре́тій

🎧 **9.4.** Listen to the cue and combine the required form of the noun **рік** *a year* with the numeral. Check yourself against the speaker.

Model. 1 - оди́н рік.

1. 12	4. 42	7. 213	10. 30	13. 53	16. 11
2. 104	5. 10	8. 94	11. 50	14. 414	17. 81
3. 24	6. 29	9. 222	12. 561	15. 77	18. 112

∩ 9.5. Write down and say these indications of age. Use the dative of the logical subject.

Model: **C** я *I*, дев'ятна́дцять *nineteen*
A Мені́ дев'ятна́дцять ро́ків. *I am nineteen years old.*

1. ти, де́в'ять
2. ми, чотирна́дцять
3. я, со́рок ві́сім
4. ви, п'ятдеся́т шість
5. їхній син, одина́дцять
6. цей поля́к, два́дцять два

7. він, чоти́ри
8. вона́, два́дцять п'ять
9. вони́, сім
10. ва́ша дочка́, два
11. моя́ по́друга, три́дцять
12. ва́ша ма́ти, шістдеся́т

Цій весе́лій школя́рці лише́ де́в'ять ро́ків.

🌐 **Завда́ння для Міжнаро́дної мере́жі**
Украї́нська Вікіпе́дія
Internet assignment Ukrainian Wikipedia

9.6. Use the Ukrainian Wikipedia to find and write in Ukrainian the answers to these questions.

Скі́льки ро́ків:

письме́нникові
Ю́рію Андрухо́вичу?

компози́торові
Мирosла́вові Ско́рику?

чемпіо́нці
Га́нні Ушені́новій?

поетові
Сергі́ю Жада́нові?

співа́чці
Русла́ні Лижичко́?

музика́нтові
Святосла́ву Вакарчуко́ві?

📅 **Note 9.6. Вік люди́ни**
Person's age

The word **рік** *year*, has three forms depending on the numeral it follows:
1) **рік** after the numeral **оди́н** *one* and those ending in **оди́н, оди́н рік** *one year*, **сто оди́н рік** *a hundred and one years*;
2) **ро́ки**, used after the numerals **два** *two*, **три** *three*, **чоти́ри** *four* and those that end in them, **два, три, чоти́ри ро́ки** *two, three, four years*, **со́рок два ро́ки** *forty-two years*
3) **ро́ків**, used after the numerals **п'ять** *five*, **шість** *six*, etc., as well as after **бага́то** *many*, **скі́льки** *how many*, **кі́лька** *several*, **п'ять, шість, сімна́дцять ро́ків.** *five, six, seventeen years*, **скі́льки ро́ків** *how many years*

What counts here is not the number you see, but the number you hear. You see the number 1 at the end of both 11 and 21, but you hear it only in *twenty-one* **два́дцять оди́н** and not in *eleven* **одина́дцять**. Therefore the numeral **одина́дцять** *eleven* is followed by **ро́ків** (not **рік**), similarly **двана́дцять** *twelve*, **трина́дцять** *thirteen*, and **чотирна́дцять** *fourteen* require the form **ро́ків** (not **ро́ки**).
For more see Note 3.17, p. 38, Lesson 11, p. 202, and Lesson 12, p. 223.

Note 9.7. Verbs with object in dative

дава́ти; да́ти щось кому́сь?
to give sth to sb (not as a present)

дарува́ти; подарува́ти щось кому́сь?
to give sth to sb (as a present)

(до)помага́ти; (до)помогти́ кому́сь?
to help sb

купува́ти; купи́ти щось кому́сь?
to buy sth to sb

пока́зувати; показа́ти щось кому́сь?
to show sth to sb

посила́ти; посла́ти щось кому́сь?
to send sth to sb

поя́снювати; поясни́ти щось кому́сь?
to explain sth to sb

ра́дити; пора́дити щось *(or inf.)* кому́? *to advise sth to sb*

Мирosла́ві Хмельни́цькій тре́ба потра́пити на залізни́чний вокза́л.

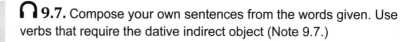

9.7. Compose your own sentences from the words given. Use verbs that require the dative indirect object (Note 9.7.)

1. Дани́ло, дава́ти пора́ди, дочка́
2. ви, пока́зувати Ки́їв, ко́жний гість
3. вчи́тель, поя́снювати, нова́ студе́нтка, текст
4. дя́дько, посила́ти, гро́ші, син
5. марко́, купува́ти, кни́жка, Мари́на
6. ми, допомага́ти, ця приє́мна кана́дка
7. тре́ба подарува́ти, украї́нський фільм, Богда́н Міщенко
8. лі́кар, ра́дити, мій хво́рий брат, поі́хати до Кри́му

9.8. Express uncertainty. Use the construction *Logical Subject in D.* + здава́тися *to seem.*

Model. 🅲 Я не впе́внений, що це на́ша ву́лиця. *I am not sure it is our street.*
🅰 Мені́ здає́ться, (що) це на́ша ву́лиця. *It seems to me that this is our street.*

1. Ми не впе́внені, що це так.
2. Ї́хня ма́ти не впе́внена, що вони́ вдо́ма.
3. Вони́ не впе́внені, що сього́дні конце́рт.
4. Її́ знайо́мий америка́нець не впе́внений, що він зна́є це мі́сто.
5. Ти не впе́внена, що Мико́ла з Ки́єва.
6. Ви не впе́внені, що це слу́шна іде́я *(good idea).*
7. Вона́ не впе́внена, що Рома́н гово́рить англі́йською мо́вою.

9.9. Express necessity. Use the construction *Logical Subject in D.* + тре́ба *to have (to do).* Note that the perfective infinitive is used to signify an action that needs to be completed.

Model. 🅲 я *I,* зроби́ти це *to do this*
🅰 Мені́ тре́ба зроби́ти це. *I need to do this.*

1. твоя́ сестра́, піти́ до лі́каря
2. її́ моло́дший брат, подзвони́ти до університе́ту
3. на́ша ма́ма, купи́ти проду́кти
4. ми, написа́ти спи́сок
5. ї́хній друг, посла́ти їм ві́дповідь
6. цей пан, знайти́ хоро́ший готе́ль
7. ва́ша виклада́чка, поясни́ти нам цей текст
8. той води́й, відпочи́ти

9.10. Form a statement that answers each of the questions.

Model.
🆀 Кому́ тре́ба спа́ти? *Who needs to sleep?* мали́й Мико́ла *little Mykola*
🅰 Мало́му Мико́лі тре́ба спа́ти. *Little Mykola needs to sleep.*

1. Кому́ здає́ться, що сього́дні неді́ля? моя́ ті́тка Стефа́нія
2. Кому́ два́дцять ро́ків? твій ста́рший брат
3. Кому́ подо́бається бага́то чита́ти? на́ша нова́ студе́нтка
4. Кому́ Марі́я ча́сто пи́ше? дя́дько Оле́г
5. Кому́ ми ма́ємо купи́ти подару́нок? їхня молодша сестра́
6. Кому́ Надія поя́снює завда́ння? украї́нець Макси́м Петре́нко

 Хто кому́ подо́бається? *Who likes whom?*

Здає́ться, що Богда́нові подо́бається Роксоля́на.

9.11. Write sentences indicating that one person likes the other.

Model.
C Павло́ *Pavlo*, Ната́ля *Natalia*
A Павло́ подо́бається Ната́лі. *Natalia likes Pavlo. (lit. Pavlo is pleasing to Natalia).*

1. Рома́н, О́льга
2. Стефа́нія, Мико́ла
3. ця украї́нка, та америка́нка
4. Петро́, Катери́на
5. наш друг, цей америка́нець
6. ваш при́ятель, їхня дочка́

9.12. React to the cue. Express a polite desire contrary to the given advice. Use the imperfective infinitive in the negative advice vs the perfective infinitive in the expression of desire.

Model.
C Не тре́ба (не слід) купува́ти ціє́ї соро́чки.
One shouldn't buy this shirt. він *he*
A А він навпаки́ хоті́в би її́ купи́ти.
And he would like to buy it nevertheless.

1. Не тре́ба чита́ти ціє́ї статті́. ми
2. Не слід дя́кувати за допомо́гу. я
3. Не тре́ба дзвони́ти до них так пі́зно. О́льга
4. Не слід писа́ти тако́го листа́. вони́
5. Не тре́ба продава́ти цього́ щеня́ти. Рома́н
6. Не слід купува́ти квитка́ так ра́но. наш знайо́мий
7. Не тре́ба домовля́тися про зу́стріч без Тетя́ни. Ігор і Кили́на
8. Не слід чека́ти його́ пора́ди. вони́
9. Не тре́ба запро́шувати Оле́га на вече́рю. Марі́чка
10. Не слід диви́тися цього́ фі́льму. на́ші ді́ти
11. Не тре́ба почина́ти нової́ спра́ви сього́дні. ми
12. Не слід зверта́тися до цього́ фахівця́. Михайло та Стефа́нія

9.13. Provide a respective ordinal numeral for each cardinal numeral. Then combine the ordinal numeral with the noun. Make sure that both agree in gender.

 Note 9.8. Як ви́словити бажа́ння How to express desire

Polite desire is expressed by **я хоті́в би** + *pf. inf.*, which is the equivalent of the English *I'd like* + *inf.* This is the conditional mood of the verb **хоті́ти** *to want* (more in Lesson 15, pp. 297-300).

Memorize identical expressions of polite desire for other persons:
m. **він (я, ти) хоті́в би** + *pf. inf.* he (I, you, sg.) would like:
Мико́ла хоті́в би прийти́. *Mykola would like to come.*
f. **вона́ (я, ти) хоті́ла б** + *pf. inf.* she (I, sg. you) would like:
Ната́ля хоті́ла б допомогти́. *Natalia would like to help.*
pl. **ми (ви, вони́) хоті́ли б** + *pf. inf.* we (pl. you, they) would like:
Дівча́та хоті́ли б трохи відпочи́ти. *The girls would like to rest a little.*

Model. **C** оди́н *one,* студе́нтка *f. student*
A пе́рша студе́нтка *the first f. student*

1. двана́дцять, *f.* ніч
2. два́дцять, *f.* ле́кція
3. чоти́ри, *nt.* а́вто
4. ві́сім, *f.* субо́та
5. сім, *m.* раз

6. три, *nt.* я́блуко
7. три́дцять шість, *m.* кіломе́т(е)р
8. сто, *m.* день
9. со́рок, *nt.* число́
10. сто два́дцять п'ять, *f.* ву́лиця

9.14. Answer the questions. Indicate the exact hour of the day. Make a note for yourself of the corresponding hour in the U.S. 12-hour frame.

Model. **Q** Котра́ за́раз годи́на? *What's the time now?* 13:00 (1:00 PM)
A За́раз трина́дцята годи́на рі́вно. *It's 1:00 PM sharp now.*

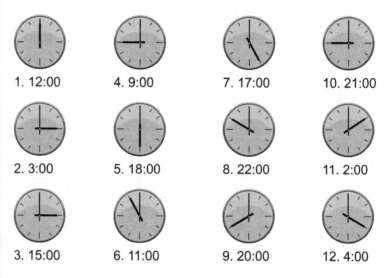

1. 12:00
4. 9:00
7. 17:00
10. 21:00

2. 3:00
5. 18:00
8. 22:00
11. 2:00

3. 15:00
6. 11:00
9. 20:00
12. 4:00

9.15. Answer the questions. Indicate the exact hour and minute. In casual speech, the words **годи́на** and **хвили́на** are often omitted. Determine the corresponding hour in the U.S. 12-hour scale.

Model.
Q Котра́ за́раз годи́на? *What's the time now?* 13:25 | *1:25 PM*
A За́раз трина́дцята годи́на два́дцять п'ять хвили́н.
It is 1:25 PM now. or За́раз трина́дцята два́дцять п'ять.

1. 1:10
2. 14:22
3. 5:19

4. 23:08
5. 18:43
6. 19:56

7. 10:15
8. 6:55
9. 8:02

10. 7:31
11. 16:17
12. 4:41

У Ки́єві за́раз п'ятна́дцята годи́на три хвили́ни.

∩ **9.16.** Engage a partner in a Q-and-A. Indicate the time of the event in the 24-hour time frame.

Model.

C Тара́с Taras, сні́дати *to have breakfast*, 8:15
Q О котрі́й сні́дає Тара́с? *At what time does Taras have breakfast?*
A О во́сьмій п'ятна́дцять. *At 8:15 AM.*

1. програ́ма, почина́тися, 19:30
2. конце́рт, закі́нчуватися, 22:20
3. мандрівники́, вече́ряти, 18:00
4. по́други, зустріча́тися, 11:45
5. магази́н, відкрива́тися, 9:15
6. Марі́я і Васи́ль, гра́ти у те́ніс, 15:50
7. по́тяг, прихо́дити, 7:37
8. ва́ші знайо́мі, ляга́ти спа́ти, 12:05
9. авто́бус, відхо́дити, 10:17
10. її консульта́нт, дзвони́ти до те́бе, 16:15

Бу́дній день vs вихідни́й   Weekday vs day off

9.17. Describe what you do on:
1) **типо́вий бу́дній день** *a typical weekday*
2) **типо́вий вихі́дний** *a typical day off*
Use the prompts below. Indicate the exact time (hour and minutes) at which you do these things. If your activity lasts for a period of time, use:

> **від** + *G.* of hour, *N.* of minute **до** + *G.* of hour, *N.* of minute

від дев'я́тої три́дцять до пе́ршої со́рок п'ять *from 9:30 to 1:45.*

прокида́тися; проки́нутися *to wake up*
збира́тися; зібра́тися на робо́ту (до університе́ту / шко́ли)
to get ready for work (university / school)
сні́дати; по~ *to have breakfast*
чита́ти; по~ і відповіда́ти; відповісти́ на листи́ *to read and answer the mail (letters)*
обі́дати; по~ *to have lunch*
йти; піти́ до спортклу́бу (до теа́тру, кіна́, па́рку, на прогу́лянку)
to go to a fitness club (theater, cinema, park, for a walk)
вече́ряти; по~ *to have dinner*
купува́ти; купи́ти проду́кти *to buy groceries*
працюва́ти; по~ у бібліоте́ці *to work in the library*
сиді́ти; по~ в мере́жі *to spend time (lit. to sit) on the Internet*
захо́дити; зайти́ до прия́теля / f. прия́тельки на ка́ву (розмо́ву, вече́рю) *to drop by a friend's place for coffee (chat, dinner)*
диви́тися; по~ телеви́ни *to watch news on TV*
роби́ти; з~ дома́шнє завда́ння *to do homework*
дзвони́ти; по~ до дру́га (по́други) *to call a friend (f. friend)*

О сьо́мій Мо́тря прокида́ється і одра́зу збира́ється до шко́ли.

У рестора́ні "Пуза́та ха́та" - украї́нські стра́ви на ко́жен смак.

Украї́нці лю́блять ї́сти сма́чно, бага́то та роби́ти це у га́рному товари́стві.

9.18. Say and write the sentences in Ukrainian. Use the vocabulary and grammar of this and previous lessons. If necessary, consult the dictionary.

1. What groceries can one buy in this grocery store?
2. Mr. Petrenko liked the new apartment very much.
3. Natalia needs to call the doctor immediately.
4. We are not sure that this is the street where Mykola lives.
5. Where can one find bread, butter, and jam here?
6. Can you show my brother where fresh fruit and vegetables are?
7. It seems to Oksana that today their friends want to have dinner at the restaurant.
8. One can pay for the products at the cash register.
9. Dear friends, it's time to call Maria and tell her about this invitation to the concert.
10. All groceries are exactly 250 hryvnias.
11. At what time does the train arrive and what time is it now?
12. They ask when I can show Kyiv to our American guest.
13. How old is this little boy?
14. We are going to meet at the post office at 1:30 PM.

9.19. Read the note on Ukrainian national cuisine below. Write out in Ukrainian the names of all the dishes and their ingredients. Using the Internet, classify the dishes by the following categories:

1. інґредіє́нти *ingredients*
2. заку́ски *appetizers*
3. пе́рші стра́ви *first courses*
4. дру́гі стра́ви *second courses*
5. десе́рт чи соло́дкі стра́ви *desserts or sweet dishes*
6. напої́ *drinks*

Украї́нська націона́льна ку́хня
Ukrainian National Cuisine

Food is an object of worship for Ukrainians. They like to eat well, a lot, and in congenial company. The absolute king of all Ukrainian dishes is **борщ** *borshch*. Its dictionary description as a *beet-and-cabbage soup* does not even hint at its rich bouquet of flavors. It is often said that there are as many borshches as there are cooks, but there can be no borshch without **буря́к** *beet*, **капу́ста** *cabbage*, **мо́рква** *carrot*, and **помідо́р** *tomato*. Optional ingredients include **квасо́ля** *beans*, **селе́ра** *celery*, **карто́пля** *potato*, **цибу́ля** *onion*, and even **чорносли́в** *prunes*, **я́блука** *apples*, and **гриби́** *mushrooms*. A good borshch is deep red in color and a bit sour with its vegetables crunchy. It is traditionally based on a meat broth (pork, chicken or veal), but can also be vegetarian. Borshch is served hot with a dollop of **смета́на** *sour cream*, **часни́к** *garlic*, and **кріп** *dill* – all fresh. It is often eaten with **пампушки́** *pampushkas*, freshly baked yeast-dough rolls bathed in a mixture of chopped garlic and **шкварки́** *fried bacon*. Another popular Ukrainian dish is **зеле́ний борщ** *green borshch*, a.k.a. **щавле́вий борщ** *sorrel soup*.

Serious contenders for the title of the second most popular Ukrainian dish are **варе́ники** *varenyks* and **голубці́** *holubtsi*. *Varenyks*, in Galicia also known as **пироги́** *pyrohy*, are dumplings made of unleavened dough and stuffed with **сир** *cottage cheese*, a mixture of **сир і карто́пля** *cheese and mashed potatoes*, **капу́ста** *fried cabbage*, or **ви́шні** *cherries*, **я́блука** *apples*, **полуни́ці** *strawberries*, or **чорни́ці** *blueberries*.

Holubtsi are cabbage rolls whose stuffing traditionally includes minced pork meat mixed with **рис** *rice* (sometimes **гре́чка** *buckwheat*), and fried chopped carrots and onions. The *holubtsi* are either boiled on a stove-top or stewed in an oven in tomato sauce. There are also meatless varieties of *holubtsi*. All are served either with fresh sour cream or a mushroom sauce.

There are dozens of other Ukrainian culinary dishes whose popularity is often limited to a particular region or a social group, such as **кулі́ш** *kulish*, **капусня́к** *kapusniak*, **деруни́** *deruns*, **галушки́** *halushkas*, **калгані́вка** *kalhanivka*, **студене́ць** *studenets*, **картопля́ники** *kartoplianyks*, **ки́шка** *kyshka*, **кисі́ль** *kysil*, **нали́сники** *nalysnyks*, **куле́ша** *kulesha*, **кров'я́нка** *krov'ianka*, **ма́цьок** *matsiok*, **кне́длі** *knedli*, **ба́бка** *babka*, **кола́чі** *kolaches*, **маківни́к** *makivnyk*, **пля́цок** *pliatsok*, **узва́р** *uzvar*, or **кутя́** *kutia*. Detailed descriptions of most of them can be found on the Internet.

А на заку́ску мо́жемо запропонува́ти вам ... сало-су́ші!

There is one component of the traditional Ukrainian cuisine that is unrivaled by any other, not even *borshch*, *varenyks*, or *holubtsi*. It defies description and comprehension by foreigners. That component is **са́ло** *pork fat*. **Са́ло** has become something of a cult among Ukrainians, involving beliefs, anecdotes, musical folklore, and even yearly festivals held all around the country. Ukrainians may have their share of differences about politics, history, or religion, but they are genuinely united by their love for **са́ло**. They consume it in all imaginable forms – fresh, salted, fried, baked, boiled, smoked, cured, and minced. It is always accompanied by bread and fresh garlic, onion, or pickled vegetables. It is seriously rumored that there is even a dessert variety of this beloved treat – **са́ло в шокола́ді** *salo coated in chocolate*. **Са́ло** is widely believed to have healing properties, particularly for those with high cholesterol (wink). Healthy or not, **са́ло** is certainly the number one Ukrainian comfort food.

На пе́ршу пода́йте мої́й по́друзі ку́рячу ю́шку, будь ла́ска, а мені́ - черво́ний борщ.

Як замо́вити ї́жу в рестора́ні
How to order food in a restaurant

🎧 **9.20.** Memorize these expressions and use them to order food in a Ukrainian restaurant.

меню́, *nt.* (дитя́че, веґетарія́нське, пісне́)	a menu (children's, vegetarian, meatless)
заку́ска, *f.* (на + *A.*) на заку́ску	appetizer, for appetizer
стра́ва, *f.* (м'ясна́, веґетарія́нська)	a dish, a course (meat, vegetarian)
пе́рша стра́ва (на + *A.*), на пе́ршу (стра́ву)	first course, for the first course
дру́га стра́ва (на + *A.*), на дру́гу стра́ву	second course, for the second course
гарні́р, *m.*, ~у (на + *A.*), на гарні́р	side dish, as a side dish
десе́рт, *m.*, ~у (на + *A.*), на десе́рт	dessert, for dessert
замовля́ти; замо́вити + *A.* (стра́ву, заку́ску, напі́й)	to order (a dish, hors-d'oeuvre, drink)
подава́ти; пода́ти + *A.* (стра́ву і т.д.)	to serve (a dish, etc.)
раху́нок, *m.*, ~у, принесі́ть раху́нок, будь ла́ска!	a check, *im.* bring the check, please!
плати́ти; заплати́ти + *A.*, раху́нок; п. за + *A.* (обі́д, вече́рю, вино́)	to pay the check; pay for (lunch, dinner, wine)

🎧 **9.21.** Listen carefully to the dialogue and answer the questions.

1. Яки́й стіл тре́ба клі́єнтові?
2. Які́ напої́ замовля́є клі́єнт?
3. Що він замовля́є на пе́ршу стра́ву?
4. Про що забу́в клі́єнт?
5. Кому́ він замо́вив на десе́рт ка́ву-еспре́со?

«У рестора́ні». At the Restaurant.

Клі́єнт. Будь ла́ска, стіл на дві осо́би.

Офіція́нт. Звича́йно. Вас влашто́вує ось цей біля вікна́?

Клі́єнт. Так, дя́кую. Біля вікна́ бу́де до́бре. Що тут пропону́ють у меню́?

Офіція́нт. Ось – заку́ски, пе́рші, дру́гі стра́ви та десе́рт. А ось напої́: безалкого́льні й алкого́ль.

Клі́єнт. Для поча́тку про́шу принести́ мені́ пля́шку мінера́льної води́. Мої́й по́друзі – пля́шку пи́ва «Черні́гівське».

Офіція́нт. До́бре. За хвили́ну.

Клі́єнт. На пе́ршу стра́ву – два борщі́. На дру́гу – шашли́к для моє́ї по́други і голубці́ для ме́не.

Офіція́нт. Яки́й гарні́р до шашли́ка?

Клі́єнт. Рис, будь ла́ска. До ре́чі, я забу́в про заку́ски. На заку́ску два сала́ти із капу́сти.

Офіція́нт. А десе́рт? Що ви хоті́ли б на десе́рт?

Клíєнт. На десе́рт, про́шу пода́ти мені́ - чо́рний чай, а їй — ка́ву-еспре́со. Це все. Дя́кую.

Офіція́нт. Пре́красно! Ва́ша вече́ря бу́де гото́ва за хвили́ну.

У Льво́ві ко́жен рестора́н особли́вий, і в ко́жному особли́ва ку́хня.

9.22. Order a Ukrainian dinner from the menu for four people. Use the dialogue in the previous exercise.

З 8:00 до 11:30 ранку!

Завітайте на сніданок,
Буде добрим кожен ранок!

Сирники із сметаною...	11,00 грн
Омлет з начинкою........	8,50 грн
Запіканка сирна.............	9,50 грн
Каша вівсяна.................	6,50 грн
Яєшня............................	6,50 грн
Деруни із сметаною......	7,00 грн

ТИПО́ВЕ МЕНЮ́
TYPICAL MENU

• Заку́ски •

асортí з горо́дини	*assorted vegetables*
ри́бне асортí	*assorted cold fish*
м'ясне́ асортí	*assorted cold cuts*
сала́т	*salad*

• Пе́рші стра́ви •

черво́ний борщ	*red borshch*
зеле́ний борщ	*green (sorrel) borshch*
капусня́к	*sauerkraut soup*
ку́ряча ю́шка	*chicken soup*
уха́	*fish soup*

Варе́ники – це дру́га стра́ва,
що особли́во популя́рна по всій
Украї́ні.

• Дру́гі стра́ви •

голубці́	cabbage rolls
варе́ники, *Gal.* пироги́	pierogi (dumplings)
деруни́	potato pancakes
шашли́к	shish kebab (of pork, veal or lamb)
котле́та по-ки́ївськи	chicken Kyiv
дома́шня ковбаса́	homemade sausage

• Гарні́ри •

сма́жена карто́пля	fried potatoes
карто́пля-фрі	French fries
товкани́ця or карtopля́не п'юре́	mashed potatoes
рис	rice
греча́на ка́ша	boiled buckwheat
о́вочі	vegetables
макаро́ни	pasta

• Десе́рт •

ті́стечко	a cake
торт	a tart
рога́лик	a croissant
пе́чиво	cookie
моро́зиво	ice-cream
фрукто́вий сала́т	fruit salad

• Напо́ї •

Безалкого́льні

чай	tea
ка́ва	coffee
вода́: мінера́льна, газо́вана, негазо́вана, джере́льна	water: mineral, carbonated, non-carbonated, spring
сік	juice

Алкого́льні

пи́во: пляшко́ве́, бочкове́	beer: bottle, on tap
вино́: бі́ле, черво́не, десе́ртне, шампа́нське	wine: white, red, dessert, sparkling
мiцні́ напо́ї: горі́лка, конья́к, бре́нді, ві́скі, джин	strong drinks: vodka, cognac, brandy, whisky, gin

9.23. Listen carefully to these questions and answer each of them using Dialogue 9.

1. Що тре́ба зроби́ти Ма́рті та Мико́лі?
2. Куди́ вони́ ду́мають іти́?
3. Як ча́сто і в яки́й день ти́жня вони́ купу́ють проду́кти?
4. Чому́ Мико́ла пропону́є Ма́рті почека́ти до субо́ти?
5. У які́й ситуа́ції кра́ще ї́сти у рестора́ні?
6. Що ма́є охо́ту зроби́ти сього́дні Ма́рта?
7. Яке́ меню́ на вече́рю пропону́є Мико́ла?
8. Про що вони́ домо́вилися?
9. У які́й підли́ві ма́є бу́ти інди́чка?
10. Які́ мо́жуть бу́ти гарні́ри в украї́нській ку́хні?
11. Які́ проду́кти ду́мають купи́ти Ма́рта й Мико́ла?
12. Що забу́ли написа́ти до спи́ску молоді́ лю́ди?
13. Які́ проду́кти за́вжди купу́єте ви?
14. Які́ проду́кти ви купу́єте рі́дко?

Мо́вні ресу́рси на мере́жі. Сино́німи
Language resources on the web. Synonyms

9.24. Find synonyms of the words below. Visit the website **Словники Украї́ни on-line**: http://lcorp.ulif.org.ua/dictua Type into its search window on the left each of the words and click. On the new screen, click **Синоні́мія** (synonyms).

украї́нська	англі́йська	сино́німи
страва		
варити		
городина		
вихідний		
будній		
навчатися		

Хо́чете покуштува́ти
на́шу нову́ стра́ву?

9.25. Enact a conversation with a partner. Use the material you have learned so far. If necessary, consult the dictionary.

Сце́нка за сцена́рієм «До суперма́ркету по проду́кти»
Scripted skit: *Buying Groceries in a Supermarket*

Kyrylo (Кири́ло) Addresses Hanna by phone. Says that he is planning to go to the supermarket. Asks whether she wants to go too.
Hanna (Га́нна): Asks whether he is planning to go today.

Kyrylo: Affirmative. Not sure exactly at what time. He has some work to do.
Hanna: Where exactly would he like to buy his groceries? Maybe at the local supermarket «Вели́ка кише́ня» *(A Big Pocket)*?

Kyrylo: Affirmative. There, he can find everything he needs and for a good price.
Hanna: The «Вели́ка кише́ня» opens at 8:00 AM and closes at 10:00 PM.

Kyrylo: Asks about the time at the moment, and answers himself that it is 3:00 PM.
Hanna: She'll be ready to go shopping at about 5:00 PM if that is OK.

Kyrylo: No problem. 5:00 PM is good for him. Suggests meeting near the entrance to the supermarket.
Hanna: Agrees. Asks whether Kyrylo remembers if one can buy fresh fish there.

Kyrylo: He does not remember, but has an ad (рекламі́вка) from the supermarket.
Hanna: Realizes that she has it too, right near the phone. Opens it and looks for the department «Дари́ мо́ря» *(Gifts of the Sea)*.

Kyrylo: He already found it. Reads «fresh fish, frozen fish». Says that they offer a good selection of fresh fish.
Hanna: Asks what specifically Kyrylo needs to buy.

Kyrylo: Practically everything, because his refrigerator is empty.
Hanna: Advises to write a list of groceries (спи́сок проду́ктів), otherwise (іна́кше) he'll have to go shopping again.

Kyrylo: He never has a list of groceries because he needs only bread, milk, cottage cheese, coffee, some ham, jam, and eggs.
Hanna: Doesn't he need vegetables too, such for example as tomatoes, cucumbers, onion? He already forgot things he needs.

Kyrylo: Says, Hanna is right and he intends to write up the list. Bids good-bye till 5:00 PM.
Anna: Confirms and adds at 5:00 PM near the entrance to the supermarket.

Ле́кція | Lesson 10

Dialogue:
Квитки́ на по́тяг до Севасто́поля
Train Tickets to Sevastopol

Grammar:
Instrumental singular
Imperfective synthetic future tense

Competencies:
Professions
Months and dates
Buying train, bus, or plane tickets
Transportation schedules
Speaking over the phone

Цим по́тягом Марі́я Новачу́к ї́здить у село́ Гли́нськ до свого́ бра́та Оле́кси.

🗨 10. Діяло́г. Квитки́ на по́тяг до Севасто́поля.

Мандрівни́к: Будь ла́ска, два квитки́ до Севасто́поля на цю се́реду.

Каси́р: Ця середа́ – це яке́ число́? Тре́тє чи четве́рте?

Мандрівни́к: Якщо́ не помиля́юся, це ма́є бу́ти тре́тє ли́пня.

Каси́р: Так, ді́йсно. Квитки́ на яки́й по́тяг ви хоті́ли б: ранко́вий, де́нний чи вечі́рній?

Мандрівни́к: Я не впе́внений, але́ ми з жі́нкою хоті́ли б приї́хати до Севасто́поля вра́нці насту́пного дня.

Каси́р: То́бто у четве́р, четве́ртого ли́пня. Зна́чить вам тре́ба ї́хати де́нним по́тягом.

Мандрівни́к: Тоді́ два купе́йні квитки́ на де́нний по́тяг на тре́тє, будь ла́ска.

Каси́р: Це кошту́ватиме вам дві́сті де́сять гри́вень за квито́к. Ра́зом чоти́риста два́дцять гри́вень.

Мандрівни́к: Ні, ні. Це на́дто до́рого. Мо́же є плацка́ртні місця́?

Каси́р: За́раз, хвили́нку. Тре́ба подиви́тися. Ні, на цей по́тяг всі плацка́ртні квитки́ прода́ли.

Мандрівни́к: А на і́нший по́тяг? Ма́є бу́ти прина́ймні ще два по́тяги до Севасто́поля.

Каси́р: Так, є плацка́ртні квитки́ на по́тяг но́мер со́рок о во́сьмій два́дцять п'ять. Сто два́дцять гри́вень за квито́к.

Мандрівни́к: Це зо́всім і́нша спра́ва. А коли́ цей по́тяг прихо́дить до Севасто́поля?

Каси́р: Об одина́дцятій нуль п'ять ра́нку четве́ртого ли́пня. Бере́те?

Мандрівни́к: Це те, що тре́ба! Беремо́!

Каси́р: Ва́ші місця́ но́мер дев'ятна́дцять та два́дцять, шо́стий ваго́н, но́мер по́тяга – со́рок.

Мандрівни́к: Чи мо́жна заплати́ти креди́тною ка́рткою?

Каси́р: На жаль, ні. Лише́ готі́вкою.

Мандрівни́к: Ось про́шу: дві́сті со́рок гри́вень за два квитки́ у плацка́ртному ваго́ні.

Каси́р: Дя́кую. А ось ва́ші квитки́. Щасли́вої вам доро́ги.

Нам тре́ба бу́ти в Маріу́полі за́втра о деся́тій ра́нку.

🗨 10. Dialogue. Train Tickets to Sevastopol.

Traveler: Two tickets to Sevastopol, for this Wednesday, please.

Ticket seller: This Wednesday, what date is it? The third or the fourth?

Traveler: If I am not mistaken, it's supposed to be July 3.

Ticket seller: Yes, indeed. Tickets for which train would you like: the morning, afternoon or evening one?

Traveler: I am not sure, but my wife and I would like to arrive in Sevastopol next day in the morning.

Ticket seller: That is to say, on Thursday, July 4. Then you should go by the afternoon train.

Traveler: Then two second-class tickets for the afternoon train of the third (of July), please.

Ticket seller:	This will cost you two hundred and ten hryvnias a ticket. All together four hundred and twenty hryvnias.
Traveler:	No, no. It's too expensive. Perhaps there are third-class seats?
Ticket seller:	Just a moment. I need to take a look. No, all third-class tickets for this train have been sold out.
Traveler:	How about a different train? There has to be at least two more trains to Sevastopol.
Ticket seller:	Yes, there are third-class tickets for train number forty at eight twenty-five. A hundred and twenty hryvnias a ticket.
Traveler:	That's an entirely different matter. And when does this train arrive in Sevastopol?
Ticket seller:	At 11:05 AM on July 4. Do you want them?
Traveler:	That's what we need! We'll take them!
Ticket seller:	Your seat numbers are nineteen and twenty, car number six. The train number is forty.
Traveler:	Can I pay by a credit card?
Ticket seller:	Unfortunately, you can't. Only in cash.
Traveler:	Here you are. Two hundred and forty hryvnias for two tickets in a third-class train car.
Ticket seller:	Thank you. And here are your tickets. Have a great trip.

Тут мо́жна купи́ти квитки́ ті́льки на по́їзд чи на літа́к і авто́бус теж?

✏ Нота́тки до діало́гу Notes on the Dialogue

по́тяг, *m*, **~а**	a train. This word is gaining in frequency and popularity as a synonym of **по́їзд**.
квито́к на + *A.* **по́тяг (літа́к, авто́бус, електри́чку)**	a train (airplane, bus, commuter train) ticket
ми з жі́нкою	my wife and I, **ми з чолові́ком (бра́том, сестро́ю, дру́гом)** my husband (brother, sister, friend) and I
ї́хати + *I.* **по́тягом** or **по́їздом (літако́м, авто́бусом, електри́чкою, а́втом, метро́м)**	to go by train, airplane, bus, commuter train, car, subway (The vehicle of locomotion is a noun in instrumental. No preposition is used with it.)
прихо́д|ити, ~ять; прий|ти, ~ду́ть	to arrive (of scheduled train, bus, boat). **Коли́ прихо́дить по́їзд з Оде́си?** *When does the train from Odesa arrive?*
спа́льний квито́к, *m.*	1st class sleeping-car ticket (two passengers in a closed compartment, each assigned a sleeping berth)
купе́йний квито́к, *m.*	2nd class ticket (four passengers in a closed compartment, each assigned a sleeping berth)
плацка́ртний квито́к, *m.*	3rd class ticket (six passengers in an open compartment, each assigned a sleeping berth)
зага́льний квито́к, *m.*	4th class ticket (twelve passengers in an open compartment, each assigned a seat)
мі́сце, *nt.*	place, *here* passenger seat or berth on train, bus, airplane, **мі́сце бі́ля** + *G.* **вікна́ (прохо́ду, авари́́йного ви́ходу)** *window (aisle, emergency exit) seat.*
плат|и́ти, плачу́, ~ять; за~ + *I.*	to pay (unlike in English, no preposition is used after the verb), **п. креди́тною ка́рткою, готі́вкою, че́ком** *to pay with a credit card, cash, check.*

Оля волі́є подорожува́ти літако́м, ніж велосипе́дом чи на́віть по́тягом.

📖 Грама́тика | Grammar

Ору́дний відмі́нок одни́ни́ Instrumental Case Singular

Instrumental case correlates with the questions
з ким? *with whom?* **з чим?** *with what?*

Фу́нкція *Function*

The instrumental case can appear on its own and with prepositions. When used on its own, it can signify:

1) an instrument of action,
   ру́чка *a pen* - **писа́ти ру́чкою** *to write with a pen*
   зо́лото *gold* - **плати́ти зо́лотом** *to pay in gold*
   ніж *a knife* - **рі́зати ноже́м** *to cut with a knife*

2) a means (vehicle) of locomotion:
   маши́на *a car* - **ї́хати маши́ною** *to drive by car*
   по́тяг *a train* - **подорожува́ти по́тягом** *to travel by train*
   чо́вен *a boat* - **пливти́ човно́м** *to sail by boat*
   літа́к *a plane* - **леті́ти літако́м** *to fly by plane*

3) a space within which a motion takes place. The noun in the instrumental usually accompanies a motion verb **ходи́ти** *to go (on foot)*, **ї́здити** *to drive*, **гуля́ти** *to walk*, **бі́гати** *to run* (For more on motion verbs see Lesson 11, pp. 203-204):
   парк *a park* - **гуля́ти па́рком** *to walk in a park*
   ву́лиця *a street* - **йти ву́лицею** *to walk along a street*
   мі́сто *a city* - **ї́хати мі́стом** *to drive through a city*
   ліс *a forest* - **бі́гти лі́сом** *to run through a forest*

In this function, the instrumental expresses the same meaning as the locative with the preposition **по** (p. 82, 84). Thus **гуля́ти па́рком** and **гуля́ти по па́рку** both mean *to walk in a park,* likewise **йти ву́лицею** and **йти по ву́лиці** both mean *to walk along a street* and so on.

When used with prepositions, the instrumental case can signify:

1) accompaniment, **друг** *a friend* - **Я зроби́ла це з дру́гом.** *I did it with a friend.* **студе́нт** *a student* - **Ми прийшли́ зі студе́нтом.** *We came with a student.*

2) a person the subject interacts with, for such verbs as
   розмовля́ти з ки́мось *to speak with sb*
   знайо́митися з ки́мось *to make an acquaintance with sb*
   пого́джуватися з ки́мось *to agree with sb*, **офіція́нт** *a waiter* -
   Яри́на розмовля́є з офіція́нтом. *Yaryna is speaking with a waiter.*

3) a static position with such prepositions as **під** *under*, **за** *behind*, **над** *above*, **між** *between, among*,
   де́рево *a tree* - **Він сиді́в під де́ревом.** *He was sitting under a tree.*

стіна́ *a wall* - **За стіно́ю хтось грав.** *Somebody was playing behind the wall.*

мі́сто *a city* - **Не́бо над мі́стом було́ чи́сте.** *The sky over the city was clear.*

ми *we* - **Хай це лиша́ється між на́ми.** *Let this stay between us.*

Утво́рення *Formation*

Іме́нники Nouns

The nominal instrumental singular endings:
~ою (~ею, ~єю), ~ю (~'ю), ~ом (~ем, ~єм), ~ям

~ою is taken by feminine and masculine nouns ending in **~a**, ру́чка *a pen* - **ру́чкою**, кни́жка *a book* - **кни́жкою**, сестра́ *a sister* - **сестро́ю**, соба́ка *a dog* - **соба́кою**;

~ею is taken by:
(a) feminine and masculine nouns ending in **~a**, and whose stem final is either **~ж, ~ч, ~ш**, or **~щ**, ї́жа *food* - **ї́жею**, зда́ча *change* - **зда́чею**, ми́ша *a mouse* - **ми́шею**, пло́ща *a square* - **пло́щею**;

(b) feminine and masculine nouns ending in **~я**: *f.* О́ля *Olia* - **О́лею**, *m.* суддя́ *a judge* - **судде́ю**;

~єю is taken by feminine and masculine nouns ending in **~'я** like **сім'я́** *a family* - **сім'є́ю** as well as those ending in **~ія**, so that the resulting sequence is **~ією**, істо́рія *a story* - **істо́рією**, олі́я *oil* - **олі́єю**, мрі́я *a dream* - **мрі́єю**;

~ю is taken by the 3rd declension feminine nouns (ending in zero), ра́дість *joy* - **ра́дістю**, мо́лодість *youth* - **мо́лодістю**.

The final stem consonant doubles before the instrumental ending **~ю** if it is preceded by a vowel,
річ *a thing* - **рі́ччю**, ніч *a night* - **ні́ччю**, сіль *salt* - **сі́ллю**, о́сінь *autumn* - **о́сінню**, мо́лодь *youth (people)* - **мо́лоддю**.

~ом is taken by masculine nouns ending in a hard consonant or in **~o** and neuter nouns ending in **~o**, брат *a brother* - **бра́том**, друг *a friend* - **дру́гом**, студе́нт *a student* - **студе́нтом**, ба́тько *a father* - **ба́тьком**, Дніпро́ *the Dnipro* - **Дніпро́м**, мі́сто *a city* - **мі́стом**, вікно́ *a window* - **вікно́м**;

~ем is taken by masculine nouns ending in a soft consonant or in **~ж, ~ч, ~ш, ~щ** and neuter nouns ending in **~e**, америка́нець *an American* - **америка́нцем**, учи́тель *a teacher* - **учи́телем**, ніж *a knife* - **ноже́м**, мо́ре *a sea* - **мо́рем**, по́ле *a field* - **по́лем**.

Note 10.1. Verbs with object in instrumental

◊ **користува́тися словнико́м (пора́дою, інтерне́том)** *to use a dictionary (a piece of advice, the Internet)*
◊ **займа́тися спо́ртом (му́зикою, фотогра́фією)** *lit. to occupy oneself with sports (music, photography)*
◊ **працюва́ти економі́стом (учи́телем, журналі́стом)** *to work as an economist (teacher, journalist)*
◊ **розмовля́ти украї́нською (англі́йською і т.д.) мо́вою** *to speak the Ukrainian (English, etc.) language*
◊ **става́ти фахівце́м (спортсме́ном)** *to become an expert (athlete)*
◊ **ціка́витися літерату́рою (кіно́м, істо́рією, теа́тром)** *to be interested in literature (cinema, history, theater)*

Ці тури́сти серйо́зно ціка́вляться старо́ю архітекту́рою Льво́ва.

Note 10.2. Motion vs. location

Some of the same prepositions, when followed by nouns in the accusative case, indicate the direction of motion as opposed to static location expressed by the instrumental case,
Він сів під (А.) де́рево. *He went and sat down under a tree.*
Вони́ схова́лися за стіну́. *They hid behind a wall.*

Ми зустріча́ємося пе́ред апте́кою-музе́єм.

 Note 10.3. Prepositions with instrumental:

◊ **за** *behind, after,* **Він сиді́в за мно́ю.** *He was sitting behind me.*

◊ **з (із, зі)** *with,* **Я познайо́мився з ново́ю ді́вчиною.** *I met a new girl.*

◊ **між** *between,* **Між ни́ми нічо́го не було́.** *There was nothing between them.*

◊ **над (на́ді)** *above, over,* **над земле́ю** *above the ground*

◊ **під (пі́ді)** *under,* **Під столо́м кіт.** *There's a cat under the table.*

◊ **пе́ред (пе́реді)** *in front of, (of time) before,* **Пе́ред вікно́м дере́ва.** *There are trees in front of the window.*

The prepositions **над**, **під**, and **пе́ред** each have an **i**-ended variant, used only before **мно́ю**, the instrumental of **я** *I:*

◊ **на́ді мно́ю** *above me*
◊ **пі́ді мно́ю** *under me*
◊ **пе́реді мно́ю** *before me*

 Note 10.4. Apostrophe in instrumental case

If the final stem consonant is **~б~**, **~п~**, **~в~**, **~ф~**, or **~м~**, it stays single but an apostrophe is inserted between it and the ending **~ю**,

любо́в *love* - **любо́в'ю**
кров *blood* - **кро́в'ю**

The instrumental singular of **ма́ти** *a mother* is **ма́тір'ю**.

~єм is taken by masculine nouns ending in **~й**, **водій** *a driver* - **водіє́м**, **музе́й** *a museum* - **музе́єм**, **ге́ній** *a genius* - **ге́нієм**, **Андрі́й** *Andriy* - **Андріє́м**;

~ям is taken by all neuter nouns ending in **~я**, **пита́ння** *a question* - **пита́нням**, **завда́ння** *an assignment* - **завда́нням**, **життя́** *a life* - **життя́м**, **теля́** *a calf* - **теля́м**, **ім'я́** *a name* - **ім'я́м** (*var.* **і́менем**).

🔊 **SOUND CHANGES** 🔊
in the instrumental singular of nouns

Dropping of ~o~ (~e~)
~o~ and **~e~** in the last syllable of 2nd declension masculine nouns are dropped in the instrumental singular,

куто́к *a corner* - **пе́ред кутко́м** *before the corner*
сон *sleep* - **пе́ред сном** *before sleep*
украї́нець *a Ukrainian* - **з украї́нцем** *with a Ukrainian*
кіне́ць *an end* - **пе́ред кінце́м** *before the end*
день *a day* - **пе́ред днем** *before the day*

Change of ~i~ to ~o~ (~e~)
~i~ changes to **~o~ (~e~)** in the final syllable in 2nd declension masculine nouns,

кіт *a cat* - **з кото́м** *with a cat*
ніс *a nose* - **з но́сом** *with a nose*
лід *ice* - **з льо́дом** *with ice*
кінь *a horse* - **коне́м** *by horse*
папі́р *a paper* - **під папе́ром** *under a paper*
but **дід** *a grandfather* - **з ді́дом** *with a grandfather*

Прикме́тники, поря́дкові числі́вники, присві́йні та вказівні́ займе́нники
Adjectives, Ordinal Numerals, Possessive, and Demonstrative Pronouns

The adjectival instrumental singular endings:
~им (~ім, ~їм), **~ою** (~ьою).

Masculine adjectives, ordinal numerals, and demonstrative, interrogative, and possessive pronouns end in:

~им for hard stems,
до́брий *good* - **до́брим**, **вели́кий** *big* - **вели́ким**, **ціка́вий** *interesting* - **ціка́вим**, **пе́рший** *first* - **пе́ршим**, **той** *that* - **тим**, **яки́й** *what (kind of)* - **яки́м**, **наш** *our* - **на́шим**;

~ім for soft stems, оста́нній *last* - оста́ннім, осі́нній *autumnal* - осі́ннім, тре́тій *third* - тре́тім, їхній *their* - ї́хнім;

~їм for soft stems ending in **~й**, мій *my* - моїм, твій *your* - твоїм, чий *whose* - чиїм.

Feminine adjectives, ordinal numerals, and pronouns end in:

~ою for hard stems,
до́бра *good* - до́брою, вели́ка *big* - вели́кою, ціка́ва *interesting* - ціка́вою, деше́ва *cheap* - деше́вою, мала́ *small* - мало́ю;

~ьою for soft stems,
оста́ння *last* - оста́нньою, осі́ння *autumnal* - осі́нньою, тре́тя *third* - тре́тьою, си́ня *blue* - си́ньою;

~єю for soft stems ending in **~й**,
моя́ *my* - моє́ю, твоя́ *your* - твоє́ю, чия́ *whose* - чиє́ю.

The stress in the instrumental of nouns, adjectives, and ordinal numerals is mostly on the same syllable as in the respective *nominative singular* as is the case in the above.

Украї́нські місяці́ Ukrainian Months

Names of months are spelled in lowercase. In numeric dates, first comes the day in Arabic numeral, followed by the month in Roman numeral, and the year in Arabic again, **28. IV. 2014** *April 28, 2014*.

	Roman numeral	мі́сяць month	G. sg. It was on the ...~th of (month)	English
1.	I.	сі́чень	Це було́ дру́гого сі́чня.	*January*
2.	II.	лю́тий	Це було́ пе́ршого лю́того.	*February*
3.	III.	бе́резень	Це було́ двадця́того бе́резня.	*March*
4.	IV.	кві́тень	Це було́ сьо́мого кві́тня.	*April*
5.	V.	тра́вень	Це було́ тре́тього тра́вня.	*May*
6.	VI.	че́рвень	Це було́ одина́дцятого че́рвня.	*June*
7.	VII.	ли́пень	Це було́ тридця́того ли́пня.	*July*
8.	VIII.	се́рпень	Це було́ п'я́того се́рпня.	*August*
9.	IX.	ве́ресень	Це було́ вісімна́дцятого ве́ресня.	*September*
10.	X.	жо́втень	Це було́ трина́дцятого жо́втня.	*October*
11.	XI.	листопа́д	Це було́ четве́ртого листопа́да.	*November*
12.	XII.	гру́день	Це було́ шо́стого гру́дня.	*December*

Note 10.5. Mixed declension nouns in instrumental singular

Second declension masculine nouns ending in **~р** can take both the ending **~ом** and **~ем** in the instrumental,
ва́рвар *a barbarian* - з ва́рваром *with a barbarian*
тре́нер *a coach* - з тре́нером *with a coach*
пасажи́р *a passenger* - з пасажи́ром *with a passenger*

but

госпо́дар *a landlord* - з госпо́дарем *with a landlord*
лі́кар *a physician* - з лі́карем *with a physician*
пе́кар *a baker* - з пе́карем *with a baker*

In these and similar cases, it is a good idea to consult the dictionary.

Note 10.6. Baby animal names in instrumental

Baby animal names like **теля́** *a calf* do not have the suffix **~ат (~ят)** in the instrumental singular, like they do in other cases,
курча́ *a chicken* - з курча́м *with a chicken*
щеня́ *a puppy* - з щеня́м *with a puppy*
котеня́ *a kitten* - з котеня́м *with a kitten*

Кі́шка Кицю́ня з котеня́м Му́рчиком

Два́дцять четве́ртого се́рпня святку́ють День незале́жности Украї́ни.

Да́ти Dates

Dates usually appear in two contexts:

1) when a date is simply stated,
Сього́дні шо́сте кві́тня дві ти́сячі трина́дцятого ро́ку. *Today is April 6, 2013.*
Such a statement correlates with the question **Яке́ сього́дні число́?** *What date is it today?*

To answer it, the combination *ordinal numeral in N. + month in G. + ordinal numeral of year in G. +* **ро́ку** is used,
Сього́дні пе́рше ли́пня дві ти́сячі деся́того ро́ку. *Today is the first of July, 2010.*

2) when a date of an event is indicated,
Фестива́ль почина́ється два́дцять пе́ршого ли́пня дві ти́сячі п'ятна́дцятого ро́ку. *The festival starts on July 21, 2015.*
Such a statement correlates with the question **Коли́ це бу́де (ста́неться, ма́тиме мі́сце)?** *When will it be (happen, take place)?*

In answer to it, both *ordinal numeral and month* are put in the genitive. Unlike in English no preposition is used:
Нови́й рік почина́ється пе́ршого сі́чня. *The new year starts on the 1st of January.*
Конце́рт бу́де тре́тього бе́резня. *The concert will be on the 3rd of March.*

In the composite ordinal numeral indicating a year, only the last word is declined,

Це ста́лося дру́гого ве́ресня ти́сяча дев'ятсо́т дев'яно́сто п'я́того ро́ку. *This happened on September 2, 1995.*

All month names with ~e~ in the final syllable lose it in oblique cases including the genitive, **сі́чень** *January* - **до сі́чня** *till January*, **пе́ред сі́чнем** *before January*, **у сі́чні** *in January*.

To indicate an event in a particular month with no specific date given, the name of that month is used in the **locative singular** with the preposition **у (в)** *in*,
у бе́резні *in March*, **у жо́втні** *in October*, **у лю́тому** *in February*.

Ukrainian equivalents of *last March, next September* are combinations of **мину́лий** *last* and **насту́пний** *next* with a month name, both in the genitive case singular,
мину́лого тра́вня *last May*, **насту́пного жо́втня**, *next October*.

A more common way of expressing similar time designations is:
у тра́вні мину́лого ро́ку *lit. in May of last year* or
торі́к у тра́вні *lit. last year in May*
у ли́пні цьо́го ро́ку *this July*
у гру́дні насту́пного ро́ку *lit. in December of next year*

Впра́ви   Exercises

🎧 **10.1.** Respond to the questions.

a) Model.

🇶 Тара́с – економі́ст? *Is Taras an economist?*
🇦 Ні, але́ він хо́че ста́ти економі́стом. *No, but he wants to become an economist.*

1. Миха́йло – журналі́ст?
2. Ігор – інжене́р?
3. Яри́на – лі́карка?
4. Ваш брат – переклада́ч?
5. Цей чолові́к – вчи́тель?
6. Рома́н – студе́нт?
7. Марі́я – вчи́телька?
8. Катери́на – письме́нниця?
9. Його́ ма́ти – акто́рка?
10. Її друг – бізнесме́н?

🔁 Change the gender of the person in each instance and use the name of the occupation that corresponds to the gender.

b) Model.

🇶 Тама́ра – економі́стка? *Is Tamara (f.) an economist?*
🇦 Ні, але́ вона́ хо́че ста́ти економі́сткою. *No, but she wants to become (f.) an economist.*

🎧 **10.2.** Answer the questions.

Model. цей пан *this getleman*, акто́р *an actor*
🇶 Ким працю́є цей пан? *What does this gentleman work as?*
🇦 Акто́ром. *As an actor.*

1. Марі́я, юри́стка
2. молоди́й чолові́к, вчи́тель
3. Іва́н, лі́кар
4. його́ брат, юри́ст
5. ва́ша сусі́дка, вчи́телька
6. Петро́ Миха́йлович, журналі́ст
7. їхня ті́тка, журналі́стка
8. Рома́н, офіція́нт

🎧 **10.3.** Answer the questions. Use the instrumental case.

Model.

🇶 Тара́с – економі́ст? *Is Taras an economist?* до́брий *good*
🇦 Ще ні, але́ коли́сь він бу́де до́брим економі́стом. *Not yet, but one day he will be a good economist.*

1. Цей хло́пець – спортсме́н? вели́кий
2. Її сусі́дка – худо́жниця? ориґіна́льна
3. Твій брат – фото́граф? ціка́вий
4. Ця па́ні – вчи́телька? добра́
5. Його́ дя́дько – такси́ст? досві́дчений
6. Ваш прия́тель – ку́хар? га́рний

Note 10.7. Як запита́ти про профе́сію How to ask about occupation

Ким вона́ працю́є? *What does she work as?*

Вона́ працю́є інжене́ром. *She works as an engineer.*

Ким працю́є Марі́я? *What does Maria work as?*

Вона́ працю́є економі́стом. *She works as an economist.*

or

Хто ви за профе́сією (фа́хом)? *What are you by occupation?*

За профе́сією я економі́ст. *By profession I am an economist.*

Хто за профе́сією ваш брат? *What is your brother by occupation?*

За профе́сією мій брат лі́кар. *By profession my brother is a physician.*

Note the difference in the word order: *subject + predicate,* when the subject is a personal pronoun,

Ким вона́ (ти, він, ви, вони́) працю́є (працю́єте, працю́ють)?

predicate + subject, when the subject is a noun or noun phrase,

Ким працю́є Марі́я Васи́лівна (його́ сестра́, їхня ма́ти, твій ба́тько)?

Улі́тку Гали́на працю́є продавце́м городи́ни.

Note 10.8. Чужі мо́ви, яки́ми розмовля́ють украї́нці

Foreign languages Ukrainians speak

англі́йська	*English*
ара́бська	*Arabic*
білору́ська	*Belarusian*
іспа́нська	*Spanish*
італі́йська	*Italian*
кита́йська	*Chinese*
німе́цька	*German*
по́льська	*Polish*
португа́льська	*Portuguese*
росі́йська	*Russian*
туре́цька	*Turkish*
францу́зька	*French*

Яко́ю мо́вою ви хо́чете навчи́тися розмовля́ти?

🎧 **10.4.** Answer the questions. Replace nouns with personal pronouns.

Model.

Q Чим ціка́виться Мари́на? *What is Maryna interested in?* украї́нська істо́рія *Ukrainian history*

A Вона́ ціка́виться украї́нською істо́рією.
She is interested in Ukrainian history.

1. Чим користу́ється Андрі́й? украї́нський словни́к
2. Чим ціка́вляться ці тури́сти? моде́рна архітекту́ра
3. Чим пи́ше Рома́н? чо́рний олі́ве́ць
4. Чим пла́тять уча́сники екску́рсії? креди́тна ка́ртка
5. Чим малю́є Окса́на? зеле́на фа́рба
6. Чим ї́здять до мі́ста ці школярі́? місь́кий авто́бус

🎧 **10.5.** First, ask what language a person can speak. Then answer for that person. Note that the feminine adjective is used as shorthand for the *adjective + noun phrase*, **украї́нська** *Ukrainian* instead of **украї́нська мо́ва** *the Ukrainian language*.

Model. ти *you*, украї́нська *Ukrainian*

Q Яко́ю мо́вою ти розмовля́єш? *What language do you speak?*

A Украї́нською (мо́вою). *Ukrainian.*

1. я, англі́йська
2. вони́, німе́цька
3. ви, італі́йська
4. Марі́я, росі́йська
5. ї́хня дочка́, ара́бська
6. ми, іспа́нська
7. ї́ ті́тка, туре́цька
8. він, кита́йська
9. ї́хні сини́, по́льська
10. мій дя́дько, португа́льська

🎧 **10.6.** Answer the questions. Use prepositions where needed and the word collocations given.

Model.

Q Чим він користу́ється? *What does he use?* твоя́ ка́рта *your map*

A Твоє́ю ка́ртою. *Your map.*

1. З ким ви познайо́милися вчо́ра? одна́ ціка́ва ді́вчина
2. Чим ми бу́демо користува́тися для пере́кладу? ї́хній нови́й словни́к
3. Де він гуля́в ці́лий день? це старе́ мі́сто
4. Чим вона́ ціка́виться? оста́нній фільм Леоні́да Оси́ки
5. З ким ти при́йдеш на день наро́дження? мій нови́й при́ятель
6. Ким ти працю́єш тут? ї́хня головна́ економі́стка
7. Чим ви поя́снюєте це? си́льний дощ і ві́тер
8. Чим вони́ займа́ються на вихідні́? моя́ музи́чна осві́та
9. Чим вони́ лю́блять малюва́ти? ця зеле́на фа́рба
10. З ким ви говори́ли про це? твоя́ моло́дша сестра́ О́ля
11. З ким мені́ тре́ба пора́дитися? моя́ знайо́ма лі́карка
12. Чим ви мо́жете заплати́ти? ї́ персона́льний чек

⌒ 10.7. Answer the questions. Use the prepositions with the instrumental case to indicate a static position.

Model.

Q Де виси́ть карти́на? *Where is (lit. hangs) the picture?*
   above стіл *a table*

A Карти́на виси́ть над столо́м? Th*e picture is above the table.*

1. Де росте́ де́рево? *behind* ха́та
2. Де лежи́ть кіт? *under* лі́жко
3. Де літа́ють птахи́? *over* парк
4. Де стої́ть ша́фа? *between* стіна́ та вікно́
5. Де лежи́ть га́рний ки́лим? *in front of* вхід
6. Де си́нє не́бо? *above* я
7. Де стої́ть а́вто? *behind* музе́й
8. Де лежи́ть ключ? *under* журна́л
9. Де росту́ть кві́ти? *between* готе́ль і рестора́н

⌒ 10.8. Fill in the blanks with either **мі́сто** *a city* or **мі́сце** *a place* in the required case form. Translate into English.

1. Ба́тько Павла́ народи́вся у старо́му га́лицькому ... .
2. Яке́ ... Украї́ни найбі́льше сподо́балося Джо́нові А́ндерсону?
3. У цьо́му га́рному ... Полта́ви стої́ть музе́й Іва́на Котляре́вського.
4. Ко́жне вели́ке чи мале́ ... Украї́ни ма́є вла́сну на́зву й істо́рію.
5. Ця кав'я́рня – їхнє улю́блене ... .
6. У старо́му кінотеа́трі Марі́я за́вжди сіда́ла на пе́рше ... у три́дцять тре́тьому ря́ді.
7. Ви́бачте, ці два ... бі́ля вас за́йняті?
8. Коли́сь на ..., де за́раз Оде́са, було́ старе́ ... Хаджибе́й.
9. У пе́ршому ря́ді є два ві́льних ... .
10. Йому́ ду́же подо́баються старі́ га́лицькі ... Дрого́бич, Стрий і Жо́вква.

⌒ 10.9. Answer the questions. Note the word order of the answer.

Model.

Q Яке́ сього́дні число́? *What date is it today?* 02.IX *Sept. 2*

A Сього́дні дру́ге ве́ресня. *Today is the 2nd of September.*

1. Яке́ сього́дні число́? 12.II.
2. Яке́ число́ бу́де за́втра? 25.V.
3. Яке́ число́ бу́де насту́пної субо́ти? 10.IV.
4. Яке́ число́ бу́де післяза́втра? 21.VII.
5. Яке́ число́ бу́де насту́пного понеді́лка? 04.VI.
6. Яке́ число́ бу́де насту́пної п'я́тниці? 3.XI.
7. Яке́ число́ бу́де насту́пного четверга́? 9.III.
8. Яке́ число́ було́ того́ дня? 11.IX.

⌖ Note 10.9. Іме́нники *мі́сто* та *мі́сце* Nouns мі́сто *vs* мі́сце

The nouns **мі́сто** *a town, city*, and **мі́сце** *a place, a seat*, are often confused by learners. Study the illustrations of their use below.

Я люблю́ жи́ти у вели́кому мі́сті. *I like to live in a big city.*
vs
Мій буди́нок стої́ть у га́рному мі́сці. *My house stands in a nice place.*

Оле́на лю́бить це мі́сто. *Olena likes this town.*
vs
Оле́на лю́бить це мі́сце. *Olena likes this place.*

The noun **мі́сто** is related by form and meaning to the adjective **міськи́й** *municipal, city, urban*, as in **міська́ ра́да** *a city council*, **міська́ культу́ра** *urban culture*, **міськи́й теа́тр** *a municipal theater*,

У Ки́єві міськи́й тра́нспорт включа́є метро́, троле́йбуси, трамва́ї та авто́буси. *In Kyiv, the city transit includes metro, trolleybuses, streetcars, and buses.*

The noun **мі́сце** correlates with the adjective **місце́вий** *local*, as in **місце́ві тради́ції** *local traditions*, **місце́вий діале́кт** *local dialect*,

Місце́вий істори́чний музе́й найкра́щий у краї́ні. *The local history museum is the best in the country.*

За о́зером їхнє га́рне се́ло Глинськ.

Note 10.10. Да́та наро́дження
Date of birth

To indicate the date of birth, the verb **наро́джуватися; народи́тися** *to be born* is used,

Q **Коли́ народи́вся Бо́дя?** *When was Bodia born?*

A **Він народи́вся сьо́мого жо́втня двоти́сячного ро́ку.** *He was born on October 7, 2000.*

Unlike in English, where the word *year* can and is often omitted, in Ukrainian dates, such an omission is typical of an informal and shorthand style and otherwise rarely occurs.

Ви́ставка скульпту́ри Олекса́ндра Архи́пенка в Украї́нському музе́ї в Нью-Йо́рку.

Завда́ння для Міжнаро́дної мере́жі
Internet assignment

10.10. Use the Ukrainian language Internet to find and write down the dates of birth and death of these great Ukrainians.

Роксола́на

профе́сія

мі́сце та да́та наро́дження

мі́сце та да́та сме́рти

Дмитро́ Бортня́нський

профе́сія

мі́сце та да́та наро́дження

мі́сце та да́та сме́рти

Мико́ла Го́голь

профе́сія

мі́сце та да́та наро́дження

мі́сце та да́та сме́рти

Ле́ся Украї́нка

профе́сія

мі́сце та да́та наро́дження

мі́сце та да́та сме́рти

Тара́с Шевче́нко

профе́сія

мі́сце та да́та наро́дження

мі́сце та да́та сме́рти

Соломі́я Крушельни́цька

профе́сія

мі́сце та да́та наро́дження

мі́сце та да́та сме́рти

Олекса́ндер Архи́пенко

профе́сія

мі́сце та да́та наро́дження

мі́сце та да́та сме́рти

Ві́ра Холо́дна

профе́сія

мі́сце та да́та наро́дження

мі́сце та да́та сме́рти

Пам'я́тник украї́нському пое́тові Тара́сові Шевче́нку пе́ред Ки́ївським націона́льним університе́том.

Іва́н Ху́ткий познайо́мився
з Мо́трею чотирна́дцятого се́рпня.

Будь ла́ска, два квитки́
на во́сьме гру́дня до У́жгорода.

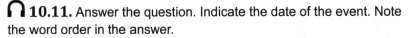

10.11. Answer the question. Indicate the date of the event. Note the word order in the answer.

Model.
Q Коли́ почина́ється семе́ст(е)р? *When does the semester start?*
02.I. *Jan. 2*
A (Семе́ст(е)р почина́ється) дру́гого сі́чня. *The semester starts on the 2nd of January.*

1. Коли́ закі́нчуються кані́кули? 14.VIII.
2. Коли́ це бу́де? 25.V.
3. Коли́ відкрива́ється фестива́ль? 18.II.
4. Коли́ вони́ йдуть на вече́рю до Рома́на? 10.IV.
5. Коли́ вона́ ї́здила до Нью-Йо́рку? 11.VI.
6. Коли́ профе́сор Шевче́нко ма́є чита́ти ле́кцію у Ґрана́ді? 13.III.
7. Коли́ Ма́рта приїжджа́є до Ло́ндона? 8.VII.
8. Коли́ почина́ється зима́? 21.XII.

10.12. Indicate the day and date you need a ticket for. Note the use of the preposition **на** + *A.*

Model.
C оди́н квито́к *one ticket*, п'я́тниця, тре́тє бе́резня *Friday, March 3*
A Будь ла́ска, оди́н квито́к на п'я́тницю, тре́тє бе́резня. *One ticket for March 3, please.*

1. оди́н квито́к, субо́та, п'я́те кві́тня
2. два квитки́, понеді́лок, деся́те ли́пня
3. три квитки́, вівто́рок, два́дцять сьо́ме лю́того
4. п'ять квиткі́в, неді́ля, трина́дцяте тра́вня
5. чоти́ри квитки́, середа́, тридця́те гру́дня
6. шість квиткі́в, п'я́тниця, шо́сте ве́ресня
7. ві́сім квиткі́в, четве́р, одина́дцяте листопа́да

10.13. Denote the start and end of a time period. Use **від** *from* **до** *to.*

Model.
Мико́ла *Mykola*, жи́ти тут *to live here*, цей понеді́лок *this Monday*, насту́пна середа́ *next Wednesday*
Q Як до́вго тут бу́де жи́ти Мико́ла? *How long will Mykola live here?*
A Від цього́ понеді́лка до насту́пної середи́. *From this Monday till next Wednesday.*

1. Марі́я, працюва́ти вдо́ма, цей вівто́рок, насту́пна п'я́тниця
2. ці англі́йці, зупиня́тися у вас, цей ти́ждень, насту́пний ти́ждень
3. Окса́на, вчи́тися, це лі́то, ця зима́
4. ті росія́ни, жи́ти у них, насту́пний жо́втень, насту́пний гру́день
5. Оле́кса, писа́ти статтю́, цей мі́сяць, насту́пний мі́сяць
6. Іва́н, подорожува́ти сві́том, тра́вень, насту́пний ве́ресень
7. Ві́ра, готува́тися до екза́мена, ця субо́та, насту́пний четве́р

🎧 **10.14.** State the departure and arrival of trains. Use 24-hour time frame.

Model. Ки́їв - Львів *Kyiv - Lviv* 5:30 PM → 6:15 AM
Q Мені́ тре́ба зна́ти ро́зклад по́тяга Ки́їв - Львів.
I need to know the schedule of the train Kyiv - Lviv.
A Він відхо́дить із Ки́єва о сімна́дцятій три́дцять і прихо́дить до Льво́ва о шо́стій п'ятна́дцять.
It departs from Kyiv at 5:30 PM and arrives in Lviv at 6:15 AM.

1. Львів - Оде́са	7:12 PM	→	4:25 AM
2. Ки́їв - Симферо́поль	1:27 PM	→	8:48 AM
3. Ха́рків - У́жгород	11:05 AM	→	5:19 AM
4. Доне́цьк - Оде́са	8:52 PM	→	10:00 AM
5. Херсо́н - Черні́гів	12:40 PM	→	3:33 AM
6. Рі́вне - Луга́нськ	9:37 PM	→	8:18 PM
7. Терно́піль - Полта́ва	11: 55 PM	→	3:00 PM
8. Львів - Вене́ція	10:00 PM	→	8:26 PM
9. Микола́їв - Лу́цьк	9:10 AM	→	8:43 PM
10. Іва́но-Франкі́вськ - Запорі́жжя	1:10 AM	→	3:28 PM
11. Маріу́поль - Ві́нниця	2:22 PM	→	1:30 AM
12. Ки́їв - Варша́ва	7:45 PM	→	9:00 PM

⏱ **Note 10.11. Train schedule**

відхо́дити з (із) + *G.* **о (об)** + *L.* to depart from a city at ⏱ o'clock
прихо́дити до + *G.* **о (об)** + *L.* to arrive in a city at ⏱ o'clock

These are set idiomatic expressions used to describe arrival and departure of trains, buses, and ships (ferries),

Коли́ прихо́дить авто́бус із Терно́поля? *When does the bus from Ternopil come?*
По́їзд до Ха́ркова відійшо́в годи́ну тому́. *The Kharkiv-bound train left an hour ago.*

To refer to people who travel by bus, train, etc. the verbs **від'їжджа́ти** *to leave* and **приїжджа́ти** *to come, arrive,* are used. Both imply motion by a vehicle (bus, train, plane, or car) and not on foot,

Яре́ма приїжджа́є за́втра вве́чері. *Yarema is arriving tomorrow evening.*

For airplanes the verbs **відліта́ти** *to depart* and **приліта́ти** *to arrive,* are used,

Мій рейс приліта́є о шо́стій. *My flight arrives at six.*

✏ **Note 10.12. Words used to describe train schedules**

залізни́ця, *f.*	railroad, **Укрзалізни́ця** the Ukrainian Railway
маршру́т, *m.,* ~**у**	a route, itinerary, **м. по́їзда** train route (itinerary)
но́мер, *m.,* ~**а**	a number, **н. по́їзда** train number, **Яки́й н. по́їзда?** What's the number?
періоди́чність, *f.*	frequency, **Яка́ п. цьо́го по́їзда?** How often does this train run?
рух, *m.,* ~**у**	a movement, **час** ~**у**, *here* duration of the trip
прибуття́, *nt.*	an arrival, **п. по́їзда** train arrival
відправлення, *nt.*	a departure, **в. по́їзда** train departure
ста́нці|я, *f.*	a station, **Скі́льки ча́су бу́де стоя́ти по́їзд на цій** ~**ї?** How long will the train be staying at this station?

🎧 **10.15** Read the schedule of the Kyiv - Berlin train *(on the next page)* and answer the questions. Write your answers in Ukrainian.

1. Яки́й но́мер по́їзда Ки́їв - Берлі́н?
2. Коли́ відхо́дить з Ки́єва цей по́їзд? (відпра́влення)
3. Коли́ прихо́дить по́їзд на ста́нцію Са́рни? (прибуття́)
4. Коли́ прихо́дить по́їзд на ста́нцію По́знань?
5. Як до́вго стої́ть по́їзд на зупи́нці «Варша́ва Центра́льна»?
6. Скі́льки раз зупиня́ється по́їзд між Ки́євом і Ягоди́ном?
7. Скі́льки ча́су трива́є по́дорож із Ки́єва до Варша́ви (час ру́ху)
8. Скі́льки ча́су трива́є по́дорож із По́знаня до Берлі́на?
9. Як назива́ється оста́ння зупи́нка по́їзда Ки́їв - Берлі́н?

КОЛІЯ TRACK	ПОЇЗД TRAIN	СПОЛУЧЕННЯ ROUTE	ПРИБУТТЯ ВІДПРАВ. ARRIVAL DEPARTURE
8	88	КИЇВ - ЛУГАНСЬК	
1	67	КИЇВ - ВАРШАВА	
10	84	КИЇВ - МАРІУПОЛЬ	
9	177	КИЇВ - КАМ. -ПОДІЛЬСЬКИЙ	16:1
2	115	ХАРКІВ - ТРУСКАВЕЦЬ	16:32 16:5
3	169	КИЇВ - ЛЬВІВ	17:0
П2	814	КИЇВ - ЗЕРНОВЕ	17:0
	154	ВІННИЦЯ - КИЇВ	17:06
6	59	КИЇВ - СОФІЯ	17:1
П1	857	КИЇВ - ХМЕРИНКА	17:1
16Z		КИЇВ - ХАРКІВ	17:3
	166	КИЇВ - ДНІПРОПЕТРОВСЬК	17:5

Маршру́т по́їзда	№ по́їзда	Періоди́чність	час ру́ху
Ки́їв - Берлі́н	29К "Кашта́н"	по 1,4,5,6 днях ти́жня	24:22

№ по́їзда	Ста́нція	Прибуття́	Відпра́влення
29К	Ки́їв-пас.		9:30
29К	Ко́ростень-пз	11:32	11:50
29К	Са́рни	14:12	14:14
29К	Ко́вель-пас.	16:18	16:38
29К	Ягоди́н	17:32	19:32
29К	Дорогу́ськ	18:50	19:45
29К	Лю́блін	21:08	21:11
29К	Варша́ва-всхо́дня	23:18	1:17
29К	Варша́ва-центра́льна	·1:25	1:30
29К	По́знань	4:53	4:58
29К	Же́пін	6:32	6:34
29К	Берлі́н остба́нгоф	8:08	8:36
29К	Берлі́н гавптба́нгоф	8:43	8:47
29К	Берлі́н зооло́гішен ґа́ртен	8:52	

Залізни́чний вокза́л у Льво́ві.

 Завда́ння для Міжнаро́дної мере́жі
Internet assignment

⌒ **10.16.** Use an Internet search engine and find the following information.

1. Які́ є по́їзди з Ки́єва до Оде́си?
2. Яки́й но́мер по́їзда «Ки́їв-Пра́га»?
3. Скі́льки ча́су йде по́їзд «Ха́рків-Ки́їв»?
4. О котрі́й годи́ні прихо́дить до Полта́ви по́їзд «Львів-Ха́рків»?
5. Яка́ оста́ння зупи́нка пе́ред Ха́рковом по́їзда «Маріу́поль-Ха́рків»?
6. О котрі́й годи́ні відхо́дить із Ки́єва по́їзд «Черні́гів-Львів»?

⌒ **10.17.** Translate into Ukrainian. Use the vocabulary and grammar of this and previous lessons.

1. We need three second-class tickets for the train Lviv-Odesa for tomorrow.
2. The bus from Kharkiv arrives late at night.
3. Can one pay with a credit card or only cash?
4. Yarema rarely uses a dictionary, instead he uses the Internet.
5. Now Mrs. Svitlychna works as an economist, but she wants to become a banker.
6. A sleeping car ticket is too much of a luxury for us. We'll travel in a third-class car.
7. I'd like to have a window seat, if one can choose.
8. We were in Kyiv on September 10. Today is October 1, and we are returning to Toronto on November 22.
9. Their daughter was born in February and their son in April.

Від середмі́стя Ки́єва до залізни́чного вокза́лу мо́жна шви́дко діста́тися метро́м.

10. Mrs. Natalia is interested in contemporary European politics.

11. At the conference I met a very interesting young Ukrainian scholar.

12. Jane already speaks fluent Ukrainian and now she'd like to learn to speak Polish.

 Note 10.13. Чолові́чі та жіно́чі профе́сії
Male and female occupations

Ukrainian names of occupations often, though not always, have a masculine and feminine variant. Both are stylistically neutral and devoid of any evaluative connotations. When a feminine variant does not exist, the masculine noun is used for both genders, **Марі́я Кухарчу́к працю́є президе́нтом ціє́ї компа́нії.** *Maria Kukharchuk works as president of the company.*

чолові́чий рід *masculine* чолові́чі профе́сії *male occupations*	жіно́чий рід *feminine* жіно́чі профе́сії *female occupations*	англі́йський відпові́дник *English equivalent* англі́йська на́зва *English name*
1. акто́р	акто́рка	*an actor, actress*
2. бібліоте́кар	бібліоте́карка	*a librarian*
3. виклада́ч	виклада́чка	*an instructor*
4. вчи́тель	вчи́телька	*a teacher, an instructor*
5. економі́ст	економі́стка	*an economist*
6. журналі́ст	журналі́стка	*a journalist*
7. консульта́нт	консульта́нтка	*a consultant*
8. лі́кар	лі́карка	*a physician, medical doctor*
9. офіція́нт	офіція́нтка	*a waiter, waitress*
10. переклада́ч	переклада́чка	*a translator, an interpretor*
11. письме́нник	письме́нниця	*a writer*
12. спортсме́н	спортсме́нка	*an athlete*
13. такси́ст	такси́стка	*a cab driver*
14. юри́ст	юри́стка	*a lawyer*

Ві́ктор був і є до́брим спортсме́ном.

∩ 10.18. Match feminine names of professions to their masculine equivalents.

Model.

C Марко́ *Marko*, рік *a year,* учи́тель *a teacher,* Світла́на *Svitlana*

A Марко́ уже́ рік працю́є учи́телем, а Світла́на лише́ ду́має ста́ти вчи́телькою. *Marko has worked as a teacher for a year already, while Svitlana is only planning to become a teacher.*

1. його́ при́ятель, мі́сяць, бібліоте́кар, Миросла́ва
2. твій моло́дший брат, три ро́ки, юри́ст, моя́ сестра́ Марі́чка
3. пан Миколайчу́к, три ти́жні, виклада́ч, па́нна Титаре́нко
4. мій при́ятель Оле́кса, два́дцять п'ять днів, такси́ст, Га́ля Кириле́нко
5. Тара́с Марчу́к, де́сять мі́сяців, журналі́ст, Валенти́на Сидоре́нко
6. цей чолові́к, п'ять ро́ків, лі́кар, його́ дружи́на

Михайло любить користуватися мобілкою.

7. наш знайо́мий канаді́єць, сім мі́сяців, офіція́нт, його́ ді́вчина
8. я, переклада́ч, чоти́ри мі́сяці, моя́ при́ятелька Лі́дія
9. їхній дя́дько, де́в'ять ти́жнів, вчи́тель, їхня ті́тка
10. ваш сусі́д, два мі́сяці, економі́ст, його́ моло́дша сестра́
11. Ві́ктор Макси́менко, шість ро́ків, консульта́нт, Ната́ля Ти́ха

Розмо́ва по телефо́ну A Telephone Conversation

∩ **10.19.** Memorize the expressions used in a phone conversation.

Альо́!	*Hello.*
Слу́хаю.	*I'm listening. (said by recipient of call)*
Хто це?	*Who's this?*
З ким ма́ю приє́мність (розмовля́ти)?	*Whom do I owe the pleasure (of this call)?*
Це кварти́ра + G. ..?	*Is this Mr. …'s apartment?*
Чи мо́жна розмовля́ти з + I. ...?	*May I speak with …*
Ні, на жаль його́ (її́) нема́ вдо́ма.	*No, unfortunately he (she) isn't home.*
Подзвоні́ть, будь ла́ска, за годи́ну.	*Please call in an hour.*
Хвили́нку.	*Just a minute.*
Я за́раз його́ (її́) покли́чу.	*I'll call him (her) right away.*
А коли́ він (вона́) бу́де?	*And when will he (she) be (home)?*
Гара́зд, я передзвоню́ пізні́ше.	*Alright, I'll call later.*
Ви хо́чете щось йому́ (їй) переказа́ти?	*Do you want to leave him (her) a message?*
Перекажі́ть йому́ (їй), будь ла́ска, що	*Please tell him (her) that …*
Ви набра́ли непра́вильний но́мер.	*You dialed the wrong number.*

∩ **10.20.** Listen to this telephone conversation and answer the questions.

1. Між ким відбува́ється розмо́ва по телефо́ну?
2. Хто дзво́нить до ко́го?
3. З ким хо́че розмовля́ти па́нна, що дзво́нить?
4. Де є за́раз Михайло?
5. Хто таки́й Оре́ст?
6. Як пропону́є Оре́ст ви́рішити пробле́му?

Телефо́нний дзвіно́к. Telephone call

А. Альо́, слу́хаю.

Б. Добри́день. Це кварти́ра Миха́йла Якове́нка?

А. Так, це його́ кварти́ра. А хто це дзво́нить?

Б. Мене́ зва́ти Окса́на Романю́к. Чи мо́жна розмовля́ти із Миха́йлом? Я коле́ґа Миха́йла із університе́ту.

А. А це брат Миха́йла Оре́ст. На жаль, Миха́йла за́раз нема́ вдо́ма. Ви хо́чете щось йому́ переказа́ти?

Б. Так. Перекажі́ть йому́, будь ла́ска, Оре́сте, що я ма́ю для ньо́го добру́ нови́ну́. Мо́же ви зна́єте, коли́ Миха́йло бу́де вдо́ма?

А. Я не впе́внений. Він не сказа́в мені́. Як хо́чете, мо́жу да́ти вам но́мер його́ мобі́лки.

Б. Так, звича́йно. Це ви́рішить пробле́му. Я гото́ва писа́ти.

А. Нуль шістдеся́т шість, три́ста п'ятдеся́т, шістна́дцять, со́рок три.

Б. Чудо́во, записа́ла. Ду́же дя́кую. До поба́чення, О́ресте.

А. Ду́же про́шу, Окса́но. На все до́бре.

 Note 10.14. Синтети́чний майбу́тній недоко́наний час
Synthetic Imperfective Future Tense

In addition to the two-word imperfective future tense (**Я бу́ду жи́ти тут**. *I'll live here*. See Lesson 7, pp. 112-113) Ukrainian has a one-word imperfective future (**Я жи́тиму тут**. *I'll live here*.). There is no difference in meaning between the two. The difference is purely in form. The synthetic imperfective future is a word, made of an imperfective infinitive and a personal ending that denotes futurity. There are six such endings:

	personal pronoun	singular	personal pronoun	plural
1st	я	~му	ми	~мемо
2nd	ти	~меш	ви	~мете
3rd	він, вона́, воно́	~ме	вони́	~муть

 The stress in the synthetic imperfective future is on the same syllable as in the infinitive. When forming the imperfective future, learners often add the ending to a truncated infinitive. Make sure the full infinitive is used,

я жи́тиму	I'll live	ми жи́тимемо	we'll live
ти жи́тимеш	you'll live	ви жи́тимете	you'll live
він жи́тиме	he'll live	вони́ жи́тимуть	they'll live

 Note 10.15. Reflexive verbs in one-word future

Reflexive verbs like **умива́тися** *to wash oneself*, **диви́тися** *to watch*, **боя́тися** *to be afraid*, form the imperfective future by inserting the endings between the suffix **~ти** and the particle **~ся**. The ending of the *3rd pers. sg.* is **~меться**, and not ~меся*:

я диви́тимуся	I'll watch	ми диви́тимемося	we'll watch
ти диви́тимешся	you'll watch	ви диви́тиметеся	you'll watch
він диви́тиметься	he'll watch	вони́ диви́тимуться	they'll watch

General question is formed either by giving a rising intonation to the affirmative statement, **Вони́ ⟋роби́тимуть завда́ння?** *Will they be doing the assignment?* or by the **чи** put at the beginning of the affirmative statement, pronounced as a question, **Чи вони́ ⟋роби́тимуть завда́ння?**

Negative statement is formed by inserting the particle **не** before the predicate in the affirmative statement, **Вони́ не ⟍роби́тимуть завда́ння.** *They will not be doing the assignment*. The negative statement is pronounced with a falling intonation.

Тиждень
укра́їнський   www.ut.net.ua
№ 23 (136), 11–17 ЧЕРВНЯ 2010 р.

Чи ви вже чита́ли журна́л "Украї́нський ти́ждень"?

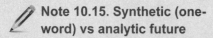

Note 10.15. Synthetic (one-word) vs analytic future

The one-word imperfective future tends to be used with verbs that are comparatively shorter,

◊ **ма́ти** *to have*, **Коли́ він ма́тиме ві́льний час**? *When will he have some free time?*

◊ **ї́сти** *to eat*, **Що ми ї́стимемо на вече́рю?** *What shall we eat for dinner?*

◊ **купува́ти** *to buy*, **Я купува́тиму проду́кти у цій крамни́ці.** *I will be buying groceries in this store.*

The two-word (or analytic) imperfective future tends to be used with longer words, five and more syllables, to avoid inordinately long formations,

◊ **відпочива́ти** *to rest, vacation*, **Де ви бу́дете відпочива́ти влі́тку?** *Where will you be vacationing in the summer?*

◊ **зупиня́тися** *to stop, stay (at hotel)*, **Тепе́р я бу́ду завжди́ зупиня́тися в цьо́му готе́лі.** *Now I'll be always staying at this hotel.*

In real life, both one- and two-word forms of the imperfective future are used interchangeably, so it is not a mistake to say **Де ви відпочива́тимете влі́тку?** and **Тепе́р я завжди́ зупиня́тимуся в цьо́му готе́лі.**

The one-word future is an originally Ukrainian form. It is not found in Polish or Russian. It should be given preference.

10.21. Answer the questions. Use the synthetic imperfective future and the suggested indications of time. Replace all nouns and nominal phrases with pronouns.

Model.

Q Чи Мико́ла вже зна́є програ́му? *Does Mykola know the program yet?* за́втра *tomorrow*

A Ще ні, але́ він зна́тиме її́ за́втра. *Not yet, but he'll know it tomorrow.*

1. Чи Юрко́ вже пи́ше впра́ву? уве́чері
2. Чи мала́ Я́рка вже вмива́ється? че́рез пів годи́ни
3. Чи Павло́ і Наді́йка вже відпочива́ють на пля́жі? насту́пного ти́жня
4. Чи ви вже йдете́ до Миха́йла й Окса́ни? че́рез годи́ну
5. Чи О́льга вже купу́є проду́кти? за́втра вра́нці
6. Чи Оре́ст і Га́ля вже переклада́ють ли́сти від Ро́берта? насту́пної п'я́тниці
7. Чи Ма́рта вже замовля́є квитки́? післяза́втра
8. Чи я вже дивлю́ся ва́ші фо́та? пі́сля пере́рви
9. Чи Марко́ та Сергі́й Козаче́нки вже про́сять їхню сестру́ допомогти́? насту́пного четверга́
10. Чи гість вже пла́тить за готе́ль? пі́сля обі́ду
11. Чи хло́пці вже ро́блять варе́ники з си́ром? пі́сля сьо́мої годи́ни ве́чора
12. Чи Лука́ш вже шука́є собі́ яку́сь робо́ту за фа́хом? одра́зу, як закі́нчить університе́т.

10.22. Answer the questions. Use the synthetic imperfective future. Replace all the nouns with pronouns.

Model.

Q Ти коли́-не́будь знав про це? *Did you ever know about it?* за́втра *tomorrow*

A Ні, я зна́тиму про це за́втра. *No, I will know about it tomorrow.*

1. Севери́н коли́-не́будь працюва́в на цій ста́нції? насту́пного мі́сяця
2. Ле́ся коли́-не́будь жила́ у цьо́му гурто́житку? насту́пного ро́ку
3. Ці ді́ти коли́-не́будь чита́ли казки́ Іва́на Франка́? у ли́пні
4. Ви коли́-не́будь писа́ли про цю пробле́му? за́втра
5. Ти коли́-не́будь говори́в про свій план? у понеді́лок
6. Ми коли́-не́будь розмовля́ли по́льською мо́вою? у Варша́ві на конфере́нції
7. Ці хло́пці коли́-не́будь вчи́лися в Ки́ївському університе́ті? че́рез три мі́сяці
8. Ми коли́-не́будь ї́здили до крамни́ці ра́зом? під час відпу́стки
9. Го́сті коли́-не́будь обі́дали у ново́му рестора́ні? цього́ вівто́рка
10. Бори́с коли́-не́будь пла́вав у Чо́рному мо́рі? насту́пного мі́сяця
11. Ми коли́-не́будь відпочива́ли на цьо́му о́зері? у се́рпні

Завда́ння для Міжнаро́дної мере́жі
Internet assignment

Пе́ред подоро́жжю тре́ба дізна́тися про пого́ду

🎧 **10.23.** Use the key words **пого́да в Украї́ні** *weather in Ukraine* and find the information on the Ukrainian language Internet to answer these questions. Refer to Notes 7.7 and 7.8, p. 120.

1. Яка́ температу́ра пові́тря вдень у Ки́єві, Ха́ркові, Симферо́полі та Льво́ві?
2. Яка́ температу́ра пові́тря вночі́ у Ки́єві, Ха́ркові, Симферо́полі та Льво́ві?
3. В яко́му мі́сті Украї́ни бу́дуть о́пади *precipitation* – дощ чи сніг?
4. В яко́му мі́сті Украї́ни бу́де со́нячно, а в яко́му – хма́рно?
5. Яка́ температу́ра води́ в Алу́шті, Євпато́рії, Ке́рчі, Севасто́полі та Я́лті?

Яка́ пого́да ма́є бу́ти за́втра в Ха́ркові?

🎧 **10.24** Listen carefully to these questions and answer each of them using Dialogue 10.

1. До ко́го зверну́вся мандрівни́к по квитки́ до Севасто́поля?
2. Яки́м по́тягом мо́жна було́ ї́хати до Севасто́поля?
3. Коли́ їм тре́ба бу́ло приї́хати до Севасто́поля?
4. Яки́м по́тягом пора́див мандрівнико́ві ї́хати каси́р?
5. З ким ще ї́хав мандрівни́к до Севасто́поля?
6. Яко́го кла́су квитки́ купи́в мандрівни́к?
7. Скі́льки кошту́вав ко́жний купе́йний квито́к?
8. Чому́ мандрівни́к не хоті́в купува́ти купе́йні квитки́?
9. Скі́льки кошту́вав ко́жний плацка́ртний квито́к?
10. Яки́м по́тягом наре́шті ви́рішив ї́хати до Севасто́поля мандрівни́к?
11. Чим хоті́в заплати́ти за квитки́ мандрівни́к?
12. Яки́м ви́дом тра́нспорту лю́бите подорожува́ти ви? Чому́?

👥 **10.25.** Enact a conversation with a partner. Use the material you learned in this and previous lessons. If necessary consult the dictionary.

Сце́нка за сце́нарієм «Квитки́ на по́їзд до Ха́ркова»
Scripted skit: *Train Tickets to Kharkiv*

Traveler (мандрівни́к): Politely says that s/he needs to get to Kharkiv.
Ticket seller (каси́р): Asks on what day (date) s/he needs to be in Kharkiv.

Traveler: Next Wednesday, September 10, before (пе́ред) 1:00 PM.
Ticket seller: Says that s/he can travel either by a night or morning train.

Тут тре́ба плати́ти лише́ готі́вкою.

У селі́ Пирого́ві під Ки́євом мандрівники́ ба́чили стари́й вітря́к.

Traveler: Inquires about the difference in ticket price for these trains.
Ticket seller: Explains that the night train is an inexpensive passenger train. The morning train is an express and therefore more expensive (доро́жчий).

Traveler: Wants to know the schedule of the night train.
Ticket seller: It departs from Kyiv at 10:33 PM and arrives in Kharkiv at 12:05 PM the following day.

Traveler: Says that the schedule suits her/him. Asks how much a 2nd class ticket for that night train is.
Ticket seller: Responds that a 2nd class ticket is HUA 150.00. (See *Ukrainian Currency,* Lesson 12, Note 12.6, p. 231.)

Traveler: Says that the price suits her/him and asks for three 2nd class tickets. Adds that he is traveling with his wife and son.
Ticket seller: Informs that three 2nd class tickets cost HUA 450.00. Asks whether or not he needs bed linen.

Traveler: S/he completely forgot. Her/his son does not seem to need a full ticket (по́вний квито́к) because he is not an adult. He is only eleven.
Ticket seller: Agrees and adds that every child from six to fourteen travels on a children's ticket (дитя́чий квито́к).

Traveler: Expresses satisfaction over the fact that s/he remembered about her/his son. Adds that s/he would need three sets (три компле́кти) of bed linen. What's the total cost?
Ticket seller: Says that one children's 2nd class ticket is HUA 100.46, and each bed linen set is HUA 18.00. Altogether HUA 604.46.

Traveler: Asks whether s/he can pay with a credit card or only cash.
Ticket seller: Says s/he can pay as s/he likes. It does not matter.

Traveler: Prefers to pay with a credit card, and offers her/his card.
Ticket seller: Asks her/him to sign. Thanks and says that here are two full and one children's 2nd class tickets for train number 64 Kyiv-Kharkiv for Wednesday, September 10.

Traveler: Thanks and complements the cashier for her/ his kindness.
Ticket seller: Says that s/he is welcome and wishes a happy journey.

Лéкція | Lesson 11

Dialogue:
Як потрáпити до музéю
How to get to the museum

Grammar:
Perfective future tense
Numerals 2, 3, and 4 + nouns
Motion verbs
Comparative and superlative adjectives
Possessive pronoun **свій** *one's own*

Competencies:
Asking for and giving directions
Street names
Colors
Comparing things

Націона́льний худо́жній музе́й розташо́вується у Музе́йному прову́лку

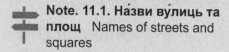

Note. 11.1. На́зви ву́лиць та площ Names of streets and squares

There are two patterns of street names:
1) *adj.* + **ву́лиця (пло́ща)**:
Володи́мирська ву́лиця *Volodymyrska Street,* **Європе́йська пло́ща** *European Square.*

The two parts can change places: **ву́лиця Володи́мирська.** Both words decline when needed, **на Володи́мирській ву́лиці** on *Volodymyrska Street,* **на ву́лиці Прорізні́й** *on Prorizna Street.*
In colloquial speech, the noun **ву́лиця** is omitted when it is clear that a street, not square, lane, or boulevard, is meant,

Він живе́ на Прорізні́й. *He lives on Prorizna Street.*

2) **ву́лиця (пло́ща)** + *noun in G.,*
ву́лиця Мазе́пи *Mazepa Street, lit. the street of Mazepa,* **пло́ща Петлю́ри** *Petliura Square.*
In this construction, only the first element is declined while the second stays in *G.,*

Кінотеа́тр є на ву́лиці Мазе́пи. *The movie theater is on Mazepa Street.*

Ми шука́ємо ву́лицю Сагайда́чного. *We are looking for Sahaidachny Street.*

Like in the former construction, the noun **ву́лиця** is often omitted, when it's self-understood,

Кінотеа́тр на Мазе́пи. *The movie theater is on Mazepa (Street).*

11. Діяло́г. Як потра́пити до музе́ю.

Гість: Скажі́ть, будь ла́ска, як потра́пити до Украї́нського музе́ю?

Кия́нка: До яко́го са́ме ви хо́чете? У Ки́єві всі музе́ї украї́нські.

Гість: А я ду́мав, що це він назива́ється так – «Украї́нський музе́й».

Кия́нка: Наскі́льки я зна́ю, музе́ю з тако́ю на́звою в столи́ці нема́є. Мо́же, ска́жете мені́ його́ адре́су?

Гість: На жаль, його́ адре́су я лиши́в на столі́ у готе́лі. Це музе́й із найбі́льшою коле́кцією украї́нського мисте́цтва, як класи́чного, так і суча́сного.

Кия́нка: Ось воно́ що! Ваш музе́й назива́ється Націона́льний худо́жній музе́й Украї́ни. Він на ву́лиці Груше́вського.

Гість: Дя́кую. Тепе́р зна́тиму, як його́ на́зву, так і адре́су.

Кия́нка: Нема́ за́ що. Отже вам тре́ба піти́ ціє́ю ву́лицею до Михайлі́вської пло́щі.

Гість: А як назива́ється ця пло́ща?

Кия́нка: Це - Софі́йська пло́ща. На Михайлі́вській пло́щі знайде́те Михайлі́вську ву́лицю.

Гість: Я що́йно там був.

Кия́нка: Михайлі́вською ву́лицею піде́те вниз до кінця́.

Гість: У кінці́ ву́лиці бу́де головна́ пло́ща Ки́єва Майда́н Незале́жности, чи не так?

Кия́нка: Пра́вильно. Тоді́ поверне́те ліво́руч і піде́те про́сто до Європе́йської пло́щі.

Гість: Як дале́ко Європе́йська пло́ща від Майда́ну Незале́жности?

Кия́нка: П'ять хвили́н пішки́. На Європе́йській знайде́те ву́лицю Груше́вського. Вона́ йде вго́ру.

Гість: Я вже її́ знайшо́в ось тут на ка́рті.

Кия́нка: На ро́зі Груше́вського та Музе́йного прову́лку бу́де ваш музе́й.

Гість: І назива́ється він Націона́льний худо́жній музе́й Украї́ни. Дя́кую вам.

Кия́нка: Про́шу. Я впе́внена, що він вам сподо́бається.

11. Dialogue. How to Get to the Museum.

Guest: Tell me, please, how to get to the Ukrainian Museum?

Kyivan: To exactly which one do you want to get? All museums in Kyiv are Ukrainian.

Guest: I thought that was what it's called *The Ukrainian Museum.*

Kyivan: As far as I know there is no museum of such a name in the capital. Maybe you'll tell me its address?

Guest: Unfortunately I left its address on the table in my hotel. This is the museum with the largest collection of Ukrainian art, both classical and contemporary.

Kyivan: That's what it is! Your museum is called the National Art Museum of Ukraine. It is on Hrushevsky Street.

Guest: Thank you. Now I'll know both its name and address.

Kyivan:	Don't mention it. So you need to go along this street to St. Michael's Square.
Guest:	And what is this square called?
Kyivan:	This is St. Sophia Square. On St. Michael's Square you'll find St. Michael's Street.
Guest:	I was there just now.
Kyivan:	You'll go down St. Michael's Street to the end.
Guest:	At the end of the street, there will be Kyiv's main square Independence Square, right?
Kyivan:	Correct. Then you'll turn left and go straight to European Square.
Guest:	How far is European Square from Independence Square?
Kyivan:	Five minutes on foot. On European (Square) you'll find Hrushevsky Street. It runs uphill.
Guest:	I have already found it right here on the map.
Kyivan:	On the corner of Hrushevsky (Street) and Museum Lane there will be the museum.
Guest:	And it's called the National Art Museum of Ukraine. Thank you.
Kyivan:	You are welcome. I am sure you will like it.

Карти́на "Маскара́д" Все́волода Максимо́вича

✏ Нота́тки до діяло́гу
Notes on the Dialogue

потра́пити, *pf.* на + *A. or* до + *G.*	to get to, **п. на Володи́мирську (на Льві́вську пло́щу)** *to get to Volodymyrska St. (to Lviv Square)* but **п. до університе́ту (ба́нку, консервато́рії)** *to get to a university (bank, conservatory).* For more see below *How to get to …* and Lesson 13, Note 13.9, p. 259.
як …, так і …	both … and …, **Як Ігор, так і Севери́н побува́ли у Полта́ві.** *Both Ihor and Severyn have been to Poltava.*
поверну́ти, *pf.*	to turn, make a turn; usually in the perfective aspect. **Тут тре́ба поверну́ти ліво́руч.** *Here, you need to turn left.*
(не)далеко від + *G.*	(not) far from… Used both on its own, as an adverb and with the preposition **від** *from*, followed by the noun in *G.*, **Це ду́же дале́ко.** *This is very far.* **Це зо́всім недале́ко.** *This is not at all far.* **Музе́й був дале́ко від ста́нції.** *The museum was far from the station.*
бульва́р, *m.*, ~у	a boulevard, a wide street typically with a pedestrian tree-flanked alley in the middle. Follows the two street name patterns (See Note 11.1): 1) **Морськи́й бульва́р** *Morsky Boulevard*, **на Морсько́му бульва́рі** *on Morsky Boulevard*; 2) **бульва́р Шевче́нка** *Shevchenko Boulevard*, **на бульва́рі Шевче́нка** *on Shevchenko Boulevard.*
проспе́кт, *m.*, ~у	an avenue, a wide and typically more important city street lined with trees. Follows the two street name patterns: 1) **Брест-Лито́вський проспе́кт** *Brest-Lytovsky Prospect*, **на Брест-Лито́вському проспе́кті** *on Brest-Lytovsky Prospect*; 2) **проспе́кт Свобо́ди** *Prospect of Liberty*, **на проспе́кті Свобо́ди** *on Prospect of Liberty.*
прову́л|ок, *m.*, ~ку	a lane, usually a short street. It is used with **у (в)** + *L.* and follows the two street name patterns: 1) **Музе́йний прову́лок** *Museum Lane*, **у Музе́йному прову́лку** *on Museum Lane*; 2) **прову́лок Стефа́ника** *Stefanyk Lane*, **у прову́лку Стефа́ника** *on Stefanyk Lane.*
р|іг, *m.*, ~о́гу	a (street) corner, **на ро́зі** + *G.* **і / та** + *G.*, **на ро́зі Хреща́тика та Проро́різної ву́лиці** *on the corner of Khreshchatyk and Prorizna Street.*

Note 11.2. Ву́лиці та пло́щі столи́ці Украї́ни
Streets and squares of the capital of Ukraine

Here are some important streets and squares of Kyiv.

Хреща́тик, *m.*	see Lesson 6, Notes on the Dialogue.
 бульва́р Шевче́нка	*Shevchenko Boulevard* is a beautiful thoroughfare with a promenade in the middle, lined with poplars. In Taras Shevchenko's poetry, the poplar symbolizes a Ukrainian girl who is waiting by the side of the road for her beloved Cossack to return from war. Among more celebrated sights of Shevchenko Boulevard are the neo-Byzantine **Володи́мирський Собо́р** *St. Volodymyr Cathedral*, **Ботані́чний сад** *the Botanical Gardens*, **Парк і́мени Шевче́нка** *the Shevchenko Park*, and the Yellow Hall of **Націона́льний університе́т і́мени Тара́са Шевче́нка** *the Taras Shevchenko National University*.
 Вели́ка Васильківська ву́лиця	*Velyka Vasylkivska Street*, one of the longest streets of the capital, is home to the biggest soccer stadium of the nation, **Олімпі́йський стадіо́н** *the Olympic Stadium*, the neo-Gothic Roman Catholic **Косте́л Свято́го Микола́я** *St. Nicholas Church*, and the prestigious concert performance venue **Пала́ц культу́ри «Украї́на»** *the Ukraina Concert Hall*.
 ву́лиця Груше́вського	*Hrushevsky Street*, runs up the hill from **Європе́йська пло́ща** *European Square*. Among its sights are: **Націона́льний худо́жній музе́й Украї́ни** *the National Art Museum of Ukraine*, **Стадіо́н «Дина́мо»** *the Dynamo soccer stadium*, **Буди́нок Уря́ду** *the House of Government* (seat of the Cabinet of Ministers), the baroque **Марі́їнський пала́ц** *Mariinsky Palace*, **Верхо́вна Ра́да** *the Supreme Rada* (Parliament of Ukraine), and **Заво́д «Арсена́л»** *the Arsenal Plant (its old building)*.
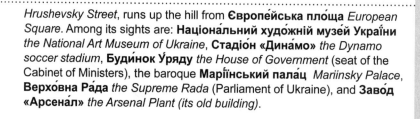 Ба́нкова ву́лиця	*Bank Street* is often used to refer to the presidential administration, which is located in the former building of the Communist Party of Ukraine Central Committee. Across the street is the famous **Буди́нок із химе́рами** the *House of Chimaeras*, an admired sample of Kyiv architectural *moderne*, sumptuously adorned with figures of mythic creatures and animals. Like *St. Nicholas Church* on Velyka Vasylkivska Street, it was designed by the architect Vladyslav Horodetsky, who is often called the Antonio Gaudí of Kyiv.
 Володи́мирська ву́лиця	*St. Volodymyr Street* lined with chestnut trees runs from the majestic 11th-century **Софі́йський Собо́р** *St. Sophia Cathedral* past **Золоті́ воро́та** *the Golden Gate*, **Націона́льна о́пера** *the National Opera House*. It is also home to the historic **Буди́нок учи́теля** *House of Teachers*, seat of the Central Rada, the first elective body of independent Ukraine in 1917-1918, and **Націона́льний університе́т і́мени Тара́са Шевче́нка** *the Taras Shevchenko National University* painted in a striking deep red.
 Андрі́ївський узві́з, на Андрі́ївському узво́зі	*St. Andrew's Street* runs downhill from the grounds of the ancient 10th-century city and **Андрі́ївська це́рква** *St. Andrew's Church* to the district of **Поді́л** *Podil* or *Lower City*. This pedestrian haven is allegedly the most romantic street of the capital, Kyiv's version of Montmartre. Artists and craftsmen from many parts of Ukraine sell all kinds of souvenirs here, such as painted Easter eggs, wood carvings, pottery, embroidered shirts, figurines, paintings, and old curiosities.

майда́н Незале́жности

Independence Square is located in the middle of Khreshchatyk. This monumental agglomeration of architectural tastelessness was made famous worldwide by the events of the 2004 **Помара́нчева револю́ція** *the Orange Revolution*. On weekends, it is the venue for pop-concerts. In the past, it hosted free performances by such pop-icons as Paul McCartney, George Michael, and Elton John, among others. The much beloved square is often referred to simply as **Майда́н** *the Square (See Ex. 11.19)*.

Євро́пейська пло́ща

European Square is located at the crossroads of Khreshchatyk, Hrushevsky Street, and St. Volodymyr Uzviz. Here one can see **Націона́льна Філармо́нія** *the National Philharmonics*, **Украї́нський Дім** *the Ukrainian Home*, a popular exhibition facility, and **Парла́ментська бібліоте́ка** *the Library of Parliament*.

Контракто́ва пло́ща

Contract Square is the heart of the old Podil District of Kyiv with the spectacular **Гости́нний Двір** *Travelers' Court*, the baroque 17th-century building of **Ки́єво-Могиля́нська Акаде́мія** *Kyiv-Mohyla Academy*, the oldest Ukrainian University and arguably one of the most prestigious schools of higher learning in the nation.

 Note 11.3. Як потра́пити на (до) …
How to get to …

потра́пити, *pf.* + **на** + *A.* **ву́лицю (пло́щу, перехре́стя, ріг; автовокза́л)** or + **до** + *G.* **музе́ю (ба́нку, крамни́ці, суперма́кету)**	to get to; is used with **на**, if it's a street, intersection, square or part of town (like **Поді́л**), *but also* **вокза́л** *station*; used with **до**, if it is a place like museum, theater, store, doctor's office, etc., or a park, village, city.
Як потра́пити до теа́тру?	How can I get to the theater?
Як потра́пити на пло́щу Франка́?	How can I get to Franko Square?
Де розташо́вується музе́й?	Where is the museum located?
іді́ть пря́мо, *im.*	go straight
іді́ть пря́мо + *I.* **ціє́ю ву́лицею**, *im.*	go straight along the street
іді́ть до + *G.* **пе́ршого перехре́стя**, *im.*	go to the first intersection
поверні́ть право́руч (ліво́руч), *im.*	turn right (left)
право́руч, *adv.*	on the right, to the right
ліво́руч, *adv.*	on your left, to the left
перехре́ст|я, *nt.*	intersection, **на ~ті** + *G.* **та** + *G.* on the intersection of … and .., **на ~і Хреща́тика та Прорі́зної** *on the intersection of Khreshchatyk and Prorizna Streets*
поба́ч/ити + *A.*, *pf.*, **-ать**	to see, **ви поба́чите** you'll see
перейді́ть + *A.* **ву́лицю (прову́лок, пло́щу)**, *im.*	cross the street (lane, square)
кварта́л, *m.*, **~у**	a block of buildings, city block, **Пройді́ть три ~и та поверні́ть ліво́руч.** Pass three blocks and turn left.

Дани́ло поба́читься з Дени́сом увече́рі на майда́ні Незале́жности і все йому́ розка́же.

📖 Грама́тика | Grammar

Майбу́тній доко́наний час   Perfective Future Tense

Фу́нкція   Function

Perfective future presents a future action as finished and emphasizes its result, **За́втра я поба́чу Мико́лу.** *Tomorrow I shall see Mykola.*

Often perfective future denotes completed action, which is followed by another action,
Я подзвоню́ до Мико́ли і запрошу́ його́ на вече́рю. *I'll call Mykola and invite him for dinner.*

Утво́рення   Formation

Perfective future uses the same set of personal endings as the present tense, which are added to the perfective stem. The verb in the perfective future follows 1st or 2nd present tense conjugation (See pp. 79-82):

пи́ти / ви́пити *to drink (1st conj.)*

pres. sg.	future pf. sg.		pres. pl.	future pf. pl.	
я п'ю	**я ви́п'ю**	I'll drink	ми п'ємо́	**ми ви́п'ємо**	we'll drink
ти п'єш	**ти ви́п'єш**	you'll drink	ви п'єте́	**ви ви́п'єте**	you'll drink
він п'є	**він ви́п'є**	he'll drink	вони́ п'ють	**вони́ ви́п'ють**	they'll drink

роби́ти / зроби́ти *to do (2nd conj.):*

pres. sg.	future pf. sg.		pres. pl.	future pf. pl.	
я роблю́	**я зроблю́**	I'll do	ми ро́бимо	**ми зро́бимо**	we'll do
ти ро́биш	**ти зро́биш**	you'll do	ви ро́бите	**ви зро́бите**	you'll do
він ро́бить	**він зро́бить**	he'll do	вони́ ро́блять	**вони́ зро́блять**	they'll do

Most other verbs follow the same conjugation patterns in the perfective future:
сказа́ти, ска́ж|уть *to say,* **поба́ч|ити, ~ать** *to see,* **почу́|ти, ~ють** *to hear,* **зрозумі́|ти, ~ють** *to understand,* **побі́гти, побіж|а́ть** *to run,* **запита́|ти, ~ють** *to ask.*

When the difference between the perfective stem and the perfective infinitive is considerable, the dictionary provides the stem of the perfective future. Here are a few such instances:
відпочи́ти, відпочи́н|уть *to rest,* **сі́сти, ся́д|уть** *to sit down, sit, take a seat,* **взя́ти, ві́зьм|уть** *to take.* They still use the personal endings of the present tense to form the future perfective,

бра́ти; взя́ти *to take* ві́зьм|уть *(1ˢᵗ conj.):*

pres. sg.	fut. pf. sg.	pres. pl.	fut. pf. pl.
я беру́	я візьму́	ми беремо́	ми ві́зьмемо
ти бере́ш	ти ві́зьмеш	ви берете́	ви ві́зьмете
він бере́	він ві́зьме	вони́ беру́ть	вони́ ві́зьмуть

Note the perfective future forms of **да́ти** *to give*

fut. pf. sg.	fut. pf. pl.
я дам	**ми дамо́**
ти даси	**ви дасте́**
він дасть	**вони́ дадуть**

Common indicators of the perfective future time are:
вже (уже́) *already,* **за́втра** *tomorrow,* **післяза́втра** *the day after tomorrow,* **ско́ро, незаба́ром** *soon,* **насту́пного ти́жня (мі́сяця, ро́ку)** *next week (month, year),* **че́рез** + *A. of time period, in, within,* **че́рез годи́ну** *in one hour,* **че́рез ти́ждень** *in one week;*

за + *A. of time period, in, within,*
за день *in one day,* **за рік** *in one year.*

 Украї́нські кольори́ | Ukrainian Colors

Color	Eng.	G. sg. of white (etc.) color
бі́лий	white	Цей сніг бі́лого ко́льору.
чо́рний	black	Цей комп'ю́тер чо́рного ко́льору.
черво́ний	red	Цей автомобі́ль черво́ного ко́льору.
жо́втий	yellow	Со́нце жо́втого ко́льору.
зеле́ний	green	Це де́рево зеле́ного ко́льору.
си́ній	blue	О́чі си́нього ко́льору.
блаки́тний	azure	Не́бо блаки́тного ко́льору.
фіоле́товий	purple	Ці кві́ти фіоле́тового ко́льору.
сі́рий	gray	Мій кіт сі́рого ко́льору.
кори́чневий	brown	Мої́ ме́блі кори́чневого ко́льору
or **бруна́тний**		Ваш стіл бруна́тного ко́льору.

Genitive or accusative are used to inquire about and denote the color of objects,

G. **Яко́го ко́льору кни́жка?** *lit. Of what color is the book?*
Кни́жка зеле́ного ко́льору. *The book is of green color* or
Кни́жка зеле́на. *The book is green.*

A. **Яка́ на ко́лір кни́жка?** *What color is the book. lit. What is the book by color?*
Кни́жка зеле́на. *The book is green.*

 Note 11.4. Яко́го ко́льору ва́ші о́чі? What color are your eyes?

When used to describe human

eyes and hair Ukrainian color nominations have certain idiosyncracies. Take a note of these set expressions.

amber eyes	буршти́нові о́чі
dark eyes	чо́рні о́чі
blue eyes	си́ні о́чі
brown eyes	ка́рі о́чі
gray eyes	сі́рі о́чі
green eyes	зеле́ні о́чі
hazel eyes	я́сно-ка́рі о́чі

Мої́ (твої́, його́, її́) о́чі ка́рі
My (your, his, her) eyes are brown.
or
У ме́не (те́бе, ньо́го, не́ї) ка́рі о́чі.
I (you, he, she) have (has) brown eyes.

Note 11.5. Яко́го ко́льору ва́ше воло́сся? What color is your hair?

blond hair	біля́ве воло́сся
black hair	чо́рне воло́сся
brown hair	ру́се воло́сся
auburn hair	кашта́нове воло́сся
grey hair	си́ве воло́сся
red hair	руде́ воло́сся
ashen gray hair	попеля́сте воло́сся

Моє́ воло́сся ру́се (руде́, кашта́нове, ко́льору блонд). *My hair is brown (red, auburn, blond).*

The English *He has blond hair.* corresponds to **Він блонди́н.** while *She has blonde hair.* is equivalent to **Вона́ блонди́нка.**

📟 Note 11.6. Numerals with оди́н *one* + *noun*

Composite numerals that end in **оди́н** *one* must agree in gender with the noun following them,

m. **кіломе́т(е)р** *a kilometer* - **сто оди́н кіломе́т(е)р** *a hundred and one kilometers*
f. **гри́вня** *a hryvnia* - **со́рок одна́ гри́вня** *forty-one hryvnias;*
nt. **ім'я́** *a name* - **два́дцять одне́ ім'я́** *twenty one names.*

Unlike in English, the noun following such **оди́н**-ended numerals is in the singular, not plural,

сто оди́н чолові́к *a hundred and one men*
два́дцять одна́ гри́вня *twenty-one hryvnias*

Столи́ця Галичини́ Льві́в – мі́сто ле́вів.

📟 Числі́вники із 2, 3 та 4 + іме́нник
Numerals with 2, 3, and 4 + Noun

The numeral **два** *two*, has two gender forms:
1) *m.* and *nt.* **два**, *m.* **два хло́пці** *two boys*, *nt.* **два міста́** *two cities*;
2) *f.* **дві**, **дві дівчи́ни** *two girls*, **дві ма́тері** *two mothers*.

In the expressions *numeral + noun* where the numeral either is, or ends in, **два (дві)**, **три**, or **чоти́ри**, the noun takes:
- ◙ the ending of the nominative plural and
- ◙ the stress of the genitive singular

provided that such an expression is used on its own or as the subject or inanimate accusative object in the sentence.

Сто со́рок два чолові́ки відві́дали музе́й. *A hundred and forty-two people visited the museum.*
Ми прочита́ємо три кни́жки. *We will read three books.*

N. sg.	G. sg.	N. pl.		num. + n.
сестра́	сестри́	се́стри	>>	дві сестри́ *two sisters*
брат	бра́та	брати́	>>	два бра́ти *two brothers*

This rule only applies if the numerals **два (дві)**, **три**, and **чоти́ри** are actually pronounced, like in **два́дцять два** *twenty-two*, **вісімдеся́т три** *eighty-three*, or **дві́сті чоти́ри** *two hundred and four*. The rule does not apply when these numerals are not pronounced, like in **12 - двана́дцять** *twelve*, **13 - трина́дцять** *thirteen*, or **114 - сто чотирна́дцять** *a hundred and fourteen*.

Exception. Nouns whose nominative plural differs from their singular form in the stem of the word, not just in the ending, take the genitive singular after **два (дві)**, **три**, and **чоти́ри**,

N. sg.	G. sg.	N. pl.		num. + n.
дити́на	дити́ни	ді́ти	>>	дві дити́ни *two children*
ді́вчина	ді́вчини	дівча́та	>>	дві ді́вчини *two girls*
люди́на	люди́ни	лю́ди	>>	три люди́ни *three people*
ім'я́	íмени	імена́	>>	чоти́ри íмени *four names*
друг	дру́га	дру́зі	>>	два дру́га *two friends*

The exception also pertains to all ~**я́нин**-type nouns,

N. sg.	G. sg.	N. pl.		numeral + n.
кия́нин	кия́нина	кия́ни	>>	два кия́нина *two Kyivans*
селя́нин	селя́нина	селя́ни	>>	три селя́нина *three peasants*

Adjectives, demonstrative, interrogative, and possessive pronouns accompanying the nouns are either in the nominative or genitive plural. There is no difference in meaning (More on *G. pl.* in Lesson 12, pp. 223-225):

(N. pl.) **ва́ші три ціка́ві кни́жки** *your three interesting books* or
   (G. pl.) **ва́ших три ціка́вих кни́жки**

(N. pl.) **ї́хні два старі́ дру́га** *their two old friends* or
   (G. pl.) **ї́хніх два стари́х дру́га**
(N. pl.) **ці дві розу́мні ді́вчини** *these two intelligent girls* or
   (G. pl.) **цих дві розу́мних ді́вчини**

Дієслова́ ру́ху Motion Verbs

In Ukrainian, verbs expressing motion stand out from the rest of
the verbs in the fact that each of them has a set of two imperfective
infinitives: 1) uni-directional and 2) multi-directional. Thus *to walk, go
on foot* is 1) **іти́ (йти)**; 2) **ходи́ти**. In the dictionary, they are assigned
the respective labels of *uni.* and *multi.* Each of them presents the act
of movement in its own specific manner.

English motion verb	uni-directional	multi-directional
to go on foot, walk	**іти́** *var.* **йти**	**ходи́ти**
to go by vehicle, drive	**ї́хати**	**ї́здити**
to run	**бі́гти**	**бі́гати**
to fly	**леті́ти**	**літа́ти**

For conjugation of these motions verbs in the present, future
perfective, and past perfective tenses consult the Appendices,
Table 16.

Uni-directional motion verbs present the motion as:

1) linear, progressing from A to B, as opposed to a round trip,
Сього́дні ми йдемо́ до теа́тру. *Today we are going to the theater.*

2) a one-time event, occurring at a specific moment as opposed to
something customary and repetitive,
Коли́ ви бу́дете леті́ти до Ки́єва? *When will you be flying to Kyiv?*
(On one specific occasion, for example, next Monday).

Multi-directional motion verbs present the motion as:

1) a circular, there-and-back trip, as opposed to linear A-to-B
progression,
Вчо́ра він ходи́в до теа́тру. *Yesterday he went to the theater.* (He
went to the theater and returned home).
2) a habitual, repetitive occurrence as opposed to a one-time,
concrete event,
Рані́ше ми за́вжди *multi.* **ї́здили до ціє́ї крамни́ці, але цьо́го
ра́зу ми** *uni.* **ї́демо до і́ншої.** *Earlier we always drove to this store,
but this time around we are driving to a different one.*

Multi-directional verbs are therefore often accompanied by such
adverbs as **за́вжди** *always,* **ніко́ли** *never,* **ча́сто** *often,* **рі́дко** *seldom,*
ко́жного понеді́лка *every Monday,* **щоти́жня** *every week* and the like,

Ми ча́сто хо́димо до басе́йну. *We often go to a swimming pool.*

Лука́ш до́бре ї́здить велосипе́дом.

Взагалі Оле́ксі Михальчуко́ві подо́бається ї́здити метро́м, але́ сього́дні він ї́де авто́бусом.

Even if no such modifier is used, the multi-directional verb alone implies such a habitual characteristic.

Multi-directional verbs are used after such verbs as:

люби́ти + *inf. to like*
подо́батися + *inf. to like*
вмі́ти + *inf. to be able*
зна́ти як + *inf. to know how*
могти́ + *inf. to be able*

Я люблю́ бі́гати. *I like to jog.*
Дитя́ ще не вмі́є ходи́ти. *The child cannot walk yet.*
Він зна́є як літа́ти де́шево. *He knows how to fly on the cheap.*

Take a look at the sentences with counter-opposed representations of what for the English is one and the same motion. A multi-directional verb presents a habitual action vs a uni-directional one that presents a one-time occurrence:

Я не люблю́ ходи́ти до о́пери, але́ сього́дні я туди́ йду.	*I don't like to go to the opera but today I am going there.*
Вони́ рі́дко ї́здять на робо́ту а́втом, але́ цього́ ра́зу вони́ ним і́дуть.	*They rarely go to work by car, but this time they are going by it.*
Він ніко́ли не бі́гає по цій ву́лиці, але́ за́раз він по ній біжи́ть.	*He never runs along this street, but now he is running along it.*
Ми рі́дко літа́ємо до Пари́жа, але́ за́втра ми туди́ летимо́.	*We seldom fly to Paris but tomorrow we are flying there.*

> ✎ **йти (ходи́ти)** *vs* **ї́хати (ї́здити)**
> Unlike in English, where *to go* can mean both *to walk on foot* and *to move by a vehicle*, Ukrainian makes a clear distinction between these two types of motion. Thus **йти** or **ходи́ти** means *to go on foot* and **ї́хати** or **ї́здити** means *to go by a vehicle* like a car, bicycle, bus or train. One cannot be used in place of the other. The sentence **Він ходи́в до Льво́ва.** means literally *He walked to Lviv on foot.*

📖 Впра́ви Exercises

∩ **11.1.** Answer the questions in the future perfective. Use indicators of future time found in this lesson. Replace nouns with personal pronouns.

Model.
Q Коли́ він ду́має писа́ти лист?
When does he plan to write the letter?

A Я впе́внений (впе́внена), що він його́ напи́ше сього́дні (за́втра, ско́ро і т.д.). *I am sure he will write it today (tomorrow, soon, etc.).*

1. Коли́ ти ду́маєш розка́зувати про цю ді́вчину?
2. Коли́ ми ду́маємо дзвони́ти до ма́тері?
3. Коли́ вони́ ду́мають диви́тися цей документа́льний фільм?
4. Коли́ ви ду́маєте ї́хати до Оле́нки Ма́рченко?
5. Коли́ ти ду́маєш вчи́ти іспа́нську грама́тику?
6. Коли́ Мари́на й Оле́г ду́мають чита́ти нову́ книжку Де́реша?
7. Коли́ Іва́н ду́має знахо́дити час на відпочи́нок?
8. Коли́ вона́ ду́має купува́ти подару́нок?
9. Коли́ Ві́ктор ду́має закі́нчувати навча́ння?
10. Коли́ Га́нна ду́має почина́ти нову́ кінокарти́ну?

∩ 11.2. Say what these people intend to do and finish doing.

Model.
C я *I, impf.* роби́ти ⇔ *pf.* зроби́ти завда́ння *to do an assignment*
A Я бу́ду роби́ти завда́ння, і зроблю́ його́ обов'язко́во.
I'll be doing the assignment and will do (finish) it by all means.

1. Марі́я, *Maria,* писа́ти ⇔ написа́ти лист *to write a letter*
2. Степа́н *Stepan,* переклада́ти ⇔ перекла́сти текст *to translate a text*
3. робі́тники, *workers* будува́ти ⇔ збудува́ти готе́ль *to build a hotel*
4. ри *we,* чита́ти ⇔ прочита́ти кни́жку *to read a book*
5. ви, *pl. you* вари́ти ⇔ звари́ти вече́рю *to cook dinner*
6. ді́ти *children,* пи́ти ⇔ ви́пити молоко́ *to drink milk*
7. ти *sg.* you, ми́ти ⇔ поми́ти а́вто *to wash a car*
8. вони́ *they,* продава́ти ⇔ прода́ти я́блука *to sell apples*

∩ 11.3. Answer the questions. Say at what time the event will start, end, or occur. Use the future perfective.

Model.
Q Ле́кція вже закі́нчи́лася? *Has the lecture already ended?*
пе́рша годи́на *the first hour*
A Ще ні, але́ вона́ закі́нчи́ться о пе́ршій годи́ні.
Not yet, but it'll end at one o'clock.

1. Фільм вже поча́вся? сьо́ма годи́на
2. Семіна́р вже закі́нчи́вся? деся́та годи́на
3. Сестра́ вже подзвони́ла? тре́тя годи́на
4. Ва́ше поба́чення вже було́? двана́дцята годи́на
5. Марко́ вже дав їм інтерв'ю́? одина́дцята годи́на
6. Ви вже порозмовля́ли з О́лею? шо́ста годи́на
7. Універма́г вже відкри́вся? чотирна́дцята годи́на
8. Го́сті вже повече́ряли? дев'ятна́дцята годи́на
9. Метро́ вже відкри́лося? п'я́та годи́на

За́втра цей відо́мий іспа́нець дасть інтерв'ю́ для украї́нського кіножурна́лу.

У моє́ї по́други Да́ни чудо́ві сі́рі о́чі.

∩ **11.4.** Answer the questions.

Model.
Q Яко́го ко́льору цей буди́нок? *What color is this building?*
фіоле́товий *purple*
A Він фіоле́тового ко́льору. *It is of purple color.*
Він фіоле́товий. *It is purple.*

1. Яко́го ко́льору ця кни́жка? си́ній
2. Яко́го ко́льору ця крава́тка? бруна́тний
3. Яко́го ко́льору це а́вто? черво́ний
4. Яко́го ко́льору ця парасо́лька? чо́рний
5. Яко́го ко́льору ці кві́ти? жо́втий
6. Яко́го ко́льору цей комп'ю́тер? бі́лий
7. Яко́го ко́льору цей стіл? сі́рий
8. Яко́го ко́льору ці штани́? кори́чневий

∩ **11.5.** Answer the questions. Use the colors you learned in this lesson. Replace nouns with personal pronouns where possible.

1. Соро́чку яко́го ко́льору шука́є Марі́я?
2. Яко́го ко́льору а́вто хо́чуть купи́ти О́льга з Ві́ктором?
3. Яко́го ко́льору о́чі подо́баються вам?
4. У які́ кольори́ ви пофарбу́єте сті́ни ново́ї кварти́ри?
5. Яки́й ко́лір за́раз тут у мо́ді?
6. Яки́м ко́льором ти лю́биш писа́ти?
7. Яко́го ко́льору воло́сся ма́є ва́ша нова́ при́ятелька?
8. Яко́го ко́льору мате́рію вони́ купи́ли на костю́ми?
9. Яко́го ко́льору (є) його́ о́чі?
10. Яки́й ко́лір воло́сся подо́бається тобі́?
11. Яки́м ко́льором ти пофарбува́ла ві́кна?
12. Яки́й ко́лір ви́йшов з мо́ди?
13. Яко́го ко́льору взагалі́ мо́жуть бу́ти о́чі?
14. Яко́го ко́льору взагалі́ мо́же бу́ти воло́сся?

∩ **11.6.** Engage in a brief Q-and-A. Use the case form required by the numeral. Follow the model below.

Model. ти *you*, 22, ти́ха годи́на, *a quiet hour*.
Q Що тобі́ тре́ба? *What do you need?*
A Мені́ тре́ба два́дцять дві ти́хі годи́ни. *I need 22 quiet hours.*

1. ми, 52, до́бра люди́на
2. ми, 302, нова́ гри́вня
3. ти, 4, ціка́ва кни́жка
4. я, 2, близьки́й друг
5. вони́, 3, смачне́ я́блуко
6. він, 24, мала́ дити́на
7. вона́, 2, пе́рше заня́ття
8. Оле́г, 3, ві́льне мі́сце
9. Мико́ла, 2, знайо́ма ді́вчина
10. ви, 4, стари́й селяни́н
11. Ната́лка, 3, лі́тній мі́сяць
12. Тара́с, 82, стара́ копі́йка
13. інжене́р, 33, оста́ння секу́нда
14. кінорежисе́р, 24, осі́нній день

⌒ 11.7. Choose either **іти́** or **ходи́ти** *to go on foot.*

1. Сього́дні ми ма́ємо іти́ / ходи́ти на вече́рю всі ра́зом.
2. Яри́на ча́сто іде́ / хо́дить до нас в го́сті.
3. Цієї п'я́тниці я іду́ / ходжу́ на заня́ття о пе́ршій годи́ні.
4. Чи ви йдете́ / хо́дите до басе́йну ко́жної неді́лі?
5. Марко́ і Ка́тря іду́ть / хо́дять на ко́жний нови́й фільм.
6. Ти іде́ш / хо́диш на сього́днішню ле́кцію?
7. Скі́льки разі́в на ти́ждень вони́ іду́ть / хо́дять до спортклу́бу?

⌒ 11.8. Choose the form of **їхати** or **ї́здити** *to ride* required by the context.

1. Улі́тку Рома́н та Оле́на їду́ть / ї́здять на пляж раз на ти́ждень.
2. Сього́дні ми не їдемо́ / ї́здимо до батькі́в.
3. Я люблю́ їхати / ї́здити мотоци́клом.
4. Ната́ля мо́же їхати / ї́здити велосипе́дом.
5. Петро́ вже їде / ї́здить до крамни́ці?
6. О котрі́й годи́ні ви їдете / ї́здите до Оде́си сього́дні?
7. Як ча́сто ва́ші батьки́ їду́ть / ї́здять на мо́ре?

⌒ 11.9. Translate into Ukrainian. Make a clear distinction between a motion on foot - **іти́ / ходи́ти** or by a vehicle - **їхати / ї́здити**.

1. I go to school every day.
2. My sister is going to Lviv tomorrow.
3. We often go by car and rarely by bus.
4. These Americans are going to the opera now.
5. Shall we walk or drive to your place (до вас)?
6. Pavlo is sick and cannot walk.
7. Do you often go to New York?
8. You need to go to the swimming-pool every day.
9. The hotel is far. We need to go there by taxi.

⌒ 11.10. React to the cue. Mind the difference between a uni-directional verb implying 'now' and a multi-directional one implying 'seldom'.

Model.
C я *I,* автомобі́ль *a car,* автобус *a bus.*
A За́раз я їду автомобі́лем, бо я рі́дко ї́жджу авто́бусом.
Right now I am going by car, because I seldom go by bus.

1. я, авто́бус, по́їзд
2. ти, метро́, маршру́тка
3. він, троле́йбус, авто́бус
4. ми, трамва́й, метро́
5. ви, велосипе́д, а́вто
6. вона́, залізни́ця, корабе́ль
7. вони́, маршру́тка, трамва́й
8. я, по́їзд, маши́на

Алла́ ча́сто хо́дить до музе́ю "Мисте́цький арсена́л".

Мину́лого лі́та Рома́н з Оле́ною ча́сто ї́здили на Бі́ле о́зеро.

11.11. Say where these people were. Use the imperfective past tense of the multi-directional verb for a round trip.

Model. *Petro went to the store. (He's back now)*
Петро́ ходи́в до крамни́ці.

1. Last year, we flew to New York.
2. Yesterday, they went to the museum.
3. You went (*f.*) to Ternopil last Wednesday.
4. Olena already drove to the station.
5. Three hours ago, I ran to the bank.
6. Last week, Ivan went to the doctor.
7. Last Thursday, our students went to this new exhibition.
8. The day before yesterday, they ran to the beach.

11.12. Ask about the location of an institution/sight. Then answer the question. Pay attention to the prepositions.

Model. університе́т *a university,*
Володи́мирська ву́лиця *Volodymyrska Street*

Q Скажі́ть, будь ла́ска, де розташо́ваний університе́т?
Tell me please where is the university located?
A З приє́мністю. Він на Володи́мирській ву́лиці.
With pleasure. It is on Volodymyrska Street.

1. Льві́вський цирк,
ву́лиця Городо́цька

2. Націона́льний банк Украї́ни,
ву́лиця Інститу́тська

3. залізни́чний вокза́л,
Привокза́льна пло́ща

4. Ки́єво-Могиля́нська акаде́мія,
Контракто́ва пло́ща.

5. пам'ятник ге́тьманові Хмельни́цькому, Софі́йська пло́ща

6. Ки́єво-Пече́рська Ла́вра, ву́лиця Іва́на Мазе́пи

7. Володи́мирський собо́р, бульва́р Шевче́нка

8. Націона́льна о́пера Украї́ни, Володи́мирська ву́лиця

9. Ки́ївська консервато́рія, майда́н Незале́жности

10. Націона́льна філармо́нія, Європе́йська пло́ща

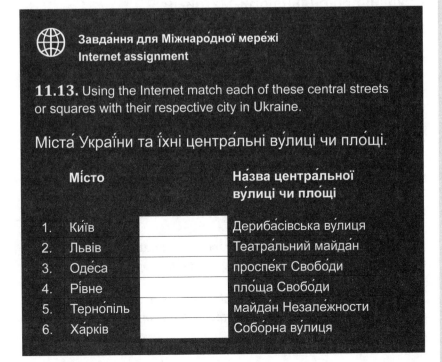

🌐 **Завда́ння для Міжнаро́дної мере́жі**
Internet assignment

11.13. Using the Internet match each of these central streets or squares with their respective city in Ukraine.

Міста́ Украї́ни та їхні центра́льні ву́лиці чи пло́щі.

Мі́сто		Назва центра́льної ву́лиці чи пло́щі
1. Ки́їв		Дериба́сівська ву́лиця
2. Львів		Театра́льний майда́н
3. Оде́са		проспе́кт Свобо́ди
4. Рі́вне		пло́ща Свобо́ди
5. Терно́піль		майда́н Незале́жности
6. Ха́рків		Собо́рна ву́лиця

✎ Note 11.7. Comparing things

When things, people, experiences, etc. are compared they can be graded along the scale of at least three measures of quality:

1) A **positive** degree simply names a given quality: *clean, long, intelligent.*

2) A **comparative** degree signifies a greater amount of the same quality relative to the positive: *cleaner, longer, more intelligent.*

3) A **superlative** degree expresses the greatest possible amount of the same quality: *the cleanest, the longest, the most intelligent.*

Ха́рків

Терно́піль

Оде́са

Львів

Ки́їв

Рі́вне

Сту́пені порі́вняння прикме́тників
Degrees of comparison of adjectives

Зна́чення   Function

Each Ukrainian adjective that denotes a quality has three respective degrees of comparison:
1) positive, a.k.a. dictionary form, **га́рний** *nice,* **смачни́й** *tasty,* **ясни́й** *clear*
2) comparative, **гарні́ший** *nicer,* **смачні́ший** *tastier,* **ясні́ший** *clearer*
3) the superlative **найгарні́ший** *the nicest,* **найсмачні́ший** *the tastiest,* **найясні́ший** *the clearest*

The **comparative degree** normally means a greater measure of quality possessed by one out of two compared objects,

Христи́на ду́має, що По́льща – ціка́ва краї́на, а Украї́на ціка́віша.
Khrystyna thinks that Poland is an interesting country, but Ukraine is more interesting.

Less commonly, the comparative degree can express a lesser measure of quality in one of the two compared objects:

Богда́н ду́має, що По́льща - ціка́ва краї́на, а Украї́на менш ціка́ва.
Bohdan thinks that Poland is an interesting country, but that Ukraine is less interesting.

Утво́рення   *Formation*

The comparative degree of adjectives is formed by the suffix **~іш~** inserted between the stem and the ending of a dictionary form of the adjective.
The superlative degree is formed by the prefix **най~** added to the comparative degree:

dictionary form	comparative degree	superlative degree
чо́рний black	**чорні́ший** blacker	**найчорні́ший** the blackest
га́рний beautiful	**гарні́ший** more beautiful	**найгарні́ший** the most beautiful
смачни́й tasty	**смачні́ший** tastier	**найсмачні́ший** the tastiest

Stress. The suffix **~іш~** normally attracts the stress both in the comparative and superlative forms of the adjective. In adjectives with more than three syllables the stress can remain unchanged,

dictionary form	comparative degree	superlative degree
впливо́вий *influential*	**впливо́віший** *more influential*	**найвпливо́віший** *the most influential*
доскона́лий *perfect*	**доскона́ліший** *more perfect*	**найдоскона́ліший** *the most perfect*

∩ 11.14. Form the comparative degree of these adjectives. Make sure that adjectives and pronouns agree with their nouns in gender. Use different intensifiers from Note 11.8.

Model. смішни́й *funny*, істо́рія *a story*
C Ця істо́рія до́сить смішна́. *This story is rather funny.*
A А та ще смішні́ша. *And that one is even funnier.*

1. ціка́вий *interesting*, рома́н *a novel*
2. га́рний *beautiful*, соро́чка *a shirt*
3. нови́й *new*, велосипе́д *a bicycle*
4. нудни́й *boring*, виклада́ч *an instructor*

 Note 11.8. Intensifiers of quality

Comparative forms of adjectives can be used with intensifiers such as:
◊ **ще** *still,*
Ця істо́рія ще смішні́ша, ніж попере́дня. *This story is still funnier than the previous one.*
◊ **набага́то** *much,*
Рома́н набага́то ста́рший, ніж його́ жі́нка. *Roman is much older than his wife.*
◊ **зна́чно** *considerably,*
Він став зна́чно серйо́знішим у́чнем. *He became a considerably more serious student.*
◊ **помі́тно** *noticeably,*
Його́ валі́зи ста́ли помі́тно тя́жчі. *His suitcases became noticeably heavier.*
◊ **дале́ко** *by far,*
Вони́ дале́ко бага́тші, як ви ду́маєте. *They are by far richer than you think.*
◊ **куди́** *colloq. way,*
Іва́н куди́ талантови́тіший, як Анато́лій. *Ivan is way more gifted than Anatoliy.*
◊ **однозна́чно** *singularly,*
Їхня кімна́та однозна́чно приє́мніша, ніж ва́ша. *Their room is singularly more pleasant than yours.*

По́други хо́чуть замо́вити найкра́щі стра́ви в меню́.

5. холо́дний *cold*, напі́й *a drink*
6. страшни́й *awful*, буди́нок *a building*
7. стари́й *old*, за́мок *a castle*
8. сумни́й *sad*, пі́сня *a song*
9. гаря́чий *hot*, ка́ва *coffee*
10. ясни́й *bright*, ко́лір *a color*
11. складни́й *complicated*, завда́ння *a task*
12. си́льний *strong*, жі́нка *a woman*
13. зручни́й *comfortable*, мі́сце *a seat*
14. ди́вний *strange*, пропози́ція *an offer*
15. щасли́вий *happy*, сім'я́ *a family*
16. сві́жий *fresh*, смета́на *sour cream*

Note 11.9. Parallel forms of adjectives

Several frequently used adjectives have two parallel comparatives and superlatives that are different in meaning:

◊ **молоди́й** *young*, *comp.* **моло́дший** *younger, junior*, **молоді́ший** *younger (if both members compared are young)*

◊ **стари́й** *old*, *comp.* **ста́рший** *older, senior, elder* and **старі́ший** *older, (if two members of comparison are both old)*

◊ **до́брий** 1) *good;* 2) *delicious;* 3) *kind*, *comp.* **кра́щий (лі́пший)** *better* and **добрі́ший** *tastier, kinder*

Take note. Some adjectives with the suffixes ~к~, ~ок~, ~ек~ form their comparative degree by replacing them with the suffix ~ш~. The same suffix is used by some other adjectives. Memorize them.

dictionary form	comparative degree	superlative degree
глибо́кий *deep*	**гли́бший** *deeper*	**найгли́бший** *deepest*
дале́кий *far*	**да́льший** *farther*	**найда́льший** *farthest*
коро́ткий *short*	**коро́тший** *shorter*	**найкоро́тший** *shortest*
м'яки́й *soft*	**м'я́кший** *softer*	**найм'я́кший** *softest*
соло́дкий *sweet*	**соло́дший** *sweeter*	**найсоло́дший** *sweetest*
тонки́й *thin*	**то́нший** *thinner*	**найто́нший** *thinnest*
широ́кий *wide*	**ши́рший** *wider*	**найши́рший** *widest*
швидки́й *fast*	**шви́дший** *faster*	**найшви́дший** *fastest*
легки́й *easy, light*	**ле́гший** *easier*	**найле́гший** *easiest*
деше́вий *cheap*	**деше́вший** *cheaper*	**найдеше́вший** *cheapest*
до́вгий *long*	**до́вший** *longer*	**найдо́вший** *longest*

Note. 11.10. Superlative degree intensifiers

Superlative adjectives can be used with their own intensifiers, such as:

◊ **абсолю́тно** *absolutely*,

Ва́ше рі́шення абсолю́тно найкра́ще.
Your solution is absolutely the best one.

◊ **без су́мніву** *no doubt*,

Оре́ст, без су́мніву, найрозумні́ший юна́к. *Orest is no doubt the most intelligent youth.*

Take note. Seven adjectives whose stems end in the ~г, ~ж, or ~з have the cluster ~жч in their comparative and superlative forms.

dictionary form	comparative degree	superlative degree
близьки́й *close*	**бли́жчий** *closer*	**найбли́жчий** *closest*
важки́й *hard*	**ва́жчий** *harder*	**найва́жчий** *hardest*
вузьки́й *narrow*	**ву́жчий** *narrower*	**найву́жчий** *narrowest*
дороги́й *dear*	**доро́жчий** *dearer*	**найдоро́жчий** *dearest*
ду́жий *strong*	**ду́жчий** *stronger*	**найду́жчий** *strongest*
низьки́й *low, small*	**ни́жчий** *lower*	**найни́жчий** *lowest*
тяжки́й *heavy*	**тя́жчий** *heavier*	**найтя́жчий** *heaviest*

Two adjectives whose stem ends in ~с have the suffix ~щ.

dictionary form	comparative degree	superlative degree
висо́кий *tall*	**ви́щий** *taller*	**найви́щий** *tallest*
товсти́й *thick*	**то́вщий** *thicker*	**найто́вщий** *thickest*

Світла́на, без су́мніву, найпракти́чніша з усі́х подру́г Ната́лі.

Take note. Like is the case with English, there are several adjectives in Ukrainian that form their degrees of comparison from stems other than their own. They need to be memorized as well.

dictionary form	comparative degree	superlative degree
до́брий *good*	**кра́щий** *better*	**найкра́щий** *best*
хоро́ший *good*	**кра́щий** *better*	**найкра́щий** *best*
пога́ний *bad*	**гі́рший** *worse*	**найгі́рший** *worst*
вели́кий *big*	**бі́льший** *bigger*	**найбі́льший** *biggest*
мали́й *small*	**ме́нший** *smaller*	**найме́нший** *smallest*

∩ 11.15. Compare the two things. Use either of the four conjunctions (prepositions) of comparison (See Note 11.11). Use different intensifiers.

Model. фільм *a film,* «Живі́» *The Living* / «Кінома́нія» *Kinomania,* ціка́вий *interesting*

Q Що ти ду́маєш про ці два фі́льми? *What do you think of these two films?*
A Фільм «Живі́» мені́ бі́льше подо́бається, бо він дале́ко ціка́віший, ніж «Кінома́нія» (or як «Кінома́нія»). *I like "The Living" more because it's by far more interesting than "Kinomania."*

1. стра́ва *dish,* голубці́ / котле́ти по-ки́ївськи, сма́чний
2. карти́на *a picture,* «Оста́ння вече́ря» / «Різдво́», оригіна́льний
3. пора́да *advice,* їхній / ваш, практи́чний *practical*
4. рестора́н, «Млин» / «Коза́цька заба́ва», деше́вий
5. ді́вчина, Тама́ра / Ма́рта, приє́мний *pleasant*
6. журна́л, «Сло́во» / «Украї́нський кур'є́р», товсти́й
7. істо́рія *story,* вчора́шній / сього́днішній, куме́дна *funny*
8. мі́сто, Полта́ва / Ха́рків, зеле́ний
9. музе́й, істори́чний музе́й / карти́нна галере́я, моде́рний
10. а́вто, «Го́нда» / «Фія́т», швидки́й
11. готе́ль, «Ге́тьман» / «Ма́ріот», комфорта́бельний
12. університе́т, Льві́вський університе́т / Оде́ський, прести́жний *prestigious*
13. село́, Рафа́лівка / Ва́раш, близьки́й

∩ 11.16. Provide the correct comparative forms of the adjectives in parentheses. Translate the sentences.

1. Мої́ батьки́ не зна́ли, що Григо́рій (стари́й) брат Оле́ни Миките́нко.
2. Софі́йський Собо́р у Ки́єві (стари́й), як Андрі́ївська це́рква.
3. Цей комп'ю́тер (нови́й і швидки́й), тому́ він (до́брий).
4. Тама́ра працю́є у цій компа́нії (молоди́й) економі́сткою.
5. Ось мої́ молоді́ дру́зі Лука́ш та Тими́ш. Як ти ду́маєш, хто із них (молоди́й)?
6. Стра́ви із сві́жої ри́би за́вжди (до́брий), як із заморо́женої.

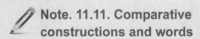

Готе́ль "Ге́тьман" помі́тно приє́мніший і деше́вший, як усі́ і́нші готе́лі мі́ста.

✎ Note. 11.11. Comparative constructions and words

There are four words in Ukrainian, which are used in comparative structures as the equivalents of the English conjunction *than.* They are:

◊ the conjunctions **ніж** and **як**, both are followed by the nominative case form, **Це де́рево ви́ще, ніж (як) той буди́нок.** *This tree is taller than the building.*

◊ the preposition **від** requires the genitive case form, **Це де́рево ви́ще від то́го буди́нку.**

◊ the preposition **за** requires the accusative case form, **Це де́рево ви́ще за той буди́нок.**

These four words have identical meaning and are interchangeable.

Залізничний вокзал у Чернівцях – один із найгарніших в Україні.

7. Михайло каже, що бабуся (добрий) до нього, ніж мама, бо завжди дає йому гроші на морозиво.
8. Будинок, у якому живе Роман із сім'єю (старий), ніж всі інші будинки на цій вулиці.

⌒ 11.17. Put the adjective in parentheses in the superlative degree. Translate the sentences into English.

Model. ⬤ (високий) дерево *a tall tree*
Ⓐ найвище дерево *the tallest tree*

1. Іван Степаненко (добрий) студент у нашій групі.
2. Чому ти вирішив вивчати (складний) предмет?
3. Сонце - це (близький) зірка до Землі.
4. Після університету Семен Максимчук працюватиме у (сучасний) лікарні Чернігова.
5. Світязь - це (великий і глибокий) українське озеро.
6. Це (короткий) дорога до старого замку.
7. Міжнародна мережа – це (простий) спосіб знайти будь-яку інформацію.
8. Я не зміг відповісти на (цікавий) питання іспиту з української історії.
9. Говерла - це (високий) гора в Україні.
10. (Вузький) вулиця у середмісті називається Підвальна.
11. Минуле літо було (гарячий) у цьому місті за останні п'ятдесят років.

⌒ 11.18. Say and write the sentences in Ukrainian. Use the vocabulary and grammar of this and previous lessons. If necessary consult the dictionary.

1. Tell me please how can I get to Khreshchatyk Street.
2. What is the color of your boyfriend's eyes?
3. His girlfriend has red hair and brown eyes. She is unbelievably beautiful.
4. We'd like to tell you about our trip to the Crimea last summer.
5. All main local banks are located downtown.
6. We'll order a taxi for 6:00 AM.
7. Your excursion around Kyiv will start on the Pryvokzalna Square and will end near St. Sophia Cathedral.
8. Every morning I walk to the University and then in the afternoon I drive to the factory.
9. She will come home, read her e-mail, write us letters, and only then have supper.
10. I'll pay you for the book tomorrow. It costs ninety-three hryvnias. I need twenty-two hryvnias more.
11. These four young Russians would like to learn Ukrainian.
12. Our plan is simple and wonderful. We'll go to Lviv, see its old architecture, walk on Rynok Square, have coffee in a nice café, visit the picture gallery, and dine in a good restaurant.

Як кияни, так і туристи люблять ходити Софійською площею.

11.19. Listen carefully to these questions and answer each of them using Dialogue 11.

1. Куди́ хо́че потра́пити гість?
2. Кого́ про́сить гість показа́ти йому́ доро́гу?
3. Чому́ між го́стем і кия́нкою ма́є мі́сце непорозумі́ння?
4. Де гість лиши́в адре́су музе́ю, до яко́го він хоті́в потра́пити?
5. Що зна́є гість про цей музе́й?
6. На які́й пло́щі Ки́єва ма́є мі́сце ця розмо́ва?
7. Де гість знайде́ Миха́йлівську ву́лицю?
8. На які́й ву́лиці щойно був гість?
9. Яка́ пло́ща є в кінці́ Миха́йлівської ву́лиці?
10. Як потра́пити від Майда́ну Незале́жности до Європе́йської пло́щі?
11. Як назива́ється головна́ пло́ща столи́ці?
12. Скі́льки ча́су тре́ба йти від Майда́ну до Європе́йської пло́щі?
13. На які́й пло́щі Ки́єва мо́жна знайти́ ву́лицю Груше́вського?
14. На ро́зі яки́х ву́лиць стої́ть Націона́льний худо́жній музе́й Украї́ни?
15. Що сказа́в гість кия́нці у кінці́ розмо́ви?
16. Що ви ро́бите, коли́ хо́чете знайти́ щось у незнайо́мому мі́сті?

> 🌐 **Мо́вні ресу́рси на мере́жі. Украї́нська Вікіпе́дія. Language resources on the web. Ukrainian Wikipedia.**
>
> **11.20.** Search the Ukrainian language **Вікіпе́дія** *Wikipedia* and do the following:
>
> 1. Find two or three museums in the cities of Ки́їв *Kyiv,* Львів *Lviv,* Оде́са *Odesa,* Ха́рків, *Kharkiv,* and Луцьк *Lutsk.* Use the key word combination **музе́ї** *museums* + **на́зва мі́ста** *name of city* in. *G.,* **музе́ї Черні́гова** *museums of Chernihiv.*
> 2. Write down the name and address of the museums you find.
> 3. Try to glean from their Internet description what kind of art each of the museums has in its collection.

11.21. Use an Internet image search or a Ukrainian language web resource to match the names of these Ukrainian castles and fortresses with the photographs.

Найбі́льше вра́ження справля́ли робо́ти украї́нського скульптора Йога́на Гео́рга Пі́нзеля.

I.

1. За́мок Люба́рта (м. Луцьк)
Liubart Castle (city of Lutsk)

II.

2. Хоти́нська форте́ця
Khotyn Fortress

Note 11.12. Possessive pronoun свій *one's own*

The possessive pronoun **свій** *one's own* has no direct equivalent in English. It signifies that the object described belongs to the person denoted by the subject of the sentence, cf.:

Мико́ла лю́бить свій комп'ю́тер.
Mykola likes his (own) computer.
Мико́ла лю́бить його́ комп'ю́тер.
Mykola likes his (somebody else's) computer.

Свій agrees with its noun in gender, case, and number, *f.* **своя́ кімна́та** *one's own room*, *nt.* **своє́ життя́** *one's own life*, *pl.* **свої́ знайо́мі** *one's own acquaintances*. It is synonymous to all other possessive pronouns with the exception of those referring to the third person singular: **його́** *his (its)*, **її́** *her*, and plural **їхній** *their*.

Я познайо́мив їх зі своє́ю (or з мо́єю) сестро́ю. *I introduced them to my sister.*

Ти чита́тимеш свої́ (твої́) ві́рші? *Will you be reading your poems?*

Ми продає́мо своє́ (or на́ше) а́вто. *We are selling our car.*

Ви до́бре зна́єте свою́ (or ва́шу) істо́рію. *You know your history well.*

However, this similarity in meaning ends with 3rd person possessive pronouns:

1) *Robert lives with his brother.* can be translated as:
Ро́берт живе́ з його́ бра́том (with somebody else's brother).
Ро́берт живе́ зі свої́м бра́том (with his very own brother).

2) *Jennifer looks at her pictures.* can be translated as:
Джені́фер ди́виться її́ сві́тлини (photos of some other woman).
Джені́фер ди́виться свої́ сві́тлини (her own photos).

3) *They came with their son.* can be translated as:
Вони́ прийшли́ із їхнім си́ном (with somebody else's son).
Вони́ прийшли́ зі свої́м си́ном (with their own son).

Unlike its synonyms **мій**, **твій**, **його́**, **її́**, etc., each of which clearly refers to a person and needs no context, **свій** can be understood only in a sentence, and has no independent meaning other than the general *one's own*.

III.

3. Оле́ський за́мок
Olesko Castle

IV.

4. Кам'яне́ць-Поді́льська форте́ця
Kamianets-Podilsk Fortress

🎧 **11.22.** Translate into Ukrainian. Use the possessive pronoun required by the context.

1. Roman speaks with his friend (John's friend).
2. We go shopping with their aunt.
3. Pavlo calls his friend (Pavlo's own friend).
4. You (ти) play the piano for our guest from Kharkiv.
5. They had lunch with their professor (those students' professor).
6. I often think about my life in the Crimea.
7. Our neighbors went to the movies with their little Ivanko (their own son).
8. You (ви) saw this film in your local cinema.
9. Natalka always consults with her sister (Maria's sister).
10. We cannot cook dinner without our own vegetables.
11. Oksana finished work thanks to the help of her elder brother (Oksana's brother).
12. These men rode their own car from Kharkiv to Odesa.

🎧 **11.23.** Answer the questions. Put the words in parentheses in the instrumental singular.

1. Ра́зом з ким прово́дить дозві́лля твій брат? (своя́ ді́вчина)
2. З ким вони́ листу́ються по інтерне́ту? (свій дире́ктор)
3. Ра́зом з ким ви бере́те у́часть у конфере́нції? (відо́мий кана́дський науко́вець)
4. З ким він ба́чився на кінофестива́лі? (одна́ знайо́ма іспа́нська кінозі́рка)
5. Ра́зом з ким Лю́ба за́вжди відпочива́є на мо́рі? (свій улю́блений пес Ру́дик)
6. З ким вече́рятимуть ва́ші го́сті за́втра? (наш головни́й економі́ст)
7. Ра́зом з ким їде Рома́н у подоро́ж до Украї́ни? (свій університе́тський прия́тель)
8. З ким домо́вилася про зу́стріч ця журналі́стка? (оди́н важли́вий полі́тик)
9. З ким ра́дився її́ чолові́к пе́ред тим, як купува́ти цей автомобі́ль? (свій меха́нік).

11.24. Translate using adverbs derived from the adjectives in parentheses. Check the stress in the adverbs.

1. It's easy (легки́й) to give advice.
2. It was boring (нудни́й) to sit and watch.
3. It will be nice (га́рний) to visit their family in Poltava.
4. It's clear (ясни́й) that they like to travel.
5. It's interesting (ціка́вий) that they are asking about it.
6. It was very strange (ди́вний) to see them together.
7. It was sad (сумни́й) to listen to his story.
8. It's wonderful (чудо́вий) that the new students from Spain will be with us.
9. It's always hard (важки́й) to translate an old text.
10. It will be good (до́брий) to see this important play for the second time.
11. It will be better (кра́щий) to tell the director about the problem now.

🌐 Завда́ння для Міжнаро́дної мере́жі

11.25. Using **Google Maps** give detailed written instructions on how to get on foot from point A to point B in these Ukrainian cities.

1. Ки́їв: (А) Центра́льний залізни́чний вокза́л - (Б) Буди́нок із химе́рами, вул. Ба́нкова, 10.

2. Льві́в: (А) Науко́ва бібліоте́ка і́мени Васи́ля́ Стефа́ника - (Б) фонта́н Адо́ніса, пло́ща Ри́нок.

3. Ха́рків: (А) Ста́нція метра́ "Центра́льний ри́нок" - (Б) Інститу́т фінана́нсів, Плетні́вський пров., 5.

4. Оде́са: (А) О́перний теа́тр, пров. Чайко́вського, 1 - (Б) Оде́ська кіносту́дія, Францу́зький бульва́р, 33.

👥 **11.26.** Enact a conversation with a partner. Use the material you have learned so far. Where necessary consult the dictionary.

Сце́нка за сцена́рієм «У по́шуках книга́рні "Є"»
Scripted Skit: *In Search of the Ye Bookstore*

Yaryna (Яри́на): Asks a passerby whether or not she knows a bookstore named *THE YE*.
Passerby (перехо́жа): Repeats the name of the bookstore and says what a strange name. She never heard of it.

Yaryna: Says it is alright. She'll ask somebody else. Approaches another person, apologizes and asks the same question.

✏️ Note 11.13. Adverbs in set expressions

Adverbs are used in the Ukrainian expressions that are equivalent to the English *It is hard (easy, interesting, necessary, etc.) + inf. or clause*.

Among the adverbs most commonly used in such expressions are:
до́бре *good, colloq.* **га́рно** *nice,* **пога́но** *bad,* **чудо́во** *wonderful,* **ціка́во** *interesting,* **ну́дно** *boring,* **ди́вно** *strange,* **тя́жко** *difficult,* **ле́гко** *easy,* **прекра́сно** *great,* **смішно** *funny,* **су́мно** *sad,*

Тя́жко жи́ти у ново́му мі́сті. *It's hard to live in a new city.*

Ціка́во чита́ти їхні листи. *It's interesting to read their letters.*

Ди́вно, що він не подзвони́в. *It's strange he didn't call.*

Ціка́во було́ зна́ти, що вони́ ду́мають. *It was interesting to know what they thought.*

Було́ ду́же ве́село на їхній вечі́рці. *Their party was a lot of fun.*

До́бре, що ви ї́дете на мо́ре. *It's good that you are going to the seaside.*

Ду́же пога́но, що вони́ не гото́ві. *It's very bad that they are not ready.*

У книга́рні "Є" ча́сто відбува́ються літерату́рні зу́стрічі й інші ціка́ві за́ходи.

Книга́рня "Є" розташо́вана на ву́лиці Мико́ли Ли́сенка за Націона́льною о́перою.

Passerby: She surely knows the place. She knows at least three such bookstores. On Lysenko, Spaska, and Saksahansky Streets.

Yaryna: She is not sure what street it is on, but she is told it is close to the National Opera House (Націона́льна о́пера).
Passerby: Says that surely this is the bookstore on Lysenko Street, a lane behind the Opera House. It is not very close to, but not very far from here (зві́дси).

Yaryna: It's no problem, she has time and desire to walk. It's a nice day today and it's always a pleasure to walk around Kyiv.
Passerby: This is the corner of Saksahansky and Vokzalna. Yaryna needs to go up Vokzalna Street, on the right side (з пра́вого бо́ку).

Yaryna: She knows the street. It runs from the Central Railway Station to Taras Shevchenko Boulevard, does it not?
Passerby: Agrees and says that, on the boulevard, Yaryna needs to cross the street, turn right, and go along the boulevard as far as (аж до) the corner with Ivan Franko Street.

Yaryna: She does not know where that street is. This is only her second time in the capital. Is there a known building there?
Passerby: There, on the corner, St. Volodymyr Cathedral is located. Yaryna will easily see it.

Yaryna: She saw it before but did not know the name of that street. All right, she is near the Cathedral, then what next?
Passerby: Yaryna needs to turn left onto Franko Street, continue straight for two blocks as far as Bohdan Khmelnytsky Street, turn right and cross the street.

Yaryna: Asks whether she will be passing anything interesting on the way to know that she is not lost.
Passerby: No, nothing particularly interesting. There is the Embassy of Austria on Franko Street. Once Yaryna is on Khmelnytsky Street, the next left turn is Lysenko Street. Cross over.

Yaryna: Now she knows where that street is. She will be right (про́сто) behind the National Opera House, will she not? But she does not remember any bookstore on that street.
Passerby: The bookstore is not on the street itself but in a courtyard. Suddenly realizes that they are very close *THE YE* Bookstore on Saksahansky Street. There it is.

Yaryna: No, that one won't do, because Yaryna does not want to buy a book. She is going to a reading (чита́ння) of a new novel by Yuri Izdryk in that very bookstore on Lysenko Street.
Passerby: Says she likes Izdryk and would like to attend the event. Suggests that they go to the reading together.

Ле́кція | Lesson 12

Dialogue:
У чернігівському готе́лі
In a Chernihiv hotel

Grammar:
Genitive plural
Expressions of quantity 5 and more + noun
Declension of family names
Cardinal numerals from 1,000 to 1,000,000
Degrees of comparison of adverbs

Competencies:
Booking a hotel
Comparing actions
Ukrainian currency and prices

Цей готе́ль назива́ється "Ґранд Готе́ль". У яко́му мі́сті Украї́ни він є?

Скажі́ть, будь ла́ска, чи у вас є ві́льні місця́?

🗨 12. Діяло́г. У чернігі́вському готе́лі.

Окса́на Коза́к: Добри́день.

Адміністра́тор: Добри́день.

Окса́на Коза́к: Чи у вас є ві́льні місця́?

Адміністра́тор: Зале́жить від то́го, які́ номери́ і на скі́льки осі́б вам тре́ба.

Окса́на Коза́к: Лише́ оди́н станда́ртний но́мер на дві осо́би із широ́ким двоспа́льним лі́жком.

Адміністра́тор: Так є. На́віть кі́лька станда́ртних кімна́т на дві осо́би. Якщо́ хо́чете, мо́жете ви́брати кімна́ту із ви́дом на рі́чку Десну́ чи на мі́сто.

Окса́на Коза́к: Ми хоті́ли б ти́ху, найтихі́шу кімна́ту із ви́дом на старе́ мі́сто. У Черні́гові так бага́то істори́чних буди́нків та церко́в!

Адміністра́тор: Кімна́та із ви́дом на старе́ мі́сто, ти́ха, на́віть із відкри́тим вікно́м, – це не пробле́ма.

Окса́на Коза́к: Чудо́во, дя́кую. Які́ по́слуги є у ва́шому готе́лі?

Адміністра́тор: Ось спи́сок по́слуг від кулі́нарних до електро́нних.

Окса́на Коза́к: Так, я ба́чу цих по́слуг до́сить бага́то. Мене́ наса́мперед ціка́вить міжнаро́дна мере́жа, але́, здає́ться, тут нема́є нія́ких інтерне́т по́слуг.

Адміністра́тор: Цей спи́сок непо́вний. Ми ма́ємо бездрото́вий зв'язо́к по всьо́му готе́лю. Крім то́го, у фоє́ є шість комп'ю́терів спеція́льно для на́ших госте́й.

Окса́на Коза́к: Дя́кую, бу́ду зна́ти. Скі́льки кошту́є наш но́мер?

Адміністра́тор: Три́ста п'ятдеся́т гри́вень за добу́, включно́ зі сніда́нком у на́шому рестора́ні «Зачаро́вана Десна́». Це вас влашто́вує?

Окса́на Коза́к: Чи ціна́ но́мера включа́є па́ркінг, бо ми приї́хали вла́сним а́втом?

Адміністра́тор: Так, звича́йно. Я зо́всім забу́в сказа́ти це. Готе́ль ма́є свій безкошто́вний па́ркінг для госте́й.

Окса́на Коза́к: Прекра́сно. Це все, що нам потрі́бно. Ва́ша ціна́ ці́лком влашто́вує нас.

Адміністра́тор: Скі́льки ча́су ви ду́маєте пробу́ти у на́шому готе́лі?

Окса́на Коза́к: Прина́ймні п'ять діб, можли́во, до́вше. Зале́жить від ситуа́ції. Я тут у спра́вах компа́нії.

Адміністра́тор: Я розумі́ю. У ко́жному ра́зі, ваш но́мер до диспози́ції до п'я́тниці, два́дцять тре́тього се́рпня.

Окса́на Коза́к: То́бто на ві́сім діб. Це бі́льше, ніж доста́тньо для нас. Ми хоті́ли б святкува́ти День Незале́жности удо́ма із сім'є́ю.

Адміністра́тор: Ось два електро́нні ключі́. Ми ра́ді віта́ти вас і бажа́ю вам приє́мно провести́ час у Черні́гові.

12. Dialogue. In a Chernihiv Hotel.

Oksana Kozak: Hello.

Receptionist: Hello.

Oksana Kozak: Do you have vacant rooms (*lit.* places)?

Receptionist: Depends on what rooms and for how many people you need.

Oksana Kozak: Only one standard room for two with a king-size bed (*lit.* a wide bed for two).

Receptionist: Yes, we do, even several standard rooms for two. If you like you can choose a room with a view of the Desna River or the city.

Oksana Kozak: We'd like a quiet, the quietest, room with a view of the old city. There are so many historic buildings and churches in Chernihiv!

Receptionist: A room with a view of the old city, quiet, even with an open window, is not a problem.

Oksana Kozak: Great, thank you. What services are there at the hotel?

Receptionist: Here is a list of services from culinary to electronic.

Oksana Kozak: Yes, I see there are quite a lot of these services. I am primarily interested in the Internet, but there seems to be no Internet services here.

Receptionist: This list is incomplete. We have a wireless connection all around the hotel. Besides, there are six computers in the lobby especially for our guests.

Oksana Kozak: Thank you. It's good to know. How much is our room?

Receptionist: Three hundred and fifty hryvnias a day, including breakfast at our restaurant The Enchanted Desna. Does this suit you?

Oksana Kozak: Does the price include parking, because we came by our own car?

Receptionist: Yes, of course. I completely forgot to say it. The hotel has its own free parking for guests.

Oksana Kozak: Excellent. This is all we need. Your price suits us perfectly.

Receptionist: How long are you going to stay at our hotel?

Oksana Kozak: At least five days, possibly longer. Depends on the situation. I am here on my company's business.

Receptionist: I see. At any rate your room is available till Friday, August 23.

Oksana Kozak: That is for eight nights. This is more than sufficient for us. We'd like to celebrate Independence Day at home with our family.

Receptionist: Here are two electronic keys. Welcome, and I wish you a pleasant time in Chernihiv.

У готе́лі мо́жна:
At a hotel one can:

жи́ти, переночува́ти, відпочи́ти	to live, spend a night, rest
зупини́тися на одну́ добу́, дві (три, чоти́ри) доби́,	to stay for a day, two (three, four) days,
на п'ять (шість і т.д.) діб.	for five (six, etc.) days.

Що ви мо́жете сказа́ти про готе́ль "Дніпро́" з інтерне́ту?

✎ Нота́тки до діяло́гу
Notes on the Dialogue

нема́ пробле́м	no problem (*lit.* there are no problems), used to indicate agreement and readiness to do sth.
зале́ж|ати, ~ать, від + G.	to depend on, **Це ~ить від пого́ди.** *It depends upon the weather.*
но́мер, *m.*, ~а	*here* hotel room, hotel accommodation, **н. на + одну́ осо́бу (дві осо́би)** a single (double) room.
вид, *m.*, ~у на + A.	a view of, **в. на мі́сто (рі́чку, мо́ре, ву́лицю)** *a view of the city (river, sea, street).*
Це вас влашто́вує?	Does that suit you? (The personal pronoun can either precede or follow the verb.)
пробу́ти, *only pf.*, пробу́д|уть, *ра.* пробули́, *intr.*	to stay (in a hotel, city, place), **Я пробу́ду тут кі́лька днів.** *I'll stay here for a few days.*
доба́, *f., G. pl.* діб	twenty-four hours, day and night, used in similar situation when day or night is used in English, **Скільки діб ви бу́дете у Ха́ркові?** *How many days will you be in Kharkiv?*

Марі́я Са́вченко ду́же хоті́ла б знайти́ недороги́й готе́ль у середмі́сті Полта́ви.

У готе́лі є такі́ по́слуги: порт'є́, рестора́н, пра́льня, спортклу́б, перука́рня, інтерне́т.	At a hotel, there are services such as: a porter, restaurant, laundry, gym, hair salon, the Internet.
У готе́лі мо́жна замо́вити: но́мер, таксі́, сніда́нок, обі́д, газе́ти	At a hotel one can order: a room, taxi, breakfast, lunch, newspapers
Но́мер у готе́лі мо́же бу́ти на: одну́ осо́бу, дві (три) осо́би.	A room in a hotel can be for: one person, for two (three) people.
посели́тися до + G. готе́лю	to check in a hotel
ви́селитися з (із) + G. готе́лю	to check out of a hotel

Піктограми

Одномісні кімнати	Можна паркувати автомобіль	Поблизу автобусна зупинка (залізнична станція)
Двомісні кімнати	Можна користуватися кухнею	Медична допомога
Тримісні кімнати	Господиня випікає хліб	Музей, історичні пам'ятки
Господар знає іноземну мову	Можна перебувати з дітьми	Ресторан, кафе, бар
Телефон	Можна їсти фрукти й овочі з городу	Магазин, базар
Ванна	У господаря є пасіка	Поблизу місце для рибалки
Душ	У господаря є корова	Можна купатися
Туалет в будинку	У господаря є коза	Можна їздити верхи
Можна дивитися телевізор	Можна привезти домашню тварину	Можна полювати
Можна користуватися пральною машиною		

По́слуги, які́ мо́жуть пропонува́ти в готе́лі.

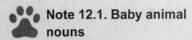

📖 Грама́тика | Grammar

Родови́й відмі́нок множини́ Genitive Case Plural

Фу́нкція   *Function*

In addition to the functions of its singular counterpart (Lesson 8), the most typical function of genitive plural is quantification, for it often denotes both an exact and an indeterminate number of objects that can be counted. When following the cardinal numerals **п'ять** *five* and higher, with the exception of the numerals ending in the words **оди́н** *one,* **два** *two,* **три** *three,* or **чоти́ри** *four* (**два́дцять оди́н** *twenty-one,* **со́рок два** *forty-two,* **сто три** *a hundred and three,* **сімдеся́т чоти́ри** *seventy-four*), it expresses an exact number of objects, **п'ять гри́вень** *five hryvnias,* **двана́дцять годи́н** *twelve hours,* **чотирна́дцять днів** *fourteen days,* **сім ноче́й** *seven nights.*

Утво́рення   *Formation*
Іме́нники Nouns

The nominal genitive plural endings:
zero, ~ів, ~ей

---

zero   is taken (1) feminine and masculine nouns ending in **~а (~я)** and (2) neuter nouns:
1) *f.* **кни́га** *a book* - **бага́то книг** *many books, f.* **ха́та** *a house* - **кі́лька хат** *a few houses, m.* **невда́ха** *a loser* - **бага́то невда́х** *many losers, m.* **задава́ка** *a braggart* - **скі́льки задава́к** *how many braggarts;*

Take note. Nouns ending in **~ія** end in **~ій** in the genitive plural, *f.* **фотогра́фія** *a photo* - **кі́лька фотогра́фій** *several photos, m.* **месі́я** *a messiah* - **бага́то месі́й** *many messiahs*

The *G. pl.* of **дівчи́на** *a girl* is **дівча́т** - **сті́льки дівча́т** *so many girls.*

2) *nt.* **я́блуко** *an apple* - **скі́льки я́блук** *how many apples,* **мі́сто** *a city* - **де́сять міст** *ten cities,* **пита́ння** *a question* - **сті́льки пита́нь** *so many questions,* **теля́** *a calf* - **кі́лька теля́т** *several calves;*

Neuter nouns with the stem ending in a double consonant (**~ння, ~ття**) have a single consonant ending in the genitive plural, **проха́ння** *a request* - **шість проха́нь** *six requests,* **завда́ння** *a task* - **кі́лька завда́нь** *several tasks.*

~ів   is taken by all **zero**- and **o**-ended masculine nouns, **студе́нт** *a student* - **бага́то студе́нтів** *many students,* **комп'ю́тер** *a computer* - **кі́лька комп'ю́терів** *several computers,* **зо́шит** *a notebook* - **ві́сім зо́шитів** *eight notebooks,* **ба́тько** *a father* - **шість батькі́в** *six fathers*

The *G. pl.* of the noun **друг** *a friend* is **дру́зів**, **кі́лька дру́зів** *several friends.*

Ці ді́ти зна́ють сті́льки суча́сних пісе́нь.

Note 12.2. Special cases with ~ів ending

The ending ~ів is also taken by some nouns of other genders:

nt. мо́ре *a sea* - п'ять морі́в *five seas,*
nt. по́ле *a field* - скі́льки полі́в *how many fields,*
f. ма́ти *a mother* - скі́льки матері́в *how many mothers,*
f. ма́ма *a mom* - шість ма́мів (*var.* мам) *six moms,*
f. ба́ба *a grandmother* - сім ба́бів (*var.* баб) *seven grandmothers.*

Note. The noun **чолові́к** *man, person* has two *G. pl.* forms with two different meanings:

чолові́ків *men* vs **чолові́к** *people,*

Нам помага́ють сім чолові́к. *Seven people help us.*

Тут п'ять чолові́ків і п'ять жіно́к. *There are five men and five women here.*

Note 12.3. Nouns with ~анин

Nouns of the ~а́нин type, shed the suffix ~ин in the genitive plural,

христия́нин *a Christian* - скі́льки христия́н *how many Christians*
мусульма́нин *a Muslim* - де́сять мусульма́н *ten Muslims*
росія́нин *a Russian* - трина́дцять росія́н *thirteen Russians*

Note 12.4. The ending ~ей is also taken by the following nouns:

статтю́ *an article* - бага́то статте́й (*var.* стате́й and статті́в) *many articles*
кінь *a horse* - сім ко́ней *seven horses*
свиня́ *a pig* - бага́то свине́й *many pigs*
о́ко *an eye* - бага́то оче́й *many eyes*
гість *a guest* - бага́то госте́й *many guests*
дити́на *a child* - бага́то діте́й *many children*
люди́на *a person* - бага́то люде́й *many people*
две́рі *a door* - бага́то дваре́й *many doors*
гро́ші *money* - бага́то гро́шей *a lot of money*

~ів is taken by the zero-ended nouns whose stem ends in ~й:
музе́й *a museum* - кі́лька музе́їв *several museums*
воді́й *a driver* - п'ять воді́їв *five drivers.*

~ей is taken by all **zero**-ended feminine nouns,
відпо́відь *an answer* - бага́то відпові́дей *many answers,*
о́сінь *autumn* - скі́льки о́сеней *how many autumns,*
річ *a thing* - кі́лька рече́й *several things,*
ніч *a night* - п'ять ноче́й *five nights.*

Commonly used quantifiers

Genitive plural expresses an indeterminate quantity after adverbs such as:

бага́то *many (much)*   кі́лька *a few, several*
ма́ло *few, little*   скі́льки *how many (much)*
сті́льки *so many (much)*   тро́хи *a little, few*

бага́то гро́шей *a lot of money*
кі́лька днів *a few days*
ма́ло годи́н *few hours*
скі́льки разі́в (*or* раз) *how many times*
сті́льки ноче́й *so many nights*

Singular only nouns

After these adverbs, uncountable nouns and nouns, which have only singular form take the genitive singular,

бага́то води́ *much water*
ма́ло ча́су *little time*
скі́льки молока́ *how much milk.*

🔊 SOUND CHANGES 🔊
in the genitive plural of nouns

Dropping of ~o~ (~e~)

~o~ and ~e~ in the last syllable of 2ⁿᵈ declension masculine nouns are dropped in the genitive plural,

куто́к *a corner* - без кутків *without corners*
сон *a dream* - без снів *without dreams*
украї́нець *a Ukrainian* - без украї́нців *without Ukrainians*
кіне́ць *the end* - без кінці́в *without ends*
день *a day* - без днів *without days*

Adding of ~o~ (~e~)

~o~ and more rarely ~e~, are inserted to avoid a consonant cluster at the end of the nouns that receive a zero ending in the genitive plural:

украї́нка *a Ukrainian woman* - кі́лька **украї́нок** *a few Ukrainian women*
копі́йка *a kopek* - кі́лька **копі́йок** *a few kopeks*
вікно́ *a window* - кі́лька **ві́кон** *a few windows*
гри́вня *a hryvnia* - кі́лька **гри́вень** *a few hryvnias*
сестра́ *a sister* - кі́лька **сесте́р** *a few sisters*
сім'я́ *a family* - кі́лька **сіме́й** *a few families*

Change of ~i~ to ~o~ (~e~)

~i~ changes to ~o~ and less frequently ~e~ in the final syllable in 2nd declension masculine and 3rd declension feminine nouns,
~i~ to ~o~
m. **стіл** *a table* - п'ять **столі́в** *five tables*
m. **кіт** *a cat* - скі́льки **коті́в** *how many cats*
f. **ніч** *a night* - бага́то **ноче́й** *many nights*

~i~ to ~e~
m. **папі́р** *a paper* - бага́то **папе́рів** *many papers*
f. **річ** *a thing* - бага́то **рече́й** *many things*
f. **піч** *a stove* - скі́льки **пече́й** *how many ovens*

Change of ~o~ to ~i~

~o~ changes to ~i~ in the final syllable that becomes closed as a result of the ending dropping in the 1st declension nouns:
доба́ *a day* - сім **діб** *seven days*
голова́ *a head* - бага́то **голі́в** *many heads*
доро́га *a road* - сті́льки **дорі́г** *so many roads*
нога́ *a leg* - деся́тки **ніг** *dozens of legs*
блоха́ *a flea* - со́тні **бліх** *hundreds of fleas*

 Note 12.5. На́зви гір
Mountain names

Names of mountain chains that are plural only nouns form their *G. pl.* by slashing the ending **~и** (~ї),

Карпа́ти *the Carpathians* -
сере́д **Карпа́т** *in the middle of the Carpathians*
А́льпи *the Alps* -
бі́ля **Альп** *near the Alps*
Балка́ни *the Balkans* -
сере́д **Балка́н** *in the middle of the Balkans*
Гімала́ї /himaláji/ *the Himalayas* -
від **Гімала́й** *from the Himalayas*
Пірене́ї /pireᵘnéji/ *the Pyrenees* -
до **Пірене́й** *to the Pyrenees*

Тимі́ш Гайдуче́нко ще ніко́ли не ба́чив А́льп.

Прикме́тники, поря́дкові числі́вники та присвійні займе́нники
Adjectives, Ordinal Numerals, and Possessive pronouns

The adjectival genitive plural endings:
~их (~іх, ~їх)

Па́нна Гали́на навча́ла багатьо́х школярі́в англі́йської мо́ви.

~их is for all hard stem adjectives,
бі́лий кінь *a white horse* - сім бі́лих ко́ней *seven white horses*
до́вга ніч *a long night* - бага́то до́вгих ноче́й *many long nights*
ціка́ве оповіда́ння *an interesting story* - сім ціка́вих оповіда́нь *seven interesting stories*;

~іх for soft stems,
оста́ннє пита́ння *the last question* - кі́лька оста́нніх пита́нь *a few last questions*, осі́нній ти́ждень *an autumn week* - шість осі́нніх ти́жнів *six autumn weeks*, си́ня су́кня *a blue dress* - без си́ніх суко́нь *without blue dresses*;

~їх for -й-ended stems,
мій друг *my friend* - кі́лька мої́х дру́зів *a few of my friends*
свій кіт *one's own cat* - шість свої́х котів *six one's own cats*
чий квито́к *whose ticket* - без чиї́х квитків *without whose tickets*.

Кі́лькісні числі́вники від ти́сячі до мілья́рда
Cardinal numerals from one thousand to a billion

English	Ukrainian
one thousand	(одна́) ти́сяча
two thousand	дві ти́сячі
three thousand	три ти́сячі
four thousand	чоти́ри ти́сячі
five thousand	п'ять ти́сяч
one million	(оди́н) мільйо́н
two million	два мільйо́ни
five million	п'ять мільйо́нів
one billion	(оди́н) мілья́рд
two billion	два мілья́рди
five billion	п'ять мілья́рдів

Cardinal numerals from 1,000 to 1,000,000 are composed of respective units, tens, hundreds, and thousands. The words ти́сяча *a thousand*, мільйо́н *a million*, and мілья́рд *a billion* decline like nouns.

Ти́сяча as a feminine noun requires the feminine forms of the numerals *one* - одна́ and *two* - дві. Thus 1,000 in Ukrainian is either одна́ ти́сяча or simply ти́сяча. 2,000 is дві ти́сячі.
The *N. pl.* ти́сячі is required after the numerals два *two*, три *three*, and чоти́ри *four*, or those composite numerals that end in these words,

2,398 дві ти́сячі три́ста дев'яно́сто ві́сім
4,000 чоти́ри ти́сячі
32,000 три́дцять дві ти́сячі
53,102 п'ятдеся́т три ти́сячі сто два.

The *G. pl.* form **ти́сяч** is used after numerals **п'ять** and more,

5,000 **п'ять ти́сяч**
12,000 **двана́дцять ти́сяч**
100,511 **сто ти́сяч п'ятсо́т одина́дцять**

Мільйо́н and **мілья́рд** are both masculine and require masculine forms of numerals **оди́н** *one* and **два** *two*. Thus 1,000,000 is either **оди́н мільйо́н** *one million*, or simply **мільйо́н** *a million*. A billion is either **оди́н мілья́рд** *one billion*, or simply **мілья́рд** *a billion* and two billion is **два мілья́рди**.

After numerals **два** *two*, **три** *three*, and **чоти́ри** *four*, or those that end in the words **два**, **три**, and **чоти́ри**, the nominative plural forms **мільйо́ни** and **мілья́рди** are used,
        чоти́ри мільйо́ни *four million*
        три́дцять два мільйо́ни *thirty-two million*
        два мілья́рди *two billion*
        со́рок чоти́ри мілья́рди *forty-four billion.*

The genitive plural forms **мільйо́нів** and **мілья́рдів** are used after numerals **п'ять** *five* and greater, **п'ять мільйо́нів** *five million* **двана́дцять мілья́рдів** *twelve billion*. For the declension of cardinal numerals see the appendices, Tables 12 and 13, pp. 324-325.

Відмі́на прі́звищ   Declension of Family Names

Ukrainian family names can be either nouns (nominal family names) or adjectives (adjectival family names). Particularly common are nominal family names ending in **~ко**, **~ук** (**~юк**),

Шевче́нко *Shevchenko*, **Петре́нко** *Petrenko*, **Ле́вченко** *Levchenko*, **Новачу́к** *Novachuk*, **Левчу́к** *Levchuk*, **Семеню́к** *Semeniuk*.

Ukrainian family names also have many other endings, no less typical, if not as common,
    ~ин as in **Павли́шин** *Pavlyshyn*, **Васили́шин** *Vasylyshyn*
    ~ів as in **Па́влів** *Pavliv*, **Іва́нів** *Ivaniv*, **Пе́трів** *Petriv*
    ~а́к as in **Петрунча́к** *Petrunchak*, **Ступа́к** *Stupak*
    ~ик as in **Дми́трик** *Dmytryk*, **Смі́лик** *Smilyk*, **До́вжик** *Dovzhyk*
    ~ій as in **Палі́й** *Paliy*, **Плохі́й** *Plokhiy*, **Черво́ній** *Chervoniy*

It is impossible to tell the gender of the person by their nominal family name alone. Unlike nouns, adjectival family names by their ending directly point to the gender of the person bearing the surname, cf.,

m. **Садови́й** *Sadovy* and *f.* **Садова́** *Sadova*
m. **Ти́хий** *Tykhy* and *f.* **Ти́ха** *Tykha*
m. **Коцюби́нський** *Kotsiubynsky* and *f.* **Коцюби́нська** *Kotsiubynska*
m. **Досві́тній** *Dosvitniy* and *f.* **Досві́тня** *Dosvitnia*
m. **Кульчи́нський** *Kulchynsky* and **Кульчи́нська** *Kulchynska*

Скі́льки чолові́ків і скі́льки чолові́к на цій світли́ні?

Ко́жен кінома́н зна́є Е́дварда Дми́трика, америка́нського режисе́ра украї́нського похо́дження.

Ми зустріча́ємося з Яре́мою Васи́льченком бі́ля па́м'ятника Про́ні Сірко́ та Свири́дові Голохво́стому. Це головні́ геро́ї фі́льму "За двома́ зайця́ми".

Indeclinable are only nominal family names ending in **~ко**, **~ук** **~**(**юк**), **~а́к**, **~ин**, **~і́й**, **~ів**, whose bearers are individuals of feminine gender. Only their first name is declined,

О́льга Васи́льченко *Olha Vasylchenko -*
G. **лист до О́льги Васи́льченко** *a letter to Olha Vasylchenko*
D. **завдяки О́льзі Васи́льченко** *thanks to Olha Vasylchenko*
A. **Я зна́ю О́льгу Васи́льченко.** *I know Olha Vasylchenko.*
I. **Я прийшо́в із О́льгою Васи́льченко.** *I came with Olha Vasylchenko.*
N. pl. **Це се́стри Васи́льченко.** *These are the Vasylchenko sisters.*

The rest of surnames are declined. They include:
1) all adjectives,
m. **Рома́н Садови́й** *Roman Sadovy,* *f.* **Іри́на Садова́** *Iryna Sadova,*
pl. **Рома́н та Іри́на Садові́** *Roman and Iryna Sadovys*
Я зна́ю Рома́на Садово́го. *I know Roman Sadovy.*
Він дру́жить з Іри́ною Садово́ю. *He is friends with Iryna Sadova.*
Ми йдемо́ до Рома́на та Іри́ни Садови́х. *We are going to Roman and Iryna Sadovys' place.*

2) nominal family names whose bearer is an individual of masculine gender,
Яре́ма Васи́льченко *Yarema Vasylchenko -*
G. **лист до Яре́ми Васи́льченка** *a letter to Yarema Vasylchenko*
D. **завдяки́ Яре́мі Васи́льченкові** *thanks to Yarema Vasylchenko*
A. **Я зна́ю Яре́му Васи́льченка.** *I know Yarema Vasylchenko.*
I. **Я прийшо́в із Яре́мою Васи́льченком.** *I came with Yarema Vasylchenko.*
N. pl. **Це брати́ Васи́льченки.** *These are the Vasylchenko brothers.*

If a nominal surname is associated with its male and female bearer at the same time (husband and wife, brother and sister), it is declined,
Це О́льга та Яре́ма Васи́льченки. *These are Olha and Yarema Vasylchenko.*
Це подру́жжя Васи́льченків. *This is the Vasylchenko couple.*

Впра́ви Exercises

Phonetics.
Drill inserting the **~o~** in the genitive plural of nouns.

⌒ **12.1.** Listen to the speaker for the cue and form the genitive plural of these nouns. Insert the **~o~** between two final consonants.

Stress Pattern A. Stress remains on the same vowel.
C бу́ква *a letter*
A скі́льки бу́ков *how many letters*

виде́лка *a fork*
запи́ска *a message*
ку́хня *a kitchen*
ло́жка *a spoon*
буха́нка *a loaf*
зни́жка *a discount*
нота́тка *a note*
пере́куска *a snack*
філіжа́нка *a cup*
несподі́ванка *a surprise*

украї́нка *a Ukrainian woman*
іспа́нка *a Spanish woman*
америка́нка *an American woman*
кана́дка *a Canadian woman*
італі́йка *an Italian woman*
кия́нка *f. citizen of Kyiv*
льві́в'я́нка *f. citizen of Lviv*
харкі́в'я́нка *f. citizen of Kharkiv*
полта́вка *f. citizen of Poltava*
селя́нка *a peasant*

12.2. Answer the questions.

Model. виде́лка *a fork*; бага́то *many*
Q Чи тут лише́ одна́ виде́лка? *Is there only one fork here?*
A Ні, навпаки́, тут бага́то виде́лок. *No, on the contrary, there are many forks here.*

1. філіжа́нка; два́дцять
2. рестора́н; кі́лька
3. а́вто; п'ять
4. ві́дповідь; бага́то
5. гість; шість
6. полта́вка; ві́сім
7. гри́вня; со́рок
8. стіл; де́в'ять
9. село́; п'ять
10. мо́ре; кі́лька
11. ма́ти; де́сять
12. ім'я́; чотирна́дцять
13. я́блуко; бага́то
14. люди́на; двана́дцять
15. доро́га; сті́льки
16. по́ле; кі́лька
17. мі́сто; одина́дцять
18. пита́ння; чотирна́дцять

Phonetics. Drill inserting the ~o~ in the genitive plural of nouns.

12.3. Listen to the speaker for the cue and form the genitive plural of these nouns. Insert the ~**o**~ between two final consonants.

Stress Pattern B. Stress shifts to the last syllable.
C су́мка *a bag*
A бага́то сумо́к *many bags*

ду́мка *a thought*
копі́йка *a kopek*
по́милка *a mistake*
тарі́лка *a plate*
соро́чка *a shirt*
щі́тка *a brush*
ю́шка *soup*

зі́рка *a star*
пля́шка *a bottle*
скля́нка *a glass*
це́рква *a church*
кни́жка *a book*
коро́бка *a box*
ми́ска *a dish, plate*

Завда́ння для Міжнаро́дної мере́жі
Internet assignment

1. Як назива́ється цей готе́ль?
2. В яко́му мі́сті він розташо́ваний?
3. Скі́льки кошту́є одна́ доба́ в готе́лі?
4. Чи ціна́ за но́мер включа́є сніда́нок?
5. Чим мо́жна плати́ти за но́мер в готе́лі?

Це коха́не дитя́
не хо́че нія́ких я́блук.

∩ 12.4. React to the statement. Use the genitive plural. Note that **жо́дний** *any* is used only in the negative statement.

Model.
C Ось нови́й студе́нт. *Here is a new student.*
A Я не зна́ю жо́дних нови́х студе́нтів. *I don't know any new students.*

1. Ось смачне́ я́блуко. Він не хо́че ...
2. Ось ціка́вий фільм. Я не дивлю́ся ...
3. Ось оста́ння нови́на. Ми не слу́хаємо ...
4. Ось спорти́вне а́вто. Він не ма́є ...
5. Ось щасли́ва сім'я́. Ми не ба́чимо ...
6. Ось америка́нський гість. Я не прийма́ю ...
7. Ось італі́йська о́пера. Я не слу́хаю ...
8. Ось украї́нський борщ. Вони́ не їдя́ть ...
9. Ось ціка́ва стаття́. Ти не чита́єш ...
10. Ось стара́ фотогра́фія. Я не шука́ю ...

Phonetics. Drill inserting the ~e~ in the genitive plural of nouns.

∩ 12.5. Listen to the speaker for the cue and form the genitive plural of these nouns. Insert the ~**e**~ between two final consonants.

Stress Pattern A. Stress remains on the same vowel.
C ви́шня *a sour cherry*
A бага́то ви́шень *many cherries*

віта́льня *a living room*	гри́вня *a hryvnia*
їда́льня *a canteen*	ліка́рня *a hospital*
спа́льня *a bedroom*	чере́шня *a sweet cherry*
сім'я́ *a family*	пра́льня *a laundry*
сестра́ *a sister*	яє́чня *an omelet*
кав'я́рня *a café*	книга́рня *a bookstore*
перука́рня *a hair salon*	коню́шня *a stable*
голя́рня *a barber's shop*	прийма́льня *reception*

Вони́ не зна́ють цих сесте́р.

∩ 12.6. Form sentences following the model. Use the genitive plural.

Model.
C ці студе́нти *these students*, бага́то *many*, складне́ завда́ння *complicated assignment*
A У цих студе́нтів бага́то складни́х завда́нь. *These students have many complicated assignments.*

1. на́ші се́стри, кілогра́м, соло́дка гру́ша
2. їхні матері́, кілька, ціка́ва фотогра́фія
3. кана́дські тури́сти, кілька, украї́нська гри́вня
4. молоді́ дівча́та, шість, вели́ка валі́за
5. симпати́чні кия́ни, де́сять, залізни́чний квито́к

6. ці щасли́ві сі́м'ї, бага́то, мала́ дити́на
7. ва́ші америка́нські дру́зі, кі́лька, потрі́бна кни́жка
8. їхні батьки́, п'ять, чудо́ва дочка́
9. мої́ ро́дичі, ві́сім, кана́дський гість
10. ті інжене́ри, бага́то, гро́ші

Phonetics. Drill changing ~o~ to ~i~ in the genitive plural of nouns.

🎧 **12.7.** Listen to the speaker for the cue and form the genitive plural of these nouns. Replace the penultimate ~**o**~ in *N. sg.* with ~**i**~ in *G. pl.* Note that the stress in *G. pl.* is on the ~**í**~.

Model.
C шко́ла *a school*
A бага́то шкіл *many schools*

пора́ *a season*	доро́га *a road*
нога́ *a leg*	боло́то *a bog*
щока́ *a cheek*	коро́ва *a cow*
бджола́ *a bee*	робо́та *work*
сльоза́ *a tear*	осо́ба *a person*
нора́ *a lair*	панчо́ха *a stocking*
гора́ *a mountain*	воро́та *gates*
брова́ *a brow*	сирота́ *an orphan*
доба́ *day and night*	голова́ *a head*
ко́ло *a circle*	сторона́ *a side*

🎧 **12.8.** Give a negative answer to each question. Change the object into the genitive plural. Use the double negation.

Model.
Q Чи Марі́я ма́є ці нові́ книжки́? *Does Maria have these new books?*
A Ні, вона́ не ма́є нія́ких нови́х книжо́к.
   No, she doesn't have any new books.

1. Чи О́ля ро́бить ці ціка́ві завда́ння?
2. Чи ви їсте́ ці до́брі ковба́си?
3. Чи ти чита́єш ці нові́ рома́ни?
4. Чи він зна́є ці ди́вні істо́рії?
5. Чи Яри́на пи́ше ці до́вгі листи́?
6. Чи вони́ пам'ята́ють ці нові́ слова́?
7. Чи ми слу́хали ці оста́нні програ́ми?
8. Чи я зна́ю ці і́нші мо́ви?
9. Чи ви лю́бите ці кана́дські фі́льми?
10. Чи ми знайшли́ ці старі́ музе́ї?
11. Чи вона́ зна́є ці америка́нські міста́?
12. Чи вони́ чита́ють ці нудні́ те́ксти?

двісті гри́вень

₴ **Note 12.6. Украї́нська валю́та**
Ukrainian currency

The Ukrainian national currency is called **гри́вня** *a hryvnia*. Its international sign is **₴**, the first letter of the word in cursive, with two horizontal lines to symbolize stability. Its code is **UAH**.

The Ukrainian equivalent of a cent is **копі́йка** *a kopek*. UAH 1.00 comprises a hundred kopeks. In designations of values and prices, **гри́вня** and **копі́йка** change their case form depending on the numeral they follow:

1) **гри́вня** and **копі́йка** after numerals ending in the word **одна́** *f. one*,

одна́ гри́вня *one hryvnia*
три́дцять одна́ гри́вня *thirty-one hryvnias*
одна́ копі́йка *one kopek*
со́рок одна́ копі́йка *forty-one kopeks;*

2) **гри́вні** and **копі́йки** after the numerals ending in the words **дві** *f. two*, **три** *three*, and **чоти́ри** *four*:

дві гри́вні *two hryvnias*
три́дцять чоти́ри гри́вні *thirty-four hryvnias*
три копі́йки *three kopeks*
дві́сті чоти́ри копі́йки *two hundred and four kopeks;*

3) **гри́вень** and **копі́йок** after all other numerals including those that have the numbers 1, 2, 3, and 4 written as words at their end but not pronounced:

п'ять гри́вень *five hryvnias*
двана́дцять гри́вень *twelve hryvnias*
сто гри́вень *a hundred hryvnias*
сім копі́йок *seven kopeks*
чотирна́дцять копі́йок *fourteen kopeks*
два́дцять копі́йок *twenty kopeks.*

Note 12.7. Ці́ни Prices

To designate a price the verb
ко́шту|вати, ~ють + *A. to cost* is used:

Квито́к ко́штує со́рок одну́ гри́вню.
A ticket costs UAH 41.00.
**Ці книжки́ ко́штують де́сять
гри́вень.** *These books cost UAH 10.00.*

No conjunction **i** *and* is used between
hryvnias and kopeks in prices.

The Ukrainian equivalent of *How much
is it?* is **Скі́льки це ко́штує?**

To indicate the price of a certain
quantity, for example, a day (in hotel), or
a kilogram (liter, etc.) one should use the
construction ***price in currency + за + A.
of quantifier***
**п'ятдеся́т гри́вень за добу́ (за ніч,
за кілогра́м, за кни́жку)** *UAH 50.00
per day (per night, per kilogram, per
book).*

Note 12.8. Decimals

Ukrainian decimals use a comma where
in English a period is used, *cf.
Eng. UAH 23.15* and *Ukr.* **23,15 грв.**,
Eng. $100.50 and *Ukr.* **100,50 до́ларів.**

Likewise a period, not a comma, is used
in Ukrainian to seperate thousands in
large numerals, *cf.*,
$2,300,700.21 and *Ukr.* **2.300.700,21
до́ларів.**

∩ 12.9. Say and write down the numerals in Ukrainian.

105; 211; 421; 390; 618; 183; 804; 571; 307; 986; 732; 1,205; 414;
5,023; 18,000; 101,000; 1,000,000.

∩ 12.10. Indicate a quantity. Put the noun phrase in the genitive plural.

Model. C ві́сім *eight*, висо́кий буди́нок *a tall building*
A ві́сім висо́ких буди́нків *eight tall buildings*

1. бага́то, кана́дська дівчина
2. кі́лька, вели́ке мі́сто
3. п'ять, знайо́мий америка́нець
4. скі́льки, ціка́ва по́дорож
5. два́дцять, украї́нська гри́вня
6. ти́сяча, америка́нський до́лар
7. сімна́дцять, до́вга годи́на
8. бага́то, важки́й рік
9. шість, оста́нній мі́сяць
10. п'ятна́дцять, лі́тній день
11. бага́то, холо́дна ніч
12. кі́лька, незнайо́ма жі́нка
13. скі́льки, мала́ дити́на
14. де́в'ять, стари́й друг

∩ 12.11. Answer the questions. Say how much the products and services cost.

Model. C ця газе́та *this newspaper*, 3,20 грн. *3.20 hryvnias*
Q Скажі́ть, будь ла́ска, скі́льки ко́штує ця газе́та?
Tell me please how much is this newspaper?
A Три гри́вні два́дцять копі́йок.
Three hryvnias and twenty kopeks.

1. ці квитки́ до теа́тру; 60,54 грн.
2. одна́ доба́ у готе́лі; 120 грн.
3. обі́д у рестора́ні; 56,97 грн.
4. ці я́блука? 24,70 грн.
5. маршру́тка? 2,50 грн.
6. лі́тер молока́? 3,14 грн.
7. буха́нка хлі́ба? 1,95 грн.
8. ця пля́шка вина́? 57,32 грн.
9. квитки́ на конце́рт? 260 грн.
10. таксі́вка? 80 грн.

Порівня́йте ці́ни на проду́кти Compare grocery prices

12.12. Compare the prices of these products in three Ukrainian supermarkets: «Глибо́ка кише́ня», «Дари́ полі́в», and «Ласу́н». Then answer the questions.

Ці́ни на де́які проду́кти в супермарке́ті:

На́зва проду́кту	Супермарке́т «Глибо́ка кише́ня»	Супермарке́т «Дари́ полі́в»	Супермарке́т «Ласу́н»
молоко́ за 1 л.	6,75 грн.	7,10 грн.	8,22 грн.
хліб за буха́нку	5,30 грн.	4,80 грн.	3,90 грн.
карто́пля за 1 кг.	5,00 грн.	5,00 грн.	6,00 грн.
цибу́ля за 1 кг.	4,80 грн.	4,50 грн.	5,20 грн.
куря́тина за 1 кг.	40,00 грн.	35.00 грн.	42.00 грн.

свини́на за 1 кг.	41,00 грн.	50,00 грн.	46,00 грн.
масло за 1 кг.	60,00 грн.	56,00 грн.	62,00 грн.
яйця за деся́ток	7,00 грн.	6,50 грн.	8,30 грн.

1. У яко́му супермаркеті буха́нка хлі́ба деше́вша?
2. Де найдеше́вші я́йця?
3. Де найдоро́жча свини́на?
4. Де карто́пля ко́штує так са́мо?
5. Порівня́йте ці́ни на свини́ну у «Глибо́кій кише́ні» та «Ласу́ні».
6. Порівня́йте ці́ни на куря́тину у супермаркеті «Дари́ полі́в» та «Глибо́ка кише́ня».

Зни́жки   Discounts

🎧 **12.13.** Study these ads of discounts offered at *Lasun Supermarket* and answer the questions.

Сир «Звенигоро́дський»   Ковбаса́ «Дрого́бич»   Майоне́з «Пісни́й»

Напі́й «Жи́вчик»   Шашли́к «Свиня́чий»   Ши́нка "Апети́тна"

1. На які́ проду́кти пропону́є зни́жки супермаркет «Ласу́н»?
2. Коли́ мо́жна купи́ти ковбасу́ «Дрого́бич» за зни́жкою?
3. Скільки ко́штує сир?
4. Що таке́ "Жи́вчик"?
5. Яки́й із цих проду́ктів найдоро́жчий?
6. Яки́й із цих проду́ктів найдеше́вший?
7. Порівня́йте ці́ни ковбаси́, шашлика́ та ши́нки.
8. За яко́ю зни́жкою продаю́ть ши́нку?

А́лла впе́внена, що її кіт Тристан – найрозумні́ший з усіх котів сві́ту.

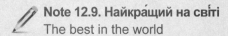

Note 12.9. Найкра́щий на сві́ті
The best in the world

To say that something is the best (worst, easiest, farthest) the construction often used is:

superlative + **з усіх** + *G. pl.*:

Це мі́сто найгарні́ше з усіх міст. *This city is the most beautiful of all cities.*
This construction can be used both with adjectives and adverbs in the superlative degree:

Ні́на була́ найкра́щою з усіх студе́нтів.
Nina was the best of all students.

Ігор працюва́в найбі́льше з усіх учасників. *Ihor worked the hardest of all participants.*

Сту́пені порі́вняння прислі́вників
Degrees of comparison of adverbs

Adverbs have the same degrees of comparison as adjectives. The only difference is that they relate not to objects but to actions, states, and qualities:

О́льга боїться літа́ти. *Olha is afraid of flying.* (positive degree)
Воло́дя боїться бі́льше, ніж О́льга. *Volodia is more afraid than Olha.* (comparative degree)
Петро́ боїться найбі́льше. *Petro is most afraid.* (superlative degree)

Утво́рення | *Formation*

The comparative degree of adverbs is formed from the comparative form of the respective adjective by replacing its ending with ~**е**,
m. **деше́вший обі́д** *a cheaper lunch* - **деше́вше пообі́дати** *to eat cheaper*
f. **важча́ пра́ця** *a harder work* - **ва́жче працюва́ти** *to work harder*
nt. **до́вше навча́ння** *a longer study* - **до́вше вчи́тися** *to study longer.*

The superlative degree is formed by adding the prefix **най~** to the comparative degree of the adverb,
їсти деше́вше *to eat cheaper* - **їсти найдеше́вше** *to eat cheapest*
працюва́ти ва́жче *to work harder* - **працюва́ти найва́жче** *to work hardest.*

comparative adjective	comparative adverb	superlative adverb
шви́дший *quicker*	**шви́дше** *more quickly*	**найшви́дше** *most quickly*
гарні́ший *more beautiful*	**гарні́ше** *more beautifully*	**найгарні́ше** *most beautifully*
смачні́ший *tastier*	**смачні́ше** *more tastily*	**найсмачні́ше** *most tastily*

12.14. Transform the sentences using comparative forms of the adverbs. Follow the word order in the model. Translate the sentences into English. Use the intensifiers from Note 11.8, p. 211.

Model.
C Після тако́го поя́снення завда́ння ле́гко зроби́ти
After such an explanation, the assignment is easy to do.
A Після тако́го поя́снення завда́ння зроби́ти набага́то ле́гше.
After such an explanation, to do this assignment is much easier.

1. Тепе́р Рома́н дале́ко живе́.
2. Тре́ба глибо́ко зрозумі́ти цей текст.
3. На нові́й робо́ті Наза́р шви́дко працю́є.
4. Хто навчи́ть мене́ де́шево жи́ти в Ки́єві?

5. Мо́жна ко́ротко говори́ти про найскладні́ші ре́чі.

6. Стефа́н живе́ тут лише́ ти́ждень, а Мари́на рік, тому́ вона́ до́бре зна́є мі́сто.

7. Ми наре́шті познайо́милися, і тому́ хоті́ли б ча́сто ба́читися з ва́ми.

8. Окса́ні слід ви́соко пові́сити карти́ну, іна́кше її тя́жко поба́чити.

9. Я не фахіве́ць з істо́рії, а ваш прові́дник ціка́во розка́же вам про мину́ле мі́ста.

10. Тре́ба ува́жно слу́хати пора́ди ва́шого лі́каря.

11. Пі́сля двох ро́ків навча́ння Ро́берт ві́льно розмовля́є і на́віть пи́ше украї́нською.

12. Насту́пного дня мандрі́вники ле́гко знайшли́ доро́гу додо́му.

Велосипе́дом, звича́йно,
бу́де шви́дше, як пі́шки.

∩ **12.15.** Express the highest degree of quality. Use the respective superlative adjectives.

Model.

Q Рома́н до́брий фахіве́ць, чи не так?

Roman is a good specialist, isn't he?

A Рома́н не про́сто до́брий, він найкра́щий з усі́х на́ших фахівці́в.

He is not simply good, he is the best of all our specialists.

1. Це складне́ завда́ння, чи не так?

2. Іва́н Миколайчу́к славе́тний украї́нський акто́р, чи не так?

3. Черні́гів вели́ке мі́сто на рі́чці Десні́, чи не так?

4. Борщ популя́рна стра́ва, чи не так?

5. Різдво́ – це весе́ле свя́то в Украї́ні, чи не так?

6. Дніпро́ – це важли́ва украї́нська рі́чка, чи не так?

7. Карпа́ти – це старі́ украї́нські го́ри, чи не так?

8. До́ктор Кириле́нко – досві́дчений лі́кар, чи не так?

∩ **12.16.** Translate the sentences into Ukrainian. Use respective superlative adverbs where adjectives are used in English.

Model. The easiest thing was to give (giving) advice.

Найле́гше було́ дава́ти пора́ди.

1. The most boring thing was to sit and watch.

2. The nicest thing was to visit (visiting) their parents in Zhytomyr.

3. The most interesting thing was that he asked nothing about them.

4. The strangest thing was to see them together.

5. The saddest thing was to meet John in the hospital.

6. The most wonderful thing will be that Larysa will be traveling with us.

7. The most complicated thing was to find the way to our hotel.

8. The funniest thing was to watch this comedy in Ukrainian.

9. The most delicious thing was to eat the salad of fresh vegetables.

∩ **12.17.** Translate the sentences into Ukrainian. Use the genitive plural after the prepositions **без** *without*, **бі́ля** *near*, **пі́сля** *after*, **для** *for*, **від** *from (person)*, and **до** *till, to*, **з (із)** *from (place)*.

У ко́жному ново́му мі́сті для нас
найціка́віше диви́тися на люде́й.

У Черні́гові бага́то стари́х церко́в.

1. He arrived in Kharkiv without the necessary papers.
2. We cannot go to the party without our new friends.
3. They stopped near a big door.
4. After the last weekend of the month we intend to call them.
5. They will live near great and beautiful lakes.
6. I will buy the tickets for their close relatives.
7. Mykola will work here till the first days of July.
8. You will receive a letter from these good specialists.
9. We traveled from Lutsk to the eastern Carpathians by bus.
10. Natalka will translate these texts for all your Russian instructors.
11. You can get from Cherkasy to Chernivtsi only by car or bus.
12. This gift is from your Canadian female friends.

12.18. Answer the questions. Where necessary, put the proper name in the required case and use the prepositions.

Model. Мико́ла Петре́нко *Mykola Petrenko* or
    О́льга Петре́нко *Olha Petrenko*
Q Кого́ ви тут зна́єте? *Who do you know here?*
A 1. Мико́лу Петре́нка. *Mykola Petrenko.*
A 2. О́льгу Петре́нко. *Olha Petrenko.*

1. Кому́ ви подару́єте кві́ти? Лари́са Бойчу́к
2. З ким він познайо́мився вчо́ра? Тара́с Ковале́нко
3. До ко́го тре́ба подзвони́ти? Яри́на Бо́ндар
4. Кому́ подаю́ть сніда́нок до кімна́ти? пан Мико́ла Павлю́к
5. З ким вони́ пора́дяться у цій спра́ві? Марі́я та Ната́лка Ковале́нко
6. Про ко́го ти хоті́в сказа́ти мені́? Ігор Бо́ндар
7. З ким ви ї́здили до Ки́єва? Рома́н Бойчу́к
8. Для ко́го цей подару́нок? Юрко́ Шевче́нко
9. Для ко́го ці гро́ші? Окса́на Шевче́нко
10. Кому́ він ку́пить квитки́? Оле́на Павлю́к
11. Про ко́го ця кни́жка? Іва́н Світли́чний
12. З ким ти на цій фотогра́фії? Наді́я Світли́чна

12.19. Answer the questions. Make sure that the noun following 2, 3, and 4 is in the required form.

Model. C 22, люди́на *person*
    Q Скі́льки тут люде́й? *How many people are here?*
    A Якщо́ не помиля́юся, тут два́дцять дві люди́ни.
    If I'm not mistaken, there are twenty-two people here.

1. 2, скля́нка
2. 23, друг
3. 63, дити́на
4. 24, кия́нин
5. 52, студе́нт
6. 183, гри́вня
7. 52, я́блуко
8. 84, дівчи́на
9. 3, ім'я́
10. 42, день
11. 74, годи́на
12. 93, хвили́на

У Черка́сах ми познайо́милися з Кили́ною Бо́ндар і Яри́ною Дома́нською.

Чита́ємо й обгово́рюємо   Reading and Discussing

🎧 **12.20.** Read and translate the questions. Listen to the text "Готе́ль Мазе́па" and answer the questions in Ukrainian.

1. Як назива́ється готе́ль?
2. У яко́му мі́сті Украї́ни розташо́ваний готе́ль?
3. У яко́му мі́сці мі́ста розташо́вується готе́ль?
4. Які́ по́слуги є в готе́лі?
5. Які́ стра́ви є в меню́ рестора́ну "Курі́нь"?
6. Що мо́жна замо́вити в готе́лі?
7. Що ще ви дізна́лися про готе́ль?

🎧 **12.21.** Read the text *The Mazepa Hotel* carefully and answer the questions in Ukrainian. Consult the dictionary, if necessary.

1. За яко́ю адре́сою розташо́ваний готе́ль «Мазе́па»?
2. Які́ по́слуги є в готе́лі?
3. Скі́льки кімна́т для госте́й є в готе́лі?
4. Які́ ти́пи кімна́т є в готе́лі?
5. У яки́й час в готе́лі мо́жна сні́дати, обі́дати та вече́ряти?
6. Які́ украї́нські стра́ви є в меню́ рестора́ну «Курі́нь»?
7. Які́ європе́йські стра́ви є в меню́ цьо́го рестора́ну?
8. Де в готе́лі мо́жна ви́пити ка́ви?
9. Які́ ти́пи квитків мо́жна купи́ти в готе́лі?

🎧 Готе́ль "Мазе́па"

"Мазе́па", нови́й готе́ль у само́му середмі́сті Полта́ви, розташо́ваний на ти́хій ву́лиці, бі́ля місько́го па́рку, за адре́сою: вул. Мико́ли Го́голя, 16. Готе́ль моде́рний і ма́є всі суча́сні по́слуги, від міжнаро́дної мере́жі та сателіта́рного телеба́чення, до спортклу́бу, сало́ну краси́ та рестора́ну із найкра́щим шеф-ку́харем у Полта́ві. Цей невели́кий та за́тишний готе́ль із дома́шньою атмосфе́рою ма́є два́дцять кімна́т чотирьо́х ти́пів:

1) шість станда́ртних кімна́т на одну́ осо́бу *(single standard)* із односпа́льним лі́жком та ду́шем. Ціна́ за добу́ 180 грн.

2) шість станда́ртних кімна́т на дві осо́би *(double standard)* із двома́ односпа́льними лі́жками (чи одни́м двоспа́льним лі́жком) та ва́нною. Ціна́ за добу́ 300 грн.

3) п'ять номе́рів напівлю́кс *(junior suite)*, у ко́жному спа́льня із вели́ким двоспа́льним лі́жком та віта́льня. Ціна́ за добу́ 580 грн.

4) три номери́ люкс *(suite)*, у ко́жному дві спа́льні із вели́ким двоспа́льним лі́жком, віта́льня та балко́н із ви́дом на парк і чудо́ву рі́чку Во́рсклу. У всіх номера́х є телефо́н, телеві́зор, холоди́льник та міні-ба́р. Ціна́ за добу́ 800 грн.

Готе́ль «Мазе́па» ма́є свій рестора́н «Курі́нь», та кав'я́рню-бар. У меню́ рестора́ну такі́ традиці́йні стра́ви украї́нської та європе́йської ку́хні, як борщ, варе́ники, голубці́, дома́шня ковбаса́, котле́та по-ки́ївськи, різо́тто, гуля́ш, пае́я, ві́денський шні́цель та і́нші. Сніда́нок із 7:30 до 10:00, обі́д з 12:30 до 15:00, вече́ря з 18:00 до 23:00. Го́сті мо́жуть замовля́ти сніда́нок до кімна́ти.

Мандрівники́ зупини́лися на ніч у готе́лі "Мазе́па".

В готе́лі мо́жна замо́вити екску́рсію мі́стом, такси́вку, найня́ти а́вто, купи́ти квитки́ на літа́к, по́їзд чи авто́бус до і́нших міст в Украї́ні та за кордо́ном, а та́кож квитки́ до теа́трів, кінотеа́трів, музе́їв та худо́жніх галере́й.

Готе́ль «Мазе́па» – це ідеа́льне мі́сце відпочи́нку як для тури́стів, так і госте́й, що приї́хали до Полта́ви у спра́вах.

12.22. Compare a single standard room and a suite in the *Mazepa Hotel* as to space, services included, and price.

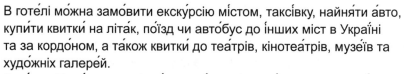

Завда́ння для Міжнаро́дної мере́жі
Internet Assignment

12.23. Find a Ukrainian hotel on the Ukrainian language Internet and provide the following information about it:

1. На́зва готе́лю та докла́дна адре́са
2. По́слуги, які́ в ньо́му пропону́ють
3. Ти́пи номе́рів та ці́ни на ко́жний
4. І́нша інформа́ція, кори́сна для міжнаро́дних тури́стів
5. Що вам подо́бається в цьо́му готе́лі, чому́?
6. Що вам не подо́бається в ньо́му, чому́?

 12.24. Say and write the sentences in Ukrainian. Use the vocabulary and grammar of this and previous lessons. If necessary, consult the dictionary.

1. When I went to Chernihiv, I always stayed at this hotel.
2. Maksym likes this hotel because it is inexpensive and has all necessary services: a restaurant, laundry, the Internet, and even a small gym.
3. We are very tired. I suggest ordering dinner to the room.
4. Do you have a vacant room for two with a view of the sea?
5. The room is alright, but the price doesn't suit us. It's too high. Do you have cheaper rooms?
6. How many days are they going to spend in the city?
7. The receptionist says that we can check out early afternoon.
8. How much money do we need to pay for six days in this hotel?
9. For our guests we bought a kilo of apples and half a kilo of sour cherries. For their children – a box of candies.
10. One U.S. dollar now costs eight hryvnias ten kopecks.
11. Can you introduce me to Ivan Vasylchenko and Natalia Tykha?
12. Our trip from New York to Kyiv lasted nine hours.
13. Their guest from Cherkasy needs to book a taxi to the airport for six o'clock tomorrow morning.
14. First Mrs. Lukashuk would like to check in at the hotel and then have her business meeting in the bank.

Го́сті ходи́ли на ду́же ціка́ву екску́рсію мі́стом Ми́ргородом.

Коли́сь Юрко́ люби́в зупиня́тися в цьо́му готе́лі.

12.25. Describe the services offered at this hotel. Use the pictograms on p. 222.

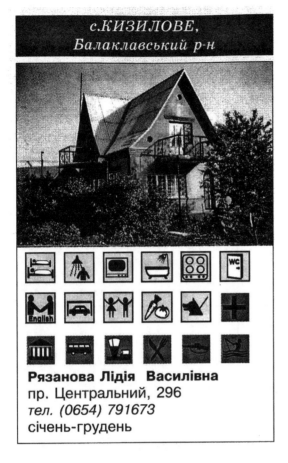

Що ви мо́жете сказа́ти про цей готе́ль?

⌒ 12.26. Listen carefully to these questions and answer each of them using Dialogue 12.

1. Де ма́є мі́сце розмо́ва у діяло́зі?
2. Скі́льки осі́б бере́ у́часть у розмо́ві?
3. Що споча́тку запи́тує в адміністра́тора готе́лю Окса́на Коза́к?
4. Яки́й но́мер хо́чуть го́сті?
5. Кімна́ту із яки́м ви́дом вибира́є Окса́на Коза́к і чому́?
6. Скі́льки ціка́вих буди́нків є в Черні́гові?
7. Які́ по́слуги пропону́ють у готе́лі?
8. Яка́ по́слуга ціка́вить Окса́ну Коза́к найбі́льше?
9. Скі́льки ко́штує станда́ртний но́мер на дві осо́би?
10. Які́ ще по́слуги включа́є ціна́ кімна́ти?
11. Чим приї́хали до Черні́гова Окса́на Коза́к із чолові́ком?
12. З яко́ю мето́ю приї́хала па́ні Коза́к?
13. Як назива́ється рестора́н у готе́лі?
14. Хто дає́ їм ключі́ до но́мера?
15. Як закі́нчується розмо́ва па́ні Коза́к із адміністра́тором?
16. Як ви шука́єте готе́ль у незнайо́мому мі́сті?
17. У яко́му готе́лі ви зупиня́лися оста́нній раз?

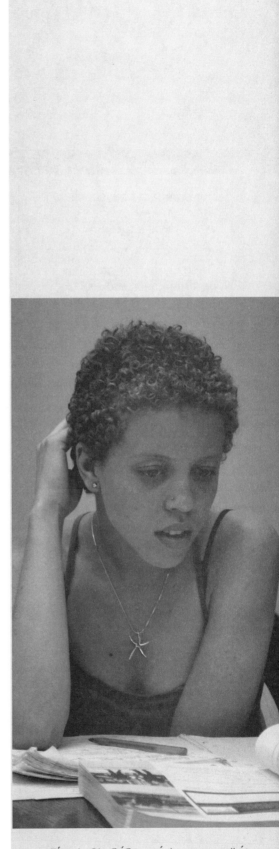

Лі́ля із Зімба́бве ви́рішила серйо́зно вивча́ти украї́нську мо́ву.

Як ви зупиня́лися в готе́лі. How you stayed in a hotel.

12.27. Engage a partner in a conversation about her / his stay in a hotel.

1) Find out each detail noted in the chart below.
2) Write them all down in Ukrainian.
3) Write a short report in Ukrainian about what you learned.
4) Be ready to present your report orally in class.

Про що дізна́тися	партне́р-1	партне́р-2	партне́р-3
До яко́го мі́ста ви ї́здили, коли́ оста́нній раз зупиня́лися в готе́лі?			
Як ви шука́ли готе́ль? (чия́сь рекоменда́ція, мере́жа, туристи́чна аге́нція, і т. п.)			
Як назива́вся готе́ль, і в які́й части́ні мі́ста він розташо́вувався?			
З яко́ю мето́ю ви приї́хали до мі́ста?			
Від яко́ї та до яко́ї да́ти ви жили́ в готе́лі?			
Чому́ ви ви́рішили зупини́тися са́ме в цьо́му готе́лі?			
Яку́ кімна́ту ви замо́вили собі́ (ціна́, по́верх, вид, і́нші дета́лі)?			
Які́ по́слуги були́ у ва́шому но́мері?			
Які́ по́слуги пропонува́ли в готе́лі? Які́ з них були́ кори́сні для вас?			
Чи сподо́балося вам жи́ти в тому́ готе́лі і чому́?			

12.28. Enact a conversation with a partner. Use the material you learned in this and previous lessons. If necessary consult the dictionary.

Сце́нка за сцена́рієм «Як замо́вити но́мер у готе́лі»
Scripted Skit: *Making a Hotel Reservation*

Tamara (Тама́ра): Calls the Hetman Hotel (Готе́ль «Ге́тьман») and verifies that it is the place she wants.
Receptionist (черго́вий): Greets her and confirms that this is indeed the Hetman Hotel. Asks how he can help.

Tamara: Says she'd like to book an accommodation for two people.
Receptionist: Asks for what date she wants the room.

Tamara: Gives the dates of arrival and departure.
Receptionist: Sums up stating the number of days (доба́) Tamara will be staying. Says that there is a room with a double bed and a separate bathroom. The rate is UAH 450 a day.

Tamara: Says this is too expensive for them. Asks if there is anything cheaper.
Receptionist: Responds that they have rooms for UAH 300 a day. They do not have a shower or a toilet.

Tamara: Asks if there are showers and bathrooms on the floor.
Receptionist: There are six showers on the third floor of the hotel and four restrooms on the first floor.

Tamara: Says this is perfectly all right and asks to book that type of a room. Stipulates she needs a quieter room.
Receptionist: Informs Tamara they will have a room looking out onto the courtyard, the quietest one.

Tamara: Appreciates it. Asks if they can use the Internet in the hotel.
Receptionist: Affirmative. There is a wi-fi connection for the guests who have their own computer.

Tamara: She says they will have no computer of their own.
Receptionist: That is no problem, for there are eight PCs in the lobby. Guests can use them for no charge.

Tamara: Expresses her satisfaction. Asks whether breakfast is included in the price of accommodation.
Receptionist: Says that indeed breakfast is included. Their restaurant serves it from 7:00 to 10:00 o'clock. One can also have lunch and dinner there. It offers traditional Ukrainian food. The chef is one of the best in town.

Tamara: Thanks him for the information, adding that both she and her husband are of the opinion that food is a serious matter.
Receptionist: Inquires whether she would like to make the reservation.

Це́рква Богда́на Хмельни́цького в селі́ Су́ботові, Черка́ської о́бласти.

Tamara: Affirmative. Asks whether they accept American Express credit cards.
Receptionist: Says they do and sums up the reservation information stating: a standard room for two guests with a double bed, no shower, breakfast included, the date of arrival and departure, the total price being UAH 1,500.

Ле́кція | Lesson 13

Dialogue:
У по́дорож до Украї́ни
On a Trip to Ukraine

Grammar:
Locative plural
Reflexive verbs
Patronymics
Motion verbs in perfective future tense
Prefixed motion verbs

Competencies:
Ukrainian honorifics
Destination, origin, and purpose of action
Planning a trip
Names of Ukrainian regions

Славе́тна ве́жа Корня́кта *Korniakt Tower*. Льві́в'яни та го́сті лю́блять ходи́ти по стари́х ву́лицях мі́ста Ле́ва.

💬 13. Діяло́г: У по́дорож до Украї́ни.

Марко́: Роксоля́но, цього́ лі́та ми з Рома́ном і́демо у по́дорож до Украї́ни.

Роксоля́на: Наре́шті, Ма́рку! Да́вно пора́! В яки́х міста́х ви ду́маєте побува́ти?

Марко́: У Льво́ві, Ки́єві та Оде́сі. Ка́жуть, у Льво́ві украї́нською розмовля́ють скрізь: у рестора́нах, у крамни́цях, на вокза́лах.

Роксоля́на: Так, це пра́вда. І не ті́льки у Льво́ві, але́ теж в і́нших міста́х, на́віть у Луга́нську, Ха́ркові чи Маріу́полі.

Марко́: Напе́вно розмовля́ють, але́ ми в цих міста́х не ду́маємо бу́ти під час ціє́ї по́дорожі.

Роксоля́на: Я почина́ла свою́ пе́ршу по́дорож до Украї́ни із Ки́єва.

Марко́: Ми споча́тку пої́демо до Льво́ва. І Рома́н, і я ма́ємо там близьки́х ро́дичів. Бу́де ціка́во побачитися з ни́ми.

Роксоля́на: Мі́сто Ле́ва - це чудо́ве мі́сто. Мені́ особи́сто найбі́льше подо́балося там про́сто ходи́ти по його́ ву́лицях, прову́лках та пло́щах.

Марко́: По́тім ми пої́демо по́їздом до Ки́єва. Я чита́в, що у столи́ці Украї́ни ду́же бага́то ціка́вих місць. Що ти ра́диш поба́чити наса́мперед?

Роксоля́на: Ра́джу побува́ти у стари́х церква́х та собо́рах.

Марко́: У яки́х, конкре́тно, бо ми про́сто не бу́демо ма́ти ча́су відві́дати всі.

Роксоля́на: У Пече́рській Ла́врі, Софі́йському, Михайлі́вському та Володи́мирському собо́рах. Вам та́кож слід піти́ на Андрі́ївський узві́з та Хреща́тик.

Марко́: До́бре, дя́кую. Ми обов'язко́во це зро́бимо. В Оде́сі ми хо́чемо відпочи́ти на пля́жі, побува́ти у худо́жніх галере́ях.

Роксоля́на: Де ви ночува́тимете в усі́х цих міста́х? Ча́сто готе́лі в Украї́ні задороги́, а в деше́вих готе́лях нема́є ві́льних місць.

Марко́: Зупиня́тися у готе́лях – це спра́вді задо́рого. Тому́ ми ночува́тимемо у студе́нтських гурто́житках, прива́тних поме́шканнях, чи на кварти́рах на́ших дру́зів.

Роксоля́на: Скі́льки ча́су ви ду́маєте провести́ в Украї́ні?

Марко́: Прина́ймні три ти́жні. Я зна́ю, що це ма́ло для тако́ї вели́кої, ціка́вої і прекра́сної краї́ни, як Украї́на.

Роксоля́на: Так і ні, бо за три ти́жні, якщо́ ма́єш бажа́ння, мо́жна ду́же бага́то поба́чити, зроби́ти і дізна́тися.

Марко́: І та́кож навчи́тися значно́ кра́ще розмовля́ти украї́нською мо́вою.

Роксоля́на: Я впе́внена, вам ду́же сподо́бається Украї́на. А ще ви бу́дете ра́ді, що вчи́ли украї́нську мо́ву ще до по́дорожі.

💬 13. Dialogue. A Trip to Ukraine.

Marko: Roksolana, this summer Roman and I are going on a trip to Ukraine.

Roksolana: Finally, Marko! High time you did! What cities are you going to visit?

Marko: Lviv, Kyiv, and Odesa. They say that in Lviv Ukrainian is spoken everywhere: in restaurants, in stores, at stations.

Roksolana: Yes, it's true. And not only in Lviv, but also in other cities, even in Luhansk, Kharkiv or Mariupol.

Marko: Surely they do, but we are not going to visit these cities during this trip.

Roksolana: I started my first trip to Ukraine from Kyiv.

Marko: We will first go to Lviv. Both Roman and I have close family there. It will be interesting to see them.

Roksolana: The City of Leo (or Lion) is a wonderful city. I personally most liked simply walking along its streets, lanes, and squares.

Marko: Then we'll travel by train to Kyiv. I read that there are very many sights in the capital of Ukraine. What do you recommend to see first of all?

Roksolana: I suggest that you visit old churches and cathedrals.

Marko: Which ones, specifically, because we simply won't have time to see them all?

Roksolana: The Pechersk Lavra and St. Sophia, St. Michael's, and St. Volodymyr Cathedrals. You should also go to St. Andrew's Street and Khreshchatyk.

Marko: Good, thank you. We'll do it by all means. In Odesa, we want to relax on the beach and to visit the art galleries.

Roksolana: Where will you be staying for the night in all these cities? Often hotels in Ukraine are too expensive, and there are no vacancies in the cheap ones.

Marko: To stay at hotels is indeed too expensive. That's why we'll be staying at student dormitories, private apartments, or in the apartments of our friends.

Roksolana: How much time are you going to spend in Ukraine?

Marko: At least three weeks. I know it is little time for such a big, interesting, and beautiful country like Ukraine.

Roksolana: Yes and no, because in three weeks, if one has the desire, one can see, do, and learn a lot.

Marko: And also (one can) learn to speak Ukrainian considerably better.

Roksolana: I am sure you'll like Ukraine very much. And also you'll be glad that you studied Ukrainian before your journey.

Андрі́ївський узві́з біжи́ть від середмі́стя Ки́єва до Контракто́вої пло́щі на Подо́лі.

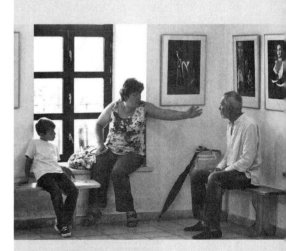

По вихідни́х ці вели́кі люби́телі мисте́цтва хо́дять по музе́ях і галере́ях Оде́си.

Миха́йлівський Золотове́рхий собо́р стоїть на Миха́йлівській пло́щі столи́ці.

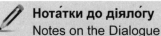

Нота́тки до діяло́гу
Notes on the Dialogue

до Украї́ни, *G. sg.*	to Ukraine, as in **по́дорож до Украї́ни** *a trip to Ukraine* or **ї́хати (поїхати) до Украї́ни** *to travel to Ukraine*. The
в Украї́ні, *L. sg.*	equivalent of the *Eng. in Ukraine* is **в Украї́ні**, **В Украї́ні є бага́то га́рних міст.** *There are many beautiful cities in Ukraine.*
на Украї́ні* *(old)* **в Украї́ну*** *(old)*	old Soviet usage implying that Ukraine is a province rather than independent nation It should be avoided as offensive or ignorant.
да́вно пора́ + *pf. inf.*	it's high time (you did it, you should have done it a long time ago); also with the logical subject in *D.* + **д. п.**, **Джо́нові д. п. навчи́тися розмовля́ти украї́нською.** *It's high time John learned to speak Ukrainian.*
побува́ти, *pf.* **у** + *L.*	to make a visit to, or see a place, city, **У яки́х міста́х Украї́ни ви вже побува́ли?** *What cities of Ukraine have you already been to?*
ка́жуть, (що) ...	*impersonal* They say …, I hear, **Ка́жуть, ви приї́хали із Доне́цька.** *They say you came from Donetsk.*
мі́сто Ле́ва	**Лев** means both *a lion* and the masculine name *Lev (Leo)* as in **князь Лев** *Prince Leo* after whom the city was named when it was founded by King Danylo of Halych in mid-13th century.
Пече́рська Ла́вра	the Monastery of the Caves, one of the holiest places of Ukrainian Christianity and a splendid monument of the architectural style known as Ukrainian, or Cossack, or Mazepa baroque.
Софі́йський собо́р	St. Sophia Cathedral, built in the 11th century by Prince Yaroslav the Wise, a.k.a. Europe's father-in-law, to imitate the Hagia Sophia in Constantinopole, this unique monument is home to a collection of frescoes and mosaics dating back to the time of its construction.
Миха́йлівський Золотове́рхий собо́р	St. Michael's Golden-Domed Cathedral was built in 1108-1113 by prince Sviatopolk II Iziaslavych in the Byzantine style. The Cathedral was demolished by the Soviet regime in the 1930s. In the 1990s it was rebuilt.
Володи́мирський собо́р	St. Volodymyr's Cathedral, the patriarchal cathedral of the Ukrainian Orthodox Church, Kyiv Patriarchate, built in 1896.
зана́дто, *adv., var.* **на́дто**	too, excessively; used with *adj., adv.,* and *v.*, **Я живу́ з. дале́ко.** *I live too far.* **з. вели́кий** *too big*.
таки́й .., як + *N.*	such ... as, **для тако́ї по́други, як Оле́на** *for such a friend as Olena*, **до таки́х дівча́т, як вони́** *to such girls as they are*. More on **таки́й** in Note 4.11, p. 53.
за + *A.*	in, over (*indicates a period of time for an action to be completed*), **Я написа́ла лист за одну́ годи́ну.** *I wrote the letter in an hour.*
якщо́, *conj.*	if, to express a real condition, **Я мо́жу допомогти́, якщо́ хо́чете.** *I can help, if you want.* More in Lesson 15.

📖 Грама́тика | Grammar

Місце́вий відмі́нок множини́   Locative Case Plural

Фу́нкція   *Function*

Locative plural is generally identical in function to the locative singular and is always used with a presposition, either **у (в)** *in*, **на** *on, upon*, and **по** *on, around, through* or some others (Lesson 6).
Days of the week and parts of the day in the locative plural after the preposition **по** *on* indicate *repetitiveness* or *frequency*. This corresponds to the *Eng. every + day of the week*:

по понеді́лках *every Monday* (*lit.* on Mondays)*,* **по вівто́рках** *every Tuesday,* **по п'я́тницях** *every Friday,* **по субо́тах** *every Saturday,* **по неді́лях** *every Sunday,* **по но́чах** *every night,* **по вечора́х** *every evening. L. pl.* of **четве́р** *Thursday* is **по четверга́х** *every Thursday.*

Утво́рення   *Formation*

Іме́нники   Nouns

The nominal locative plural endings are:
~ах (~ях)

~ах is for hard-stem nouns of all genders,
кімна́та *a room* - **у кімна́тах** *in rooms,* **парк** *a park* - **у па́рках** *in parks,* **стіл** *a table* – **на стола́х** *on tables,* **мі́сто** *a city* - **по міста́х** *through cities,* **пло́ща** *a square* - **по пло́щах** *through squares,* **студе́нт** *a student* - **на студе́нтах** *on students,* **сестра́** *a sister* - **на се́страх** *on sisters*

~ях is used for soft-stem nouns of all genders,
прия́тель *a friend* - **на прия́телях** *on friends,* **лі́кар** *a physician* - **на лікаря́х** *on physicians,* **готе́ль** *a hotel* - **у готе́лях** *in hotels,* **поли́ця** *a shelf* - **на поли́цях** *on shelves,* **ву́лиця** *a street* - **по ву́лицях** *along streets*

 The stress in the locative plural is usually on the same syllable as in the nominative plural,

сестра́ *a sister* - *N. pl.* **се́стри** *sisters* – *L. pl.* **на се́страх** *on sisters*
ба́тько *a father* - *N. pl.* **батьки́** *fathers* – *L. pl.* **на батька́х** *on fathers*
мі́сто *a city* - *N. pl.* **міста́** *cities* – *L. pl.* **у міста́х** *in cities*
    but
річ *a thing* - *N. pl.* **ре́чі** *things* – *L. pl.* **у реча́х** *in things.*

 Note 13.1. Ukrainian honorifics

Ukrainian honorifics are:
пан *mister (Mr.)*
пані *mistress (Mrs.)* for married women
па́нна *miss (Ms.)* for unmarried women.

Each can be used with a (name and) family name conveying the highest degree of formality:

пан Тиміш Іваничу́к *Mr. Tymish Ivanychuk* or **пан Іваничу́к** *Mr. Ivanychuk*

пані Яри́на Михайле́нко *Mrs. Yaryna Mykhailenko* or **пані Михайле́нко** *Mrs. Mykhailenko*

па́нна Соломі́я Коза́к *Ms. Solomia Kozak* or **па́нна Коза́к** *Ms. Kozak*

Unlike their English equivalents, all three honorifics can also be used with only a first name for a less formal way of addressing or referring to a person:

пан Тиміш (*lit. Mr. Tymish*), **пані Яри́на** (*lit. Mrs. Yaryna*), **па́нна Соломі́я** (*lit. Ms. Solomia*)

The Ukrainian for 'Ladies and Gentlemen!' is **Пані та пано́ве!**

A polite way of addressing a stranger, like the *Eng.* Sir! or Madam! is **добро́дію!** (*lit. benefactor*) addressed to a man, and **добро́дійко!** (*lit. benefactress*) to a woman. In real life situations, the functional equivalent of *Sir!* or *Madam!* is **ви́бачте, будь ла́ска!** *lit. excuse me, please!* followed by a question or request,

Ви́бачте, будь ла́ска, де тут банк?
Excuse me, Sir/Madam, where is a bank here?

Note 13.2. Locative plural of irregular nouns

The nouns with stem differences between *N. sg.* and *N. pl.*, derive their *L. pl.* from the *N. pl.*:

друг *a friend* - *N. pl.* **дру́зі** *friends*
   L. pl. **на дру́зях** *on friends*

люди́на *a person* - *N. pl.* **лю́ди** *people*
   L. pl. **на лю́дях** *on people; in public*

дити́на *a child* - *N. pl.* **ді́ти** *children*
   L. pl. **на ді́тях** *on children*

о́ко *an eye* - *N. pl.* **о́чі** *eyes*
   L. pl. **на оча́х** *on the eyes*

кия́нин *a Kyivan* - *N. pl.* **кия́ни** *Kyivans*
   L. pl. **на кия́нах** *on Kyivans*

росія́нин *a Russian* - *N. pl.* **росія́ни** *Russians*
   L. pl. **на росія́нах** *on Russians*

🔊 SOUND CHANGES 🔊
in the locative plural of nouns

Dropping of ~o~ (~e~)
~o~ and ~e~ in the last syllable of 2nd declension masculine nouns are dropped in the locative plural:
   куто́к *a corner* - **у кутка́х** *in corners*
   сон *a dream* - **у́ві снах** *in dreams*
   украї́нець *a Ukrainian* - **на украї́нцях** *on Ukrainians*
   кіне́ць *the end* - **у кінця́х** *in the ends*

Change of ~i~ to ~o~ (~e~)
~i~ changes to ~o~ (~e~) in the final syllable in 2nd declension masculine and 3rd declension feminine nouns:
   m. **стіл** *a table* - **на стола́х** *on tables*
   m. **кіт** *a cat* - **на кота́х** *on cats*
   m. **папі́р** *a paper* - **у папе́рах** *in papers*
   f. **річ** *a thing* - **у реча́х** *in things*
   f. **ніч** *a night* - **у ноча́х** *in the nights*

Прикме́тники   Adjectives

The adjectival locative plural endings:
~их (~ix)

~их is for all hard-stem adjectives regardless of gender,
вели́ке мі́сто *a big city* - **у вели́ких міста́х** *in big cities*,
мала́ ву́лиця *a small street* - **на мали́х ву́лицях** *on small streets*,
украї́нський словни́к *a Ukrainian dictionary* - **в украї́нських словника́х** *in Ukrainian dictionaries*

~ix is for all soft-stem adjectives,
си́ній зо́шит *a blue notebook* - **у си́ніх зо́шитах** *in blue notebooks*, **оста́нній по́тяг** *the last train* - **в оста́нніх по́тягах** *in the last trains*

The *L. pl.* of **весь (уве́сь)** *all, whole, entire* is **всіх (усі́х)**.

Зворо́тні дієслова́   Reflexive verbs

Reflexive verbs are easy to recognize by the particle **~ся** (~self) at the end. They denote:

1) an action whose performer is also its recipient. They correspond to the English verbs used with the pronoun *oneself* and its variants (*myself, yourself, himself, herself, ourselves*, etc.),

зва́тися *to be called (lit. to call oneself)*, **умива́тися** *to wash oneself*

На цих чолові́ках о́дяг спра́вжніх ба́йкерів.

Ukrainian reflexive verbs can also correlate with the English intransitive verbs that have no pronoun *oneself*,
Я верта́юся за́втра. *I am returning tomorrow.* **Він помили́вся.** *He made a mistake.*

2) a reciprocal action that involves two or more participants. In this case, the verb is followed by the preposition **з** (**із**) *with* and a noun in *I.*,
   знайо́митися з + *I.* to get acquainted with one another
   ба́читися з + *I.* to see one another
   листува́тися з + *I.* to correspond with one another
   спереча́тися з + *I.* to argue with one another

Reflexive verbs normally cannot take a direct object, for their object is also the doer (subject) of the action, cf.,
Учи́тель поча́в ле́кцію. *The instructor began the lecture.* and
Ле́кція почала́ся *The lecture began (lit. … began itself).*

The only reflexive verb that can take a direct accusative object is **диви́тися** *to watch.* It can be used both without and with a preposition,

диви́тися програ́му (фільм, виста́ву) *to watch a show (film, play)*
диви́тися на карти́ну (світли́ну, люди́ну) *to look at a picture (photo, person)*

3) an action that describes or is directed at the subject even though it does not originate in the subject,

жури́тися *to worry*, **хвилюва́тися** *to be nervous*

Some verbs have only reflexive forms,
   диви́тися (на) + *A.* to look at
   здава́тися to seem
   смія́тися to laugh
   подо́батися to be liked
   боя́тися + *G.* to fear, be afraid of
   користува́тися + *I.* to use
   листува́тися з (із) + *I.* to correspond with sb

When conjugated, reflexive verbs have the same forms as their regular counterparts plus the particle **~ся**, cf.,
роби́в *he made* ⇔ **роби́вся** *he became, transformed himself*
вона́ знайо́мить *she introduces (sb to sb)* ⇔ **вона́ знайо́миться** *she gets herself acquainted*

The only exception is 3rd person singular of the present tense of the **~уть/~ють** verbs, when **~ть~** is inserted between the personal ending **~е/~є** and the particle **~ся**:
він ми́є *he washes* - **він ми́ється** *he washes himself*

Note 13.3. Transitive vs reflexive verbs

A transitive verb that takes a direct object often has a reflexive form as well, cf.:
почина́ти *to start sth*
   почина́тися *to start (oneself)*

закі́нчувати *to finish sth*
   закі́нчуватися *to finish (oneself*

продо́вжувати *to continue sth*
   продо́вжуватися *to continue (oneself)*

ми́ти *to wash sth*
   ми́тися *to wash oneself*

знайо́мити *to familiarize sb with sth*
   знайо́митися *to get acquainted*

ціка́вити *to interest sb*
   ціка́витися *to be interested in sb/sth*

Thus a number of frequently used English verbs have two Ukrainian counterparts. One is transitive and the other reflexive:

The story began a long time ago.
refl. **Ця істо́рія почала́ся давно́.**
She began the novel last year.
tran. **Вона́ поча́ла рома́н торі́к.**

Ivan returned on Sunday.
refl. **Іва́н поверну́вся у неді́лю.**
He returned the money yesterday.
tran. **Він поверну́в гро́ші вчо́ра.**

Other such verbs are:

to change, intr., impf. **міня́тися**; *pf.* **зміни́тися** and *tran., impf.* **міня́ти**; *pf.* **зміни́ти**;

to meet, intr., impf. **зустріча́тися**; *pf.* **зустрі́тися** and *tran., impf.* **зустріча́ти**; *pf.* **зустрі́ти**;

to stop, intr., impf. **зупиня́тися**; *pf.* **зупини́тися** and *tran., impf.* **зупиня́ти**; *pf.* **зупини́ти.**

Ори́ся Кра́вченко вже два ро́ки займа́ється фотогра́фією.

Note 13.4. Some irregular patronymics

Special cases of patronymics are:
Лука́ *Luka* - *m.* Луки́ч *Lukych*, *f.* Лукі́вна *Lukivna*

Яків *Yakiv* - *m.* Я́кович *Yakovych*, *f.* Яківна *Yakivna*

Микола *Mykola* - *m.* Микола́йович *Mykolaiovych*, *f.* Микола́ївна *Mykolaïvna* (Both these forms are derived not from **Мико́ла** but from its variant **Миколай**.)

Григо́рій *Hryhoriy* - *m.* Григо́рович *Hryhorovych*, *f.* Григо́рівна *Hryhorivna* (These are derived not from **Григо́рій** but from its variant **Гри́гір**.)

Оста́п Яросла́вович Мудра́к дуже любить рідну природу.

По ба́тькові Patronymics

Фу́нкція Function

The patronymic is a person's middle name meaning "the son or daughter of father." It is used after a person's first name (never with surname) as a formula of calling or referring to the person,

Мико́ла **Васи́льович** *Mykola Vasyliovych (Mykola, Vasyl's son)*
Марі́я **Миха́йлівна** *Maria Mykhailivna (Maria, Mykhailo's daughter)*

As any other proper name the patronymic is always capitalized. When used alone, the patronymic is a familiar, and, in a workplace, a quasi-formal address or reference. The person called only by the patronymic would be otherwise referred to by the speaker as **ви**, not **ти**.

Васи́льовичу, що ви сказа́ли? *Vasyliovych, what did you say?*
Миха́йлівно, що ново́го? *Mykhailivno, what's new?*

Утво́рення Formation

Masculine patronymics are derived from the father's name by adding the following suffixes:

~ович for all hard stems,
Іва́н *Ivan* - *m.* Іва́нович *Ivanovych*, Миха́йло *Mykhailo* - *m.* Миха́йлович *Mykhailovych*, Сергі́й *Serhiy* - *m.* Сергі́йович *Serhiyovych*.

~ьович for soft stems,
Васи́ль *Vasyl* - *m.* Васи́льович *Vasyliovych*

Feminine patronymics are also derived from the father's name by adding the suffix:

~івна for all types of stems,
Іва́н *Ivan* - *f.* Іва́нівна *Ivanivna*, Миха́йло *Mykhailo* - *f.* Миха́йлівна *Mykhailivna*, Сергі́й *Serhiy* - *f.* Сергі́ївна *Serhiyivna*, Васи́ль *Vasyl* - *f.* Васи́лівна *Vasylivna*.

To enquire about a person's patronymic one asks: **Як вас (тебе́, його́) по ба́тькові?** *What's your (sg. your, his) patronymic?*
The answer is: **По ба́тькові мене́ (його́)** *m.* **Іва́нович.** *My (his) patronymic is Ivanovych.*

The stress in a patronymic is usually where it is in the respective first name. Exceptions include **Павло́** *Pavlo* - **Па́влович** *Pavlovych*, **Па́влівна** *Pavlivna*; **Дмитро́** *Dmytro* - **Дми́трович** *Dmytrovych*, **Дми́трівна** *Dmytrivna*, **Марко́** *Marko* - **Ма́ркович** *Markovych*, **Ма́рківна** *Markivna*.

Дієслова́ ру́ху у майбу́тньому доко́наному
Motion Verbs in Perfective Future

To form the perfective future of the motion verbs the prefix **по~** is added to a respective uni-directional infinitive:

uni-directional infinitive		perfective infinitive
іти́	to go on foot, walk	піти́
ї́хати	to go by a vehicle, drive	пої́хати
бі́гти	to run	побі́гти
леті́ти	to fly	полеті́ти

За́втра Ната́ля, Ле́ся та Мо́тря піду́ть на конце́рт.

Their endings in the perfective future are the same as in the present tense. Note the change of stress pattern in the future forms.

present sg.		perfective future sg.		present pl.		perfective future pl.	
я іду́	I go	я піду́	I'll go	ми ідемо́	we go	ми пі́демо	we'll go
ти іде́ш	you go	ти пі́деш	you'll go	ви ідете́	you go	ви пі́дете	you'll go
він іде́	he goes	він пі́де	he'll go	вони́ іду́ть	they go	вони́ пі́дуть	they'll go

These particular perfective future forms of motion verbs can denote:

1) a future event viewed as one-time completed action like the ones described in these sentences

За́втра вона́ пої́де на мо́ре відпочива́ти. *Tomorrow she will travel to the sea to rest.*
Коли́ ви полетите́ до Оде́си? *When will you fly to Odesa?*
Ми побіжимо́ до па́рку ра́зом. *We shall run to the park together.*
Дру́зі піду́ть до теа́тру в насту́пний четве́р. *The friends will go to the theater next Thursday.*

2) one, often initial, action in a chain of future actions, each viewed as completed,

Вона́ пої́де на мо́ре і га́рно відпочи́не. *She will go to the sea and have a good rest.*
Ми полетимо́ до Оде́си, побува́ємо в о́пері та відві́даємо дя́дька Василя́. *We'll fly to Odesa, go the opera, and visit Uncle Vasyl.*
За́втра Марі́я пі́де до крамни́ці і ку́пить хлі́ба, молока́ та ка́ви. *Tomorrow Maria will go to the store and buy some bread, milk, and coffee.*
Пі́сля робо́ти ми поверне́мося додо́му, зро́бимо смачні́ шашлики́, запро́симо Кухарчукі́в і чудо́во відпочи́немо всі ра́зом. *After work, we shall return home, make delicious shish kebabs, invite the Kukharchuks, and have a great time all together.*

✏️ **Note 13.5. На́зви регіо́нів Украї́ни** Names of Ukrainian Regions

Гуцу́льщина – це украї́нський край, де живу́ть гуцу́ли.

Typically Ukrainian provinces and counties are named along the model: ***adjective*** + **о́бласть** *province* or **райо́н** *district, county*. The adjective is derived from the name of the respective city by the suffix **-ськ**, **Ки́їв** *Kyiv* - **Ки́ївська о́бласть** *the Kyiv Province*, **Ки́ївський райо́н** *the Kyiv District. The administrative map of Ukraine above gives names of all Ukrainian provinces.*

Ukrainian has also a more compact way of naming a region or territory around a particular city by adding the suffix **~щина** to the stem of the respective city name. The derived name can mean: 1) an administrative unit, province or district; 2) an area around a city having nothing to do with the administrative division of the country. Most typically these region names are derived from names of provincial capitals,

Ки́їв *Kyiv* - **Ки́ївщина** *the Kyiv Province (area around Kyiv)*
Львів *Lviv* - **Льві́вщина** *the Lviv Province (area around Lviv)*
Ха́рків *Kharkiv* - **Ха́рківщина** *the Kharkiv Province (or area around Kharkiv)*
Херсо́н *Kherson* - **Херсо́нщина** *the Kherson Province (or area around Kherson)*

Less commonly such derivatives are formed from names of district centers or simply of other historically, culturally, or economically important cities,

Косто́піль *Kostopil* - **Косто́пільщина** *the Kostopil District*
Перея́слав *Pereiaslav* - **Перея́славщина** *the Pereiaslav District*
Берди́чів *Berdychiv* - **Берди́чівщина** *the Berdychiv District*
Some city names do not yield themselves to the formation of such territorial designators. Thus instead of **Лу́ччина*** (from the provincial capital of Volhynia **Лу́цьк** *Lutsk*) **Воли́нь** or **Воли́нська о́бласть** is used. Instead of **Запорі́жчина*** (from the provincial capital **Запорі́жжя** *Zaporizhia*) **Запорі́зька о́бласть** is used.
Take a note of these forms of the region names:
Ві́нниця *Vinnytsia* - **Ві́нничина** *the Vinnytsia Province*
Доне́цьк *Donetsk* - **Доне́ччина** *the Donetsk Province*
Рі́вне *Rivne* - **Рі́вненщина** (*var.* **Рі́венщина**) *the Rivne Province*
Хмельни́цький *Khmelnytsky* - **Хмельни́ччина** *the Khmelnytsky Province*

📖 Впра́ви Exercises

Phonetics. Drill dropping the ~o~ in the locative plural

🎧 **13.1.** Listen carefully and repeat. Practice dropping the vowel ~o~ in the final syllable of the consonant-ended masculine nouns in the locative plural. Take note of the *L. pl.* stress.

Model.
Stress Pattern A. Stress remains on the same vowel.
Ⓒ ви́нято́к *an exception*, у *in*
Ⓐ у ви́нятках *in exceptions*

буди́нок *a building*, у *in*
прову́лок *a lane*, у *in*
спи́сок *a list*, у *in*
сніда́нок *a breakfast*, у *in*
гурто́житок *a dormitory*, у *in*
подару́нок *a gift*, у *in*

ґа́нок *a doorstep*, на *on*
ри́нок *a market*, на *on*
ко́рок *a cork*, на *on*
ту́рок *a Turk*, на *on*
я́рмарок *a fair*, на *on*
понеді́лок *Monday*, по *on*

Stress Pattern B. Stress is on the last syllable.
Ⓒ місто́к *a little bridge*, на *on*
Ⓐ на містка́х *on little bridges*

тано́к *a dance*, у *in*
сон *a dream*, уві *in*
огіро́к *a cucumber*, у *in*
лісо́к *a grove*, у *in*
замо́к *a lock*, у *in*

куто́к *a corner*, у *in*
свисто́к *a whistle*, у *in*
като́к *a skating rink*, на *on*
квито́к *a ticket*, на *on*
листо́к *a sheet, leaf*, на *on*

Ціка́во, що мо́же бу́ти в таки́х ди́вних буди́нках, як цей.

✏️ **Донба́с** *Donbas*, an abbreviation of **Доне́цький басе́йн** *the Donets River Basin*, is a region of Ukraine that includes the easternmost provinces of Donetsk **Доне́цька** and Luhansk **Луга́нська о́бласті**.

🎧 **13.2.** Answer the questions. Use the locative plural with **по** *along, around*.

Model.
Ⓠ Де ви ходи́ли? *Where have you been? (lit. Where did you go?)*
    ву́лиці Ха́ркова *streets of Kharkiv*.
Ⓐ По ву́лицях Ха́ркова. *Through the streets of Kharkiv.*

1. Де вони́ ї́здили? міста́ Галичини́
2. Де гуля́ла молода́ япо́нка Йо́ко? ву́лиці Оде́си
3. Де ти ходи́в? крамни́ці мі́ста
4. Де ходи́в ваш друг? ба́нки Ки́єва
5. Де ї́здили ці студе́нти? се́ла Воли́ні
6. Де гуля́ли ва́ші ді́ти? па́рки та пло́щі Симферо́поля
7. Де ходи́ли їхні ро́дичі? магази́ни та книга́рні Ха́ркова
8. Де ходи́ли твої́ го́сті? галере́ї Ки́єва
9. Де ходи́ли Сте́фко та Марко́? кав'я́рні та рестора́ни Льво́ва
10. Де ї́здила ця гру́па інжене́рів? заво́ди та фа́брики Донба́су

Япо́нка Йо́ко живе́ в Ки́єві та захо́плено вивча́є украї́нську мо́ву.

Львів – столи́ця Галичини́. Що зна́чить цей кола́ж худо́жника Євге́на Ра́вського?

Phonetics. Drill dropping the ~e~ in the locative plural

⋒ **13.3.** Listen carefully and repeat. Practice dropping the vowel ~**e**~ in the final syllable of the consonant-ended masculine nouns when forming the locative plural. Take note of the *L. pl.* stress.

Model.
Stress Pattern A. Stress remains on the same vowel.
С ні́м**е**ць *a German man*, на *on*
A на ні́мцях *on German men*

та́нець *a dance*, у *in*   науко́вець *a scientist*, на *on*
хло́пець *a boy*, на *on*   у́чень *a pupil*, на *on*
украї́нець *a Ukrainian*, на *on*   ду́рень *a dumbhead*, на *on*
рі́вень *a level*, на *on*   кита́єць *a Chinese*, на *on*
пі́вень *a rooster*, на *on*   ста́рець *a beggar*, на *on*

Stress Pattern B. Stress is on the last syllable.
С речен**е́**ць *a deadline*, у *in*
A у реченця́х *in the deadlines*

гамане́ць *a wallet*, у *in*   кіне́ць *an end*, на *on*
гребіне́ць *a comb*, на *on*   день *a day*, на *on*
млине́ць *a pancake*, у *in*   фахіве́ць *a specialist*, на *on*
оліве́ць *a pencil*, в *in*   горобе́ць *a sparrow*, на *on*
покупе́ць *a buyer*, на *on*   продаве́ць *a salesman*, на *on*

⋒ **13.4.** Give a short answer to each question. Pay attention to prepositions.

Model.
Q У яки́х крамни́цях ви це купи́ли? *What stores did you buy it in?*
вели́кий *big*
A У вели́ких. *In big (ones).*

1. У яки́х рестора́нах мо́жна знайти́ су́ші? япо́нський
2. На яки́х екску́рсіях були́ ці італі́йці? ціка́вий
3. По яки́х части́нах Украї́ни подорожува́ли ці тури́сти? за́хідний та півні́чний
4. На яки́х зупи́нках продаю́ть квитки́ на авто́бус? авто́бусний
5. У яки́х ка́сах мо́жна взя́ти ро́зклад поїзді́в? залізни́чний
6. По яки́х па́рках гуля́ли по́други? стари́й і га́рний
7. На яки́х ву́лицях є світлофо́ри? весь центра́льний
8. По яки́х міста́х Фра́нції ви ї́здили? півде́нний та схі́дний
9. У яки́х магази́нах мо́жна знайти́ цю кни́жку? букіністи́чний
10. У яки́х теа́трах побува́ли ва́ші студе́нти? о́перний і драмати́чний

Phonetics. Drill shifting ~i~ to ~o~ (~e~) in the locative plural

🎧 **13.5.** Listen carefully and react to the cue changing ~**i**~ to ~**o**~ in the locative plural. Check yourself against the speaker.

Model.
Stress Pattern A. Stress remains on the same vowel.
C *m.* брід *a ford*, по *on*
A по бро́дах *on fords*

m. твір *a work*, у *in*	*m.* порі́г *a doorstep*, на *on*
f. сіль *salt*, у *in*	*m.* ви́хід *an exit*, на *on*
m. сік *a juice*, у *in*	*m.* вхід *an entrance*, на *on*
m. полі́т *a flight*, у *in*	*m.* ріг *a street corner*, на *on*
m. ви́бір *a choice*, у *in*	*m.* гість *a guest*, на *on*

Stress Pattern B. Stress shifts to the last syllable.
C *m.* кіт *a cat*, на *on*
A на кота́х *on cats*

m. ко́лір *a color*, у *in*	*m.* о́стрів *an island*, на *on*
m. двір *a courtyard*, у *in*	*m.* баті́г *a whip*, на *on*
m. рід *a gender*, у *in*	*m.* стіл *a table*, на *on*
m. рік *a year*, у *in*	*m.* віз *a wagon*, на *on*
m. живі́т *a stomach*, у *in*	*m.* плід *a fruit*, на *on*
m. пирі́г *a pie*, у *in*	*m.* ве́чір *an evening*, по *on*
m. ніс *a nose*, у *in*	*m.* бік *a side*, по *on*

i/e change:
f. річ *a thing* - у реча́х *in things*
f. піч *an oven* - у печа́х *in ovens*
m. ко́рінь *a root* - у ко́ренях *in roots*
m. папі́р *a paper* - у папе́рах *in papers*

Насту́пного лі́та Оле́сь пої́де до Криму. Він лю́бить ходи́ти по висо́ких гора́х.

🎧 **13.6.** Indicate the frequency of action. Use the *L. pl.* with the preposition **по**.

Model.
Q Як ча́сто Макси́м ди́виться фі́льми? *How often does Maksym watch films?* п'я́тниця *Friday*.
A По п'я́тницях. *Every Friday.*

1. Як ча́сто її́ брат хо́дить до бібліоте́ки? неді́ля
2. Як ча́сто Ната́ля займа́ється англі́йською мо́вою? субо́та та середа́
3. Як ча́сто у цьо́му музе́ї вихідни́й день? вівто́рок
4. Як ча́сто він ба́чить профе́сора Кириле́нка? понеді́лок
5. Як ча́сто Степа́н дзво́нить ма́тері? четве́р
6. Як ча́сто вони́ розмовля́ють? ве́чір

Бібліоте́ка Ки́ївського університе́ту працю́є і по бу́дніх, і по вихідни́х днях.

Note 13.6. Assimilation of ш /sh/ in reflexive verbs

The consonant ш /sh/ becomes a soft /s'/ before ~ся /s'a/ in the 2nd pers. sg. of the present tense. The result is a lengthened soft /s's'/. Thus the consonant cluster ~шс~ is pronounced as /s's'/:

дивитися *to look* - ти дивишся /dývy^{e}s's'a/ *you are looking*

сміятися *to laugh* - ти смієшся /s'mijés's'a/ *you are laughing*

сумніва́тися *to doubt* - ти сумніва́єшся /sumn'iváje^{y}s's'a/ *you doubt*

боя́тися *to be afraid* - ти бої́шся /bo^{u}jís's'a/ *you are afraid*

помиля́тися *to be wrong* - ти помиля́єшся /po^{u}myl'ájes's'a/ *you are wrong*

Note 13.7. Assimilation of ~ть~ /t'/ in reflexive verbs

The soft consonant ~ть~ /t'/ before ~ся /s'a/ in the 3rd pers. sg. and pl. of the present tense becomes soft /ts'/. The result is a lengthened soft /ts'ts'/. The speaker, instead of fully pronouncing the first /ts'/, presses the tip of the tongue against the upper gum, and then pronounces only the second /ts'/. The lengthened /ts'/ in reality is *a stop* ¬ + /ts'/:

3rd *pers. sg*:

він дивиться /dývy^e¬ts'a/ *he is looking*

він сміється /s'mije¬ts'a/ *he is laughing*

він сумнівається /sumn'iváje¬ts'a/ *he doubts*

він боїться /bo^{u}jí¬ts'a/ *he's afraid*

він помиля́ється /po^{u}my^{e}l'áje¬ts'a/ *he's wrong*

3rd *pers. pl*:

вони́ ди́вляться /dývl'a¬ts'a/ *they are looking*

вони́ смію́ться /s'miju¬ts'a/ *they are laughing*

вони́ сумніва́ються /sumn'iváju¬ts'a/ *they doubt*

вони́ боя́ться /bo^{u}já¬ts'a/ *they are afraid*

вони́ помиля́ються /po^{u}myl'áju¬ts'a/ *they are wrong*

∩ 13.7. Change the locative singular into plural.

Model.

C Наші ді́ти вча́ться у цій шко́лі. *Our children study in this school.*

A Наші ді́ти вча́ться у цих шко́лах. *Our children study in these schools.*

1. На́ші дру́зі працю́ють на вели́кій фа́бриці.
2. Ма́рки мо́жна купи́ти на на́шій по́шті.
3. Сма́чно пої́сти мо́жна у тому́ рестора́ні.
4. Інтерне́т є в університе́тській бібліоте́ці.
5. Поміня́ти до́лари на гри́вні мо́жна у націона́льному ба́нку.
6. Катери́на ба́чила таку́ соро́чку на молодо́му кия́нинові.
7. Кві́ти стоя́ть на ново́му столі́.
8. Го́сті ї́здили по дале́кому селу́.
9. Іва́н лю́бить гуля́ти по зеле́ному по́лю.
10. Ми до́вго ходи́ли по книжко́вому магази́ну.
11. Вони́ живу́ть у суча́сній кварти́рі.
12. Лі́фти за́вжди є у багатоповерхо́вому буди́нку.

∩ 13.8. Provide the required present tense form of the reflexive verb.

I. Подо́ба|тися (~ються). 1. Вона́ мені́ подо́ба~ ____ . 2. Чи я вам подо́ба~ ____ ? 3. Так ви мені́ ду́же подо́ба~ ____ , але́ вони́ не подо́ба~ ____ .

II. Знайо́м|итися (~ляться). 1. Я знайо́м~ ____ з ним. 2. Він знайо́м~ ____ з на́ми. 3. Ми знайо́м~ ____ з не́ю. 4. Вони́ знайо́м~ ____ зі мно́ю. 5. Ви знайо́м~ ____ з ни́ми.

III. Ціка́в|итися (~ляться). 1. Чим ти ціка́в~ ____ ? 2. Я ціка́в~ ____ матема́тикою. 3. А вони́ чим ціка́в~ ____ ? 4. Не зна́ю. А ми ціка́в~ ____ фі́зикою. 5. Вона́ теж ціка́в~ ____ фі́зикою. 6. Я зна́ю, що ви ціка́в~ ____ архітекту́рою.

IV. Листу́|ва́тися (~ються). 1. З ким ти листу́~ ____ ? 2. Я листу́~ ____ із дру́гом. 3. А з ким ви листу́~ ____ 4. Ми листу́~ ____ з одніє́ю жі́нкою. 5. Чи вони́ теж листу́~ ____ з ки́мось? 6. Ні, але́ ви листу́~ ____ .

V. Боя́|тися (~яться). 1. Чого́ вони́ бо~ ____ ? 2. Нічо́го. Але́ я бо~ ____ спе́ки. А ви? 3. Ми теж бо~ ____ 4. А вона́ не бо~ ____ 5. Ти бо~ ____ ? 6. Ні, ми всі її́ не бо~ ____ .

∩ 13.9. Provide the Ukrainian equivalent of the English verb in parentheses. Translate each sentence.

1. За́втра (begin) лі́тні кані́кули.
2. Нам тре́ба (to change) всі на́ші пла́ни.
3. Виста́ва (ended) о дев'я́тій годи́ні ве́чора.
4. За оди́н рік моя́ ситуа́ція цілко́м (changed).
5. Ми попроси́ли їх (to meet) з на́ми бі́ля бібліоте́ки.

6. Я чув, що пого́да ма́є (to change).
7. Ми ці́лий день (prepared) до подоро́жі.
8. На цій ста́нції по́їзд не (stop).
9. Ви мо́жете (stop) авто́бус? Мені́ тре́ба ви́йти.
10. Я (shall see) із Сашко́м за́втра вве́чері.
11. Ми ма́ємо (prepare) все дома́шнє завда́ння на п'я́тницю.
12. Вчо́ра ми не змогли́ (see) цей нови́й украї́нський фільм.

🎧 **13.10.** Say and write these sentences in Ukrainian. Pay attention to the difference in meaning between transitive verbs and their reflexive counterparts.

1. The film started at seven o'clock.
2. He started to watch the film.
3. The train does not stop here.
4. Our trip will start in Kyiv and end in Odesa.
5. When will Maria finish the new project?
6. We stopped for lunch between Ternopil and Vinnytsia.
7. Can you stop the car please?
8. The conversation will continue next Tuesday.
9. I want to continue this interesting discussion later.
10. We see each other often.
11. My wife saw this program on TV.
12. They met at an international conference last year.
13. He introduced me to his fiancée.
14. Can you meet me at the railway station at nine o'clock?
15. Now these old friends rarely meet.
16. This historical period interests Mykola.
17. Nadia is interested in modern architecture.
18. Five years passed and this city has not changed.
19. We need to change the departure date.

🎧 **13.11.** State the patronymic of the person.

Їхнє знайо́мство почало́ся на кораблі́, що плив зачаро́ваною Десно́ю.

Model.

m. 🅲 Це Іва́н Ковальчу́к, а то його́ ба́тько Миха́йло. *This is Ivan Kovalchuk, and that is his father Mykhailo.*
🅰 Зна́чить, його́ по ба́тькові Миха́йлович. Він – Іва́н Миха́йлович Ковальчу́к. *Hence his patronymic is Mykhailovych. He is Ivan Mykhailovych Kovalchuk.*

f. 🅲 Це О́льга Ковальчу́к, а то її́ ба́тько Миха́йло. *This is Olha Kovalchuk, and that is her father Mykhailo.*
🅰 Зна́чить, її́ по ба́тькові Миха́йлівна. Вона́ – О́льга Миха́йлівна Ковальчу́к. *Hence her patronymic is Mykhailivna. She is Olha Mykhailivna Kovalchuk.*

1. Це Миха́йло Якове́нко, а то його́ ба́тько Петро́.
2. Це Васи́ль Хмельничу́к, а то його́ ба́тько Павло́.
3. Це Павло́ Івани́шин, а то його́ ба́тько Тара́с.
4. Це Тара́с Петрусе́нко, а то його́ ба́тько Богда́н.
5. Це Іри́на Миките́нко, а то її́ ба́тько Андрі́й.

Ша́тські озе́ра *the Shatsk Lakes* are a group of spectacularly beautiful lakes in north-western Ukraine that includes **Світязь** *the Svitiaz*, the biggest fresh water lake in Ukraine.

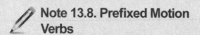 **Note 13.8. Prefixed Motion Verbs**

Prefixes added to the motion verbs make them perfective and modify their meaning.

The **по~** added to a unidirectional verb has the meaning of *"setting out, leaving, moving away,"*

Васили́ни нема́ вдо́ма. Вона́ побі́гла до ба́нку. *Vasylyna is not home. She ran to the bank. (She left.)*

The prefix **при~** has the opposite meaning of *"coming to, arriving at"* or *"returning, getting back,"*

Богда́н приї́хав зі Льво́ва вчо́ра. *Bohdan arrived from Lviv yesterday.*

Take a note of these **по~** / **при~**prefixed motion verbs:

іти́ - піти́ *to go (on foot)* - **прийти́** *to come (on foot)*

бі́гти - побі́гти *to run* - **прибі́гти** *to come running*

ї́хати - пої́хати *to go (by a vehicle)* - **приї́хати** *to come (by a vehicle)*

леті́ти - полеті́ти *to fly* - **прилеті́ти** *to come flying*

6. Це Ната́ля Яре́менко, а то її ба́тько Володи́мир.

7. Це Катери́на Олі́йник, а то її ба́тько Дени́с.

8. Це Наді́я Козаче́нко, а то її ба́тько Степа́н.

13.12. Answer the questions. Pay attention to prepositions and the changed verb aspect. Then replace the verb **побува́ти** with the prefixed motion verbs **пої́хати** *to go (by car, train)* or **полеті́ти** *to fly*.

Model.

Q Ти вже бува́в у Я́лті? *Have you already been to Yalta?*
02.II. *February 2.*

A 1) Ще ні, але́ я наре́шті побува́ю там дру́гого ли́пня. *Not yet, but I will finally visit it on the 2nd of July.*
2) Ще ні, але́ я наре́шті пої́ду (полечу́) туди́ дру́гого ли́пня. *Not yet, but I will finally go (fly) there on the 2nd of July.*

1. Ви вже бува́ли у Терно́полі? 12.I.

2. Яри́на вже бува́ла в У́жгороді? 30.XII.

3. Брати́ Мельниче́нки вже бува́ли в Оде́сі? 5.IV.

4. Тара́с уже́ бува́в у Ха́ркові? 23.XI.

5. Ви з дру́гом уже́ бува́ли на Чо́рному мо́рі? 10.VII.

6. Ната́ля вже бува́ла на Ша́тських озе́рах? 19.V.

7. Ти вже бува́в у Карпа́тах? 11.X.

13.13. Translate these sentences into the future perfective. Use the motion verbs with **по~**.

1. Tomorrow their Polish friends will fly to Symferopol.

2. Next Monday all the students will go to the lecture of professor Kozachenko.

3. Next month we will finally travel to New York and visit its museums.

4. I'll run to the bank and exchange some money.

5. This Saturday, Roman and Olha will go to the gallery and see a new exhibit.

6. When will they go to Kyiv and visit the Ukrainian Museum of Western Art?

7. I will finish the assignment, run to the store, and buy today's newspapers.

8. On the weekend, we will go to the restaurant for a nice dinner.

9. Who will travel with me to Lviv and show me the city?

10. Petro will run to the hotel and invite them to our party.

13.14. Read the sentences and choose the right motion verb. Translate them.

1. Мико́ли нема́є на заня́ттях. Йому́ ста́ло пога́но, і він пішо́в / прийшо́в додо́му лікува́тися.

2. Оле́на побі́гла / прибі́гла до крамни́ці. Вона́ за́раз поверне́ться.

3. Мари́ни ще нема́є. Вона́ ма́є полеті́ти / прилеті́ти з Ха́ркова о пе́ршій годи́ні.

4. Я піду́ / прийду́ і допоможу́ їм.

5. Це швидки́й по́тяг, і ми пої́демо / прийде́мо до Терно́поля за дві годи́ни.

6. Куди́ мо́жна піти́ / прийти́ на та́нці у цьо́му мі́сті?

7. На скі́льки ча́су пої́хали / прийха́ли до нас ці англі́йці?

8. У нас не працю́є телефо́н, тому́ Павло́ побі́г / прибі́г до сусі́дів, щоб подзвони́ти.

9. Брат пішо́в / прийшо́в до університе́ту. Він піде́ / прийде́ додо́му уве́чері.

10. Тара́с і Ната́лка обіця́ли піти́ / прийти́ в го́сті до нас ціє́ї п'я́тниці.

11. Він побі́г / прибі́г на по́шту, відісла́в гро́ші і побі́г / прибі́г додо́му.

🎧 13.15. Express a destination of motion or action. Choose either **на** + *A.*, or **до** + *G.*, or both.

Model.

Q Куди́ ви ї́дете? *Where are you going (by car)?* ле́кція *a lecture,* Ки́ївський університе́т. *Kyiv University*

A На ле́кцію до Ки́ївського університе́ту. *To a lecture to Kyiv University.*

1. Куди́ ви ду́маєте запроси́ти ва́ших ро́дичів? вече́ря, рестора́н

2. Куди́ ти хо́чеш потра́пити? пошта́мт, майда́н Незале́жности.

3. Куди́ його́ дру́зі йду́ть за́втра вве́чері? істори́чний музе́й, нова́ ви́ставка

4. Куди́ тобі́ тре́ба потра́пити? нови́й італі́йський фільм, кінотеа́тр "Украї́на"

5. Куди́ вони́ пої́дуть на кані́кули? Оде́са, відпочи́нок

6. Куди́ ви побіжите́ вве́чері? наш універма́г, вели́кий розпро́даж

7. Куди́ Юрко́ полети́ть насту́пного ти́жня? Ха́рків, міжнаро́дна конфере́нція

8. Куди́ Сергі́й запро́шує Ле́сю? нова́ кав'я́рня, розмо́ва

9. Куди́ ва́ші го́сті ходи́ли мину́лої субо́ти? Хреща́тик, фестива́ль "День Євро́пи"

10. Куди́ Оле́кса з О́лею ї́дуть на вихідні́? ми, шашлики́

Оле́кса Романи́шин запроси́в свої́х по́друг на моро́зиво.

Note 13.9. Призна́чення дії
Destination of action

To express destination of action or motion with verbs such as:

потра́пити *or* **діста́тися** *to get to*
запроси́ти *to invite to*
купи́ти квито́к на *to buy a ticket to a performance*
іти́ (**ходи́ти, піти́**) *to go to*
бі́гти (**бі́гати, побі́гти**) *to run to*

two prepositions can be used:

1) **на** + *A.*
2) **до** + *G.*

  The preposition на + *A.* is used when the destination is an event, such as a lecture, concert, opera, performance, coffee, drink, dinner, and the like,

Як потра́пити на ле́кцію (**конце́рт, о́перу, виста́ву**)? *How to get to a lecture (concert, opera, performance)?*

  The preposition до + *G.* is used when the destination is a physical object, building, city, a home or a person's residence,

Вона́ пої́хала до музе́ю (**Ки́єва, університе́ту, них**). *She went to a museum (Kyiv, university, their place).*

Note these special cases: **іти́** *to go to*

на фа́брику (**заво́д**) *to a factory (plant)*
на ста́нцію (**вокза́л**) *to a station*
на по́шту *to a post office*

The two types of destinations can both appear in the same sentence, as in

За́втра Тара́с піде́ на виста́ву до теа́тру. *Tomorrow Taras will go to a performance at the theater.*

Ви при́йдете до нас на обі́д? *Will you come to our place for dinner?*

  If the destination is a street, square or part of town, the preposition **на** + *A.* is used,

Коли́ ми пої́демо на Хреща́тик? *When shall we go to Khreshchatyk?*

Як потра́пити на Льві́вську пло́щу? *How to get to Lvivska Square?*

Note 13.10. Зві́дки? Where from?

Where from? in Ukrainian corresponds to the interrogative word **зві́дки**:

Зві́дки ва́ші сусі́ди? *Where are your neighbors from?*
Зві́дки ти йде́ш? *Where are you coming from?*
Зві́дки у вас ця га́рна карти́на? *Where is this nice picture of yours from?*

In answer to such questions, two prepositions can be used, **з (із, зі)** + *G.* and **від** + *G.* Both are translated as *from.*

з (із, зі) is used with inanimate nouns (cities, places, or buildings), **На́ші сусі́ди зі Льво́ва.** *Our neighbors are from Lviv.* **Ця га́рна карти́на із Ри́му.** *This nice picture is from Rome. (We brought it from there.)*

Від is used with animate nouns, usually indicating somebody's home or a person: **Я йду́ від батькі́в.** *I am coming from my parents' place.* **Ця га́рна карти́на від Рома́на.** *This nice picture is from Roman. (He gave it to us.)*

 13.16. Use either **з (із)** or **від** *from* depending on the context. Translate into English.

1. Скі́льки ча́су тре́ба йти _____ Марі́ї до середмі́стя?
2. Га́ля поверну́лася _____ по́дорожі до По́льщі мину́лого ти́жня.
3. Батьки́ ча́сом прино́сять нам вече́рю _____ рестора́ну.
4. Всі світли́ни на стіні́ _____ моїх стари́х університе́тських дру́зів.
5. Коли́ Андрі́й Микола́йович ма́є поверну́тися _____ конфере́нції у Лу́цьку?
6. Я чека́ю важли́ві папе́ри _____ ба́нку _____ головно́го еконо́міста.
7. Переказу́йте різдвяні́ і новорі́чні віта́ння ва́шим батька́м _____ всіє́ї сім'ї́ Максимчукі́в.
8. Ці кві́ти для вас _____ Марка́ Скри́пченка _____ Черні́гова.
9. Ми вече́рятимемо в І́горя Прихо́дька і _____ ньо́го пі́демо на конце́рт.
10. Це проха́ння прийшло́ _____ яко́гось па́на А́ндерсона _____ Ло́ндона.
11. Вам дзвони́ла па́нна Ори́ся _____ Коломи́йського університе́ту

⊕ **Завда́ння для Міжнаро́дної мере́жі**
Internet Assignment

Істори́чні місця́ Украї́ни *Historical Sights of Ukraine*

13.17. Use the Ukrainian language Internet and provide answers to these questions.
1. У яко́му мі́сті Украї́ни розташо́ваний парк «Софі́ївка»?
2. Де є па́м'ятник архітекту́ри «Ласті́вчине гні́здо» *(Swallow's Nest)*?
3. Як зва́ти архіте́ктора, що зроби́в Буди́нок з химе́рами *(House with Chimeras)*?
4. Яка́ адре́са Буди́нку з химе́рами?
5. Чим відо́ме село́ Кере́лівка?

Парк "Софі́ївка"

"Ласті́вчине гні́здо"

Буди́нок з химе́рами

село́ Кере́лівка

13.18. Answer the questions. Express the purpose using the perfective infinitive introduced by **щоб**.

1. З яко́ю мето́ю дзвони́ли ва́ші батьки́?
   To wish me a Happy Birthday.
2. З яко́ю мето́ю ви ходи́ли до мі́ста?
   To buy groceries for the weekend.
3. З яко́ю мето́ю Рома́н поміня́в кварти́ру?
   To live closer to work.
4. З яко́ю мето́ю дире́ктор компа́нії лети́ть до Я́лти?
   To take part in an international conference.
5. З яко́ю мето́ю їхні знайо́мі приї́хали до Льво́ва?
   To get acquainted with its beautiful old architecture.
6. Наві́що вони́ розказа́ли мені́ цю істо́рію?
   To explain to you what happened.
7. Наві́що ці студе́нти приї́хали до Оде́си?
   To see the only picture by Caravaggio in Ukraine.
8. Наві́що Васи́ль чита́є цю газе́ту?
   To know the latest news from Ukraine.
9. Наві́що Оре́ст дав вам ці гро́ші?
   To pay for my work.
10. Наві́що Оле́на купи́ла цю карти́ну?
    To hang it in her living-room.
11. Наві́що вам тре́ба подиви́тися цей німи́й фільм?
    To prepare for the discussion tomorrow.
12. Наві́що Степа́н пита́є все це?
    To see whether she is telling the truth.
13. З яко́ю мето́ю Васи́ль вивча́є гре́цьку мо́ву?
    To be able to read Homer (Гоме́р) in the original.
14. З яко́ю мето́ю Ма́рта купи́ла всі ці проду́кти та вино́?
    To cook a festive dinner for Tetiana's birthday.

13.19. Choose a pair of cities from the chart on the next page. Explore transportation options between them. Use the Internet. Discuss each transportation option in Ukrainian as to convenience, price, length of travel, etc. **Як мо́жна заї́хати з одно́го мі́ста до і́ншого?** *How can one get from one city to another?*

Model. Маршру́т: Вене́ція, Іта́лія - Маріу́поль, Украї́на
Route: Venice, Italy - Mariupol, Ukraine.
З Вене́ції до Маріу́поля мо́жна заї́хати:
From Venice to Mariupol one can get by:

1) а́втом (тре́ба ї́хати А́встрією, Слова́ччиною чи Уго́рщиною і всіє́ю Украї́ною)
2) корабле́м (оби́два мі́ста розташо́вані на мо́рі, переса́дка в Стамбу́лі)
3) по́тягом (переса́дка у Ві́дні, Льво́ві та Ки́єві)
4) літако́м (переса́дка у Варша́ві та Ки́єві)
Ві́дстань 1.944 кіло́метри. *Distance 1,944 kilometers*

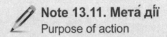

Note 13.11. Мета́ дії
Purpose of action

To express the purpose of an action, perfective infinitive is used with the conjunction **щоб** *in order to (so as to)*,
Марко́ подзвони́в, щоб розказа́ти нам нови́ни. *Marko called in order to tell us the news.*
Щоб зрозумі́ти цей текст, тре́ба зна́ти істо́рію. *To understand the text one needs to know history.*

To learn about the purpose of somebody's action, one asks:

З яко́ю мето́ю ...? *With what purpose?*
Наві́що (для чо́го) ..? *Why (what for)..?*

Q **З яко́ю мето́ю вони́ збира́ють гро́ші?** *With what purpose are they collecting money?*
A **Щоб купи́ти нови́й комп'ю́тер.** *So as to buy a new computer.*
Q **Наві́що Ні́на дала́ йому́ гро́ші?** *What has Nina given him the money for?*
A **Щоб помогти́ йому́.** *In order to help him.*

звідки / куди	Ки́їв	Льві́в	Оде́са	Ха́рків	Я́лта
Нью-Йо́рк					
Торо́нто					
Варша́ва					
Стамбу́л					
Ло́ндон					
Ки́їв					
У́жгород					
Херсо́н					
Доне́цьк					

⌒ **13.20.** Listen carefully to the text «Запро́шуємо у подо́рож». Provide answers to these questions in Ukrainian.

1. Куди́ запро́шує у по́дорож тури́стична аґе́нція «Ма́ндри»?
2. На́зви яки́х міст Украї́ни ви почу́ли?
3. Як назива́ється корабе́ль?
4. Де почина́ється тур?
5. Де закі́нчується цей тур?

⌒ **13.21.** Read the **реклама́вка** (flyer) of the *Mandry Travel Agency* and provide detailed answers to these questions.

1. Що ви дізна́лися про корабе́ль «Таври́да»?
2. У яки́х міста́х зупиня́тиметься тур?
3. Що поба́чать тури́сти, які́ ку́плять цей тур?
4. Чим відо́мий о́стрів Хо́ртиця?
5. Стра́ви яко́ї ку́хні обіця́є аґе́нція «Ма́ндри»?
6. Де відпочи́нуть тури́сти?
7. Скі́льки ко́штує тур?
8. Що включа́є ціна́ ту́ру?
9. Яки́х по́слуг ціна́ ту́ру не включа́є?
10. Скі́льки ча́су трива́тиме тур?
11. Що включа́є зупи́нка в мі́сті Запорі́жжі?
12. У яко́му мі́сті тури́сти проведу́ть найбі́льше ча́су?

13. Яку́ о́перу подивля́ться тури́сти в Оде́сі?

14. Як мо́жна поверну́тися з Оде́си до Ки́єва?

Запро́шуємо у подоро́ж

Десно́ю та Дніпро́м

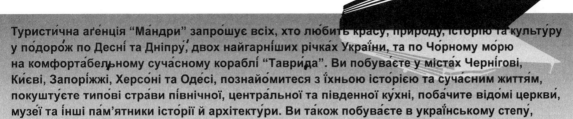

Туристи́чна аге́нція "Ма́ндри" запро́шує всіх, хто лю́бить красу́, приро́ду, істо́рію та культу́ру у подоро́ж по Десні́ та Дніпру́, двох найгарні́ших річка́х Украї́ни, та по Чо́рному мо́рю на комфорта́бельному суча́сному кораблі́ "Таври́да". Ви побува́єте у міста́х Черні́гові, Ки́єві, Запорі́жжі, Херсо́ні та Оде́сі, познайо́митеся з їхньою істо́рією та суча́сним життя́м, покушту́єте типо́ві стра́ви півні́чної, центра́льної та півде́нної ку́хні, поба́чите відо́мі це́ркви, музе́ї та і́нші па́м'ятники істо́рії й архітекту́ри. Ви та́кож побува́єте в украї́нському степу́, огля́нете легенда́рний о́стрів Хо́ртицю, батьки́вщину запоро́зьких козакі́в, відпочи́нете на пля́жах Чо́рного мо́ря.

На кораблі́ "Таври́да" до ва́ших по́слуг три рестора́ни, чоти́ри ба́ри, дискоте́ка та басе́йн. Ціна́ ту́ру, **2.500 грв.**, включа́є прожива́ння, сніда́нок, обі́д та вече́рю на кораблі́ «Таври́да» та в готе́лі «Паса́ж» в Оде́сі, квито́к до Оде́ської націона́льної о́пери на о́перу «Запоро́жець за Дуна́єм». Трива́лість ту́ру **де́сять діб** (ві́сім на кораблі́ та дві доби́ в готе́лі "Паса́ж", в Оде́сі).

Тур почина́ється у **Черні́гові 12-го ли́пня** та закі́нчується в **Оде́сі 21-го ли́пня**.

Зупи́нки: у Ки́єві 12-13-го ли́пня, у Запорі́жжі 15-го ли́пня з екску́рсією на о́стрів Хо́ртиця, у Херсо́ні 16-го ли́пня з екску́рсією у степ, та в Оде́сі 19-21-го ли́пня.
З Ки́єва до Черні́гова мо́жна діста́тися по́їздом, авто́бусом, маршру́ткою та а́втом.
З Оде́си до Ки́єва мо́жна діста́тися літако́м, по́їздом, авто́бусом та а́втом.

 Завда́ння для Міжнаро́дної мере́жі
Internet Assignment

13.22. Visit the webpage of the *Passage Hotel* in Odesa. Use its Ukrainian language version and find out all you can about the hotel.

In your Internet search, use the key words **готель Паса́ж Одеса**

Розмо́ва. Conversation.

13.23. Engage a partner in a conversation in Ukrainian about a recent memorable trip.

1. Find out each detail noted in the chart below.
2. Write them all down in Ukrainian.
3. Report in Ukrainian what you learned from your conversation.

Про що дізна́тися	партне́р-1	партне́р-2	партне́р-3
Куди́ їзди|в, ~ла?			
Коли́ їзди|в, ~ла?			
Як подорожува|в, ~ла (тип тра́нспорту)?			
Скі́льки ча́су подорожува|в, ~ла?			
У яки́х міста́х побува|в, ~ла?			
Які́ ціка́ві місця́ поба́чи|в, ~ла?			
Де зупиня|вся, ~лася на ніч?			
Скі́льки ко́штувала по́дорож?			
Що сподо́балося і чому́?			
Що не сподо́балося і чому́?			

13.24. Write the sentences in Ukrainian. Where required consult the dictionary.

1. On a journey to what country would you like to go first?
2. It's high time they learned to cook Ukrainian borshch and varenyky.
3. Ladies and Gentlemen, what cities of Ukraine would you like to visit this summer?
4. My wife corresponds with them on the Internet for many years.
5. Excuse me, Madam, you don't need to worry. Your husband is only five minutes late.
6. Yurko always worked a lot and slept very little.
7. We'll quickly finish the conversation and immediately ring you up.
8. Andriy knows your colleague at work sufficiently well.
9. Perhaps you think that I lost the money on purpose.
10. It's not important where and how but we need to quickly arrange for a meeting.

11. Next Wednesday, Mr. and Mrs. Khomenko will fly to Toronto for an international conference.

12. Tomorrow I will go to their place for dinner to tell them what happened in the mountains.

Марко́ та Рома́н завжди́ хоті́ли поїхати у по́дорож до Украї́ни та наре́шті поба́чити чудо́ве мі́сто Ки́їв і рі́чку Дніпро́.

🎧 **13.25.** Listen carefully to these questions and answer each of them using Dialogue 13.

1. Хто пої́де в по́дорож до Украї́ни цього́ лі́та?
2. Кому́ розка́зує Марко́ про свої́ пла́ни?
3. Коли́ рані́ше бува́в в Украї́ні Марко́?
4. У яки́х міста́х Украї́ни побува́ють хло́пці?
5. Де розмовля́ють украї́нською мо́вою?
6. Чому́ Роксоля́ні подо́бається Львів?
7. До яко́го мі́ста споча́тку пої́дуть Марко́ з Рома́ном?
8. Куди́ пої́дуть хло́пці пі́сля Льво́ва?
9. З яко́го мі́ста почина́ла свою́ по́дорож Роксоля́на?
10. Де са́ме у Ки́єві ра́дить побува́ти Роксоля́на?
11. Що хо́чуть роби́ти хло́пці в Оде́сі?
12. Де вони́ ночува́тимуть в цих трьох міста́х?
13. Чому́ хло́пці бу́дуть ра́ді, що вчи́ли украї́нську мо́ву?
14. Скі́льки ча́су вони́ ду́мають провести́ в Украї́ні?
15. По яки́х міста́х ї́здили ви?
16. У яки́х міста́х Украї́ни хоті́ли б побува́ти ви?

👥 **13.26.** Enact a conversation with a partner. Use the material you learned in this lesson. If necessary consult the dictionary.

Сце́нка за сцена́рієм «Майбу́тня по́дорож»
Scripted Skit: *A Future Trip*

Йога́н Гео́рг Пі́нзель,
Святи́й Ю́рій Зміебо́рець,
мі́сто Льві́в, собо́р Св. Ю́ра.

Oksana is talking during her flight with a fellow passenger Borys who happens to be Ukrainian and lives in Kyiv.

Oksana (Окса́на): Says she always wanted to make a trip to Kyiv.
Borys (Бори́с): Does this mean she has never been to Kyiv?

Oksana: No, she lived there and left it ten years ago.
Borys: Asks why she does not live in Kyiv any more.

Oksana: When she was eighteen she became a student at Lviv University, moved to Lviv and lived there for five years.
Borys: But she said she had not been to Kyiv for ten years.

Oksana: Then she found work in Berlin. She started traveling around Europe and the world.
Borys: Asks what countries she visited when she lived in Berlin.

Oksana: She always wanted to see France, Italy, and Egypt.
Borys: Why specifically these countries and not, for example, Spain, United States, or Brazil.

Oksana: France has excellent cuisine and Oksana likes it very much, more than any other.
Borys: Assumes Oksana did (таки́) visit France, Italy, and Egypt finally.

Oksana: Affirmative and adds that she is now ready to see Kyiv again.
Borys: Oksana will not recognize the city.

Oksana: She will be flying by plane. Asks for advice on how to get from the Boryspil International Airport to Mazepa Street.
Borys: He does not know. His friends always meet him at the airport, so he gets to downtown by their car.

Oksana: Asks what other ways there are besides a car. She has friends in Kyiv, but they have no cars.
Borys: By taxi or by bus going from the airport to the closest metro station.

Oksana: Approximately how much is a taxi from Boryspil to downtown Kyiv?
Borys: He is not sure, but a year ago it was about HUA 300.

Oksana: Asks how much the bus costs and what metro station it goes to. She can go by bus.
Borys: The bus is much cheaper, and quicker. It goes to the Kharkivska Metro Station.

Лéкція | Lesson 14

Dialogue:
Візи́т до лі́каря
A Visit to a Doctor

Grammar:
Accusative plural
Genitive singular of quantity
Modal verb **могти́** *to be able*
Imperative mood

Competencies:
Health problems
Parts of the human body
Requests
Too much of something

Що вас боли́ть?

🗨 14. Діяло́г. Візи́т до лі́каря.

Хво́рий: Добри́день лі́карю, я ма́ю поба́чення з ва́ми на деся́ту годи́ну.

Лі́кар: Добри́день. Вас зва́ти Оле́г Ткаче́нко, чи не так?

Хво́рий: Са́ме так, й оста́нні два дні я не найкра́ще себе́ почува́ю. Мені́ здає́ться, я хво́рий.

Лі́кар: До́бре, що ви одра́зу ви́рішили зверну́тися до лі́каря.

Хво́рий: Я ду́же рі́дко хворі́ю і коли́ переступа́жуюся, то це швидко прохо́дить. Але́ цього ра́зу мені́ щодня́ гі́рше. Тому́ я зверну́вся до вас.

Лі́кар: За́раз я вас огля́ну і призна́чу лікува́ння. Споча́тку скажі́ть мені́, що вас боли́ть?

Хво́рий: Голова́. Я сто́млений, со́нний, не ма́ю апети́ту.

Лі́кар: Мо́же ви переступи́лися чи з'ї́ли щось?

Хво́рий: Позавчо́ра я був у дру́зів на вече́рі. Вони́ роби́ли су́ші. Вдо́ма мені́ ста́ло недо́бре. Я блюва́в.

Лі́кар: Я ба́чу, що у вас тиск кро́ви зна́чно ви́щий, ніж норма́льний, і температу́ра три́дцять де́в'ять і шість.

Хво́рий: Це й не ди́вно, бо мене́ теж моро́зить і ну́дить.

Лі́кар: Мій пе́рший дія́гноз – отру́єння. Але́ споча́тку ми зро́бимо ана́лізи, щоб напе́вно зна́ти, що з ва́ми.

Хво́рий: Чи мо́жете да́ти мені́ щось уже́ тепе́р і не чека́ти результа́тів ана́лізів?

Лі́кар: Звича́йно. Ми почнемо́ лікува́ти вас нега́йно. Ось реце́пт на лі́ки. Вам слід пи́ти їх по дві табле́тки вра́нці та вве́чері.

Хво́рий: Це – антибіо́тики? Бо я ма́ю алергі́ю на антибіо́тики.

Лі́кар: Не журі́ться, це не антибіо́тики. Ви ка́жете, що вас моро́зить?

Хво́рий: Так лі́карю, мене́ моро́зить вже два дні. Чи мо́жете теж приписа́ти мені́ щось від гаря́чки?

Лі́кар: Від гаря́чки вам слід пи́ти звича́йну аспіри́ну. Її мо́жна купи́ти без реце́пту у ко́жній апте́ці.

Хво́рий: Як до́вго я ма́ю пи́ти ці лі́ки?

Лі́кар: Табле́тки за реце́птом слід пи́ти де́сять днів. Уже́ за́втра ви ма́єте почува́тися кра́ще.

Хво́рий: Дя́кую, лі́карю. Мені́ вже кра́ще.

Лі́кар: Бажа́ю вам шви́дко оду́жати. До поба́чення.

🗨 14. Dialogue. A Visit to a Doctor.

Patient: Hello, doctor, I have a ten o'clock appointment with you.

Physician: Hello. Your name is Oleh Tkachenko, isn't it?

Patient: Exactly and for the last two days I haven't felt the best. I think I am sick.

Physician: It's good you immediately decided to see a doctor.

Patient: I very rarely get sick and when I get a cold, it quickly passes. But this time around I am feeling worse every day. That's why I came to see you.

Physician: I'll examine you now and assign you a treatment. First tell me what bothers you?

Patient: My head. I am tired and sleepy. I have no appetite.

Physician: Maybe you caught a cold or ate something (bad)?

Patient: The day before yesterday I was at my friends' place for dinner. They made sushi. At home I felt sick. I vomited.

Physician: I see your blood pressure is considerably higher than the norm and your temperature is above a hundred and three (39.6 C = 103.28 F).

Patient: That is not surprising because I also have feverish chills and feel nauseous.

Physician: My first diagnosis is food poisoning. But first we'll do some tests so as to know for sure what's with you.

Patient: Can you give me something already now and not wait for the test results?

Physician: Of course. We'll start treating you at once. Here's a prescription for medicine. You should take two pills, mornings and nights.

Patient: Are these antibiotics? Because I am allergic to antibiotics.

Physician: Don't worry, these are not antibiotics. You are saying that you are having the chills?

Patient: Yes, doctor. I've had feverish chills for two days already. Can you also prescribe me something for the fever?

Physician: For the fever you should take a regular aspirin. You can buy it over the counter in any pharmacy.

Patient: For how long do I need to take this medicine?

Physician: The precription pills should be taken for ten days. By tomorrow you should feel better.

Patient: Thank you, doctor. I am already feeling better.

Physician: I wish you a speedy recovery. Goodbye.

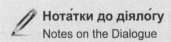

Нота́тки до діало́гу
Notes on the Dialogue

болі|ти, ~я́ть, *impf. + A.*	to ache, hurt; **Що вас боли́ть?** *What bothers you?* **Мене́ боли́ть голова́ (го́рло, се́рце, шлу́нок).** *I have a headache (sore throat, heartache, stomach ache).*
перестуд|и́тися, ~я́ться, *pf.*	to catch a cold, **ду́же п.** to catch a nasty cold
недо́бре, *adv.*	sick, nauseous; **Мені́ недо́бре.** *I feel sick.* **Мені́ ста́ло недо́бре.** *I began to feel sick.*
отру́ї|тися, ~ться, *pf.*	*here* to get food poisoning.
отру́єння, *nt.*	food-poisoning, **У ме́не всі симпто́ми о.** *I have all symptoms of food poisoning.*
моро́з|ити, ~ять *impf. + A.*	to have feverish chills, **Мене́ моро́зить.** *I have feverish chills.*
ну́д|ити, ~ять, *impf. + A.*	to feel nauseous, sick, **Мене́ ну́дить.** *I feel nauseous.*
реце́пт, ~у, на + *A.*	prescription for; **р. на снодíйне (знебо́лююче)** *prescription for sleeping pills (painkiller)*
лі́ки, *only pl.*, **на** + *A.*	*medicine, medication, drugs for*; **пи́ти л.** *to take medicine;* **л. на го́рло (температу́ру, головни́й біль, безсо́ння)** *medication for sore throat (fever, headache, insomnia)*

Ля́на та Воло́дя рі́дко переступджу́ються.

В апте́ці мо́жна купи́ти потрі́бні лі́ки.

почува́	тися, *impf.,* ~ються	to feel, **п. кра́ще (гі́рше)** *to feel better (worse)*
D. бу́ти кра́ще (гі́рше)	to feel better (worse); **Мені́ кра́ще.** *I am feeling better.* **Йому́ було́ гі́рше.** *He was feeling worse.*
D. ста́ти, *pf.* кра́ще (гі́рше)	to become better (worse); **Мені́ ста́ло кра́ще.** *I started feeling better.* **Йому́ ста́не гі́рше.** *He'll start feeling worse.*
ма́ти (висо́ку) температу́ру	to have a (high) fever

📖 Грама́тика | Grammar

Знахі́дний відмі́нок множини́ Accusative Case Plural

Фу́нкція *Function*

The accusative plural case is similar in function to the accusative singular (Lesson 7).

Утво́рення *Formation*

Іме́нники Nouns
The accusative plural for all inanimate nouns coincides with the nominative plural (Lesson 5):
N. pl. **Це потрі́бні лі́ки.**
These are necessary drugs (medicine).
A. pl. **Мико́ла купу́є потрі́бні лі́ки.**
Mykola buys necessary drugs.
N. pl. **Це соло́дкі я́блука.**
These are sweet apples.
A. pl. **Яри́на лю́бить соло́дкі я́блука.**
Yaryna likes sweet apples.

For animate nouns, the accusative plural coincides with the genitive plural (Lesson 12), *cf.,*
N. pl. **На́ші коле́ґи розмовля́ють.**
Our colleagues are talking.
G. pl. **Бага́то на́ших коле́ґ були́ на екску́рсії.**
Our many colleagues were on the excursion.
A. pl. **Ми чу́ємо на́ших коле́ґ.**
We hear our colleagues.

N. pl. **На́ші америка́нські го́сті лю́блять украї́нську ку́хню.**
Our American guests like the Ukrainian cuisine.
G. pl. **Це подару́нок від на́ших америка́нських госте́й.**
This is a present from our American guests.
A. pl. **Яри́на ду́має про на́ших америка́нських госте́й.**
Yaryna is thinking about our American guests.

✏️ **Note 14.1. Adjectives in accusative plural**

The accusative plural adjectives take the ending **~i** and are identical to the nominative plural when they modify inanimate nouns:

чита́ти ціка́ві рома́ни *to read interesting novels*
шука́ти старі́ книжки́ *to look for old books*

They take the ending **~их (~ix)** and are identical to the genitive plural when they modify animate nouns:

Він зна́є цих росі́йських дівча́т.
He knows these Russian girls.
Ми слу́хаємо нови́х студе́нтів.
We listen to the new students.

Родови́й відмі́нок одни́ни кі́лькости
Genitive Singular of Quantity

Used with uncountable nouns, the genitive means a limited quantity of something and corresponds to the English *some, a little*, e.g.,
Рома́н ма́є купи́ти ка́ви та молока́. *Roman is supposed to buy some coffee and milk.*

The uncountable nouns that follow the quantifiers **бага́то** *much* and **ма́ло** *little* are always in the genitive singular, e.g.,
У ме́не бага́то робо́ти. *I have a lot of work.*
Тут ма́ло мі́сця. *There's little room here.*

These quantifiers can be used with the intensifier **ду́же** *very*, e.g.,
У ме́не ду́же бага́то робо́ти. *I have very much work.*
Тут ду́же ма́ло мі́сця. *There's very little room here.*

Надмі́рна я́кість
Excessive quantity
Excessive quantity can be expressed in two ways:
1) by a separate word **на́дто**, *var.* **зана́дто** *too,* which precedes the adjective or adverb,
Це мі́сто зана́дто вели́ке. *This city is too big.*
Ми на́дто до́вго чека́ємо. *We have been waiting for too long.*

2) by the prefix **за~** added to the adjective or adverb,
Ця кни́жка задо́вга. *This book is too long.*
Він зашви́дко гово́рить. *He speaks too fast.*

Мода́льне дієсло́во могти́ /змогти́
Modal Verb **могти́ /змогти́** can, be able to

The modal verb **могти́ /змогти́** expresses a capacity to do something. In the imperfective aspect, **могти́** corresponds to the English *can, to be able to*,
Ця дити́на вже мо́же говори́ти. *This baby is already able to speak.*

In the perfective aspect **змогти́**, can also mean *to manage, to do something despite a shortage of time, to succeed*,
Я зміг допомогти́ вам. *I managed to help you.*
Вони́ змо́жуть знайти́ доро́гу без на́шої допомо́ги.
They'll manage to find the way without our help.

In the present tense, **могти́** follows the **уть**-conjugation pattern:

я мо́жу *I can*	**ми мо́жемо** *we can*
ти мо́жеш *you can*	**ви мо́жете** *you can*
вона́ мо́же *she can*	**вони́ мо́жуть** *they can*

In the future perfective, it uses the identical set of endings:

я змо́жу *I'll be able*	**ми змо́жемо** *we'll be able*
ти змо́жеш *you'll be able*	**ви змо́жете** *you'll be able*
вона́ змо́же *she'll be able*	**вони́ змо́жуть** *they'll be able*

Здає́ться, що ці ко́ні мо́жуть розмовля́ти.

Note 14.2. Imperative Mood

The imperative mood has three forms:
1) addressed to 2nd *pers. sg.* **ти**, **скажи́!** *tell!* **напиши́!** *write!,* **послу́хай!** *listen!,* **поста́в!** *put!*

2) addressed to 2nd *pers. pl.* **ви**, **скажі́ть!** *tell!,* **напиші́ть!** *write!,* **послу́хайте!** *listen!,* **поста́вте!** *put!*

3) addressed to 1st *pers. pl.* **ми**, **скажі́мо!** *let's tell!,* **напиші́мо!** *let's write!,* **послу́хаймо!** *let's listen!,* **поста́вмо!** *let's put!*

Formation of the imperative mood follows a complex set of rules as to the endings and stress pattern. The dictionary provides the first two forms of the imperative for every verb at the end of their description. Each is marked by the exclamation point:

чу́|ти, ~ють; по~, *tran.* + *A.* to hear; (по)чу́й! ~те!

Скажі́ть, будь ла́ска, який зуб вас боли́ть.

In the past imperfective and perfective, **могти́ / змогти́** has these respective forms:

я (ти, він) **міг / зміг**	*m. I was (you were, he was) able*
я (ти, вона́) **могла́ / змогла́**	*f. I was (you were, she was) able*
воно́ **могло́ / змогло́**	*nt. it was able*
ми (ви, вони́) **могли́ / змогли́**	*pl. we (you, they) were able*

Проха́ння, ви́ражене могти́ + інфініти́в
Request expressed by **могти́** + *infinitive*

A request to do something can be expressed by the interrogative constructions with a perfective infinitive:

Ти мо́жеш + *pf. infinitive Can you do it?*	for 2nd *pers. sg.*
Ви мо́жете + *pf. infinitive Can you do it?*	for 2nd *pers. pl.*
Дава́й + *pf. future tense Let's do it?*	for 2nd *pers. sg.*
Дава́йте + *pf. future tense Let's do it?*	for 2nd *pers. pl.*

Thus a functional equivalent of the English *Say it!* is the Ukrainian **Ти мо́жеш сказа́ти це?** *Can you say it?* Being a question rather than an imperative, this formula is much more polite. It is a periphrastic request that can be used in situations where imperative is used, such as asking for directions, advice, help, etc.

The respective negative construction **Ти не мо́жеш сказа́ти це?** *Can't you say it?* conveys the same request to do something but with an even greater degree of politeness. Politeness of the request can be enhanced by the expression **будь ла́ска** *please,* used either at the beginning or at the end of the question,
Ти мо́жеш сказа́ти це, будь ла́ска? *Can you say it please?*
Будь ла́ска, ти мо́жеш сказа́ти це? *Please, can you say it?*

A request not to do sth is conveyed by the expressions with a negated imperfective infinitive:

Ти мо́жеш + **не** + *impf. inf. Can you not do it!*	for 2nd *pers. sg.*
Ви мо́жете + **не** + *impf. inf. Can you not do it!*	for 2nd *pers. pl.*
Дава́й + **не** + *impf. inf. Let's not do it!*	for 2nd *pers. sg.*
Дава́йте + **не** + *impf. inf. Let's not do it!*	for 2nd *pers. pl.*

Thus a functional equivalent of the English *Don't say it!* is the Ukrainian:

Ти мо́жеш не каза́ти цього́? *Can you not say it?*
addressed to the 2nd *pers. sg. It excludes the speaker.*
Ви мо́жете не каза́ти цього́? *Can you not say it?*
addressed to the 2nd *pers. pl. It excludes the speaker.*
Дава́й не каза́ти цього́! *Let's not say it!*
addressed to the 2nd *pers. sg. It includes the speaker.*
Дава́йте не каза́ти цього́! *Let's not say it!*
addressed to the 2nd *pers. pl. It includes the speaker.*

A request to do something uses the perfective aspect, while a request not to do something uses the imperfective aspect. As any general question, these types of requests are pronounced with a rising tone,

Ти ↗ мо́жеш допомогти́ мені́?! *Can you help me?!*
Ви не ↗ мо́жете почека́ти?! *Can't you wait?!*

 Впра́ви Exercises

Цих талано́витих акто́рок і акто́рів запроси́ли гра́ти в ново́му українському фі́льмі

∩ **14.1.** Provide full answers to the questions. Practice the accusative plural. Use one pair of words at a time.

Model.
C Що ти ма́єш? *What do you have?* францу́зький журна́л *a French magazine*
A Я ма́ю францу́зькі журна́ли. *I have French magazines.*

1. Що ви сього́дні ро́бите? це завда́ння, граматична впра́ва, англійський пере́клад
2. Що Марі́я лю́бить пи́ти? фрукто́вий сік, безалкого́льний напі́й
3. Що ви тут купу́єте? сві́жа ви́шня, рі́зний йо́ґурт, італі́йське вино́, українська газе́та
4. Кого́ він уже́ зна́є? цей тури́ст, америка́нський гість, нови́й сусі́д, на́ша ді́вчина, ваш хло́пець
5. Що ви за́раз їсте́? смачни́й бутербро́д, дома́шня ковбаса́, соло́дке я́блуко
6. Кого́ ми ба́чимо? наш студе́нт, мала́ дити́на, молоди́й кана́дець, незнайо́мий росія́нин
7. Кого́ він огляда́є? та люди́на, цей хво́рий, нови́й паціє́нт
8. Кого́ слу́хає Окса́на? її ба́тько, ва́ша ма́ма, знайо́мий львів'я́нин, америка́нська по́друга

∩ **14.2.** Give full answers. Practice the accusative plural after **про** *about* and **на** *at*. Use one pair of words at a time.

Model.
C Про що ти ду́маєш? *What are you thinking about?* ва́ше сло́во *your word*
A Я ду́маю про ва́ші слова́. *I'm thinking about your words.*

1. Про що вона́ розповіла́? своя́ хворо́ба, міська́ шко́ла, ця істо́рія.
2. Про ко́го ти ду́маєш? симпатична жі́нка, їхня ба́ба, стара́ ті́тка.
3. Про що ви пам'ята́єте? ва́ше проха́ння, те дале́ке село́.
4. Про ко́го вони́ розповіли́? ди́вна студе́нтка, льві́вський спортсме́н.
5. Про що ти поду́мала? важке́ завда́ння, дома́шня впра́ва, весь той архітекту́рний пам'ятник.
6. Про ко́го ти пам'ята́єш? наш ро́дич, той досві́дчений акто́р.
7. На що він ди́виться? ця карти́на, смішна́ світли́на, поро́жня ву́лиця.

Сього́дні у Тара́са забага́то рі́зного завда́ння, щоб іти́ на яку́сь заба́ву.

8. На ко́го вони́ ди́вляться? свій друг, по́льська подру́га, ки́ївський лі́кар.

 14.3. Answer the questions. Indicate a small quantity using the genitive.

Model.
Q Що вам тре́ба до ка́ви? *What do you need for coffee?* цу́кор *sugar*
A Цу́кру. *Some sugar.*

1. Що Ната́лці тре́ба? молоко́
2. Що ви хо́чете на сніда́нок? чай
3. Що нам купи́ти на обі́д? ковбаса́ та хліб
4. Що вам принести́ на вече́рю? бі́ле вино́
5. Що тобі́ да́ти пи́ти? я́блучний сік
6. Що вам звари́ти на обі́д? черво́ний борщ
7. Чого́ попроси́в гість до ю́шки? пе́рець і сіль

14.4. Express excessive quantity. Use **на́дто бага́то (забага́то)** *too much (many)* or **на́дто ма́ло (зама́ло)** *too little (few)* + G. sg.

Model.
C Я *I*, бага́то *much*, нудна́ робо́та *boring work*
A У ме́не на́дто бага́то нудно́ї робо́ти. *I have too much boring work.*

1. Ти, ма́ло, ві́льний час
2. Ви, бага́то, складне́ завда́ння
3. Вони́, ма́ло, чи́ста вода́
4. Він, ма́ло, ціка́ва інформа́ція
5. Ми, бага́то, смачна́ ковбаса́
6. Вона́, ма́ло, сві́жа ка́ва
7. Тара́с, ма́ло, органі́чна городина

Note 14.3. Пробле́ми зі здоро́в'ям
Health problems

бу́ти хво́р|им на + *A.*	1) to be ill, to be sick with; **Ніхто́ не лю́бить бу́ти ~им.** *Nobody likes to be sick.* 2) to be sick with, **Ви зна́єте, на що ви ~і?** *Do you know what you are sick with?*
хворі́|ти, ~ють + *I.* or на + *A.*	1) *intr.* to be sick; **Чи вона́ ще ~є?** *Is she still sick?* 2) to be ill with sth, **Він ~в гри́пом (на грип) ці́лий ти́ждень.** *He has been ill with the flu for a whole week.*
бу́ти здоро́в|им	to be healthy, to be in good health; **Вона́ цілко́м ~а.** *She is quite well.*

захворі́|ти, **~ють**, *pf.*, *intr.* + *I.* or **на** + *A.*	(used mostly in perfective aspect) 1) to fall ill; **Коли́ він ~в?** *When did he fall ill?* 2) to fall ill with sth; **Вона́ ~ла бронхі́том.** *She fell ill with bronchitis.*
лама́|ти, **~ють**; **з~**, *tran.*	to break (a limb, etc.), **Він упа́в і злама́в па́льця.** He fell and broke his finger.
хворо́ба, *f.* + *G.*	illness, sickness, disease. **У ньо́го х. се́рця.** He has a heart disease.
ангі́на, *f.*	tonsillitis
грип, *m.*, **~у**	influenza
засту́да, *f.*	a cold; **си́льна з.** *a bad cold*
температу́ра, *f.*	temperature; **норма́льна (висо́ка, низька́) т.** *normal (high, low) temperature.* On the Celsius scale used in Ukraine, the normal body temperature is around +36.6º C, high temperature is +38.0º C and higher.
тиск, *m.*, **~у**	pressure; **висо́кий (низьки́й, норма́льний) тиск кро́ви** high (low, normal) blood pressure.
мі́ря|ти, **~ють**; **по~**, *tran.* температу́ру (тиск) + *D.*	to take sb's temperature; **Мені́ тре́ба помі́ряти вам температу́ру (тиск).** *I need to take your temperature (blood pressure).*
дія́гноз, *m.*, **~у**	a diagnosis; **ста́вити; по~ д.** + *D.* to make sb a diagnosis; **Рома́нові шви́дко поста́вили д.** *They made Roman a quick diagnosis.*
симпто́м, *m.*, **~у**	a symptom; **Ви мо́жете описа́ти ва́ші ~и?** *Can you describe your symptoms?*
вто́млен|ий, *adj.*, *var.* **сто́млений**	tired; **Я ду́же в.** *I am very tired.*
втомлю́|ватися, **~ються**, *var.* **стомлюватися**, *refl.*	to get tired; **Я шви́дко ~юся.** *I get tired quickly.*
запа́лення, *nt.*	inflammation; **з. го́рла (ву́ха, легені́в)** *inflammation of throat, (ear, lungs)*
ка́шля|ти, **~ють**, *impf.*	to have a cough, to cough. **Я ду́же ~ю.** *I have a bad cough.*
не́жить, *m.*, **~ю**	catarrh, runny nose
зга́г|а, *f.* or **печі́|я**, *f.*	heartburn, **си́льна (нестерпна) з.** *a severe (unbearable) heartburn*
проно́с, *m.*, **~у**	diarrhea
ро́злад шлу́нка	indigestion, stomach upset
о́пік, *m.*, **~у**	a burn, **си́льний о.** *a severe burn*
прохо́д|ити, **~ять**; **пройти́, пройд|у́ть**	(of sickness) to pass, disappear, **Його́ ка́шель не прохо́див ти́ждень.** *His cough would not pass for a week.*
виду́жу|вати, **~ють**; **виду́жа|ти**, **~ють**	to recover, get well; **Він шви́дко виду́жав.** *He quickly recovered.*
серце́вий на́пад, *m.*, **~у**	a heart attack, **ма́ти с. н.** to have a heart attack; **Торі́к його́ дід мав с. н.** *Last year his grandfather had a heart attack.*
інсу́льт, *m.*, **~у**	a stroke, **ма́ти і.** *to have a stroke*
швидк|а́ (допомо́га, *f.*)	an ambulance, **виклика́ти ~у́** to call an ambulance; **Тре́ба нега́йно ви́кликати ~у́.** *You need to call an ambulance at once.*

Ле́сі тре́ба було́ нега́йно ви́кликати швидку́.

🎧 **Note 14.4. Части́ни ті́ла люди́ни** Parts of the human body (*sg. and pl.*)

голов|а́, *f.*, ~и	a head
обли́чч|я, *nt.*, ~я	a face
ву́х|о, *nt.*, ~а, *var.* у́ші	an ear
рот, *m.*, ~и́	a mouth
щок|а́, *f.*, ~и	a cheek
доло́н|я, *f.*, ~і	a palm
го́рл|о, *nt.*, ~а	a throat
па́л|ець, *m.*, ~ьці	a finger, toe
ног|а́, *f.*, ~и	a leg, foot
колі́н|о, *nt.*, ~а	a knee
н|іс, *m.*, ~оси́	a nose
губ|а́, *f.*, ~и	a lip
зуб, *m.*, ~и	a tooth
воло́сся, *nt.*, *only sg.*	hair (collective)
ні́г|оть, *m.*, ~ті	a nail
шкі́ра, *f.*, *only sg.*	skin
ши́|я, *f.*, ~ї	a neck
рук|а́, *f.*, ~и	an arm, hand
спин|а́, *f.*, ~и	a back
плеч|е́, *nt.*, ~і	a shoulder
жив|і́т, *m.*, ~оти́	stomach (belly)
м'яз, *m.*, ~и	a muscle
се́рц|е, *nt.*, ~я	a heart
леге́н|я, *f.*, ~і	a lung
печі́нк|а, *f.*, ~и	a liver
ни́рк|а, *f.*, ~и	a kidney
шлу́н|ок, *m.*, ~ки	a stomach (digestive organ)

🎧 **14.5.** Translate the questions into English.

1. Що тебе́ боли́ть?
2. Як почува́ється ва́ша ма́ма?
3. Чому́ Андрі́я моро́зить?
4. Яка́ норма́льна температу́ра ті́ла?
5. Чому́ О́льга ці́лу ніч не спа́ла?
6. Чому́ лі́кар ду́має, що Оле́кса отру́ївся?
7. Що тре́ба ма́ти, щоб купи́ти антибіо́тики?
8. Як почува́ється люди́на, коли́ переступа́жується?
9. Що ви роби́ли, коли́ ма́ли висо́ку температу́ру?
10. Як ча́сто ви хворі́єте?
11. На що ви ма́єте алерґі́ю?
12. Як ча́сто тре́ба пи́ти ці лі́ки?

14.6. Provide full answers to the questions in the previous exercise. Replace nouns for pronouns where possible. Find the right prompt below.

Model. Він злама́в но́гу. *He broke his leg.*
Q Чому́ Бори́с ви́кликав швидку́? *Why did Borys call an ambulance?*
A Бори́с ви́кликав її́, бо він злама́в но́гу. *He called it because he broke his leg.*

Prompts

1. голова́ й о́чі
2. ма́є висо́ку температу́ру.
3. ду́же болі́в шлу́нок.
4. реце́пт від лі́каря
5. ма́є температу́ру і ка́шляє.
6. на антибіо́тики
7. три́дцять шість і шість гра́дусів Це́льсія
8. зна́чно кра́ще
9. блюва́в і мав проно́с.
10. раз чи два ра́зи на рік я ма́ю засту́ду.
11. одра́зу зверну́лася до лі́каря
12. три ра́зи, ко́жні ві́сім годи́н

🎧 **14.7.** Match the English equivalent to each Ukrainian statement.

1. Мені́ здає́ться, що я хво́ра.	1. She rarely has headaches.
2. Його́ ду́же боли́ть зуб.	2. They have a bad cough.
3. Лі́кар обсте́жить хво́рого за́втра.	3. I think I am sick.
4. Їм ста́ло набага́то кра́ще.	4. He has a bad toothache.
5. Її́ рі́дко боли́ть голова́.	5. You need to take something for diarrhea.

6. Я ви́дужав за три дні.	6. The doctor will examine the patient tomorrow.
7. У не́ї були́ хво́рі ни́рки.	7. Their daughter is never sick.
8. Їхня дочка́ ніко́ли не хворі́є.	8. She had kidney problems.
9. Вони́ си́льно ка́шляють.	9. They began to feel much better.
10. Тобі́ тре́ба ви́пити щось від проно́су.	10. I recovered in three days.

В апте́ці продаю́ть рі́зні лі́ки.

∩ **14.8.** Study carefully the Notes on the Dialogue, Notes 14.2, and 14.3. Answer these questions.

1. Що мо́же болі́ти?
2. Де мо́жна купи́ти лі́ки?
3. Хто мо́же обсте́жувати хво́рих?
4. Що мо́жна злама́ти?
5. До ко́го мо́же зверну́тися по допомо́гу хво́ра люди́на?
6. Хто випи́сує реце́пт на лі́ки?
7. На які́ хворо́би чи симпто́ми мо́жуть бу́ти лі́ки?
8. Що тре́ба зроби́ти, щоб ви́кликати швидку́?
9. Коли́ лю́ди виклика́ють швидку́, а не йдуть до лі́каря самі́?
10. Як ча́сто ви мі́ряєте собі́ тиск?
11. Як ча́сто ви мі́ряєте собі́ температу́ру?
12. Що ви ро́бите, коли́ переступ́джуєтеся?
13. На що люди́на мо́же ма́ти алергі́ю?

14.9. Fill out the table. Explain in Ukrainian what you do in each of these situations.

Що ви ро́бите, коли́ вас щось боли́ть?
What do you do when something ails you?

Пробле́ма зі здоро́в'ям	ви́пити лі́ки на + *A.*	зверну́тися до лі́каря	ви́кликати швидку́
боли́ть голова́			
висо́ка температу́ра			
ро́злад шлу́нка			
боля́ть зу́би			
не́жить			
боли́ть се́рце			
безсо́ння			
ви злама́ли ру́ку			
ви отру́їлися			

Га́нна не змо́же пої́хати з на́ми до Я́лти, бо зніма́тиме свій нови́й фільм.

⌒ 14.10. Express a person's inability in the past to do something. Use imperfective past tense form of **могти́** *to be able*. Translate.

1. Мину́лого ро́ку це дитя́ ще не … говори́ти.
2. Ці жінки́ були́ за́йняті і не … прийти́ на конце́рт.
3. Іва́н не … знайти́ відповіді на це пита́ння.
4. На́ша сусі́дка не … сказа́ти йому́ про це.
5. Мої́ знайо́мі поля́ки працюва́ли і не … подзвони́ти вам.
6. Я зна́ю, що Ната́лка не … написа́ти мені́ таки́й лист.
7. Він не … зна́ти про це.
8. Вчо́ра Петре́нки не … допомогти́ нам.

⌒ 14.11. Indicate a person's ability to do something now. Use the respective present tense form of **могти́** *to be able*.

1. Я … помогти́ тобі́.
2. Марі́я … чита́ти кита́йські те́ксти.
3. Ти … пора́дити мені́ у цій спра́ві.
4. Мої́ батьки́ … да́ти нам гро́ші на це.
5. Ви … не поспіша́ти.
6. Плато́н … знайти́ для нас деше́вий готе́ль.

⌒ 14.12. Explain future inability to do something due to the excess or shortage of something. Use **змогти́** *to be able, manage*.

Model.
C Васи́ль *Vasyl*, да́ти їй гро́ші *to give her money*,
    ма́ло заробля́ти *to earn little*
A Васи́ль не змо́же да́ти їй гро́ші, бо він зама́ло заробля́є.
    *Vasyl won't be able to give her the money, because he earns
    too little.*

1. Я, допомогти́ тобі́, у ме́не ма́ло ча́су
2. Ти, піти́ на конце́рт, ти ма́єш бага́то робо́ти
3. Ми, прочита́ти цей рома́н, текст є складни́й
4. Марко́, зароби́ти на подо́рож, тепе́р тя́жко знайти́ робо́ту
5. Ви, зупини́тися у цьо́му готе́лі, він дороги́й
6. Ці італі́йці, поба́чити Оде́су, у них коро́тка відпу́стка

Розмо́ва Conversation

⌒ 14.13. Engage a partner in a conversation in Ukrainian about the last time they were sick.

1. Find out each detail noted in the table below
2. Write them all down in Ukrainian
3. Report in Ukrainian about what you learned from your conversation

Про що дізна́тися	партне́р-1	партне́р-2	партне́р-3
Де ви були́, коли́ захворі́ли?			
Коли́ са́ме це було́?			
Що са́ме вас болі́ло?			
Куди́ ви зверта́лися по допомо́гу?			
Як і скі́льки ча́су ви лікува́лися?			
Як ча́сто ви хворі́єте?			
Коли́ виліку́єтеся самі́?			
Коли́ зверта́єтеся до лі́каря?			

14.14. Express a polite request directed at **ти** or **ви**. Use **могти́** + *pf. inf.*

Model.
C Ти *you (sg.),* сказа́ти це *to say it*
A Ти мо́жеш сказа́ти це, будь ла́ска! *Can you say it, please!*

C Ви *you (pl.),* сказа́ти це *to say it*
A Ви мо́жете сказа́ти це, будь ла́ска! *Can you say it, please!*

1. Ти, запита́ти про це
2. Ви, показа́ти нам доро́гу
3. Ти, взя́ти гро́ші
4. Ви, повтори́ти це
5. Ви, зачини́ти две́рі
6. Ви, подзвони́ти до готе́лю
7. Ти, заплати́ти за вече́рю
8. Ви, знайти́ до́брий рестора́н
9. Ти, послу́хати про пого́ду
10. Ви, купи́ти ка́рту
11. Ти, поверну́ти право́руч
12. Ти, допомогти́

14.15. Express exhortation directed at *ти* and then *ви*. Use **дава́й / дава́йте** + *pf. future.*

Model.
C сказа́ти це *to say it*
A Дава́й (дава́йте) ска́жемо це! *Let's say it!*

Ви мо́жете відпові́сти на моє́ пита́ння?

1. подиви́тися ро́зклад поїздів
2. прочита́ти цей текст
3. зачини́ти две́рі
4. подзвони́ти до Мико́ли
5. заплати́ти за по́слуги
6. закі́нчити пакува́тися
7. знайти́ банкома́т
8. запита́ти про це
9. купи́ти щось ї́сти
10. поверну́ти ліво́руч
11. перейти́ ву́лицю
12. замо́вити но́мер у готе́лі

Дава́йте займа́тися спо́ртом,
щоб ніко́ли не хворі́ти.

∩ **14.16.** Ask not to do something. Use **могти́** + **не** + *impf. inf.*

Model.
C ти, *you (sg.),* не каза́ти цього́ *not to say it*
A Ти мо́жеш не каза́ти цього́! *Can you not say it!*

C ви *you (pl.),* не каза́ти цього́ *not to say it*
A Ви мо́жете не каза́ти цього́! *Can you not say it!*

1. ти, не пита́ти про це
2. ви, не чита́ти листа́
3. ти, не бра́ти гро́шей
4. ти, не забува́ти її́
5. ви, не зачиня́ти двере́й
6. ви, не дзвони́ти до готе́лю
7. ти, не плати́ти за вече́рю
8. ти, не слу́хати про пого́ду
9. ви, не купува́ти ка́рти мі́ста
10. ти, не допомага́ти
11. ви, не повто́рювати цього́
12. ти, не дава́ти їм гро́шей

∩ **14.17.** Express negative exhortation directed at **ви**. Use **дава́йте** + **не** + *impf. inf.* Replace the perfective aspect of the verb with the imperfective. Put the negated object in the genitive.

Model.
C Дава́йте ска́жемо це! *Let's say it!*
A Дава́йте не каза́ти цього́. *Let's not say it.*

1. Дава́йте поди́вимося ро́зклад поїздів.
2. Дава́йте прочита́ємо цей те́кст.
3. Дава́йте зачи́нимо ті две́рі.
4. Дава́йте пока́жемо їм мі́сто.
5. Дава́йте розка́жемо цю істо́рію.
6. Дава́йте спаку́ємо на́ші ре́чі.
7. Дава́йте знайде́мо найбли́жчий банкома́т.
8. Дава́йте запита́ємо доро́гу.
9. Дава́йте ку́пимо лі́ки від гаря́чки.
10. Дава́йте пове́рнемо батька́м ключі́ до кварти́ри.
11. Дава́йте перейде́мо ту ву́лицю.
12. Дава́йте замо́вимо окре́мі номери́ у готе́лі.

∩ **14.18.** Say and write the sentences in Ukrainian. Use the vocabulary and grammar of this and previous lessons. If necessary, consult the dictionary.

1. I have a bad headache. It seems I caught a nasty cold.
2. Petro says that he has feverish chills.

What drugs can you recommend for him?

3. If a person is nauseous, has a stomach ache and a high fever, it's probably food poisoning.

4. One can't buy this medicine without a prescription. You need to call your doctor immediately.

5. Can you tell me the latest news from our family in Kyiv? Is Grandpa feeling better now?

6. Let us not do these assignments today. They can wait a few days.

7. Can you send me the money, six hundred hryvnias exactly? I will return it to you next month.

8. Can they explain to her what the problem is?

9. The plane is two hours late. What do you propose to do?

10. They'd like to visit her in the hospital. Would you like to come along with them?

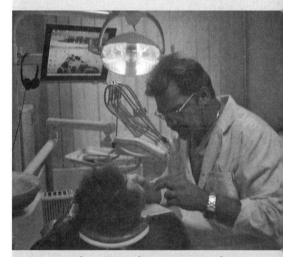

Оле́на зверну́лася до свого́ данти́ста, бо її́ поча́в болі́ти зуб.

⌂ 14.19. Listen carefully to the questions. Answer each of them using Dialogue 14.

1. Чому́ Оле́г зверта́ється до лі́каря?
2. Що його́ боли́ть?
3. Скі́льки днів пога́но почува́вся Оле́г?
4. Яки́й тиск кро́ви і температу́ра ті́ла в Оле́га?
5. Що роби́в Оле́г позавчо́ра?
6. Чому́ захворі́в Оле́г?
7. Що тре́ба було́ зроби́ти, щоб напе́вно зна́ти, чим він захворі́в?
8. Як ча́сто пи́ти лі́ки сказа́в Оле́гові лі́кар?
9. Чому́ не Оле́г пи́ти антибіо́тиків?
10. Які́ лі́ки від температу́ри пора́див Оле́гові лі́кар?
11. Скі́льки днів ма́є Оле́г пи́ти лі́ки від отру́єння?
12. Які́ лі́ки мо́жна купи́ти без реце́пту лі́каря?
13. Коли́ Оле́г ма́є почува́тися кра́ще?
14. Коли́ і де ви оста́нній раз хворі́ли?
15. Що ви роби́ли, щоб шви́дко одужа́ти?

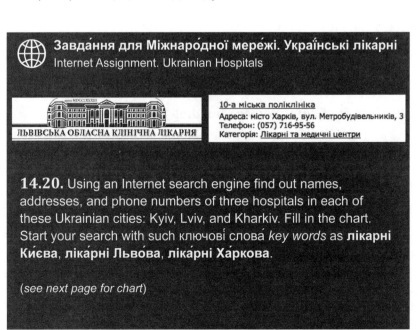

🌐 **Завда́ння для Міжнаро́дної мере́жі. Украї́нські ліка́рні**
Internet Assignment. Ukrainian Hospitals

ЛЬВІВСЬКА ОБЛАСНА КЛІНІЧНА ЛІКАРНЯ

10-а міська поліклініка
Адреса: місто Харків, вул. Метробудівельників, 3
Телефон: (057) 716-95-56
Категорія: Лікарні та медичні центри

14.20. Using an Internet search engine find out names, addresses, and phone numbers of three hospitals in each of these Ukrainian cities: Kyiv, Lviv, and Kharkiv. Fill in the chart. Start your search with such ключові слова́ *key words* as **лікарні Ки́єва**, **ліка́рні Льво́ва**, **лі́ка́рні Ха́ркова**.

(see next page for chart)

Назва ліка́рні	адре́са	но́мер телефо́ну
Ки́їв		
1.		
2.		
3.		
Льві́в		
1.		
2.		
3.		
Ха́рків		
1.		
2.		
3.		

Подві́йне запере́чення   Double Negation

Review *"How to Be Negative" in Lesson 8.*

🎧 **14.21.** Say that nobody does this. Practice the double negation with **ніхто́** *nobody.*

Model. **Q** Хто розмовля́є росі́йською? *Who speaks Russian?*
A Ніхто́ не розмовля́є росі́йською. *Nobody speaks Russian.*

1. Хто лю́бить ра́но встава́ти у неді́лю?
2. Хто ма́є телевізі́йну програ́му на насту́пний ти́ждень?
3. Хто до вас дзво́нить щодня́?
4. Хто бу́де на їхній вечі́рці крім нас?
5. Хто пропону́є допомогти́?
6. Хто відпочива́є в Бердя́нську цього́ лі́та?
7. Хто зна́є ві́дповідь на це пита́ння?
8. Хто лю́бить ко́ка-ко́лу?
9. Хто п'є чо́рну ка́ву?
10. Хто пока́зує їм доро́гу до музе́ю?

Чита́ємо і обгово́рюємо   Reading and Discussing

14.22. Read these accounts of people dealing with sickness from an Internet forum for contemporary parents «Інтерне́т-фо́рум для суча́сних батькі́в». Find and write down:

1) на́зви хворо́б
2) симпто́ми хворо́б
3) на́зви лі́ків
4) імена́ хво́рих

Лукаша́ ніко́ли нічо́го не боли́ть,
бо він гра́є у футбо́л.

Інтерне́т-фо́рум для суча́сних батькі́в

📄 **30.10.2014 01:03**

Мари́на Т.

Реєстра́ція: 30.10.14
Зві́дки ви: Полта́ва
Вік: 39
До́писи: 299

У нас 22-го жо́втня захворі́в ста́рший син Сашко́ - ра́птом уночі́ температу́ра 39,5. Він ніко́ли ранí́ше не мав тако́ї висо́кої температу́ри. В неді́лю вра́нці поїхали до мо́їх батькі́в, ви́кликали туди́ лі́каря. Бо я не ві́рю на́шому місце́вому лі́кареві. Лі́кар батькі́в огля́нув як мо́їх обо́х діте́й, так і до́чку сестри́. Вона́ теж захворі́ла в той са́мий час. Лі́кар сказа́в, що це засту́да і призна́чив лікува́ння. Табле́тки від температу́ри, пи́ти по одні́й три ра́зи на день. Прийма́ти вітамі́н C, пи́ти бага́то води́ і лежа́ти в лі́жку, ніку́ди не ходи́ти. Я запита́ла лі́каря, чи це мо́же бу́ти грип. Він відпові́в, що ні, бо доро́слі у на́шій сім'ї́ не хворі́. Три дні у мого́ ста́ршого си́на була́ температу́ра: з неді́лі до вівто́рка. У вівто́рок вра́нці я сама́ проки́нулася із температу́рою 39,4.

Тако́ї температу́ри я не ма́ла 10 ро́ків!!!

До ве́чора моло́дший син Оле́кса мав таку́ са́му висо́ку температу́ру. Ко́жен з нас прові́в три дні у лі́жку з температу́рою. Табле́тки, що приписа́в лі́кар ма́ло допомага́ли. По́тім ко́жного з нас почало́ болі́ти го́рло, почали́ся не́жить і ка́шель. В цей час захворі́ла моя́ сестра́ Ні́на та її́ 7-рі́чна дочка́ Миро́ся. Ми живемо́ в рі́зних місця́х, працю́ємо в рі́зних організа́ціях, на́ші ді́ти хо́дять до рі́зних шкіл. Че́рез три дні пі́сля ме́не захворі́ли мої́ батьки́. Коли́ зно́ву звернули́ся до лі́каря і спита́ли чи це грип, він наре́шті сказа́в, що так, це всі типо́ві симпто́ми гри́пу.

Я й сама́ зрозумі́ла тоді́, що ми всі захворі́ли на грип, а не на звича́йну засту́ду. Я поду́мала, до́бре, що це не запа́лення леге́нів. На шо́стий день ми всі ма́ли ускла́днення. У ста́ршого си́на теж почала́ся анги́на, а в моло́дшого й у ме́не - бронхі́т.

📄 **09.11.2014 14:22**

Миха́йло Я.

Реєстра́ція: 09.11.14
Зві́дки ви: Я́лта
Вік: 27
До́писи: 114

Я серйо́зно захворі́в на грип і до́вго не міг ходи́ти на робо́ту. Це ста́лося 2-го листопа́да, за ти́ждень до поча́тку епіде́мії гри́пу в на́шому мі́сті. В понеді́лок у ме́не була́ температу́ра 37, а насту́пні три дні бу́ла ма́йже 40 і ні́чого з цим не мо́жна було́ зроби́ти. Два ти́жні я пробу́в до́ма в лі́жку. Єди́ні лі́ки, що допомага́ли – це парацетамо́л та анальгі́н. Я не зверта́вся до лі́каря, бо знав, що він мені́ ска́же, і які́ табле́тки призна́чить. Торі́к я теж хворі́в на грип але́ ме́нше ча́су. Мо́же, мені́ тре́ба було́ піти́ до лі́каря. Цього́ ра́зу, крім гаря́чки, я мав ду́же си́льний ка́шель. Живі́т так болі́в, ні́би я займа́вся ці́лий день у спортклу́бі. Ї́сти не хотів, мене́ весь час нуди́ло. Ті́льки хотів пи́ти. Че́рез шість днів температу́ра прийшла́ до но́рми. По́тім я ще ти́ждень лікува́в ускла́днення - бронхі́т.

🎧 **14.23.** Answer the questions in Ukrainian based on the information posted on the Internet forum from the previous exercise.

1. Хто мав температу́ру ма́йже со́рок гра́дусів?
2. Чому́ Мари́на Т. ви́кликала лі́каря, коли́ поїхала до батькі́в?
3. Кого́ огля́нув лі́кар у батькі́в?
4. Яки́й дія́гноз поста́вив їм лі́кар?
5. Чи пра́вильний дія́гноз поста́вив лі́кар і чому́?
6. Чому́ лі́кар ду́мав, що це не грип?

7. Яке́ лікува́ння призна́чив лі́кар?

8. Скі́льки ча́су Сашко́ мав висо́ку температу́ру?

9. Коли́ захворі́ла сама́ Мари́на Т.?

10. Хто ще захворі́в в той са́мий день?

11. Як допомогли́ у лікува́нні табле́тки, що приписа́в лі́кар?

12. Коли́ захворі́ли батьки́ Мари́ни Т.?

13. Яки́й дру́гий дія́гноз поста́вив їм лі́кар?

14. Що поду́мала Мари́на Т., коли́ почу́ла дія́гноз лі́каря?

15. Які́ усклада́ння ма́ли Мари́на та її́ ді́ти?

16. Які́ симпто́ми мав Миха́йло Я.?

17. Чому́ Миха́йло не зверну́вся до лі́каря?

18. Скі́льки ча́су хворі́в Миха́йло?

∩ 14.24. Number the statements in the order the events unfold in the case of Maryna T.'s family as described in 14.22. Narrate the story in the past perfective. To link the events, use the adverbs **споча́тку** *first*, **тоді́** (**по́тім**, **пі́сля того́**) *then*, **наре́шті** *finally*, **наса́мкінець** *at the end*.

No.		No.
1.	Лі́кар поста́вив дія́гноз грип.	
2.	Батьки́ Мари́ни Т. захворі́ли.	
3.	Мари́ну та її́ діте́й почало́ болі́ти го́рло.	
4.	Мари́на Т. захворі́ла.	
5.	Лі́кар поста́вив дія́гноз засту́да.	
6.	В Оле́кси поча́вся бронхі́т.	
7.	Сашко́ захворі́в.	
8.	Мари́на Т. ви́кликала лі́каря до батькі́в.	
9.	Мари́на Т. зрозумі́ла, що це не засту́да, а грип.	
10.	У Сашка́ почала́ся ангі́на.	
11.	Ні́на з Миро́сею захворі́ли.	

∩ 14.25. Compare and discuss with a partner the situations and behavior of Maryna T. and Mykhailo Ya. in 14.22 Use the contrasting conjunction **a** *while*. See Note 1.7.

1. З ким були́ Мари́на Т. та Миха́йло Я., коли́ вони́ захворі́ли?

2. Що вони́ зна́ли про свою́ хворо́бу?

3. Як вони́ зверта́лися по допомо́гу до лі́каря ?

4. Як вони́ лікува́лися?

5. Як до́вго вони́ хворі́ли?

6. Які́ усклада́ння вони́ ма́ли пі́сля гри́пу?

7. У яки́х міста́х Украї́ни живу́ть Мари́на та Миха́йло?

8. Коли́ (да́та і час) ко́жен із них написа́в про свою́ істо́рію на інтерне́т-фо́румі?

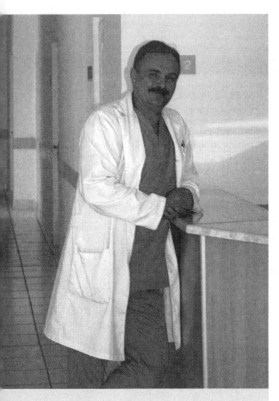

За́раз вас огля́не досві́дчений лі́кар.

14.26. Open the parentheses and put each phrase within in the required case form.

Model. **C** А́лла ма́є (бага́то, кіт і пес).
A А́лла ма́є бага́то коті́в і псів.
Alla has many cats and dogs.

1. Окса́на отри́мувала листи́ від (бага́то, своя́ по́друга).
2. Профе́сор Богда́ненко написа́в (бага́то, популя́рна кни́жка).
3. Я́ків Онищу́к не знайшо́в тут (бага́то, симпати́чна люди́на)
4. Працюва́ти було́ ле́гко завдяки́ (бага́то, ко́рисна програ́ма) в ново́му комп'ю́тері.
5. У цьо́му буди́нку жило́ (бага́то, відо́мий вче́ний).
6. Мандрівники́ шука́ли доро́гу че́рез го́ри протя́гом (бага́то, холо́дна годи́на).
7. Гали́на чи́тала цю новину́ у (бага́то, газе́та).
8. (Бага́то, до́брий письме́нник) ніко́ли не вивча́ло літерату́ри чи мо́ви.
9. Для пере́кладу Марко́ Павлю́к користува́вся (бага́то, словни́к).
10. (Бага́то, економі́ст) тре́ба було́ слу́хати нови́й університе́тський курс.

14.27. Enact a conversation with a partner. Use the material you learned in this and previous lessons. If necessary, consult the dictionary.

Сце́нка за сцена́рієм «У лі́каря»
Scripted Skit: "At Doctor's Office"

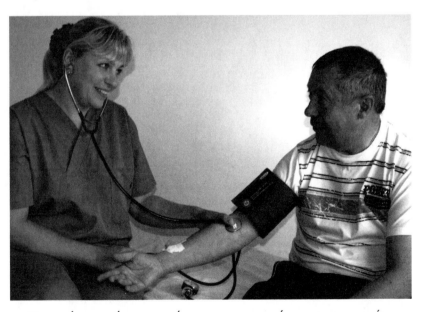

Не журі́ться, за́раз я помі́ряю вам тиск кро́ви та температу́ру.

Patient (Хво́рий): Expresses suspicion that s/he is ill.
Physician (Лі́кар): Asks for the reasons of such a suspicion.

Patient: Describes symptoms: headache, tiredness, lack of appetite.
Physician: Asks about a cough.

Note 14.5 Cardinal numeral бага́то *many, much*

The numeral **бага́то** *many, much* requires that the noun or phrase following it be in the genitive plural, if this word combination is the subject (a) or inanimate accusative object (b) of a sentence,

(a) **Бага́то мої́х дру́зів ніко́ли не були́ за кордо́ном.** *Many of my friends have never been abroad.*
(b) **Наза́р чита́в бага́то їхніх статте́й (or стате́й).** *Nazar read many of their articles.*

The numeral **бага́то** declines as any other cardinal numeral. Its case forms are:

G. **багатьо́х**, *D.* **багатьо́м**, *A. anim.* **багатьо́х**, *inan.* **бага́то**, *I.* **багатьма́**, *L.* **на багатьо́х**,
G.: **Її́ слова́ були́ несподі́ванкою для багатьо́х слухачі́в.** *Her words were a surprise for many listeners.*
D.: **Цей факт здава́вся ди́вним багатьо́м уче́ним.** *The fact seemed strange to many scientists.*
L.: **На багатьо́х уча́сниках були́ костю́ми.** *There were suits on many participants.*

Note that, when the phrase **бага́то** + *noun* is the subject of a sentence, it often requires that the predicate be in the singular for the present (a) and future (b) tense, and singular neuter for the past (c) tense:
(a / b) **Цей фільм лю́бить (люби́тиме) бага́то люде́й.** *Many people like (will like) the movie.*
(c) **Тут жило́ бага́то іспа́нців.** *Many Spanyards lived here.*

Христи́на і Ка́тери́на не ма́ють
жо́дних пробле́м зі здоро́в'ям.

Patient: Negative. No cough but a sore throat.
Physician: Asks when these symptoms started.

Patient: Not sure. Some two to three days ago. First s/he thought that they would pass. They didn't.
Physician: Inquires whether or not s/he has a fever now.

Patient: Just forgot to mention it. During the day it seems s/he does not, but at night s/he feels s/he has a fever.
Physician: Will examine her/his throat now, take her temperature and blood pressure.

Patient: Asks what the diagnosis is.
Physician: With inflammation of throat and fever, in his opinion, it is a common cold. Nothing terribly serious.

Patient: Expresses relief. Asks what treatment to take.
Physician: He will write a prescription for antibiotics. They can be bought in any drugstore.

Patient: Asks how often s/he needs to take them.
Physician: One pill three times a day after meals with water, not with milk or juice. Wishes her a quick recovery.

Ле́кція | Lesson 15

Dialogue:
Щось на зга́дку з Украї́ни
A Memento of Ukraine

Grammar:
Dative plural
Instrumental plural
Impersonal sentences
Conditional mood

Competencies:
Personal opinion
Asking to repeat
Assumptions, wishes, and hypothetical situations
University studies

Народна кераміка - чудовий подарунок кожному на згадку з України.

Ярема Мирний обіцяв поділитися враженнями від футбольного чемпіонату "Євро-2012".

15. Діялог. Щось на згадку з України.

Марта: Пане Василю, ми з Романом їдемо до Канади і хотіли би привезти нашим друзям щось на згадку з України.

Пан Василь: Це чудова ідея, Марто. Отримати гарний український сувенір у подарунок приємно кожному.

Марта: Чи можете порадити нам, де у Києві можна купити гарні сувеніри?

Пан Василь: О, із сувенірами проблем нема. Зараз продають багато всього. Які сувеніри ви маєте на думці?

Марта: Ну, наприклад, фотоальбом про цікаві місця України.

Пан Василь: Альбоми із фотографіями українських міст є у кожній великій книгарні.

Марта: Так, я знаю. Але ми хотіли б фотоальбом із текстом кількома мовами: українською, англійською та французькою.

Пан Василь: Зараз українські фотоальбоми звичайно виходять кількома мовами. Тому що так їх купують як наші, так і міжнародні туристи.

Марта: Батькам наших друзів ми думали подарувати щось із українського народного мистецтва.

Пан Василь: Україна відома своїми писанками, вишиванками та рушниками. Взяти, наприклад, писанки. Кожна – це витвір мистецтва.

Марта: Так, я цілком згідна. Кожна писанка неповторна, кожна розказує власну історію. Писанки подобаються навіть найвибагливішим любителям мистецтва.

Пан Василь: Все це можна купити на Андріївському узвозі у Києві.

Марта: Друзям у Монреалі ми хочемо привезти компакт-диски із українськими фільмами. Обов'язково з англійськими чи французькими субтитрами.

Пан Василь: На жаль, знайти такі компакт-диски – непроста справа.

Марта: Це правда, але нам із Романом пощастило знайти на інтернеті надзвичайно цікавий диск «Волоцюги» із незалежними фільмами.

Пан Василь: Так, дещо справді можна купити на інтернеті. Я теж знаю напевно, що українські фільми продають на ринку «Петрівка».

Марта: Ми вже раз їздили туди. Він величезний і ми швидко заблудилися.

Пан Василь: Звичайно, бо треба було знати, де ятки з українськими фільмами.

Марта: Наступного разу ми саме так і зробимо – спочатку довідаємося про такі ятки.

Пан Василь: До речі, я чув, що недавно видали компакт-диск із фільмом Юрія Іллєнка «Білий птах з чорною ознакою». Він з англійськими, французькими та німецькими субтитрами.

Марта: Невже!? Це чудовий подарунок усім любителям українського кіна. Пане Василю, дякуємо за інформацію.

Пан Васи́ль: Неха́й щасти́ть вам і ва́шим кана́дським дру́зям. Сподіва́юся, що ви поді́литеся з на́ми вра́женнями від Кана́ди пізні́ше, як поверне́теся додо́му.

 ## 15. Dialogue. A Memento of Ukraine.

Marta: Mr. Vasyl, Roman and I are going to Canada and would like to bring our friends a memento of Ukraine.

Mr. Vasyl: That is a wonderful idea, Marta. A nice Ukrainian souvenir as a present is a pleasure for everyone.

Marta: That's right. Can you advise us where in Kyiv one can buy nice souvenirs?

Mr. Vasyl: Well, there is no problem with souvenirs. They sell a lot of everything now. What souvenirs are you looking for?

Marta: Well, for instance, a photo album about the sights of Ukraine.

Mr. Vasyl: There are albums with pictures of Ukrainian cities in any large bookstore.

Marta: Yes, I know. But we'd like a photo album with the text in several languages: Ukrainian, English, and French.

Mr. Vasyl: Now Ukrainian photo albums usually come out in several languages. Because that way both our and international tourists buy them.

Marta: We were going to give our friends' parents some Ukrainian folk art.

Mr. Vasyl: Ukraine is famous for its painted Easter eggs, embroidered shirts, and embroidered towels. Painted Easter eggs, for example. Each is a work of art.

Marta: Yes, I totally agree. Each painted Easter egg is inimitable, and tells its own story. Even the most discriminating art lovers like painted Easter eggs.

Mr. Vasyl: One can buy all this on St. Andrew's Street in Kyiv.

Marta: We want to bring our friends in Montreal DVDs with Ukrainian films. By all means with English or French subtitles.

Mr. Vasyl: Unfortunately, to find such DVDs is not an easy matter.

Marta: That's true, but Roman and I were lucky to find on the Internet an extremely interesting DVD *The Rascals* with independent films.

Mr. Vasyl: Yes, something can indeed be bought on the Internet. I also know for certain that they sell Ukrainian films in the Petrivka Market.

Marta: Once we already went there. It's huge and we quickly got lost.

Mr. Vasyl: Certainly, because you needed to know where kiosks with Ukrainian films were.

Marta: Next time we'll do exactly that - first we'll find out about such kiosks.

Mr. Vasyl: By the way, I heard that recently they released a DVD with the Yuri Illienko film *The White Bird with a Black Mark*. It has English, French, and German subtitles.

Marta: Really!? That is a great gift to all lovers of Ukrainian film. Mr. Vasyl, thanks for the information.

Mr. Vasyl: Good luck to you and your Canadian friends. I hope that you share your impressions of Canada with us later, when you return home.

 ### Нота́тки до діало́гу
Notes on the Dialogue

ми з Рома́ном	Roman and I.
щось на зга́дку з + *G.* **from** or **про** + *A.* about	a souvenir (*lit.* something for remembrance of); **Це вам на зга́дку про ме́не.** *This is something to remember me by.*
пора́д|ити, ~ять, *pf.* + *A.*	to advise, recommend to do sth, suggest doing sth, **Що ви нам пора́дите зроби́ти?** *What will you suggest that we do?*
ціка́ве мі́сце, *nt.*	a sight, interesting place, **Ця кни́жка про ціка́ві місця́ Украї́ни.** *This book is about the sights of Ukraine.*
ко́жний, *var.* **ко́жен,** *pron. and n.*	every, any; when used as a noun it is equivalent to the *Eng.* everybody, anybody, **Ко́жен зна́є, що ...** *Everybody knows that …*
бу́ти відо́м|им + *I.*	to be known, famous for sth, **Украї́нська ку́хня відо́ма борще́м, голубця́ми та варе́никами.** *Ukrainian cuisine is known for its borshch, cabbage rolls, and dumplings.*
уда́чі + *D., phr.*	Good luck!, **У. тобі́ (вам)!** *Good luck to you!,* **Він поба́жав нам уда́чі.** *He wished us good luck.*

Багатьо́м студе́нтам Колумбі́йського університе́ту ціка́во вивча́ти украї́нську.

📖 Грама́тика | Grammar

Дава́льний відмі́нок множини́ Dative Case Plural

Фу́нкція *Function*

Dative case plural is identical in function to dative case singular (see Lesson 9).

Утво́рення *Formation*

Іме́нники Nouns

The nominal dative plural endings: ~ам (~ям)

~ам is used for hard-stem nouns of all genders, **сестра́** *a sister* - **писа́ти се́страм** *to write to sisters*, **ба́тько** *a father* - **дарува́ти батька́м** *to give (presents) to parents*, **студе́нт** *a student* - **поя́снювати студе́нтам** *to explain to students*

~ям is used for soft-stem nouns of all genders, **прия́тель** *a friend* - **допомага́ти прия́телям** *to help friends*, **у́чень** *a pupil* - **поя́снювати у́чням** *to explain to pupils*, **лі́кар** *a physician* - **дзвони́ти лікаря́м** *to ring up physicians*.

🔊 SOUND CHANGES 🔊
in the dative plural of nouns

Dropping of ~о~ (~е~)
~о~ and ~е~ in the last syllable of 2nd declension masculine nouns are dropped in the dative plural,
    куто́к *a corner* - **кутка́м**
    день *a day* - **дням**
    украї́нець *a Ukrainian* - **украї́нцям**
    кіне́ць *the end* - **кінця́м**

Change of ~і~ to ~о~ (~е~)
~і~ changes to ~о~ (~е~) in the final syllable in 2nd declension masculine and 3rd declension feminine nouns,
    m. **кіт** *a cat* - **кота́м**
    m. **папі́р** *a paper* - **папе́рам**
    f. **річ** *a thing* - **реча́м**
    f. **ніч** *a night* - **ноча́м**

 The stress in the dative plural of nouns is usually on the same syllable as in the nominative plural,

N. sg. **сестра́** *a sister* - *N. pl.* **се́стри** *sisters* - *D. pl.* **се́страм**
N. sg. **ба́тько** *a father* - *N. pl.* **батьки́** *fathers* - *D. pl.* **батька́м**

✏️ Note 15.1. Dative Plural of Irregular Nouns

Nouns whose nominative plural differ in stem from singular, derive their dative plural from the nominative plural,

N. sg.	N. pl.	D. pl.
друг *a friend*	дру́зі	дру́зям
люди́на *a person*	лю́ди	лю́дям
дити́на *a child*	ді́ти	ді́тям
дівчина *a girl*	дівча́та	дівча́там
о́ко *an eye*	о́чі	оча́м
кия́нин *a Kyivan*	кия́ни	кия́нам
росія́нин *a Russian*	росія́ни	росія́нам

N. sg. **мі́сто** *a city* - *N. pl.* **міста́** *cities* - *D. pl.* **міста́м**

But *N. sg.* **річ** *a thing* - *N. pl.* **ре́чі** *things* - *D. pl.* **реча́м**
N. sg. **ніч** *a night* - *N. pl.* **но́чі** *nights* - *D. pl.* **ноча́м**

Прикме́тники Adjectives

The adjectival dative plural endings: ~им (~ім)

~им for hard-stem adjectives, **вели́кий** *big* - **вели́ким**, **мали́й** *small* - **мали́м**, **украї́нський** *Ukrainian* - **украї́нським**

~ім for soft-stem adjectives, **си́ній** *blue* - **си́нім**, **оста́нній** *last* - **оста́ннім**, **неда́вній** *recent* - **неда́внім**

Цим музи́кам тре́ба бага́то працюва́ти, щоб могти́ так га́рно гра́ти класи́чні тво́ри.

Ору́дний відмі́нок множини́ Instrumental Case Plural

Фу́нкція Function

The instrumental plural is identical in function to *I. sg.* (Lesson 10). Besides it can denote a future, repetitive, or protracted action as in:

дня́ми *soon, in the next few days (future action)*
вечора́ми *at night, every evening (repetitive action)*
годи́нами *for (many) hours (protracted action)*
місяця́ми *for (many) months (protracted action)*,

Він годи́нами розмовля́є по телефо́ну. *He speaks on the phone for hours.*
Дня́ми бу́де йти нови́й фільм. *Soon there'll be a new film on.*
Ми лю́бимо диви́тися на мо́ре вечора́ми. *We like to look at the sea at night.*

Утво́рення Formation

Іме́нники Nouns

The nominal instrumental plural endings: ~ами (~ями)

~ами for hard-stem nouns of all genders,
ру́чка *a pen* - **писа́ти ру́чками** *to write with pens*
ніж *a knife* - **рі́зати ножа́ми** *to cut with knives*
маши́на *a car* - **ї́здити маши́нами** *to drive by cars*
по́тяг *a train* - **подорожува́ти по́тягами** *to travel by trains*
літа́к *a plane* - **літа́ти літака́ми** *to fly by planes*
парк *a park* - **гуля́ти па́рками** *to walk in parks*
мі́сто *a city* - **ї́хати міста́ми** *to drive through cities*
ліс *a forest* - **бі́гти ліса́ми** *to run through forests*

Дени́с хоті́в пройти́ пі́шки всіма́ ци́ми се́лами Черка́щини.

Львів сла́виться свої́ми шокола́дними цуке́рками на всю Украї́ну.

~ями for soft-stem nouns of all genders,
ву́лиця *a street* - йти ву́лицями *to walk along streets*
америка́нець *an American* - знайо́митися з америка́нцями *to get acquainted with Americans*
учи́тель *a teacher* - листува́тися з учителя́ми *to correspond with teachers*
стіле́ць *a chair* - між стільця́ми *between chairs*
мо́ре *a sea* - за моря́ми *over the seas*
музе́й *a museum* - ходи́ти музе́ями *to walk from museum to museum*
Андрі́й *Andriy* - ба́читися з Андрі́ями *to see Andriys*

🔊 SOUND CHANGES 🔊
in the instrumental plural of nouns

Dropping of ~o~ (~e~)
~o~ and ~e~ in the last syllable of 2nd declension masculine nouns are dropped in the instrumental plural,

куто́к *a corner* - кутка́ми
день *a day* - дня́ми
сон *a dream* - сна́ми
украї́нець *a Ukrainian* - украї́нцями
кіне́ць *the end* - кінця́ми
поча́ток *a beginning* - поча́тками

Change of ~i~ to ~o~ (~e~)
~i~ changes to ~o~ (~e~) in the final syllable in 2nd declension masculine and 3rd declension feminine nouns,
m. кіт *a cat* - кота́ми
m. ніс *a nose* - носа́ми
m. папі́р *a paper* - папера́ми
f. річ *a thing* - реча́ми
f. ніч *a night* - ноча́ми

✏ Note 15.2. Instrumental Plural of Irregular Nouns

Nouns whose nominative plural differ in stem from the singular, derive their instrumental plural from the nominative plural stem,

N. sg.	N. pl.	I. pl.
друг *a friend*	дру́зі	дру́зями
ді́вчина *a girl*	дівча́та	дівча́тами
кия́нин *a Kyivan*	кия́ни	кия́нами
росія́нин *a Russian*	росія́ни	росія́нами

✏ Note 15.3. Irregular Forms of Instrumental Plural

Memorize these forms of instrumental plural:
гро́ші *money* - гроши́ма or грішми́
две́рі *door(s)* - дверми́а or дверми́
лю́ди *people* - людьми́
ді́ти *children* - дітьми́
о́чі *eyes* - очи́ма
пле́чі *shoulders* - плечи́ма
штани́ *pants* - штана́ми or штаньми́

 The stress in the instrumental plural is usually identical to that of the locative plural,

N. sg. стіл *a table* - *L. pl.* на стола́х *on tables* - *I. pl.* під стола́ми *under tables*

N. sg. по́ле *a field* - *L. pl.* на поля́х *on fields* - *I. pl.* над поля́ми *over fields*

N. sg. сестра́ *a sister* - *L. pl.* на се́страх *on sisters* - *I. pl.* ра́зом із се́страми *together with sisters*

N. sg. ба́тько *a father* - *L. pl.* на батька́х *on fathers* - *I. pl.* з батька́ми *with fathers* (or *with parents*).

Прикме́тники Adjectives

The adjectival instrumental plural endings:
~ими (~іми)

~ими for hard-stem adjectives,
вели́кий *big* - **вели́кими**, **мали́й** *small* - **мали́ми**, **украї́нський**
Ukrainian - **украї́нськими**

~іми for soft-stem adjectives,
си́ній *blue* - **си́німи**, **оста́нній** *last* - **оста́нніми**,
неда́вній *recent* - **неда́вніми**

When forming the instrumental plural of adjectives, use the nominative
singular stem. For the instrumental plural of pronouns consult the
appendices (Tables 6-10).

Впра́ви Exercises

15.1. Answer the questions. Use expressions of personal opinion.

Model.

Q Кому́ дівча́та купу́ють кві́ти? *Whom are the girls buying flowers
for?* америка́нці *Americans*

A Я гада́ю, що америка́нцям. *I think for the Americans.*

1. Кому́ украї́нці дару́ють альбо́м? кана́дки.
2. Кому́ дру́зі дзво́нять? батьки́.
3. Кому́ профе́сор поя́снює пра́вило? студе́нти.
4. Кому́ сестра́ посила́є гро́ші? брати́.
5. Кому́ паціє́нти пи́шуть? лікарі́.
6. Кому́ кия́ни подо́баються? льві́в'яни.

15.2. Answer the questions. Make sure that the verb
подо́батися agrees with its subject (for *pres. sg.* **подо́бається** and
for *pres. pl.* **подо́баються**)

Model.

Q Що на́ші украї́нці ду́мають про кіно́? *What do our Ukrainians
think about cinema?*

A Кіно́ подо́бається на́шим украї́нцям. *Our Ukrainians like cinema.*

1. Що їхні дру́зі ду́мають про ці сувені́ри?
2. Що на́ші батьки́ ду́мають про італі́йські фі́льми?
3. Що його́ студе́нтки ду́мають про украї́нську мо́ву?
4. Що твої́ брати́ ду́мають про францу́зьку ку́хню?
5. Що її́ го́сті ду́мають про стари́й Львів?
6. Що мої́ при́ятелі ду́мають про моде́рну архітекту́ру?

 Note 15.4. Особи́ста ду́мка
Personal opinion

На мою́ (твою́, його́, її́, на́шу, ва́шу, їхню) ду́мку	*In my (your, his, her, our, your, their) opinion*
Я гада́ю (вони́ гада́ють), що	*I think (they think) ...*
Я вважа́ю (вони́ вважа́ють), що	*I think (they think) ...*
Я раху́ю (вони́ раху́ють), що	*I reckon (they reckon) ...*
Як на ва́шу ду́мку, це ціка́ва кни́жка?	*In your opinion, is this an interesting book?*
Як ти вважа́єш, нам тре́ба написа́ти їм?	*Do you think we need to write them?*
Як вона́ раху́є, це до́бра пора́да?	*Does she think it is a good advice?*

⌒ 15.3. Pose three questions to each statement. Give a short answer to each of the questions.

Model 1.
Ⓠ Кому́ подо́бається кіно́? *Who likes the cinema?*
Ⓐ На́шим украї́нцям. *Our Ukrainians.*

Model 2.
Ⓠ Чиї́м украї́нцям подо́бається кіно́? *Whose Ukrainians like cinema?*
Ⓐ На́шим. *Ours.*

Model 3.
Ⓠ Що подо́бається на́шим украї́нцям? *What do our Ukrainians like?*
Ⓐ Кіно́. *The cinema.*

1. Їхнім дру́зям подо́баються сувені́ри з Ко́сова.
2. На́шим батька́м подо́баються америка́нські фі́льми.
3. Його́ студе́нткам подо́бається по́льська мо́ва.
4. Твої́м брата́м подо́бається кита́йська ку́хня.
5. Її́ го́стям подо́бається стари́й Луцьк.
6. Мої́м при́ятелям подо́бається стара́ архітекту́ра.

⌒ 15.4. Answer the questions. Indicate the need to do something. Use **тре́ба** + *logical subject in the dative plural.*

Model.
Ⓠ Кому́ тре́ба купи́ти квитки́? *Who needs to buy tickets?*
  украї́нські тури́сти *Ukrainian tourists*
Ⓐ Украї́нським тури́стам. *Ukrainian tourists (do).*

1. Кому́ тре́ба пи́ти молоко́? малі́ ді́ти
2. Кому́ тре́ба зна́ти фі́зику? хоро́ші інжене́ри
3. Кому́ тре́ба ї́сти городину́? старі́ лю́ди
4. Кому́ тре́ба займа́тися спо́ртом? молоді́ дівча́та
5. Кому́ тре́ба розмовля́ти украї́нською мо́вою? нові́ акто́ри
6. Кому́ тре́ба поба́чити Оде́су? по́льські го́сті
7. Кому́ тре́ба купи́ти а́вто? мої́ сусі́ди
8. Кому́ тре́ба подиви́тися цей фільм? на́ші да́вні при́ятелі
9. Кому́ тре́ба ви́вчити украї́нську? росі́йські студе́нтки
10. Кому́ тре́ба замо́вити готе́ль? англі́йські лікарі́

⌒ 15.5. Answer the questions. Put the noun in the dative plural. Then replace it with a corresponding pronoun.

Model 1.
Ⓠ Кому́ дзво́нить Мико́ла? *Whom does Mykola call?* батьки́ *parents*
Ⓐ Він *дзво́нить батька́м. He calls his parents.*
  Він *дзво́нить їм. He calls them.*

1. Кому́ пи́ше лист О́льга? близькі́ по́други

Цим двом чоловіка́м тре́ба
поговори́ти про нови́ни.

2. Кому́ вони́ допомага́ють? старі́ дру́зі
3. Кому́ ти хо́чеш сказа́ти пра́вду? їхні матері́
4. Кому́ купу́є штани́ Марі́я? малі́ ді́ти
5. Кому́ вона́ посила́є гро́ші? на́ші ро́дичі
6. Кому́ ви дає́те пора́ду? знайо́мі львів'я́ни

15.6. Give short answers. Use only adjectives or possessive pronouns in the dative plural.

Model.

Q Яки́м дру́зям дзво́нить Мико́ла? *What friends does Mykola call?*
близьки́й *close*
A Близьки́м. *Close (ones).*

1. Яки́м студе́нтам ка́же про це профе́сор? оста́нній
2. Яки́м дівча́там ти подо́баєшся? розу́мна і га́рна
3. Яки́м ді́тям лише́ оди́н рік? ця мала́
4. Чиї́м брата́м тре́ба працюва́ти? їхній
5. Чиї́м тітка́м ми допомо́жемо за́втра? ва́ша
6. Яки́м чоловіка́м ти не ві́риш? незнайо́мий
7. Яки́м тури́сткам тре́ба поясни́ти це? америка́нська та кана́дська
8. Яки́м лю́дям він дає́ інформа́цію? літній

15.7. Engage in an exchange using the vocabulary given.

Model.

Q Ці чоловіки́ – економі́сти? *Are these men economists?*
A Ні, але́ вони́ хо́чуть ста́ти економі́стами.
No, but they want to become economists.

1. Ті кия́ни – журналі́сти?
2. Ва́ші сусі́ди – інжене́ри?
3. Марі́я та Яри́на – вчительки́?
4. Їхні знайо́мі – письме́нниці?
5. Її́ брати́ – лікарі́?
6. Ці молоді́ матері́ – акто́рки?
7. Твої́ при́ятелі – харків'я́ни?
8. Його́ сини́ – худо́жники?
9. Ці дівча́та – експе́рти?
10. Ті жінки́ – офіція́нтки?

15.8. Answer the questions. Use the instrumental plural.

Model.

Q Ті чоловіки́ – економі́сти? *Are those men economists?*
До́брий *good*
A Ще ні, але́ вони́ коли́сь ста́нуть до́брими економі́стами.
Not yet, but one day they will become good economists.

1. Ці хло́пці – бізнесме́ни? бага́тий
2. Ці пані́ – вчительки́? чудо́вий
3. Її́ сусі́дки – худо́жниці? оригіна́льний
4. Його́ дядьки́ – такси́сти? га́рний
5. Твої́ брати́ – фото́графи? ціка́вий
6. Ва́ші при́ятелі – ку́харі? славе́тний

Note 15.5. Повторі́ть, будь ла́ска. Come again, please.

Memorize the expressions used to solicit a repetition of what has been said:

Дару́йте! *Gal.* **Про́шу!**	*Come again! (used as a request to repeat what was said; pronounced with a rising intonation)*
Повторі́ть, будь ла́ска.	*Repeat please; come again, please.*
Що ви сказа́ли?	*What did you say?*
Ви́бачте, я не почу́в. (*f.* **почу́ла**)	*Sorry, I did not hear you.*
Ви́бачте, я вас не зрозумі́|в. (*f.* **зрозумі́ла**)	*Sorry, I didn't understand you.*
Gal. **Перепро́шую, що ви сказа́ли?**	*Excuse me, what did you say?*

Його́ оде́ські по́други хо́чуть ста́ти акто́рками теа́тру.

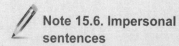

Note 15.6. Impersonal sentences

The impersonal sentence of the type *They sell vegetables here.* is equivalent to the Ukrainian sentence that has no subject and starts with an adverbial modifier of place or of time, that usually completes the English sentence,

Тут продаю́ть горо́дину. *They sell vegetables here.*

The absence of subject means that the sentence does not refer to anybody in particular and is a general characteristic of some place. Other examples of impersonal sentences:

У цій шко́лі вча́ть бага́то мов. *They study many languages at this school.*
Мину́лого ро́ку тут готува́ли чудо́ву їжу. *Last year, they made great food here.*
На фестива́лі бу́дуть пока́зувати лише́ нові́ фі́льми. *They will show only new films at the festival.*

У цій кна́йпі подаю́ть найсмачні́ше у мі́сті пи́во.

7. Ці америка́нки – мандрі́вниці? вели́кий
8. Ці дівча́та – акто́рки? популя́рний

15.9. Give a complete answer to each question. Use the instrumental plural.

Model.
Q Чим ви ціка́витеся? *What are you interested in?*
україн́ські пісні́ *Ukrainian songs*
A Я ціка́влюся українськими пісня́ми.
I am interested in Ukrainian songs.

1. Чим ти користу́єшся? їхні улю́блені словники́
2. Чим вони́ ціка́вляться? його́ старі́ ме́блі
3. Чим Рома́н пи́ше? свої́ чо́рні олівці́
4. Чим ми пла́тимо? твої́ украї́нські гро́ші
5. Чим ви малю́єте? ті зеле́ні фа́рби
6. Чим вони́ їздять? ці си́ні автобуси
7. Ким він ціка́виться? мої́ япо́нські знайо́мі
8. Чим заробля́є на життя́ Наді́я? письмо́ві пере́клади
9. Чим отру́ївся Павло́ Москале́нко? яки́сь гриби́
10. Ким назва́ла Ле́ся Яросла́ва і Тара́са спра́вжні дру́зі

15.10. Say and write the sentences in Ukrainian. Make sure that:

1) no subject is used;
2) the end of the English sentence is the beginning of the Ukrainian one.

Model.
C *They study many languages at this university.*
A У цьо́му університе́ті вивча́ють бага́то мов.

1. They sell meat in these stores.
2. They buy groceries in those supermarkets.
3. They show wonderful films in these movie theaters.
4. They offer inexpensive rooms in those new dormitories.
5. They rent out different cars there.
6 They sing very nice songs in these regions of the country.
7. They prepared good experts at Kyiv National University.
8. They like to eat a lot in their country.
9. They pay only with cash in those restaurants.
10. They serve very good beer in Lviv bars.
11. They will always help at these tourist agencies.
12. They speak Ukrainian and English in these banks.
13. They will always show you the way on the streets of Kyiv.
14. Once they taught many foreign languages at this school.
15. They do not play American football in this part of the world.
16. Many years ago they knew all Italian operas in his home village.
17. Earlier they did not accept credit cards in theses stores.
18. They don't stop at such a wonderful hotel for only one day, do they?

15.11. Say and write the sentences in Ukrainian. Use the vocabulary and grammar of this and previous lessons. If necessary, consult the dictionary.

1. We'd like to give this album to our new Italian friends as a memento of their trip to Ukraine.
2. Can you give my parents advice on where to find some information about the sights of Galicia?
3. Everybody knows that Ukrainians who live in the region of the Carpathian Mountains are called the *Hutsuls.*
4. The region of Poltava is famous for delicious pears, the region of Kherson for its sweet watermelons, and the region of Nizhyn for its wonderful cucumbers.
5. Oleksa called his sisters and wished them good luck at their photo exhibition.
6. In my opinion we need to buy train tickets and book hotels now.
7. I think that, at this agency, they help tourists to find inexpensive accommodation.
8. They do not accept credit cards in this supermarket.
9. Thanks to your recommendations and very good tourist maps we easily found all museums and galleries.
10. For one month, they wrote their close friends about their travels through cities and villages of Ukraine.

Украї́нців, що живу́ть у Карпа́тах, назива́ють гуцу́лами.

15.12. Listen carefully to the questions and answer each of them using Dialogue 15.

1. Куди́ ско́ро пої́дуть Ма́рта з Рома́ном?
2. Що хо́чуть привезти́ вони́ свої́м кана́дським дру́зям?
3. До кого́ зверта́ється Ма́рта по пора́ду?
4. Що ду́має про украї́нські сувені́ри у подару́нок пан Васи́ль?
5. Яки́й фотоальбо́м шука́ють Ма́рта з Рома́ном?
6. У яки́х магази́нах мо́жна знайти́ фотоальбо́ми Украї́ни?
7. Чому́ такі́ фотоальбо́ми звича́йно видаю́ть кількома́ мо́вами?
8. Що хо́чуть подарува́ти Ма́рта з Рома́ном батька́м свої́х кана́дських дру́зів?
9. Яки́м мисте́цтвом відо́ма Украї́на у сві́ті?
10. Чому́, на ду́мку Ма́рти, писанки́ подо́баються на́віть найвиба́гливішим люби́телям мисте́цтва?
11. Де у Ки́єві мо́жна купи́ти ви́роби наро́дного мисте́цтва?
12. Що вони́ хо́чуть подарува́ти свої́м дру́зям в Монреа́лі?
13. Із яки́ми субти́трами шука́ють вони́ украї́нські фі́льми?
14. Де у Ки́єві мо́жна знайти́ украї́нські фі́льми?
15. Чому́ Ма́рта з Рома́ном загуби́лися пе́рший раз на Петрі́вці?
16. Яки́й фільм неда́вно ви́дали на компа́кт-ди́ску?
17. Що ду́має Ма́рта про цей фільм?
18. Які́ подару́нки ви купи́ли свої́м дру́зям на уроди́ни?

 Note 15.7. Conditional Mood

The condition under which something can take place, is expressed in a two-part sentence. One part, called the main clause, describes an action. The other, called the subordinate clause, lays out the condition under which it can take place,
(1) Robert reads the newspapers if (2) there is no work to be done.

The two clauses are always linked by a conjunction of condition *(if.., provided that.., on the condition that.., etc.).*

There are two types of condition in Ukrainian:
1) the real and possible condition
2) the hypothetical and impossible condition

Note 15.8. Real possible condition

A real possible condition indicates that the action can take place if certain realistic terms are met. The main clause refers either to the present or future, but never to past time. The conditional clause can refer to the past, present, and future. For examples take a look at the chart on the right part of page.

main clause	conj.	conditional clause
pres. **Мо́жете купи́ти комп'ю́тер,**	**якщо́**	*pres.* **ма́єте гро́ші.**
You can buy a computer	*if*	*you have money.*

main clause	conj.	conditional clause
pres. **Мо́жете купи́ти комп'ю́тер,**	**якщо́**	*pa.* **ви ще не купи́ли його́.**
You can buy a computer	*if*	*you have not yet bought it.*

main clause	conj.	conditional clause
fut. **Я куплю́ комп'ю́тер**	**якщо́**	*fut.* **ма́тиму гро́ші.**
I will buy a computer	*if*	*I have money.*

Note 15.9. Conjunctions of Real Condition

The conjunctions of the real and possible condition are:

якщо́ *if, colloq.* **як** *if,* **коли́** *when,*
як ті́льки *as soon as*
form. **за умо́ви, що ...** *on the condition that ...*

Note 15.10. Future Condition

If the real and possible condition refers to the future time, the Ukrainian conditional clause is also in the future, not in the present, as is the case in English,

Петро́ поя́снить вам пра́вила, якщо́ ви попро́сите.
Petro will explain the rules to you, if you ask (lit. if you will ask).

Ти ско́ро ви́дужаєш, якщо́ не бу́де ускла́днень.
You'll soon recover, if there are no complications (lit. if there will be no complications).

Я напишу́ вам, як знайду́ відповідь.
I will write you if I find the answer (lit. if I will find the answer).

Наші студе́нти за́вжди сиді́ли до кінця́ ле́кції, якщо́ вона́ була́ ціка́вою.

🎧 **15.13.** Translate the sentences of real possible condition into English. Pay attention to the tense of the conditional clause.

1. Не жур́іться, якщо́ ви не закі́нчили робо́ти.
2. Ната́ля поя́снить завда́ння, якщо́ ви не були́ на ле́кції.
3. Я принесу́ моро́зива, якщо́ ви лю́бите десе́рт.
4. Стефа́н подзво́нить пізні́ше, якщо́ хо́чете.
5. Ми ви́беремо подару́нки за́втра, якщо́ це зручні́ше для вас.
6. Кра́ще одягну́ти щось те́пле, якщо́ ви вечеря́тимете надво́рі.
7. Я користува́тимуся інтерне́том, якщо́ це бу́де потрі́бно.
8. Хло́пці змо́жуть подиви́тися цей фільм, якщо́ вони́ його́ не ба́чили.
9. Купі́ть мені́ газе́ти, якщо́ ма́тимете можли́вість.
10. Ми не зустріча́тимемося, якщо́ бу́де дощ.
11. Тре́ба обов'язко́во поїхати до Оде́си, якщо́ вони́ там ніко́ли не бува́ли.
12. Ми бу́демо ра́ді, якщо́ ви не запі́знитеся.

15.14. Transform these pairs of sentences into one sentence expressing a real and possible condition. Determine the tense to which the main and conditional clauses refer. Translate.

Model.

🅲 Я покажу́ Окса́ні Ки́їв. *I'll show Oksana Kyiv.* Вона́ хо́че. *She wants.*

🅐 Я покажу́ Окса́ні Ки́їв, якщо́ вона́ хо́че. *I'll show Oksana Kyiv, if she wants.*

1. Ма́рта закі́нчить робо́ту. Ми всі їй допомо́жемо.
2. Марко́ почека́є два́дцять хвили́н. Ми бу́демо запізнюватися.
3. Ми прийде́мо до вас в го́сті. Ви нас запро́сите.
4. Іва́н чита́є нови́ни. Марі́я не розмовля́є по телефо́ну.
5. Бори́с піде́ на ви́ставку. Ви пошле́те йому́ запро́шення.
6. Ната́ля зве́рнеться до лі́каря. Її до́нці ста́не гі́рше.
7. Ми ку́пимо всі потрі́бні проду́кти. Богда́н зро́бить вече́рю.
8. Іва́н за́вжди посила́є гро́ші сестрі́. Вона́ про́сить допомогти́.
9. Га́ля і́ноді пока́зувала го́стям мі́сто. Була́ до́бра пого́да.
10. Я дочита́ю кни́жку. Я ма́тиму час і бажа́ння.
11. Перекажі́ть віта́ння батька́м. Ви ба́читимете їх на Різдво́.
12. Ви мо́жете зупини́тися у нас. Ви не хо́чете жи́ти в готе́лі.

🎧 **15.15.** Engage your partner in an exchange in Ukrainian.

Model.

🅲 Вони́ іду́ть до теа́тру. *They are going to the theater.*
Там бу́де ціка́ва п'є́са. *There'll be an interesting play there.*

🆀 Це пра́вда, що вони́ йду́ть до теа́тру?
Is it true that they are going to the theater?

🅐 Так, пра́вда, але́ ті́льки якщо́ там бу́де ціка́ва п'є́са.
Yes, it is, but only if there's an interesting play there.

1. Ма́рта сього́дні закі́нчить робо́ту. Ми їй допомо́жемо.
2. Марко́ нас почека́є. Ми не бу́демо до́вго у ліка́рні.
3. Петре́нки при́йдуть до них в го́сті. Ви теж при́йдете.
4. Іва́н гра́є на скри́пці. В ха́ті ніко́го нема́є.
5. Бори́с пої́де до Ха́ркова. Він зна́йде там деше́вий готе́ль.
6. Ната́ля вече́рятиме вдо́ма. Вони́ з чолові́ком не пі́дуть до рестора́ну.
7. Стрі́льчуки ку́плять нову́ ха́ту. Вони́ прода́дуть стару́ кварти́ру.
8. Іва́н чита́тиме нам пое́зію. Всі його́ слу́хатимуть і не розмовля́тимуть.
9. Вона́ пока́же го́стям мі́сто. Не бу́де дощу́.
10. О́ля дочита́є кни́жку до суббо́ти. Вона́ ма́тиме час.
11. Ви з дру́зями диви́тиметеся нову́ виста́ву Андрі́я Жо́лдака в теа́трі "Березі́ль". Ми змо́жемо діста́ти квитки́.
12. У суббо́ту ти зро́биш чудо́ву вече́рю для всіє́ї роди́ни. Хтось із вас допомо́же мені́ на ку́хні.

Людми́ла пої́де з Іва́ном на мо́ре, якщо́ він пообіця́є, що бу́де че́мним.

Йо́сип Марчу́к обов'язко́во пі́де з дівча́тами по я́годи, якщо́ бу́де до́бра пого́да.

Note 15.11. Hypothetical and impossible condition

A hypothetical and impossible condition indicates that:

1) the action is presented as hypothetical and could still take place, if certain terms were met, *She would help John if John asked her.*

2) the action could have taken place but never did, because the conditions for it were never met, or cannot be met, *She would have helped John if John had asked her (It's too late now).*

In Ukrainian, only the context can help make a distinction between the hypothetical *(would do)* and unreal impossible *(would have done)* condition.

The conditional clause is linked with the main one by the conjunction **якби** *if*. The verb in the main clause is in the past perfective or imperfective plus the particle **б (би)** immediately after it, while the verb in the conditional clause is in the past tense,

main clause	conj.	conditional clause
Він купи́в би комп'ю́тер	**якби**	(він) мав гро́ші.
He would buy a computer	*if*	*he had money. (hypothetical)*
He would have bought a computer	*if*	*he had had money. (unreal)*

Note 15.12. Word Order in Conditional Sentences

The main and conditional clauses can exchange places in a sentence, with no significant change of meaning,
Він зрозумі́є, якщо́ ви поя́сните.
He'll understand, if you explain.
Якщо́ ви поя́сните, він зрозумі́є.
If you explain, he'll understand.
Іва́н купи́в би це, якби́ він мав гро́ші. *Ivan would buy it if he had the money.* **Якби́ Іва́н мав гро́ші, він купи́в би це.** *If Ivan had the money he would buy it.*

Якби́ Оле́сь спра́вді коха́в мене́, він би ...

⌒ 15.16. Transform the real condition into a hypothetical one. Translate into English.

Model.
C Він зрозумі́є план, якщо́ ви поя́сните.
He will understand the plan, if you explain.
A Він зрозумі́в би план, якби́ ви поясни́ли.
He would understand the plan, if you explained.

Note 15.13. Hypotheses

Unreal condition is used to describe hypothetical or imagined situations,
hypothesis
Якби́ ми вчи́лися ра́зом, ми ста́ли б найкра́щими дру́зями. *If we studied together, we would become best friends.*
wish
Якби́ ті́льки він прийшо́в. *If only he came.* **Якби́ лише́ ви знали, як це ва́жко.** *If only you knew how hard it is.*

1. Офіція́нтка принесе́ ка́ву, якщо́ ви її замо́вите.
2. Оле́на пої́де до крамни́ці, якщо́ у нас закі́нчилися проду́кти.
3. Стефа́н подзво́нить пізні́ше, якщо́ О́ля хо́че.
4. Ми ви́беремо подару́нки за́втра, якщо́ ви ще нічо́го не купи́ли.
5. Го́сті одя́гнуть щось те́пле, якщо́ вони́ відпочива́тимуть надво́рі.
6. Я користува́тимуся інтерне́том, якщо́ це бу́де потрі́бно.
7. Хло́пці змо́жуть подиви́тися цей фільм на компа́кт-ди́ску, якщо́ вони́ його́ не ба́чили.
8. Сергі́й ку́пить мені́ газе́ти, якщо́ він ма́тиме таку́ можли́вість.
9. Ми не зустріча́тимемося, якщо́ бу́де дощ.
10. Ми пої́демо до Оде́си, якщо́ зна́йдемо квитки́ на вечі́рній по́тяг.
11. Ді́ти боя́лися ходи́ти па́рком, якщо́ вони́ були́ без батькі́в.
12. Юрко́ подзво́нить їй, якщо́ він не забу́де.

Ми теж пішли́ б на заба́ву, якби́ не ма́ли так бага́то завда́ння від професора́ Шевче́нка.

15.17. Transform the sentences in the previous exercise so that the conditional clause comes before the main one.

15.18. Complete the sentences and describe an imagined situation.

1. Якби́ ти мене́ люби́ла (люби́в), …
2. Якби́ всі студе́нти до́бре вчи́лися, …
3. Якби́ Петро́ й Іри́на працюва́ли ра́зом над проє́ктом, …
4. Якби́ Семе́н закі́нчив університе́т цього́ ро́ку, …
5. Якби́ виклада́ч задава́в нам ме́нше завда́ння, …
6. Якби́ ви хоті́ли святкува́ти уроди́ни, …
7. Якби́ ця кни́жка кошту́вала ме́нше, …
8. Якби́ Тама́ра Михальчу́к знайшла́ пра́цю, …
9. Якби́ я ви́грав (ви́грала) лотере́ю, …
10. Якби́ я був (була́) Президе́нтом Украї́ни, …

Вишива́нки в нас традиці́йно одяга́ють на свя́то.

Якби́ ви чу́ли, як га́рно співа́ють різдвя́ні коля́дки ці пластуни́ із Нью-Йо́рку!

 Завда́ння для Міжнаро́дної мере́жі

15.19. Using the Internet, search these key words in Ukrainian **пи́санка, кра́шанка, вишива́нка, украї́нський рушни́к** and provide answers to the questions.

1. Що таке пи́санка?
2. Чим відрізня́ється пи́санка від кра́шанки?
3. Що таке украї́нський рушни́к?
4. Що таке́ вишива́нка чи вишива́на соро́чка?

15.20. Enact a conversation with a partner. Use the material you learned in this and previous lessons. If necessary consult the dictionary.

Сце́нка за сцена́рієм «Поку́пки»
Scripted Skit: *"Shopping"*

John (Джон): Would like to know where one can buy clothes and Ukrainian souvenirs.
Valentyna (Валенти́на): Asks exactly what clothes he needs.

John: Some shirts and pants for winter.
Valentyna: Suggests visiting the Central Department Store and the Ukraina Department Store. Kyiv is famous for these two stores.

John: Asks about their location and how to get to them.
Valentyna: The Central Department Store is on the corner of Khreshchatyk and Bohdan Khmelnytsky Streets. One can get there by metro, the stop is called Khreshchatyk.

John: He lives close to the metro station called *the Ukraina Palace of Culture* (Пала́ц культу́ри «Украї́на»). It is a direct line to Khreshchatyk. Asks about prices at the Central Department Store.
Valentyna: Generally it is not very cheap. Clothes from Europe can be quite expensive.

John: Thanks for the advice and asks where one can buy souvenirs, something that is typically Ukrainian.
Valentyna: Ukraine is known for folk embroidery, wood-carving, pottery, and painted Easter eggs. People like to give them as presents or mementos of Ukraine.

John: This is exactly what he wants. Asks whether they sell these things in those two department stores.
Valentyna: Responds that maybe they do, but the best place to buy them is St. Andrew's Street. It's a street market (ву́личний ри́нок).

John: Asks about its hours of operation.
Valentyna: It is open every day of the week from nine o'clock till the evening.

John: Asks whether or not one can find there anything else interesting besides the traditional Ukrainian souvenirs.
Valentyna: They also sell antiques, old books, magazines, photographs, coins, and many other strange things. Lots of modern kitsch (кіч), particularly paintings.

John: This place seems interesting and he intends to visit it, if the weather is fine.
Valentyna: The street is famous not only for its art, but its cafés, restaurants, and particularly for the vendors who come from all the corners of Ukraine.

John: Asks whether Valentyna can show him St. Andrew's Street.
Valentyna: She will do it with pleasure. It's been a long time since she was there.

У Чернівецькому національному університеті
імени Юрія Федько́вича ціка́во навча́тися.

Навча́ння в університе́ті University Studies

15.21 Listen carefully to the text online and summarize its contents in English. Rely on the points below.

1. Про що оповіда́ння?
2. Хто головни́й геро́й оповіда́ння? Що ви про ньо́го дізна́лися?
3. Де та коли́ відбува́ється ця істо́рія?

15.22. Fill the blanks with either **вивча́ти** or **навча́тися.** Translate the completed sentences.

1. Мій прия́тель _____ істо́рію Украї́ни.
2. Вони́ ма́ють _____ ці пра́вила на насту́пне заня́ття.
3. Щоб розмовля́ти украї́нською тре́ба _____ п'ятсо́т слів.
4. У яко́му університе́ті _____ цей юна́к?
5. Які́ предме́ти ти _____ на пе́ршому ку́рсі?

Note 15.14. How to say STUDY

The verbs **вивча́ти** and **навча́тися** are both translated as *to study*, but they mean different things.

⭐ **Вивча́ти** and its colloquial synonym **вчи́ти** are transitive. Both require a direct object in the accusative and are used to say WHAT one studies,

Торі́к ми вивча́ли (вчи́ли) істо́рію.
Last year we studied history.
Вона́ лю́бить вивча́ти (вчи́ти) чужі́ мо́ви. *She likes to study foreign languages.*
Both have the perfective form **ви́вчити**, which is used to signify that a rule, text, or other limited amount of information was or will be learned (memorized),
На за́втра я ма́ю ви́вчити два́дцять нови́х слів. *For tomorrow, I need to learn twenty new words.*
Мо́жна вивча́ти (вчи́ти) украї́нську літерату́ру все життя́ і ніко́ли її́ не ви́вчити. *One can study Ukrainian literature all life long and never learn it all.*

⭐ **Навча́тися** and its synonym **вчи́тися,** are intransitive and are never followed by a direct accusative object. They are used to say WHERE, WHEN, or HOW one studies,
Де (як) він навча́ється (вчи́ться)?
Where (how) does he study?
Він навча́ється (вчи́ться) у Ха́рківському університе́ті. *He studies at Kharkiv University.*
Він ду́же до́бре навча́ється (вчи́ться). *He studies very well.*

Both **навча́тися** and **вчи́тися** have the perfective form **навчи́тися** + inf., which is used to signify *to learn, master doing sth,*
Він ра́но навчи́вся чита́ти. *He learned to read early.* **Коли́ ти навчи́вся танцюва́ти та́нго?** *When did you learn to dance the tango?*

6. Мали́й Петро́ вже _____ писа́ти.

7. Я за́вжди́ хоті́ла _____ літерату́ру, щоб ста́ти письме́нницею.

8. Хто тут _____ геогра́фію?

9. У цьо́му університе́ті _____ украї́нський письме́нник Іва́н Франко́.

15.23. Skim the text «Лука́ш Нова́чу́к – майбу́тній журналі́ст» on the next page, find Ukrainian equivalents of these expressions and write them down in their dictionary form.

1. a second-year student
2. to work in school for three years
3. to decide to become a journalist
4. to consist of two semesters
5. all this means, that
6. to start at nine in the morning
7. one of the best universities of Ukraine
8. to study interesting subjects
9. not the most interesting instructors
10. Wi-Fi network
11. on the condition that
12. to do interviews with boring people

Льві́вський націона́льний університе́т – оди́н із найстарі́ших і найпрести́жніших в Украї́ні.

🌐 **Завда́ння для Міжнаро́дної мере́жі**

15.24. Find official websites of at least three Ukrainian universities. Try to find the following information about each of them and fill out the questionnaire in Ukrainian.

На́зва університе́ту	Адре́са та телефо́н	Факульте́ти

⌒ **15.25.** Answer these questions and provide a maximum number of words that can be used in combination with the ones given below in bold. Consult the dictionary if need be.

Model.

Q Де мо́жна **відпочива́ти**? *Where can one vacation?*

A. **Відпочива́ти** мо́жна: на мо́рі, на рі́чці, на о́зері, на пля́жі, у го́рах і т. д. *One can vacation: by the sea, by a river, by a lake, on a beach, in the mountains, etc.*

1. Що мо́жна **вивча́ти** в університе́ті?
2. Які́ **ку́рси** мо́жуть бу́ти?
3. Де мо́жна **навча́тися**?
4. Які́ **програ́ми навча́ння** мо́жуть бу́ти?
5. Ким за фа́хом мо́жна **ста́ти**?
6. Що **мо́жна роби́ти** в міжнаро́дній мере́жі?
7. Що **мо́жна роби́ти** на вихідні́?
8. Чим **мо́жна займа́тися** у спортклу́бі?
9. Де мо́жна ціка́во **провести́** ві́льний час?

Лише́ че́рез ві́сім ро́ків Марко́, Га́нна та Андрі́й посту́плять до університе́ту.

⌒ **15.26.** Read the text below then answer these questions.

1. У яко́му університе́ті навча́ється Лука́ш?
2. У яко́му університе́ті він закі́нчив бакала́врську програ́му?
3. З яко́го предме́ту спеціялізува́вся Лука́ш на бакала́врській програ́мі?
4. Що він роби́в після закі́нчення бакала́врської програ́ми?
5. Як до́вго трива́є навча́льний рік у Льві́вському університе́ті?
6. Які́ предме́ти вивча́є Лука́ш тепе́р?
7. Як звича́йно він прово́дить свої́ зимо́ві вака́ції?
8. Що він роби́тиме на зимо́ві вака́ції цьо́го ра́зу?
9. Яки́й ро́зклад ма́тиме Лука́ш у цьо́му семе́стрі?
10. Скі́льки заня́ть ма́є Лука́ш щодня́?
11. Що подо́бається Лукаше́ві у його́ тепе́рішньому житті́?
12. Чим займа́вся Лука́ш в газе́ті «Нови́ни Галичини́»?
13. З ким він роби́в інтерв'ю́ для ціє́ї газе́ти мину́лого лі́та?
14. З яко́ю мето́ю він пої́де в Карпа́ти?
15. За яко́ї умо́ви пої́де у Карпа́ти Лука́ш?
16. Чим займа́ється Лука́ш в університе́тському спортклу́бі?
17. Де збира́ються студе́нти журналі́стики на ка́ву у ві́льний час?

Лука́ш Новачу́к – майбу́тній журналі́ст.

Лука́ш Новачу́к навча́ється у Льві́вському націона́льному університе́ті і́мени Іва́на Франка́. За́раз він – студе́нт дру́гого ку́рсу маґі́стерської програ́ми журналі́стики. Бакала́врську програ́му він закі́нчив у Остро́зькій акаде́мії зі спеція́льности украї́нська літерату́ра та мо́ва. Він три ро́ки працюва́в у шко́лі, а пото́м ви́рішив ста́ти журналі́стом і поступи́в до Льві́вського університе́ту. Навча́льний рік тут склада́ється із двох семе́стрів: осі́ннього та весня́ного. Навча́ння почина́ється пе́ршого ве́ресня і трива́є до кінця́ тра́вня. Після осі́ннього семе́стру прихо́дять зимо́ві вака́ції, а після весня́ного – лі́тні.

У цьо́му семе́стрі Лука́ш записа́вся на п'ять ку́рсів, а са́ме: істо́рія журналі́стики, мо́ва украї́нської пре́си, європе́йська літерату́ра двадця́того столі́ття, англі́йська мо́ва та класи́чна філосо́фія. Все це зна́чить, що Лука́ш ма́тиме ду́же бага́то робо́ти. Щодня́ у ньо́го бу́де по три, а ча́сом на́віть чоти́ри заня́ття, п'ять днів на ти́ждень. Ле́кції почина́тимуться о дев'я́тій ра́нку та з пере́рвами трива́тимуть до тре́тьої, а ча́сом на́віть до сьо́мої годи́ни ве́чора. Але́ таки́й ро́зклад не пробле́ма для Лука́ша. Йому́ ду́же подо́бається вчи́тися в одно́му із найкра́щих університе́тів Украї́ни, вивча́ти ціка́ві предме́ти, ма́ти спра́ву із чудо́вими викладача́ми та жи́ти у чарі́вному мі́сті Льво́ві. На жаль, у його́ ро́зкладі є та́кож нудні́ заня́ття із не найціка́вішими викладача́ми. Це нічо́го, бо він не за́вжди хо́дить на такі́ заня́ття.

Лука́ш прово́дить бага́то ча́су в бібліоте́ці, чита́є, сиди́ть у мере́жі, шука́є та вивча́є потрі́бні матерія́ли. Для цьо́го мо́жна користува́тися університе́тськими комп'ю́терами, або́ свої́м вла́сним, бо скрізь в університе́ті є бездро́това мере́жа.

Зимо́ві вака́ції Лука́ш звича́йно прово́дить з батька́ми у рі́дному мі́сті Лу́цьку. Проте́ ціє́ї зими́ він пої́де з дру́зями на ли́жі у Карпа́ти, за умо́ви, що бу́де сніг. Тому́ що до сих пір сні́гу в Карпа́тах ще не було́. Під час оста́нніх лі́тніх вака́цій Лука́ш працюва́в журналі́стом у газе́ті «Нови́ни Галичини́», писа́в статті́ про життя́ Льво́ва. Для цьо́го йому́ тре́ба було́ бага́то чита́ти, ходи́ти на прес-конфере́нції, роби́ти інтерв'ю́ ча́сом із ціка́вими, а ча́сом із нудни́ми людьми́.

Ча́сто пі́сля заня́ть Лука́ш прово́дить кі́лька годи́н в університе́тському спортклу́бі, щоб відпочи́ти, погра́ти у футбо́л чи те́ніс. На вихідні́ він лю́бить бува́ти у теа́трі, кіні́, чи на конце́ртах популя́рної му́зики. Якщо́ в мі́сті нема́є нічо́го ціка́вого, вони́ з і́ншими студе́нтами журналі́стики про́сто збира́ються на ка́ву і розмо́ви у своє́му улю́бленому "Музе́ї іде́й" на ву́лиці Валові́й у середмі́сті Льво́ва. Там за́вжди мо́жна ціка́во провести́ ві́льний час і дізна́тися щось нове́.

∩ **15.27.** Correct these statements based on the text above.

1. Головно́го геро́я оповіда́ння зва́ти Левко́ Нови́цький.
2. За́раз головни́й геро́й – студе́нт четве́ртого ку́рсу.
3. Він навча́ється на бакала́врській програ́мі Оде́ського університе́ту.
4. Він хо́дить на всі заня́ття – ціка́ві й нудні́.
5. Головни́й геро́й звича́йно прово́дить зимо́ві вака́ції на мо́рі.
6. Його́ рі́дне мі́сто назива́ється Чернівці́.
7. Мину́лого лі́та він працюва́в фото́графом у журна́лі «Університе́тське життя́».
8. Щоб відпочи́ти, Лука́ш і́нколи гра́є в те́ніс.
9. Якщо́ у Льво́ві нема́є нічо́го ціка́вого, то Лука́ш сиди́ть вдо́ма і ди́виться телеві́зор.
10. «Музе́й іде́й» розташо́ваний на ву́лиці Зеле́ній у ново́му Льво́ві.

Але́ найкра́щий відпочи́нок для Лукаша́ – це велоси́пед, або́ "ро́вер", як ка́жуть у Льво́ві.

Розмо́ва   Conversation

∩ **15.28.** Engage a partner in a conversation in Ukrainian about university studies.

1. Find out each detail noted in the chart below.
2. Write them all down in Ukrainian.
3. Report in Ukrainian what you learned.

Про що дізна́тися	партне́р-1	партне́р-2	партне́р-3
Де, коли́ і скі́льки ча́су ви навча́лися?			
Які́ ку́рси ви слу́хали?			
Хто виклада́в ко́жен курс?			
Яка́ бу́ла ва́ша спеціялізáція?			
Де ви жили́ в студе́нтські ро́ки?			
Що ви роби́ли в час, ві́льний від заня́ть?			
Які́ ку́рси вам найбі́льше подо́балися та чому́?			
Які́ ку́рси вам найме́нше подо́балися та чому́?			
Що ціка́вого ви роби́ли у вихідні́?			
Як ви прово́дили зимо́ві та лі́тні вака́ції?			

Напе́вно, ця студе́нтка ма́є
ду́же ціка́ві професі́йні пла́ни на
майбу́тнє.

15.29. Write an essay entitled "The Story of My Life in 300 Words".
Try to use the material you learned in the textbook. Be sure to include
information about:

- where you come from;
- your family;
- what you like to do in your free time;
- your university studies;
- your most memorable trip;
- your professional and personal plans for the future.

Appendices

Basic Linguistic Terms Used in the Textbook

Accusative case *(A.), see* **Case**.

Adjective *(adj.)* is a word that describes a quality of an object, **нови́й** костю́м *a **new** suit*, **до́вга** ву́лиця *a **long** street*, **мале́** село́ *a **small** village*. Adjective corresponds to the question **яки́й?** *what (kind of)?* In a sentence, it is almost always an attribute and therefore modifies a noun, with which it agrees in gender, case, and number. It can also be linked to the noun by the verbs **бу́ти** *to be,* **става́ти, роби́тися** *to become,* when it is part of the predicate, Він був **щасли́вий.** *He was **happy.*** Вода́ ста́ла **соло́на.** *The water became **salty**.* Dictionary ending of adjectives are **~ий** or, less commonly, **~ій**. Adjective has a set of its case, gender, and number endings. *See* **Declension**.

Adverb *(adv.)* is a word that describes an action or quality. It corresponds to the questions **як?** *how?*, **де? куди́?** *where?* and **коли́?** *when?*. Adverbs can modify: 1) a verb, either preceding or following it, **бага́то ї́сти** *to eat much*, **диви́тися ско́са** *to look askance*, **приї́хати за́втра** *to come tomorrow*; 2) an adjective, **страше́нно приє́мний** *awfully pleasant*; 3) another adverb, **ду́же дале́ко** *very far*. Adverbs are often derived from adjectives and in that case have the dictionary endings **~о** and, less commonly, **~е**. Adverbs are indeclinable.

Adverbial modifier is a part of a sentence that modifies a verb. It can be one word or a group. *Adverbial modifier of manner* describes the manner of action, **Він шви́дко закі́нчив робо́ту.** *He quickly finished work. Adverbial modifier of place* denotes the place of action, **Він навча́ється в морські́й акаде́мії.** He studies in a naval academy. *Adverbial modifier of time* expresses the time or frequency of the action, **Ми ду́же рі́дко хо́димо до теа́тру.** *We very seldom go to the theater.* There are also adverbial modifiers of reason, cause, and condition.

Analytic form is the form consisting of more than one word as opposed to a **synthetic,** or one-word form. The comparative degree of the adjective **досві́дчений** *experienced* has both its analytic (two-word) form, **бі́льш досві́дчений**, and synthetic (one-word) form, **досві́дчені́ший**, both meaning *more experienced. Also see* **Synthetic.**

Animate noun *(anim.)* denotes a human being or animal and requires a different form of the accusative for masculine gender, which coincides with the genitive, **брат** *a brother* - **про бра́та** *about the brother. See* **Inanimate noun**.

Aspect of a verb presents its action either as a process with no regard to its completion, **imperfective aspect** *(impf.),* **Я чита́в кни́жку.** *I read a book.*, or as an accomplished deed, with emphasis on the completion and its result, **perfective aspect** *(pf.),* **Я вже прочита́в кни́жку.** *I have already read the book.* Most verbs have both aspects: *impf.* **пи́ти** - *pf.* **ви́пити** *to* drink, *impf.* **ї́сти** - *pf.* **з'ї́сти** *to* eat. Perfective aspect pertains only to the past and future tense. Imperfective pertains to past, present and future. A small number of words lack one of the aspects: *only impf.* **бу́ти** *to be,* **ма́ти** *to have,* **жи́ти** *to live; only pf.* **пробу́ти** *to stay.*

Attribute is a member of the sentence that modifies (describes) a noun. It can be an adjective, a possessive pronoun or an ordinal numeral, **Цьому́ молодо́му** студе́нтові подо́бається **наш нови́й** гуртожи́ток. ***This young*** *student likes **our new** dormitory.*

Cardinal numeral *(card.)* denotes the quantity of objects that can be enumerated. They are used in counting, **оди́н** *one,* **два** *two,* **три** *three, …* **де́сять** *ten, etc.* and modify nouns that can be counted: **оди́н рік** *one year*, **два ро́ки** *two years*, **сто днів** *a hundred days*, **три́ста кіло́метрів** *three hundred kilometers. Also see* **Numeral** and **Ordinal numeral**.

Case is a form of a noun, adjective, or pronoun that signifies how each of them relates to other words in the sentence. There are seven cases in Ukrainian. Each case expresses at least one, but more often a number of such principal relationships. The **nominative** case *(N.)* signifies that the word is the subject of the sentence (for nouns) or describes the subject (for adjectives and pronouns). This case is never used with prepositions. The **genitive** case *(G.)* expresses relationships of possession, part and a whole, origin, direction, anteriority, posteriority, frequency, and other. It is used both without and with prepositions. The **dative** case *(D.)* signifies the person or thing that receives something from the action or experiences a particular state. More often than not it is used without prepositions. Indirect objects in the sentence are usually in the dative case. The **accusative** case *(A.)* marks the direct object of a transitive verb when used without prepositions, and the object of conversation with prepositions **про** *about, of* or **за** *colloq. about*. The **instrumental** case *(I.)* signifies the tool of action, its accompaniment or counterpart of interaction. It can be used both with and without prepositions. The **locative** case *(L.),* sometimes also known as the prepositional case because it cannot be used without prepositions, signifies a location in space or time. The **vocative** case *(V.)* signifies that the person or personified object is being spoken to. It is used without prepositions.

Closed syllable, *see* **Syllable.**

Conjugation of the verb is a set of endings the verb takes in the sentence that signify the person, gender, and number of the doer of action for the present and future tenses, and the gender and number for the past tense. There are two verb conjugations in the present tense. The **first conjugation** has the 3rd *pers. pl.* endings **~уть** or **~ють** and the connector-vowel **~e~**. The **second conjugation**, respectively **~ать** or **~ять** and the connector-vowel **~и~**. *Also see* **Verb.**

Conjunction *(conj.)* is an auxiliary word that connects words, parts of a sentence, or two smaller sentences (clauses) within a bigger one. The most common conjunctions are **і (й, та)** *and,* **a** *but, and,* **але́** *but,* **що** *that,* **яки́й** *that, which,* **чи, або́** *or,* **ніж** *than,* and **як** *than.*

Consonant is a sound created by putting an obstacle (tongue, teeth, or lips) to the flow of air from the lungs, while speaking. There are thirty-two consonants in Ukrainian expressed by the letters **б, в, г, ґ, д, ж, з, й, к, л, м, н, п, р, с, т, ф, х, ц, ч, ш, щ,** and by the combinations **дз** and **дж**. Consonants can be voiced and voiceless. **Voiced consonants** are pronounced with participation of the voice. **Voiceless consonants** involve no participation of the voice. Most of them are paired as (voiced-voiceless) **б-п, в-ф, г-х, ґ-к, д-т, ж-ш, з-с, дж-ч,** and **дз-ц**. In Ukrainian, voiced consonants do not become voiceless at the end of word or syllable. The voiced **й, л, м, н,** and **р** have no voiceless counterparts. The voiceless **щ** does not have a voiced match. Consonants can be **hard** and **soft**. The consonants **б, п, в, м, ф, р, г, ґ, х, к, ж, ш, ч,** and **ж** are always hard, while the **й** is always soft. *Also see* **Soft consonant.**

Countable nouns *(count.)* is a class of nouns that can be enumerated and, therefore, can follow cardinal numerals. In English, they correlate with the question *how many?* (**стіл** *a table,* **гри́вня** *a hryvnia,* **гра́дус** *a degree,* **люди́на** *a person). See* **Uncountable nouns**.

Dative case *(D.), see* **Case.**

Declension is a set of case endings a noun (adjective, pronoun, numeral) has when it is used in a sentence. There are four noun declensions, each determined by the gender and ending of the noun. *See* Note 4.7, pp. 50-51.

Demonstrative pronoun *(dem.)* is a class of pronouns that point to somebody or something. They are few, highly frequent, and counter-opposed by the degree of relative proximity to the speaker of the thing they point out to: **цей (оце́й)** *m. this, f.* **ця (оця́),** *nt.* **це (оце́), ці (оці́)** *pl. these* vs **той (отой)** *m. that, f.* **та (ота́),** *nt.* **те (оте́), ті (оті́)** *pl. those.*

Dictionary form is the form in which the word is registered in dictionaries. For *nouns* it is the nominative case singular, for *adjectives*, *possessive pronouns*, and *ordinal numerals* it is the masculine gender of the nominative case singular, and for *personal pronouns* and *cardinal numerals* it is the nominative case. For *verbs* it is the infinitive, imperfective and perfective.

Direct object is the noun part of the sentence at which the action of the predicate is directed. It is always in the accusative and without preposition, Він читає **газету**. *He reads a* ***newspaper***. To make full sense of its meaning, a transitive verb, by definition, requires a direct object, *cf.* Він купує. *He buys.* and Він купує **комп'ютер**. *He buys* ***a computer***. In the dictionary the label *tran.* is used.

Ending is the changeable final part of a word that expresses number, gender, case, tense, and other components of meaning, as opposed to the word stem which stays unchanged. In the dictionary, the two are separated by a vertical bar: **батьк|о** *a father*, **дівчин|а** *a girl*, **співа|ють** *they sing*, **мал|ий** *small*. *Also see* **Zero ending**.

Gender is an important characteristic of most Ukrainian nouns. They are either masculine *(m.)*, feminine *(f.)*, or neuter *(nt.)*. It determines the form of adjectives, possessive and other pronouns as well as past tense predicates used with it. The nouns, that lack the singular form, have no gender and are marked as *only pl.,* **воро́та** *gate*, **две́рі** *a door*.

Genitive case *(G.), see* **Case**.

Imperfective aspect *(impf.), see* **Aspect**.

Impersonal sentence is a sentence that has no subject, its predicate is in the third person plural and it expresses a situation pertaining to no specific person, **Тут не па́лять.** *They don't smoke here.*

Infinitive is the dictionary form of the verb ending in **~ти** that has no tense, voice, person, gender or number. Most infinitives have both imperfective and perfective aspectual forms, *impf.* сіда́**ти** - *pf.* сі́**сти** *to sit down, impf.* відкрива́**ти** - *pf.* відкри́**ти** *to open*. Infinitives of **reflexive verbs** have the ending **~тися** or *colloq.* **~ться**, боя́**тися** *to be afraid*, прокида́**тися** *to wake up*.

Inanimate noun *(inan.)* denotes an object that is not a living being and requires a form of the accusative for masculine gender that coincides with the nominative, **подару́нок** *a gift -* **А. про подару́нок** *about the gift. Also see* **Inanimate noun**.

Indeclinable *(indecl.)* is a word whose ending does not change. Such words are: 1) nouns of neuter gender borrowed from some foreign languages and ending in **~і, ~е, ~є, ~іо, ~у, ~ю: колі́брі** *a hummingbird*, **кабаре́** *a cabaret*, **кольє́** *a necklace*, **ра́діо** *a radio*, **рандеву́** *a meeting*, **меню́** *a menu*; 2) noun surnames of women ending in **~ко, ~ук, ~юк, ~ак, ~ин, ~ій**; 3) adverbs.

Indirect object indicates to whom or for whom the action of the verb is done and who is receiving the direct object, Він купує комп'ютер **для свого́ сина**. *He buys a computer* ***for his son***.

Instrumental case *(I.), see* **Case**.

Labialized sound is a consonant or vowel pronounced by protruding and rounding the lips, or labia in Latin. In Ukrainian, the consonant **в** /v/ is thus labialized in the word and syllable final position, **люби́в** /l'ubý^w/ *he loved*, **навко́ло** /nawkólo/ *around*, as well as the vowel **о** /o/ when not under the stress, thus resembling the vowel /u/, **торі́к** /to^urík/ *last year*.

Locative case *(L.), see* **Case**.

Modal word *(mod.)* expresses possibility, permission (**мо́жна)**, prohibition (**не мо́жна**), necessity (**тре́ба**), assumption (**можли́во**), advice (**слід**), obligation (**му́сити**), expectation (**ма́ти** + *inf.*) and similar relationships.

Nominative case *(A.), see* **Case**.

Noun *(n.)* is a part of speech that names objects (**телефо́н** *telephone*, **кни́жка** *book*, **де́рево** *tree*), people (**студе́нтка** *female student*, **юна́к** *young man*, **маля́** *baby*), animals (**кінь** *horse*, **пта́шка** *bird*, **теля́** *calf*), natural phenomena (**дощ** *rain*, **бу́ря** *storm*), abstract notions (**іде́я** *idea*, **конфлі́кт** *conflict*), or states (**ща́стя** *happiness*, **ю́ність** *youth*). A noun correlates with a question **хто?** *who?* or **що** *what?* and can be either animate (names of living beings) or inanimate (*see* **Animate noun** *and* **Inanimate noun**). Most nouns have singular and plural form (*sg.* **де́рево** *a tree* and *pl.* **дере́ва** *trees)* Some have only one and not the other (*sg. only* **молоко́** *milk, pl. only* **две́рі** *a door) (see* **Number**). All nouns have a gender *(see* **Gender**). In the sentence, nouns are most typically subjects and objects. Combined with other words they can also play other roles, like adverbial modifiers: на насту́пний **день** *next **day**.*

Number is a binary opposition between word forms refering to a single entity (person or thing) or a plurality thereof. There is singular and plural number. It can describe nouns (*sg.* **хло́пець** *a boy* and **хло́пці** *boys*), pronouns (*sg.* **я** *I*, **він** *he* and *pl.* **ми** *we*, **вони́** *they*), adjectives (*sg.* **вели́кий** *big* and *pl.* **вели́кі** *big*), and verbs (*sg.* **зро́бить** *he'll do* and *pl.* **зро́блять** *they'll do*).

Numeral *(num.), see* **Cardinal numeral** *and* **Ordinal numeral**.

Oblique case is any case other than the nominative or vocative.

Object is the part of a sentence onto which the action of the predicate is directed - Я завжди́ ра́джуся **з бра́том**. *I always consult **with my brother**. See* **Direct object** and **Indirect object**.

Open syllable, *see* **Syllable**.

Ordinal numeral *(ord.)* is a class or words that indicate position in an order of objects. They correlate by their meaning with **cardinal numerals** and, with few exceptions, are derived from them. They have adjectival endings and, like adjectives, they agree with the nouns they modify in gender, case, and number: *m.* **пе́рший** день *the first day, f.* **во́сьма** годи́на *the eighth hour, nt.* **тре́тє** вікно́ *the third window*.

Perfective aspect *(pf.), see* **Aspect**.

Person indicates who performs the action: 1) 1st person is the speaker, *sg.* **я** *I, pl.* **ми** *we*; 2) 2nd person, is somebody directly addressed by the speaker, *sg.* **ти** *you, pl.* **ви** *you*; 3) 3rd person is a third party, other than the two directly participating in communication, *sg.* **він** *he*, **вона́** *she*, **воно́** *it*, and *pl.* **вони́** *they.*

Personal pronouns point to a specific person and correspond to the question **хто?** *who?* They are: 1st *pers.* **я** *I,* **ми** *we,* 2nd *pers. sg.* **ти** *you, pl.* **ви** *you*, and 3rd *pers. sg.* **він** *he*, **вона́** *she*, **воно́** *it*, and *pl.* **вони́** *they.* Each has a respective possessive pronoun. *See* **Possessive pronoun**.

Possessive pronouns *(poss.)* express who something belongs to. They correspond to the question **чий?** *whose?*. They are: **мій** *my*, **наш** *our*, **твій** *sg. your*, **ваш** *pl. your*, **його́** *his,* **її** *her*, **їхній** *their*. Much like adjectives, they agree with the nouns they describe in gender, case, and number.

Predicate is the part of a sentence, most commonly a verb, that expresses the action performed by the subject, Студе́нти **вивча́ють** мо́ви. *Students study languages.* Predicates can be: 1) simple verbal, expressed by one verb, Іва́н **живе́** тут. *Ivan lives here.*; 2) compound verbal, expressed by two verbs, Вона́ **мо́же чита́ти** китайською. *She can read Chinese.*; 3) compound nominal predicate, expressed by a link-verb **бу́ти** *to be*, **ста́ти** *to become*, **лиша́тися** *to continue to be*, **працюва́ти** *to work as* and a noun or adjective, called *the predicative*, Торі́к він **став журналі́стом**. *Last year, he **became a journalist**.* A predicate often appears with other words, **objects** and **adverbial modifiers**, that further describe it, Він **зроби́в всі поку́пки за годи́ну**. *He **made all purchases within an hour**. See **Subject**.*

Prefix is the part of a word that is added to the beginning of its root or stem, to produce a new word, хід *movement* - **ви́**хід *exit*, or a grammatical form of the same word, *impf.* чита́ти *to read* - *pf.* **про**чита́ти *to have read. See **Suffix, Root, Ending**.*

Preposition *(prep.)* is an auxiliary word usually preceding a noun or a pronoun and expressing their relationship to another word in a phrase or sentence, **під столо́м** *under a table*, **для них** *for them*. Each preposition requires its noun or noun phrase to be in a specific case. *See **Appendices, Table 4. Prepositions and Cases**.*

Pronoun *(pron.)* is a class of words used to replace a noun *(personal pronoun)* or a phrase *(demonstrative pronoun)* to avoid repetition. A special class of pronouns signifies possession. *See **Demonstrative pronoun, Personal pronoun, Possessive pronoun.***

Question is a sentence asking for information. There are four basic types of questions: 1) **general** requiring a yes or no answer; 2) **special**, beginning with a question word like **хто?** *who?*, **що?** *what?*, **коли́?** *when?*, **де?** *where?*, etc.; 3) **alternative**, asking to choose; 4) **disjunctive**, stating the fact and soliciting agreement. Its marker is the tag **Чи не так?** *isn't it?, don't they?, shouldn't we?*, etc. *See **Lesson 6**.*

Reflexive verb *(refl.)* expresses an action that is done by *and* directed at its performer. The formal indicator of such a verb is the particle **~ся**, attached to its ending. Ukrainian reflexive verbs correspond either to an English verb with the reflexive pronoun *oneself (myself, himself,* etc.), Він **вмива́ється**. *He washes himself.*, or to an intransitive verb without such a pronoun, Нови́й рік **поча́вся** вчо́ра. *A new year **started** yesterday.*

Root is the most basic and obligatory part of a word, minus prefix and/or suffix, that is present in all its forms. It is used to produce derivatives, as is the case with the root **~роб~** and its derivatives **робо́та** *work*, **роб**и́ти *to do*, за**роб**и́ти *to earn*, **роб**і́тник *a worker*, **роб**о́чий *working*, за**роб**і́тчанин *a guest worker*.

Soft consonant is pronounced by lifting the tongue to the roof of the mouth. To mark softness in transcription, the sign /...'/ is used here, /s'/, /t'/, /l'/. In writing, a letter is soft before: 1) the soft sign **~ь**, па́лець *a finger*; 2) **~я, ~ю, ~є**, and **~і**, дя́кую /d'ákuju/ *thank you*, сюди́ /s'udý/ *here*, *nt.* да́внє /dáwn'e/ *ancient*, лі́то /l'ito/ *summer. Also see **Consonant**.*

Stem is the word minus its ending. Stems can coincide with the entire word, when the word has a zero ending, куто́к *a corner*, студе́нт *a student*, or with the root, when the word has no prefixes and suffixes, стіл *a table*. There are three types of stems: 1) **hard stems** end in a hard consonant, дя́дько *an uncle;* 2) **soft stems** end in a soft consonant, пита́ння *a question;* 3) **mixed stems** end in the consonants **~р, ~ж, ~ч, ~ш**, and **~щ**, лі́кар *a physician*, това́риш *a friend*, прі́звище *a surname*, плече́ *a shoulder*, ї́жа *food. See **Ending, Root, Prefix**, and **Suffix**.*

Subject is the part of a sentence that denotes the performer of the action of the predicate. The performer can be a person or a thing. The subject is expressed by a noun or pronoun and is by definition in the nominative case, Ці **мандрівники́ (вони́)** хо́чуть відпочи́ти. *These **travelers (they)** want to take a rest.* In Ukrainian impersonal sentences, the subject is necessarily absent, **Тут ча́сто продаю́ть кві́ти**.*They often sell flowers here.*

Suffix is the part of a word added at the end of the root or stem to produce a new word, **Львів** *Lviv* - львів'я́нин *a citizen of Lviv,* or a grammatical form of the same word, **купи́ти** *pf. to have bought* - купува́ти *impf. to buy.*

Syllable is a part of a word consisting of a vowel that may be accompanied by one or more consonants. A syllable can consist of: only a vowel (V), **але** *but*; a consonant and vowel (CV), **але**, a vowel and consonant (VC), **як** *how*; several consonants variously combined with one vowel, **ліс** *a forest* (CVC), **стіл** *a table* (CCVC), **злість** *anger* (CCVCC), etc. There are as many syllables in a word as there are vowels. An **open syllable** ends in a vowel; **мама** *a mom* has two open syllables **ма-ма** (CV-CV). A **closed syllable** ends in a consonant, **балкон** *a balcony* has two closed syllables **бал-кон** (CVC-CVC).

Synthetic form is a one-word form as opposed to an **analytic** form (more than one word). For example, the Ukrainian imperfective future has both these forms, the analytic **буду жити** and the synthetic **житиму** *I shall live*. The two forms have the same meaning. *See* **Analytic**.

Tense is a characteristic of a verb that signifies when the action expressed by it takes place relative to the moment of speaking. There are three tenses in Ukrainian: **минулий** *past*, **теперишній** *present*, and **майбутній** *future*. Each correlates with its own group of **adverbial modifiers of time.**

Uncountable noun *(uncount.)* is a class of nouns that cannot be enumerated. They are names of substances: **вода** *water*, **сніг** *snow*, **вино** *wine*, **повітря** *air*; or materials: **дерево** *wood*, **метал** *metal*, **золото** *gold*. They cannot immediately follow cardinal numerals. In English, they correlate with the question *how much? See* **Countable nouns**.

Velar consonant is one of the four consonants that are pronounced in the soft palate of the mouth, called *the velum*. They are **г** /h/- **х** /kh/, **ґ** /g/ - **к** /k/. In the position before the vowel -**і**, they tend to change (or shift) and transform into other consonants, **г** to **з**, **х** to **с**, **ґ** to **дз**, and **к** to **ц**.

Verb *(v.)* is a word that signified an action and corresponds to the question **що робити?** *(impf.) or* **що зробити?** *(pf.) what to do?* Ukrainian verb has three tenses and two aspects *(see* **Tense, Aspect**). In the sentence the verb most typically is the predicate. *(See* **Predicate**). Dictionaries register the verb in the form of its infinitive, easily identifiable by its suffix ~**ти**: **думати** *to think*, **жити** *to live*, **кохати** *to love*, **мати** *to have*, **хотіти** *to want. See* **Infinitive**.

Vocative case *(V.), see* **Case**.

Vowel is a sound created by the vibration of vocal chords only. There are no obstacles to the flow of air from the lungs. There are six vowel sounds in Ukrainian, represented by ten letters: /a/ by **а** and **я**, /o/ – **о**, /u/ – **у** and **ю**, /e/ – **е** and **є**, /y/ – **и**, /i/ – **і** and **ї**. Ukrainian vowels, with the exception of /e/, /y/, and /o/, are pronounced in full both in stressed and unstressed positions. An unstressed vowel /e/ is pronounced close to /y/. An unstressed /y/ is pronounced closed to /e/, **перебити** /pe^{y}re^{y}bу́ty^e/ *to interrupt*, **мерехтіти** /me^{y}re^{y}khtíty^e/ *to twinkle*, **вибирати** /vy^{e}by^{e}rату́^{e}/ *to select*. The /e/ - /y/ convergence is a salient feature of Ukrainian. An unstressed vowel /o/ is labialized, i.e., the lips protrude, giving it a shade of the vowel /u/, **молоко** /mo^{u}lo^{u}ко́/ *milk*, **колосок** /ko^{u}lo^{u}sо́k/ *an ear (of rye)*, **сороковий** /so^{u}ro^{u}ко́vyj/ *fortieth. See* **Syllable, Consonant**, and **Soft consonant**.

Zero ending (ø) is the absence of an ending in a noun. It typically occurs in the nominative singular of the masculine nouns of the second declension (**хліб** *bread*, **рік** *year*) and feminine nouns of the third declension (**любов** *love*, **ніч** *night*). It is counter-opposed to the real ending in other case forms of the same noun (note for instance the instrumental case endings in the same nouns **хлібом, роком, любов'ю, ніччю**).

Граматичні таблиці Grammar Tables

Іменники Nouns

The nominal declension tables are based on correlations between nominative case endings and others. For example, if a masculine noun has **~a** in the nominative (1st declension), then its genitive, accusative, dative, instrumental, locative, and vocative endings are respectively **~и**, **~у**, **~і**, **~ою**, **~і**, **~о**, and so on. By the same logic the **~ія** ending in the nominative correlates respectively with **~ії**, **~ію**, **~ії**, **~єю**, **ії**, and **~іє**.

Table 1. First and Third Declension Feminine and masculine nouns ending in **~a/~я/~ія** (1st declension) and feminine nouns ending in **zero** (3rd declension). In this declension type, feminine and masculine nouns both take the same endings.

	singular				plural			
N.	~a	~я	~ія	~ø	~и	~і	~ї	~і
	хата	земля	історія	ніч	хати	землі	історії	ночі
G.	~и	~і	~ії	~і (~и¹)	~ø	~ø (~ь)	~ø (~й)	~ей
	хати	землі	історії	ночі	хат	земель	історій	ночей
D.	~і	~і	~ії	~і	~ам	~ям	~ям	~ам
	хаті	землі	історії	ночі	хатам	землям	історіям	ночам
A.	~у	~ю	~ію	~ø	~и	~і	~ії	~і
	хату	землю	історію	ніч	хати	землі	історії	ночі
I.	~ою	~ею	~ією	~ю	~ами	~ями	~іями	~ами
	хатою	землею	історією	ніччю²	хатами	землями	історіями	ночами
L.	~і	~і	~ії	~і	~ах	~ях	~іях	~ах
	у хаті	на землі	в історії	у ночі	у хатах	на землях	в історіях	у ночах
V.	~о	~е	~іє	~е	~и	~і	~ії	~і
	хато!	земле!	історіє!	ноче!	хати!	землі!	історії!	ночі!

Table 2. Fourth Declension Neuter nouns with **~ат/~ят** (4th declension)

This declension type consists of names of baby animals and stands out by the suffix **~ат** (**~ят**) that appears in all case forms with the exception of the accusative and vocative, which is the same as nominative, and the instrumental singular cases. The neuter noun **ім'я** *name*, though without the suffix **~ат** (**~ят**), is also part of the 4th declension.

	singular			plural		
N.	~a	~я	ім'я	~ата	~ята	
	курча	дитя		курчата	дитята	імена
G.	~ати	~яти	імени	~ат	~ят	
	курчати	дитяти		курчат	дитят	імен
D.	~аті	~яті	імені	~атам	~ятам	
	курчаті	дитяті		курчатам	дитятам	іменам
A.	= N. sg.			= N. pl.		
I.	~ам	~ям	ім'ям, *var.*	~атами	~ятами	
	курчам	дитям	іменем	курчатами	дитятами	іменами
L.	~аті	~яті	в імені	~атах	~ятах	
	на курчаті	на дитяті		на курчатах	на дитятах	в іменах
V.	= N. sg.			= N. pl.		

---

1 The exception to the rule is the group of nouns that take the **~и** instead of **~і**. These are 3rd declension nouns ending in two consonants, **совість** *conscience* – **совісти**, **молодість** *youth*– **молодости**, and the five other nouns: **сіль** *salt* – **соли**, **кров** *blood* – **крови**, **любов** *love* – **любови**, **осінь** *autumn* – **осени**, **Русь** *Rus* – **Руси**.

2 If the noun ends in a consonant preceded by a vowel, the consonant doubles in the instrumental, **річ** *a thing* – **річчю**. If it ends in two consonants or in **б**, **п**, **в**, **м**, **ф**, and **р**, no doubling occurs, **юність** *youth* – **юністю**, **любов** *love* – **любов'ю**.

Table 3. Second Declension Masculine nouns ending in **zero** or **~o** and neuter nouns ending in **~o**, **~e**, **~ння** (**~ття**, **~лля**) (2nd declension)

For this declension type it is important to differentiate between animate masculine on the one hand, and inanimate masculine and neuter nouns on the other hand. The two classes have different sets of endings in the accusative, dative, and locative cases. The animate noun endings are given in the top line and the inanimate in the line below. It is helpful to remember that the accusative of animate masculine nouns is identical with their genitive, while the accusative of the inanimate masculine and neuter nouns is the same as their nominative.

	masculine						neuter				
	singular			plural			singular			plural	
N.	~ø (~о) дід стіл театр	~ø (~ь) вчитель	~й водій музей	~и діди́ столи́ театри	~і вчителі	~ї водії́ музеї	~о мі́сто	~е мо́ре	~я пита́ння	~а міста́	~я моря́ пита́ння
G.	~а діда	~я вчи́теля водія́		~ів дідів	~ів вчителів	~їв водії́в	~а мі́ста	~я моря́, пита́ння		~ø міст морі́в*	~ø (~ь) пита́нь
	~а стола́ ~у теа́тру	~я стільця́ ~ю музе́ю		~ів столі́в, стільці́в теа́трів		~їв музе́їв					
D.	~ові ді́дові	~еві вчи́телеві	~єві воді́єві	~ам діда́м	~ям вчителя́м, водія́м		~у мі́сту	~ю мо́рю пита́нню		~ам міста́м	~ям моря́м, пита́нням
	~у столу́ теа́тру	~ю музе́ю		~ам стола́м теа́трам	~ям музе́ям						
A.	= G. sg.			=G.pl.							
	= N.sg.			=N.pl.			= N. sg.			= N. pl.	
I.	~ом ді́дом столо́м теа́тром	~ем вчи́телем	-єм воді́єм	~ами діда́ми стола́ми теа́трами	~ями вчителя́ми, водія́ми		~ом мі́стом	~ем мо́рем	~ям пита́нням	~ами міста́ми	~ями моря́ми пита́ннями
L.	~ові на ді́дові	~еві на вчи́телеві	-єві на воді́єві	~ах на діда́х	~ях на вчителя́х, на водія́х		~і у мі́сті, у мо́рі, у пита́нні			~ах у міста́х	~ях у моря́х, у пита́ннях
	~і[3] у столі́ у теа́трі	~ї у музе́ї		~ах у стола́х	~ях у музе́ях						
V.	~у ді́ду!	~ю вчи́телю!	~ю воді́ю!	= N.pl.			= N. sg.			= N.pl.	

---

3 Inanimate masculine and neuter nouns that take the **~і** ending in the *L. sg.*, when used with the preposition **по** take the **~у** ending, cf., **у столі́** *in a table* - **по столу́** *on the table*, **у теа́трі** *at a theater* - **по теа́тру** *around a theater*, **у мі́сті** *in a city* - **по мі́сту** *through a city*, **у по́лі** *in a field* - **по по́лю** *along a field*, **у не́бі** *in the sky* - **по не́бу** *on the sky*.

Table 4. Prepositions and Cases This table describes the meaning of most common prepositions and the case forms of nouns and pronouns that they require.

preposition	case	meaning	English equivalent	Illustration
без	+ G.	absence of sth	without	**Він працює без комп'ютера.** *He works without a computer.*
біля	+ G.	proximity in place,	near	**Це місто біля Києва.** *This city is near Kyiv.*
		in time,	close to	**Ми зустрілися біля третьої години.** *We met at about three o'clock.*
		in quantity	about approximately	**Я маю біля двадцяти гривень.** *I have approximately twenty hryvnias.*
в	+ L.	static location in or within sth.	in, at	**в університеті** *at a university* **уві сні** *in a dream*
		time (with names of months)	in	**у квітні (лютому)** *in April (February)*
var. **у, уві**	+ A.	time (with days of week)	on	**у суботу (понеділок)** *on Saturday (Monday)*
		direction of motion in or into a space	in, into	**Він зайшов у кімнату.** *He went into the room.*
	+ G.	location in sb's place, being in sb's possession	at	**Ольга живе у батьків.** *Olha lives at her parents'.* **У мене є трохи часу.** *I have some time.*
від	+ G.	starting point in place or time	since, from	**Я не працюю від понеділка.** *I haven't worked since Monday.* **від Львова до Венеції** *from Lviv to Venice*
		origin involving a person	from	**Цей подарунок він Романа.** *This gift is from Roman.*
для	+ G.	person viewed as destination of action	for	**Ми купили це для вас.** *We bought this for you.*
до	+ G.	1) destination of motion or action; 2) final point in distance or time; 3) priority in time	to till before	1) **Ми підемо до музею.** *We'll go to a museum.* 2) **Ми попрощалися до наступного понеділка.** *We parted till next Monday.* 3) **Хто тут жив до нас?** *Who lived here before us?*
з *var.* **із, зі, зо, ізі**	+ G.	origin involving a city starting point	from since	**З якого він міста?** *What city is he from?* **з раннього ранку** *since early morning*
	+ I.	accompaniment, togetherness	with	**разом з другом** *together with a friend*

за	+ I.	position behind or following sth in place or time	behind after	за стіно́ю *behind a wall* **За понеді́лком йде вівто́рок.** *After Monday comes Tuesday.*
	+ A.	in place of sb, instead of sb, in compensation for sth	for instead of, in place of, in lieu of *colloq.* about	**Я бага́то заплати́в за кни́жку.** *I paid a lot for the book.* **Вона́ працю́є за сестру́.** *She works instead of her sister.* **За що ти жу́ришся?** *What do you worry about?*
завдяки́	+ D.	due to, owing to	thanks to	**завдяки́ мої́й ка́рті** *thanks to my map*
між	+ I.	static position between two points in place or time	1) between … and … 2) among	1) **Я поста́вила стіл між вікно́м і ша́фою.** *I put the table between the window and the wardrobe.* 2) **між людьми́** *among people*
на	+ L.	static location: 1) on a surface	on	**Кни́жка на столі́.** *A book is on the table.*
	+ L.	2) at or in some institutions	at	**Він працю́є на по́шті (вокза́лі, заво́ді, фа́бриці).** *He works at a post-office (station, plant, factory).*
	+ A.	direction of motion, destination of action: 1) to an event; 2) on or onto a surface	1) to for 2) on, onto	1) **Він ходи́в на ле́кцію.** *He went to a lecture.* **Лукаша́ запроси́ли на вече́рю.** *Lukash was invited for dinner.* 2) **Він покла́в це на стіл.** *He put it onto the table.*
	+ A.	temporal destination, time for or by which sth is done	for, by	**Мені́ тре́ба зроби́ти це на пе́рше тра́вня.** *I need to do it for (by) May 1.* **квито́к до Я́лти на се́реду** *a ticket to Yalta for Wednesday* **завда́ння на за́втра** *assignment for tomorrow*
над, *var.* на́ді, по́над	+ I.	1) position above sth 2) object of work	over, above at, on	**Карти́на виси́ть над столо́м.** *The picture is above the table.* **на́ді мно́ю** *above me* **Я працю́ю над но́вою кни́жкою.** *I'm working on a new book.*
	+ A.	3) toward or by a point in time 4) exceeding a quantity	by above	**над ве́чір** *by the evening,* **над ра́нок** *towards morning* **над мі́ру** *above measure,* **над усе́** *above all*
о *var.* об	+ L.	specific hour in designations of time by the clock	at	**о пе́ршій годи́ні** *at one o'clock* **об одина́дцятій п'ятна́дцять** *at eleven fifteen*
пе́ред *var.* пе́реді	+ I.	position in time or place preceding a given point	in front of before	**пе́ред буди́нком** *in front of a house,* **пе́реді мно́ю** *in front of (before) me* **пе́ред поча́тком фі́льму** *before the beginning of the film*

під *var.* піді	+ I.	static position under sth	under, below	**Газе́та лежи́ть під кни́жкою.** *The newspaper is under the book.* **піді мно́ю** *under me*
	+ A.	direction of motion toward or close to a moment in time	under, below toward, by	**Я покла́в газе́ту під кни́жку.** *I put the newspaper under the book.* **Ми закі́нчили робо́ту під ра́нок.** *We finished work by the morning.*
після	+ G.	position in time after a given point	after, past	**Після нас хоч пото́п.** *After us the deluge.* **Лиші́ть повідо́млення після сигна́лу.** *Leave your message after the beep.*
по	+ L.	motion within, along or across space	along, in, around, across, through	**Він хо́дить по цій ву́лиці щодня́.** *He goes along this street every day.* **Я люблю́ гуля́ти по па́рку.** *I like to walk in (around) the park.*
	+ L. pl.	repetition in time	on, every	**по субо́тах** *on Saturdays,* **по вечора́х** *every evening*
	+ A.	object of action or motion	*paraphrase or* for	**Васи́ль пішо́в по молоко́.** *Vasyl went to buy (get) milk.* **Вони́ прийшли́ по пора́ду.** *They came for advice.*
повз	+ A.	motion past an object	by, past	**Вони́ проїжджа́тимуть повз стари́й за́мок.** *They will be passing by an old castle.*
по́за	+ I.	outside of, beyond (*opposite to* within)	outside, out of, beyond, without	**по́за ко́нкуренцією** *outside competition,* **по́за вся́ким су́мнівом** *without (beyond) any doubt*
про	+ A.	object of narration, thought	about, on	**Ця стаття́ про мисте́цтво.** *The article is about art.*
про́тягом	+ G.	length, duration of time period	for, for the duration of	**про́тягом ці́лого мі́сяця** *for an entire month or* **ці́лий мі́сяць** **про́тягом двох ти́жнів** *for the duration of two weeks or* **два ти́жні**
се́ред	+ G.	in the middle (midst) of	1) in the middle of … 2) among, in the midst of …	1) **се́ред дня** *in the middle of the day* 2) **се́ред мої́х дру́зів** *among my friends*
усу́переч, *var.* всу́переч	+ D.	contrary to some circumstances	contrary to, despite, in spite of	**Яре́ма зроби́в це всу́переч їхнім рекоменда́ціям.** *Yarema did it contrary to their recommendations.*
че́рез	+ A.	1) motion across sth 2) cause of sth/sb 3) after period of time	1) across 2) because of 3) in	1) **Зупи́нка таксі́вки че́рез ву́лицю.** *The taxi stand is across the street.* 2) **Че́рез те́бе ми запізни́лися.** *Because of you we are late.* 3) **Він закі́нчить робо́ту че́рез годи́ну.** *He will finish work in an hour.*

Table 5. Sound Change Distribution within Nominal Declension

Case/ sound change	velar consonant shift г *to* з, к *to* ц, х *to* с	dropping of **o/e** adding of **o/e**	change of **i** to **o/e**
N. sg.	нога́, рука́, му́ха, по́верх	ні́мець, буди́нок	ніс, міст, річ
N. pl.	* * *	ні́мець – ні́мці, буди́нок – буди́нки	ніс – носи́, міст – мости́, річ – ре́чі
G. sg.	* * *	ні́мець – ні́мця, буди́нок – буди́нку	ніс – но́са, міст – мостá, річ – ре́чі
G. pl.	* * *	ні́мець – ні́мців, буди́нок – буди́нків **o/e**-*adding* кни́жка – книжо́к, сім'я́ – сіме́й	ніс – носі́в, міст – мостíв, річ – рече́й
D. sg.	нога́ – нозí рука́ – руцí му́ха – му́сі	ні́мець – ні́мцеві, буди́нок – буди́нку	ніс – но́су, міст – мо́сту, річ – ре́чі
D. pl.	* * *	ні́мець – ні́мцям, буди́нок – буди́нкам	ніс – носа́м, міст – мостáм, річ – реча́м
A. sg.	* * *	ні́мець – ні́мця	* * *
A. pl.	* * *	ні́мець – ні́мців, буди́нок – буди́нки	ніс – носи́, міст – мости́, річ – ре́чі
I. sg.	* * *	ні́мець – ні́мцем буди́нок – буди́нком	ніс – но́сом, міст – мо́сто́м
I. pl.	* * *	ні́мець – ні́мцями буди́нок – буди́нками	ніс – носа́ми, міст - мостáми річ – реча́ми
L. sg.	нога́ – на нозí рука́ – на руцí по́верх – на по́версі	ні́мець – на ні́мцеві буди́нок – у буди́нку	ніс – на но́сі, міст – на мо́сту́ річ – на ре́чі
L. pl.	* * *	ні́мець – на ні́мцях буди́нок – у буди́нках	ніс – на носá́х, міст – на мостá́х, річ – на реча́х
V. sg.	* * *	ні́мець – ні́мцю! буди́нок – буди́нку!	ніс – но́се! міст – мо́сте! річ – ре́че!
V. pl.	* * *	ні́мець – ні́мці! буди́нок – буди́нки!	ніс – носи́! міст – мости́! річ – ре́чі!

Table 6. Personal Pronouns[4]

Case	sg. I	sg. you	sg. he / it	sg. she	pl. we	pl. you	pl. they
N.	я	ти	він/воно́	вона́	ми	ви	вони́
G.	мене́ / до ме́не	тебе́ / до те́бе	його́ / до ньо́го	її́ / до не́ї	нас	вас	їх / до них
D.	мені́	тобі́	йому́	їй	нам	вам	їм
A.	мене́ / про ме́не	тебе́ / про те́бе	його́ / про ньо́го	її́ / про не́ї	нас	вас	їх / про них
I.	мно́ю	тобо́ю	ним	не́ю	на́ми	ва́ми	ни́ми
L.	на мені́	на тобі́	на ньо́му	на ній	на нас	на вас	на них

Table 7. Possessive Pronouns

Eng.	sg. m.	sg. f.	sg. nt.	sg. pl.	Eng.	pl. m.	pl. f.	pl. nt.	pl. pl.
my	мій	моя́	моє́	мої́	**our**	наш	на́ша	на́ше	на́ші
your	твій	твоя́	твоє́	твої́	**your**	ваш	ва́ша	ва́ше	ва́ші
his	його́				**their**	і́хній	і́хня	і́хнє	і́хні
her	її́				**their**	і́хній	і́хня	і́хнє	і́хні
its	його́				**their**	і́хній	і́хня	і́хнє	і́хні

Table 8. Possessive Pronouns мій my, наш our, твій sg. your, ваш pl. your, і́хній their

Case	мій my, sg. m.	f.	nt.	pl.	наш our, pl. m.	f.	nt.	pl.
N.	мій	моя́	моє́	мої́	наш	на́ша	на́ше	на́ші
G.	мого́	моє́ї	= m.	мої́х	на́шого	на́шої	= m.	на́ших
D.	моє́му	мої́й	= m.	мої́м	на́шому	на́шій	= m.	на́шим
A.[5]	мій / мого́	мою́	моє́	мої́ / мої́х	наш / на́шого	на́шу	на́ше	на́ші / на́ших
I.	мої́м	моє́ю	= m.	мої́ми	на́шим	на́шою	= m.	на́шими
L.	у моє́му	у мої́й	= m.	у мої́х	у на́шому	у на́шій	= m.	у на́ших

4 In the cells with lighter shading, the first form of the personal pronoun is used without prepositions, **Він мене́ не зна́є.** *He doesn't know me.* Note that the stress is on the final syllable. The second form is used with prepositions. Note that the stress shifts to the initial syllable, **Він писа́в до ме́не.** *He wrote to me.* The darker shading of the cells indicates stress shift and initial syllable mutation both of which occur in the *A.* and *G. sg.* of the pronouns **він** and **вона́** when used with a preposition, cf., no preposition, **Він його́ (її́) не зна́є.** *He doesn't know him (her).* with preposition, **Він писа́в до ньо́го (не́ї).** *He wrote to him (her).*

5 In the shaded cells for the accusative, the first accusative form identical with the nominative is used with the inanimate masculine nouns, **Він ба́чить мій буди́нок.** *He sees my house.* The second form, which is identical with the genitive, is used with the animate masculine nouns, **Богда́н слу́хає мого́ ба́тька** *Bohdan is listening to my father.*

	твій *your, sg.*				ваш *your, pl.*			
Case	*m.*	*f.*	*nt.*	*pl.*	*m.*	*f.*	*nt.*	*pl.*
N.	твій	твоя́	твоє́	твої́	ваш	ва́ша	ва́ше	ва́ші
G.	твого́	твоє́ї	= *m.*	твої́х	ва́шого	ва́шої	= *m.*	ва́ших
D.	твоє́му	твої́й	= *m.*	твої́м	ва́шому	ва́шій	= *m.*	ва́шим
A.	твій / твого́	твою́	твоє́	твої́ / твої́х	ваш / ва́шого	ва́шу	ва́ше	ва́ші / ва́ших
I.	твої́м	твоє́ю	= *m.*	твої́ми	ва́шим	ва́шою	= *m.*	ва́шими
L.	у твоє́му	у твої́й	= *m.*	у твої́х	у ва́шому	у ва́шій	= *m.*	у ва́ших

 Note! The possessive pronouns **його́** *his* and **її́** *her* are the same in all cases.

	їхній *their, sg.*			їхні *their, pl.*
Case	*m.*	*f.*	*nt.*	*for all genders*
N.	і́хній	і́хня	і́хнє	і́хні
G.	і́хнього	і́хньої	= *m.*	і́хніх
D.	і́хньому	і́хній	= *m.*	і́хнім
A.	і́хній / і́хнього	і́хню	і́хнє	і́хні / і́хніх
I.	і́хнім	і́хньою	= *m.*	і́хніми
L.	у і́хньому	у і́хній	= *m.*	у і́хніх

Table 9. Demonstrative Pronouns *цей* this, *ці* these, *той* that, and *ті* those

	цей *this, sg.*			ці *these, pl.*
Case	*m.*	*f.*	*nt.*	*for all genders*
N.	цей	ця	це	ці
G.	цього́	цє́ї *or* ціє́ї	= *m.*	цих
D.	цьому́	цій	= *m.*	цим
A.	цей / цього́	цю	це / цього́	ці / цих
I.	цим	цє́ю *or* ціє́ю	= *m.*	ци́ми
L.	у цьо́му	у цій	= *m.*	у цих

	той *that, sg.*			*plural -* ті *those*
Case	*m.*	*f.*	*nt.*	*for all genders*
N.	той	та	те	ті
G.	того́	тіє́ї *or* то́ї	= *m.*	тих
D.	тому́	тій	= *m.*	тим
A.	той / того́	ту	те / того́	ті / тих
I.	тим	тіє́ю *or* то́ю	= *m.*	ти́ми
L.	у то́му / у тім	у тій	= *m.*	у тих

Table 10. Interrogative Pronouns

The pronouns **який** *what (kind of)* and **котрий** *which, what*
are declined in all their gender forms as **той** *that*

	чий whose, *sg.*			**чиї** whose, *pl.*
Case	m.	f.	nt.	for all genders
N.	чий	чия́	чиє́	чиї́
G.	чийо́го	чиє́ї	= m.	чиї́х
D.	чийо́му	чи́й	= m.	чиї́м
A.	чий / чийо́го	чию́	чиє́ / чийо́го	чиї́ / чиї́х
I.	чиї́м	чиє́ю	= m.	чиї́ми
L.	у чийо́му / у чиї́м	у чиї́й	= m.	у чиї́х

Table 11. Adjectives and Ordinal Numerals

	masculine and neuter		feminine		plural	
Case	hard stem	soft stem	hard stem	soft stem	hard stem	soft stem
N.	*m.* ~**ий**, *nt.* ~**е** нови́й нове́	*m.* ~**ій**, *nt.* ~**є** оста́нній оста́ннє	~**а** нова́	~**я** оста́ння	~**і** нові́	оста́нні
G.	~**ого** ново́го	~**ього** оста́ннього	~**ої** ново́ї	~**ьої** оста́нньої	~**их** нови́х	~**іх** оста́нніх
D.	~**ому** ново́му	~**ьому** оста́нньому	~**ій** нові́й оста́нній		~**им** нови́м	~**ім** оста́нньому
A.	= N. sg *for inan. m. and all nt.* = G. sg. *for anim. m.*		~**у** нову́	~**ю** оста́нню	= N. pl. *for inan.* = G. pl. *for anim.*	
I.	~**им** нови́м	~**ім** оста́ннім	~**ою** ново́ю	~**ьою** оста́нньою	~**ими** нови́ми	~**іми** оста́нніми
L.	~**ому** (~**ім**) на ново́му (нові́м)	~**ьому** (~**ім**) на оста́нньому (оста́ннім)	~**ій** на нові́й на оста́нній		~**их** на нови́х	~**іх** на оста́нніх
V.	= N. sg.				= N. pl.	

Table 12. Cardinal Numerals

Numeral **оди́н** *one* is declined like a masculine adjective with a hard stem. The stress in all forms stays on the second syllable. Numerals from **де́в'ять** *nine* through **два́дцять** *twenty*, and **три́дцять** *thirty*, follow the declension of the numeral **п'ять** *five*. In all numerals from **одина́дцять** *eleven* to **дев'ятна́дцять** *nineteen*, the stress is on the ~**на**~. **Шістдеся́т** *sixty*, **сімдеся́т** *seventy*, **вісімдеся́т** *eighty* and **дев'ятдеся́т** *ninety* are declined like **п'ятдеся́т** *fifty*. The variant **дев'яно́сто** *ninety* is declined like **сто** *a hundred*. Numerals **шістсо́т** *six hundred*, **сімсо́т** *seven hundred*, **вісімсо́т** *eight hundred*, and **дев'ятсо́т** *nine hundred* follow the declension of **п'ятсо́т** *five hundred*. Vocative case forms for all cardinal numerals are identical to their nominative case.

The shaded form of the accusative is used when the numeral is modified by an animate masculine noun, **Я зна́ю цих чотирьо́х хло́пців**. *I know these four guys.*

Два - вісім *two* through *eight*

Case	two	three	four	five	six	seven	eight
N.	*m.* два, *f.* дві	три	чоти́ри	п'ять	шість	сім	ві́сім
G.	двох	трьох	чотирьо́х	п'ятьо́х п'яти́	шести́ шістьо́х	семи́ сімо́х	восьми́ вісьмо́х
D.	двом	трьом	чотирьо́м	п'ятьо́м п'яти́	шістьо́м шести́	семи́ сімо́м	восьми́ вісьмо́м
A.	*m.* два, *f.* дві **двох**	три **трьох**	чоти́ри **чотирьо́х**	п'ять **п'ятьо́х**	шість **шістьо́х**	сім **сімо́х**	ві́сім **вісьмо́х**
I.	двома́	трьома́	чотирма́	п'ятьма́ п'ятьо́ма	шістьма́ шістьо́ма	сіма́ сімо́ма	вісьма́ вісьмо́ма
L.	у двох	у трьох	у чотирьо́х	у п'ятьо́х у п'яти́	у шістьо́х шести́	у сімо́х семи́	у вісьмо́х у восьми́

Table 13. Со́рок 40, **п'ятдеся́т** 50, **сто** 100, **дві́сті** 200, **три́ста** 300, **чоти́риста** 400, and **п'ятсо́т** 500

Case	fourty	fifty	a hundred	200, 300, and 400	five hundred
N.	со́рок	п'ятдеся́т	сто	дві́сті три́ста чоти́риста	п'ятсо́т
G.	сорока́	п'ятдесятьо́х	ста	двохсо́т трьохсо́т чотирьохсо́т	п'ятисо́т
D.	сорока́	п'ятдесятьо́м	ста	двомста́м трьомста́м чотирьомста́м	п'ятиста́м
A.	со́рок	п'ятдеся́т / п'ятдесятьо́х	сто	дві́сті / двохсо́т три́ста / трьохсо́т чоти́риста / чотирьохсо́т	п'ятсо́т
I.	сорока́	п'ятдесятьма́	ста	двомаста́ми трьомаста́ми чотирмаста́ми	п'ятиста́ми
L.	у сорока́	у п'ятдесяти́ у п'ятдесятьо́х	у ста	у двохста́х у трьохста́х у чотирьохста́х	у п'ятиста́х

Дієвідмі́на дієсло́ва Verb Conjugation

Table 14. First Conjugation in *~уть (~ють)*

a) Hard stem *~уть* endings, *жи́ти* to live

person	singular		example	plural		example
1st	**я**	**~у**	я живу́	**ми**	**~емо**	ми живемо́
2nd	**ти**	**~еш**	ти живе́ш	**ви**	**~ете**	ви живете́
3rd	**він**	**~е**	він живе́	**вони́**	**~уть**	вони́ живу́ть

b) Soft stem ~ють endings, знати to know

person	singular		example	plural		example
1st	я	~ю	я знаю	ми	~ємо	ми знаємо
2nd	ти	~єш	ти знаєш	ви	~єте	ви знаєте
3rd	він	~є	він знає	вони	~ють	вони знають

c) Reflexive verb endings, умиватися to wash oneself

person	singular		example	plural		example
1st	я	~юся	я умиваюся	ми	~ємося	ми умиваємося
2nd	ти	~єшся	ти умиваєшся	ви	~єтеся	ви умиваєтеся
3rd	він	~ється	він умивається	вони	~ються	вони умиваються

Table 15. Second Conjugation in ~ать (~ять)

a) ~ать endings, бачити to see

person	singular		example	plural		example
1st	я	~у	я бачу	ми	~имо	ми бачимо
2nd	ти	~иш	ти бачиш	ви	~ите	ви бачите
3rd	вона	~ить	він бачить	вони	~ать	вони бачать

b) ~ять endings, говорити to speak, talk

person	singular		example	plural		example
1st	я	~ю	я говорю	ми	~имо	ми говоримо
2nd	ти	~иш	ти говориш	ви	~ите	ви говорите
3rd	він	~ить	він говорить	вони	~ять	вони говорять

c) Reflexive verb endings, знайомитися to get acquainted

person	singular		example	plural		example
1st	я	~юся	я знайомЛюся	ми	~имося	ми знайомимося
2nd	ти	~ишся	ти знайомишся	ви	~итеся	ви знайомитеся
3rd	він	~иться	він знайомиться	вони	~яться	вони знайомЛяться

Table 16. Motion Verbs

uni-directional	multi-directional	future pf. (of uni-directional)	pa. pf. (of uni-directional)
іти to go on foot	ходити	піти	
я йду	я ходжу	я піду	пішов, m.
ти йдеш	ти ходиш	ти підеш	пішла, f.
він йде	він ходить	він піде	пішло, nt.

ми йдемо́	ми хо́димо	ми пі́демо	пішли́, *pl.*
ви йдете́	ви хо́дите	ви пі́дете	
вони́ йдуть	вони́ хо́дять	вони́ пі́дуть	

і́хати *to go (by vehicle)*   **і́здити**   **пої́хати**

я і́ду	я і́жджу	я пої́ду	пої́хав, *m.*
ти і́деш	ти і́здиш	ти пої́деш	пої́хала, *f.*
він і́де	він і́здить	він пої́де	пої́хало, *nt.*
ми і́демо	ми і́здимо	ми пої́демо	пої́хали, *pl.*
ви і́дете	ви і́здите	ви пої́дете	
вони́ і́дуть	вони́ і́здять	вони́ пої́дуть	

бі́гти   *to run*   **бі́гати**   **побі́гти**

я біжу́	я бі́гаю	я побіжу́	побі́г, *m.*
ти біжи́ш	ти бі́гаєш	ти побіжи́ш	побі́гла, *f.*
він біжи́ть	він бі́гає	він побіжи́ть	побі́гло, *nt.*
ми біжимо́	ми бі́гаємо	ми побіжимо́	побі́гли, *pl.*
ви біжите́	ви бі́гаєте	ви побіжите́	
вони́ біжа́ть	вони́ бі́гають	вони́ побіжа́ть	

летí́ти *to fly*   **літа́ти**   **полетí́ти**

я лечу́	я літа́ю	я полечу́	полетí́в, *m.*
ти лети́ш	ти літа́єш	ти полети́ш	полетí́ла, *f.*
він лети́ть	він літа́є	він полети́ть	полетí́ло, *nt.*
ми летимо́	ми літа́ємо	ми полетимо́	полетí́ли, *pl.*
ви летите́	ви літа́єте	ви полетите́	
вони́ летя́ть	вони́ літа́ють	вони́ полетя́ть	

Украї́нські імена́ та на́зви міст Ukrainian Names of People and Cities

Table 17. Де́які типо́ві украї́нські імена́ Some Common Ukrainian Names

а) **Чолові́чі імена́** Male Names

Украї́нське ім'я́ Ukrainian name (in nominative case and its vocative case ending)	Англі́йська транслітера́ція English transliteration	Англі́йський відпові́дник English etymological or semantic equivalent	Пестли́ва фо́рма Affectionate or familiar form	По ба́тькові, що похо́дить від і́мени Patronymic derived from the name
Андрі́й, ~ю	*Andrii*	*Andrew*	Андрі́йк|о, ~у	Андрі́|йович ~ївна
Анато́лі|й, ~ю	*Anatolii*	*Anatole*	То́лик, ~у	Анато́лі|йович, ~ївна

Богда́н, ~е	Bohdan	Theodore	Да́нк|о, ~у	Богда́н|ович, ~івна
Васи́л|ь, ~ю	Vasyl	Basil	Васи́льк|о, ~у	Васи́л|ьович, ~івна
Ві́ктор, ~е	Viktor	Victor	Ві́т|я, ~ю	Ві́кторович, ~івна
Володи́мир, ~е	Volodymyr	n/a	Воло́д|я, ~ю	Володи́мир|ович, ~івна
Григо́рі|й, ~ю	Hryhorii	Gregory	Гриц|ь, ~ю	Григо́р|ович, ~івна
Дани́л|о, ~е	Danylo	Daniel	Дани́лк|о, ~у	Дани́л|ович, ~івна
Дени́с, ~е	Denys	Denis	Дени́ск|о, ~у	Дени́с|ович, ~івна
Дмитр|о́, ~е	Dmytro	Dimitrius	Дми́трик, ~у	Дми́тр|ович, ~івна
Євге́н, ~е	Yevhen	Eugene	Ге́н|я, ~ю	Євге́н|ович, ~івна
Іва́н, ~е	Ivan	John, Ian	Іва́нк|о, ~у	Іва́н|ович, ~івна
І́гор, ~ю; G. ~я	Ihor	Igor	Іго́рк|о, ~у	І́гор|евич, ~івна
Кири́л|о, ~е	Kyrylo	Cyril	Кири́лк|о, ~у	Кири́л|ович, ~івна
Лука́ш, ~е	Lukash	Lucas	Лука́шик, ~у	Лука́ш|евич, ~івна
Любоми́р, ~е	Liubomyr	n/a	Лю́бко, ~у	Любоми́р|ович ~івна
Макси́м, ~е	Maksym	Max	Макси́мк|о, ~у	Макси́м|ович, ~івна
Марк|о́, ~у	Marko	Mark	Ма́рцьо, ~ю	Ма́рк|ович, ~івна
Матві́|й, ~ю	Matvii	Matthew	Матві́йк|о, ~у	Матві́|йович, ~ївна
Мико́л|а, ~о	Mykola	Nicholas	Мико́лк|а, ~о	Микола́|йович, ~ївна
Миха́йл|о, ~е	Mykhailo	Michael	Миха́сик, ~у	Миха́йл|ович, ~івна
Наза́р, ~е	Nazar	n/a	Наза́рк|о, ~у	Наза́р|ович, ~івна
Оле́кс|а, ~о	Oleksa	Alexis	Лес|ь, ~ю	Оле́кс|ович, ~івна
Олекса́нд|ер, ~ре	Oleksander	Alexander	Сашк|о́, ~у	Олекса́ндр|ович, ~івна
Оре́ст, ~е	Orest	Orestes	О́рк|о, ~у	Оре́ст|ович, ~івна
Павл|о́, ~е	Pavlo	Paul	Па́влик, ~у	Па́вл|ович, ~івна
Петр|о́, ~е	Petro	Peter	Пе́трик, ~у	Петр|о́вич, ~і́вна
Рома́н, ~е	Roman	Roman	Ро́мк|о, ~у	Рома́н|ович, ~івна
Сергі́|й, ~ю	Serhii	Sergio	Сергі́йко, ~у	Сергі́|йович, ~ївна
Степа́н, ~е	Stepan	Stephen	Степа́нк|о, ~у	Степа́н|ович, ~івна
Стефа́н, ~е	Stefan	Stephan	Сте́фк|о, ~у	Стефа́н|ович, ~івна
Тара́с, ~е	Taras	Terry	Тара́сик, ~у	Тара́с|ович, ~івна
Ю́рі|й, ~ю	Yurii	George	Юрк|о́, ~у	Ю́рі|йович, ~ївна
Я́к|ів, ~ове	Yakiv	Jacob	Я́сик, ~у	Я́к|ович, ~івна
Яре́м|а, ~о	Yarema	Jeremy	Яре́мк|о, ~у	Яре́м|ович, ~івна
Яросла́|в, ~е	Yaroslav	Jerry	Славк|о́, ~у	Яросла́в|ович, ~івна

b) **Жіно́чі імена́** Female names

Украї́нське ім'я́ Ukrainian name and vocative ending	Англі́йська транслітера́ція English transliteration	Англі́йський відпові́дник English etymological or semantic equivalent	Пе́стлива фо́рма Affectionate or familiar form
Богда́н|а, ~о	Bohdana	Theodora	Да́н|а, ~о
Валенти́н|а, ~о	Valentyna	Valentine	Ва́л|я, ~ю
Вікто́рі|я, ~є	Viktoria	Victoria	Ві́т|а ~о
Ві́р|а, ~о	Vira	Faith	Ві́рц|я, ~ю
Гали́н|а, ~о	Halyna	Galina	Га́л|я, ~ю

Га́нн|а, ~о	Hanna	Anna, Hanna	Га́н|я, ~ю
Катери́н|а, ~о	Kateryna	Catherine	Ка́т|я, ~ю, Катру́с|я, ~ю
Іва́нн|а, ~о	Ivanna	Joanna	Іва́нк|а, ~о
Іри́н|а, ~о	Iryna	Irene	Ірц|я, ~ю
Ї́вг|а, ~о	Ïvha	Eugenia	Ге́н|я, ~ю
Лари́с|а, ~о	Larysa	Lara	Ле́с|я, ~ю
Лі́ді|я, ~є	Lidiya	Lydia	Лі́д|а, ~о
Любо́в, ~е	Liubov	n/a	Лю́б|а, ~о
Мар'я́н|а, ~о	Mariana	Marianne	Мар'я́нк|а, ~о
Мари́н|а, ~о	Maryna	Marina	Мари́нк|а, ~о
Марі́|я, ~є	Maria	Maria	Марі́йк|а, ~о, Мару́с|я, ~ю
Ма́рт|а, ~о	Marta	Martha	Марту́с|я, ~ю
Мела́ні|я, ~є	Melania	Melanie	Мала́нк|а, ~о
Миросла́в|а, ~о	Myroslava	Mira	Сла́вк|а, ~о, Миро́с|я, ~ю
Наді́|я, ~є	Nadia	Hope	На́д|я, ~ю, Наді́йк|а, ~о
Ната́лі|я, ~є	Natalia	Natalie	Ната́л|я, ~ю, Ната́лк|а, ~о
Окса́н|а, ~о	Oksana	n/a	Окса́нк|а, ~о
Олекса́ндр|а, ~о	Oleksandra	Alexandra	Ле́с|я, ~ю
О́льг|а, ~о	Olha	Olga	О́л|я, ~ю
Оле́н|а, ~о	Olena	Helen	Оле́нк|а, ~о
Ори́с|я, ~ю	Orysia	n/a	Ри́с|я, ~ю
Роксола́н|а, ~о	Roksolana	Roxana	Ла́н|а, ~о
Світла́н|а, ~о	Svitlana	Lucia	Ла́н|а, ~о
Соломі́|я, ~є	Solomiya	Salome	Со́л|я, ~ю, Соло́х|а, ~о
Софі́|я, ~є	Sofia	Sophia	Со́н|я, ~ю
Стефа́ні|я, ~є	Stefania	Stephanie	Сте́ф|а, ~о
Тама́р|а, ~о	Tamara	Tamara	То́м|а, ~о, То́мк|а, ~о
Тетя́н|а, ~о	Tetiana	Tatiana	Та́н|я, ~ю
Яри́н|а, ~о	Yaryna	Irene	Я́рк|а, ~о

Table 18. Де́які типо́ві украї́нські прі́звища   Some Common Ukrainian Family Names

Nominal family names with suffixes **~ук (~юк)** and **~ко** are declined only if their proprietor is a man, Я зна́ю Оре́ста **Козаче́нка.** *I know Orest Kozachenko.* They are indeclinable if their proprietor is a woman, Я зна́ю О́льгу **Козаче́нко.** *I know Olha Kozachenko.* If the family name is an adjective, its feminine ending is **~а (~я)** and it is declined both for men and women: Він лю́бить Петра́ **Ху́ткого.** *He likes Petro Khutky.* and Він лю́бить Яри́ну **Ху́тку.** *He likes Yaryna Khutka.* Adjectival declinable family names are shaded in this table.

Ім'я́ Name	Англі́йська трансліте́рація *English transliteration*	Жіно́ча фо́рма Feminine form
Авра́менко, *n.*	Avramenko	Авра́менко, *indecl.*
Бойчу́к, *n.*	Boichuk	Бойчу́к, *indecl.*
Бо́ндар, *n.*	Bondar	Бо́ндар, *indecl.*

Васи́льченк|о, *n.*	Vasylchenko	Васи́льченко, *indecl.*
Григоре́нк|о, *n.*	Hryhorenko	Григоре́нко, *indecl.*
Денисе́нко, *n.*	Denysenko	Денисе́нко, *indecl.*
Дмитру́к, *n.*	Dmytruk	Дмитру́к, *indecl.*
Дома́нськ|ий, *adj.*	Domansky	Дома́ньск|а, *decl.*
Задоро́жн|ий, *adj.*	Zadorozhny	Задоро́жн|а, *decl.*
Івани́шин, *n.*	Ivanyshyn	Івани́шин, *indecl.*
Калю́жн|ий, *adj.*	Kaliuzhny	Калю́жн|а, *decl.*
Ковале́нк|о, *n.*	Kovalenko	Ковале́нко, *indecl.*
Ковальчу́к, *n.*	Kovalchuk	Ковальчу́к, *indecl.*
Козаче́нк|о, *n.*	Kozachenko	Козаче́нко, *indecl.*
Миките́нк|о, *n.*	Mykytenko	Миките́нко, *indecl.*
Му́др|ий, *adj.*	Mudry	Му́др|а, *decl.*
Новакі́вськ|ий, *adj.*	Novakivsky	Новакі́вськ|а, *decl.*
Новачу́к, *n.*	Novachuk	Новачу́к, *indecl.*
Олі́йник, *n.*	Oliinyk	Олі́йник, *indecl.*
Павли́шин, *n.*	Pavlyshyn	Павли́шин, *indecl.*
Па́влів, *n.*	Pavliv	Па́влів, *indecl.*
Павлю́к, *n.*	Pavliuk	Павлю́к, *indecl.*
Палі́й, *n.*	Palii	Палі́й, *indecl.*
Пе́вн|ий, *adj.*	Pevny	Пе́вн|а, *decl.*
Петре́нк|о, *n.*	Petrenko	Петре́нко, *indecl.*
Петрунча́к, *n.*	Petrunchak	Петрунча́к, *indecl.*
Петрусе́нк|о, *n.*	Petrusenko	Петрусе́нко, *indecl.*
Пінчу́к, *n.*	Pinchuk	Пінчу́к, *indecl.*
Пилипе́нк|о, *n.*	Pylypenko	Пилипе́нко, *indecl.*
Полі́щу́к, *n.*	Polishchuk	Полі́щу́к, *indecl.*
Садов|и́й, *adj.*	Sadovy	Садов|а́, *decl.*
Світли́чн|ий, *adj.*	Svitlychny	Світли́чн|а, *decl.*
Тарасю́к, *n.*	Tarasiuk	Тарасю́к, *indecl.*
Ти́х|ий, *adj.*	Tykhy	Ти́х|а, *decl.*
Хмельничу́к, *n.*	Khmelnychuk	Хмельничу́к, *indecl.*
Хмельни́цьк|ий, *adj.*	Khmelnytsky	Хмельни́цьк|а, *decl.*
Шевче́нк|о, *n.*	Shevchenko	Шевче́нко, *indecl.*
Шевчу́к, *n.*	Shevchuk	Шевчу́к, *indecl.*
Яво́рськ|ий, *adj.*	Yavorsky	Яво́рськ|а, *decl.*
Якове́нк|о, *n.*	Yakovenko	Якове́нко, *indecl.*
Яре́менк|о, *n.*	Yaremenko	Яре́менко, *indecl.*

Table 19. Важли́ві міста́ Украї́ни Important Cities of Ukraine

Each city listed below is the capital of a respective Ukrainian province or **о́бласть**. The exceptions are the important sea ports or recreation centers of **Маріу́поль** *Mariupol*, **Севасто́поль** *Sevastopol*, and **Я́лта** *Yalta*. Where the root ~**i**~ changes to ~**o**~ (~**e**~) or some other sound change occurs, the genitive case form is also given, **Ка́нів**, *m.*, **Ка́нева**. The adjective derived from a provincial capital name is also the first part of the name of that province, **Вінниця** *Vinnytsia* – **Вінницька область** *Vinnytsia Province*, **Рівне** *Rivne* – **Рівненська область** *Rivne Province*. The exceptions are **Ужгород** *Uzhhorod* the capital of **Закарпатська область** *Trans-Carpathian Province*, **Луцьк** *Lutsk*, the capital of **Волинська область** *Volhynia Province*, and **Симферополь** *Symferopol*, the capital of **Кримська автономія** *the Crimean Autonomy*.

Місто та англійська транслітерація City and its English transliteration	Похідний прикметник Derived adjective	Водойма, на якій розташоване Body of water on which it is located
Вінниц|я, *f. Vinnytsia*	вінницький	р. Південний Буг *the Southern Buh River*
Дніпропетровськ[6], *т. Dnipropetrovsk*	дніпропетровський	р. Дніпро *the Dnipro River*
Донецьк, *т. Donetsk*	донецький	р. Кальміус *the Kalmius River*
Житомир, *т. Zhytomyr*	житомирський	р. Тетерів *the Teteriv River*
Запоріжжя, *nt. Zaporizhia*	запорізький	р. Дніпро *the Dnipro River*
Івано-Франківськ[7], *т. Ivano-Frankivsk*	івано-франківський	р. Бистриця Надвірнянська та Бистриця Солотвинська *the Bystrytsia Nadvirnianska and the Bystrytsia Solotvynska rivers*
Кам'янець-Подільський, *т.,* Кам'янця-Подільського *Kamianets-Podilskyi*	кам'янець-подільський	р. Смотрич *the Smotrych River*
Київ, *т.,* Києва *Kyiv*	київський	р. Дніпро *the Dnipro River*
Кіровоград, *т. Kirovohrad*	кіровоградський	р. Інгул *the Inhul River*
Кременчук, *т.,* ~á *Kremenchuk*	кременчуцький	р. Дніпро *the Dnipro River*
Кривий Ріг, *т.,* Кривого Рогу *Kryvyi Rih*	криворізький	р. Інгулець *the Inhulets River*, р. Саксагань *the Saksahan River*
Луганськ, *т. Luhansk*	луганський	р. Вільхівка та Лугань *the Vilkhivka and Luhan rivers*
Луцьк, *т. Lutsk*	луцький *but* Волинська область	р. Стир *the Styr River*
Львів, *т.,* Львова *Lviv*	львівський	р. Полтва *the Poltva River*
Маріупол|ь, *т. Mariupol*	маріупольський	Азовське море *the Sea of Azov*
Микола|їв, *т.,* ~єва *Mykolaiv*	миколаївський	р. Дніпро та р. Південний Буг *the Dnipro and the Southern Buh River*
Ніжин, *т. Nizhyn*	ніжинський	р. Остер *the Oster River*
Одес|а, *f. Odesa*	одеський	Чорне море *the Black Sea*
Полтав|а, *f. Poltava*	полтавський	р. Ворскла *the Vorskla River*
Рівн|е, *adj., nt.,* ~ого *Rivne*	рівненський	р. Устя *the Ustia River*
Севастопол|ь, *т. Sevastopol*	севастопольський	Чорне море *the Black Sea*
Симферопол|ь, *т. Symferopol*	симферопольський, *but* Кримська автономія	р. Салгир *the Salhyr River*

---

6 Many nationally conscious Ukrainians call the city Січеслав *Sicheslav* (*lit.* glory of the Sich), a reference to the Zaporozhian Sich, the citadel of Ukrainian Cossacks, who hold a special place in Ukrainian mythology as protectors of the motherland from foreign invaders in the 16th-18th centuries

7 In Ukrainian Galicia, this city is still often referred to by its original name Станіслав *Stanislav* or Станіславів *Stanislaviv*. In 1962, the Soviet regime renamed it, ostensibly to honor the Ukrainian writer Іван Франко *Ivan Franko*. This remains its official name today.

Су́ми, *pl.*, Сум *Sumy*	су́мський	р. Псол та р. Су́мка *the Psol River and Sumka River*
Терно́п|іль, *m.*, ~оля *Ternopil*	терно́пільський	р. Се́рет *the Seret River*
У́жгород, *m. Uzhhorod*	у́жгородський, *but* Закарпа́тська о́бласть	р. Уж *the Uzh River*
Черка́си, *pl.*, Черка́с *Cherkasy*	черка́ський	р. Дніпро́ *the Dnipro River*
Чернівці́, *pl.*, Чернівці́в *Chernivtsi*	чернівє́цький	р. Прут *the Prut River*
Черні́гів, *m.*, Черні́гова *Chernihiv*	черні́гівський	р. Десна́ *the Desna River*
Ха́рків, *m.*, Ха́ркова *Kharkiv*	ха́рківський	р. Ха́рків та р. Ло́пань *the Khrakiv and Lopan rivers*
Херсо́н, *m. Kherson*	херсо́нський	р. Дніпро́ *the Dnipro River*
Хмельни́цьк|ий, *adj.*, ~ого, *Khmelnytsky*	хмельни́цький	р. Півде́нний Буг *the Southern Buh River*
Я́лт|а, *f. Yalta*	я́лтинський	Чо́рне мо́ре *the Black Sea*

Subject Index

Dictionary
Ukrainian-English & English-Ukrainian

Словни́к
Украї́нсько-англі́йський та а́нгло-украї́нський

How to Use the Dictionary

This dictionary introduces the learner to the core Ukrainian word-stock that: 1) has the highest frequency of usage in everyday communication; 2) is stylistically neutral; 3) is more likely used in spoken rather than written speech. Its acquisition and creative utilization will ensure adequate communication in all major everyday situations of most informal and some formal settings. It is a learner's dictionary and, unlike any other Ukrainian dictionary published so far, it gives essential information needed in order to use every given word in actual communication. The dictionary is made up of two interrelated parts, Ukrainian-English and English-Ukrainian.

The presentation of each word includes:

1) its phonetic description, i.e., stress, stress shifts (**сестр|а́** sister, *pl.* **~и**), phonetic variants (**вчи́тель** teacher, *var.* **учи́тель**), phonetic mutations (**ніч** *vs.* **ночі** night, presented as **н|іч**, *f.* **~очі** night);
2) morphological description, i.e., the endings it takes in specific positions in a sentence;
3) description of the word meaning, usually a number of its most frequent meanings;
4) some most common idiomatic expressions it is used in; these are marked by the ♦;
5) simple illustrations of the word's usage;
6) stylistic and functional characteristics of the word where pertinent, such as informal, formal, colloquial, Kyiv standard, and Galician standard, *fam.* **Васи́ль** *Vasyl (first name)* vs. *form.* **пан Васи́ль** *Mr. Vasyl**; *colloq.* **нема́** vs *form.* **нема́є** *there isn't*; *Galician standard* vs *Kyiv standard, Gal.* **прошу́** vs. *Kyiv* **будь ла́ска** *please, here you are.*

Each description follows the same pattern for a given part of speech. The vertical bar (|) divides the stem or unchanging part of the word from its ending. The unchanging part is omitted in description. When it is used in its dictionary form as part of an expression, it is represented by its initial letter and a period, **весн|а́**, *f.* spring, **ра́ння (пі́зня) в.** early (late) spring. When it is used in a form different from its dictionary form, it is represented by a tilde and the ending: **весн|а́**, *f.* spring … ♦ **до ~и́ / ~о́ю** which stands for **до весни́** *by spring* and **весно́ю** *in spring* respectively. If the stem undergoes consonant shifts or vowel changes the relevant form is presented as follows: **р|ік**, *m.*, **~о́ку** year, *L.* **у ~о́ці**, when **~о́ку** stands for the genitive singular **ро́ку**, and *L.* **у ~о́ці** - for locative singular **у ро́ці**. When the productive stem of the word occurs in a form other than the dictionary one the inserted vertical bar | will mark it as the one that should be used for declension (if its a noun, adjective, etc.) or conjugation (if its a verb). Thus for the item appearing here under the entry **г|ість**, *m.*, **~о́стя** guest, the productive form is not **гість** but **г~** which is used for other case forms: **го́стя, го́стеві, го́стем, го́сті, госте́й, го́стям**, etc. So if your come across a word whose stem is divided by the |, you can be sure that it undergoes sound changes in its stem, **книж|ка**, *f.* book, **товста́ к.** thick book. *L.* **у ~ці** (у кни́жці), *G. pl.* **~ок** (кни́жок). In the English explanations, the articles are often omitted.

    Noun (n.) is given in the nominative singular, followed by the label for its grammatical gender *m.* (masculine), *f.* (feminine), or *nt.* (neuter) in the Ukrainian-English dictionary, and by the label *n.* (noun) in the English-Ukrainian dictionary. The singular case forms are indicated only by the respective capital letter, as in *L.* for locative singular, or *I.* for instrumental singular. By contrast, the plural case forms are represented by *pl.* following the capital initial letter of the case, as in *G. pl.* for genitive plural, etc. The gender label is absent after the nouns used only in plural, instead *only pl.* is used: **две́рі**, *only pl.* door; *only sg.* follows the nouns used only in singular: **моро́зиво**, *only sg.* ice-cream. Also given is the case form that differs in stem or stress from the nominative singular, **дру|г**, *m.* friend, *N. pl.* **~зі**. Being problematic for native speakers of Ukrainian, the *genitive singular* form is always given for the inanimate masculine nouns of 2nd declension and sometimes for nouns of other declensions. It follows their dictionary form immediately after a comma and has no label of *G.*: **буди́н|ок**, *m.*, **~ку** house. After the description of meaning, other case endings that deviate from the rule are given. Most often it is the ending of the *locative singular (L.)* with the preposition **у (в)** or **на** which corresponds to the English *in, inside, at,* and forms a set expression with the noun. It is best memorized, cf. **у магази́ні** *in a store*, but **на по́шті** *at a post office*, **в університе́ті** *at a university* but **на факульте́ті** *at a (university) department*. Where appropriate, a frequently used phraseological expression with the respective word is furnished, **вих|ід**, *m.*, **~оду** exit, way-out, ♦ **нема́є ~оду** no exit.

    Adjective (adj.) is introduced by its masculine nominative singular form, followed by the label *adj.*: **жо́вт|ий**, *adj.* yellow; **си́н|ій**, *adj.* blue. The stem is also marked by the vertical bar |. The learner is expected to know that the feminine adjectives end in **~а** for hard stems, **жо́вта кві́тка** *a yellow flower*, and **~я** for soft stems, **си́ня фа́рба** *a blue paint*, the neuter ends in **~е** for hard stems, **жо́вте а́вто** *a yellow car*, or **~є** for soft stems, **си́нє не́бо** *a blue sky*, and all plural adjectives without exception end in **~і**, **жо́вті кві́тки** *yellow flowers*, **си́ні фа́рби** *blue paints*. For adjectives with irregular forms of comparative degree only the *comparative degree (comp.)* is given, the expectation being that the learner can easily coin the superlative by adding the prefix **най~** to the comparative form: **вели́кий**, *adj.* big, large, great; *comp.* **бі́льший** bigger, *superlative* **найбі́льший** the biggest.

    Adverb (adv.) is normally given as a separate entry in those cases when it is not derived from a respective adjective: **взагалі́**, *adv.* in general, generally speaking; or when the meaning of the adverb is different from that of the cognate adjective, cf.: **га́рний**, *adj.* beautiful, pleasant and **га́рно**, *adv., colloq.* alright, fine, OK. The learner is also expected to know that the comparative and superlative forms of all adverbs take the ending **~е**: **до́вго** *for a long time* - **до́вше** *for a longer time* - **найдо́вше** *for the longest time*.

    Cardinal numerals (card.). The genitive case form of the cardinal numeral is given and the case form of the noun following it when this *numeral + noun* combination either stands on its own or is used as the subject or inanimate object of the sentence: **чоти́р|и**, *card.*, **~ьох** four, + *N. pl.*; **в|ісім**, *card.*, **~осьми́** eight + *G. pl.* This is to say that, after these numerals, the nouns are to be in the *N. pl.* and *G. pl.* respectively: **чоти́ри гри́вні** *four hryvnias* and **ві́сім гри́вень** *eight hryvnias*. Declension tables of cardinal numerals can be found in the Appendices, pp. 324-325.

    Ordinal numerals (ord.) take the same case endings as adjectives: for masculine **~ий**, **пе́рший** first, or **~ій**, **тре́тій** *third*; for feminine **~а**, **пе́рша** or **~я**, **тре́тя**, and for neuter **~е**, **пе́рше** or **~є**, **тре́тє**. An ordinal numeral is normally derived from its cardinal counterpart by adding the adjectival ending **~ий** (**~а**, **~е** or **~і**), **п'ять** five - **п'я́тий** *fifth*. Ordinal numerals are given as a separate entry only in cases when they do not follow the general rule of formation, *card.* **один** *one* - *ord.* **перший** *first*; or have mutations even if they follow the rule, **сім** *seven* - **сьомий** *seventh*. The learner is expected to know that they decline like adjectives and like adjectives they have three gender forms with the same set of adjectival endings for singular and one genderless for plural, **~і**.

Verb (*v.*). The imperfective infinitive as the basic form of the verb is given first. It is followed only by the 3rd person plural ending (for **вони** *they*) of the present tense, if the verb conjugates by the general rules. When the stem mutation affects other present tense forms, these forms are also given in the following sequence: 1st person singular, 2nd person singular, and 3rd person plural: **люб|ити, ~лю, ~иш, ~лять** ... to like, love. (The forms of 3rd *pers. sg.*, 1st and 2nd *pers. pl.* are omitted when their stems are identical with that of the 2nd *pers. sg.* Hence the complete present tense conjugation of the verb **роб|ити** *to do*, **я роблю** *I do*, **ти робиш** *you do*, **він робить** *he does*, **ми робимо** *we do*, **ви робите** *you do*, **вони роблять** *they do*, will be presented only as **роб|ити, ~лю, ~иш, ~лять**; ... to do. Then, after the semicolon in bold (;) the perfective infinitive is given either in full, **поясню|вати, ~ють; поясн|ити, ~ять** to explain, or represented only by the prefix, if the perfective forms differ from the imperfective conjugation only by the prefix, **чита|ти, ~ють; про~** to read. This means that in its future perfective conjugation, it takes the present tense endings. Then the information on how the verb combines with nouns is given - the label *tran.* for transitive verbs which take a direct accusative object, and *intr.* for intransitive, *refl.* for reflexive ones, etc. In exceptional cases when the transitive verb takes a noun in the genitive the case symbol will be given after *tran.* + *G.* The case forms of its objects, with prepositions where required, are also indicated as + *D.* for the dative, + *I.* for the instrumental and so on: **рад|ити, ~жу, ~ять; по~**, *tran.* to advise sth to sb + *A.* + *D.*

If the perfective form of the verb has a different conjugation pattern, its 3rd person plural form is furnished: **назива|ти, ~ють; назв|ати, ~уть**, *tran.* to name, give a name to sb or sth + *I.* For verbs that are irregular, all their tense forms are spelled out: **їсти, їм, їси, їсть, їмо, їсте, їдять; з'~**; *ра.* **їв, їла, їло, їли**, *tran.* to eat. Minimal word combinations or short sentences as illustrations of specific usage are often given.

The past participle form of each verb follows the description of its meaning. It is marked by the label *pa. pple.*, its English equivalent is given: **переклада|ти, ~ють; перекласти, переклад|уть**, *tran.* + *A.* to translate, etc. [...], *pa. pple.* **перекладений** translated; [...]. Sometimes the meaning of the *pa. pple.* considerably differs from that of its infinitive: **запитати**, *tran.* + *A.* to ask; *pa. pple.* **запитаний** asked; requested; in demand.

The imperative mood of each verb is given at the end of its description. An exclamation mark singles it out. Imperfective imperative comes first and in two forms. One is addressed to the 2nd person singular **ти** *you*, **пиш|и!** *write!* It is used in familiar, informal communication or when one chooses to be impolite with a stranger. Following it is the ending of the 2nd person plural imperative, used in polite or formal communication, **~іть!** representing the form **пишіть!** After these two forms of the imperfective imperative, come two respective forms of the perfective imperative. Because for the verb **писати** these forms differ from the imperfective only by the prefix **на~**, they are represented only by that prefix, which the learner should add to the stems of the imperfective forms. Thus the abbreviated description of the imperative of **писати** is **(на)пиш|и! ~іть!**. instead of its full description: *impf.* **пиши! пишіть!**; *pf.* **напиши! напишіть!** If the stress in not on the ending it means that it stays on the same syllable of the 2nd person singular. The learner is expected to know that the omitted imperative form addressed to 1st person plural and corresponding to the English *let us* + *infinitive* (*Let's write!*) is derived by adding the ending **~мо** to the imperative 2nd person singular stem if it ends in a consonant, **їж!** - **їжмо!** *let's eat!*, and **~імо**, if it ends in the vowel **~и**, **скаж|и!** - **скажімо!** *let's say!*

Perfective infinitive of each verb is listed separately and alphabetically in the body of the Ukrainian-English Dictionary with reference to a full description under the imperfective infinitive: **помогти**, *pf.*, see **помагати** or **взяти**, *pf.*, see **брати**. If no perfective infinitive is listed that means that the verb is irregular and does not have it: **бути**, *pres.* for all persons **є**; *no pf.*; *fut.* **буд|уть**, *intr.* to be; **буд|ь! ~те!**

Preposition (prep.). It is important to bear in mind that the meaning of Ukrainian prepositions in *verb + noun collocations* often depends on whether static or dynamic relations are expressed. One and the same preposition often requires the noun after it to be in one case if the static position is denoted and in a different case when motion is involved. Two labels are used to distinguish between these situations only when they require different case forms: *posn.*, short for 'a static position', and *dir.*, short for 'direction of motion'. The rule of thumb is that the static position (*posn.*) is expressed by *preposition + noun in the locative*: Книжка **на столі**. *The book is on the table*. The direction (*dir.*) is expressed by the same *preposition + noun in the accusative*: Поклади книжку **на стіл**. *Put the book on the table*. The relations of static position and direction can also be expressed by other prepositions requiring other case forms. This information is offered in the description of the respective word.

Synonyms and antonyms The dictionary entry often refers the learner to other words that have an identical (synonyms) or opposite (antonyms) meanings. The reference *See* directs the learner to the synonym that should be given preference of the two, while *Also see* refers to the synonym used in actual speech but not preferable.

The Ukrainian-English and the English-Ukrainian parts of the dictionary are connected and it is a good strategy always to look up the same item in both these parts to get the fullest information about it: **airplane**, should be followed by reading the description of its Ukrainian equivalent in the Ukrainian-English Dictionary, **літак**. The learner should make it a habit to use the dictionary not only while doing translation exercises but also when creating with language and generating one's own Ukrainian speech. When in the slightest unsure, always consult the dictionary.

Ukrainian Alphabet

No.	Letter	Cursive	Its name	English spelling equivalent	No.	Letter	Cursive	Its name	English spelling equivalent
1.	А, а	А, а	/a/	A, a	18.	Н, н	Н, н	/en/	N, n
2.	Б, б	Б, б	/be/	B, b	19.	О, о	О, о	/o/	O, o
3.	В, в	В, в	/ve/	V, v	20.	П, п	П, п	/pe/	P, p
4.	Г, г	Г, г	/he/	H, h	21.	Р, р	Р, р	/er/	R, r
5.	Ґ, ґ	Ґ, ґ	/ge/	G, g	22.	С, с	С, с	/es/	S, s
6.	Д, д	D, д	/de/	D, d	23.	Т, т	Т, т	/te/	T, t
7.	Е, е	Е, е	/e/	E, e	24.	У, у	У, у	/u:/	U, u
8.	Є, є	Є, є	/je/	Ie, ie	25.	Ф, ф	Ф, ф	/ef/	F, f
9.	Ж, ж	Ж, ж	/zhe/	Zh, zh	26.	Х, х	Х, х	/kha:/	Kh
10.	З, з	З, з	/ze/	Z, z	27.	Ц, ц	Ц, ц	/tse/	Ts, ts
11.	И, и	И, и	/y/	Y, y	28.	Ч, ч	Ч, ч	/che/	Ch, ch
12.	І, і	І, і	/i/	I, i	29.	Ш, ш	Ш, ш	/sha/	Sh, sh
13.	Ї, ї	Ї, ї	/ji/	I, i	30.	Щ, щ	Щ, щ	/shcha/	Shch, shch
14.	Й, й	Й, й	/jot/	I, i	31.	..., ь	..., ь	znak mjákshennia	-
15.	К, к	К, к	/ka/	K, k	32.	Ю, ю	Ю, ю	/ju/	Iu, iu
16.	Л, л	Л, л	/el/	L, l	33.	Я, я	Я, я	/ja/	Ia, ia
17.	М, м	М, м	/em/	M, m					

Українсько-англійський словник
Ukrainian-English Dictionary

A

а, *conj.* 1) and *(expresses opposition)*, **Мене́ зва́ти Юрко́, а тебе́?** My name is Yurko, and yours? 2) but, **не вели́кий, а мали́й** not big, but small; 3) whereas, while, **Яри́на живе́ у Ки́єві, а Катери́на – у Льво́ві.** Yaryna lives in Kyiv whereas Kateryna lives in Lviv.

або́, *conj.* or *(expresses the alternative based on options of no difference)*, **На вихідні́ Макси́м ди́виться телеві́зор а. слу́хає му́зику.** On weekends Maksym watches TV or listens to music; *Cf.* **чи**, *conj.*

австрі́|єць, *m.* Austrian, **На літаку́ він познайо́мився з одни́м ~йцем.** He met an Austrian on board the plane. *N. pl.* **~йці, Ці мандрі́вники всі ~йці.** These travelers are all Austrians.; *f.* **~йка** Austrian woman; *L.* **на ~йці**, *G. pl.* **~йок.**

австрі́йськ|ий, *adj.* Austrian, **Ми летíли ~ими авіялі́ніями.** We flew by Austrian Airlines.

А́встрі|я, *f.,* **~ї** Austria, **Я ніко́ли в житті́ не був в ~ї.** I have never been to Austria in my life.

а́вт|о, *nt.,* **~а** car, automobile; **~ом** by car; *G. pl.* **авт.**

авто́бус, *m.,* **~а** bus; **~ом** by bus; ♦ **сіда́ти на а.** to take a bus.

авто́бусн|ий, *adj.* bus, **~а зупи́нка** bus stop.

автовокза́л, *m.,* **~у** a bus station *(usually larger in size)*; *L.* **на ~і**, *dir.* **на а.**

аге́нці|я, *f.,* **~ї** agency; **тур-а.** travel agency; **а. нови́н** news agency. *L.* **в ~ї.**

адвока́т, *m.,* lawyer, attorney, counsel; **вчи́тися на ~а** be trained as a lawyer; **зверта́тися до** + *G.* **(найма́ти** + *A.*) **~а** turn to (hire) a lawyer, **працюва́ти ~ом** work as a lawyer.

адміністра́тор, *m.* 1) an administrator, manager (in hotel); 2) receptionist (in hotel), **Я замо́вив кімна́ту в ~а готе́лю.** I booked a room with the hotel administrator. *N. pl.* **~и.**

адре́с|а, *f.* address, **дома́шня а.** residential address, **а. відпра́вника (отри́мувача)** sender's (receiver's) address; *dir.* **писа́ти на ~у** write to an address, **За яко́ю ~ою ви живете́?** What address do you live at?

аеропо́рт, *m.,* **~у** airport, **міжнаро́дний а. «Бори́спіль»** Boryspil International Airport; *L.* **в ~і**; **таксі́вка до ~у** taxi to the airport. *See* **летови́ще.**

Азо́вськ|е мо́р|е, *nt.,* **~ого ~я** the Sea of Azov; *L.* **на ~ому ~і** on the Sea of Azov; **на А. м.** to the Sea of Azov.

акаде́мі|я, *f.* academy; **Націона́льний університе́т «Ки́єво-Моги́лянська А.» (НаУКМА)** the National University of Kyiv Mohyla Academy; **Націона́льна А. Нау́к Украї́ни (НАНУ)** the National Academy of Sciences of Ukraine.

акто́р, *m.,* **~а** actor, **а. кіна́ (теа́тру)** film (theater) actor; **провідни́й а.** leading man, **а. дру́гого пла́ну** supporting actor; *f.,* **~ка** actress, **провідна́ ~ка** leading lady; *L.* **на ~ці**, *G. pl.* **~ок.**

але́, *conj.* but, however, **Я мо́жу, а. не хо́чу.** I can but I don't want to.

алергі́|я, *f.,* **~ї** allergy; **ма́ти ~ю на** + *A.* to be allergic to sth, **Він ма́є ~ю на антибіо́тики.** He's allergic to antibiotics.

Аме́ри|ка, *f.* America; **Сполу́чені Шта́ти ~ки** the United States of America; *L.* **в ~ці.**

америка́н|ець, *m.,* **~ця** American; *L.* **на ~цеві**, *N. pl.* **~ці; ~ка**, *f.* American woman; *L.* **на ~нці**, *G. pl.* **~нок.**

америка́нськ|ий, *adj.* American; **~а мрі́я** the American dream.

ана́ліз, *m.,* **~у** 1) analysis; 2) text, **а. кро́ви** blood test.

англі́|єць, *m.,* **~йця** Englishman; *L.* **на ~йцеві**; *f.,* **~йка** Englishwoman; *L.* **на ~йці**, *G. pl.* **~йок**

англі́йськ|ий, *adj.* English, **~а мо́ва** English language; **розмовля́ти ~ою** to speak English.

антибіо́тик, *m.,* **~а** antibiotic; **прийма́ти ~и** to take antibiotics.

апети́т, *m.,* **~у** appetite; **ма́ти а. на** + *A.,* to have an appetite for sth, **Я ма́ю а. на ка́ву.** I feel like a cup of coffee. **Він не ма́є ~у.** He has no appetite.

апте́|ка, *f.* pharmacy, **цілодобо́ва а.** twenty-four hour pharmacy, **Місце́ва а. працю́є без пере́рви на обі́д.** The local pharmacy works without a lunch break.; *L.* **в ~ці.**

ара́бськ|ий, *adj.* Arab, Arabic, **~а мо́ва** Arabic language.

а́ркуш, *m.,* **~а** sheet (of paper), **~і папе́ру** sheets of paper, ♦ **почина́ти з чи́стого ~а** to turn a new page.

археоло́г, *m.* archeologist, **Він завжди́ хотів ста́ти ~ом.** He has always wanted to become an archeologist.

архіте́ктор, *m.,* **~а** architect.

архітекту́р|а, *f.* architecture, **моде́рна (стара́) а.** modern (old) architecture; **Вона́ ціка́виться старо́ю ри́мською ~ою.** She iss interested in old Roman architecture.

архітекту́рн|ий, *adj.* architectural, **а. анса́мбль (стиль)** architectural ensemble (style), **~а па́м'ятка** architectural sight.

атмосфе́р|а, *f.* 1) atmosphere; 2) mood, tone, **У цьо́му готе́лі приє́мна а.** This hotel has a pleasant atmosphere.

Б

ба́б|а, *f.*, **~и** 1) grandmother; 2) *vulg.* woman; ♦ **база́рна б.** a gossip, chatterbox; *N. pl.* **~и**, *G. pl.* **баб** or **~ів**.

бага́ж, *m.*, **~у́** luggage, baggage; **мі́сце ~у́** piece of luggage, **реєстра́ція ~у́** luggage check-in; **ручни́й б.** carry-on luggage; *I. sg.* **~ем**.

бага́т|ий, *adj.* rich, wealthy; *comp.* **~ший**.

бага́т|о[1], *adv.* + *G.* a lot of, many, **б. днів** many days; much, **б. робо́ти** a lot of work; **б. ча́су** much time; **б. гро́шей** much money, *comp.* **бі́льше** more.

бага́т|о[2], *num.* a lot of, many, *G. and L.* **-ьо́х**, **Він дзвони́в до ~ьо́х фахівці́в.** He called many specialists.; *D.* **~ьо́м**, **Фільм сподо́бався ~ьо́м гляда́ча|м.** Many viewers liked the film.; *I.* **~ьма́, Ми познайо́милися з ~ьма́ ціка́вими людьми́.** We met many interesting people.

багатоповерхо́в|ий, *adj.* multistory, having several floors, **б. буди́нок** a multistory building.

бажа́нн|я, *nt.* wish, desire, **новорі́чні б.** New Year wishes; **ма́ти б.** to have a wish.

бажа́|ти, **~ють**; **по~** + *G.* + *D.* to wish; ♦ **~ю вам уда́чі.** I wish you good luck.; ♦ **б. всьо́го найкра́щого** to wish all the best; *pa. pple.* **ба́жаний** desired; **(по)бажа́й! ~те!**

база́р, *m.*, **~у** a bazaar; *L.* **на ~і**, *N. pl.* **~и**

байду́же, *adv.* with indifference, indifferently; ♦ **Мені́ б.** I don't care.

байду́ж|ий, *adj.* indifferent; **бу́ти ~им до** + *G.* to be indifferent to sth/sb; **Вона́ до цьо́го ці́лком ~а.** She is completely indifferent to it.

бакалавра́т, *m.*, **~у** bachelor's program, bachelor's studies; **б. з** + *G.* bachelor's degree in; **Він навча́вся на ~і в Оде́ському університе́ті.** He did his bachelor's studies at Odesa University.

бакала́врськ|ий, *adj.* bachelor's, pertaining to bachelor's degree, **б. сту́пінь** bachelor's degree, **~а програ́ма** bachelor's program.

бале́т, *m.*, **~у** ballet, **ходи́ти на б.** to go to the ballet.

балко́н, *m.*, **~у** balcony; *L.* **на ~і**, **Він лю́бить спа́ти на ~і.** He likes to sleep on the balcony.

банду́р|а, *f.* bandura *(Ukrainian national musical instrument)*; **гра́ти на ~і** to play the bandura; **~и́ст**, *m.* bandura player.

банк, *m.*, **~у** bank; **Націона́льний Б. Украї́ни** the National Bank of Ukraine; *L.* **у ~у**.

банкі́р, *m.*, **~а** banker, *N. pl.* **~и**.

банкома́т, *m.*, **~у** ATM machine; **вийма́ти гро́ші з ~у** to get money from an ATM; *N. pl.* **~и**.

бар, *m.*, **~у** bar, **мі́ні-б.** mini-bar, **со́ковий б.** juice bar.

ба́рв|а, *f.* color, **рі́зні ~и** various colors.

басе́йн, *m.*, **~у** swimming pool; **ходи́ти до ~у** to go to swimming pool; **пла́вати у ~і** to swim in swimming pool.

баскетбо́л, *m.*, **~у** basketball; **гра́ти в б.** to play basketball.

батьківщи́н|а, *f.* fatherland, homeland, mother country; *L.* **на ~і**.

ба́тьк|о, *m.* father, *N. pl.* **~и** 1) fathers; 2) parents, **Мої́ ~и живу́ть на селі́.** My parents live in the countryside.

ба́ч|ити, **~ать**; **по~**, *tran.* to see, **Я ба́чив це уві сні.** I saw it in a dream.; *pa. pple.* **(по)ба́чений** seen; **(по)бач! ~те!**

ба́читися; **по~**, *intr.* + **з/із** + *I.* 1) to see each other, **Поба́чимося за́втра.** I'll see you tomorrow.; 2) to go out with sb, **Оле́кса Нова́чук ба́читься з не́ю мі́сяць.** Oleksa Novachuk has gone out with her for a month.; **(по)бач|ся! ~теся!**

без, *prep.*, without + *G.*, **б. робо́ти** without work, **б. су́мніву** without a doubt, **б. ме́не** without me.

безалкого́льн|ий, *adj.* nonalcoholic; **б. напі́й** a nonalcoholic drink.

бездрото́в|ий, *adj.* having no wires, wireless, **б. інтерне́т (зв'язо́к)** Wi-Fi Internet (connection), **~а мере́жа** Wi-Fi network.

безкошто́вн|ий, *adj.* free of charge, gratis, at no cost; **~е навча́ння** free education, **б. квито́к (прої́зд, дзвіно́к)** a free ticket (trip, phone call), **~і по́слуги** free services.

безкошто́вно, *adv.* for free, gratis, at no cost.

безпере́чно, *adv.* undoubtedly, surely, without a doubt.

бе́ре|г, *m.*, **~а** a coast (of sea), river bank; *L.* **на ~зі**, *N. pl.* **~ги**.

бе́резе|нь, *m.*, **~ня** March, **Він народи́вся пе́ршого ~ня.** He was born on March 1; *L.* **у ~ні**.

бібліоте́|ка, *f.* library, **дитя́ча (електро́нна, науко́ва, публі́чна, університе́тська) б.** children's (electronic, scientific, public, university) library; *L.* **у ~ці**.

бібліоте́кар, *m.*, **~я** librarian, **Він працю́є ~ем.** He works as a librarian.; *f.*, **~ка, Пані́ Скори́на – досві́дчена ~ка.** Mrs. Skoryna is an experienced librarian.; *L.* **на ~ці**, *G. pl.* **~ок**.

бі́га|ти, **~ють**, *intr., multi.* to run, jog, **Він лю́бить б. уранці́.** He likes to jog in the morning.; **Тут ніко́ли ніхто́ не ~є.** Nobody ever runs here.; **бі́гай! ~те!**

бі́|гти, **~жа́ть**; **по~**, *intr., uni.* to run, jog, **Куди́ це він ~жить?** Where is he running to?; **біжи́! ~іть!** *see multi.* **бі́гати.**

бі́дн|ий, *adj.* 1) poor; 2) unfortunate.

бізнесме́н, *m.*, **~а** businessman; *L.* **на ~ові**; *f.* **~ка** businesswoman; *L.* **на ~ці**, *G. pl.* **~ок**.

б|ік, *m.*, **~о́ку** side, **лі́вий (пра́вий) б.** left (right) side; ♦ **з одного́ ~у .., з і́ншого ~у** on the one hand ... on the other hand; **на ~о́ці** on the side.

бі́л|ий, *adj.* white; ♦ **б. як сніг** snow-white, **~а соро́чка (су́кня)** white shirt (dress); ♦ **се́ред ~ого дня** in plain daylight.

білору́с, *m.* a Belarusian man; *f.* **~ка** a Belarusian woman; *L.* **на ~ці**, *G. pl.* **~ок**.

Білору́с|ь, *f.* Belarus; **у ~і** in Belarus; **до ~и** to Belarus.

білору́ськ|ий, *adj.* Belarusian, **~а мо́ва** Belarusian language.

біль

біль, *m.*, ~**о́лю** pain, ache; **зубни́й б.** toothache, **головни́й б.** headache; **з ~о́лем** with pain.

бі́льше, *adv.*, *comp.* 1) more, **набага́то б.** much more, **значно́ б.** considerably more; 2) any more *in neg. sentences*, **Він б. не працю́є тут.** He doesn't work here any more.; ♦ **чим б., тим кра́ще** the more the better. *Also see* **бага́то**.

бі́льш|ий, *adj.*, *comp. of* **вели́кий** 1) bigger, larger, greater; **набага́то б.** much bigger; *in comp. structures* **б. ніж** (*or* **як**) + *N.*, **б. за** + *A.*, **б. від** + *G.* more than; **Ця спа́льня ~а., ніж та́ (як та́, за ту, від тіє́ї).** This bedroom is bigger than that one.

бі́ля, *prep.* + *G.* 1) near, close to, **б. мі́ста** near the city; 2) about, approximately, **б. десяти́ гри́вень** about ten hryvnias.

блаки́тн|ий, *adj.* 1) sky-blue, azure, ~**е не́бо** azure sky; 2) one of the two Ukrainian national colors; ♦ **жо́вто-б.** yellow and blue; ♦ ~**а мрі́я** cherished dream.

бли́зьк|ий, *adj.* close, near, **Ми ~і дру́зі.** We are close friends.; *comp.* **бли́жчий**.

бли́зько, *adv.* + *G.* 1) close, nearby; **Ста́нція метра́ б. мого́ до́му.** The subway station is near my house.; 2) approximately, about, **б. ста гри́вень** about a hundred hryvnias.

бо, *conj.*, *colloq.* because, for, as (cause), **Зроби́ це за́раз, б. за́втра бу́де пі́зно.** Do it now because it'll be too late tomorrow.

бог, *m.*, ~**а**, god; ♦ **Б. зна́ що** God knows what; *N. pl.* ~**и́**, *V.* **Бо́же!** Oh God! ♦ **не дово́дь Бо́же!** God forbid!

бол|і́ти, ~**я́ть**, *intr.*, *A.* + to ache, hurt, **Іва́на ~и́ть голова́.** Ivan has a headache. **Що вас ~и́ть?** What ails you?; **бол|и́! ~і́ть!**

борщ, *m.*, ~**у́**, borshch, beet and cabbage soup (a beloved Ukrainian national dish). *N. pl.* ~**і́**.

бо|я́тися, ~**ю́ся**, ~**і́шся**, ~**я́ться**, *intr.* + *G.* to be afraid of, fear sth; **Він ~ї́ться літакі́в.** He is afraid to fly.; **бі́й|ся! ~теся!**

бра́м|а, *f.* gate, **че́рез ~у** through the gate; ~**ка**, *f.* wicket-gate.

брат, *m.* 1) a brother; **рі́дний б.** a brother by birth (*as opposed to a cousin*), **двоюрі́дний б.** a cousin; 2) brother (*intimate form of address to man*); *N. pl.* ~**и**.

бра́ти, **бер|у́ть**; **взя́ти**, ~**у́**, **ві́зьм|уть**, *tran.* 1) to take, **Вона́ завжди́ бере́ з собо́ю телефо́н.** She always takes her phone along.; 2) to get, procure, obtain, **Ціка́во, де це він бере́ гро́ші.** I'm curious where he gets the money. ♦ **Зві́дки він взяв, що … (Рома́н одру́жений)?** What makes him think that … (Roman is married)?; ♦ **б.** + *A.* **за ду́рня** (*f.* **дуре́пу**) to take sb for a fool; **Він завжди́ брав Іва́на за ду́рня.** He has always taken Ivan for a fool.; *pa. pple.* **взя́тий** taken; **бер|и́, ~і́ть; візьм|и́! ~і́ть!**

бруна́тн|ий, *adj.* brown, **те́мно-б. ділови́й костю́м** dark brown business suit; *Also see* **кори́чневий**.

бува́|ти, ~**ють**; **по~** *intr.* to visit, frequent, **у (в)** + *L.*, **Де ви ~ли в Украї́ні?** Where in Ukraine have you been?, **Я хо́чу по~ у Льво́ві.** I want to visit Lviv.; **б. на** + *L.* attend (a lecture, concert); **(по)бува́й! ~те!** ♦ **бува́й (здоро́в|ий, ~а)!** or **бува́йте (здоро́ві)!** so long, take care.

буди́н|ок, *m.*, ~**ку** a house, building, edifice; *L.* **у ~ку**.

ва́нна

буд|и́ти, ~**жу́**, ~**я́ть**; **роз~**, *tran.* to wake sb up, **Коли́ вас розбуди́ти?** When do you want me to wake you up?; *pa. pple.* **розбу́джений** woken; **(роз)буд|и́! ~і́ть!**

буд|и́тися, ~**жу́ся**, ~**я́ться**; **з~**, *refl.* to wake (oneself) up, **Коли́ ти ~ишся?** When do you wake up?; **буд|и́ся! ~ться!**

бу́дн|ій, *adj.* everyday, **б. день** weekday.

буду|ва́ти, ~**ють**; **з-**, *tran.* to build, construct; *pa. pple.* **збудо́ваний** built; **(з)буду́й! ~те!**

будь- *indef. part.* any, ever (*expresses vagueness or indifference with pronouns and adverbs*); **б.-хто** anybody, **б.-що** whatever, **б.-коли** any time, whenever, **б.-де** wherever, **б.-як** whichever way, carelessly.

будь ла́ска, ♦ please (*lit. im.* be kind!), **скажі́ть, б. л.** tell me, please; ♦ **ось, б. л.** here you are.

бу́к|ва, *f.* letter; ♦ **писа́ти з вели́кої (мало́ї) ~ви** to write in upper (lower) case; *G. pl.* ~**ов**.

букіністи́чн|ий, *adj.* second-hand (bookstore); pertaining to rare books, ~**а книга́рня** second-hand bookstore.

бульва́р, *m.*, ~**у** boulevard, wide street typically lined with trees with a promenade in the middle, **б. Тара́са Шевче́нка** Taras Shevchenko Boulevard; *L.* **на ~і**; *N. pl.* ~**и**.

бурштино́в|ий, *adj.*, amber, of amber yellow color; made of amber.

бутербро́д, *m.*, ~**у** a sandwich, **роби́ти б. із ши́нки, помідо́ра та цибу́лі** to make a sandwich of ham, tomato, and onion; *See* **кана́пка**.

бу́ти, *pres. for all persons* **є**; *no pf.*; *fut.* **бу́д|уть**, *intr.* to be, **Учо́ра він ~в на конце́рті.** Yesterday, he was at a concert.; ♦ **Б. чи не б.?** To be or not to be?; **будь! ~те!**; ♦ **бу́дьте здоро́ві!** Bless you! (*in response to somebody sneezing, lit. be healthy*); ♦ *im.* ~**дьмо, гей!** cheers!, to our health! (*popular Ukrainian drinking toast repeated three times*).

буха́н|ка, *f.* loaf (of bread), **б. жи́тнього (пшени́чного) хлі́ба** loaf of rye (wheat) bread, *L.* **на ~ці**, *G. pl.* ~**ок**.

В

в, *prep.*, *var.* **у, у́ві** 1) in, at (with *L.* location inside), **в університе́ті** in/at university; 2) on (with *A.* of week days), **у неді́лю** on Sunday; 3) into, to (+ *A.* direction of motion), **поста́вити у кімна́ту** to put into a room.

ваго́н, *m.*, ~**а** train car, **пасажи́рський в.** passenger car, **купе́йний (плацка́ртний, зага́льний) в.** second-(third-, fourth-) class car, **спа́льний в.** sleeping car.

важк|и́й, *adj.* heavy, hard, difficult, ~**а́ валі́за** heavy suitcase, ~**е завда́ння** a hard task, *comp.* **важчий**.

важли́в|ий, *adj.* important, significant; ~**о зроби́ти це на за́втра.** It's important to do it by tomorrow.

вака́ці|ї, *only pl.* vacation, holidays; **на в.** for holidays; **на ~ях** during / on vacation. *Also see* **кані́кули**.

валі́з|а, *f.* suitcase, trunk, **пакува́ти ~у** to pack a suitcase.

валю́т|а, *f.* currency; **обмі́нна в.** convertible currency; ~**ою** in currency; **обмі́н ~и** currency exchange; **міня́ти ~у** to exchange currency.

ва́нн|а, *f.* 1) bathroom (with shower, sink); 2) bathtub.

варе́ник, *m.*, ~**a** 1) dumpling stuffed with potato, cottage cheese or fruit *(Ukrainian national dish)*, normally in *pl.*; 2) pierogi, **З чим сього́дні ~и?** What are the pierogis with today?. *Also see* **піріг.**

вар|и́ти, ~**ю́**, ~**ять**; **з~**, *tran.* to cook, prepare food; *also* **в. ї́сти**; **в. вече́рю** to make dinner; **в. я́йця** to boil eggs; *pa. pple.* **зва́рений** cooked, boiled; **(з)вари́! ~іть!**

ва́рто, *mod.* + *pf. inf.* it's worth doing sth., **В. купи́ти цю кни́жку.** This book is worth buying.; **не в.** + *impf. inf.* it's not worth doing, **не в. роби́ти цього́.**

ваш, *poss. pron.*, *m.* your, yours, **в. син** your son; *f.* ~**а**, *nt.* ~**е**, *pl.* ~**і.**

вважа́|ти, ~**ють**, *only impf.* to be of the opinion, to think; **я ~ю, що ...** I think that, **Він так не ~є.** He doesn't think so.; ♦ **вважа́й! ~те!** watch out!, be careful!

ввесь, *adj.*, *m.*, *var.*, *see* **весь.**

вве́чері, *adv.*, *var.* **уве́чері** in the evening, at night (before midnight); ♦ **сього́дні в.** tonight.

вго́ру, *adv.*, *var.* **уго́ру** up, upwards.

вдо́ма, *adv.*, *var.* **удо́ма, до́ма**, *posn.* at home, home, **Марі́ї нема́є в.** Maria is not home; **у** + *G. of pers. pron.* + **в.** at sb's place, **у ме́не (те́бе, не́ї,** etc.) **вдо́ма** at my (your, her, etc.) place.

вез|ти́, ~**у́ть**, *uni.*; **за~** , *tran.* 1) to drive, take sb/sth by vehicle, **За́втра він завезе́ нас до Оде́си.** Tomorrow he'll drive us to Odesa.; 2) to cart; *also see multi.* **вози́ти**; *pa. pple.* **заве́зений** delivered, carried to; **(за)вези́! ~іть!**

Вели́кдень, *m.*, **Вели́кодня** Easter *(lit. the great day)*; **на В.** for Easter, on Easter.

великодн|ій, *adj.* Easter, pertaining to Easter, ~**і вака́ції** Easter holidays, ~**я пи́санка** Easter egg, ~**ій обі́д** Easter dinner.

вели́к|ий, *adj.* big, large; great, ~**е мі́сто** a big city, **в. актор** great actor; *comp.* **бі́льший.**

велосипе́д, *m.*, ~**a**, a bicycle, **ї́здити** ~**ом** to ride a bicycle.

ве́рес|ень, *m.*, ~**ня** September; *L.* **у** ~**ні.**

верну́ти, *also var.* **поверну́ти**, *pf.*, *see* **верта́ти.**

верта́|ти, ~**ють**; **(по)верн|у́ти**, ~**уть**, 1) *tran.* to return sb sth, give sth back to sb, + *A.* **і** *D.*, **Він верну́в гро́ші бра́тові.** He returned his brother the money.; 2) *intr.* to return, turn back, **Вони́ зупини́лися і поверну́ли наза́д.** They stopped and turned back.; *pa. pple.* **пове́рнутий**, *var.* **пове́рнений** returned; **верта́й! ~те!; (по)верни́! ~іть!**

верта́|тися, ~**ються**; **(по)верн|у́тися**, ~**уться**, *refl.* to return, come back, **Коли́ ти поверне́шся?** When will you be back?

весе́л|ий, *adj.* merry, happy.

ве́село, *adv.* merrily, happily; ♦ **Нам було́ ду́же в.** We had a lot of fun.

весн|а́, *f.* spring, **ра́ння (пі́зня) в.** early (late) spring; ♦ ~**о́ю** *or* **на** ~**і** in spring.

весня́н|ий, *adj.* spring, pertaining to spring, **в. день** spring day, ~**і кані́кули** spring break, ~**е со́нце** spring sun.

весь, *adj.*, *m.*, **вс|ього́**; *var.*, **ввесь** and **уве́сь**; *f.* **вся**, *var.* **уся**; *nt.* **все**, *var.* **усе**; *pl.* **всі**, *var.* **усі** all, whole, entire; + *A. (in indications of time period)* **в. день** all day long, **в. час** all the time, all along, ~**ю ніч** all night long.

вече́р|я, *f.* dinner, supper, **Що у нас на** ~**ю?** What do we have for dinner?; **вари́ти** ~**ю** to cook dinner; *G. pl.* **вече́р.**

вече́ря|ти, ~**ють**; **по~** *intr.* to have dinner (supper); *or* + *I.*, **Він повече́ряв борще́м і варе́никами.** He ate borshch and dumplings for dinner.; **(по)вече́ряй! ~те!**

ве́ч|ір, *m.*, ~**ора** evening; **до́брий в.!** good evening!; **від ра́нку до** ~**ора** from morning till night; *N. pl.* ~**ори́.**

вечі́р|ка, *f.* party, reception; **роби́ти** ~**ку** to throw a party, **запро́шувати на** ~**ку** to invite to a party; *L.* **на** ~**ці**, *G. pl.* ~**ок.**

вечі́рн|ій, *adj.* evening (paper, train), ~**і нови́ни** evening news.

вже, *adv.*, *var.* **уже́** already; **Я в. був там.** I have already been there., **Він в. їв.** He already ate.

взагалі́, *adv.*, *var.* **зага́лом** 1) in general, on the whole; ♦ **в. і зокрема́** in general and in particular; ♦ **в. ка́жучи** generally speaking; 2) at all, not at all *(for emphasis in negative statements)*, **Я не зна́ю Ки́єва в.** I don't know Kyiv at all.

взає́мно, *adv.* ♦ the same to you *(response to a wish)*.

взи́мку, *adv.*, *var.* **узи́мку** in winter.

взуття́, *nt.* footwear, shoes, **ві́дділ в.** shoe department.

взя́ти, *pf.*, *var.* **узя́ти** *see* **бра́ти.**

ви, *pers. pron.*, 2ⁿᵈ *pers. pl.*, **вас** you, **Що в. ду́маєте про це?** What do you think about it?

виба́глив|ий, *adj.* demanding, whimsical, **в. смак** discriminating taste.

виба́ча|ти, ~**ють**; **ви́бач|ити**, ~**ать**, *tran.* to forgive sb sth, pardon, excuse, + *D.* **Він ви́бачив О́льзі її кри́тику.** He forgave Olha her criticism.; *pa. pple.* **ви́бачений** forgiven; **вибача́й! ~те!; ви́бач! ~те!**

ви́бачити, *pf.*, *see* **вибача́ти.**

вибира́|ти, ~**ють**; **ви́брати, ви́бер|уть**, *tran.* to choose, select; *pa. pple.* **ви́браний** chosen, select; **вибира́й! ~те!; ви́бер|и! ~іть!**

вивча́|ти, ~**ють**; **ви́вч|ити**, ~**ать**, *tran.* to study (subject), learn, memorize, **Що ти вивча́єш?** What do you study?; *pa. pple.* **ви́вчений** learned; **вивча́й! ~те! ви́вч|и! ~іть!**

ви́вчити, *pf. see* **вивча́ти** and **вчи́ти.**

вид, *m.*, ~**у** 1) view, **в. на** + *A.* view of sth, **кімна́та із** ~**ом на мо́ре** a room with a view of the sea; 2) type, sort, **в. тра́нспорту** type of transportation, **Яки́м** ~**ом тра́нспорту ти лю́биш ї́здити?** What type of transportation do you like to go by?

вида|ва́ти, ~**ю́ть**; **ви́дати** *(for conjugation see* **да́ти**), *tran.* to publish (book, film); *pa. pple.* **ви́даний** published, issued; **видава́й! ~те!; ви́дай! ~те!**

ви́дати, *pf.*, *see* **видава́ти.**

ви́дужати, *pf.*, *see* **виду́жувати.**

виду́жувати   **відо́мий**

виду́жу|вати, ~ють; **виду́жа|ти**, ~ють, *intr.* to get well; recover from sickness, **від** + *G.* from, **Він до́вго не міг виду́жати від ка́шлю.** He took a long time to recover form cough.; **виду́жуй! ~те!; виду́жай! ~те!;** ♦ **виду́жуйте скорі́ше!** get well soon!

ви́йти, *pf., see* **вихо́дити.**

виклада́|ти, ~ють; **ви́класти**, *see* **кла́сти**, *tran.* + *D.* 1) *only impf.* to teach sth to sb, **Що він ~є?** What does he teach?; 2) to put out, **Вона́ ви́клала всі ре́чі на стіл.** She put all her things out on the table.; *pa. pple.* **ви́кладений** put out; **виклада́й! ~те!; ви́клад|и! ~іть!**

виклада́ч, *m.,* ~á instructor *(at university as opposed to* **вчи́тель** *high school teacher)*, **в. істо́рії** history instructor; *L.* **на ~éві**, *N. pl.* ~í; *f.* ~ка; *L.* **на ~ці**, *G. pl.* ~ок.

ви́кликати, *pf., see* **виклика́ти.**

виклика́|ти, ~ють; **ви́кликати**, **ви́клич|уть**, *tran.* to call *(an ambulance)*, **Швидку́ допомо́гу мо́жна ви́кликати за но́мером 103.** The ambulance can be called by dialing 103.; *pa. pple.* **ви́кликаний** summoned; **виклика́й! ~те!; ви́клич! ~те!**

вимика́|ти, ~ють; **ви́мкн|ути**, ~уть, *tran.* to turn off *(light, radio)*; *pa. pple.* **ви́мкнений** or **ви́мкнутий** turned off; **вимика́й! ~те!; ви́мкн|и! ~іть!**

ви́мкнути, *pf, see* **вимика́ти.**

вин|о́, *nt.* wine, **черво́не (бі́ле) в.** red (white) wine. *N. pl.* ~а.

ви́прати, *pf., see* **пра́ти.**

ви́пуск, *m.,* ~у 1) graduation class; 2) edition (of printed matter, newscast); *L.* **у ~у.**

ви́раз, *m.,* ~у expression, **фразеологі́чний в.** phraseological expression, **в. обли́ччя** facial expression.

ви́рішити, *pf., see* **виріша́вати.**

вирішу́|вати, ~ють; **ви́ріш|ити**, ~ать, *tran.* to decide, resolve; make up one's mind; *pa. pple.* **ви́рішен|ий** decided; **виріша́й! ~те!; ви́ріш|и! ~іть!**

ви́рости, *pf., see* **рости́.**

ви|сі́ти, ~шу́, ~си́ш, ~си́ть, ~ся́ть, *only impf., intr.* to hang, **Ця карти́на за́вжди тут висі́ла.** This picture has always hung here.

висо́к|ий, *adj.* high, tall, ~а температу́ра high temperature, ~а я́кість high quality; *comp.* **ви́щий.**

виста́в|а, *f.* 1) performance, show, theater play; **театра́льна в.** theater performance; **іти́ на ~у** to go to a performance; 2) art exhibit; *L.* **на ~і.**

ви́став|ка, *f.* exhibition (of art, industrial products, etc.), *L.* **на ~ці**, *G. pl.* ~ок.

ви́тв|ір, *m.,* ~ору work (of art, literature), creation, **Це справжні́й в. мисте́цтва.** This is a true work of art.; *N. pl.* ~ори.

ви|хід, *m.,* ~оду exit, way out, **з (із)** + *G.,* **в. з буди́нку (кімна́ти)** exit from building (room); **У нас нема́є ~оду.** We have no way out, *N. pl.* ~оди.

вихідн|ий, *n.* day off; ♦ **у ~і** on weekend, **Що ти роби́тимеш у ~і?** What will you do on the weekend? **на ~і** for weekend, **На ~і ми ду́маємо піти́ до о́пери.** For the weekend, we plan to go the opera; *adj.* non-working (of day, week), **в. день** day off.

вихо́д|ити, ~жу, ~ять; **ви́йти**, **ви́йд~уть**, *intr.* 1) to exit, go out; ♦ **в. з мо́ди** to go out of fashion; 2) get off (bus, etc.), **Ви ~ите на насту́пній зупи́нці?** Are you getting off at the next stop?; 3) to get published, **Ця газе́та ~ить по субо́тах.** This newspaper comes out on Saturdays.; **виходь! ~те!; ви́йд|и! ~іть!**

вишива́н|ка, *f.* tradional Ukrainian embroidered shirt; *L.* **у ~ці**; *G. pl.* ~ок.

ви́ш|ня, *f.* sour cherry, *G. pl.* ~ень.

ви́щий, *adj.* higher, taller; *comp. of* **висо́кий.**

вівто́р|ок, *m.,* **вівті́рка**, *var.* ~ка Tuesday, **у в.** on Tuesday.

від, *prep.* + *G.* 1) *with anim. n.* from (origin), **Це в. Іва́на.** This is from Ivan.; 2) from (time), **в. понеді́лка до середи́** from Monday to Wednesday; 3) (in comparison) than, **Те а́вто нові́ше в. цього́.** That car is newer than this one.; 4) against, from, for (remedy), **Ви ма́єте щось в. ка́шлю?** Do you have anything for a cough?

відві́дати, *pf., see* **відві́дувати.**

відві́ду|вати, ~ють; **відві́да|ти**, ~ють, *tran.* 1) to visit sth/sb, **Ми відві́дали Са́шка у ліка́рні.** We visited Sashko in the hospital.; 2) to attend, **Він регуля́рно ~є її ле́кції.** He regularly attends her lectures.; *pa. pple.* **відві́даний** visited; **відві́дуй! ~те!; відві́дай! ~те!**

відгада́ти, *pf., see* **гада́ти.**

відійти́, *pf., see* **відхо́дити.**

від'їжджа́|ти, ~ють; **від'ї́хати**, **від'ї́д|уть**, *intr.* 1) to depart, leave (by a vehicle, not on foot), **Ми ~ємо за́втра вра́нці.** We are leaving tomorrow morning.; 2) to drive away; **від'їжджа́й! ~те! від'ї́дь! ~те!**

від'ї́зд, *m.,* ~у a departure (by a vehicle), **зустрі́тися пе́ред ~ом** to meet before the departure.

від'ї́хати, *pf., see* **від'їжджа́ти.**

відкрива́|ти, ~ють; **відкри́|ти**, ~ють, *tran.* 1) to open sth, **Чи мо́жна відкри́ти вікно́?** May I open the window? 2) to discover; *pa. pple.* **відкри́тий** opened; **відкрива́й! ~те!; відкри́й! ~те!**

відкрива́|тися, ~ються; **відкри́|тися**, ~ються, *refl.* to open, **Фестива́ль відкрива́ється за́втра.** The festival opens (starts) tomorrow.

відкри́ти, *pf., see* **відкрива́ти.**

відкри́т|ий, *pa. pple.* open, opened; working (of store, library); **Ви ~і?** Are you open (of a store, office)?

відкри́тися, *pf., see* **відкрива́тися.**

відлеті́ти, *pf., see* **відліта́ти.**

відлі́т, *m.,* ~ьо́ту departure (of flight, airplane), **До ~у її ре́йсу лиша́ється три годи́ни.** Three hours are left before the departure of her flight.

відліта́|ти, ~ють; **відлеті́ти**, **відлечу́**, ~я́ть, *intr.* to leave, depart (of a plane, birds), **Коли́ він відліта́є до Нью-Йо́рка?** When is he leaving (by plane) for New York?; **відліта́й! ~те! відлети́! ~іть!**

відо́м|ий, *adj.* well-known, renowned, **в. письме́нник** well-known writer; ♦ **бу́ти ~им** + *I.* to be known for sth **Украї́нці ~і своє́ю гости́нністю.** Ukrainians are known for their hospitality.

відповіда|ти, **~ють**; **відпові́|сти**, **відповім**, **~си**, **~сть**, **~мо**, **~сте**, **~дять**, *intr.*, to answer, respond, **на + A., в. на пита́ння** answer a question; **відповіда́й! ~те!**; *no pf. im., instead* **дай! ~те відпові́дь!**

відпові́д|ь, *f.* answer, response; **у в. на + A.** in answer to; *I.* **~дю.**

відпочива|ти, **~ють**; **відпочи́ти**, **відпочи́н|уть**, *intr.* 1) to rest, relax, **Тобі́ тре́ба відпочи́ти.** You need some rest; 2) to vacation, be on holidays, **Де ви відпочива́ли влі́тку?** Where did you vacation in the summer?; ♦ **ї́здити відпочива́ти** to go for vacations; **відпочива́й! ~те!**; **відпочи́нь! ~те!**

відпочи́н|ок, *m., only sg.,* **~ку** 1) rest; 2) free time, leisure; ♦ **на ~ку** on holiday.

відпочи́ти, *pf., see* **відпочива́ти.**

відпу́ст|ка, *f. (only relative to work, not studies)* a leave, vacation, holidays, **(п)іти́ у ~ку** to go on a leave; **Як ви прове́ли ~ку?** How did you spend your holidays?; *L.* **у ~ці** on leave; *G. pl.* **~ок.** *Cf.* **кані́кули.**

відрізни́ти, *pf., see* **відрізня́ти.**

відрізни́тися, *pf., see* **відрізня́тися.**

відрізня́|ти, **~ють**; **відрізн|и́ти**, **~я́ть**, *tran.* to tell sth from sth, **від + G., відрізни́ти Оле́ну від Ольги.** to tell Olena from Olha.; *pa. pple.* **відрі́знений** told apart; **відрізня́й! ~те!**; **відрізн|и́! ~і́ть!**

відрізня́|тися, **~ються**; **відрізн|и́тися**, **~я́ться**, *intr.* **+ від** *G. (usually impf.)* to be different from, differ from, **Чим ~є́ться америка́нський футбо́л від європе́йського?** What's the difference between American and European football?

відсвяткува́ти, *pf., see* **святкува́ти.**

відхо́д|ити, **~жу**, **~ять**; **відійти́**, **відійд|у́ть**, *intr.* to depart, leave (of train, bus, ship), **Коли́ ~ить авто́бус до Оде́си?** When does the Odesa-bound bus leave?; **відхо́дь! ~те!**; **відійд|и́! ~і́ть!**

відчини́ти, *pf., see* **відчиня́ти.**

відчиня́|ти, **~ють**; **відчин|и́ти**, **~ю́**, **~ять**, *tran.* to open *(usually something that is locked)*, **Коли́ ~ють гастроно́м.** When do they open the grocery store. *pa. pple.* **відчи́нений** opened, unlocked; **відчиня́й! ~те!**; **відчин|и́! ~і́ть!** *Cf.* **відкрива́ти.**

ві́з|а, *f.* visa, **туристи́чна (студе́нтська, ділова́) в.** tourist (student, business) visa.

війти́, *pf., var.* **вві́йти** and **уві́йти,** *see* **вхо́дити.**

вікн|о́, *nt.* window; *N. pl.* **~а.**

ві́льн|ий, *adj.* 1) free, available; 2) vacant, not occupied; **в. день** day off, **Це мі́сце ~е?** Is this seat vacant?; ♦ **у в. час** in one's free time.

ві́льно, *adv.* fluently, **Він в. розмовля́є по́льською.** He speaks fluent Polish.

вімкну́ти, *pf., see* **вмика́ти.**

він *pers. pron., m.* he; it *(as substitute for inan. m. sg. nouns),* **Ось авто́бус, в. зру́чний.** Here's a bus, it is comfortable.; *G.* **його́.**

ві́р|ити, **~ять**; **по~**, *intr.* **+ D.** to believe sb., trust; **Я не ~ю йому́.** I don't believe him.; **(по)ві́р! ~те!**

вірш, *m.,* **~а** poem, verse; *N. pl.* **~і.**

ві́сім, *card.,* **восьми́** eight + *G. pl.,* **в. гри́вень** eight hryvnias.

вісімдеся́т, *card.,* **~и** eighty + *G. pl.,* **в. днів і ноче́й** eighty days and nights.

вісімна́дцять, *card.,* **~и** eighteen + *G. pl.,* **в. ро́ків** eighteen years.

вісімсо́т, *card.,* **восьмиста́** eight hundred + *G. pl.,* **в. гра́мів ри́су.** eight hundred grams of rice.

віта́л|ьня, *f.* living room, drawing room; *G. pl.* **~ень.**

віта́н|ня, *nt., often in pl.* greeting, **різдвя́ні (новорі́чні, великодні) в.** Christmas (New Year, Easter) greetings, **в. з днем наро́дження** birthday greetings; ♦ **перека́зувати в.** to pass greetings (regards), **Перека́зуйте мої́ в. батька́м.** Pass my regards to your parents.; *G. pl.* **~ь.**

віта́|ти, **~ють**; **при~**, *tran.* 1) to greet, welcome, salute; 2) to congratulate sb on sth, **+ A. + з (із) + I.,** **Він привіта́в її́ з перемо́гою.** He congratulated her on her victory.; **Тре́ба при~ Рома́на із днем наро́дження.** We need to greet Roman on his birthday.; *no pa. pple.,* **поздоро́влен|ий** *is used instead*; **(при)віта́й! ~те!**

ві́т|ер, *m.,* **~ру** wind; *N. pl.* **~ри́.**

ві́трян|ий, *adj.* windy, **в. день** windy day, **~а пого́да** windy weather.

включа́|ти, **~ють**; **включ|и́ти**, **~у́**, **~ать**, *tran.* to include, **Ціна́ ~є послу́ги переклада́ча.** The price includes translator's services.; *pa. pple.* **включе́ний** included; **включа́й! ~те**; **включ|и́! ~і́ть!**

включи́ти, *pf., see* **включа́ти.**

включно з (із), *adv.* including, **+ I., всі, в. з ді́тьми.** everybody includuing the children.

вла́сн|ий, *adj.* own, one's own, **Це його́ ~а кварти́ра.** This is his own apartment.; ♦ **~е!** indeed, exactly, yes.

влашто́ву|вати, **~ють**; **влашту́|вати**, *tran.* 1) to arrange, organize, set up sth (meeting), **Мо́жете в. мені́ зустрі́ч із не́ю?** Can you arrange me a meeting with her?; 2) to suit sb., **Цей готе́ль нас не ~є.** This hotel doesn't suit us.; *pa. pple.* **влашто́ваний** arranged; **влашто́вуй! ~те!**; **влашту́й! ~те!**

влаштува́ти, *pf., see* **влашто́вувати.**

влі́тку, *adv., var.* **улі́тку** in the summer.

вмива́тися, *var., see* **умива́тися.**

вмика́|ти, **~ють**; **вімкн|у́ти**, **~у́ть**, *tran.* to turn on (lights, radio); *pa. pple.* **вімкну́тий**, *var.* **ві́мкнений** switched on; **вмика́й! ~те!**; **вімкн|и́! ~і́ть!**

вми́тися, *var., see* **уми́тися.**

вмі́ти, *var, see* **умі́ти.**

вниз, *adv., var.* **уни́з,** *dir.* downward, down; **іти́ в.** go down.

внизу́, *adv., var.* **унизу́,** *posn.* 1) *posn.* down, in the lower part; 2) downstairs.

вод|а́, *f.* water, **питна́ в.** potable water, **прі́сна в.** fresh water, **мінера́льна в.** mineral water, **джере́льна в.** spring water; *A.* **~у**, *N. pl.* **~и.**

водíй   гáрно

водí|й, *m.*, ~я driver, chauffeur, **Він працює ~єм.** He works as a driver, *N. pl.* ~í.

возúти, **вожý**, **воз|ять**, *multi.*; **по~** *tran.* to drive, take sb/sth by vehicle, to cart, **Він возитиме нас до Одеси щодня.** He'll drive us to Odesa everyday.; *uni.* **везти**; *pa. pple.* **завéзений** delivered; **(по)воз|ú!**; ~íть!

вокзáл, *m.*, ~у bus station, train station or airport *(usually larger in size than* **стáнція** station); *dir.* **на в.**; **Менí трéба на залізничний в.** I need to get to the railway station.; *L.* **на ~і.**

волейбóл, *m.*, ~у volleyball; ♦ **грáти у в.** to play volleyball.

Волúн|ь, *f.* Volhynia or Volyn *(historical region of north-western Ukraine comprising modern provinces of Lutsk, Rivne, and parts of Zhytomyr and Ternopil provinces. Lutsk is the capital of Volhynia.)*; *I.* ~ню.

волиня́|к, *m.*, ~кá person born in Volhynia; *f.*, ~чка, *L.* **на ~чці**, *G. pl.* ~чок.

волí|ти, ~ють, *only impf., tran.* + *A* + **пéред** *I.* to prefer, **Він ~є ïсти салáти, ніж м'ясо.** He prefers to eat salads rather rather than meat.

волóсс|я, *nt., only sg.* hair, **дóвге (корóтке) в.** long (short) hair.

вóл|я, *f., only sg.* freedom, liberty, **на ~і** free.

вонá, *pers. pron., f.*, ïї she; it *(as substitute for inan. f. sg. nouns)*, **Ось книжка, в. тонкá.** Here's a book, it is thin.

вонú, *pers. pron., pl.*, ïх they, **Ось книжки, в. цікáві.** Here are books, they are interesting.

вонó, *pers. pron., nt.*, **йогó** it; **Ось áвто, в. новé.** Here's a car, it is new.

вор|óта, *m., only pl.*, ~íт gates; *I. pl.* ~óтами or ~íтьми.

впéвнен|ий, *adj.* sure, certain, **у** *I*, **в** + *L.* of sth / sb, **Я в. у цьóму.** I'm sure of this; *var.* **упéвнений**.

впрáв|а, *f.* exercise, drill, **робити ~и** to do exercises.

врáжен|ня, *nt.* impression, **в. від** + *G.* impression of, **справля́ти в.** to make an impression, **ділúтися ~нями** share impressions; *G. pl.* ~ь.

врáнці, *adv., var.* **урáнці** in the morning, **рáно в.** early in the morning, **сьогóдні (зáвтра, вчóра) в.** this (tomorrow, yesterday) morning.

вс|е, *var.* **усé** *pron., nt.*, ~ьóго all, everything, the whole lot, **Це в.?** Is that all?, **В., що він сказáв – дурнúці.** All he said is nonsense.; *adj. nt. of* **ввесь**, **В. життя́ я подорожувáв.** All my life I traveled.; *adv. colloq.* all the time, constantly, **Він в. дýмає про тéбе.** He thinks of you all the time.; ♦ **в. однó**, *adv.* all the same, still, **Я в. однó дізнáюся.** I'll find out all the same.

вс|і, *adj., pl.*, ~ix, *var.* **усí**, *see* **весь**, **в. моï друзí** all my friends.

встигá|ти, ~ють; **встигн|ути**, ~уть, *intr.* + *inf.* to have enough time to do sth, make it on time, manage, **Він ледве встиг на робóту.** He hardly made it to work on time.

встúгнути, *pf., see* **встигáти**.

вступá|ти, ~ють; **вступúти**, ~ю, **вступл|ять**, *intr.* to enter, enroll in (university, party) **до** + *G.*; **вступáй! ~те!**; **вступ|ú!** ~íть!

вступúти, *pf, see* **вступáти**.

вс|ьóго, *G. of* **весь (увéсь, ввесь)** or **все**; *colloq.* **в.-на-всьóго** nothing but, only, **Це в.-на-всьóго копія.** This is nothing but a replica. **Нам трéба в.-на-всьóго сто грúвень.** We need a measely hundred hryvnias.

вс|я, *adj., f., var.* **уся** *see* **весь**; **В. ця істóрія здається дúвною.** This whole story seems strange.; *G.* ~iéï.

вузьк|úй, *adj.* narrow; *comp.* **вужчий**.

вулиц|я, *f.* street; ~ею along the street, **Люблю́ гуля́ти цією ~ею.** I like to walk along this street.; **центрáльна в.** the main street; **на ~і** outdoors; on the street.

ву́|хо, *nt., var.* **ухо**, ~а ear; *L.* **у ~сі**, *N. pl.* **(в)уха**, *var.* **(в)уші**.

вх|ід, *m.*, ~ду entrance, way-in, **до** + *G.* to, **в. до кінотеáтру (крамнúці)** cinema (store) entrance; ♦ ~у немáє no entrance; **при ~і** near (at) the entrance.

вхóд|ити, ~жу, ~ять; **війти, війд|ýть**, *intr.* to enter, to come in, **до** + *G.*, **Богдáн війшов до кімнáти.** Bohdan walked into the room.; **входь! ~те!**; **війд|ú! ~íть!**

вчéн|ий, *m., var., see* **учéний**.

вчúтель, *m., var., see* **учúтель**.

вчúтелька, *f., var.,* see **учúтелька**.

вчúти, *v., var. see* **учúти**.

вчúтися, *v., var. see* **учúтися**.

вчóра, *adv., var.* **учóра** yesterday.

Г

гадá|ти, ~ють; **від~** 1) *only impf., intr.* to think, guess, reckon, to be of the opinion; ♦ **я гадáю, що** ... I think that; 2) *tran.* to guess, conjure, figure out, **відгадáти загáдку** to guess a riddle; *pa. pple.* **відгáданий** guessed; **(від)гадáй! ~те!**

газéт|а, *f.* newspaper, **щодéнна г.** daily newspaper.

галерé|я, *f.* gallery, **картúнна (мистéцька) г.** picture (art) gallery,

галицьк|ий, *adj.* Galician, pertaining to **Галичинá** Ukrainian Galicia, **Це стáра ~а традиція.** This is an old Galician tradition.

галичáнин, *m.* man of Ukrainian Galician identity; *N. pl.* **галичáни**, *G. pl.* **галичáн**.

галичáн|ка, *f.* woman of Ukrainian Galician identity, *L.* **на ~ці**, *G. pl.* ~ок.

Галичин|á, *f.* Galicia *(three provinces of Western Ukraine, Lviv, Ternopil, and Ivano-Frankivsk, lands that were part of the 12th century Principality of* **(Гáлич)** *Halych)*.

гарáзд, *adv.* alright, fine, OK *(to express agreement)*.

гáрн|ий, *adj.* nice, pretty, fine, beautiful.

гарнíр, *m.*, ~у side dish, garnish; **на г.** as side dish.

гáрно, *adv.* 1) nice, nicely, pleasantly, great, **У ньóго зáвжди г.** It's always nice at his place.; 2) *colloq.* fine, OK, alright *(to express agreement or approval)*.

га́ряче, *adv.* 1) hotly, **Окса́ні було́ г. у кімна́ті.** Oksana felt hot in the room.; 2) warmly; passionately, **Госте́й г. зустрі́ли у Льво́ві.** The guests were warmly welcomed in Lviv.

гаря́ч|ий, *adj.* 1) hot, **Був г. день.** It was a hot day; 2) heated, **Ми ма́ли до́сить ~у розмо́ву.** We had a rather heated conversation.

гастроно́м, *m.*, **~у** a smaller grocery store.

ге́ні|й, *m.*, **~я** genius.

генія́льн|ий, *adj.* **бу́ти ~им** to be a genius of …, **Ле́ся - ~а пое́тка.** Lesia is a genius of a poet.

геро́|й, *m.* 1) character in a story, **головни́й г. опові́дання** the protagonist of a story, leading character; 2) hero; *N. pl.* **~ї**.

геть, *adv.*, *colloq.* completely, at all *(with neg. statements)*, **Я г. стоми́вся.** I got completely tired., **Він вас г. не зрозумі́в.** He did not understand you at all.

ге́тьман, *m.* hetman, supreme military commander, **г. Богда́н Хмельни́цький** Hetman Bohdan Khmelnytsky.

гірк|и́й, *adj.* bitter, **г. смак** bitter taste, **~е розчарува́ння** bitter disappointment, **Це я́блуко ~е на смак.** This apple tastes bitter.

гі́рш|ий, *adj.*, worse, *comp. of* **пога́ний**.

г|іс́ть, *m.*, **~о́стя** guest, visitor; *N. pl.* **~о́сті**; ♦ **піти́ у ~о́сті до** + *G.* to go visit sb; *G. pl.* **~осте́й**, *D. pl.* **~о́стям**, *I. pl.* **~і́стьми́**.

гіта́р|а, *f.* guitar, **гра́ти на ~і** to play the guitar, **~и́ст** guitar player.

глибо́к|ий, *adj.* deep, profound; *comp.* **гли́бший**.

говор|и́ти, **~ю́**, **~я́ть**; **сказа́ти**, **~у́**, **ска́ж|уть**, *tran.* 1) to say, **Він говори́ть ціка́ві ре́чі.** He is saying interesting things.; 2) to speak (a language) + *I.*, **г. украї́нською мо́вою** to speak Ukrainian; ♦ **г. пра́вду** to tell the truth; *pa. pple.* **ска́заний** said, pronounced; **говор|и́! ~і́ть!; скаж|и́! ~і́ть!**

годи́н|а, *f.* hour, **Котра́ г.?** What time is it?, **О котрі́й ~і?** At what time?

годи́нник, *m.*, **~а** 1) clock; 2) wrist-watch; ♦ **за ~ом** by the clock.

голов|а́, *f.* 1) head; **поверну́ти ~у** to turn one's head; 2) chairman, **г. коміте́ту** chair of the committee; *G. pl.* **голі́в**.

головн|и́й, *adj.* 1) main, principal, **~а ву́лиця** the main street; 2) chief, leading, **г. еконо́міст** chief economist; 3) head, pertaining to head, **г. біль** headache.

голо́дн|ий, *adj.* hungry.

голуб|е́ць, *m.*, **~ця́** cabbage roll *(traditional Ukrainian food made of rice, minced meat and other ingredients rolled in a cabbage leaf and boiled or stewed)*, often in pl. **~і**.

гор|а́, *f.* mountain; *posn.* **у ~ах** in the mountains, **Тепе́р вони́ живу́ть у ~ах.** They live in the mountains now.; *dir.* **у ~и**; *L.* **на ~і**, *N. pl.* **~и**.

горо́д, *m.*, **~у** vegetable garden.

городин|а, *f.*, *coll.*, *only sg.* vegetables, **сві́жа (заморо́жена) г.** fresh (frozen) vegetables, **з ~ою** with vegetables. *Also see* **о́воч**.

го́сті, *n. pl.*, *see* **гість**, **ходи́ти (піти́) в г. до** + *G.* to visit, **Ми ходи́ли в г. до дру́зів.** We visited our friends., **Приходь(те) до нас в г.** Come to visit us.

готе́л|ь, *m.*, **~ю** hotel, *L.* **у ~і.**

готі́в|ка, *f.* ready money, cash; *L.* **у ~ці**; ♦ **плати́ти ~ою** to pay in cash.

гото́в|ий, *adj.* ready, prepared.

готу|ва́ти, **~ють**; **при~**, *tran.* 1) to prepare; 2) cook food; *pa. pple.* **пригото́ваний** prepared; **(при)готу́й! ~те!**

гр|а, *f.*, **~и́** game; *N. pl.* **і́гри**, **гра́ти в комп'ю́терні і́гри** to play computer games; *G. pl.* **і́гор.**

грам, *m.*, **~а** gram (one thousandth of a kilogram), **сто ~ів** a hundred grams.

гра́|ти, **~ють**; **по~** 1) to play (a game), **г. в/у** + *A.*, **Ми гра́ємо у футбо́л.** We play soccer.; 2) play (an instrument), **г. на** + *L.* to play an instrument, **Він до́бре ~є на гіта́рі.** He plays the guitar well.; 3) act, play on stage or in film, *pf.* **зігра́ти**; **(по)грай! ~те!**

гриб, *m.*, **~а** mushroom, **бі́лий г.** porcini mushroom; ♦ **збира́ти ~и́** to gather mushrooms; *N. pl.* **~и́.**

грибо́в|ий, *adj.* mushroom, of mushrooms; **~а підли́ва (ю́шка)** mushroom sauce (soup).

гри́в|ня, *f.* hryvnia *(Ukrainian national currency unit)*, **дві́, три́, чоти́ри ~ні** two, three, four hryvnias; *G. pl.* **гриве́нь, сто п'ять ~ень** twenty-five hryvnias.

грип, *m.*, **~у** influenza, flu, **У не́ї г.** She has the flu; ♦ **захворі́ти на г.** to go down with the flu.

гро́ш|і, *only pl.*, **~ей** money, **папе́рові г.** paper money; *I.* **грі́шми** or **~и́ма.**

гру́де|нь, *m.*, **~ня** December, **у ~ні** in December; **Він народи́вся тре́тього ~я.** He was born on December 3.

гру́п|а, *f.* group, **г. люде́й (тури́стів)** a group of people (tourists).

гру́ш|а, *f.*, **~і**, *var.* **~ка** 1) pear; 2) peartree.

гру́ш|ка, *f.*, *var.* **~а** 1) a pear; 2) peartree; *L.* **на ~ці**, *N. pl.* **~ки**, *G. pl.* **~ок.**

губ|а́, *f.* lip; *N. pl.* **~и**, *G. pl.* **губ** or **~ів.**

губ|и́ти, **~лю́**, **~иш**, **~лять**; **за~**, *var.* **з~**, *tran.* 1) to lose, **Я загуби́в запи́сник.** I lost my notebook.; 2) to waste (time); *pa. pple.* **загу́блений** lost, **~а наго́да** a lost opportunity; **(за)губ|и́! ~і́ть!**

губ|и́тися, **~лю́ся**, **~ишся**, **~иться**, **~ляться**; **за~** *refl.* + *A.* to lose one's way, go astray, get lost, **Тут ле́гко за~.** It's easy to get lost here.; **(за)губ|и́ся! ~і́ться!**

гуля́|ти, **~ють**; **по~** *intr.* to walk, take a walk, go for a walk, saunter, **Я люблю́ г. у (по) па́рку.** I like to walk in (around) the park.; **г. по ву́лиці** or **ву́лицею** to walk along a street; **(по)гуля́й! ~те!**

гуртожи́т|ок, *m.*, **~ку** dormitory; hostel, **студе́нтський г.** student dormitory; *L.* **у ~ку.**

Ґ

ґа́н|ок, *m.*, **~ку** 1) doorstep; 2) porch; *L.* **на ~ку.**

ґрунт | **дивно**

ґрунт, *m.*, ~**у** soil, earth, ground.

ґу́дзик, *m.*, ~**a** button; *L.* **на** ~**у**.

Д

да|ва́ти, ~**ють**; **да́ти, дам, даси́, дасть, дамо́, дасте́, даду́ть**, *tran.* + *D.* 1) to give, **Він дав ма́пу Оле́гові.** He gave the map to Oleh.; 2) + *inf.* to let, allow, permit, **Він не дає́ мені́ зроби́ти це.** He doesn't allow me to do it.; 3) *impf. im.* let us (*exhortation to do sth*), **Дава́йте роби́ти це ра́зом.** Let's do it together.; *pa. pple.* **да́ний** given; this; **дава́й!** ~**те!**; **дай!** ~**те!**

да́вн|ій, *adj.* 1) old, **Він мій д. друг.** He is an old friend of mine.; 2) ancient, **у** ~**ій Гре́ції** in ancient Greece.

давно́, *adv.* a long time ago; for a long time, **Ми д. не ба́чилися.** We haven't seen each other for a long time.; ♦ **коли́сь давни́м д.** once upon a time; ♦ **д. пора́** high time; **Вам д. пора́ познайо́митися.** It's high time you met each other.

дале́к|ий, *adj.* far, distant, remote, **д. ро́дич** a distant relative, **Як** ~**о зві́дси він живе́?** How far from here does he live?; *comp.* **да́льший**.

данти́ст, *m.* dentist.

дару|ва́ти, ~**ють**; **по**~, *tran.* 1) to give as present + *D.*, **Він подарува́в це щеня́ сестрі́.** He gave the puppy to his sister.; 2) forgive, excuse in ♦ **дару́й(те)!** excuse me! (*said to draw attention*); *pa. pple.* **(по)даро́ваний** given as gift; **(по)дару́й!** ~**те!**

да́т|а, *f.* date, day of month and year, **Яка́ сього́дні д.?** What date is it today? *Also see* **число́**.

да́ти, *pf., see* **дава́ти**.

дв|а, *card., m.*, ~**ox** two (for two *m. nouns*) + *N. pl.* **д. хло́пці** two boys, **д. дні** two days. *Also see* **дві**.

два́дцят|ь, *card.*, ~**и** twenty + *G. pl.*, **д. копі́йок** twenty kopeks.

двана́дцят|ь, *card.*, ~**и** + *G. pl.* twelve, **д. юнакі́в** twelve youths.

две́р|і, *n., only pl.*, ~**ей** door, **Він підійшо́в до** ~**ей.** He came up to the door.; *I.* ~**има** or ~**ями**; ♦ **сту́кати у д.** to knock on the door.

дв|і, *card., f.*, ~**ox** two (for two *f. nouns*) + *N. pl.* **д. се́стри** two sisters, **д. кни́жки** two books.

двір, *m.*, **дво́р|у** court; *L.* **у** ~**і**, ♦ **надво́рі** outdoors.

дві́сті, *card.*, **двохста́** two hundred + *G. pl.*, **д. гра́мів** two hundred grams.

двохсо́т|ий, *ord.* two hundredth.

де, *adv.* where, **Д. він живе́?** Where does he live?; ♦ *colloq.* **Та д.?** Really? You don't say so?

дев'яно́ст|о, *card.*, ~**a** ninety + *G. pl.*, **д. гра́дусів** ninety degrees. *See* **дев'ятдеся́т**.

дев'ятдеся́т, *card.*, ~**и** *Gal. var.* **дев'яно́сто** ninety + *G. pl.*

дев'ятна́дцят|ь, *card.*, ~**и** nineteen + *G. pl.*, **д. мі́сяців** nineteen months.

дев'ятсо́т, *card.*, ~**иста́** nine hundred + *G. pl.*, **д. сторі́нок** nine hundred pages.

дев'ят|ь, *card.*, ~**и** nine + *G. pl.*, **д. ти́жнів** nine weeks.

деі́льк|а, *pron.*, ~**ox** + *G. pl.* a few, several (*for count.*), *var. See* **кі́лька**.

де-не́будь, *adv.* somewhere, some place.

де́нн|ий, *adj.*, day, daytime, afternoon; **д. по́їзд** afternoon train; ~**а температу́ра** daytime temperature.

день, *m.*, **дн|я**, day; ♦ **з** ~**я на день** from day to day; **щодня́** every day; *N. pl.* ~**і**; *G. pl.* ~**ів** or **д., сім** ~**ів** seven days, **ві́сім д.** eight days.

де́рев|о, *nt.* tree; *N. pl.* **дере́ва**.

десе́рт, *m.*, ~**у** dessert; ♦ **на д.** for dessert.

Десн|а́, *f.* the Desna (*a left tributary of the Dnipro*); ♦ **зачаро́вана Д.** the enchanted Desna; **Мі́сто Черні́гів стої́ть на** ~**і.** The city of Chernihiv is situated on the Desna.; *L.* **на** ~**і**.

деся́т|ок, *m.*, ~**ка** 1) ten, + *G. pl.*, **Нам тре́ба купи́ти два** ~**ки яє́ць.** We need to buy twenty eggs; 2) dozen, ~**ки ти́сяч** dozens of thousands; *L.* **у** ~**ку**.

деся́т|ь, *card.*, ~**и** ten, **д. годи́н** ten hours.

десь, *adv.* 1) somewhere, some place, **Він живе́ д. бі́ля Оде́си.** He lives some place near Odesa.; 2) *colloq.* about, approximately, **Мені́ тре́ба д. дві годи́ни.** I need about two hours.

деше́в|ий, *adj.* 1) cheap, 2) poor quality; *comp.* ~**ший**.

де́як|ий, *pron., usually in pl.* 1) some, certain, + *G. pl.* ~**им лю́дям подо́бається зима́.** Some people like winter.; 2) select, particular, **Ось спи́сок цін на** ~**і проду́кти.** Here is the price list for select products.

джаз, *m.*, ~**у** jazz, **слу́хати д.** to listen to jazz.

джем, *m.*, ~**у** marmalade, jam.

джерел|о́, *nt.* 1) a spring (of water, etc.); 2) source, **д. інформа́ції** source of information.

джере́льн|ий, *adj.* spring, from a spring, ~**а вода́** spring water.

джи́нс|и, *only pl.*, ~**ів** jeans; ~**ов|ий**, *adj.* denim, ~**ова ку́ртка** denim jacket.

джин, *m.*, ~**у** gin, **д. з то́ніком** gin and tonic.

дзвон|и́ти, ~**ять**; **по**~, *intr.* + *D.* or **до** + *G.* to call sb., telephone sb, **Він** ~**ить мені́ (до ме́не) щодня́.** He calls me every day.; **Кому́ (до ко́го) ти** ~**иш?** Who are you calling?; **(по)дзвони́!** ~**і́ть!**

див|и́тися, ~**лю́ся**, ~**ишся**, ~**ляться**; **по**~ 1) *tran.* to watch (a film, program), **Яки́й фільм ви** ~**и́лися вчора́?** What film did you watch yesterday? *in pf.* to look through (a book, paper, magazine), **Я подивлю́ся цей альбо́м по́тім.** I'll look through the album later.; *no pa. pple., instead* **поба́чений** watched, *is used*; 2) *intr.* **на** + *A.* to look at, take a look at, **Він** ~**иться на те́бе.** He's looking at you.; **подиви́ся! ~іться!** take a look!

ди́вн|ий, *adj.* strange, unusual.

ди́вно, *adv.* strange(ly), unusually, **Д., що він гово́рить це.** It's strange he should say it.; **D.+ д., Мені́ ду́же д. це чу́ти.** It's very strange for me to hear this.; ♦ **не д., що ...** it's not surprising that.., it's little wonder that ... .

диспозиці|я

диспози́ці|я, *f.* disposition, ♦ **бу́ти до ~ї** to be available, **Він зара́з не до ~ї, подзвоні́ть пізні́ше.** He is not available now, call later.

дити́н|а, *f.* child, baby; *pl.* **ді́ти**; *G. pl.* **діте́й**; **скі́льки діте́й?** how many children?; *I. pl.* **ді́тьми**, *L. pl.* **на ді́тях.**

дитя́, *nt.,* **~ти** child, baby; *I.* **~м**, *N. pl.* **~та**; *G. pl.* **~т.**

дівча́та, *n., f., N. pl., see* **ді́вчина.**

дівч|ина, *f.* 1) girl; 2) girlfriend, **Чи він ма́є ~ину?** Does he have a girlfriend?; *N. pl.* **~а́та**; *G. pl.* **~ча́т.**

дід, *m.,* **~а** 1) grandfather; 2) *colloq.* old man; *N. pl.* **~и́.**

дізна|ва́тися, **~ю́ться**; **дізна́тися, дізна|ю́ться**, *intr.* to find, learn, **про** + *A.* about, **Тре́ба дізна́тися, яка́ там пого́да.** We need to find out what the weather is like there.; **дізнава́й|ся! ~теся!; дізна́й|ся! ~теся!**

дізна́тися, *pf., see* **дізнава́тися.**

ді́йсно, *adv.* really, indeed, truly.

дім, *m.,* **до́м|у** 1) house, **Бі́лий Д.** the White House, **Бі́ля на́шого ~у був парк.** There was a park near our house.; 2) a home, **Мій д. за́вжди відкри́тий для друзі́в.** My home is always open for friends.; *N. pl.* **~и́.** *Cf.* **буди́нок** and **ха́та.**

діста|ва́ти, **~ю́ть**; **діста́ти, діста́н|уть**, *tran.* 1) to obtain, procure sth, **Я ма́ю діста́ти росі́йську ві́зу.** I have to obtain a Russian visa.; 2) to get, receive, **Ти діста́неш цей паке́т за ти́ждень.** You'll get the package in a week.; *no pa. pple.* **діставай! ~те!; діста́нь! ~те!**

діста|ва́тися, **~ю́ться**; **діста́тися, діста́н|уться**, *intr.* to get (from / to a point), **від** + *G.* ... **до** + *G.* from ... to, **Як діста́тися від аеропо́рту до мі́ста?** How do you get from the airport to the city?; **дістава́й|ся! ~теся!; діста́нь|ся! ~теся!**

діста́ти, *pf. see,* **діставати.**

діста́тися, *pf. see,* **діставатися.**

ді́ти, *N. pl., see* **дити́на.**

ді́|яти, **~ють**, *intr. only impf.* to act, **Тре́ба нега́йно д.** We need to act immediately.

для, *prep.* + *G.* for, **це д. вас** this is for you; **Це тре́ба д. робо́ти.** This is needed for work.

Дніпр|о́, *m.,* **~а** the Dnipro (*main river in Ukraine*); *L.* **на ~і.**

до, *prep.* + *G.* 1) *dir.* to, **до Ки́єва** to Kyiv; 2) before, **Д. поча́тку виста́ви п'ять хвили́н.** Five minutes are left before the start of the show; 3) until, till, **Д. цьо́го ча́су він не дзвони́в.** Up until now, he hasn't called.

доб|а́, *f.* 1) day and night, twenty-four hours, **Він прові́в ~у в літаку́.** He spent twenty-four hours in the airplane.; 2) day, **На скі́льки діб ви приї́хали?** For how many days have you come?; *G. pl.* **діб.**

добра́ніч, ♦ good night! *Also var.* **на добра́ніч.**

до́бре, *adv.* 1) well, **Я ду́же д. зна́ю це.** I know it very well.; 2) alright, OK, yes (*expression of agreement*).

добри́день, ♦ good day, good afternoon; *colloq. var.* of **добрий день**; (used in the afternoon and any other time of day as informal greeting).

до́бр|ий, *adj.* 1) good, **Він д. вчи́тель.** He is a good teacher., *comp.* **кра́щий**; 2) kind, **Вона́ ма́є ~е се́рце.** She has a kind heart, *comp.* **~іший**; 3) tasty, **Його́ борщ за́вжди д.** His borshch is always tasty., *comp.* **~іший.**

добро́ді|й, *m.,* **~я** gentleman (*form of reference*), **Я зна́ю цьо́го ~я.** I know this gentleman.; *V.* **~ю!** *or* **па́не ~ю!** (*polite form of address to male strangers*).

добро́дій|ка, *f.* madam, lady (*form of reference*), **Вас хо́че ба́чити яка́сь д.** A lady wants to see you; *L.* **на ~ці,***V.* **~ко!** *or* **па́ні ~ко!** (*polite form of address to female strangers*), *G. pl.* **~ок.**

до́вг|ий, *adj.* long, extended; *comp.* **~ший.**

до́вго, *adv.* for a long time, **Він д. не писа́в.** He hasn't written for long.

додо́му, *adv., dir.* home, to one's home, **іти́ д.** to go home.

дозві́лл|я, *nt.* leisure, free time, **на ~і** in one's free time.

дозво́лити, *pf., see* **дозволя́ти.**

дозволя́|ти, **~ють**; **дозво́л|ити**, **~ять**, *tran.* to allow, permit; *pa. pple.* **дозво́лений** allowed; **дозволя́й! ~те!; дозво́ль! ~те!**, **Дозво́льте предста́вити – мій брат Рома́н.** Allow me to introduce to you, my brother Roman.

докуме́нт, *m.,* **~а** document.

документа́льн|ий, *adj.* documentary, **д. фільм** documentary film.

до́лар, *m.,* **~а** a dollar, **оди́н д.** one dollar, **два (три, чоти́ри) ~и** two (three, four) dollars, **п'ять ~ів** (five and more) dollars.

доло́н|я *f.* palm (*of hand*).

до́ма, *adv., var.* **вдо́ма, удо́ма** at home, home.

дома́шн|ій, *adj.* home; homemade; domesticated (animal), **~є завда́ння** home assignment, **~я ковбаса́** homemade sausage, **~я ку́хня** home cooking.

домовля́|тися, **~ються**; **домо́в|итися**, **~люся, ~ишся, ~иться, ~ляться**, *intr.* to come to an agreement on sth.; **про** + *A.*, to arrange for (*meeting, consultation, assistance*), **Ми домови́лися про консульта́цію.** We agreed to meet for a consultation.; ♦ **Домови́лися!** It's a deal!; **домовля́й|ся! ~теся! домо́в|ся! ~теся!**

Донба́с, *m.,* **~у** Donbas (the Donets River Basin, historical part of south-eastern Ukraine comprising modern provinces of Luhansk and Donetsk); *L.* **на (у) ~і, по ~у** around Donbas.; *dir.* **на Д.** to Donbas.

до́нь|ка, *f.,* **~и**, *colloq.* daughter; *L.* **на ~ці**, *N. pl.* **~ки**; *G. pl.* **~ок.**

до поба́чення, *cliché* goodbye!

допомага́|ти, **~ють**; **допомогти́, допомо́ж|уть**, *intr.* + *D.* to help sb, assist, **Вам допомогти́?** Do you need help?; **допомага́й! ~те! допомо́ж|и! ~іть.**

допомо́|га, *f.* help, assistance; ♦ **на ~гу** to the rescue; *L.* **у ~зі.**

допомогти́, *pf., see* **допомага́ти.**

доро́|га, *f.* way, road; ♦ **по ~зі додо́му** on the way home; **пока́зувати ~гу** to show the way; ♦ **Щасли́вої ~ги!** Have a nice trip!; *L.* **на ~зі**; *G. pl.* **дорі́г.**

дорогий   жоден

дорог|и́й, *adj.* 1) dear, darling, beloved; 2) expensive, dear, high-priced; *comp.* **дорожчий**.

до́рого, *adv.* dearly, expensively, *comp.* **доро́жче**.

досві́дчен|ий, *adj.* experienced.

до́сить, *adv.*1) (with *adj.* and *adv.*) rather, fairly, **Цей готе́ль д. дороги́й**. This hotel is rather expensive., **Він д. до́брий музика́нт.** He's a fairly good musician.; 2) enough, sufficiently, **У нас д. гро́шей.** We have enough money.; ♦ **д. сказа́ти, що …** suffice it to say …; ♦ **цьо́го д.?** will that do?

до сих пір, *adv.* still, until now, up until today, **Він д. с. п. не навчи́вся пла́вати.** He still has not learned to swim.

доста́тн|ій, *adj.* sufficient.

доста́тньо, *adv.* enough, sufficiently, **Я д. до́бре зна́ю це мі́сто.** I know this city well enough.

доч|ка́, *f., ~и́* daughter; *L.* **на ~ці**, *N. pl.* **~ки́**; *G. pl.* **~о́к**.

дощ, *m., ~у́* rain, *I.* **~е́м; у д.** in the rain; **Йде д.** It's raining.

драмати́чн|ий, *adj.* dramatic, **д. теа́тр** drama theater.

дру́г, *m., ~га* close friend, **Рома́н – мій спра́вжній (да́вній) д.** Roman is my true (old) friend; *N. pl.* **~зі́**, *G. pl.* **~зі́в**, *I. pl.* **~зя́ми.** *Cf.* **подру́га, прия́тель, прия́телька.**

дру́г|ий, *ord.* second, **~е мі́сце** second place, **Це на́ша ~а по́дорож.** This is our second trip.

друж|и́ти, *only impf., ~ать, intr.* to be friends **з (із)** + *I.,* with sb., **Вони́ ~а́ть з дити́нства.** They've been friends since childhood.; **~и́! ~і́ть!**

дру́зі, *N. pl., see* **друг.**

ду́же, *adv.* very, very much (*used with adj., adv., and v.*), **Вона́ д. га́рна.** She's very pretty., **Він живе́ д. дале́ко.** He lives very far., **Я д. люблю́ це.** I like it a lot.

ду́ма|ти, *~ють; по~, intr.* 1) to think, **про** + *A.* about, **Я ~ю про Марі́ю.** I am thinking about Maria.; 2) be of opinion; ♦ **Як ти ~єш?** What do you think?; 3) *colloq.* **д.** + *inf.* to intend, plan, be going to do sth, **Він давно́ ~в зроби́ти це.** He has wanted to do it for a long time.; **(по)ду́май! ~те!**

ду́м|ка, *f., ~ки* 1) thought; 2) opinion; ♦ **на мою́ ~ку** in my opinion; ♦ **ма́ти на ~ці** to mean, **Що вона́ ма́є на ~ці?** What does she mean?; *L.* **на ~ці**; *N. pl.* **~и́, *G. pl.* ~о́к.**

дя́дьк|о, *m., ~а* uncle, father's or mother's brother; *N. pl.* **~и.**

дя́ку|вати, *~ють; по~, intr.* to thank sb + *D.* **за** + *A.* for sth, **дя́кую тобі́ / вам** thank you; **(по)дя́куй! ~те!**

дя́кую, *cliché* thank you; **ду́же д.** thanks a lot.

Е

екза́мен, *m., ~у* examination (*at school*), **з (із)** + *G.* in (*subject*), **е. з украї́нської** Ukrainian language exam; **склада́ти е.** to take an exam, **скла́сти е.** to pass an exam. *Also see* **і́спит.**

економі́ст, *m.* male economist; *f., ~ка* woman economist, *L.* **на ~ці.**

екску́рсі|я, *f., ~ї* excursion, organized sightseeing, **іти́ на ~ю** to go on an excursion.

експе́рт, *m.* expert, specialist, **з (із)** + *G.* in, **е. з істо́рії мисте́цтва** expert in art history. *Also see* **фахі́вець.**

електри́ч|ка, *f.,* electric suburban train, **~кою** by suburban train, **сіда́ти на ~ку** to take a suburban train.

електро́нн|ий, *adj.* electronic, **~а по́шта** e-mail.

есе́|й, *m., ~ю* essay.

Є

є, *v., pres. of* **бу́ти** am, are, is; ♦ **хто є хто?** who is who?

є́вр|о, *nt.* euro, **два ~а** two euros, **де́сять євр** ten euros.

Євро́п|а, *f.* Europe, **За́хідна (Схі́дна, Центра́льна) Є.** Western (Eastern, Central) Europe.

європе́|єць, *m., ~йця* European man; *f. ~йка,* European woman; *L.* **на ~йці**, *G. pl.* **~йок.**

європе́йськ|ий, *adj.* European.

єди́н|ий, *adj.* 1) only, **Вона́ була́ ~ою дити́ною.** She was an only child.; 2) single, **~а валю́та** the single currency.

Ж

жал|ь, *m., ~ю* pity; ♦ **на ж.** unfortunately; ♦ *D.* + **бу́ти ж.** + *A.* to feel sorry for sb, **Мені́ їх ду́же ж.** I feel very sorry for them.

жарт, *m., ~у* joke, **розповіда́ти ~и** to tell jokes.; ♦ **Це не ~и.** This is not a laughing matter.

жарту|ва́ти, *~ють; по~, intr.* to joke, **з (із)** + *I.*; ♦ **ви ~єте** you're kidding; **(по)жартуй! ~те!**

жив|и́й, *adj.* 1) alive; 2) live, **ж. му́зика** live music.

живі́т, *m., ~ота́* stomach, abdomen, **Мене́ боли́ть ж.** I have a stomachache.; *L.* **у ~оті́**; *N. pl.* **~оти́.**

жи́ти, **живу́ть**; *про~; pa. m.* **жи|в**, *f.* **~ла́**, *nt.* **~ло́**, *pl.* **~ли** 1) *intr.* to live, exist; reside, **Він ще ~е.** He is still alive., **Він ~е у Лу́цьку.** He lives in Lutsk.; 2) *tran. in pf.* to live a life, **Я прожи́в все життя́ тут.** I lived my whole life here.; *pa. pple.* **прожи́тий** lived (through); **(про)жив|и́! ~і́ть!**

житл|о́, *nt.* accommodation; place of residence; **ж. і харчі́** room and board.

життя́, *nt., ~я́* 1) life; **на все ж.** for all life long; 2) lifetime, **ніко́ли в ~і́** never in a lifetime; *G. pl.* **~і́в.**

жін|ка, *f., ~ки* 1) woman, **Ця висо́ка ж. – Мари́на.** This tall woman is Maryna; 2) *fam.* wife, female spouse, **Його́ ж. з Сока́ля.** His wife is from Sokal.; *L.* **на ~ці**, *N. pl.* **~ки**, *G. pl.* **~о́к.**

жіно́ч|ий, *adj.* female, women's; for women (*department, clothes, washroom*), **~е взуття́** women's footwear, **~і студі́ї** women's studies.

жо́вт|ень, *m., ~ня* October, **Заня́ття почну́ться пе́ршого ~ня.** Classes will start on October 1.; *L.* **у ~ні.**

жо́вт|ий, *adj.* yellow, **жо́вто-блаки́тний пра́пор** yellow-and-blue flag (national flag of Ukraine).

жо́ден, *adj., m., var., see* **жо́дний.**

жо́дн|ий, *adj., var. m.* **жо́ден** none, not a single (*in negated sentence*), **Я не чита́в ~ої статті́.** I didn't read a single article.; **жо́дного ра́зу** not once; **ж. з нас** none of us (*for all m.*), **~а з нас** (for all *f.*)

жур|и́тися, **~я́ться**; **за~** *intr. + I.* 1) to worry over sth, get concerned, **Я ~ю́ся, що ми не всти́гнемо на конце́рт.** I am worried that we won't make it to the concert.; 2) *pf.* to become concerned, worried, sad, **Він послу́хав нови́ни і зажури́вся.** He listened to the news and grew sad.; ♦ **не жур|и́ся! ~і́ться!** don't worry!

журна́л, *m.*, **~у** 1) magazine, **ж. мо́ди** fashion magazine, **жіно́чий ж.** women's magazine; 2) newsreel.

журналі́ст, *m.* journalist, **Він хо́че ста́ти ~ом.** He wants to become a journalist.; *f.* **~ка**, **Вона́ вчи́ться на ~ку.** She studies to become a journalist.; *L.* **на ~ці**, *G. pl.* **~ок**.

журналі́сти|ка, *f.* journalism; *L.* **у ~ці**.

З

з, *prep., var.* **із**, **зі**, 1) from (in relations of place) + *G.*, **з Ки́єва** from Kyiv; 2) from, since (in relations of time) + *G.*, **із насту́пної субо́ти** from next Saturday; 3) with (in relations of accompaniment) + *I.*, **з дру́гом** with a friend. *Also see* **зі** *and* **із**.

за, *prep.* 1) *posn.* behind + *I.*, **Я сиджу́ з. не́ю.** I am sitting behind her.; 2) *dir.* behind + *A.*, **Я сів з. не́ї.** I took a seat behind her.; 3) in, within (*period of time*) + *A.*, **Ми зроби́ли це з. годи́ну.** We did it in one hour.; 4) than + *A.* (*in comparison*), **Ця кни́жка деше́вша з. ту.** This book is cheaper than that one.; 5) *colloq.* about, **Ми говори́ли з. життя́.** We talked about life. *See* **про**.

за~, *pref.* too (excessive quality, combines with *adj.* and *adv.*), **задороги́й** too expensive, **задале́ко** too far.

заба́в|а, *f.* party, entertainment, **на ~і** at a party; **роби́ти ~у** to have a party; **Ми до́бре погуля́ли у ньо́го на ~і.** We had a lot of fun at his party.

заблуди́ти, *v., var., see* **заблуди́тися**.

заблу́джу|ватися, **~ються**; **заблуд|и́тися**, **~я́ться**, *intr.* to get lost, lose one's way, **У цьо́му мі́сті ле́гко заблуди́тися.** It's easy to get lost in this city.; **заблуджу́й|ся! ~теся!; заблуд|и́ся! ~і́ться!**

заблуди́тися, *pf., see* **заблу́джуватися**.

забува́|ти, **~ють**; **забу́ти, забу́д|уть**, *tran., + A.* 1) to forget, **Я зовсі́м забу́в про це.** I completely forgot about it.; 2) to leave behind, **Він за́вжди забува́є гро́ші вдо́ма.** He always leaves the money home.; *pa. pple.* **забу́тий** forgotten; **забува́й| ~те! забу́дь| ~те!**

забу́ти, *pf., see* **забува́ти**.

завда́нн|я, *nt.* assignment, task, **дома́шнє з.** home assignment, **задава́ти (роби́ти) з.** to give (do) assignment.

завдяки́, *prep.* thanks to + *D.* **З. їй у нас є що ї́сти.** Thanks to her we have food.

за́вжди, *adv.* always, all the time; **як з.** as always.

заво́д, *m.*, **~у** plant, factory, works; *L.* **на ~і**.

за́втра, *adv.* tomorrow, **з. вра́нці (вве́чері)** tomorrow morning (evening), **відкла́сти на з.** to put sth off till tomorrow.

зага́льн|ий, *adj.* general, common, **~а ду́мка** general opinion; **з. квито́к** fourth class train ticket with no assigned seat.

заголо́в|ок, *m.*, **~ку** title (*of article, text*), headline, heading, **з. статті́ (те́ксту)** title of the article (text), **під ~ом** under the title. *Cf.* **назва**.

загуби́ти, *var.* **згуби́ти**, *pf., see* **губи́ти**.

зада|ва́ти (*see* **дава́ти**); **зада́ти** (*see* **да́ти**), *tran.* to give an assignment, to assign (work), **Що вам зада́ли на за́втра?** What homework were you assigned for tomorrow?; *pa. pple.* **за́даний** assigned; **задава́й! ~те!; зада́й! ~те!**

зада́ти, *pf., see* **зада́ти**.

займа́|ти, **~ють**; **зайня́ти**, **займ|у́ть**, *tran.* 1) to occupy (a place), **Тре́ба зайня́ти місця́.** We need to occupy (take) our seats.; 2) to take up time, **Подоро́ж до мі́ста займа́є пів годи́ни.** A trip downtown takes a half hour; *fig.* to waste sb's time, **Не займа́йте мені́ ча́су!** Don't waste my time!; *pa. pple.* **за́йнятий** occupied, busy (*of a person, seat*); **займа́й! ~те! займ|и́! ~і́ть!**

займа́|тися, **~ються**; **зайня́тися, займ|у́ться**, *intr. + I.* 1) to occupy oneself with, **Чим ти лю́биш з. на дозві́ллі?** What do you like to do in your free time?; 2) to engage in, train oneself in (music, sports), **Він займа́ється футбо́лом уже́ три ро́ки.** He has played football for three years already.; 3) to practice (playing an instrument), prepare assignment, **Студе́нти займа́ються.** The students are studying.; **займа́й|ся! ~теся!; займ|и́ся! ~і́ться!**

за́йнят|ий, *pa. pple.* busy, taken, occupied, **Я ці́лий день був ду́же з.** I've been very busy all day., **Це мі́сце ~е?** Is this place taken?

закі́нчити, *pf., see* **закі́нчувати**.

закі́нчу|вати, **~ють**; **закі́нч|ити**, **~ать**, *tran. or impf. inf.*, to finish, complete, get done with, **Коли́ він закі́нчив навча́ння?** When did he finish his studies?; *pa. pple.* **(за)кі́нчений** finished; **закі́нчуй! ~те!; закі́нч|и! ~іть!**

закі́нчуватися; **закі́нчитися**, *intr.* to end (in sth), finish, be over, **Кані́кули закі́нчуються за́втра.** Holidays end tomorrow..

закрива́|ти, **~ють**; **закри́|ти**, **~ють**, *tran.* to close sth, shut, shut down, **Тре́ба закри́ти вікно́.** The window needs to be closed.; *pa. pple.* **закри́тий** shut, closed; **закрива́й! ~те!; закри́й! ~те!**

закрива́|тися; **закри́тися**, *intr.* to close, shut, shut down, **Ми ~є́мося ра́но.** We close early., **Коли́ закри́ється суперма́ркет?** When will the supermarket close?

закри́т|ий, *adj.* 1) closed, shut; 2) off limits, inaccessible.

заку́пи, *pl.*, **~ів** purchases; ♦ **роби́ти з.** to make purchases; ♦ **іти́ на з.** to go shopping; **з. проду́ктів** grocery shopping.

заку́с|ка, *f.* 1) hors d'oeuvre, appetizer, **сала́т на ~ку** salad for hors d'oeuvre; 2) snack, **легкі́ ~ки** light snacks; *L.* **у ~ці**, *G. pl.* **~ок**.

зале́ж|ати, **~ать**, *no pf., intr.* to depend, **від** + *G.* on, ♦ **~ить** it depends., **Вони́ ні від ко́го не ~ать.** They do not depend on anybody.; **зале́ж! ~те!**

залиша́ти

залиша́|ти, *var.* **лиша́|ти**, **~ють**; **залиши́ти**, *var.* **лиши́|ти**, **~ать**, *tran.* to leave, **Я залиши́ла кви́тки на столі́.** I left the tickets on the table., **з. повідо́млення** to leave a message; *pa. pple.* **зали́шений** left, abandoned; **залиша́й! ~те!**; **залиш|и́! ~і́ть!**

залиша́тися, *var.* **лиша́тися**; **залиши́тися**, *var.* **лиши́тися**, *intr.* to stay, remain, to be left, **Він ~и́ться тут на два дні.** He'll stay here for two days., **Скі́льки ча́су ~и́лося?** How much time is left?; **залиша́й|ся! ~теся!**; **залиш|и́ся! ~і́ться!**

залиши́ти, *pf.*, *see* **залиша́ти**.

залиши́тися, *pf.*, *see* **залиша́тися**.

залізни́ц|я, *f.*, **~і** railroad, **і́хати ~ею** to go by train.

залізни́чн|ий, *adj.* pertaining to railroad or train, **з. квито́к** train ticket, **~а ка́са** train ticket-office, **з. вокза́л** train station.

замо́вити, *pf.*, *see* **замовля́ти**.

замовля́|ти, **~ють**; **замо́в|ити**, **~лю**, **~иш**, **~лять**, *tran.* to order, place an order for sth, book, **Тре́ба замо́вити таксі́вку.** We need to order a taxi.; *pa. pple.* **замо́влений** ordered, booked; **замовля́й! ~те!**; **замо́в! ~те!**

за́м|ок¹, *m.*, **~ку** castle, **стари́й (зруйно́ваний) з.** old (ruined); *L.* **в ~ку**; *G. pl.* **~ків**.

зам|о́к², *m.*, **~ка́** lock; *N. pl.* **~ки́**, *G. pl.* **~кі́в**.

заморо́жен|ий, *adj.* frozen, **~а ри́ба** frozen fish, **~і фру́кти й о́вочі** frozen fruit and vegetables.

зана́дто, *adv.*, *var.* **на́дто** too, excessively.

заня́тт|я, *nt.* 1) pastime, occupation, **улю́блені з.** favorite pastimes; 2) (generic for) class, lecture, seminar; **на ~і** in (during) class; **з. з (із) + G.** practice in music (singing, language), **У нас за́раз з. з істо́рії.** We have a class in history now.

записа́ти, *pf.*, *see* **запи́сувати**.

записа́тися, *pf.*, *see* **запи́суватися**.

запи́с|ка, *f.* note, **лиша́ти ~ку** to leave a note; *L.* **у ~ці**; *G. pl.* **~ок**.

запи́су|вати, **~ють**; **записа́ти**, **запи́ш|уть**, *tran.* to write sth down, make a note, **Він лю́бить з. ціка́ві ду́мки.** He likes to write down interesting thoughts.; *pa. pple.* **запи́саний** written down, recorded; **запи́суй! ~те!**; **запиш|и́! ~і́ть!**

запи́су|ватися, **~ються**; **записа́тися**, **запи́ш|уться**, *refl.* to enroll, sign up, **на + A.** for (course); **запи́суй|ся! ~теся!**; **запиш|и́ся! ~і́ться!**

запита́ти, *pf.*, *see* **запи́тувати**.

запи́ту|вати, **~ють**; **запита́|ти + A.** to ask sb, **про + A.** about sth; ask (a question), to inquire, **Мо́жна запита́ти, де метро́?** May I ask (you) where the subway is?; *pa. pple.* **запи́таний** asked, posed (of question); **запи́туй! ~те! запита́й! ~те!**

запізни́тися, *pf.*, *see* **запі́знюватися**.

запі́зню|ватися, **~ються**; **запізн|и́тися**, **~яться**, *refl.*, **на + A.** to be (come) late, **По́їзд ~є́ться на пів годи́ни.** The train is half an hour late.; **запі́знюй|ся! ~теся!**; **запізн|и́ся! ~і́ться!**

збудува́ти

заплати́ти, *pf.*, *see* **плати́ти**.

запропонува́ти, *pf.*, *see* **пропонува́ти**.

запроси́ти, *pf.*, *see* **запро́шувати**.

запро́шенн|я, *nt.* an invitation; ♦ **на з.** on invitation; **без з.** without invitation.

запро́шу|вати, **~ють**; **запроси́ти**, **запрошу́**, **запро́с|ять**, *tran.* invite, (to a building or home) **до + G.**, **Він запроси́в І́горя до се́бе (рестора́ну).** He invited Ihor to his place (restaurant).; (to event, performance) **на + A.**, **Мене́ запроси́ли на ціка́ву ви́ставку (ле́кцію, вече́рю).** I was invited to an interesting exhibit (lecture, dinner); *pa. pple.* **запро́шений** invited; **запро́шуй! ~те!**; **запроси́! ~і́ть!**

за́раз, *adv.* now, at present; **з. же** right away.

зароби́ти, *perf*, *see* **заробля́ти**.

заробля́|ти, **~ють**; **зароб|и́ти**, **~лю́**, **~иш**, **~лять**, *tran.* to earn (money, salary), **Скі́льки він заробля́є?** How much does he earn?, **Тут бага́то не заро́биш.** You won't earn much here.; **до́бре (пога́но) з.** to earn well (little); *pa. pple.* **заро́блений** earned; **заробля́й! ~те!**; **зароб|и́! ~і́ть!**

засма́га|ти, **~ють**; **засма́гн|ути**, **~уть**, *m. pa.* **засма́г** *or* **засма́гнув**, *intr.* to get suntanned, **Вона́ га́рно засма́гла.** She got a nice suntan.; *pa. pple.* **засма́гл|ий** suntanned; **засма́гай! ~те!**; **засма́гн|и! ~і́ть**

засма́гнути, *pf.*, *see* **засма́гати**.

зате́, *conj.* but then, however, **Це ну́дно, з. кори́сно для здоро́в'я.** It's boring but then it is good for your health.

зати́шн|ий, *adj.* quiet, cozy, comfortable.

зафільмува́ти, *pf.*, *see* **фільмува́ти**.

захворі́|ти, **~ють**, *pf. intr.* to fall ill, become sick, **на + A.** with, **Іва́н ~ів на грип.** Ivan got sick with the flu.; *Also see* **хворі́ти**; **захворі́й! ~те!**

за́х|ід, *m.*, **~оду**, west, *dir.* **на з. від + G.** to the west of; *posn.* **на ~оді + G.** in the west of, **на ~оді Украї́ни** in the west of Ukraine.

за́хідн|ий, *adj.* western, **~а Євро́па** Western Europe.

захо́плення, *nt.* hobby, passion, **Моє́ найбі́льше у житті́ з. – це німе́ кіно́.** My greatest hobby in life is silent cinema.

зацı́кавити, *pf.*, *see* **ціка́вити**.

зацı́кавитися, *pf.*, *see* **ціка́витися**.

зачиня́|ти, **~ють**; **зачин|и́ти**, **~ять**, *tran.* to close, shut sth; *pa. pple.* **зачи́нений** closed, shut; **зачиня́й! ~те!**; **зачин|и́! ~і́ть!**

зачиня́|тися; **зачин|и́тися**, *intr.* to close, shut, **Крамни́ця вже зачини́лася.** The store is already closed.

збира́|тися, **~ються**; **зібра́тися**, **збер|у́ться**, *intr.* 1) **+ inf.** to intend, be going to, plan, **Ми збира́лися дзвони́ти вам.** We were going to call you.; 2) to get oneself ready; **з. у доро́гу** to get ready, pack for the road; 3) to get together; **збира́й|ся! ~теся!**; **збер|и́ся! ~і́ться!**

збудува́ти, *pf.*, *see* **будува́ти**.

зва|ти, ~уть; на~, *tran.* to call by name, give name to, name; as part of set expression **Мене́ зва́ти Юрко́.** My name is Yurko.; **Як тебе́ зва́ти?** What is your name?; *pa. pple.* **на́званий** named, **на́званий брат** adopted brother; **(на)зв|и́! ~і́ть!**

звerr...

звернути, *pf., see* зверта́ти.

зверну́тися, *pf., see* зверта́тися.

зверта́|ти, ~ють; зверн|у́ти, ~уть, *tran.* 1) to turn, **з. право́руч / ліво́руч** to turn right / left; 2) **з. ува́гу** to pay attention; *pa. pple.* **зве́рнутий** directed to (of attention); **звертай! ~те!; зверн|и́! ~іть!**

зверта́тися; зверн|у́тися, *intr.* to address sb, **до +** G.; **по +** A. to turn to sb for help (advice), **Він ~у́вся до неї по пора́ду.** He turned to her for advice.

звика́|ти, ~ють; зви́кн|ути, ~уть, *pa.* звик, зви́кли, *intr.* to get accustomed, **до +** G. to, **Він шви́дко звик до но́вого мі́сця.** He got quickly accustomed to the new place.; *pa. pple.* **звикл|ий** accustomed; **звика́й! ~те! звикн|и́! ~іть!**

зви́кнути, *pf., see* звика́ти.

звича́йно, *adv.* 1) of course, certainly; clearly, **Деше́вші квитки́, з., кра́щі.** Cheaper tickets are, of course, better. 2) usually, as a rule, **Він з. працю́є до во́сьмої.** Usually he works till eight.

зви́ч|ка, *f.* habit, **шкідли́ва з.** bad habit, **ма́ти ~ку + *inf.*** to be in the habit of, **Він ма́є з. прихо́дити без запро́шення.** He is in the habit of coming uninvited.; *L.* **у ~ці,** *G. pl.* **~ок.**

зві́дки, *adv.* where from, **З. вона́?** Where is she from?; **З. ти зна́єш?** How do you know?

зв'яз|о́к, *m.,* ~ку́ connection.

зга́д|ка, *f.* mention; ♦ **на зга́дку про +** A as a memento of. *L.* **у ~ці,** *G. pl.* **~ок.**

зга́ду|вати, ~ють; згада́|ти, *tran.* 1) to recall, recollect, remember, **про +** A. about, **Я не мо́жу згада́ти її но́мера.** I can't recall her number.; 2) to reminisce, look back on, **Ми лю́бимо згаду́вати дити́нство.** We like to reminisce about childhood.; *pa. pple.* **зга́даний** recollected, remembered; **згаду́й! ~те!; згада́й! ~те!**

згі́дн|ий *adj.* in agreement, *var.* **зго́ден; бу́ти ~им з (із) +** I. to agree with, **Я цілко́м з. з ва́ми.** I quite agree with you.

зго́д|а, *f.* 1) agreement, consent, **дава́ти ~у на +** A. to give one's consent to sth; 2) alright, fine, **Я розкажу́ вам пото́му, з.?** I'll tell you later, alright?

зго́ден, *adj., see* згі́дний.

зда|ва́тися, ~ються; зда́тися, здаду́|ться, *intr.* 1) to seem to sb + *D.,* **мені́ здає́ться, що ...** it seems to me that ...; seem to be sth / sb, **Він здавася мені́ приє́мною люди́ною.** He seemed to be a pleasant person.; 2) to surrender, give up; **здава́й|ся! ~теся! здай|ся! ~теся!**

зда́тися, *pf, see* здава́тися.

зда́ч|а, *f.,* ~і change (*rest of money paid*), **Ось ва́ша з.** Here's your change.

здоро́в|ий, *adj.* 1) healthy, **Тепе́р він почува́ється цілко́м ~им.** Now he feels quite healthy.; 2) *colloq.* big, stupendous, **Вони́ ма́ють ~у кварти́ру.** They have a big apartment.

здоро́в'|я, *nt., only sg.* health; ♦ **на з.!** to your health! (*as toast*).

зеле́н|ий, *adj.* 1) green; 2) *fig.* young, immature, inexperienced; 3) not ripe.

зем|ля́, *f.* 1) earth, soil, ground; 2) **З.** planet Earth; *N. pl.* **~лі,** *G. pl.* **~е́ль.**

зим|а́, *f.* winter; **~о́ю** in winter, **мину́лої (ціє́ї, насту́пної) ~и́** last (this, next) winter.

зі, *prep., var., see* **з;** used before **мно́ю** and consonant clusters, which include **з, с, ш: з. стра́ху** with fear, **з. шко́ли** from school, **з. зло́сти** with anger, **з. мно́ю** with me. *Also see* **із.**

зібра́тися, *pf, see* збира́тися.

зіпсува́ти, *pf., see* псува́ти.

зіпсува́тися, *pf., see* псува́тися.

зі́р|ка, *f.* 1) a star; 2) *fig.* a celebrity, famous person, **з. кіна́** or **кінозі́рка** film star; *L.* **на ~ці;** *N. pl.* **~ки,** *G. pl.* **~ок.**

з'ї́сти, *pf. see* ї́сти.

злама́ти, *pf., see* лама́ти.

злама́тися, *pf., see* лама́тися.

злови́ти, *pf., see* лови́ти.

знайо́м|ий, *adj.* familiar, known; *n.* acquaintance, **да́вній з.** old acquaintance, **О́льга моя́ ~а.** Olha is an acquaintance of mine.

знайо́м|ити, ~лю, ~иш, ~лять; по~, *tran.* to introduce sb to sb, **з (із) +** I. **Він познайо́мив Сергі́я з Па́влом.** He introduced Serhiy to Pavlo; *pa. pple.* **познайо́млений** familiar with sb or sth; **(по)знайо́м! ~те!**

знайо́м|итися; по~, *intr.* 1) to meet sb, **з (із) +** I., **Вона́ наре́шті познайо́милася з Оле́ною.** She finally met Olena.; 2) to familiarize oneself with, study sth, **Мені́ тре́ба по~ із но́вими докуме́нтами.** I need to familiarize myself with the new documents.

знайо́мств|о, *nt.* acquaintance, the act of getting acquainted with sb / sth.

знайти́, *pf., see* знахо́дити *and* шука́ти.

знамени́т|ий, *adj.* 1) *colloq.* wonderful, great, **Це ~а іде́я!** This is a great idea!; 2) famous, celebrated, renowned. *Also see* **сла́ветний.**

зна́н|ий, *adj.* known, well-known, **Він з. фото́граф.** He is a well-known photographer.; **бу́ти ~им +** I. to be famous for sth, **Херсо́нщина завжди́ була́ ~а свої́ми кавуна́ми.** The Kherson Province has always been famous for its watermelons.

зна́|ти, ~ють; пі~, *tran.* 1) *impf.* to know, **Я не ~ю** I don't know; 2) *pf.* to learn, to get to know (a person), **Тя́жко пізна́ти люди́ну.** It's hard to get to know a person.; *pa. pple.* **зна́ний** (well) known; **(пі)знай! ~те!**

знахо́д|ити, ~жу, ~ять; знайти́, знайд|у́ть, *pa. pf.* **знайш|о́в, ~ли,** *tran.* to find, locate sb or sth, **Як знайти́ деше́вий готе́ль?** How can you find a cheap hotel?; *pa. pple.* **зна́йден|ий** found; **знахо́дь! ~те!; знайд|и́! ~іть!**

знахо́ди|тися, *only impf., intr.* to be located, **Де ~ться суперма́ркет?** Where is the supermarket located? *See* **розташо́вуватися.**

значення   італієць

зна́ченн|я, *nt.* meaning, sense; ♦ **не ма́є з.** it doesn't matter, **перено́сне з.** figurative sense, **у прямо́му ~і** in a direct sense, literally, **у яко́му ~і?** in what sense?

зна́ч|ити, **~ать** *intr.* to mean, **Що ~ить це сло́во?** What does this word mean?

зна́чить, *adv.* hence, so, that means, consequently. *Also see* **отже**.

значн|и́й, *adj.* considerable, noticeable, **з. ро́змір (успіх)** considerable size (success).

зна́чно, *adv.* considerably, **Він з. ста́рший, ніж вона́.** He is considerably older than her.

зни́ж|ка, *f.* discount, **за ~кою** at a discount, **Які́ ~ки пропону́ють сього́дні?** What discounts do they offer today?; *L.* **у ~ці**, *G. pl.* **~ок.**

зно́ву, *adv.* again.

зну́дити, *pf., see* **ну́дити**.

зо́всім, *adv.* 1) completely, entirely, fully, **За день він з. втоми́вся.** He got completely tired over the day.; 2) at all (*in neg.*), **Я з. не зна́ю її.** I don't know her at all.

золот|и́й, *adj.* gold, golden, **~а середи́на** golden mean.

зо́лот|о, *nt.* gold.

зоопа́рк, *m.*, **~у** zoo; *L.* **у ~у**; **ходи́ти до ~у** to go to the zoo.

зо́шит, *m.*, **~а** notebook.

зроби́ти, *pf. see* **роби́ти**.

зрозумі́ти, *pf. see* **розумі́ти**.

зручн|и́й, *adj.* comfortable, cozy, convenient, suitable, **Це крі́сло ~е.** This chair is comfortable.

зру́чно, *adv.* conveniently, comfortably, suitably, **Тут ду́же з. працюва́ти.** It's very comfortable to work here.

зуб, *m.*, **~а** a tooth, **Мене́ ду́же боли́ть з.** I have a bad toothache.

зумі́ти, *pf., see* **умі́ти**.

зупи́н|ка, *f.* stop, **кінце́ва з.** the final stop; *L.* **на ~ці**, **На які́й ~ці мені́ тре́ба зійти́?** At what stop do I need to get off?; *G. pl.* **~ок.**

зупиня́|ти, **~ють; зупин|и́ти**, **~ять**, *tran.* to stop sb / sth, **Вони́ зупини́ли прое́кт посереди́ні.** They stopped the project in the middle.; *pa. pple.* **зупи́нений** stopped; **зупиня́й! ~те!; зупи́н|и́! ~і́ть!**

зупиня́|тися; зупини́тися, *refl.* 1) to stop (oneself), **На цій ста́нції по́їзд не ~є́ться.** The train does not stop at this station.; 2) to stay (*at a hotel*), **Я люблю́ з. у цьо́му готе́лі.** I like to stay at this hotel.

зустрі́(ну)ти, *pf., see* **зустріча́ти**.

зустрі́(ну)тися, *pf., see* **зустріча́тися**.

зу́стріч, *f.*, **~і** meeting, rendezvous; **домовля́тися про з.** to agree to meet; **іти́ на з.** to go to a meeting.

зустріча́|ти, **~ють; зустрі́(ну)ти, зустрі́н|уть;** *pa.* **зустрі́в** *or* **~нув**, *tran.* to meet sb / sth.; **Він зустрі́не вас на перо́ні.** He'll meet you on the platform.; *pa. pple.* **зустрі́нутий** met, encountered; **зустріча́й! ~те!; зустрі́нь! ~те!**

зустріча́|тися; зустрі́(ну)тися, *intr.* з + *I.* 1) to meet each other, **Де ви ~є́теся?** Where are you meeting?; 2) to go out with one another, date, **Вони́ ~ються два ро́ки.** They have gone out for two years.

І

і, *conj.* and, *var.* **й** (used between vowels, **Мико́ла й Оле́г**), **Степа́н і Ори́ся** Stepan and Orysia; **і ..., і** both ..., and, **Тре́ба купи́ти і молока́, і хлі́ба.** We need to buy both milk and bread. *Also see conj.* **та**.

ідеа́льн|ий, *adj.* ideal, **Мої́ ~і вака́ції – це те́пле мо́ре та добра́ пого́да.** My ideal vacation is warm sea and good weather.

іде́|я, *f.*, **~ї** an idea, **Це чудо́ва і.!** It's a great idea!

із, *prep., var. see* **з** (used between consonants, after, and before consonant clusters), **і. Брази́лії** from Brazil, **і. крамни́ці** from a store, **Він і. прия́телем.** He is with a friend. *Also see* **зі**.

ім'я́, *nt.*, **іме́н|и** name (*only of a person*), **Як твоє́ (ва́ше) і.?** What is your name?, **Яке́ твоє́ і.?** What kind of name do you have?; *I.* **ім'я́м** *or* **~ем**, *N. pl.* **~а**, *G. pl.* **іме́н.** *Cf.* **на́зва**.

іна́кше, *adv.* 1) otherwise, **Тре́ба купи́ти ка́рту мі́ста, і. ми заблу́димося.** We need to buy a city map, otherwise we'll get lost.; 2) differently, **Пропону́ю зроби́ти це і.** I suggest that we do it differently.

іна́кш|ий, *adj., var., see* **і́нший**.

інґредіє́нт, *m.*, **~а** ingredient, **Ця стра́ва склада́ється із п'ятьо́х ~ів.** This dish consists of five ingredients.

інжене́р, *m.*, **~а** engineer, **і.-меха́нік** mechanical engineer.

і́нколи, *adv.* sometimes, every now and then.

і́ноді, *adv.* sometimes, every now and then.

інтерв'ю́, *nt., indecl.* interview, **дава́ти (роби́ти) і.** to give (do) an interview, **Тара́с зроби́в з ним і.** Taras did an interview with him.

інтерне́т, *m.*, **~у** the Internet, **користува́тися ~ом** to use the Internet, **і.-кафе́** Internet café, **і.-по́слуги** Internet services; *L.* **на ~і** on the Internet.

інформа́ці|я, *f.* information, data.

і́нш|ий, *adj.* other, another, different, **Він зо́всім ~а люди́на тепе́р.** He is a completely different person now.; **~им ра́зом** another time.

іспа́нськ|ий, *adj.* Spanish, **~а мо́ва** the Spanish language.

і́спит, *m.*, **~у** examination, test, **склада́ти (скла́сти) і. з (із) + G.** to take (pass) an exam in. *Also see* **екза́мен**.

істо́рик, *m.* historian.

істори́чн|ий, *adj.* historical, historic, **і. музе́й** a historical museum, **~а зу́стріч** historic encounter.

істо́рі|я, *f.*, **~ї** 1) story, tale, **Це і. мого́ життя́.** That's the story of my life.; **Оце́ так і.!** That's quite a story!; 2) history (discipline), **світова́ і.** world history, **музе́й ~ї** museum of history.

італі́|єць, *m.*, **~йця** Italian man; **~йка**, *f. L.* **на ~йці**, *G. pl.* **~йок.**

італі́йськ|ий, *adj.* Italian, **~а мо́ва** the Italian language, **розмовля́ти ~ою** to speak Italian.

Іта́лі|я, *f.*, **~ї** Italy, **ї́хати до ~ї** to go to Italy.

іти́, **ід|у́ть; п~; ра. ишо́в**, **~ла́**, **~ло́**, **~ли́**, *uni.*, *intr.* 1) go, come, walk (on foot), **Ти ~е́ш зі мно́ю?** Are you coming along?; 2) leave, **Я вже ма́ю і.** I need to leave; 3) *(of film, play)* to be on the program, **Що сього́дні іде́ у кінотеа́трі?** What is on in the movie theater today? *Also see multi.* **ходи́ти; (п)ід|и́! ~і́ть!**

Ї

їв, *ра.*, *m.*, *see* **ї́сти.**

ї́да|льня, *f.* canteen, eatery, diner *(normally with self-service)*; *G. pl.* **~ень.**

ї́ж|а, *f.*, **~і**, *only sg.* food, meals; *I.* **~ею.**

ї́ї, *pers. pron.*, *A. of* **вона́**, when used without preposition, **Я ї. зна́ю.** I know her.; *poss. pron.*, *f.* her (does not decline), **Це ї. батьки́.** These are her parents.

ї́зд|ити, **ї́жджу**, **~иш**, **~ять; з’~**, *multi.*, *intr.* to drive, go by a vehicle, travel, **Я ча́сто ї́жджу до Ри́му.** I often travel to Rome. *Also see uni.* **ї́хати; (з’)ї́зди́! ~і́ть!**

ї́сти, **їм**, **їси́**, **їсть**, **їмо́**, **їсте́**, **їдя́ть; з’~; ра. їв**, **ї́ла**, **ї́ло**, **ї́ли; з’~**; *tran.* to eat; ◆ **вари́ти ї.** to cook, **хоті́ти ї.** to be hungry; *pa. pple.* **з’ї́дений** eaten; **(з’)їж! ~те!**

ї́х, *pers. pron. A. of* **вони́**, when used without preposition, **Я ба́чив ї. учо́ра.** I saw them yesterday.

ї́хати, **ї́д|уть; по~**, *intr.*, *uni.* to drive, go by a vehicle, travel, **За́втра він ї́де до Мадри́ду.** Tomorrow he is going to Madrid. *Also see multi.* **ї́здити; (по)ї́дь! ~те!**

ї́хн|ій, *pers. pron.* **~я**, **~є**, **~і** their, theirs, **Усі́ ~і ді́ти вже доро́слі.** All their children are already grown-up.

Й

й, *conj.* and, *var.*, *see* **і** (used between vowels), **Мико́ла й О́льга** Mykola and Olha.

його́, *pers. pron.*, *A. of* **він**, when used without preposition, **Я й. ду́же добре зна́ю.** I know him very well.; *poss. pron.* his (does not decline), **й. брат** his brother.

йо́ґурт, *m.*, **~у** yogurt.

йти, *var.*, *see* **іти́.**

К

ка́в|а, *f.* coffee, **чо́рна к.** black coffee, **к. з молоко́м** coffee with milk.

каву́н, *m.*, **~а́** watermelon; *N. pl.* **~и́.**

кав’я́р|ня, *f.* coffee-house, café; *G. pl.* **~ень.**

каза́ти, **ка́ж|уть; с~**, *tran.* to say, **про + A.** about sth, **Ка́жуть, ви лю́бите о́перу.** They say you like opera, **Мені́ (нам) сказа́ли, що ...** I was (we were) told that ..., **Що він сказа́в вам?** What did he say to you?; *pa. pple.* **ска́заний** said; **(с)кажи́! ~і́ть!**

каз|ка́, *f.* fairy tale, **розпові́дати ~ку** to tell a fairy tale; ◆ **розка́зувати ~ки** to spin a yarn; *N. pl.* **~ки́**, *G. pl.* **~о́к.**

Кана́д|а, *f.* Canada.

кана́д|ець, *m.*, **~ця** Canadian man; *L.* **на ~цеві.**

кана́д|ка, *f.* Canadian woman; *L.* **на ~ці**, *G. pl.* **~ок.**

кана́дський, *adj.* Canadian.

кана́п|ка, *f. Gal.* sandwich; *L.* **на ~ці**, *G. pl.* **~ок.**

кані́кул|и, *only pl.*, **кані́кул** *(only relative to studies, not work)* vacation, holidays, **зимо́ві (лі́тні, різдвя́ні) к.** winter (summer, Christmas) vacation; *L.* **на ~ах** on vacation. *Cf.* **відпу́стка.** *Also see* **вака́ції.**

ка́р|ий, *adj. (of eyes only)* brown, **~і о́чі** brown eyes; ◆ **каро́ок|ий** brown-eyed (person).

Карпа́т|и, *only pl.*, **Карпа́т** the Carpathian Mountains; *L. pl.* **у ~ах.**

ка́рт|а, *f.* 1) map; 2) playing card; ◆ **гра́ти в ~и** to play cards; *L.* **на ~і.**

карти́н|а, *f.* 1) picture, painting; 2) film. *Also see* **кінокарти́на.**

ка́рт|ка, *f.* card, **креди́тна к.** a credit card; **плати́ти креди́тною ~ою** to pay with a credit card.; *L.* **на ~ці**, *G. pl.* **~ок.**

карто́пл|я, *f.*, *only sg.*, *coll.* potato, **кілогра́м ~і** a kilogram of potatoes, **сма́жена (ва́рена, пе́чена) к.** fried (boiled, baked) potatoes, **к.-фрі** French fries.

ка́с|а, *f.* 1) ticket office, box office, **залізни́чна к.** railroad ticket office, **театра́льна к.** box-office; 2) cash register, **плати́ти в ~і** to pay at the cash register.

каси́р, *m.*, **~а** cashier, ticket seller; *L.* **на -о́ві.**

кашта́нов|ий, *adj. (of hair color)* auburn, of chestnut color, **~е воло́сся** auburn hair.

ка́ш|ель, *m.*, **~лю** cough, **си́льний к.** bad cough.

ка́шля|ти, **~ють**, *intr.* to cough, to have a cough; **кашля́й! ~те!**

кварта́л, *m.*, **~у** block of buildings, city block, **Пройді́ть три ~и та поверні́ть ліво́руч.** Pass three blocks and turn left.

кварти́р|а, *f.*, **~и** apartment, flat, **найма́ти ~у** to rent an apartment.

квит|о́к, *m.*, **~ка́** ticket, **к. до теа́тру (кіна́, музе́ю)** theater (movie, museum) ticket, **к. на конце́рт (футбо́л)** ticket to a concert (soccer match), **к. на + A. по́їзд (авто́бус, літа́к)** train (bus, plane) ticket; *L.* **на ~ку**, *N. pl.* **~ки́.**

кві́т|ень, *m.*, **~ня** April, **Він народи́вся п’я́того ~ня.** He was born on April 5.; *L.* **у ~ні.**

кві́т|ка, *f.* flower, *L.* **на ~ці**, *N. pl.* **~ки́**, *G. pl.* **~о́к.**

кві́т|и, *only pl.*, **~ів** flowers, **Він за́вжди купу́є їй к.** He always buys her flowers. *See* **кві́тка** *for sg.*

ке́пськ|ий, *adj.* bad, of poor quality, poor, **к. вчи́тель** bad teacher, **~а пого́да** bad weather, **~е здоро́в’я** poor health.

Ки́їв, *m.*, **Ки́єв|а** Kyiv (the capital of Ukraine); *L.* **у ~і.**

ки́ївськ|ий, *adj.* Kyivan, pertaining to Kyiv, **К. націона́льний університе́т** Kyiv National University; **К. торт** Kyiv cake *(brand name of a popular cake).*

ки́лим, *m.*, ~а carpet, rug, kilim; *N. pl.* ~и́.

ки́сл|ий, *adj.* sour, **к. смак** sour taste, **~ий ви́раз** sour countenance.

кита́|єць, *m.*, ~йця Chinese man.

Кита́|й, *m.*, ~ю China; *L.* у ~ї.

кита́й|ка, *f.* Chinese woman; *L.* на ~ці, *G. pl.* ~ок.

кита́йськ|ий, *adj.* Chinese.

кише́н|я, *f.* pocket; ♦ **бу́ти по ~і** to be within one's means, **Мені це не по ~і.** I cannot afford it.

кия́нин, *m.*, **кия́н|ина** Kyivan, male citizen of Kyiv, *N. pl.* ~и, *G. pl.* **киян**; **~ка**, *f.* female Kyivan; *L.* на ~ці, *G. pl.* ~ок.

кілогра́м, *m.*, ~а kilogram; **два (три, чоти́ри) ~и** two (three, four) kilos, **п'ять ~ів** five (*six, and more*) kilos.

кіломе́т|(е)р, *m.* ~ра kilometer; **два (три, чоти́ри) ~ри** two (three, four) kilometers, **п'ять ~рів** (*six, and more*) five kilometers.

кільк|а́, *pron.*, ~о́х several, a few, a number of (with *count.*) + *G. pl.* **к. днів** a few days.

кімна́т|а, *f.* room, chamber, **к. на одно́го (двох, трьох)** room for one (two, three) persons.

кінемато́граф, *m.*, ~а the art of filmmaking, the film; **украї́нський к.** the Ukrainian cinema. *Also see* **кіно**.

кін|е́ць, *m.*, ~ця́ end, finish, **до само́го ~ця** till the very end, **при ~ці** and **у ~ці** + *G.* at the end of.

кін|о́, *nt.*, ~а́ 1) movie theater, **до ~а́** or **у ~і** to / at the cinema, **ходи́ти у к.** go to the movies; 2) *colloq.* cinema (as art), **украї́нське кіно** Ukrainian cinema.

кіноакто́р, *m.*, ~а film actor; **~ка**, *f.* actress; *L.* на ~ці, *G. pl.* ~ок.

кінокарти́н|а, *f.* film, movie, picture, **худо́жня (документа́льна, повнометра́жна, короткометра́жна) к.** feature (documentary, full-length, short) film. *Also see* **фільм**.

кінорежисе́р, *m.* film director; *N. pl.* ~и.

кіношко́л|а, *f.* film school.

кінотеа́тр, *m.*, ~у movie theater, movies, cinema house.

кінча́|ти, ~ють; **скінчи́|ти**, ~у, ~ать, *tran. or only impf. inf.* to finish, end, complete, **Він кінча́є робо́ту о шості́й.** He finishes work at six.; **скі́нчений** finished; **кінча́й! ~те!; скінчи́! ~і́ть!** *var., also see* **закі́нчувати**.

кінча́|тися; скінчи́|тися, *intr.* to be over, come to an end, **Виста́ва ско́ро ~лася.** The show ended quickly. *Also see* **закі́нчуватися**.

кінчи́ти, *pf., var.* **скінчи́ти** and **закінчи́ти**, *see* **кінча́ти** and **закі́нчувати**.

кінь, *m.*, **кон|я́** horse; *N. pl.* ~і́, *G. pl.* ~е́й, *I. pl.* **кі́ньми** or ~я́ми.

кіт, *m.*, **кот|а́** a cat; *N. pl.* ~и́.

клас, *m.*, ~у 1) class, grade, form, **У яко́му ~і навча́ється ї́хній син?** In what grade is their son?; 2) classroom; 3) class, quality, **Він перекла́дач висо́кого ~у.** He is a high class translator.

кла́сти, клад|у́ть; по~ ; *pa.* **кла|в, ~ли**, *tran.* 1) to put sth (in prone position *as opposed* to **ста́вити** to put in upright position), **Він покла́в гро́ші на стіл.** He put the money on the table.; 2) deposit (money), **Мені́ тре́ба по~ гро́ші до ба́нку.** I need to put money into my bank.; *pa. pple.* **покла́дений** put, deposited; **(по)клади́! ~і́ть!**

кли́кати, кли́ч|уть; по~, *tran.* 1) to call, **Він кли́че її́ по і́мені.** He calls her by name.; 2) *colloq.* invite, **Вони́ покли́кали нас на вечі́рку.** They invited us to their party.; *pa. pple.* **покли́каний** called; **(по)клич! ~те!**

ключ, *m.*, ~а́ key; *N. pl.* ~і́, **Ось ва́ші ~і́.** Here are your keys.

кна́йп|а, *f.*, Gal., *colloq.* restaurant, hang-out.

кни́|га, *f.* book (*usually big or important*), **Бі́ла к.** The White Book, **куха́рська (телефо́нна) к.** cook (phone) book; *L.* у ~зі. *Also see* **кни́жка**.

книга́р|ня, *f.* a bookstore; *G. pl.* ~ень.

кни́ж|ка, *f.* book; *L.* ~ці.; *G. pl.* ~ок; *Cf.* **кни́га**.

ковбас|а́, *f.* sausage, **дома́шня к.** homemade sausage; *N. pl.* **ковба́си**.

ко́жен, *adj., var., see* **ко́жний**; **К. зна́є, що …** Everybody knows that …

ко́жн|ий, *adj.* each, every; **~ого** + *noun* (*to express repetition*), **~ого дня (но́чі, ти́жня, мі́сяця, і т.д.)** every day (night, week, month, etc.).

коза́к, *m.*, ~а́ Cossack.

коле́|ґа, *m. and f. var.* **коле́га**, colleague, **Ю́рій – мій к.** Yuri is my colleague., **Ната́ля – моя́ к.** Natalia is my colleague.; *L.* на ~зі.

колекціоне́р, *m.* collector; *N. pl.* ~и; *f.* ~ка, female collector, *L.* на ~ці.; *G. pl.* ~ок.

коле́кці|я, *f.* collection, **к. мисте́цтва** art collection, **Музе́й ма́є бага́ту ~ю скульпту́ри.** The museum has a rich collection of sculpture.

коли́, *adv.* when; **К. він при́йде?** When will he come?

коли́-не́будь, *adv.* 1) at some point, some day, **Я сподіва́юся, що ми к. зустрі́немося.** I hope we meet some day.; 2) any time, **Мо́жеш дзвони́ти мені́ к.** You can call me any time.

коли́сь, *adv.* some day, one day.

колі́н|о, *nt.* knee; *G. pl.* **колі́н**.

ко́л|ір, *m.*, ~ьору color, **Яко́го ~ьору її́ о́чі?** What color are her eyes?; *N. pl.* ~ьори.

комерці́йн|ий, *adj.* commercial.

компа́кт-ди|ск, *m.*, ~а CD, compact disk; *L.* на ~у.

компа́ні|я, *f.*, ~ї 1) company, enterprise; 2) company, group (of friends).

компле́кт, *m.*, ~у set, **к. о́дягу (біли́зни)** set of clothes (bed linen).

компози́тор, *m.*, ~а composer.

комп'ю́тер, *m.*, ~а computer, **персона́льний к.** PC.

комп'ю́терн|ий, *adj.* computer, **к. ві́рус** computer virus, **~і техноло́гії** computer technologies.

комфорта́бельний   **ку́хар**

комфорта́бельн|ий, *adj.* comfortable.

консервато́рі|я, *f.*, ~ї conservatory, music academy.

консульта́нт, *m.* consultant, з (із) + *G.* **к. з безпе́ки** security consultant.

конфере́нці|я, *f.*, ~ї conference, **бра́ти у́часть у ~ї** to take part in a conference, **міжнаро́дна к.** international conference; *L.* **на ~ї**.

конце́рт, *m.*, ~у 1)concert, **іти́ на к.** to go to a concert, **на ~і** at a concert; 2) concerto.

копі́й|ка, *f.* kopeck *(one hundredth of the Ukrainian currency unit hryvnia)*; *L.* **у ~ці**, *N. pl.* ~ки, *G. pl.* ~о́к.

кораб|е́ль, *m.*, ~ля́ ship, ~ле́м by ship; *L.* **на ~лі́**.

кордо́н, *m.*, ~у border, frontier; *posn.* **за ~ом** abroad, **Скі́льки ча́су ви жи́ли за ~ом?** How much time did you live abroad?; *dir.* **за к.**, **Вона́ ча́сто ї́здить за к. у спра́вах.** She often goes abroad on business.

кори́сн|ий, *adj.* useful, beneficial, ~а пора́да a useful piece of advice.

користу|ва́тися, ~ються; **скориста́|тися**, ~ються, *intr. + I.* 1) *usually impf.* to use sth, **Я ~юся но́вим словнико́м.** I use a new dictionary; 2) *pf.* to take advantage of, **Він не скориста́вся мо́єю пора́дою.** He hasn't taken advantage of my advice.; **користу́й|ся! ~теся!; скориста́й|ся! ~теся!**

кори́чнев|ий, *adj.* brown. *See* **бруна́тний**.

коро́б|ка, *f.* box; *L.* **у ~бці**; *N. pl.* **коро́бки**, *G. pl.* ~о́к.

коро́ткий, *adj.* short, brief; *comp.* **коро́тший**.

костю́м, *m.*, ~а suit, **ділови́й к.** business suit, **Вона́ лю́бить носи́ти ~и.** She likes to wear suits.

котеня́, *nt.*, ~ти kitten; *I.* ~м, *N. pl.* ~та.

котле́т|а, *f.* meat patty; **к. по-ки́ївськи** chicken Kyiv.

котр|и́й, *pron.* which, what, ~а́ годи́на? What time is it?, ~и́й з вас Степа́н? Which one of you is Stepan?

коха́н|ий, *adj.* beloved, dear *(as form of address)*; *colloq. (of people, pets)* wonderful, **Він ~а люди́на.** He's a wonderful person.; *n.* beloved, boyfriend, **Це подару́нок від мого́ ~ого.** This is a gift from my beloved; ~а girlfriend.

коха́нн|я, *nt.* love, physical love, **к. з пе́ршого по́гляду** love at first sight, **істо́рія ~я** love story.

коха́|ти, ~ють; **по~**, *tran.* 1) *impf.* to love (romantically), adore; 2) *pf. + A.* to fall in love with, **Він її́ покоха́в.** He fell in love with her.; *pa. pple.* **зако́ханий** in love, enamored; **(по)коха́й! ~те!**

кошту́|вати, ~ють, *only impf.* 1) *intr.* to cost; **Скі́льки це ~є?** How much is it?; 2) *tran.* to cost (a certain amount) *+ A.* **Це ~є одну́ гри́вню (вели́ку су́му гро́шей; бага́то).** This costs one hryvnia (a large sum of money; a lot); **кошту́й! ~те!**

крава́т|ка, *f.* tie, **одягну́ти (носи́ти) ~ку** to put on (wear) tie; *L.* **на ~ці**; *G. pl.* ~о́к.

краї́н|а, *f.* country, nation, land, **з усіє́ї ~и** from all over the country, **по всій ~і** all over the country, **у ко́жній ~і** in every country; ♦ **на́ша к.** this country, **подорожува́ти ~ою** to travel around the country, **рі́дна к.** homeland.

крамни́ц|я, *f.* store, shop *(often small)*; *Cf.* **магази́н**.

крас|а́, *f.* beauty, ♦ **Що за к.!** How beautiful!; **сало́н ~и** beauty parlor.

кра́щ|ий, *adj.* better, *comp. of* **до́брий**.

кра́ще *adv.* better, *comp. of* **до́бре**; ♦ **К. пі́зно, ніж ніко́ли.** Better late than never., ♦ **К. подзвони́ти до ба́тька увве́чері.** Better to call the father in the evening.

креди́тн|ий, *adj.* credit, ~а ка́ртка credit card, **плати́ти ~ою ка́рткою** to pay with credit card.

Крим, *m.*, ~у the Crimea (peninsula and autonomous republic in the south of Ukraine); *L.* **у ~у́**.

крім *prep.+ G.*, besides, **Хто ще к. Павла́ зна́є про це?** Besides Pavlo who else knows about it?, ♦ **к. того́** besides, in addition.

кров, *f.*, ~и, *only sg.* blood; *I.* ~'ю; **з ~'ю** medium rare.

куди́, *adv.* where to *(dir.)*, **К. ви ї́здили?** Where did you drive (go) to?

куди́-не́будь, *adv., dir.* wherever to, anywhere, somewhere, **Дава́йте пі́демо к.** Let's go some place.

куди́сь, *adv., dir.* to someplace, somewhere, **Марко́ к. побі́г.** Marko ran some place.

кулі́нарн|ий, *adj.* culinary, ~і по́слуги culinary services.

культу́р|а, *f.* culture.

куме́дн|ий, *adj.* funny, comic.

купа́|ти, ~ють; **ви~**, *tran.* to bathe sb, **Вони́ ~ють мало́го Іва́нка щодня́.** They bathe little Ivanko every day.; *pa. pple.* **ви́купаний** bathed; **(ви)купа́й! ~те!**

купа́|тися, ~ються; **ви~**, *refl.* to bathe (oneself), **В Я́лті дру́зі бага́то купа́лися у мо́рі.** In Yalta the friends bathed a lot in the sea.; **(ви)купа́йся! ~теся!**

купе́йн|ий, *adj.* **к. квито́к** train ticket for a sleeping compartment shared by four passengers; second class train ticket; **к. ваго́н** second-class train car.

купи́ти, *pf.*, *see* **купува́ти**.

купу́|вати, ~ють; **куп|и́ти**, куплю́, ~иш, ~ить, ~лять, *tran. + D.* to buy, purchase, **Ми ку́пимо Мико́лі га́рну крава́тку.** We'll buy Mykola a nice tie.; *pa. pple.* **ку́плений** bought; **купу́й! ~те!; куп|и́! ~і́ть.**

курс, *m.*, ~у 1) course *(in a discipline)*, з (із) + *G.*, **к. з матема́тики** course in math, **записа́тися на к.** to enroll in a course, **слу́хати к.** take a course, **Скі́льки ~ів він прослу́хав?** How many courses has he taken?; 2) year of studies at university, **Тоді́ вона́ була́ студе́нткою пе́ршого ~у.** Then she was a first-year student. **На яко́му ти ~і?** What year (of studies) are you?

курча́, *nt.*, ~ти (baby) chicken; *I.* ~м, *N. pl.* ~та, *G. pl.* ~т.

куря́тин|а, *f.*, *only sg.* chicken meat.

кут|о́к, *m.*, ~ка́ corner *(of room)*; *L.* **у ~ку́**, **У ~ку́ стоя́в стіл.** There was a table in the corner.

ку́хар, *m.*, ~я cook, **Він до́брий к.** He is a good cook.; *N. pl.* ~і; ~ка, *f.* female cook, **Моя́ ма́ма – чудо́ва ~ка.** My mom is a wonderful cook.; *L.* **на ~ці**, *G. pl.* ~о́к.

ку́хня

ку́х|ня, *f.* 1) kitchen, **Ми лю́бимо ї́сти на ~ні.** We like to eat in the kitchen.; 2) cuisine, **Борщ – це пе́рша стра́ва украї́нської ~ні.** Borshch is the primary dish of the Ukrainian cuisine.; *L.* **на ~ні**; *G. pl.* **~онь**.

кошту|ва́ти, **~ють**; **по~** or **с~**, *tran.* to taste, **За́вжди ціка́во к. нові́ стра́ви.** It's always interesting to taste new dishes.; *pa. pple.* **покушто́ваний** tasted; **(по)кошту́й! ~те!**

Л

лаго́дити, **~жу, лаго́д|ять; по~** *tran.* to repair, fix, **Чи мо́же хтось по~ замо́к?** Can somebody repair the lock?; *pa. pple.* **полаго́джений** repaired; **(по)лаго́дь! ~те!**

лама́ти, **~ють; з~** *tran.* to break, **л. но́гу (ні́готь, две́рі)** break a leg (nail, door), **Іри́на злама́ла но́гу.** Iryna broke her leg.; *pa. pple.* **зла́маний** broken; **(з)лама́й! ~те!**

лама́тися, **~ються; з~** *intr.* to break, **На́ше а́вто злама́лося.** Our car broke down.; **(з)лама́й|ся! ~теся!**

ласка́во, *adv.* kindly; ♦ **Л. про́симо!** Welcome!

легк|и́й, *adj.* 1) light (of weight), **~а́ валі́за** light suitcase; 2) easy, **~е́ завда́ння** easy assignment; *comp.* **ле́гший**.

леж|а́ти, **~а́ть**, *intr.* to lie (*as opposed to* **стоя́ти** be standing); **На столі́ ~и́ть газе́та.** There is a newspaper on the table., **На підло́зі ~ли́ га́рні кили́ми.** There were nice carpets lying on the floor.; **леж|и́! ~і́ть!**

ле́кці|я, *f.* 1) lecture, **з (із) +** *G.* in, **л. з істо́рії мисте́цтва** a lecture in art history; **про +** *A.* about, **л. про Іва́на Франка́** a lecture on Ivan Franko; 2) (*chapter in textbook*) lesson; **(про)чита́ти ~ю** to give a lecture; *L.* **на ~ї**.

лет|і́ти, **лечу́, ~и́ш, ~я́ть; по~** *uni., intr.* to fly, **Насту́пної середи́ ми ~имо́ до Украї́ни.** Next Wednesday we're flying to Ukraine; **(по)лет|и́! ~і́ть!** *Also see multi.* **літа́ти**.

лето́вищ|е, *nt.* airport, **Міжнаро́дне л. «Бори́спіль»** Boryspil International Airport (*Ukraine's most important airport*), **ї́хати на л.** to go to the airport, **Чи вас хтось зустріча́тиме на ~і?** Will anybody be meeting you at the airport?; *L.* **на ~і**, *N. pl.* **~а.** *Also see* **аеропо́рт**.

ли́ж|а, *f.* ski,. **ї́здити на ~ах** to ski; **ї́здити на ~і** to go skiing; *N. pl.* **~і**.

ли́п|ень, *m.*, **~ня** July, **Ва́ля прийде́ во́сьмого ~ня.** Valia will arrive on July 8.; *L.* **у ~і**.

лист, *m.*, **~а́** 1) letter (*message*), **л. додо́му** a letter home, **писа́ти л.** or **~а** to write a letter; 2) sheet (*of paper*), 3) leaf. *Also see* **а́ркуш**.

листі́в|ка, *f.* postcard, **Він отри́мав ~ку від сестри́.** He received a postcard from his sister.; *L.* **у ~ці**, *G. pl.* **~ок**.

лист|о́к, *m.*, **~ка́** 1) sheet, **л. папе́ру** sheet of paper; *also see* **а́ркуш**; 2) a leaf (of plant).

листопа́д, *m.*, **~а** November, **Моя́ по́друга Наді́йка народи́лася во́сьмого листопа́да.** My friend Nadiyka was born on November 8.; *L.* **у ~і**.

листу|ва́тися, **~ються**, *only impf., intr.* to correspond with, write letters to, **з (із) +** *I.* with, **Він ~є́ться з не́ю.** He corresponds with her.; **листу́й|ся! ~теся!**

лиша́ти, *impf., var., see* **залиша́ти**.

лиша́тися, *impf., var., see* **залиша́тися**.

любитель

лише́, *adv.* only, **Я ма́ю л. одну́ гри́вню.** I have only one hryvnia. *Also see* **ті́льки**.

лиши́ти, *pf., var., see* **залиши́ти**.

лиши́тися, *pf., var., see* **залиши́тися**.

лі́в|ий, *adj.* 1) left, lefthand; 2) left wing.

ліво́руч, *adv.* to the left, on the left; **поверн|и́, ~і́ть л.** turn left, **л. від +** *G.* to the left of, **Л. від вікна́ стоя́в стіл.** Left of the window there was a table.

лі́ж|ко, *nt.* bed, **застеля́ти л.** to make a bed; *L.* **на ~ку**, *N. pl.* **~ка**, *G. pl.* **~ок**.

лі́кар, *m.*, **~я** physician, **л.-терапе́вт** general practitioner; **зубни́й л.** dentist; *N. pl.* **~і**; **~ка**, *f.* female physician; *L.* **на ~ці**; *G. pl.* **~ок**.

лі́кар|ня, *f.* hospital; *L.* **у ~і**, *G. pl.* **~ень**.

лі́к|и, *only pl.*, **~ів** drugs, medicine, **від +** *G.* for, **Мені́ тре́ба л. від температу́ри.** I need some remedy for fever.

лікува́|ння *nt.* medical treatment, **л. від +** *G.* treatment for sth, **признача́ти л.** to give treatment, **Яке́ л. вам призна́чили?** What treatment were you given?, **прохо́дити л.** undergo treatment.

ліку|ва́ти, **ліку́|ють; ви~**, *tran.* 1) to treat sth with sth, **від +** *G.* from, **Чим ви ліку́єте грип?** What do you treat the flu with?; 2) *pf.* to cure sb, bring back to health, **Він її́ ско́ро ви́лікував.** He soon cured her.; *pa. pple.* **ви́лікуваний** cured; **(ви)ліку́й! ~те!**

ліс, *m.*, **~у** forest, woods; *L.* **у ~і**.

літа́к, *m.*, **~а́** airplane, aircraft, **квито́к на л.** airplane ticket, **~о́м** by plane, **сіда́ти на (у) л.** to take a plane; *L.* **на ~у́**.

літа́|ти, **~ють**, *multi., intr. + I.* to fly, **Він за́вжди ~є ци́ми авіалі́ніями.** He always flies by these airlines.; *uni.* **леті́ти**; **літа́й! ~те!**

лі́тер|а, *f.* letter (in alphabet), **~а л. алфаві́ту** the first letter of alphabet.

літерату́р|а, *f.* literature, **худо́жня (класи́чна, суча́сна) л.** fiction (classical, contemporary) literature.

лі́тн|ій, *adj.* 1) summer (of season, clothes), **л. о́дяг** summer clothes; 2) old, aged, **~я люди́на** old person.

лі́т|о, *nt.* summer, **спеко́тне (холо́дне, дощове́) л.** hot (cold, rainy) summer, **мину́лого (насту́пного) ~а** last (next) summer.

ліфт, *m.*, **~а** elevator, **ї́хати ~ом** to go by elevator, **сіда́ти на л.** take an elevator, **У моє́му буди́нку нема́є ~а.** There is no elevator in my building.

лов|и́ти, **ловлю́, ~иш, ло́влять; з~**, *tran.* to catch, **л. пташо́к** catch birds, **л. ри́бу** go fishing, **Ма́рко лю́бить л. ри́бу.** Marko likes to go fishing.; *pa. pple.* **зло́влений** caught; **(з)лов|и́! ~і́ть!**

ло́ж|ка, *f.* spoon; *L.* **у ~ці**, *G. pl.* **~ок**.

лю́б|ий, *adj.* dear, beloved; (as form of address) darling, honey, sweetheart, **~а сестро́!** dear sister!, **~і дру́зі!** dear friends!

люби́тел|ь, *m.* 1) lover (of art, literature, etc.), **Він пристра́сний л. кі́на.** He is a passionate lover of movies.; 2) amateur, **Я ра́дше л., ніж фахіве́ць з архітекту́ри.** I'm rather an amateur than specialist in architecture.

люб|и́ти, ~лю́, ~иш, ~лять; по~, *tran.* 1) to like, love; 2) *pf.* to fall in love, come to love (like); *pa. pple.* **полю́блений** loved; **(по)люби́! ~і́ть!** *Cf.* **коха́ти**.

любо́в, *f.*, ~и (spiritual) love, affection; *I.* ~'ю. *Cf.* **коха́ння**.

лю́ди, *pl.*, *see* **люди́на**.

люд|и́на, *f.* person, human being; **приє́мна л.** pleasant individual, **до́бра л.** kind person; *N. pl.* ~и, *G. pl.* ~е́й, *I. pl.* ~ьми́, ♦ **на ~ях** publicly.

лют|ий, *m.*, ~ого February, **Він пока́зуватиме цей фільм двадця́того ~ого.** He will be screening this film on February 20.; *L.* у ~ому *or* ~ім; *adj.* fierce; angry, **л. моро́з** bitter cold.

ляга́|ти, ~ють; **лягти́**, **ля́ж|уть**; *pa.* ліг, лягли́; *intr.* 1) to lie, lie down, **л. спа́ти** go to bed; 2) go to bed, **Вони́ ра́но ляга́ють.** They go to bed early.; **ляга́й! ~те!; ляж! ~те!**

Льв|і́в, *m.*, ~о́ва Lviv *(the capital of Ukrainian Galicia)*.

львів'я́н|ин, *m.*, ~ина citizen of Lviv; *N. pl.* ~и, *G. pl.* **львів'я́н**; ~ка, *f.* female citizen of Lviv; *L.* **на ~ці**, *G. pl.* ~ок.

М

ма́буть, *adv.* maybe, perhaps, probably.

магази́н, *m.*, ~у store, shop; **іти́ до ~у** to go shopping, **продукто́вий м.** grocery store. *Also see* **гастроно́м** *and* **крамни́ця**.

магісте́ріум, *m.*, ~а master's program, **м. з (із)** + *G.* master's program in, **Він поступи́в на м. з соціоло́гії.** He enrolled in a MA program in sociology.

магі́стерськ|ий, *adj.* master's, pertaining to master's degree, **м. ступінь** master's degree, ~а **програ́ма** master's program.

майбу́тн|є, *nt.*, *(declines like adj.)* future, **без ~ього** without a future, **на м.** for the future, **у ~ьому** in future.

майбу́тн|ій, *adj.* future, **м. час** future tense, **Це її м. чоловік.** This is her future husband.

майда́н, *m.*, ~у square, **М. Незале́жности** Independence Square *(the central square of Kyiv)*.

ма́йже, *adv.* almost, nearly, **Він м. закі́нчив чита́ти.** He almost finished reading.

мале́ньк|ий, *adj.*, *dimin.*, *var. of* **мали́й** small, little.

мал|и́й, *adv.* small, little; *comp.* **ме́нший**.

ма́ло, *adv.* + *G.* 1) little, few, **м. робо́ти** little work, **м. ча́су** little time, **м. люде́й** few people; 2) not enough *with D.*, **Йому́ м. зіпсува́ти всім настрій.** It's not enough for him to spoil it for everybody.

малю́|вати, ~ють; на~, *tran.* 1) to draw, **Він га́рно малює́.** He is a good drawer., **Ти мо́жеш на~ план кімна́ти?** Can you draw a plan of the room? 2) *Gal.* to paint; *pf.* по~, **Ми помалюва́ли сті́ну у си́ній ко́лір.** We painted the wall blue.; **намальо́ваний** drawn; **(на)малю́й! ~те!**

ма́м|а, *f.*, *fam.* mommy, mom, mama; *N. pl* ~и́, *G. pl.* **мам** *or* ~ів.

мандрівни́|к, *m.* traveler, wayfarer; ~ця, *f.*

ма́р|ка, *f.* 1) postal stamp, **пошто́ва м.**; 2) brand, trademark, **Яко́ї ~и це а́вто?** What make is this car?; *L.* **на ~ці**, *G. pl.* ~ок.

маршру́т, *m.*, ~у route, itinerary, **На цьо́му ~і нема́є прями́х ре́йсів.** There are no direct flights on this route.

маршру́т|ка, *f.* shuttle bus *(passenger minivan running both within cities and between)*, **сіда́ти на ~ку** to take the minivan, **іха́ти ~кою** to go by the minivan; *L.* **у ~ці**; *G. pl.* ~ок.

ма́сл|о, *nt.* butter, **хліб з ~ом** bread and butter.

мате́рі|я, *f.* cloth, fabric, material.

ма́т|и¹, *f.*, ~ері, mother; *A.* ~ір, *D.* ~ері, *I.* ~ір'ю, *N. pl.* ~ері, *G. pl.* ~ерів, *I. pl.* ~еря́ми.

ма́|ти², ~ють, *only impf.*, *tran.* 1) to have, possess, **Сього́дні я ~ю вихідни́й.** Today I have a day-off.; **м. мі́сце** to take place, **Де мала мі́сце зу́стріч?** Where did the meeting take place?; 2) *mod.* + *inf.* to have to, need to do sth, to be supposed to do sth (obligation to do sth due to necessity, agreement or expectation), **Він ~є купи́ти це.** He is supposed to buy it.; *no pa. pple.*; **май! ~те!**

маши́н|а, *f.* car, automobile, ~ою by car. *Also see* **а́вто**.

ме́бл|і, *only pl.*, ~ів furniture, **спа́льні м.** bedroom furniture; *L. pl.* **на ~ях**.

ме́неджер, *m.*, ~а manager, **Я хо́чу розмовля́ти з ва́шим ~ом.** I want to talk with your manager.

ме́нш|ий, *adj.*, *comp.*, *see* **мали́й**, **м. брат** younger brother, ~а **сестра́** younger sister.

меню́, *nt.*, *indecl.* menu, **у м.** on the menu, **попроси́ти м.** to ask for a menu.

ме́реж|а, *f.*, ~і 1) network; chain *(of restaurants, stores)*; 2) the Internet, **у ~і** on the Internet.

мереже́в|ий, *adj.* Internet, pertaining to the Internet, ~а **публіка́ція (сторі́нка)** Internet publication *(page)*.

мет|а́, *f.* purpose, aim, goal, **З яко́ю ~о́ю ви пи́шете йому́?** What's the purpose of your writing him?

ме́т|ер, *m.*, ~ра, *var.* **ме́тр** meter *(international unit of measure)*, **два ~и** two meters, **де́сять ~ів** ten meters.

метр, *. var.*, *see* **ме́тер**.

метр|о́, *nt.*, ~а subway, metro, ~о́м by subway, **Ми зустріча́ємося біля ~а.** We are meeting near the subway station.

меха́нік, *m.* mechanic, **інжене́р-м.** mechanical engineer.

ми, *pers. pron.*, **нас** we, **М. тут живемо́.** We live here.

ми́л|о, *nt.* soap, **шмато́к ~а** a bar of soap.

мина́|ти, ~ють; **мин|у́ти**, ~у́ть 1) *intr.* to pass *(of time)*, **Лі́то мину́ло шви́дко.** The summer passed quickly.; 2) *tran.* to pass by sth + *A.*, **Він мина́є бібліоте́ку доро́гою додо́му.** He passes the library on his way home.; *pa. pple.* **мину́лий** passed, last; **минай! ~те!; мин|и́! ~і́ть!**

мину́л|е, *nt.*, ~ого the past; *L.* **у ~ому**, **Все це вже у ~ому.** All this is already in the past.

мину́л|ий, *adj.* 1) last, ~ого **ти́жня (мі́сяця, лі́та, ро́ку)** last week (month, summer, year), ~ої **о́сени (весни́, зими́)** last autumn (spring, winter); 2) past, ~і **ро́ки** past years.

мину́ти   **му́сити**

мину́ти, *pf. see* **мина́ти**.

мисте́цтв|о, *nt.* art, **моде́рне м.** modern art.

ми́|ти, ~**ють**; **по**~, *tran.* to wash *(body, dishes)*, clean *(floor)*; *pa. pple.* **поми́тий** cleaned, washed; **(по)ми́й! ~те!**

ми́ш|а, *f.*, ~**і** mouse.

міжнаро́дн|ий, *adj.* international, ~**і відно́сини** international relations.

мій, *poss. pron. m.*, **мого́** my, mine, **Марко́ – м. стари́й друг.** Marko is an old friend of mine.

мільйо́н, *m.*, ~**а** million, + *G. pl.*, **де́сять ~ів гри́вень** ten million hryvnias.

мілья́рд, *m.*, ~**а** billion, + *G. pl.*, **три ~и до́ларів** three billion dollars.

міня́|ти, ~**ють**; **по**~, *tran.* 1) to change, alter sth., **м. адре́су** change address; 2) to exchange currency, **Мені́ тре́ба по~ валю́ту.** I need to exchange currency.; *pa. pple.* **змі́нений** changed; **(по)міня́й! ~те!**

міня́|тися, ~**ються**; **по**~ *intr.* to change, become different, **Він зо́всім не поміня́вся.** He hasn't changed at all.; **(по)міня́й|ся! ~теся!**

мі́ст|о, *nt.* 1) city, town, **Він лю́бить жи́ти в ~і.** He likes to live in the city.; 2) downtown; ♦ **іти́ до ~а** to go downtown; *N. pl.* ~**á**.

мі́сц|е, *nt.*, ~**я** 1) place, **ціка́ве м.** sight; 2) seat, **м. бі́ля вікна́** window seat, **м. багажу́** piece of luggage; *N. pl.* ~**я́**.

місце́в|ий, *adj.* local, ~**і зви́чаї** local customs.

місьќ|и́й, *adj.* urban, municipal, city, **м. парк** city park, ~**á ра́да** city hall, **м. тра́нспорт** urban transportation.

мі́сяц|ь, *m.*, ~**я** 1) month, ♦ **медо́вий м.** honey moon; 2) the moon; **по́вний м.** full moon; *L.* **у ~і**; *N. pl.* ~**і**.

млине́ць, *m.*, **млинця́** pancake, blintz.

мобі́л|ка, *f. colloq.* mobile phone, **з ~ки** from a mobile phone, **по ~ці** over a mobile phone; *L.* **у ~ці**.

мо́в|а, *f.* language; **розмовля́ти украї́нською (мо́вою)** to speak Ukrainian (language); ♦ **про що м.?** What are you (they, we) talking about?; *G. pl.* **мов, Скі́льки мов ти зна́єш?** How many languages do you know?

могти́, **мо́ж|уть**; **з**~; *pa.* **міг, могли́** + *inf.* 1) be able to do sth., can, **Я мо́жу допомогти́.** I can help., **Він не змо́же прийти́.** He won't be able to come. 2) *pf.* to manage, succeed, **Мико́ла зміг попереди́ти нас.** Mykola succeeded in warning us.

мо́д|а, *f.* fashion, vogue, **оста́ння м.** latest fashion, **за оста́нньою ~ою** in the latest fashion, **бу́ти (не) у ~і** to be in (out of) fashion, **вихо́дити з ~и** go out of fashion.

моде́рн|ий, *adj.* modern, contemporary.

мо́дн|ий, *adj.* fashionable, in vogue, **м. о́дяг** fashionable clothes.

мо́дно, *adv.* fashionably, **Він за́вжди́ м. вдяга́ється.** He always dresses fashionably.

мо|є́, *poss. pron., nt.*, ~**го́** my, mine, **м. мі́сто** my city, **Це нове́ а́вто м.** This new car is mine.   **мо́же**, *mod.* perhaps, maybe *(expression of uncertainty or approximation)*, **М., ви зна́єте це.** Maybe you know it.

можли́в|ий, *adj.* possible, **Це м. ви́хід.** It's a possible solution.

можли́в|ість, *f.*, ~**ости** possibility, opportunity, **виняткова́ м.** exceptional opportunity, **ма́ти м.** + *inf.* to have an opportunity to do sth, **Я не ма́ю найме́ншої ~ости зроби́ти це.** There's no chance I can do it.

мо́жна, *mod.* + *inf.* 1) to be possible, **Квитки́ м. купи́ти у ка́сі.** Tickets can be bought in the ticket-office. 2) to be allowed (used with *D.* of logical subject), **Мико́лі теж м. прийти́.** Mykola can also come.

мої́, *poss. pron., pl.*, ~**x** my, mine, **м. давні дру́зі** my old friends, **Ці гро́ші м.** This money is mine.

мо́кр|ий, *adj.* 1) wet, **Взуття́ було́ все ~им.** The shoes were all wet.; 2) rainy, **м. клі́мат** rainy climate; *adv.* ~**о**, **Надво́рі було́ ~о і хо́лодно.** It was wet and cold outside.

молод|и́й, *adj.* young, *comp.* ~**і́ший** younger *(out of those who are all young)*; ~**ший** younger or junior in rank *(out of those who are not necessarily young)*; ~**ша сестра́** younger sister.

мо́лод|ість, *f., only sg.*, ~**ости** youth, young years, young age, **Сімдеся́ті - це роки́ моє́ї ~ости.** The seventies are the years of my youth; *I.* ~**істю**.

мо́лод|ь, *f., only sg.* youth, young people, **На зу́стрічі було́ бага́то ~і.** There were a lot of young people at the meeting.; *I.* ~**дю**.

молоќ|о, *nt.* milk, **ка́ва з ~м** coffee with milk, **тро́хи ~а** a little milk.

моло́чн|ий, *adj.* milk, dairy, **м. кокте́йль** milk shake, **м. ві́дділ** dairy department, ~**і проду́кти** dairy products.

моме́нт, *m.*, ~**у** moment, **у цей м.** at this moment.

мо́р|е, *nt.*, ~**я** sea; **на ~і** by the sea; **ї́хати на м.** to go to the sea-shore; **Ми лю́бимо відпочива́ти на ~і.** We like to vacation by the sea. *N. pl.* ~**я́**, *G. pl.* ~**і́в**.

моро́зив|о, *nt.* ice-cream, **Найбі́льше йому́ подоба́ється шокола́дне м.** Most of all he likes chocolate ice-cream.

моро́з|ити, **моро́жу**, ~**ять**; **за**~, *tran.*, + *A.* 1) to freeze sth; 2) (with logical subject in *D.*) to suffer from feverish chills, **Мене́ ду́же ~ить.** I have sever feverish chills.; *pa. pple.* **заморо́жений** frozen; **(за)моро́зь! ~те!**

мотоци́кл, *m.*, ~**а** motocycle, **ї́здити ~ом** to ride a motocycle.

мо|я́, *poss. pron., f.*, ~**є́ї** my, mine, **Знайо́мтеся – це м. сестра́ Ната́ля.** Meet my sister Natalia.; *N. pl.* ~**ї**.

музе́|й, *m.*, ~**ю** museum, **худо́жній (істори́чний) м.** art (history) museum; *L.* **у ~ї**.

му́зи|ка, *f.*, music, **джа́зова (класи́чна, хорова́, наро́дна, популя́рна) м.** jazz (classic, choir, folk, popular) music; *L.* **у ~ці**.

музика́нт, *m.*, ~**а** musician, **Він відо́мий м.** He is a well-known musician.

музи́чн|ий, *adj.* musical, pertaining to music, **м. інструме́нт** musical instrument.

му́с|ити, **му́шу**, ~**иш**, ~**ять** + *inf.* to have to, be obliged or compelled to do, **Ви не ~ите це роби́ти.** You don't have to do it.

м'як|и́й, *adj.* soft, mild, gentle; *comp.* **м'я́кший**.

м'ясн|и́й, *adj.* meat, **м. ві́дділ** butcher's department.

м'я́с|о, *nt., only sg.* meat; **ку́ряче (свиня́че, теля́че, ялови́че) м.** chicken (pork, beef, veal) meat.

м'яч, *m.,* **~а** ball, **футбо́льний (баскетбо́льний, те́нісний) м.** soccer, (basketball, tennis) ball.

Н

на, *prep.* 1) *dir.* on, to, into, + *A.,* **ста́вити н. стіл** to put on a table, **н. пі́вніч** to the north, **їхати н. ста́нцію** to go to a station; ♦ **н. мою́ ду́мку** in my opinion; 2) *posn.* in, at + *L.,* **н. столі́** on a table, **н. ри́нку** in the market place, **н. пі́вночі** in the north, **н. ста́нції** at a station; 3) *(of time)* for + *A.,* **н. лі́то** for summer, *(duration of action),* **Ми приї́хали н. два дні.** We came for two days., *(time destination)* for, by, **Тре́ба зроби́ти це на понеді́лок.** We need to do it by Monday.

на! *inter.* take it, here, here you are (said when you offer sb to take sth from you); *pl.* **на́те!**

набира́|ти, **~ють**; **набра́ти**, **набер|у́ть**, *tran.+ A.* (но́мер) to dial a number; ♦ **набра́но непра́вильний но́мер** wrong number; *pa. pple.* **на́браний**; **набира́й! ~те!**; **набер|и́! ~і́ть!**

набра́ти, *pf., see* **набира́ти**.

нава́житися, *pf., see* **нава́жуватися**.

нава́жуватися, **нава́жу|ються**; **нава́житися**, **нава́ж|аться**, *intr.* to dare, have courage, **на** + *A.* for or + *inf.,* **Я не нава́жуюся сказа́ти їй.** I don't dare tell her., **Сергі́й наре́шті нава́жився на подоро́ж літако́м.** Serhiy finally mustered the courage for a trip by airplane.

наві́ть, *adv.,* even, **Н. Рома́н прийшо́в на зу́стріч.** Even Roman came to the meeting.

наві́що, *adv.* what for, why, **Н. це тобі́?** What do you need it for? *Also see* **на́що**.

на все до́бре, *cliché* Take care! (*lit.* for all the best).

навми́сно, *adv., var.* **навми́сне** deliberately, on purpose, expressly, **Він н. сказа́в вам про це.** He told you about it on purpose.

навпаки́, 1) *adv.* on the contrary, quite the opposite, **Хто сказа́в, що я про́ти? Н., я за цю пропози́цію.** Who said I was against? On the contrary, I am in favor of this proposal.; 2) the other way around, **Він все зроби́в н.** He did everything the other way around.

навча́льн|ий, *adj.* pertaining to studies, **н. рік** academic year.

навча́|тися, **~ються**; *no. pf., intr.* to study (where, how), **Де (як) він ~ється?** Where (how) does he study?; **навча́й|ся! ~теся!** *Also see* **учи́тися**. *Cf.* **навчи́тися**.

навча́нн|я, *nt., only sg.* studies, a course of studies.

навчи́тися, *pf., see* **вчи́тися** + *G. or impf. inf.* to learn to do sth, **Коли́ він навчи́вся говори́ти украї́нською?** When did he learn to speak Ukrainian?; **навч|и́ся! ~і́ться!**

над, *prep.* + *I., var.* **на́ді** (*before* **мно́ю**) above, over, **Н. столо́м виси́ть годи́нник.** There's a clock (hanging) over the table.; **н. усе́** above all, **Н. усе́ він лю́бить подорожува́ти.** Above all he likes to travel.

надво́рі, *adv.* outdoors, **Ми прово́димо бага́то ча́су н.** We spend much time outdoors.

на́дто, *adv., var.* **зана́дто** too, overly (used before *adj., adv.* or *v.* to express excessive quality), **н. вели́кий** too big, **н. пові́льно** too slowly, **н. стара́тися** try too much. *Also see* **за~** prefix.

на́зв|а, *f.* name (*only of inan. object*), title (*of book*), **Яка́ н. ціє́ї кни́жки?** What's the title of the book? **під ~ою** under the title of, **Його́ стаття́ ви́йшла під ~ою "Дити́нство".** His article came out under the title of *Childhood*.; *G. pl.* **назв.** *Cf.* **заголо́вок** *and* **ім'я́**.

на́зван|ий, *adj.* 1) named; 2) **н. брат (ба́тько)** step-brother (-father), **~а сестра́** step-sister.

назва́ти, *pf., see* **назива́ти**.

назва́тися, *pf., see* **назива́тися**.

назива́|ти, **~ють**; **назв|а́ти**, **~у́ть**, *tran.* 1) to name, give a name to sb or sth + *I.,* **Си́на назва́ли Оре́стом.** They named their son Orest.; 2) to call sb sth, **Вона́ назва́ла Іва́на справжні́м дру́гом.** She called Ivan a true friend.; *pa. pple.* **на́званий** named; **назива́й! ~те!**; **назв|и́! ~і́ть!**

назива́|тися; **назва́тися**, *intr.* 1) to be called, to have the name of; **Як ~ється це мі́сто?** What is this city called? 2) to call oneself + *I.,* **Він назва́вся Миха́йлом.** He said his name was Mykhailo.; **назива́й|ся! ~теся!**; **назв|и́ся! ~і́ться!**

найбі́льш|ий, *adj.* the biggest, largest, greatest, *super.* of **вели́кий**; *adv.* **~е** most of all.

найкра́щ|ий, *adj.* best, *super.* of **до́брий**; **нагоро́да за н. фільм** the best film award.

найма́|ти, **~ють**; **найня́ти**, **найм|у́ть**, *tran.* to rent, hire; *pa. pple.* **на́йнятий** hired, rented; **найма́й! ~те!**; **найм|и́! ~і́ть!**

найня́ти, *pf., see* **найма́ти**.

намага́|тися, **~ються**; *no pf., intr.* to try, **Він ~ється не ї́сти пі́сля шо́стої.** He tries not to eat after six (o'clock).; **намага́й|ся! ~теся!** *Also see* **стара́тися**.

намалюва́ти, *pf., see* **малюва́ти**.

напа́м'ять, *adv.* by heart, **ви́вчити (зна́ти) н.** to learn (know) by heart.

напе́вне, *adv., var., see* **напе́вно**.

напе́вно, *adv., var.* **пе́вно**, **пе́вне** 1) perhaps, probably, maybe, **Н., вони́ не прийду́ть.** Probably they won't come. 2) surely, certainly, **Я ці́лком н. знайду́ вас у Ки́єві.** I shall most certainly find you in Kyiv.

напі́|й, *m.,* **~ою** drink, **(без)алкого́льний н.** (non) alcoholic drink; *N. pl.* **~ої**.

напри́клад, *adv.* for example, for instance.

нарече́н|ий, *m.,* **~ого** fiancé; boyfriend; **~а**, *f.* fiancée; girlfriend (both *m.* and *f.* decline as adjectives).

наре́шті, *adv.* finally, at last.

наро́д, *m.,* **~у** nation, people, folk.

наро́дженн|я, *nt.* birth; **день н.** birthday; **подару́нок на день н.** birthday present; **мі́сце (да́та) н.** place (date) of birth. *See* **уроди́ни**.

наро́джувати   **ні́готь**

наро́джу|вати, **~ють**; **народ|и́ти**, **~жу́**, **~ять**, *tran.* to give birth to sth / sb; *pa. pple.* **наро́джений** born; **наро́джуй! ~те!**; **народ|и́! ~і́ть!**

наро́джу|ватися; **народ|и́тися**, *refl.* to be born; **Коли́ він народи́вся?** When was he born?

народи́ти, *pf.*, *see* **наро́джувати**.

народи́тися, *pf.*, *see* **наро́джуватися**.

наро́дн|ий, *adj.* people's, folk, **~а му́дрість (пі́сня)** folk wisdom (song).

наса́мперед, *adv.* first of all, above all, most of all.

настава́ти, **наста|ю́ть**; **наста́ти**, **наста́н|уть**, *intr. (of period)* to come, arrive, **Настала зима́.** Winter arrived.

наста́ти, *pf.*, *see* **настава́ти**.

насту́пн|ий, *adj.* next, coming, following; **~ого понеді́лка** next Monday, **~ої о́сени** next autumn.

ната́мість, *adv.* instead, **Не поя́снюйте, допоможі́ть н.** You don't explain, help (me) instead.

нау́|ка, *f.* 1) science, **н. і те́хніка** science and technology, **гуманіта́рні (суспі́льні) ~ки** humanities (social sciences); 2) lesson, experience, **Це ста́ло для ньо́го ~ою.** This taught him a lesson.; *L.* **у ~ці.**

науко́в|ець, *m.*, **~ця** scientist, scholar *(used both for m. and f.)*, **Вона́ відо́мий н.** She is a well-known scientist. *N. pl.* **~ці.**

науко́в|ий, *adj.* scientific, scholarly, **~і да́ні** scientific data, **~е това́риство і́мени Шевче́нка (НТШ)** the Shevchenko Scientific Society.

націона́льн|ий, *adj.* 1) national, **Ки́ївський ~ий університе́т** Kyiv National University; 2) public.

на́че, *conj., var., see* **нена́че**.

наш, *poss. pron.*, **~ого** our, ours, **н. університе́т** our university, **~а мо́ва** our language, **~і батьки́** our parents.

на́що, *adv., fam.* what for, why, **Я не зна́ю, н. йому́ це.** I don't know what he needs it for. *Also see* **наві́що.**

не, *neg. part.* 1) not (used before a word to negate it), **Я н. зна́ю.** I don't know., **Ми пи́шемо н. лист, а листі́вку.** We are not writing a letter but a postcard., **Ця ха́та була́ н. нова́, а стара́.** This house was not new but old.; 2) no, **Н. пали́ти!** No smoking!, **Сього́дні спра́ви н. кра́щі.** Things are no better today.; 3) **н. .., н. ...** neither .., nor.., **Це н. вода́ і н. сік.** This is neither water, nor juice.

-не́будь, *part.* some *(expresses vagueness with pron. and adv.)* **хто-не́будь** somebody, **де-не́будь** somewhere, **як-не́будь** somehow, **що-не́будь** something. *Also see* **~сь.**

неда́вн|ій, *adj.* recent.

неда́вно, *adv.* not long ago, recently, lately; **Ми н. ба́чили його́.** We saw him recently.; *var.* **нещода́вно.**

недале́к|ий, *adj.* 1) close, nearby, not distant; 2) *fig.* narrow-minded, **Він ~а люди́на.** He is a narrow-minded person.

недале́ко, *adv.* not far, nearby, **Я живу́ зо́всім н.** I don't live far at all.

неді́л|я, *f.* Sunday, **у ~ю** on Sunday.

не́жит|ь, *m.*, **~ю** cold, catarrh, **У ньо́го вже два дні н.** He's had a cold for two days.; *I.* **~тем.**

незаба́ром, *adv.* soon, **Н. бу́де лі́то.** There'll be summer soon.; ♦ *(in film ads)* **н.** coming to your screens.

незабу́тн|ій, *adj.* unforgettable, **~і вра́ження** unforgettable impressions.

незале́жн|ий, *adj.* independent.

незале́жність, *f.* independence, **день незале́жности** independence day.

незнайо́м|ець, *m.*, **~ця** stranger; **~ка**, *f. L.* **на ~ці**, *G. pl.* **~ок.**

незнайо́м|ий, *adj.* unknown, unfamiliar, **~а мо́ва** unknown language, **~а люди́на** unknown person, stranger.

нема́(є), *pred.* there is no, there are no + *G.*, **Тут н. готе́лю.** There is no hotel here., **У ме́не н. гро́шей.** I have no money; *fut.* **н. бу́де**; *pa.* **н. було́.**

нема́ за що, *cliché* don't mention it, sure *(in response to* **дя́кую!** thanks!).

ненави́ді|ти, **~жу**, **~ять**, *tran. or impf. inf.* to hate, **Він ~ить молоко́.** He hates milk., **Ма́рта ~іла ра́но встава́ти.** Marta hated to rise early.

нена́вист|ь, *f.* hatred, **глибо́ка н.** deep hatred, **У її́ оча́х не було́ ~и.** There was no hatred in her eyes.

нена́че, *conj., var.* **на́че** as if, as though, **Н. ти не зна́єш.** As if you don't know. *Also see* **на́че** *or* **ні́би.**

непо́вн|ий, *adj.* incomplete, unfinished.

неповто́рн|ий, *adj.* inimitable, unique, incomparable.

непога́но, *adv.* not bad, decent, good, **Він н. співа́є.** He is a pretty good singer.

непорозумі́нн|я, *nt.* misunderstanding, **при́кре н.** unfortunate misunderstanding, **Це я́кесь н.** This must be a misunderstanding; **ма́ти н. з (із)** + *I.* to have a misunderstanding with sb.

несподі́ван|ка, *f.* surprise, **вели́ка н.** a great surprise, **Його́ слова́ були́ для всіх по́вною ~кою.** His words were a total surprise for all.; *L.* **у ~ці**; *G. pl.* **~ок.**

нести́, **нес|у́ть**; **за~** *uni., tran.*, to carry, bring along *(on foot as opposed to* **везти́** carry by a vehicle), **Григо́рій несе́ додо́му кві́ти.** Hryhoriy is carrying flowers home.; *pa. pple.* **зане́сений** carried away; **(по)неси́! ~і́ть!** *Also see multi.* **носи́ти.**

нещода́вно, *var., form., see* **неда́вно.**

низьк|и́й, *adj.* low, small *(of height, not tall)*, **н. на зріст** of small height, *comp.* **ни́жчий.**

ні, *adv.*, no *(used as negative answer to question, opposite of* **так** yes), **Н., я не зна́ю її́.** No, I don't know her., **так чи н.** yes or no.

ні.., ні..., *conj.* neither ... nor ... **Я не купи́в н. молока́, н. хлі́ба.** I bought neither milk nor bread.

ні́би, *conj.* as if, as though, **Він говори́в (так), н. нічо́го не ста́лося.** He spoke as if nothing had happened. *Also see* **нена́че** *or* **на́че.**

ні́г|оть, *m.*, **~тя** fingernail, toenail; *N. pl.* **~ті**, *I. pl.* **~тя́ми.**

ні|ж¹, *m.*, **~ожа́** knife, **кухо́нний н.** kitchen knife; *I.* **~оже́м**; *N. pl.* **~ожі**.

ніж², *conj.* than, + *N.* (*in comparison*), **Він працю́є бі́льше, н. вона́.** He works more than she does. *Also see* **як**, **від**, *and* **за**.

ні́м|ець, *m.*, **~ця** German man. *N; pl.* **~ці**.

німе́цьк|ий, *adj.* German.

німке́н|я, *f.* German woman. *G. pl.* **~ь**.

н|іс, *m.*, **~о́са** nose; ♦ **Не пхай ~о́са до чужо́го про́са.** Don't poke your nose into other people's business; *N. pl.* **~оси**.

н|іч, *f.*, **~о́чі** night, **те́мна н.** dark night, **Ми все зро́бимо до ~о́чі.** We'll do everything by nightfall., **~оча́ми** by night; *I.* **~і́ччю** night.

ніщо́, *pron.* **ніч|о́го** nothing; ♦ **~о́го собі́!** Imagine that!, **Я ~о́го не зна́ю.** I know nothing.

нов|и́й, *adj.*, new; **Н. Рік** New Year; ♦ **Щасли́вого -о́го Ро́ку!** A Happy New Year!, *comp.* **~і́ший**.

нови́н|а, *f.* piece of news, news; *N. pl.* **нови́ни**, **оста́нні ~и** the latest news.

но|га́, *f.* leg, foot; *L.* **на ~зі**; *N. pl.* **~ги**, *G. pl.* **ніг**.

но́мер, *m.*, **~а** 1) number, **н. телефо́ну (буди́нку, кварти́ри)** phone (building, apartment) number; 2) hotel room, **ві́льний (за́йнятий) н.** vacant (occupied) room; *N. pl.* **~и́**.

носи́ти, **ношу́, но́с|ять; по~** *multi.*, *tran.* 1) to carry, bring along (*on foot as opposed to* **везти́**), **Ві́ктор за́вжди ~ить кві́ти свої́й дружи́ні.** Victor always brings flowers for his wife.; 2) to wear, **Оре́ст лю́бить н. джи́нси.** Orest likes to wear jeans.; *pa pple.* **поно́шений** worn out; **(по)носи́! ~і́ть!** *Also see uni.* **нести́**.

нота́т|ка, *f.* note, brief comment; *often in pl.*, **роби́ти ~ки** to take notes; *L.* **у ~ці**, *G. pl.* **~ок**.

ночу́|ва́ти, **~ють; пере~**, *intr.* to spend the night, to stay for the night, **Де ви бу́дете н.?** Where will you be staying for the night?

ну́д|ити, **~жу, ~иш, ~ять; з~**, *tran.* 1) to bore sb.; 2) *with logical subject in A.* to feel nauseous, to feel like vomiting, **Мико́лу ~ить.** Mykola feels sick; 3) cause aversion, **від** + *G.*, **Від ньо́го мене́ ну́дить.** He makes me sick.; 4) *pf.* to vomit, **Оле́ну знуди́ло.** Olena threw up.; *pa. pple.* **знуджений** bored; **(з)нудь! ~те!**

нудн|и́й, *adj.*, boring, tedious.

ну́дно, *adv.*, boringly, tediously, **Тут так н.** It's so boring here; ♦ **Мені́ н.** I am bored *or* I feel sick.

нул|ь, *m.*, **~я** zero; **ви́ще (ни́жче) ~я** above (below) zero.

Нью-Йо́рк, *m.*, **~а** *or* **~у**, New York, **Коли́ ви ї́дете до ~у?** When do you go to New York?; *L.* **у ~ку**.

О

о, *prep.*, *var.* **об** (*before vowels*) + *L.* at (*in designations of time by the clock*), **о пе́ршій годи́ні** at one o'clock; **об одина́дцятій** at eleven o'clock.

об, *prep.* + *A.* 1) against, on, **би́ти об стіл** to hit against the table; 2) *var.*, *see* **о**, *prep.*

обі́д, *m.*, **~у** 1) lunch; **на о.** for lunch, **Що у ти їв на о.?** What did you have for lunch?; 2) *colloq.* afternoon, **пі́сля ~у** *or* **по ~і** in the afternoon.

обі́да|ти, **~ють; по~**, *intr.* + *A.* to have lunch, **Ми за́вжди ~ємо пі́зно.** We always have a late lunch.; **(по) обі́дай! ~те!**

обіця́н|ка, *f.* promise; *L.* **у ~ці**, *G. pl.* **~ок**.

обіця́|ти, **~ють; по~**, *tran.* to promise sth + *D.*, **Він пообіця́в нам подзвони́ти ба́тькові.** He promised us to call his father.; *pa. pple.* **(по)обі́цяний** promised; **(по) обіця́й! ~те!**

об'ї́зд, *m.*, **~у** detour, **роби́ти о.** make a detour.

обласн|и́й, *adj.* provincial, pertaining to a province; **Лу́цьк – це о. цент(е)р Воли́ні.** Lutsk is the provincial center of Volhynia. *Also see* **о́бласть**.

о́бласт|ь, *f.*, **~ти** (*in Ukraine*) oblast, province (*administrative unit, one of twenty-four provinces of the nation*) **Ха́рківська о.** the Kharkiv Province; *L.* **в ~і**.

обли́чч|я, *nt.* face, **весе́ле о.** happy face; ♦ **про́сто в о.** right to the face; *G. pl.* **облич**.

обмі́н, *m.*, **~у** exchange, **о. валю́ти** currency exchange, **о. ду́мками** exchange of opinions.

обмі́ню|вати, **~ють; обміня́|ти**, *tran.*, + *A* to exchange, **о. до́лари на гри́вні** to exchange dollars for hryvnias.

обміня́ти, *pf.*, *see* **обмі́нювати**.

обов'язко́во, *adv.* by all means, certainly, of course.

обслуго́вуванн|я, *nt.* service, **рестора́н швидко́го о.** fast food restaurant.

обслуго́ву|вати, **~ють; обслуж|и́ти, ~у́, ~ать**, *tran.* to service sb, serve sb / sth, **У цьо́му рестора́ні пові́льно обслуго́вують.** The service is slow in this restaurant.; *pa. pple.* **обслу́жений** serviced; **обслуго́вуй! ~те!; обслуж|и́! ~і́ть!**

обслужи́ти, *pf*, *see* **обслуго́вувати**.

обхо́д|итися, **~жуся, ~яться; обійти́ся, ~у́ся, обі́йд|уться: без** + *G.* to do without, manage without, **Я обійшо́вся без його́ допомо́ги.** I did without his help.; **обхо́дь|ся! ~теся!; обі́йд|ися! ~іться!**

о́воч, *m.*, **~а** vegetable, *N. pl.* **~і**; *adj.* **~евий** vegetable, **~евий сала́т** vegetable salad. *Also see* **городи́на**.

огір|о́к, *m.*, **~ка́** a cucumber, **ні́жинські ~ки́** Nizhyn gherkins; *L.* **в ~ку́**.

огляда́|ти, **~ють; огля́н|ути, ~уть**, *tran.* 1) to examine (*a patient*), to give a medical examination, **Лі́кар огля́не вас за́втра.** The doctor will examine you tomorrow.; 2) to see, look over (exhibit, museum), **Він огля́нув усю́ виста́вку.** He saw the entire exhibit.; *pa. pple.* **огля́нутий** *or* **огля́нений** examined; **огляда́й! ~те!; огля́нь! ~те!**

огля́нути, *pf.*, *see* **огляда́ти**.

Оде́с|а, *f.* Odesa (*port city in Ukraine on the Black Sea*), **в ~і** in Odesa, **до ~и** to Odesa.

одеси́т, *m.*, **~а** a male citizen of Odesa; **~ка**, *f.* female citizen of Odesa.; *L.* **на ~ці**, *G. pl.* **~ок**.

оде́ський   пам'ята́ти

оде́ськ|ий, *adj.* pertaining to Odesa, **Оде́ська о́бласть** the Odesa Province, **~ий гу́мор** Odesa sense of humor, **~а о́пера** Odesa Opera House.

оди́н, *card. m.*, **одн|ого́** 1) one, **о. квито́к** one ticket, 2) certain, some, **Вас шука́ли ~і чолові́ки.** Some (unknown) men were looking for you. *Also see* **одна́, одне́, одні́.**

одина́дцять, *card.*, **~ох** + *G. pl.* eleven, **о. днів** eleven days.

одн|а́, *card. f.*, **~іє́ї** one, **о. гри́вня** one hryvnia; *See* **оди́н.**

одна́ков|ий, *adj.* the same, identical, **за ~у ці́ну** for the same price.

одн|е́, *card. n.*, **~ого́** one, **о. я́блуко** one apple; *See* **оди́н.**

одн|і́, *card. m.*, **~и́х** ones; certain; *See* **оди́н.**

одра́зу, *adv.* at once, immediately, **Я о. все зрозумі́в.** I understood everything at once.

оду́жати, *pf., see* **оду́жувати.**

оду́жу|вати, **~ють; оду́жа|ти**, **~ють**, *intr.* to get well, **о. від** + *G.* recover from illness; **оду́жуй! ~те!; оду́жай! ~те!**

о́дяг, *m., only sg.*, **~гу** clothes, **лі́тній (зимо́вий) о.** summer (winter) clothes; *L.* **в ~зі.**

одяга́|ти, **~ють; одягн|у́ти**, **~у́, ~у́ть**, *tran.* 1) to put on, **Я одягну́ нову́ су́кню.** I'll put on my new dress.; 2) to dress in sth. **в / у** + *A.*, **Її одягну́ли у чо́рний костю́м.** They dressed her in a black suit.; *pa. pple.* **одя́гнутий**, *var.* **одя́гнений** dressed; **одяга́й! ~те!; одягн|и́! ~іть!**

одяга́|тися, **~ються; одягн|у́тися**, **~у́ся, ~у́ться**, *refl.* to dress (oneself) **в / у** + *A.*, **Він одяга́ється зі сма́ком.** He dresses tastefully.; **одяга́й/ся! ~теся!; одягн|и́ся! ~іться!**

одягну́ти, *pf., see* **одяга́ти.**

одягну́тися, *pf., see* **одяга́тися.**

о́зер|о, *nt.* lake; *L.* **на ~і**, *N. pl.* **озе́ра.**

о́к|о, *nt.*, **~а** eye; ♦ **каза́ти у ві́чі** to say straight to sb's face.; *N. pl.* **о́чі**, *G. pl.* **оче́й.**

окре́м|ий, *adj.* separate, **~а кімна́та** separate room, **Це ~е пита́ння.** This is a separate question.

олів|е́ць, *m.*, **~ця́** pencil, **писа́ти (малюва́ти) ~це́м** write (draw) with a pencil; *N. pl.* **~ці́.**

олі́|я, *f.* (food) oil, **оли́вкова о.** olive oil, **соня́шникова о.** sunflower oil.

ону́к, *m.* grandson; **~а**, *f.* granddaughter.

о́пер|а, *f.* opera, **йти на ~у** to go to the opera.

о́перн|ий, *adj.* opera, **о. теа́тр** opera house.

о́пік, *m.*, **~у** a (skin) burn, scald, **си́льний о.** severe burn, **отри́мати о.** to burn oneself.

оповіда́нн|я, *nt.* 1) story, narrative; *pf.* **розказа́ти о.** to tell a story; 2) short story, **Він бі́льше лю́бить о., ніж рома́ни.** He likes short stories more than novels.

ориґіна́л, *m.*, **~у** original, **Це о. чи ко́пія?** Is this the original or a copy?, **в ~і** in the original.

ориґіна́льн|ий, *adj.* original, authentic.

осві́т|а, *f.* education, **ви́ща о.** higher education.

осі́нн|ій, *adj.*, fall, autumnal; **о. семе́стр** fall semester.

ос|і́нь, *f.*, **~ени** fall, autumn, *I.* **~і́нню** in the autumn.

осо́б|а, *f.* person, individual, **Він ціка́ва о.** He's an interesting individual, **ду́же важли́ва о.** VIP; *G. pl.* **осі́б, Скі́льки осі́б мо́же сі́сти за цей стіл?** How many people can sit at this table?

особли́в|ий, *adj.* special; original, **Рома́н – ду́же ~а люди́на.** Roman is a very special person.

особли́во, *adv.* particularly, especially, **Він о. лю́бить готува́ти.** He is especially fond of cooking.

оста́нн|ій, *adj.* last, **о. раз** (for) the last time; **~ім ча́сом** lately.

о́стр|ів, *m.*, **~ова** island, isle, **бага́то ~ові́в** many islands; *L.* **на ~ові** on island, *N. pl.* **~ови.**

ось, *adv.* here, here is (used to point to sb/sth), **О. моя́ сестра́.** Here's my sister.

отри́мати, *pf., see* **отри́мувати.**

отри́му|вати, **~ють; отри́ма|ти**, **~ють**, *tran.* to get, receive, **Коли́ він отри́мав цю нови́ну?** When did he receive this news?; *pa. pple.* **отри́маний** received; **отри́муй! ~те!; отри́май! ~те!** *Also see* **діста́вати.**

отру́є́нн|я, *nt.* poisoning, food poisoning, **У ме́не о.** I have food poisoning.

отру́ї́тися, *pf., see* **отру́юватися.**

отру́ю|ватися, **~ються; отру|ї́тися**, **~ю́ся, ~я́ться**, *refl.* + *I.* to poison oneself, **Я чи́мось отру́ївся.** I have a food-poisoning.; **отру́юй|ся! ~теся!; отру́ї|ся! ~ться!**

о́фіс, *m.*, **~у** office.

офіція́нт, *m.* waiter; **~ка**, *f.* waitress; *L.* **на ~ці**, *G. pl.* **~ок.**

охо́т|а, *f.* inclination, mood; **ма́ти ~у на** + *A.* or *inf.* to be in the mood for, to feel like, **Я ма́ю ~у побі́гати па́рком.** I feel like jogging in the park.

очи́щу|вати, **~ють; очи́стити, очи́щу, очи́ст|ять**, *tran.* to clean, clear, **Ми очи́стили сад від ли́стя.** We cleaned the garden of leaves.

о́чі, *nt., pl., see* **о́ко.**

П

паку́|ватися, **~ються; с~**, *intr.* to pack, pack up *(for a trip)*, **Ви вже спакува́лися?** Have you already packed up?; **(с)паку́й|ся! ~теся!**

па́л|ець, *m.*, **~ьця** finger, toe; ♦ **подорожува́ти на п.** to hitchhike; *L.* **на ~ьці**; *N. pl.* **~ьці.**

пам'я́та|ти, **~ють; за~**, *tran.* 1) to remember, **Він до́бре пам'я́тає свою́ пе́ршу подоро́ж.** He clearly remembers his first trip.; 2) *pf.* memorize, commit to memory, **Рані́ше він все шви́дко запам'ято́вував.** Earlier he was quick to memorize everything.; *no pa. pple.* **(за)пам'ятай! ~те!**

па́м'ятник, *m.*, ~а monument + *D.* to sb, **Пропону́ю зустрі́тися бі́ля ~а Тара́сові Шевче́нкові.** I suggest meeting near the Taras Shevchenko monument.

па́м'ять, *f.*, memory; ♦ **Якщо́ мені́ не зра́джує п.** If my memory doesn't fail me.

пан, *m.*, ~а 1) mister *(form of address or polite reference to a man used with surname and / or name, less formal)*, **П. Петре́нко вже це зна́є.** Mr. Petrenko already knows it.; *V.* ~е; 2) gentleman, **Цей п. пита́в про вас.** This gentleman asked about you. *N. pl.* ~и, *var.* ~о́ве.

па́н|і, *f.* 1) Mrs. *(form of address to a woman used with surname and/or name, less formal)*, **Я подзвоню́ п. Па́влів за́втра.** I'll ring up Mrs. Pavliv tomorrow; 2) lady, **Для вас лист від яко́їсь п.** There's a letter for you from some lady.; *V.* п.!, *N. pl.* ~і, *G. pl.* ~ь, *D. pl.* ~ям, *A. pl.* ~ь, *I. pl.* ~ями, *V. pl.* ~і!

па́нн|а, *f.*, 1) Ms., miss *(form of address to an unmarried woman used with surname and / or, less formal, with name)*; *V.* ~о; 2) young lady, **Ці ~и дуже допомогли́ нам.** These young ladies helped us a lot.

пано́ве, *m., pl., used only in N. and V.* gentlemen *(form of address to men)*; **Пані і п.!** Ladies and Gentlemen!

папі́р, *m.*, ~е́ру 1) paper; 2) document, **Він загуби́в свої́ ~ери.** He lost his documents. *L.* на ~е́рі.

парасо́ль|ка, *f.*, umbrella, **складна́ п.** folding umbrella *L.* на ~ці, *G. pl.* ~ок.

Пари́ж, *m.*, ~а *or* ~у Paris; **у ~і** in Paris, **до ~а** to Paris.

парк, *m.*, ~у park; *L.* у ~у.

па́ркінг, *m.*, ~у parking, parking lot, **Де тут п.?** Where's the parking here?; *L.* на ~у.

парку|ва́ти, ~ють; за~ , *tran.* to park (a car), **Чи тут поблизу́ мо́жна за~ авто́?** Can one park a car nearby?; *pa. pple.* запарко́ваний parked; **(за)паркуй!; ~те!**

паропла́в, *m.*, ~а a passenger ship, large passenger boat, **пливти́ ~ом** to sail by ship.

па́руб|ок, *m.*, ~ка 1) young man; 2) bachelor; single man; ♦ **одру́жений чи п.** married or single. *N. pl.* ~и.

пасажи́р, *m.*, ~а passenger; *N. pl.* ~и; ~ка, *f. L.* на ~ці, *G. pl.* ~ок.

па́спорт, *m.*, ~а passport, **закордо́нний (вну́трішній) п.** foreign (internal) passport.

пацíє́нт, *m.*, ~а patient *(in hospital)*; ~ка, *f. L.* на ~ці, *G. pl.* ~ок. *Also see* **хво́рий**.

пе́вно, *adv.*, *var.* пе́вне, *var.*, *see* напе́вно.

перебива́|ти, ~ють; переби́ти, переб'|ю́ть, *tran.* to interrupt, **Не люблю́, як мене́ перебива́ють.** I don't like to be interrupted; *pa. pple.* переби́тий interrupted; **перебива́й! ~те! переби́й! ~те!**

переби́ти, *pf.*, *see* перебива́ти.

перебува́нн|я, *nt.* stay *(in a city, country)*, visit, stop-over, **Протягом всьо́го п. тут ми листува́лися.** During my entire stay here we corresponded.

перебува́|ти, ~ють; *only impf.*, *intr.* to stay, **Коли́ Іва́н у Ки́єві, в яко́му готе́лі він ~є?** When Ivan is in Kyiv, what hotel does he stay in?; ~й! ~те!

пе́ред, *prep.*, *var.* пе́реді *(only before* мно́ю) + *I.* 1) in front of, **П. університе́том був парк.** There was a park in front of the university; 2) before, earlier than, **Ми приї́хали п. ни́ми.** We arrived before them.

переда́ч|а, *f.*, ~і 1) *(TV, radio)* broadcast, transmission, show, **Це моя́ улю́блена п.** This is my favorite show.; 2) sth delivered, handing over, **Я ма́ю для вас ~у з Ки́єва.** I have a package from Kyiv for you.

перейти́, *pf.*, *see* перехо́дити.

пере́клад, *m.*, ~у translation, interpretation, **у ~і** in translation, **п. украї́нською** translation into Ukrainian.

переклада́|ти, ~ють; перекла́сти, переклад|у́ть; *pa.* перекла́|в, *tran.* + *A* to translate, interpret. + *I.* into, **Вона́ ~ла текст украї́нською мо́вою.** She translated the text into Ukrainian; *pa. pple.* перекла́дений translated; **перекладай! ~те!; переклад|и́! ~іть!**

перекла́сти, *pf.*, *see* переклада́ти.

пере́кус|ка, *f.* snack, bite of food, **легкі́ ~ки** light snacks; ♦ **на ~ку** for snack; *L.* у ~ці; *G. pl.* ~ок. *Also see* **заку́ска**.

перекуси́ти, *pf.*, *see* переку́шувати.

переку́шу|вати, ~ють; перекуси́ти, перекушу́, пере́кус|ять 1) *intr.* to have a snack + *I.*, **Я не голо́дний, я перекуси́в трохи си́ром.** I'm not hungry, I had some cheese for a snack; 2) *tran.* to bite sth into two parts, *pa. pple.* переку́шений bitten into two; **переку́шуй! ~те!; перекус|и́! ~іть!**

переночува́ти, *pf.*, *see* ночува́ти.

пере́рв|а, *f.* break, interval, **на ~і** at (during) a break, **без ~и** without any break, not-stop, **п. на ка́ву** coffee break; *G. pl.* пере́рв.

переса́д|ка, *f.* change, transfer *(from one train, bus, etc. to another)* **на + *A.*, **п. на і́нший рейс** change to a different flight *(bus, train, boat)*, **без ~и** nonstop, **Чи мо́жна дої́хати з Пра́ги до Ки́єва без ~ки?** Can one get from Prague to Kyiv nonstop?; *L.* на ~ці, *G. pl.* ~ок.

пересіда́ти, *see* сіда́ти; пересі́сти, *see* сі́сти, *intr.* 1) to change seats, **Тут нічо́го не мо́жна поба́чити, дава́й пересяде́мо.** I can't see anything here, let's change seats.; 2) to change *(bus, train, flight, etc.)* з (із) + *G.* from, **на + *A.* to, **Тут він переся́де із по́їзда «Варша́ва-Львів» на по́їзд «Львів-Ки́їв».** Here he will change from the Warsaw-Lviv train to the Lviv-Kyiv train.; **пересіда́й! ~те!; пересядь! ~те!**

пересіка́|ти, ~ють; пересікти́, пересіч|у́ть, *tran.*+ *A.* to cross, traverse *(a street, field, etc.)*, **Які́ ву́лиці пересіка́ють цей бульва́р?** What streets cross the boulevard?; *pa. pple.* пересі́чений crossed; **пересіка́й! ~те!; пересіч|и́! ~іть!**

пересіка́|тися, ~ються; пересікти́ся, пересіч|у́ться, *intr.* to cross (a street, field, etc.), **У цьо́му мі́сці пересіка́ються п'ять ву́лиць.** Five streets cross in this place.

пересі́сти, *pf.*, *see* пересіда́ти.

переста́|вати, ~ють; переста́ти, переста́н|уть, *intr.* to stop, cease doing something *(only with impf. inf.)*, **Я переста́в ба́читися з не́ю.** I stopped seeing her.; **переставай! ~те!; переста́нь! ~те!**

переста́ти, *pf.*, *see* переста́вати.

перестуджуватися

переступджу|ватися, ~ються; **перестуд|итися**, ~жуся, ~ишся, ~яться, *intr.* to catch a cold, **дуже п.** to catch a bad cold; **перестуджуй|ся! ~теся! перестуд|ися! ~іться!**

перестудитися, *pf., see* **перестуджуватися**.

переход|ити, **переходжу**, **переход|ять**; **перейти**, **перейд|уть**, *tran.* 1) (of people) to cross, walk across, traverse (street), **Вважайте, як переходите вулицю!** Watch out crossing the street!; 2) switch to, **Коли в Україні переходять на літній час?** When do they switch to the summer time in Ukraine?; *pa. pple.* **перейдений** crossed over; **переход|ь! ~те!; перейд|и! ~іть!**

перехрест|я, *nt.* crossing (*of streets*), intersection; *L.* **на ~і, Цей будинок стоїть на ~і (вулиць) Підвальної і Мазепи.** The building is on the intersection of Pidvalna and Mazepa streets.

пер|ець, *m.*, ~цю pepper, **щипка ~ю** a pinch of pepper.

пер|о, *nt.* pen, ink-pen, **Я любив писати ~ом.** I liked to write with an ink pen.; *N. pl.* ~**а.** *Also see* **ручка**.

персональн|ий, *adj.* personal, **п. чек** personal check.

перукар|ня, *f.* barber's shop, hairdresser's; *G. pl.* ~**ень.**

перш|ий, *ord.* first, **п. раз** (for) the first time, **Зараз ~а година рівно.** It's one o'clock sharp now.

пес, *m.*, **пс|а** dog.

п'єс|а, *f.* play.

пив|о, *nt.* beer, **бочкове п.** beer on tap.

писан|ка, *f.* Easter egg (*traditional Ukrainian folk art*); *L.* **на ~ці**; *N. pl.* ~**и**, *G. pl.* ~**ок.**

писа|ти, **пиш|уть**; **на~** + *A.* 1) to write, **Я пишу їй щотижня.** I write her every week.; 2) *fam.* to be about, **У цьому тексті пише про погоду.** This text is about the weather.; *pa. pple.* **написаний** written; **(на)пиш|и! ~іть!**

письменник, *m.* male writer, **В Україні багато молодих і цікавих ~ів.** There are many young and interesting writers in Ukraine.

письменниц|я, *f.* female writer, **Ця п. мені дуже подобається.** I like this (f.) writer very much.

питанн|я, *nt.* question; **задавати (ставити) п.** to pose a question; **Це слушне п.** It's a good question.

пита|ти, ~**ють**; **за~ y** + *G.*, to ask sb, **Ми маємо за~ у професора.** We should ask the professor.; *pa. pple.* **запитаний** asked; requested; in demand, **Він людина запитана.** He is a sought after person.; **(за)питай! ~те!**

пити, **п'|ють**; **ви~** + *A.* 1) to drink, **Я часом п'ю червоне вино до вечері.** I sometimes drink red wine with dinner.; 2) to abuse alcohol, **Це правда, що він пив?** Is it true that he abused alcohol?; *pa. pple.* **випитий** (of a drink) drunk, consumed; **(ви)пий! ~те!**

пів, *part.* + *G. sg.* 1) a half, **п. дня** half a day, **п. року** half a year; *also see* **половина**; 2) a half hour (*in time by clock*), **п. на** + *A.* half past (the hour), **о п. на третю** at half past two.

півгодини, *adv.* half hour, **Він дзвонив п. тому.** He called half an hour ago.

півд|ень, *m.*, ~**ня**, *only sg.* south, **на п. від** + *G.* to the south of, **на ~ні** + *G.* in the south of.; *I.* ~**нем.**

південн|ий, *adj.* southern; ~**о-західний** south-western.

півн|іч, *f.*, ~**очі**, *only sg.* north, **на п. від** + *G.* to the north of, **на ~і** + *G.* in the north of; *I.* ~**іччю.**

північн|ий, *adj.* northern; ~**о-східний** north-eastern.

під, *prep.* 1) *posn.* + *I.* under, below, beneath, **Кіт п. столом.** The cat is under the table.; near, **Вони живуть п. Луцьком.** They live near Lutsk.; 2) *dir.* + *A.* under, below, beneath, **Кіт сховався п. стіл.** The cat hid under the table.; 3) + *A.* (of time) by, toward, **п. вечір** by the evening, **П. ранок стало холодно.** It got cold towards the morning.

під'їзд, *m.*, ~**у** entryway, entrance (*in a multistoried building*), **Наша квартира була у третьому ~і.** Our apartment was in the third entryway.

підло|га, *f.* floor (*of a room*), **Килим треба покласти на ~у.** The carpet should be put on the floor.; *L.* **на ~зі.**

під час, *prep.* + *G.* during, **п. ч. подорожі** during a trip.

пізно, *adv.* late, belatedly; ♦ **Краще п., ніж ніколи.** Better late than never.

після, *prep.* + *G.* after, **п. вас** after you; ♦ **П. нас хоч потоп.** After us the deluge.; *var.* **опісля.**

піс|ня, *f.* song, **весела (народна, сумна, улюблена) п.** happy (folk, sad, favorite) song; *N. pl.* ~**ні**, *G. pl.* ~**ень.**

піти, *pf., see* **іти.**

пішки, *adv.* on foot, **іти / ходити п.** to go on foot, **Звідси до музею п'ять хвилин п.** The museum is a five-minute walk from here.

піаніст, *m., var.* **піаніст** piano-player; ~**ка**, *f.*; *L.* **на ~ці**, *G. pl.* ~**ок.**

плава|ти, ~**ють**, *multi., intr.* to swim; sail, float, **Ви завжди ~єте на початку травня?** Do you always sail in early May?; **Щосереди вона ~ла у басейні.** Every Wednesday she swam in the swimming pool.; **плавай! ~те!** *Also see uni.* **пливти.**

план, *m.*, ~**у** plan, **Які у вас (тебе) ~и на завтра?** What are your plans for tomorrow?

плат|ити, **плачу**, ~**ять**; **за~**, *tran.* + *D.* to pay sb sth, **Я заплатив йому сто гривень.** I paid him a hundred hryvnias.; to pay for sth **за** + *A.*, **Де тут платять за покупки?** Where do they pay for purchases here?; *pa. pple.* **заплачений** paid for; **(за)плат|и! ~іть!**

платт|я, *nt.* dress, robe; *G. pl.* ~**ів.** *Also see* **сукня.**

плацкартн|ий, *adj.* in **п. квиток** train ticket for a reserved seat.

плеч|е, *nt.*, ~**а**, shoulder; *N. pl.* ~**і**, *G. pl.* ~**ей**, *var.* **пліч**, *I. pl.* ~**има.**

плив|ти, ~**уть**; **по~** *uni., intr.* to swim; sale, float, **Човен плив до берега.** The boat sailed to the shore.; **(по)плив|и! ~іть!** *Also see multi.* **плавати.**

площ|а, *f.*, ~**і** 1) square, **Львівська п.** Lvivska Square; 2) *math.* area; *L.* **на ~і** on a square.

пляж, *m.*, ~**у** beach, **Ми завжди їздимо на п.** We always go to the beach.; *L.* **на ~і.**

пляш|ка, *f.*, bottle; *L.* **у пляшці**; *N. pl.* ~**и**; *G. pl.* ~**ок.**

по, *prep.* 1) + *L.* *(indicates motion within space)* on, **ходити п. мокрій підлозі** to walk on a wet floor; along, **їхати п. вулиці** to drive along a street; through, **йти п. місту** to walk through a city; in, around, **гуляти п. парку** to walk in (around) a park; 2) + *L.* via, through, over, **розмовляти п. телефону** to talk over the phone; **дзвонити п. комп'ютеру** to phone via computer; 3) + *A.* *(denotes a goal)* for, **іти по воду** to go for water; 4) *(in quantification)* for, **п. три гривні за кілограм** (for) three hryvnias a kilogram.

побажати, *pf.,* *see* **бажати**.

по батькові, ♦ patronymic, **Як вас по батькові?** What's your patronymic?

побаченн|я, *nt.* meeting, get-together, rendezvous, **йти на п.** to go to a meeting, **домовитися про п.** to arrange for a meeting; **до п.!** good-bye!

побачити, *pf.,* *see* **бачити**.

побігти, *pf., see* **бігти**.

поблизу, *adv.* nearby, near, not far, **Чи десь тут п. можна повечеряти?** Can one have dinner somewhere nearby?

побувати, *pf., see* **бувати**.

повернути, *pf., see* **повертати**.

поверта|ти, ~**ють**; **поверн|ути**, ~**уть** 1) *intr.* to turn, make a turn *(also* **звертати**), **п. праворуч (ліворуч)** to turn right (left); 2) *tran.* to return sth, give sth back, **Він обіцяв повернути книжку у четвер.** He promised to return the book on Thursday.; *pa. pple.* **повернутий**, *var.* **повернений** returned; **повертай!** ~**те!**; **поверн|и!** ~**іть!**

поверта|тися, ~**ються**; **поверн|утися**, ~**уться**, *var.,* *see* **вертатися**; **повертай|ся!** ~**теся!**; **поверн|ися!** ~**іться!**

повер|х, *m.,* ~**у** floor, story; *L.* **на** ~**сі**.

повз, *prep.* + *A.* by, past; **п. бібліотеку** past library.

повинн|ий, *adj.* obliged; **Я п. це зробити.** I must do it.; *var.* **повинен**.

повідомленн|я, *nt.* 1) message, **Хтось залишив вам п.** Somebody left a message for you.; 2) announcement, **п. уряду** government announcement.

повільн|ий, *adj.* slow, **п. потяг** slow train.

поворот, *m.,* ~**у** turn, bend, corner *(of street)*, crossroads.

повторю|вати, ~**ють**; **повтор|ити**, ~**ять**, *tran.* 1) to repeat, **повторіть!** come again! repeat!; 2) *(of learned material)* to review, revisit, **Я повторюю правила на наступне заняття.** I'm reviewing the rules for the next class.; *pa. pple.* **повторений** repeated; reviewed; **повторюй!** ~**те!**; **повтор|и!** ~**іть!**

поган|ий, *adj.* 1) bad, **п. настрій** low spirits, ~**е здоров'я** poor health, ~**а погода** nasty (weather); *comp.* **гірший**.

погод|а, *f.* weather, **прогноз** ~**и** weather forecast.

погоджу|ватися, ~**ються**; **погод|итися**, ~**жуся**, ~**ишся**, ~**яться**, to agree, **з (із)** + *I.* with sth / sb, **Я не погоджуюся.** I don't agree.; **погоджуй|ся! ~теся!**; **погодь|ся! ~теся!**

погодитися, *pf., see* **погоджуватися**.

пода|вати, ~**ють**; **подати**, **подам**, **подаси**, **подасть**, **подамо**, **подасте**, **подадуть**, *tran.* + *A* 1) to serve (food). + *D.*, **Що** ~**ють у ресторані?** What do they serve in the restaurant?; 2) hand over, pass. sth over, **Подайте сіль, будь ласка.** Pass the salt please.; *pa. pple.* **поданий** served *(of food)*; **подавай!** ~**те!**; **подай!** ~**те!**

подарувати, *pf., see* **дарувати**.

подарун|ок, *m.,* ~**ка** present, **п. на день народження** birthday present; *L.* **у** ~**ку**.

подати, *pf., see* **подавати**.

подзвонити, *pf., see* **дзвонити**.

подивитися, *pf., see* **дивитися**.

поді|я, *f.* event, development, occurrence, **важлива (міжнародна) п.** important (international) event.

подіяти, *pf., see* **діяти** *(in sense 2)*.

подоба|тися, ~**ються**; **с~** *intr.* + *D.* to like sth or sb, to like doing sth *(with logical subject in D.)*, **Мені** ~**ється танцювати.** I like to dance.; **Миколі** ~**ється тут.** Mykola likes it here.; **Я знаю, що він їй сподобається.** I know she will like him.; **(с)подобай|ся! ~теся!**

подорож, *f.,* ~**і** journey, voyage, trip; **їхати у п.** to go on a trip, **п. за кордон** trip abroad; *I.* ~**жю**.

подорожу|вати, ~**ють**, *only impf., intr.* + *I.* to travel, **п. Україною** to travel around Ukraine; + *I.* travel by sth, **п. автом (потягом)** travel by car (train); **подорожуй!** ~**те!**

подру|га, *f., (female)* friend; *L.* **на** ~**зі**.

подружж|я, *nt.* married couple, matrimony.

подумати, *pf., see* **думати**.

подякувати, *pf., see* **дякувати**.

поезі|я, *f.,* ~**ї** 1) poem, verse; 2) poetry.

поет, *m.,* ~**а** male poet; ~**ка**, *f. L.* **на** ~**ці**, *G. pl.* ~**ок**.

пожартувати, *pf., see* **жартувати**.

позавчора, *adv.* the day before yesterday.

познайомитися, *pf., see* **знайомитися**.

поїзд, *m.,* ~**а** train; **сідати на п.** to catch a train; *See* **потяг**.

поїхати, *pf., see* **їхати**.

показати, *pf., see* **показувати**.

показу|вати, ~**ють**; **показати**, **пока́ж|уть**, *tran.* 1) to show, **п. дорогу** to show the way; 2) to screen *(a film)*, **Що показували в кіні?** What was on in the movies?; *pa. pple.* **показаний** shown; **показуй!** ~**те!**; **покаж|и!** ~**іть!**

покликати, *pf., see* **кликати**.

покуп|ка, *f.,* purchase, **робити** ~**ки** to go shopping, make purchases, **Ми зробили всі** ~**ки на лінії.** We did all the shopping online; *L.* **у** ~**ці**, *G. pl.* ~**ок.** *See* **закупи**.

покуштувати, *pf., see* **куштувати**.

полагодити, *pf., see* **лагодити**.

пол|е, *nt.,* ~**я** field, **п. зору** field of vision; *N. pl.* ~**я**; *L. pl.* **на** ~**ях** in the margins *(of page)*.

полетіти   пофарбувати

полеті́ти, *pf.*, *see* **леті́ти**.

поли́ц|я, *f.*, ~і shelf; *dir.* **Поста́в кни́жку на ~ю.** Put the book on the shelf., **книжко́ва п.** book-shelf; *L.* **на ~і.**

полі́тик, *m.* politician, **впливо́вий п.** influential politician.

полі́ти|ка, *f.*, *only sg.* politics, policy, **міжнаро́дна (вну́трішня) п.** international (internal) politics; *L.* **у ~ці.**

політи́чн|ий, *adj.* political, **~а поді́я (ситуа́ція, кри́за)** political event (situation, crisis).

полови́н|а, *f.* half; + *G.*; **п. мі́сяця** half of the month. *Also see* **пів.**

по́луд|ень, *m.*, ~ня noon, midday, **до ~ня** before the noon, **о ~ні** at noon.

поля́к, *m.* Pole, Polish man.

по́ль|ка, *f.* Polish woman; *L.* **на ~ці**, *G. pl.* ~ок.

по́льськ|ий, *adj.* Polish, **~а мо́ва** the Polish language.

По́льщ|а, *f.*, ~і Poland, **по́їхати до ~і** to travel to Poland.

помага́|ти, ~ють; **помогти́**, ~у́, ~еш, **помо́ж|уть**, *var.* **допомага́ти**, *intr.* + *D.* to help, assist, **Тре́ба помогти́ йому́.** We need to help him.; **помага́й! ~те!; поможи́! ~іть!**

поме́шканн|я, *nt.* accommodation, apartment, home.

помили́тися, *pf.*, *see* **помиля́тися**.

по́ми́л|ка, *f.* mistake, error; **гру́ба п.** bad mistake, **зроби́ти ~ку** to make a mistake; *L.* **у ~ці**, *N. pl.* ~ки, *G. pl.* ~ок.

помиля́|тися, ~ються; **поми́л|итися**, ~юся, ~яться, *refl.* to make a mistake, err, to be wrong; **помиля́й|ся! ~теся!; помил|и́ся! ~іться!**

поми́ти, *pf.*, *see* **ми́ти.**

помідо́р, *m.*, ~а tomato, **сти́глий п.** ripe tomato.

поміня́ти, *pf.*, *see* **міня́ти.**

помогти́, *pf.*, *see* **помага́ти.**

понеді́л|ок, *m.*, ~ка Monday, **у п.** on Monday; *N. pl.* ~ки.

пообі́дати, *pf.*, *see* **обі́дати.**

попливти́, *pf.*, *see* **пливти́.**

поп-му́зи|ка, *f.* pop music; *L.* **у ~ці.**

пополу́дні, *adv.* in the afternoon, **ра́но (пі́зно) п.** early (late) afternoon.

по-по́льському, *adv.*, *var.* **по-по́льськи** in a Polish way, **говори́ти п.** to speak Polish.

попроси́ти, *pf.*, *see* **проси́ти.**

популя́рн|ий, *adj.* popular, **Яка́ му́зика за́раз ~а в Украї́ні?** What kind of music is popular in Ukraine now?

пор|а́, *f.* time, season, **п. ро́ку** season of the year; *D.* + **п.** + *inf.* it's time, **Мені́ п. йти** It's time for me to go.; *N. pl.* ~и, *G. pl.* пір.

пора́д|а, *f.*, advice, **дава́ти ~у** to give advice, **зверта́тися по ~у** to turn for advice.

пора́дити, *pf.*, *see* **ра́дити.**

пора́дитися, *pf.*, *see* **ра́дитися.**

поремонтува́ти, *pf.*, *see* **ремонтува́ти.**

поро́жн|ій, *adj.* empty, void, **За́ла була́ цілко́м ~я.** The hall was completely empty.

по-росі́йському, *adv.*, *var.* **по-росі́йськи** in a Russian way, **говори́ти п.** to speak Russian.

португа́льськ|ий, *adj.* Portuguese.

посели́тися, *pf.*, *see* **поселя́тися.**

поселя́|тися, ~ються; **посел|и́тися**, ~ю́ся, ~яться, *refl.* to take up residence, settle; check in (at a hotel), **Ви мо́жете посели́тися пі́сля тре́тьої (годи́ни).** You can check in after three o'clock.; **поселя́й|ся! ~теся!; посел|и́ся! ~іться!**

посила́|ти, ~ють; **посла́ти**, **пошл|ю́ть**, *tran.* to send, mail, **Він посла́в по допомо́гу.** He sent for help.; *pa. pple.* **по́сланий** sent, mailed; **посила́й! ~те!; пошли́! ~іть!**

посла́ти, *pf.*, *see* **посила́ти.**

послу́г|а, *f.* 1) service, *usually pl.*; **пошто́ві (кулínáрні) ~ги** postal (culinary) services; 2) favor; **роби́ти ~гу** to do a favor; *L.* **у ~зі.**

поспіша́|ти, ~ють; **поспіш|и́ти**, ~а́ть, *intr.* to hurry, to be in a hurry, **Я не люблю́ п.** I do not like to be in a hurry; **поспіша́й! ~те!; поспіш|и́! ~іть** hurry up!

постара́тися, *pf.*, *see* **стара́тися.**

по́ст|іль, *f.*, ~е́лі 1) bed, **(за)стели́ти п.** to make a bed; 2) bed linen, **~і́льна білизна́** bed linen; *I.* **~і́ллю** or **~е́лею.**

по́суд, *m.*, ~у, *only sg.*, *coll.* dishes, plates, **ми́ти п.** to wash dishes.

потво́рн|ий, *adj.* ugly, repulsive, awful.

по́тім, *adv.* then, afterwards, later, **Він ви́рішив подзвони́ти їм п.** He decided to call them later.

потра́пити, *pf.*, *see* **потрапля́ти.**

потрапля́|ти, ~ють; **потра́п|ити**, ~лю, ~иш, ~лять, *intr.* to get somewhere *(street, square)*, **на** + *A.* **Як потра́пити на Хреща́тик?** How do you get to Khreshchatyk?, **п. до** + *G. (building, institution)*, **~ити до ба́нку** to get to a bank; **потрапля́й! ~те!; потра́п! ~те!**

потребува́ти, *only impf.*, **потребу́|ють**, *tran.* or + *inf.* to need, **Він ~є зроби́ти це якнайшви́дше.** He needs to do it as quickly as possible.

потрі́бн|ий, *adj.* necessary, *var.* **потрі́бен** + *D.*, **Тури́стові п. путівни́к.** A tourist needs a guidebook.; **~а річ** a useful thing.

потрі́бно, *pred.* to be necessary *(logical subject in D.)* + *D.* + *inf.*, **Їй п. знайти́ час.** She needs to find the time.

по́тяг, *m.*, ~а train; **сіда́ти на п.** to catch a train; *L.* **на потя́зі.** *Also see* **по́їзд.**

по-украї́нському, *adv.*, *var.* **по-украї́нськи** 1) in a Ukrainian manner; 2) *(to write, speak)* Ukrainian, **Він гово́рить п.** He speaks Ukrainian.

пофарбува́ти, *pf.*, *see* **фарбува́ти.**

похму́р|ий, *adj.* 1) gloomy, sullen, **Він був ~ою на ви́гляд люди́ною.** He was a person of gloomy appearance.; 2) sunless, overcast, **Два оста́нні дні були́ мо́крими та ~ими.** The last two days were wet and gloomy.

похму́ро, *adv.* 1) gloomily, sullenly, **Роксоля́на ду́же ~о подиви́лася на сво́го хло́пця.** Roksolana gave her boyfriend a very gloomy look.; 2) *(in weather descriptions)* cloudy, overcast, **Було́ хо́лодно і п.** It was cold and cloudy.

поча́ти, *pf., see* **почина́ти**.

поча́тися, *pf., see* **почина́тися**.

поча́т|ок, *m.,* **~ку** a beginning, start; **від ~у до кінця́** from start to finish; **з са́мого ~ку** from the very beginning; *L.* **на ~ку.**

почека́ти, *pf., see* **чека́ти**.

почина́|ти, **~ють; поча́ти, почн|у́ть,** *tran. or impf. inf.* to start, begin, initiate; *pa. pple.* **поча́тий** begun; **почина́й! ~те!; почн|и́! ~іть!**

почина́|тися, **~ються; поча́тися, почн|у́ться** *intr.* to start, begin, initiate, **Коли́ почне́ться конце́рт?** When will the concert begin?; **почина́й|ся! ~теся!; почн|и́ся! ~іться!**

почува́|тися, **~ються; no pf.,** *intr.* to feel; **почува́йся! ~теся!**

почу́ти, *pf., see* **чу́ти**.

по́шт|а, *f.* 1) post-office, **головна́ п.** main post-office; 2) mail, **авіа-п.** air mail, **електро́нна п.** e-mail, **~ою** by mail; *L.* **на ~і.**

пошта́мт, *m.,* **~у** post-office, the main post-office; **Головпошта́мт** the Central Post-Office in Kyiv on Independence Square; *L.* **на ~і.**

пошто́в|ий, *adj.* postal, pertaining to mail, **~а ма́рка** postal stamp, **~і по́слуги** postal services.

по́шук, *m.,* **~у** search, ♦ **бу́ти у ~у** + *G.* to be in search of sth, **Він за́вжди у ~у нови́х іде́й.** He is always in search of new ideas.; **вести́ п.** to conduct a search; *adj.* **~о́вий, ~о́вий двигу́н** search engine.

пощасти́ти, *pf., see* **щасти́ти**.

поя́сненн|я, *nt.* explanation, **дава́ти п.** to give an explanation; *N. pl.* **поя́снень.**

поясню́|вати, **~ють; поясн|и́ти, ~ю́, ~я́ть,** *tran.* explain sth + *D.* to sb, **Він пояснив це сло́во Ро́бертові.** He explained this word to Robert.; *pa. pple.* **поя́снений** explained; **поясню́й! ~те!; поясн|и́! ~іть!**

поясни́ти, *pf., see* **поя́снювати**.

пра́вд|а, *f.* the truth; ♦ **п. ж?** right?, correct?, true?, *(synonymous with question tags after a statement asking for its confirmation)*, **Твоє́ ім'я́ Петро́, п. ж?** Your name is Petro, isn't it?; **Це п.?** Is it true?

пра́вил|о, *nt.* rule, **як п.** as a rule; ♦ **дотри́мувати(ся) пра́вил** to abide by the rules, **пору́шувати ~а** to break the rules, **бра́ти за п.** + *inf.* to make it a rule.

пра́вильн|ий, *adj.* correct, right, **це ~а ві́дповідь** it's the right answer.

пра́вильно, *adv.* correctly, rightly, **Тре́ба п. писа́ти адре́су.** One should write the address correctly.

право́руч, *adv.* right, to the right; ♦ **поверн|и́, ~і́ть п.** turn right, **п. від** + *G.* to the right of, **П. від вхо́ду виси́ть карти́на.** To the right of the entrance there hangs a picture.

практи́чн|ий, *adj.* practical.

пра́л|ьня, *f.* laundry, laundromat, launderette; *G. pl.* **~ень.**

пра́ти, пер|у́ть; ви~, *tran.* to wash clothes, do laundry, **Ми пере́мо раз на два ти́жні.** We do the laundry once every two weeks.; *pa. pple.* **ви́пран|ий** washed, clean (of clothes); **(ви́)пер|и́! ~іть!**

працю́|вати, **~ють; no pf. intr.** 1) work, **над** + *I.* on sth, **Він ~є над нови́м рома́ном.** He's working on a new novel.; 2) function, operate *(of equipment)*; **Холоди́льник не працю́є.** The fridge is broken.; **працю́й! ~те!**

предме́т, *m.,* **~а** 1) subject, discipline, **Які́ ~и ти вивча́єш?** What subjects do you study?; 2) object, material thing.

прибира́|ти, **~ють; прибра́ти, прибер|у́ть,** *tran.* to clean, tidy up, **Я прибира́ю у ха́ті раз на ти́ждень.** I clean my home once a week.; **прибира́й! ~те!; прибер|и́! ~іть!**

прибра́ти, *pf., see* **прибира́ти**.

прива́тн|ий, *adj.* private, **~а розмо́ва** a private conversation.

привезти́, *pf, see* **приво́зити**.

приво́з|ити, привожу́, ~иш, ~ять; привез|ти́, ~у́ть, *tran.* to bring *(by a vehicle, over a distance, or from a trip)*, **Тре́ба привезти́ їй подару́нок.** We need to bring her a gift.; *pa. pple.* **приве́зений** brought; **привози́! ~те!; привез|и́! ~іть!**

приві́т, *inter., colloq.* hi, hello.

приготува́ти, *pf., see* **готува́ти**.

приє́мн|ий, *adj.* pleasant, agreeable, nice.

приє́мн|ість, *f.,* **~ости** pleasure; **з ~істю** gladly, with pleasure.

приє́мно, *adv.* pleasantly, agreeably, nicely; ♦ **п. познайо́митися** it's nice to meet you.

прийма́|ти, **~ють; прийня́ти, ~у́, прийм|у́ть,** *tran.* 1) to receive, see (visitors), **Коли́ ви прийма́єте хво́рих?** When do you see patients?; 2) accept *(argument)*; *pa. pple.* **прийня́тий** received, accepted; **прийма́й! ~те!; прийм|и́! ~іть!**

прийня́ти, *pf., see* **прийма́ти**.

прийти́, *pf., see* **прихо́дити**.

приїжджа́|ти, **~ють; приї́хати, приї́д|уть,** *intr.* to come, arrive (by a vehicle, not on foot), **Ми приї́демо до Я́лти вве́чері.** We'll come to Yalta in the evening.; **Чи вони́ вже приї́хали?** Have they arrived yet?; **приїжджа́й! ~те!; приї́дь! ~те!**

приї́зд, *m.,* **~у** arrival, coming *(by a vehicle)*.

приї́хати, *pf., see* **приїжджа́ти**.

при́клад, *m.,* **~у** example, **дава́ти п.** to give an example.

прилеті́ти, *pf., see* **приліта́ти**.

прилі́т | профе́сія

приліт|т, *m.*, ~ьо́ту arrival *(of plane, flight)*, **П. ре́йсу із Ки́єва запі́знюється че́рез пого́ду.** The arrival of the flight from Kyiv is being delayed because of the weather.

приліта|ти, ~ють; **прилеті́ти, прилечу́, прилет**|я́ть, *intr.* 1) *(of people)* to come or arrive *(by airplane)*, **Ми прилети́мо за́втра вве́чері.** We'll come tomorrow evening; 2) *(of birds, airplanes, etc.)* to come, arrive.

прина́ймні, *adv.* at least, **Мені́ тре́ба п. ти́сяча гри́вень.** I need at least a thousand hryvnias.

принести́, *pf., see* **прино́сити.**

принос|ити, **прино́шу, ~иш, ~ять; принес**|ти́, ~у́ть, *tran.* to bring, fetch, **Алла принесла́ цуке́рок.** Alla brought some candies.; *pa. pple.* **прине́сений** brought along; **принось! ~те!; принес|и́! ~і́ть!**

припини́ти, *pf., see* **припиня́ти.**

припиня|ти, ~ють; **припини́ти, ~ю, припи́н|ять,** *tran. or inf.* to discontinue, stop, cease, **Тре́ба припини́ти диску́сії і ді́яти.** We need to stop discussions and act., **Припині́ть розмовля́ти!** Stop talking!; *pa. pple.* **припи́нений** stopped, discontinued; **припиня́й! ~те!; припин|и́! ~і́ть!**

При́п'ят|ь, *f.,* ~і the Prypiat River *(the largest right tributary of the Dnipro);* **I. ~тю, L. на ~і.**

приро́д|а, *f.* nature.

присни́тися, *pf., see* **сни́тися.**

прихо́д|ити, ~жу, ~ять; **прийти́, прийд|у́ть,** *intr.* to come, arrive, **Коли́ прихо́дить по́їзд із Ки́єва?** When does the train from Kyiv arrive?; **прихо́дь! ~те!; прийд|и́! ~і́ть!**

при́ятел|ь, *m.* friend, **Він мій да́вній п.** He is my old friend; **~ка,** *f.* female friend, **Окса́на й Ната́ля ~ки.** Oksana and Natalia are friends.; *L.* **на ~ці,** *G.* **~ьок.**

прі́звищ|е, *nt.* family name, **Як його́ п.?** What's his family name?; *N. pl.* **~а.**

про, *prep.* + *A.* about, **П. яку́ нови́ну́ ви гово́рите?** What news are you talking about?

пробле́м|а, *f.* problem, **У чо́му тут п.?** What's the problem here?, **п. в то́му (тім), що ...** the problem is that ..., **нема́ пробле́м!** no problem!

пробу́в|ати, ~ють; **с~,** *tran.* to try, attempt; **Я пробува́в дзвони́ти їм.** I tried to call them.; **(с)пробу́й! ~те!**

пробу́ти, *only pf.,* **пробу́д|ути,** *pa.* **пробули́,** *intr.* to stay *(in a hotel, city, place)*, spend, **Я пробу́в у Лу́цьку два дні.** I stayed in Lutsk for two days.

прове́сти́, *pf., see* **прово́дити.**

провідни́|к, *m.* conductor *(in a train);* guide of a tourist group; **Я бу́ду ва́шим ~о́м по Ки́єву.** I'll be your guide around Kyiv.; **~ця,** *f.* **Коли́сь О́ля працюва́ла провідни́цею.** Once Olia worked as a conductor.

прово́д|ити, ~жу, ~ять; **прове́сти́, прове́д|уть,** *pa. pf.* **прові́в, прове́ли,** *tran.* 1) to pass time; **га́рно (ве́село) п. час** to have a good time; **Ната́лю, як ти провела́ вихідні́?** Natalia, how did you spend the weekend? 2) see sb off, **Я проведу́ вас на по́їзд.** I'll see you off to the train.; *pa. pple.* **прове́дений** spent *(of time)*; **прово́дь! ~те!; провед|и́! ~і́ть!**

прову́л|ок, *m.,* ~ку lane, narrow short street, *L.* **у ~ку.**

програ́м|а, *f.,* 1) program, **у ~і** in the program; 2) computer software.

прогу́лян|ка, *f.* walk, stroll; **йти на ~ку** to go for a walk. *L.* **на ~ці.**

прода|ва́ти, ~ю́ть; **прода́|ти, ~м, ~си, ~сть, ~ду́ть,** *tran.* to sell, **Дава́й подиви́мося, що тут продаю́ть.** Let's see what they're selling here.; *pa. pple.* **про́даний** sold; **продава́й! ~те!; прода́й! ~те!**

прода́ти, *pf. see* **продава́ти.**

продо́вжити, *pf., see* **продо́вжувати.**

продо́вжу|вати, ~ють; **продо́вж|ити, ~ать,** *tran.* 1) + *A.* or *only impf. inf.* to continue sth, **Він продо́вжує працюва́ти тут.** He continues to work here; 2) + *A.* to extend sth (a stay, trip, leave), **Ми продо́вжили подоро́ж ще на ти́ждень.** We extended our trip for another week; *pa. pple.* **продо́вжений** continued, extended; **продо́вжуй! ~те!; продо́вж|и! ~і́ть!**

продо́вжу|ватися, ~ються; **продо́вж|итися, ~аться,** *refl.* 1) to last, go on, continue + *only impf. inf.,* **Нови́й проє́кт продо́вжується вже рік.** The new project has already lasted for a year.; 2) to resume *(after interruption),* **Виста́ва продо́вжиться пі́сля коро́ткої пере́рви.** The show will resume after a brief intermission; **продо́вжуй|ся! ~теся!; продо́вж|ися! ~иться!**

проду́кт, *m.,* ~у product; *N. pl.* ~и foodstuffs, produce, **купува́ти ~и** to buy groceries.

продукто́в|ий, *adj.* pertaining to groceries, ~**а крамни́ця** grocery store.

прокида́|тися, ~ються; **проки́н|утися, ~уться,** *intr.* to wake up, **Степа́н проки́нувся ра́но.** Stepan woke up early.; **прокида́й|ся! ~теся!; проки́нь|ся! ~теся!**

проки́нутися, *pf., see* **прокида́тися.**

проно́с, *m.,* ~у diarrhea.

пропону́|вати, **пропону́|ють; за~,** *tran.* 1) to suggest, **Він запропонува́в зроби́ти це поті́м.** He suggested doing it later.; or + *pf. inf.* ~ю **написа́ти до них.** I suggest we write to them; 2) to offer *(money, help, advice),* **п. допомо́гу** offer help; *pa. pple.* **запропоно́ваний** proposed; **(за)пропону́й! ~те!**

прос|и́ти, **прошу́, ~ять; по~,** *tran.* 1) to ask, request, **Марі́я попроси́ла допомогти́ їй.** Maria asked to help her.; 2) to invite, **Вони́ ~ять нас в го́сті до се́бе.** They are inviting us to their place; *pa. pple.* **попро́шений** asked, requested; **(по)прос|и́! ~і́ть!**

проспе́кт, *m.,* ~у avenue, a wide street, **п.** + *G.* of n. *(in street names),* **П. Свобо́ди** Liberty Avenue *(main drag in Lviv);* **L. на ~і.**

прости́й, *adj.* simple.

про́сто, *adv.* 1) simply, merely, **Я п. пита́ю вас.** I am simply asking you.; 2) straight, **Іди́ (~і́ть) п.** Go straight.

про́ти, *prep.* against + *G.,* **п. ві́тру** against the wind; *adv.* against; **бу́ти п.** + *G,* to oppose, be against sb / sth, **Ви не п., якщо́ я відкри́ю вікно́?** Do you mind if I open the window?

про́тягом, *prep.* + *G.* during, for, for the duration of, **п. годи́ни** for one hour.

профе́сі|я, *f.,* ~ї profession, occupation, **за ~єю** by profession. *See* **фах.**

профе́сор

Різдво́

профе́сор, *m.*, ~**a** professor; *N. pl.* ~**и**.

проха́нн|я, *nt.* request, **на п.** at the request.

прох|ід, *m.*, ~**о́ду** passage, passageway; aisle (in aircraft, theater); **мі́сце бі́ля** ~**о́ду** aisle seat.

про́шу, ♦ *Gal.* please, here you are (in response to **дя́кую** thank you).

прям|и́й, *adj.* straight, direct, **п. рейс** direct flight, ~**а вули́ця** straight street.

пря́мо, *adv.* directly, straight, *imp.* **Іді́ть п.** Go straight. *Also see* **про́сто**.

псу|ва́ти, ~**ю́ть; зі**~, *tran.* 1) to break sth, cause sth to break, **Він не знав, як користува́тися комп'ю́тером і зіпсува́в його́.** He didn't know how to use the computer and broke it.; 2) spoil (event, children), **Ма́рко зіпсува́в вечі́рку для всіх.** Marko spoiled the party for everybody. *pa. pple.* **зіпсо́ваний** broken, spoiled, **зіпсо́вана дити́на** spoiled child; **(зі)псуй!** ~**те!**

псува́тися, **псу|ю́ться; зі**~, *intr.* 1) to spoil, **Ця ри́ба шви́дко псу́ється.** This fish quickly spoils.; 2) *refl.* to break, become broken, stop functioning, **Годи́нник зіпсува́вся.** The watch broke down; **(зі)псуй|ся! ~теся!**

птах, *m.*, ~**a** bird; *L.* **на** ~**ові**, *N. pl.* ~**и́**, *G. p.* ~**ів**.

путівни́к, *m.*, ~**a** guidebook, **п. по Ки́єву / Ки́євом** guidebook of Kyiv; *L.* **у** ~**у́**.

п'ятдеся́т, *card.*, ~**ьо́х** + *G. pl.* fifty, **п. гри́вень** fifty hryvnias.

п'ятна́дцять, *card.*, ~**ох** + *G. pl.* fifteen, **п. хвили́н** fifteen minutes.

п'ятсо́т, *card.*, ~**иста́** + *G. pl.* five hundred, **п. до́ларів** five hundred dollars.

п'ять, *card.*, ~**ох** + *G. pl.* five, **п. чолові́к** five people.

Р

ра́д|а, *f.* council, **Верхо́вна Р.** the Supreme Rada (Parliament of Ukraine); ♦ **На то нема́** ~**и.** There's nothing doing.

ра́д|ий, *adj.* glad, content, pleased; ♦ **р. знайо́мству** *m.* glad to meet you.

ра́д|ити, ~**жу**, ~**ять; по**~, 1) *tran.* + *D.* to advise sth. to sb., give advice, to recommend, **Ра́джу вам замо́вити готе́ль сього́дні.** I advise you to book the hotel today.; 2) *pf.* to undo damage, remedy, help, **Тут вже нічи́м не пора́диш.** There's no remedy here.; **(по)ра́дь! ~те!**

ра́д|итися, ~**жуся**, ~**яться; по**~, *intr.* 1) to consult, **з (із)** + *I.* with sb, **Я завжди́ ра́джуся з ним.** I always consult with him.; 2) get sb's advice, **Нам тре́ба по**~ . **(по)ра́дь|ся! ~теся!**

ра́діо, *nt., indecl.* radio, radio set, **по р.** on the radio.

ра́ді|сть, *f.*, ~**ости** joy, happiness; ♦ **на р.** + *D.* to sb's joy; **з** ~**істю** gladly.

раз, *m.*, ~**у** time, occasion, **пе́рший р.** (for) the first time, ♦ **у тако́му** ~**і** in that case; *N. pl.* **рази́**, **з пе́ршого** ~**у** at first go; *G. pl.* ~**ів** *or* **раз.**

ра́зом *adv.* together, at the same time, **р. з на́ми** together with us.

райо́н, *m.*, ~**у** 1) district, borough (of city), **Поді́л – це р. мі́ста, де я живу́.** Podil is the city borough I live in.; 2) (in Ukraine) unit of administrative division below **о́бласть** province, equivalent to county in USA, **Володими́рецький р.** Volodymyrets District.

ра́но, *adv.* early, **Я люблю́ р. встава́ти.** I like to rise early.; ♦ **р. чи пі́зно** sooner or later; *comp.* **рані́ше.**

ра́н|ок, *m.*, ~**ку** morning, **з** ~**ку до ве́чора** from morning till night.

ранко́в|ий, *adj.* morning (paper, train), ~**а газе́та** morning newspaper.

ра́птом, *adv.* suddenly, all of a sudden.

раху́|ва́ти, **раху́|ють; по**~, *tran.* 1) to count, **Він все раху́є зда́чу.** He always counts the change; 2) think, be of opinion, **я раху́ю, що …** I think that …; *pa. pple.* **пора́хований** counted, calculated; **(по)раху́й!** ~**те!**

раху́н|ок, *m.*, ~**ку** check, bill (in restaurant).

регіо́н, *m.*, ~**у** region, part of a country, **за́хідний р.** a western region, **у цьо́му** ~**і** in this region.

режисе́р, *m.*, ~**a** film (theater) director.

ремонту́|ва́ти, ~**ють; по**~, *tran.* to repair, fix, **Чи ви мо́жете по**~ **стіле́ць?** Can you repair the chair?; *pa. ppla.* **поремонто́ваний** repaired; **(по)ремонту́й!** ~**те!**

результа́т, *m.*, ~**у** result.

рейс, *m.*, ~**у** flight, bus, train, boat, **Він ї́де ранко́вим** ~**ом.** He is taking a morning flight (bus, train, boat).

рестора́н, *m.*, ~**у** restaurant.

реце́пт, *m.*, ~**a** 1) medical prescription, **Ці лі́ки продаю́ть лише́ за** ~**ом.** This medicine is sold only by prescription. 2) recipe, **Це борщ за** ~**ом мо́є́ї бабу́сі.** This borshch is made by my granny's recipe.

речене́|ць, *m.*, ~**ця** deadline, **За́втра р., тре́ба поспіша́ти.** Tomorrow is the deadline, we need to hurry up.

рече́н|ня, *nt.* sentence, utterance; *G. pl.* ~**ь.**

ре́шт|а, *f.* rest, remaining part + *G.*, **Він дав мені́** ~**у молока́.** He gave me the rest of the milk.

ри́б|а, *f.* fish, **сві́жа (моро́жена) р.** fresh (frozen) fish; **лови́ти** ~**у** to fish; ♦ **як р. у воді́** in one's element.

рин|ок, *m.*, ~**ку** market, market place; *L.* **на** ~**ку.**

рис, *m.*, ~**у** rice, **ва́рений р.** boiled rice.

рі́вно, *adv.* 1) evenly; ♦ **все р.** all the same; 2) exactly, **Зара́з пе́рша (годи́на) р.** It's one o'clock sharp now.

р|іг, *m.*, ~**о́гу** corner (of street, building), **за** ~**о́гом** behind the corner; *L.* **на** ~**о́зі**, *N. pl.* ~**о́ги.**

рі́дко, *adv.* rarely, seldom, **Ми р. ба́чимося тепе́р.** We seldom see each other now.; *comp.* ~**ше.**

рі́дн|ий, *adj.* 1) own (by blood), **р. брат** brother as opposed to cousin; 2) native, home **р. край** homeland, ~**е мі́сто** hometown; 3) dear, beloved, ~**і мо́ї** my dear ones.

Різдв|о́, *nt.*, Christmas, **на Р.** for Christmas, **у Р.** on Christmas; ♦ **Весе́лого** ~**а!** Merry Christmas! *religious greeting* **Христо́с рожда́ється!** Christ is born! **Сла́вімо його́!** Praise be to him!

різний   салат

рı́зн|ий, *adj.* 1) different, differing, **Це зо́всім ~і питáння.** These are completely different issues.; 2) various, **Тут продаю́ть ~і ви́ди ри́би.** They sell various types of fish here.

рı́зни|ця, *f.* difference, **р. за вı́ком** age difference; **нема́є ~і** it makes no difference, **Я не ба́чу ~і між нови́м і стари́м пла́ном.** I see no difference between the new and the old plan.

р|ік, *m.*, **~о́ку** year; **цього́ ~о́ку** this year, **Ми познайо́милися у дві ти́сячі четве́ртому ~о́ці.** We met in the year 2004.; ♦ **р. за ~о́ком** year after year; **~ока́ми** for years; *L.* **у ~о́ці**, *N. pl.* **~оки.**

р|іч, *f.*, **~е́чі** thing; ♦ **до ~е́чі** by the way; ♦ **пе́вна р.** certainly; ♦ **р. у тı́м (тому́), що** ... the thing is that ...; *I.* **~ı́ччю**, *N. pl.* **~е́чі**, *G. pl.* **~ече́й.**

рı́ч|ка, *f.*, **~ки** river, **Дніпро́ - це найважливı́ша р. Украı́ни.** The Dnipro is the most important river of Ukraine.; *L.* **у ~ці**, *N. pl.* **~ки.**

роб|и́ти, **роблю́**, **~иш**, **ро́блять**; **з~**, *tran.* 1) to do, act, **Що ти ~и́в учора́?** What did you do yesterday? 2) to make, manufacture; **Нам треба зроби́ти це на за́втра.** We need to make this for tomorrow; **р. ви́няток** to make an exception; *pa. pple.* **зро́блений**; **зро́блено в Украı́ні** made in Ukraine; **(з)роб|и́! ~іть!**

робı́тни|к, *m.* male worker, **Тара́с – до́брий р.** Taras is a good worker.; *N. pl.* **~и́;**

робı́тни|ця, *f.* female worker, **Надı́я – р. на цьо́му заво́ді.** Nadia is a worker at this plant.

робо́т|а, *f.* work, job, **на ~і** at work, **дома́шня р.** home work, **ха́тня р.** work around the house.

робо́ч|ий, *adj. (of day)* working, **р. день** working day.

ро́дич, *m.*, **~а** relative, family, **близьки́й (дале́кий) р.** close (distant) relative; **бу́ти р. + D.** to be sb's relative, **Миха́йло нам близьки́й р.** Mykhailo is our close relation.; *N. pl.* **~і.**

ро́дич|ка, *f.* female relative, **бу́ти р. + D.** to be sb's relative, **Мари́на йому́ не ~ка.** Maryna is not his relative.; *L.* **на ~ці**, *G. pl.* **~ок.**

розка́зу|вати, **~ють**; **розказа́ти**, **розка́ж|уть**, *tran.* to tell *(a story)*; ♦ **р. ба́йки** to tell old wives' tales; *pa. pple.* **розка́заний** told; **розка́зуй! ~те!**; **розка́ж|и! ~іть!**

ро́зк|іш, *f.*, **~оші** luxury, extravagance; **це завели́ка р.** it's too much of a luxury.

ро́зклад, *m.*, **~у** timetable, schedule *(of trains)*, **р. заня́ть** class schedule, **р. поı́здів (літакı́в, авто́бусів)** train (airplane, bus) schedule, **за ~ом** on schedule.

розмо́в|а, *f.* conversation, a talk, **до́вга (неприє́мна) р.** long (unpleasant) talk.

розмовля́|ти, **~ють**; **по~**, *intr.* to speak *(language)* + *I.*, **він розмовля́є англı́йською** he speaks English; 2) talk, have a conversation, **Про що ви розмовля́ли?** What did you talk about?; **(по)розмовля́й! ~те!**

розповіда́|ти, **~ють**; **розповı́|сти**, **розповı́м**, **~си́**, **~сть**, **~мо**, **~сте**, *no 3rd pers. pl. form, instead* **розка́жуть** *is used, tran.* to tell, narrate *(a story)*, **Він лю́бить р. цю істо́рію.** He likes to tell this story.; *pa. pple.* **розка́заний** told, *for im. see* **розка́зувати.**

ро́зповідь, *f.* story, narrative.

розповı́сти, *pf., see* **розповіда́ти.**

ро́зпро́даж, *m.*, **~у** sale; **на ~і** on sale, **р. сезо́ну (ро́ку)** the sale of the season (year).

розташо́ван|ий, *adj.* situated, located, **бу́ти ~им** to be located.

розташо́ву|ватися, **~ються**; **розташува́тися**, *intr.* + *L. (usually impf.) (of building, city)* to be located, be situated, **Нови́й ко́рпус університе́ту ~ється у па́рку.** The new university hall is located in a park.

розумı́|ти, **~ють**; **з~**, *tran.* to understand, **Ви мене́ розумı́єте?** Do you understand me?, **Я нічо́го не ~ю.** I don't understand anything., **Ми наре́шті все зрозумı́ли.** We finally understood everything.; *pa. pple.* **зрозумı́лий** understood, clear; **(з)розумı́й! ~те!**

розу́мн|ий, *adj.* wise, clever, intelligent.

рома́н, *m.*, **~у** 1) novel; 2) love affair.

росı́йськ|ий, *adj.* Russian, **~а мо́ва** Russian language.

Росı́|я, *f.*, **~ï** Russia; *L.* **у ~ï.**

росія́н|ин, *m.* Russian man; *N. pl.* **~и**, *G. pl.* **росія́н.**

росія́н|ка, *f.* a Russian woman; *L.* **на ~ці**, *G. pl.* **~ок.**

рост|и́, **~у́ть**; **ви~**, *pa.* **ви́ріс**, **ви́росли**, *intr.* 1) to grow, **Під де́ревом ~у́ть квı́ти.** There are flowers growing under the tree.; 2) grow up, **Він ви́ріс у Володи́мирці.** He grew up in Volodymyrets.; **(ви)рост|и́! ~іть!**

рот, *m.*, **~а** mouth; *N. pl.* **~и́.**

руд|и́й, *adj. (of hair color)* red, **~оволо́сий** red-haired.

ру|ка́ *f.*, **~ки́** hand, arm; *L.* **у ~ці́**, *N. pl.* **~ки**, *L. pl.* **на ~ка́х.**

ру́с|ий, *adj. (only of hair color)* brown, **~оволо́сий** brown-haired.

Рус|ь, *f.*, **~и** Rus, old historical name of Ukrainian lands in early Middle Ages; *poet.* Ukraine *also* **Украı́на-Русь.**

ру́ськ|ий, *adj.* old Ukrainian, pertaining to the medieval principality of Kyivan Rus, **~а мо́ва** Old Ukrainian before 14th century.

рух, *m.*, **~у** 1) *(physical and political)* movement, **р. за права́ люди́ни** human rights movement; 2) traffic, **У цей час у мı́сті за́вжди вели́кий р.** At this time there is a lot of traffic in the city.; *cliché* **ро́зклад ~у поı́здів (авто́бусів, літакı́в)** train (bus, airplane) schedule.

ру́ч|ка, *f.* 1) pen; *also see* **перо́**; 2) handle; *L.* **у ~ці**, *N. pl.* **ру́чки**, *G. pl.* **~ок**; 3) little hand; *N. pl.* **~ки**, *etc.*

рушни́|к, *m.*, **~á** 1) towel; 2) traditional Ukrainian embroidered towel; *L.* **на ~у** or **~о́ві.**

ряд, *m.*, **~у** row *(in theater)*, **Ді́ти лю́блять сидı́ти у пе́рших ~ах.** Children like to sit in the first rows.; 2) aisle *(in a supermarket)*; *L.* **у ~і** and **~у**, *N. pl.* **~и́.**

С

сад, *m.*, **~у** garden, orchard, **ботанı́чний с.** botanical garden; *L.* **у ~у**, *N. pl.* **~и́.**

сала́т, *m.*, **~у** salad, **з (із)** + *G.* of, **с. з капу́сти** cabbage salad, **с. з огı́рків і помı́дорів** cucumber and tomato salad.

сам, *adj., m., var.* **самий** *(rarely used)* 1) alone; on one's own, **Він не с.** He is not alone.; 2) without anybody's help, **Іван с. написав це.** Ivan wrote it himself.; 3) oneself *(myself, yourself, etc.)*, **Марко с. не знає що робити.** Marko himself does not know what to do.

сам|а, *adj., f., see* **сам, Вона с. не хотіла нікуди йти.** She herself did not want to go anywhere.

сам|е, *adj., nt., see* **сам, С. це питання було дивне.** This very question was strange.

саме, *emph. part., indecl.* exactly, specifically *(follows, more rarely precedes, interr. words that are emphasized)*, **Де с. ви читали про це?** Exactly where did you read about it?, **Хто с. це зробив?** Who specifically did that?

свинин|а, *f., sg. only* pork meat, pork, **тушкована с.** pork stew.

свиняч|ий, *adj.* pork, **~е м'ясо** pork meat, **~а котлета** pork patty.

свіж|ий, *adj.* fresh *(of food, air)*.

св|ій, *pron.,* **~ого** or **~ойого** one's own *(concretized in translation as my, your, his, her, our, your, their, depending on the person referred to by the subject)*, **Я знаю свого брата.** I know my brother., **Вона знає свого брата.** She knows her (own) brother.

світ, *m.,* **~у** the world, **на ~і** in the world, **на всьому ~і** in the whole world.

світл|ий, *adj.* light, full of light; bright.

світлин|а, *f.* photograph, **на ~і** in the photo, **робити (проявляти) ~у** to take (develop) a photo. *Also see* **фотографія.**

світл|о, *nt.* light, **денне с.** daylight, **вімкнути (вимкнути) с.** to turn on (off) the light, *also* **запалити (згасити) с.**

світлофо́р, *m.,* **~а** traffic light, **На третьому ~і поверніть ліворуч.** At the third light, turn left.

світов|ий, *adj.* 1) world, **с. чемпіонат** world championship; 2) global, **~а криза** global crisis.

своєрідн|ий, *adj.* original, peculiar, singular.

святков|ий, *adj.* festive, **с. настрій** festive mood, **~а вечеря** festive dinner; **с. день** holiday, day-off.

святку|ва́ти, **~ють**; **від~**, *tran.* to celebrate, **Як ви думаєте с. День Незалежности?** How are you going to celebrate Independence Day with? *pa. pple.* **відсвяткований** celebrated *(of a holiday)*; **(від) святкуй! ~те!**

свят|о, *nt.* holiday, day off work, **Що ви робили на Різдвяні ~а?** What did you do for Christmas holidays?; **Найбільше свят у січні.** The greatest number of holidays is in January.; *N. pl.* **свята**, *G. pl.* **свят.**

себе, *pron., G.* oneself *(concretized in translation as myself, yourself, themselves, etc.)*, **для себе** for oneself; **Він с. дуже любить.** He loves himself a lot. *D.* **собі**, *I.* **собою**, *L.* **на собі.**

секретар, *m.,* **~я** secretary; *N. pl.* **~і**; **~ка**, *f.* female secretary; *L.* **на ~ці**, *G. pl.* **~ок.**

секунд|а, *f.* second; **(Почекайте) ~у** (Wait) one second; *G. pl.* **секунд.**

сел|о, *nt.,* **~а** 1) village, **До найближчого ~а десять кілометрів.** It's ten kilometers to the nearest village.; 2) countryside, province *(as opposed to city)*; *L.* **на ~і** in the country, *N. pl.* **~а**, *G. pl.* **сіл.**

селян|ин, *m.* peasant, villager; *N. pl.* **~и**, *G. pl.* **селян.**

селян|ка, *f.,* female peasant, villager; *L.* **на ~ці**; *G. pl.* **~ок.**

семест|(е)р, *m.,* **~ру** semester, **осінній (весняний) с.** fall (spring) semester; *N. pl.* **~ри.**

семінар, *m.,* **~у** seminar, **з (із)** + *G. pl.* **с. з історії** seminar in history; *L.* **на ~і**, *N. pl.* **~и.**

серед|а, *f.* Wednesday, **у середу** on Wednesday.

середин|а, *f.* middle, ♦ **золота с.** the golden mean, **с. місяця (року)** middle of the month (year); *L.* **по ~і** in the middle.

середміст|я, *nt.,* **~я** downtown, **Звідси до с. п'ять хвилин пішки.** It's a five-minute walk from here to downtown.; *L.* **у ~і**, *G. pl.* **~ь.**

середн|ій, *adj.* middle, **~я школа** high school, secondary school.

серп|ень, *m.,* **~ня** August, **День Незалежности святкують двадцять четвертого ~я.** Independence Day is celebrated on August 24.; *L.* **у ~і.**

сер|це, *nt.,* **~ця** heart, ♦ **від усього ~я** from the heart; **~цевий напад** heart attack; *N. pl.* **~ця**, *G. pl.* **~дець** or **~ць.**

сест|ра, *f.,* **~ри** 1) sister; 2) female medical nurse; *N. pl.* **~ри.** *G. pl.* **~ер.**

сид|іти, **~жу**, **~ять**; **по~**, *intr.* to sit, be seated; *pf.* to sit for a limited time; **сиди! ~іть!**

сильн|ий, *adj.* strong, powerful, great.

симпатичн|ий, *adj.* likable, agreeable, nice, **Він дуже ~а людина.** He is a very nice person.

симптом, *m.,* **~у** symptom *(of sickness)*.

син, *m.,* **~а** son, **єдиний (молодший, старший) с.** only (younger, elder) son. *N. pl.* **~и.** *Cf.* **дочка.**

син|ій, *adj.* blue, darker blue.

сир, *m.,* **~у** cheese, cottage cheese; *N. pl.* **~и.**

ситуаці|я, *f.* situation, **складна (сімейна) с.** difficult (family) situation, **Моя с. цілком змінилася.** My situation has completely changed.

сіда|ти, **~ють**; **сісти, ся́д|уть**; *pa.* **сі|ли**, *intr.* + **на** + *A.* to sit down, sit, take a seat; ♦ **с. на автобус (поїзд, літак)** to take a bus (train, airplane); **сідай! ~те!; сядь! ~те!**

с|ік, *m.,* **~оку** juice, **фруктовий (овочевий) с.** fruit (vegetable) juice; *L.* **у ~оці / ~оку**; *N. pl.* **~оки.**

с|іль, *f.,* **~оли** salt, **без ~оли** without salt; *I.* **~іллю.**

с|ім, *card.,* **~еми** + *G. pl.* seven, **с. братів** seven brothers.

сімдеся́т, *card.,* **~и** + *G. pl.* seventy, **с. осіб** seventy people.

сімнадцят|ь, *card.,* **~и** + *G. pl.* seventeen, **с. жінок** seventeen women.

сімсот

сімсо́т, *card.*, **семиста́** + *G. pl.* seven hundred, **с. ро́ків** seven hundred years.

сім|'я́, *f.*, ~'ї family, **У ньо́го вели́ка с.** He has a large family.; *N. pl.* ~'ї, *G. pl.* ~е́й.

сі́р|ий, *adj.* 1) gray, **Він лю́бить носи́ти сі́ре.** He likes to wear gray.; 2) plain, boring, **Вона́ ~а і неціка́ва люди́на.** She is a gray and boring person.

сі́сти, *pf.*, see **сіда́ти**.

сі́ч|ень, *m.*, ~ня January, **У нас Різдво́ сьо́мого ~я.** We have Christmas is on January 7.; *L.* у ~і.

сказа́ти, *pf.*, see **каза́ти** and **говори́ти**.

скасо́ву|вати, ~ють; **скасу́|вати**, ~ють, *tran.* 1) to cancel, **Вони́ скасува́ли вечі́рку в са́му оста́нню хвили́ну.** They canceled the party at the very last moment.; 2) to validate a ticket *(on city bus, etc.)*; *pa. pple.* **скасо́ваний** validated *(ticket)*, cancelled *(event)*; **скасо́вуй! ~те!; скасу́й! ~те!**

скасува́ти, *pf.*, see **скасо́вувати**.

скі́льки, *adv.* + *G.* how many, how much, **С. хлі́ба ти ма́єш?** How much bread do you have?

скінчи́ти, *pf.*, *var.*, see **кінча́ти** and **закі́нчувати**.

склада́|тися, ~ються, *intr.* to consist **з (із)** + *G.* of, **Рік ~є́ться з двана́дцяти мі́сяців.** A year consists of twelve months.; **склада́й|ся! ~теся!**

складн|и́й, *adj.* complicated, hard; **Це ~е́ пита́ння.** This is a complicated question.

скл|о́, *nt.*, *only sg.* (material) glass, **зі ~а** of glass, **розби́те с.** broken glass; *var.*, *colloq.* **шкло**.

скля́н|ка, *f.*, ~ки glass + *G.*, **с. води́** glass of water; *L.* у ~ці, *N. pl.* ~ки, *G. pl.* ~ок.; *var. colloq.* **шкля́нка**.

ско́р|ий, *adj.* fast, rapid, **с. по́їзд** fast train.

скориста́тися, *pf.*, see **користува́тися**.

ско́ро, *adv.* soon, quickly, **С. бу́де Нови́й рік.** Soon it will be the New Year.

скри́п|ка, *f.* violin, **гра́ти на ~ці** to play the violin; *L.* на ~ці, *G. pl.* ~ок.

скрізь, *adv.* everywhere.

слаб|ки́й, *adj.* weak, feeble *(of voice, influence)*; *comp.* ~ши́й.

славе́тн|ий, *adj.* famous, celebrated.

слід, *mod.* + *inf.* should *(in expressions of advice, obligation, with logical subject in D.)*, **Вам с. сказа́ти їй про це.** You should tell her about it.

словни́|к, *m.*, ~а dictionary, vocabulary, **украї́нсько-англі́йський с.** Ukrainian-English dictionary; *L.* у ~у́.

сло́в|о, *nt.*, ~а a word, ♦ **~ом** in short, in a word, ♦ **с. че́сти!** on my word!; *N. pl.* ~а́, *G. pl.* **слів**.

слу́ха|ти, ~ють; **по~** + *A.* 1) to listen to *(no prep.)*, **с. му́зику** to listen to music; 2) to obey, to be obedient to, **Він не завжди́ слу́хає ма́тір.** He does not always obeys his mother.; *pa. pple.* **послу́ханий** *also* **прослу́ханий** listened to **(по)слу́хай! ~те!**

спе́ка

сма|к, *m.*, ~у́ taste, **на ко́жний с.** to every taste; **до́брий с.** good taste, **вибагли́вий с.** discriminating taste; **бу́ти соло́дким (гірки́м, соло́ним) на с.** to taste sweet (bitter, salty); *N. pl.* ~и́.

смачн|и́й, *adj.* tasty, delicious, ~а́ **стра́ва** tasty dish; ♦ **смачно́го!** bon appétit! *Also see* **до́брий**.

сма́чно, *adv.* deliciously; **с. пої́сти** to have a delicious meal.

смішн|и́й, *adj.* funny, comical; *Also see* **куме́дний**.

смі|я́тися ~ю́ться, *intr.* 1) to laugh, **Вони́ ве́село ~я́лися.** They laughed cheerfully. 2) to laugh at sb, ridicule sb, **з (із)** + *G.* at, **Не ду́майте, що ми сміємо́ся з ньо́го.** Don't think that we are laughing at him.; **смі́й|ся! ~теся!**

сн|и́тися, ~я́ться; **при~**, *intr.* (with subject in D.) to dream of sth, see sth in a dream, **Що вам (при)сни́лося мину́лої но́чі?** What did you dream of last night?; **(при) сн|и́ся! ~и́ться!**

сніг, *m.*, ~у snow, **бага́то ~у** much snow, **Па́дає с.** It's snowing.; *L.* у ~у́, *N. pl.* ~и́.

сніда́н|ок, *m.*, ~ку breakfast, **на с.** for breakfast.

сніда́|ти, ~ють; **по~**, *intr.* to have breakfast, **с.** + *I.* to have sth for breakfast, **Оле́на за́вжди сніда́є ка́вою з рога́ликом.** Olena always has coffee with croissant for breakfast.; **(по)сніда́й! ~те!**

соба́|ка, *m.*, dog; *L.* на ~ці.

собо́р, *m.*, ~у cathedral, **Софі́йський с.** St. Sophia Cathedral, **С. Св. Ю́ра** St. George's Cathedral.

соло́д|кий, *adj.* sweet *(of taste)*; *comp.* ~ший.; *as n.* ~е dessert, **моро́зиво на ~е** ice-cream for dessert.

соло́н|ий, *adj.* salty, ~а **вода́** salty water.

с|он, *m.*, ~ну sleep, dream; *N. pl.* ~ни.

со́нн|ий, *adj.* sleepy; **бу́ти ~им (~ою)** to be sleepy.

со́нце, *nt.*, ~я the sun, **на ~і** in the sun; ♦ **за ~ем** clockwise, **про́ти ~я** counterclockwise; *G. pl* **сонць**.

соня́чн|ий, *adj.* 1) sunny ~а **пого́да** sunny weather; 2) solar, ~а **батаре́я (ене́ргія)** solar battery (energy), ~а **систе́ма** the Solar System.

со́рок, *card.* ~а́ + *G. pl.* forty, **с. до́ларів** forty dollars.

соро́ч|ка, *f.* shirt; *L.* на ~ці, *N. pl.* ~ки, *G. pl.* ~ок.

со́т|ий, *ord.* one hundredth.

спакува́тися, *pf.*, see **пакува́тися**.

спа́льн|ий, *adj.* sleeping, **с. ваго́н (мішо́к)** sleeping car (bag).

спа́|льня, *f.* bedroom; *G. pl.* ~ень.

спаси́бі, *nt.*, *indecl.* thank you; **вели́ке с.** thanks a lot. *Also see* **дя́кую**.

спа́ти, **сплю, спи|ш, ~мо́, ~те́, сплять; по~**, *intr.* to sleep, **до́бре с.** to sleep well; **(по)сп|и́! ~іть!**

спе́|ка, *f.* heat, hot weather, heat wave; **у спе́ку** in hot weather; *L.* на ~ці.

спеціяльн|ий, *adj.* special.

спеціяльн|ість, *f.*, **~ости** speciality, **Хто він за ~істю?** What is he by speciality?

спеціялізу|ватися, **~ються**, *no pf., intr.* to specialize, **з (із)** + *G.* in, **Вона ~ється з історії мистецтва.** She specializes in art history.; **~йся! ~йтеся!**

спин|а, *f.*, **~и** back *(of a person)*; **за ~ою** behind one's back; *N. pl.* **~и.**

спис|ок, *m.*, **~ку** list, **с. учасників** list of participants, **чорний с.** black list; *L.* **у ~ку** on the list.

співа|к, *m.* singer, **талановитий с.** talented singer.

співа|ти, **~ють; про~**, *tran.* to sing; *pa. pple.* **проспіваний** sung; **(про)співай! ~те!**

співа|чка, *f.* female singer; *L.* **на ~ці;** *G. pl.* **~ок.**

сподобатися, *pf., see* **подобатися.**

спорт, *m., sg. only,* **~у** sport, **займатися ~ом** to do sports.

спортивн|ий, *adj.,* sports, pertaining to sports, **с. клуб** sports club.

спортклуб, *m.,* **~у** fitness club, **ходити до ~у** to go to a fitness club, **займатися у ~і** to work out in fitness club.

спортсмен, *m.* male athlete, sportsman; **~ка**, *f.* female athlete; *L.* **на ~ці,** *G. pl.* **~ок.**

спос|іб, *m.,* **~обу** manner, way, **у такий с.** this way, in such a manner.

спочатку, *adv.* first, at the beginning; at first.

справ|а, *f.* matter, business; ♦ **Не твоя (ваша) с.** None of your business; ♦ **Як ~и?** How are things?; ♦ **у ~ах** on business, **Він приїхав до міста на відпочинок чи у ~ах?** Has he come to our city for pleasure or on business?; **Це інша с.** It's a different matter; ♦ **мати ~у з** + *I.* to deal with.

справа, *adv.* on the right, **с. від** + *G.* to the right of. *Also see* **праворуч.**

справді, *adv.* really, indeed.

спробувати, *pf., see* **пробувати.**

ста|вати, **~ють; стати, стан|уть**, *pa.* **ста|ли**, *intr.* 1) to become, + *I.,* **с. фахівцем** to become a professional; *D.* + **с. краще (гірше)** to feel better (worse), **Марії стало краще.** Maria felt better.; 2) to stand, take a place somewhere; ♦ **с. у чергу** to line up, join the queue; **ставай! ~те!; стань! ~те!**

ста|ватися, **~ються; статися, стан|уться**, *pa.* **ста|ли**, *intr.* to happen, occur, take place, **Це сталося другого червня.** This happened on June 2.

ста|вити, **~лю, ~иш, ~лять; по~**, *tran.*+ *A.* to put, place, set *(in upright position)* as opposed to **класти** *(to put in prone position),* **по~ стіл посередині** to put a table in the middle, **с. на стіл** to put on a table; *pa. pple.* **поставлений** put; **(по)став! ~те!**

стадіон, *m.,* **~у** stadium; *L.* **на ~і** at a stadium.

стандартн|ий, *adj.* standard, regular, **~а кімната на дві особи** a standard room for two.

станці|я, *f.,* **~ї** station *(usually smaller)*, **залізнична (автобусна) с.** train (bus) station; *L.* **на ~ї.** *Cf.* **вокзал.**

стара|тися, **~ються; по~** , *intr.* 1) to try, attempt, make an effort, **Хома старався ходити на всі його лекції.** Thomas tried to attend all his lectures.; 2) *pf.* to do one's best, **Я постараюся закінчити роботу до середи.** I'll do my best to finish the job by Wednesday.; **(по)старайся! ~теся!**

стар|ий, *adj.* old, **Люда – моя ~а подруга.** Liuda is my old friend. *Also see* **старіший** and **старший.**

старіш|ий, *adj., comp.* of **старий** older out of those who are all old, **У цьому старому подружжі жінка ~іша за чоловіка.** In this old marriage, the wife is older than the husband.

старш|ий, *adj., comp.* of **старий** older, senior out of those who are not necessarily old; **~ий брат** older brother.

стати, *pf., see* **ставати.**

статися, *pf., see* **ставатися.**

статт|я, *f.,* **~і** article *(newspaper)* **Вона прочитала цю ~ю вчора.** She read the article yesterday.; *I.* **~ею,** *L.* **у ~і,** *G. pl.* **~ей.**

степ, *m.,* **~у** steppe, **Я їздив у подорож українськими ~ами.** I went on a journey through Ukrainian steppes.; *L.* **у ~у,** *N. pl.* **~и.**

ст|іл, *m.,* **~ола** and **~олу** table; ♦ **щось до ~у** sth to eat; *N. pl.* **~и.**

стіл|ець, *m.,* **~ьця** chair; *N. pl.* **~і.**

стільки, *adv.* + *G.* so much, so many; in such quantity, **с. часу** so much time, **У нас с. роботи.** We have so much work.

стін|а, *f.,* **~и** wall, **На ~і висить картина.** There is a picture on the wall.; *N. pl.* **~и.**

ст|о, *card.,* **~а** one hundred, **Він має біля ~а опублікованих статтей.** He has about a hundred published articles. *G., D., I. and L.* **~а.**

столиц|я, *f.* capital *(city)*, **Київ – с. України.** Kyiv is the capital of Ukraine.

століт|тя, *nt.* century, **двадцять перше с.** twenty-first century, **У якому ~і це сталося?** In what century did it happen?; **~ями** for centuries; *L.* **у ~і.**

стомлен|ий, *adj.* tired.

сторін|ка, *f.* page, **У цій книжці триста сторінок.** There are three hundred pages in this book.; *L.* **на ~ці** on page; *N. pl.* **~ки,** *G. pl.* **~ок.**

сто|яти, **~ять**, *intr.* 1) to stand, **Ваза ~їть на столі.** The vase is on the table.; 2) be situated, **Рівне ~їть на Усті.** Rivne is situated on the Ustia River.; **стій! ~те!**

страв|а, *f.* 1) dish, **Джонові подобаються українські ~и.** John likes Ukrainian dishes.; 2) course *(in a meal)*, **перша (друга) с.** first (second) course; ♦ **на першу ~у** for the first course.

студент, *m.* student *(of college and higher, never of high school)*. *Cf.* **учень.**

студент|ка, *f.* female student *(of college and higher, never of high school)*; *L.* **на ~ці,** *G. pl.* **~ок.** *Cf.* **учениця.**

студе́нтський

студе́нтськ|ий, *adj.* student, having to do with students, **~а газе́та** student newspaper, **с. гурто́житок** student dormitory.

субо́т|а, *f.*, Saturday, **у ~у** on Saturday.

субти́тр, *m.*, **~у** subtitle *(in a film)*, ususally in pl.; **англі́йські ~и** English subtitles.

сувені́р, *m.*, **~а** souvenir, keepsake, memento.

су́к|ня, *f.* dress, **весі́льна (вечі́рня) с.** wedding (night) dress; *G. pl.* **~онь**. *Also see* **пла́ття**.

су́м|ка, *f.* bag, handbag; *L.* **у ~ці**, *N. pl.* **су́мки**, *G. pl.* **~о́к**.

су́мнів, *m.*, **~у** doubt; **ма́ти ~и** to have doubts.

суперма́ркет, *m.*, **~у** supermarket.

сусі́д, *m.*, **~а** neighbor; **~ка**, *f.* female neighbor; *L.* **на ~ці**, *G. pl.* **~ок**.

суча́сн|ий, *adj.* modern, contemporary, **~е мисте́цтво** contemporary art.

суча́сни|к, *m.* contemporary, **~ця**, *f.*, **Вона́ була́ ~цею Тара́са Шевче́нка.** She was a contemporary of Taras Shevchenko's.

су́ші, *nt.*, *indecl.* sushi (Japanese raw fish dish), **сма́чне с.** a delicious sushi.

сфотографува́ти, *pf.*, *see* **фотографува́ти**.

сх|ід, *m.*, **~о́ду**, east, **на с. від** + *G.* to the east of, **на ~о́ді** + *G.* in the east of, **Луга́нськ на ~о́ді Украї́ни.** Luhansk is in the east of Ukraine.

схі́дн|ий, *adj.* eastern, **півні́чно-с.** north-eastern.

сюди́, *adv.*, *dir.* here, to this place, **іди́** or **ходи́ с.** come here. *Cf.* **тут**.

сього́дні, *adv.* today, **с. вве́чері** tonight.

сього́днішн|ій, *adj.* today's, contemporary, **~я газе́та** today's newspaper.

сьо́м|ий, *ord.* seventh, **За́раз ~а годи́на рі́вно.** It is seven o'clock sharp now.

Т

та, *dem. pron.*, *f.* that, **т. кни́жка** that book.

та, *conj.*, *form.* 1) and, **купи́ти ка́ви т. молока́,** to buy some coffee and milk. *Also see* **і** and **й**; 2) but, **ти́хий, т. небезпе́чний** quiet but dangerous. *Also see* **але́**.

табле́т|ка, *f.* pill, **по ~ці кожні три годи́ни** one pill every three hours; *L.* **у ~ці**, *G. pl.* **~ок**.

так, *part.* yes, affirmative answer to a question, opposite of **ні** no; ♦ **т. чи ні?** yes or no?

так, *adv.* so, in such a way, so much, **Чому́ ти т. ди́вишся?** Why are you looking so?; ♦ **т. і не іна́кше** this and no other way, **Це т. тяжко́ чита́ти.** This is so difficult to read., **Йому́ це т. подо́бається.** He likes it so.

так|и́й, *adj.*, such, **Я зна́ю ~о́го фахівця́.** I know such an expert., **~і фі́льми завжди ціка́ві.** Such films are always interesting.; **т. ... як** + *N.* such ... as, **Ми побува́ли у таки́х міста́х, як Ки́їв, Оде́са та Ха́рків.** We have visited such cities as Kyiv, Odesa, and Kharkiv.

тако́ж, *adv.*, *form.* also, as well, too, **Оре́ст т. хо́че поба́чити Володи́мира.** Orest also wants to see Volodymyr. *Also see* **теж**.

такси́ст, *m.*, **~а** taxi-driver.

таксі́, *nt. indecl.* taxi, taxi-cab, **Пої́демо (на) т.** We'll go by taxi., **замо́вити т. по телефо́ну** to order a taxi by phone. *Also see* **таксі́вка**.

таксі́в|ка, *f.* taxi, taxi-cab, **Пої́демо ~кою.** We'll go by taxi.: **замо́вити ~ку** to order a taxi; *L.* **у ~ці**, *G. pl.* **~ок**.

талано́ви́т|ий, *adj.* talented, gifted.

там, *adv.* there, **Я чека́тиму там, бі́ля вхо́ду.** I'll be waiting there, near the entrance. *Cf.* **туди́**.

та́н|ець, *m.*, **~цю** dance, **наро́дний т.** folk dance; ♦ **(п)іти́ на ~ці** to go dancing, **Він лю́бить ходи́ти на ~ці.** He likes to go dancing.

танцю́|ва́ти, **~ють**; **про~**, *tran.* to dance, **Він ду́же до́бре ~є та́нго.** He dances the tango very well.; *pa. pple.* **протанцьо́ваний** danced; **(про)танцю́й! ~те!**

тарі́л|ка, *f.* plate, dish; *L.* **на ~ці**, *N. pl.* **~ки**, *G. pl.* **~о́к**.

та́т|о, *m. fam.* dad; *V.* **~у**, *N. pl.* **~и**.

твари́н|а, *f.* animal, **дома́шня (ди́ка) т.** domestic (wild) animal.

тверд|и́й, *adj.* 1) hard *(not soft)*, solid, **~е́ лі́жко** hard bed; 2) unshakable, unwavering.

тв|і́й, *poss. pron.*, *m.*, **~ого́** your, yours, **т. друг** your friend, **з ~ого́ дозво́лу** with your permission, **Цей комп'ю́тер т.?** Is this computer yours?

тво|є́, *poss. pron.*, *nt.*, **~ого́** your, yours, **т. а́вто** your car, **Це а́вто т.?** Is this car yours?, **Він пої́хав ~ім а́втом.** He went by your car.

тво|ї́, *poss. pron.*, *pl.*, **~ї́х** your, yours, **т. батьки́** your parents, **Ті пита́ння т.?** Are those questions yours?, **Я не зна́ю ~ї́х браті́в.** I don't know your brothers.

тво|я́, *poss. pron.*, *f.* , **~є́ї** your, yours, **т. сестра́** your sister, **Це су́кня ~є́ї ма́тері?** Is this your mother's dress?

т|е, *dem. pron.*, *nt.*, **~ого́** that, **т. мале́ дитя́** that little child, **для ~ого́ дитя́ти** for that child.

теа́тр, *m.*, **~у** theater, **до ~у** to the theater, **драмати́чний (музи́чний) т.** drama (music) theater.

теж, *adv.* also, as well, *var. of* **тако́ж**.

текст, *m.*, **~у** text, **Про що цей т.?** What is the text about?

тексту́|ва́ти, **~ють**; **за~** *tran.* to text, send a text message; **Я зате́ксту́ю їм цю інформа́цію, як ті́льки змо́жу.** I'll text them this information as soon as I can.

телеві́зор, *m.*, **~а** television set; **по ~у** on TV.

телефо́н, *m.*, **~у** telephone, phone; **по ~у** over the phone, **мобі́льний (стільнико́вий) т.** mobile (cellular) phone. *Also see* **мобі́лка**.

теля́, *nt.*, **~ти** calf; *I.* **~м**, *N. pl.* **~та**.

темни́й

те́мн|ий, *adj.* 1) dark, unlit, **~а кімна́та** dark room; 2) dark, deep *(of colors)*, **~е воло́сся** dark hair.

те́мно, *adv.* 1) dark, **Тут т.** It's dark here.; 2) deep *(of colors)*, **т.-зеле́ний** dark green.

те́ніс, *m.*, **~у** tennis, **гра́ти в т.** to play tennis, **Петро́ ча́сто гра́є в т.** Petro often plays tennis.

тепе́р, *adv.* now; **Т. чи ніко́ли.** It's now or never; ♦ **і то т.** right now, at once.

тепе́рішн|ій, *adj.* 1) present-day, present, **т. час** present tense, **у ~ьому ча́сі** in the present tense; 2) current **т. стан справ**, the current state of affairs.

те́пл|ий, *adj.* 1) warm, **т. клі́мат** warm climate; 2) cordial, **Атмосфе́ра на зу́стрічі була́ ~ою.** The atmosphere of the meeting was cordial.

ти, *pers. pron. inform.* you (2nd *pers. sg.*), **Т. зна́єш?** You know?, **Що т. ду́маєш?** What do you think?

ти́ж|день, *m.*, **~ня** a week, **цьо́го (насту́пного, мину́лого) ~ня** this (next, last) week; *N. pl.* **~ні**, *G. pl.* **~нів**.

типо́в|ий, *adj.* typical, common.

ти́х|ий, *adj.* quiet, calm, placid.

т|і, *dem. pron., pl.*, **~их** those, **т. ди́вні лю́ди** those strange people, **для ~их жіно́к** for those women.

ті́льки, *adv.* only, **Т. Рома́н розумі́є її́.** Only Roman understands her., **т. за запро́шенням** by invitation only. *Also see* **лише́**.

ті́т|ка, *f.* 1) aunt, **моя́ т. Мару́ся** my aunt Marusia; 2) *colloq. derogatory* woman; *L.* **на ~ці**, *N. pl.* **~ки**, *G. pl.* **~ок**.

то, *dem. pron.* that *(as in that is)*; is combined with verbs, **То була́ Ма́рта.** That was Marta., **То співа́є Іва́н.** That's Ivan singing.

то́бто *conj.* that is, i.e., I mean *(as a parasitic phrase)*.

товари́ств|о, *nt.* 1) company, **у ~і дру́зів** in the company of friends; ♦ *fam.* **пано́ве т.!** Gentlemen!; 2) society, company.

това́р, *m.*, **~у** merchandise, goods, *also pl.*, **продово́льчі ~и** foodstuffs, **промисло́ві ~и** manufactured goods.

това́риш, *m.*, **~а** friend, companion; *N. pl.* **~і**; **~ка**, *f.* female friend; *L.* **на ~ці**, *N. pl.* **~ки**, *G. pl.* **~ок**.

товст|и́й, *adj.* 1) thick, 2) *(of person)* fat, obese.

тоді́ *adv.* 1) then, after that; 2) in that case.

т|ой, *dem. pron., m.*, **~ого́** that; **т. га́рний хло́пець** that handsome guy, **пі́сля ~ого́ ве́чора** after that evening, **пе́ред ~им конце́ртом** before that concert.

тому́[1], *adv.* ago, back, preceded by *n. in A.*, **рік т.** a year ago, **Вони́ пішли́ годи́ну т.** They left an hour ago.

тому́[2], *adv.* 1) that's why, therefore, **Ти лиша́єшся, т. я ра́дий.** You're staying that's why I am glad.; 2) **т. що** because, **Поясни́ мені́, т. що я не розумі́ю.** Explain to me because I don't understand. *Also see* **бо**.

тонк|и́й, *adj.* 1) thin, 2) *(of taste, etc.)* refined, subtle.

тра́в|ень, *m.*, **~ня** May, **Фільм ви́йшов во́сьмого ~ня.** The film was released on May 8.; *L.* **у ~ні**.

традиці́йн|ий, *adj.* traditional.

трамва́|й, *m.*, **~я** streetcar, **~єм** by streetcar; *N. pl.* **~ї**.

тра́нспорт, *m.*, **~у** transportation, transit, transport, **місь́кий т.** municipal transit.

трапи́тися, *pf.*, *see* **трапля́тися**.

трапля́|тися, **~ються**; **трап|итися**, **~люся**, **~ишся**, **~ляться**, *intr.* to happen, occur, **Що трапи́лося?** What happened?; ♦ **Нічо́го, трапля́ється!** It's alright, it happens!; **трапля́й|ся! ~теся!**; **трап|ся! ~теся!**

тре́ба, *mod.* it is necessary; expresses need, necessity to do sth., when negated (**не тре́ба** + *impf. inf.*) expresses advice not to do sth, **Не т. пла́кати.** You shouldn't cry.; *D.* + **т.**, **Іва́нові т. йти.** Ivan needs to go.

тре́т|ій, *ord., f.*, **~я**, *nt.*, **~є** third, **Зара́з ~я годи́на.** It's three o'clock now.

тр|и, *card.*, **~ьох** three + *N. pl.*, **т. весе́лих хлопці́** three merry boys, **з ~ьома гри́внями в кише́ні** with three hryvnias in pocket.

трива́|ти, **~ють**; **про~**, *intr.* to last, continue, go on; **Різдвя́ні вака́ції звича́йно ~ють два ти́жні.** Christmas vacation usually lasts two weeks.; **(про) трива́й! ~те!**

три́дцят|ь, *card.*, **~и́** thirty + *G. pl.*, **т. до́вгих днів** thirty long days; **із ~ьма́ кі́ньми** with thirty horses.

трина́дцят|ь, *card.*, **~ьо́х** thirteen + *G. pl.*, **т. щасли́вих квиткі́в** thirteen lucky tickets, **подзвони́ти ~ьом лю́дям** to call thirteen people.

три́ста, *card.*, **трьохст|а́** three hundred + *G. pl.*, **т. незабу́тніх годи́н** three hundred unforgettable hours, **із ~ами́ є́врами** with three hundred euros.

троле́йбус, *m.*, **~а** trolley-bus, **~ом** by trolley-bus, **Тут зупиня́ється т. но́мер сім?** Does trolley-bus number seven stop here?

тро́хи, *adv.* 1) a little, somewhat, a bit, + *G.*, **т. гро́шей** a little money, **т. молока́** some milk, **Я т. бою́ся.** I'm afraid a little; 2) almost, *with negated pa. pf. verbs*, **Я т. не спізни́вся на по́тяг.** I almost missed the train.

трьохсо́тий, *ord.* three hundredth.

туале́т, *m.*, **~у** restroom, lavatory, bathroom, **грома́дський (пла́тний) т.** public (paid) restroom, **користува́тися ~ом** to use a bathroom.

туди́, *adv., dir.* there, in that direction *(direction with motion verbs)*, **Він піде́ т. за́втра.** He'll go there tomorrow. *Cf.* **там**.

тур, *m.*, **~у** 1) tour, **Ця аге́нція пропону́є ціка́ві ~и За́хідною Украї́ною.** The agency offers interesting tours of Western Ukraine; 2) package tour, **Їхній т. включа́є подоро́ж літако́м та готе́ль.** Their package tour includes airfare and a hotel accommodation.

туре́цьк|ий, *adj.* Turkish, **~а мо́ва** the Turkish language, **розмовля́ти ~ою** to speak Turkish.

тури́ст, *m.*, **~а** tourist, **міжнаро́дний т.** international tourist; **~ка**, *f.*; *L.* **на ~ці**, *G. pl.* **~ок**.

туристи́чн|ий, *adj.* tourist, pertaining to tourism.

туркен|я́, *f.* Turkish woman.

ту́р|ок, *m.*, **~ка** Turk, **Гусе́йн – т. за націона́льністю.** Huseyin is a Turk by nationality.

тут   фарбува́ти

тут, *adv., posn.* here, **Т. ніко́го нема́є.** There's nobody here. *Cf.* **сюди́**.

тяжк|и́й, *adj* 1) heavy, **~а́ валі́за** heavy suitcase; 2) hard, difficult, **~і часи́** hard times; 3) complicated, **~е пита́ння** complicated issue; *comp.* **тя́жчий**.

тя́жко, *adv.* 1) difficult, hard, **Зроби́ти це бу́де т.** It will be hard to do it.; 2) gravely (sick), **Він т. хво́рий.** He's gravely sick.

У

у, *prep., var.* **в** 1) + *L.* in (location in space), **у мі́сті** in the city; 2) + *G. of anim. n.* at sb's place, possession, **У Марі́ї було́ дві кімна́ти.** Maria had two rooms; at somebody's place, **Вони́ живу́ть в Оле́га.** They live at Oleh's place., **У ко́го ви жили́ у Терно́полі?** At whose place did you live in Ternopil?

уве́сь *adj., m., var., see* **ввесь**.

уве́чері, *adv., var., see* **вве́чері**.

у́ві, *prep., var. of* **у** used in **у́ві сні** in a dream.

увійти́, *var., see* **війти́**.

уда́ч|а, *f.,* **~і** luck, good fortune; ♦ **~і тобі́ (вам)!** good luck to you!; **(по)ба́жати ~і** to wish good luck.

удо́ма, *adv., var.* **вдо́ма** at home, home *posn.,* **Чи він у.?** Is he home?; *colloq.* ♦ **У те́бе що, не всі вдо́ма?** Are you nuts?

уже́, *adv., var., see* **вже**.

Украї́н|а, *f.* Ukraine, **ї́хати до ~и** travel to Ukraine, *poetic var.* **Вкраї́на**; *L.* **в ~і**.

украї́н|ець, *m.,* **~ця** Ukrainian man; *L.* **на ~еві**.

украї́н|ка, *f.* Ukrainian woman; *L.* **на ~ці**, *G. pl.* **~ок**.

украї́нськ|ий, *adj.* Ukrainian, **~а мо́ва** the Ukrainian language, **розмовля́ти ~ою** to speak Ukrainian.

улі́тку, *adv., var., see* **влі́тку**.

улю́блен|ий, *adj.* favorite, **~е заня́ття** favorite pastime; **у. письме́нник** a favorite writer.

умива́|тися, **~ються**; **уми́|тися**, **~ються** *refl.* to wash oneself *(face and hands)*; **умива́й|ся! ~теся!**; **уми́й|ся! ~теся!**

уми́сно, *adv., var.* **уми́сне**, *see* **навми́сно**.

уми́тися, *pf., see* **умива́тися**.

умі́|ти, *impf., var.* **вмі́ти**, **~ють** + *impf. inf.* to be able to do sth, to know how, **Він ~є пла́вати.** He can swim.; **умі́й! ~те!**

універма́|г, *m.,* **~гу** department store, **Центра́льний у.** the Central Department Store; *L.* **в ~зі**.

університе́т, *m.,* **~у** university, **У яко́му ~і ти навча́єшся?** What university do you study at?, **до ~у** to a university, **За́втра я не піду́ до ~у.** I won't go to the university tomorrow.

університе́тськ|ий, *adj.,* university, pertaining to a university, **~а бібліоте́ка** university library.

упе́внен|ий, *adj., var., see* **впе́внений**.

ура́нці, *adv., var., see* **вра́нці**.

уроди́н|и, *only pl.* birthday, **на у.** for / on birthday; **святкува́ти у.** to celebrate one's birthday.

усе́, *adv., pr. and adj., var., see* **все**.

усі́, *adj., pl. var., see* **всі**.

ускла́дненн|я, *nt.* complication, **Він мав серйо́зні у. пі́сля хворо́би.** He had serious complications after his illness.

уся́, *adj., f. var., see* **вся**.

ухо́дити, *var., see* **вхо́дити**.

у́хо, *var., see* **ву́хо**.

уча́сник, *m.* participant + *G.,* **~и конфере́нції прие́хали із рі́зних краї́н.** Conference participants came from various countries.; **уча́сниця**, *f.*

у́част|ь, *f.,* **~и** participation, **бра́ти у.** to take part, **Мину́лого мі́сяця він взяв у. у ціка́вій конфере́нції.** Last month he took part in an interesting conference.; **Вони́ не беру́ть ~и в жо́дній політи́чній кампа́нії.** They do not participate in any political campaign.

уче́н|ий, *n., m.,* **~ого** scholar, scientist; *adj.* learned, **~а люди́на** an educated person, learned man.

у́ч|ень, *m.,* **~ня** 1) pupil, student *(only of high school, not university)*, **Мико́ла – у́чень сере́дньої шко́ли №2.** Mykola is a student in High School No 2.; 2) *fig.* student; *N. pl.* **~ні**. *Cf.* **студе́нт**.

учи́тел|ь, *m.,* **~я** 1) male teacher, instructor *(usually in high school)*; 2) *fig.* teacher; *N. pl.* **~і**.

учи́тель|ка, *f.* female teacher + *G.,* **у. літерату́ри (істо́рії)** a literature (history, etc.) teacher; *L.* **на ~ці**, *N. pl.* **~ки**, *G. pl.* **~ок**.

уч|и́ти, **~а́ть**; **ви́вч|и́ти**, *tran.* 1) study sth, learn sth, **Він ~ить істо́рію та літерату́ру.** He studies history and literature.; 2) *fam.* to teach sb, *pf.* **навчи́ти**, **Він ~ить мене́ співа́ти.** He teaches me to sing., **Хто його́ навчи́в чита́ти?** Who taught him to read?; *pa. pple.* **ви́вчений** learned; **(ви)вч|и́! ~іть!**; *var.* **вчи́ти**.

уч|и́тися, **~а́ться**; **ви́вч|итися**, *intr.* to study somewhere or in a certain way (well, poorly), **Де ~иться ваш син?** Where does your son study?, **Я добре ~уся.** I am a good student; ♦ **в. на** + *A.* to study to become *(profession)*, **Він ~ться на лі́каря.** He studies to become a physician.; *var.* **вчи́тися**.

учо́ра, *adv., var.* **вчо́ра** yesterday; **у. вве́чері (вдень, вра́нці)** yesterday evening (afternoon, morning).

Ф

фа́бри|ка, *f.* factory, plant, works; *L.* **на ~ці**.

факульте́т, *m.,* **~у** department *(at university)*, **істори́чний ф.** department of history; *L.* **на ~і**, **Він навча́ється на ~і соціоло́гії.** He studies at the Department of Sociology.

фа́рб|а, *f.* paint, **акваре́льна ф.** watercolor, **олі́йна ф.** oil paint.

фарбу́|вати, **~ють**; **по ~**, *tran.* to paint, **Він хо́че по~ а́вто у черво́ний ко́лір.** He wants to paint the car red.; *pa. pple.* **пофарбо́ваний** painted; **(по)фарбу́й! ~те!**

фах, *m.,* **~у** profession, speciality; professional occupation, **за ~ом** by trade, **Хто він за ~ом?** What is he?; *L.* **у ~у.**

фахів|ець, *m.,* **~ця** expert, specialist, **з (із)** + *G.* in, **Вона провідний ф. з історії театру.** She is a leading expert in theater history.

фестива́л|ь, *m.,* **~ю** festival, **кінофестива́ль** film festival; *L.* **на ~і.**

фі́зик, *m.* physicist, **Вона́ вчи́ться на ~а.** She studies to be a physicist.

фі́зи|ка, *f., only sg.* physics; *L.* **у ~ці.**

філіжа́н|ка, *f.* cup, coffee-cup, **Дві ~ки ка́ви, будь ласка.** Two cups of coffee please.; *L.* **у ~ці,** *G. pl.* **~ок.**

фільм, *m.,* **~у** film, **худо́жній (докумен та́льний, короткометра́жний) ф.** feature (documentary, short) film; **зніма́ти (показувати) ф.** to shoot (screen) a film; *L.* **у ~і.**

фільму|ва́ти, **~ють;** **за~**, *tran.* to shoot a film, to film + *A.,* **Я хочу за~ всю на́шу подоро́ж.** I want to film our entire trip., **ф. кінокарти́ну (сце́ну, епізо́д, ви́ступ)** to shoot a film (scene, episode, performance).

фіоле́тов|ий, *adj.* violet, purple.

фоє́, *nt., indecl.* a lobby, **у вели́кому ф. готе́лю** in the large hotel lobby.

фортеп'я́н|о, *nt.,* **~а** piano, **гра́ти на ~і** to play the piano.

фо́т|о, *nt.,* **~а**, photo, picture, **Хто на цьо́му ~і?** Who is in this picture?, **Він приніс кілька фот.** He brought several photos. *Also see* **фотогра́фія** *and* **світли́на.**

фотоальбо́м, *m.,* **~у** photo album.

фото́граф, *m.* photographer.

фотогра́фі|я, *f.,* **~ї** photograph, **на ~ї** in the picture, **чорно-бі́ла ф.** black and white photo, **кольоро́ва ф.** color photo. *Also see* **світли́на.**

фотографу|ва́ти, **~ють;** **с~**, *tran.* to photograph, take a picture, **Він сфотографува́в нас.** He took a picture of us.; *pa. pple.* **сфотогра́фований** photographed; (**с**) **фотографу́й! ~те!**

Фра́нці|я, *f.* France, **у ~ї** in France, **до (із) ~ї** to (from) France.

францу́з, *m.* Frenchman, **Ґасто́н – мій знайо́мий ф.** Gaston is a Frenchman I know.

францу́з|ка, *f.* Frenchwoman; *L.* **на ~ці,** *G. pl.* **~ок.**

францу́зьк|ий, *adj.* French, **~а (мо́ва)** the French language.

фрукт, *m.,* **~а** a fruit, *N. pl.* **~и.,** **свіжі (заморо́жені) ~и** fresh (frozen) fruit.

фрукто́в|ий, *adj.,* fruit, **ф. сала́т (сік)** fruit salad (juice).

футбо́л, *m.,* **~у** soccer; **гра́ти у ф.** to play soccer, **америка́нський ф.** American football.

X

хай щасти́ть! *cliché* good luck! *var.* **неха́й щасти́ть!**

Ха́рк|ів, *m.,* **~ова** Kharkiv *(second largest city in Ukraine)*, **у ~ові** in Kharkiv, **до ~ова** to Kharkiv.

ха́рківськ|ий, *adj.* Kharkiv, pertaining to Kharkiv, **Х. університе́т** Kharkiv University.

харків'я́н|ин, *m.,* **~ина** citizen of Kharkiv; *N. pl.* **~и,** *G. pl.* **харків'я́н;** **~ка,** *f. L.* **на ~ці,** *G. pl.* **~ок.**

ха́т|а, *f.,* **~и** house, *colloq.* a home, **Я йду до ха́ти.** I am going home.; ♦ **у себе в ~і** at one's place; *L.* **у ~і,** *N. pl.* **ха́ти.**

хвили́н|а, *f.* minute; **одну́ ~у** just a moment; **за ~у** in a moment.

хвилю|ва́тися, **~ються,** *only impf., intr.* to be nervous, worry, be concerned, be anxious, **Ми завжди ~ємося перед виста́вою.** We are always nervous before the show.; **хвилю́|йся! ~йтеся!** *Also see* **журитися.**

хво́р|ий, *adj.* ill, sick, **Васи́ль почува́вся ~им.** Vasyl felt to be sick.; *n.* patient *(declines like adj.);* **~а,** *f.,* **Лі́кар рете́льно огля́нув ~у.** The physician gave the *(f.)* patient a thorough examination. *Also see* **пацієнт.**

хворі́ти, **~ють;** **за~,** *intr.* to be sick, **на** + *A.* **(за) хворі́й! ~те!** *Also see* **захворі́ти.**

хворо́б|а, *f.* illness, sickness, malaise, **невиліко́вна х.** incurable desease, **х. се́рця (ни́рок, шлу́нка)** heart (kidney, stomach) desease.; *G. pl.* **хворо́б.**

хіба́, *part.* 1) *(used in questions with negated predicate, corresponds to don't, doesn't, didn't, won't, shan't, haven't, etc.)* **Х. він не зна́є цього́?** Doesn't he know this?, **Х. Оля не каза́ла вам?** Hasn't Olia told you?; 2) *(used in general questions, implies disbelief or a negative answer),* **Х. тут мо́жна спа́ти?** Can one sleep here? *Also see* **чи.**

хі́мік, *m.* chemist, **Вона́ хо́че ста́ти ~ом.** She wants to become a chemist.

хі́мі|я, *f.* 1) chemistry, **Вона́ вивча́є ~ю.** She studies chemistry; 2) *fig.* **Між Олего́м й Ігорем не було́ нія́кої хі́мії.** There was no chemistry between Oleh and Ihor.

хліб, *m.,* **~а** bread, **буха́нка (ски́бка) ~а** loaf (slice) of bread.

хло́п|ець, *m.,* **~ця** 1) boy, guy, chap; 2) boyfriend, **Як зва́ти її́ хло́пця?** What's her boyfriend's name?; *V.* **~че** *(fam. form of address),* *N. pl.* **~ці.**

хма́рн|ий, *adj.* cloudy.

ход|и́ти, **~жу́, ~иш, ~ять,** *multi.,* 1) to go *(as to the movies),* **Ми ~имо до спортклу́бу три рази на ти́ждень.** We go to a fitness club three times a week.; 2) attend *(university, lecture),* **Я ~жу́ на всі заня́ття.** I attend all classes.; **ход|и́! ~іть!** *Also see* **uni. йти (іти́).**

хо́лод, *m.,* **~у** cold, **на ~і** in the cold.

холоди́льник, *m.,* **~а** refrigerator; *L.* **у ~у.**

холо́дн|ий, *adj.* cold, **~а пого́да** cold weather.

хо́лодно, *adv.* cold, **На дворі́ х.** It's cold outdoors.

хорово́|ий, *adj.* of choir singing and choral music.

хотíти, хо́ч|уть; за~, *tran. or inf.* to want, **Що ти хо́чеш робити на вихідні?** What do you want to do on the weekend?; ♦ **х. ї́сти (пити)** to be hungry (thirsty); *pa. pple.* **ба́жаний** desired, preferred; **(за)хоч! ~те!**

християн|ин *m.,* ~ина Christian; *N. pl.* ~и, *G. pl.* **християн**; ~ка, *f. L.* **на ~ці**, *G. pl.* **~ок.**

хто, *pron.,* к|ого́ who, **Х. там?** Who's there?, **До ~ого він зверта́вся?** Who did he turn to?, **З ~им ви ра́дилися?** Whom did you consult with?

хто-небудь, *pron.,* к|ого́-небудь somebody, someone, anybody, **Мо́жна з ~им-небудь прийти́.** You can come with anybody.

хтось, *pron.,* к|ого́сь somebody, someone, anybody, **Чи ви тут з ~имось знайо́мі?** Are you familiar with anybody here?; *D.* **~омусь**, *L.* **на ~омусь.**

худо́жн|ій, *adj.* art, artistic, **х. фільм** feature film, **х. музе́й** art museum, **~я літерату́ра** fiction literature.

худо́жник, *m.,* ~а artist, painter; *L.* **на ~ові.**

худо́жниця, *f.* artist, painter, **Оле́на дуже провокати́вна х.** Olena is a very provocative artist.

Ц

це, *dem. pron. nt.* 1) *see* **цей**; 2) this; it *(as in this is / was)*, **Це була́ моя́ поми́лка.** It was my mistake.

цей, *dem. pron., m.,* ц|ьо́го this, *f.* **ця**, *nt.* **це**, *pl.* **ці**, **Ц. рік шви́дко пройшо́в.** This year quickly passed.

цент|(е)р, *m.,* ~у center; *L.* **у ~рі.**

центра́льн|ий, *adj.* central, **ц. вокза́л** central station.

це́рк|ва, *f.,* ~ви church, **ходи́ти до ~ви** to go to church, **Андрі́ївська ц.** St. Andrew's Church; *N. pl.* ~и, *G. pl.* **~ов.**

цибу́л|я, *f., only sg.* onion, **сма́жена ц.** fried onion.

ц|і, *dem. pron. pl.,* ~их these, **ц. америка́нці** these Americans. *Also see* **цей.**

ціка́в|ий, *adj.* interesting, **Це ~а ду́мка.** This is an interesting thought.

цікави́н|ка, *f.* curious fact or thing, **тури́сти́чна ц.** tourist sight, **пока́зувати ~и міста** to show the sights of the city; *L.* **у ~ці**, *G. pl.* **~ок.**

ціка́в|ити, ~лю, ~иш, ~лять; за~, *tran.* to interest sb, **Історія дуже ціка́вить Петра́.** History interests Petro very much.; *pa. pple.* **заціка́влений** interested; **(за) ціка́в! ~те!**

ціка́в|итися, ~люся, ~ишся, ~ляться; за~, *intr.* to take interest, be interested + *I.* in sth, **Ірина ~иться літерату́рою.** Iryna is interested in literature.

ці́л|ий, *adj.* entire, whole, all, *(followed by n. in A. when denoting duration)*, **~у субо́ту** all Saturday long, **ц. рік** all year long.

цілко́м, *adv.* quite, completely, fully *(in affirmative sentences)*, **Я ц. погоджуюся.** I fully agree. *Cf.* **зовсім.**

цін|а́, *f.,* ~и price, **за яку́ ~у** at what price, **висо́кі ~и** high prices.

цуке́р|ка, *f.* candy, **Він лю́бить шокола́дні ~и.** He likes chocolate candies.; *L.* **у ~ці**, *N. pl.* **~ки**, *G. pl.* **~ок.**

цу́к|ор, *m., only sg.* ~ру sugar, **з ~ом** with sugar, **ча́йна ло́жка ~ру** teaspoon of sugar.

ц|я, *dem. pron., f.,* ~іє́ї this, **ц. жі́нка** this woman, **Він завжди́ подорожує з ~іє́ю лі́тньою осо́бою.** He always travels with this elderly person. *Also see* **цей.**

Ч

ча|й, *m.,* ~ю tea, **ч. з молоко́м** tea with milk, **міцни́й (слабки́й, чо́рний) ч.** strong (weak, black) tea, **ч. на тра́вах** herbal tea.

чарівн|и́й, *adj.* 1) charming, fascinating, **Він про́сто ~а люди́на.** He is simply a charming person.; 2) magic, ♦ **~а па́личка** magic wand.

час, *m.,* ~у time, **Я не ма́ю ~у на це.** I have no time for this., **Скі́льки ~у вам тре́ба?** How much time do you need?, **ч. від ~у** from time to time, **під ч.** + *G.* during.

ча́сом, *adv.* 1) sometimes, at times, **Ч. я дивлю́ся телеві́зор.** Sometimes I watch TV.; 2) by any chance *(in neg. questions)*, **Він ч. не з Терно́поля?** Is he from Ternopil by any chance?

части́н|а, *f.,* part, **виста́ва у двох ~ах** performance in two parts.

ча́сто, *adv.* often, frequently, **Він на́дто ч. хворі́є.** He is too often sick.; ♦ *fam.* **ч.-гу́сто** often.

чек, *m.,* ~а bank check, **ч. на** + *A.* check for, **Він ви́писав ч. на три́ста гри́вень.** He wrote out a check for three hundred hryvnias., **персона́льний ч.** personal check, **плати́ти ~ом** to pay by check.

чека́|ти, ~ють; по~, *tran.* to wait, **Я не люблю́ ч.** I don't like waiting., **Ми почека́ли тро́хи і пішли́.** We waited a while and left; **(по)чека́й! ~те!**

че́рв|ень, *m.,* ~ня June, **Він закі́нчує шко́лу дру́гого ~ня.** He finishes school on June 2.; *L.* **у ~і.**

червон|ий, *adj.* red, **~е вино́** red wine.

че́рез, *prep.* + *A.* 1) through, **ч. усю́ краї́ну** through the whole country; 2) because of, due to, **ч. пога́ну пого́ду** because of nasty weather; 3) after *(time)*, **ч. годину** in an hour.

четве́рт|ий, *ord.* fourth; **Зустрі́немося о ~ій годи́ні.** We'll meet at four o'clock.

чи 1) *conj.* or, *(expresses alternative of mutually exclusive options)*, **Це чолові́к ч. жі́нка?** Is it a man or a woman?, **за́раз ч. пі́зніше** now or later; *Cf.* **або́**; 2) *interr. part.* in yes / no-questions, **Ч. він тури́ст?** Is he a tourist?; 3) whether, **Він пита́є, ч. ви прийдете.** He's asking whether you'll come.

чи не так? *(lit.* Isn't it so?) *equivalent to Eng.* isn't it? don't you? won't they? etc., *asking for confirmation of what is stated,* **Ви з Нью-Йо́рка, ч.?** Your are from New York, aren't you?, **Він дзвони́в вам, ч.?** He called you, didn't he?

чиє́, *poss. pron., nt.* whose, **Ч. а́вто у гаражі́?** Whose car is the garage?

чи|й, *poss. pron., m.* whose, *f.* ~я, *nt.* ~є, *pl.* ~ї, **Ч. він друг?** Whose friend is he?

чиї́, *poss. pron., pl.* whose, **Ч. це ре́чі?** Whose things are these?

чис|ло́, *nt.*, ~ла́ 1) number, **ч. телефо́ну** phone number; 2) date *(of month)*, **Яке́ сього́дні ч.?** What date is it today?; **по па́рних (непа́рних) ~ла́х** on even (odd) dates; *N. pl.* ~а́, *G. pl.* ~ел.

чи́ст|ий, *adj.* 1) *(of air, water, etc.)* clean, ~і ру́ки clean hands; 2) *(of sky)* cloudless; 3) *(of page)* blank, ~а сторі́нка blank page.

чи́ст|ити, чи́щу, ~иш, ~ять; по~, *tran.* +*A.* to brush *(teeth, clothes, shoes)*, **Я чи́щу зу́би дві́чі на день.** I brush my teeth twice a day.; *pa. pple.* **почи́щений** cleaned, brushed; **(по)чи́сти! ~іть!**

чита́|ти, ~ють; про~, *tran.* to read, **ч. вго́лос (про себе)** read aloud (quietly); *pa. pple.* **прочи́таний** read; **(про)чита́й! ~те!**

чи|я́, *poss. pron.*, *f.* whose, **Ч. це газе́та?** Whose newspaper is it?

чо́в|ен, *m.*, ~на boat, rowing boat, **ката́тися на ~ні** to go boating; *I.* ~ном, *N. pl.* ~ни.

чого́, *pron. G. sg.* of **що** what; *adv. colloq.* why, **Ч. вони́ не прийшли́?** Why didn't they come? *Cf.* **чому́**.

чолові́к, *m.*, ~а 1) man, male; 2) husband, spouse; 3) *G. pl.* **чолові́к** persons of both genders, **У на́шій гру́пі сім ч.** There are seven people in our group.; *G. pl.* ~і́в men, husbands, **Скі́льки ~і́в і жіно́к працю́є тут?** How many men and women work here?; *N. pl.* ~и́.

чому́, *adv.* why, for what reason, **Ч. ви пита́єте?** Why are you asking? *Also see* **чого́**, **наві́що**, and **на́що**.

Чо́рн|е мо́р|е, *nt.* the Black Sea; *L.* **на ~ому ~і** at the Black Sea; *dir.* **на Ч. м.** to the Black Sea.

чо́рн|ий, *adj.* black; ♦ ~а невдя́чність rank ingratitude; ♦ *(of eye color)* ~і о́чі dark eyes.

чоти́р|и, *card.*, ~ьо́х + *N. pl.* four, **ч. америка́нці** four Americans.

чоти́риста, *card.*, **чотирьохста́** + *G. pl.* four hundred, **ч. сто́млених чолові́к** four hundred tired people.

чоти́рна́дцят|ь, *card.*, ~и + *G. pl.* fourteen, **ч. соло́дких я́блук** fourteen sweet apples.

чотирьохсо́т|ий, *ord.* four hundredth.

чудо́в|ий, *adj.* wonderful, great, delightful, **ч. день** a wonderful day, ~а іде́я a great idea.

чудо́во, *adv.* 1) wonderfully, superbly, **Ю́рій ч. співа́є.** Yuri is a superb singer. 2) perfectly, **Ми все ч. розумі́ємо.** We understand everything perfectly well.; *interj.* **ч.!** great!, wonderful!, super!

чуж|и́й, *adj.* foreign, ~а мо́ва (культу́ра) foreign language (culture).

чу́|ти, ~ють; по~, *tran.* to hear; **Ви мене́ до́бре ~єте?** Do you hear me well?, **Я ~в, що ви зна́єте цю кра́їну.** I heard that you know this country., **Він слу́хає мене́, але́ нічо́го не ~є.** He is listening to me but he does not hear anything.; *pa. pple.* **почу́тий** heard; **(по)чуй! ~те!**

Ш

шано́вн|ий, *adj.* esteemed, respected; **Ш. па́не (~а па́ні)** + *N.* of name or surname…   Dear Mr. (Mrs.) *(form of address in letters)*.

ша́ф|а, *f.* wardrobe, dresser.

шашли́|к, *m.*, ~а́ shish kebab; ♦ ~и́ barbecue, **роби́ти ~и́** to do a barbecue.

швидк|и́й, *adj.* fast, quick, swift; ♦ ~а́ (допомо́га) ambulance, **(по)дзвони́ти на ~у́** to call an ambulance. *Also see* **виклика́ти**; *comp.* **шви́дший.**

шви́дк|ість, *f.*, ~ості speed, velocity; ♦ **на вели́кій (ма́лій) ~ості** at high (low) speed; *I.* ~істю.

шви́дко, *adv.* fast, quickly, swiftly; ♦ **шви́дше за все** most probably (likely).

ши́н|ка, *f.* ham; *L.* **у ~ці**, *G. pl.* ~ок.

ши́р|окий, *adj.* wide, ~о́ка ву́лиця wide street; *comp.* ~ший.

ши|я́, *f.*, ~ї neck, **до́вга ш.** long neck; ♦ **по ~ю в борга́х** up to the ears in debt.

шістдеся́т, *card.*, ~ьо́х, *var.* ~и́ sixty + *G. pl.*, **ш. ціка́вих сторі́нок** sixty interesting pages.

шістна́дцят|ь, *card.*, ~ьо́х, *var.* ~и́ sixteen + *G. pl.*, **ш. холо́дних діб** sixteen cold days.

шістсо́т, *card.*, **шестисо́т** six hundred + *G. pl.*, **ш. є́вр** six hundred euros.

шість, *card.*, ~ьо́х, *var.* **шести́** six + *G. pl.*, **ш. вели́ких кімна́т** six large rooms.

шкір|а, *f.* 1) skin, **її ш. га́рно засма́гла.** Her skin is nicely suntanned.; 2) leather, **Він не купу́є нічо́го, зро́бленого зі ~и.** He doesn't buy anything made of leather.

шкло, *var.*, *colloq.*, *see* **скло**.

шкля́нка, *var.*, *colloq.*, *see* **скля́нка**.

шко́л|а, *f.* school *(usually elementary or high school)*, **сере́дня ш.** high school, **ви́ща ш.** school of higher learning; *L.* **у ~і.**

школя́р, *m.*, ~а́ schoolboy, high school student *(as opposed to college of university student)*; *N. pl.* ~і́; ~ка, *f.* *L.* **на ~ці**, *G. pl.* ~ок. *Cf.* **студе́нт**.

шлу́н|ок, *m.*, ~ка stomach *(digestive organ)*, **ро́злад ~а** indigestion; *L.* **у ~у.** *Cf.* **живі́т**.

шлюб, *m.*, ~у marriage; ♦ **вступа́ти в ш. з** + *I.* to marry sb.; **розі́рвати ш.** break up a marriage.

шо́ст|ий, *ord.*, ~ого sixth, **о ~ій годи́ні** at six o'clock.

штан|и́, *only pl.*, ~і́в. pants, trousers, **дво́є ~і́в** two pants; *D.* ~а́м *or* ~я́м, *I.* ~а́ми *or* ~я́ми *or* ~ьми́, *L.* **у ~а́х** *or* ~я́х.

шука́|ти, ~ють *impf.* to look for, search, seek; *pf.* **знайти́, знайд|у́ть** to find; *pa.* **знайшо́в, знайшли́**, **Де мо́жна знайти́ до́брий рестора́н?** Where can I find a good restaurant?, **Ми шука́ли готе́ль «Мазе́па» і наре́шті знайшли́.** We looked for the Mazepa Hotel and finally found it.; *pa. pple.* **зна́йдений** found; **шука́й! ~те!; знайди́! ~іть!**

Щ

щасли́в|ий, *adj.* happy; ♦ ~ої подоро́жі! Have a nice trip!

щáст|я, *nt.* happiness; ♦ **на щ.** luckily, fortunately; for good luck.

ще, *adv.* 1) still *(in affirmative statements)*, **Він щ. працює.** He is still working.; 2) more, **Нам треба щ.** We need more; 3) yet *(in negative sentences)*, **Він щ. не знáє.** He doesn't know yet.

щеня́, *nt.,* **~ти** a puppy; *N. pl.* **~та**, *I.* **~м.**

щíт|ка, *f.* brush; **зубнá щ.** toothbrush; *L.* **на ~ці**, *N. pl.* **~ки**, *G. pl.* **~ок.**

що, *pron.,* **чогó** what, **Щ. це (такé)?** What is it?; **Чогó там нема?** What is not there?

що~ *pref.* + *n.* in *G.* every, *forms adverbs of frequency when added to nouns denoting time periods,* **щохвилини** every minute, **щогодини** every hour, **щодня** every day, **щопонеділка** every Monday, etc.

щоб, *conj.* in order to, so as *(used to introduce infinitive of purpose,* **Щ. зробити це, треба багáто чáсу.** In order to do it we need a lot of time., **Він подзвонив, щ. запросити нас на лéкцію.** He called to invite us to the lecture.

щóйно, *adv.* just, just now, a moment ago, **Він щ. закінчив роботу.** He just finished work.

щок|á, *f.* a cheek; *N. pl.* **~и**, *G. pl.* **щік.**

що-нéбудь, *pron.,* **чогó-н.** something, anything, **Скажíть щ.!** Say something!

щось, *pron.,* **чогóсь** something, **Тебé щ. жýрить.** Something worries you.

Ю

юнáк, *m.,* **~á** young man, youth; *N. pl.* **~и.**

юнáч|ка, *f.* young woman; *L.* **на ~ці**; *G. pl.* **~ок.**

юри́ст, *m.* a lawyer, law expert; *f.* **~ка**, female lawyer; *L.* **на ~ці**, *G. pl.* **~ок.**

юш|ка, *f.* soup; broth; **кýряча ю.** chicken soup (broth); *L.* **у юшці**; *N. pl.* **~и**, *G. pl.* **~ок.** *Also see* **суп.**

Я

я, *pers. pron., 1ˢᵗ pers. sg.,* **менé**, **Я живý тут** I live here.

я́блук|о, *nt.* apple; ♦ **я. незгóди** apple of discord; *L.* **у ~ку.**

я́блучн|ий, *adj.* apple, **я. (пирíг) сік** apple (pie) juice.

яє́ш|ня, *f., var.* **яє́чня** fried eggs, omelet, **смáжити (пряжити) ~ю** make an omelet; *G. pl.* **~ень.**

я|йцé, *nt.,* **~йця́** an egg, **кýряче (качи́не, інди́че) я.** chicken (duck, turkey) egg; *N. pl.* **~йця**, *G. pl.* **~є́ць.**

як 1) *adv.,* how, **Я. ти це знáєш?** How do you know this?, **Я. це далекó?** How far is it?; 2) *conj.* than (in comparison) + *N.,* **Ці яблука смачнíші я. ті.** These apples are tastier than those ones.; **я. ..., так і ...** both ... and, **Я. він, так і його жíнка – лікарí.** Both he and his wife are physicians.; *colloq. var., see* **якщо**, **Я. хóчеш, я допоможý.** If you want I'll help.

як|á, *pron., f.,* **-óї** what, which, **Я. цікáва кни́жка!** What an interesting book!, **Я. з цих фотогрáфій крáща?** Which one of these photos is better?

якби́, *conj.* if (in hypothetical or unreal conditions), **Він допомíг би, я. його попроси́ли.** He would help if they asked him.

як|é, *pron., nt.,* **~óго** what, which, **Я. сьогóдні число?** What date is it today?

як|и́й, *pron. m.,* **~óго** what, which, **Я. сьогóдні день?** What day is it today?

як|и́й-нéбудь, *pron., m.* some, any; whatever, whichever, **Нас влаштýє я. путівни́к.** Any guidebook will do for us. *Also see* **будь-яки́й.**

яки́йсь, *pron. m.,* **якáсь** *f.,* **якéсь** *nt.,* **якíсь** *pl.* some, some kind of, **Їй дзвони́в я. добрóдій.** Some man called her.

як|í, *pron., pl.,* **~и́х** what, which, **Я. гáрні квíти!** What beautiful flowers! *Also see* **яки́й, яка́, якé.**

якщó, *conj.* if *(in real possible conditions),* **Я. бýде дощ, ми лиши́мося вдóма.** If it rains we'll stay home.

япóн|ець, *m.,* **~ця** a Japanese man.

Япóні|я, *f.* Japan, **Я нікóли не був у ~ї.** I have never been to Japan.

япóн|ка, *f.* a Japanese woman; *L.* **на ~ці**; *G. pl.* **~ок.**

япóнськ|ий, *adj.* Japanese, **Япóнське мóре** the Sea of Japan, **~а мóва** Japanese language.

я́рмар|ок, *m.,* **~ку** a fair, market; *L.* **на ~у.**

я́сн|ий, *adj.* 1) clear, understood, **Ситуáція цілкóм ~а.** The situation is quite clear.; 2) light, bright (of color); ♦ **~і зóрі й ти́хі вóди** the bright stars and the quiet waters *(a traditional reference to Ukraine and its yellow and azure national colors).*

я́сно, *adv.* 1) clear; **Менí стáло все я.** It all became clear to me; ♦ **Я.?** Do you understand? **Я., як Бóжий день.** Clear as a day; 2) light, bright (of color); **Їй подóбається я.-зелéний колір.** She likes a bright green color.

я́т|ка, *f.* a kiosk, stall, fruit-stand; *L.* **у ~ці**, *G. pl.* **~ок.**

English-Ukrainian Dictionary
Англо-українськи́й словни́к

A

a, *an article* either not translated or rendered by які́йсь, оди́н (certain, some, one); **An acquaintance told me that.** Оди́н (які́йсь) знайо́мий сказа́в мені́ це.

able, *adj.* зда́тний, спромо́жний; **to be a.** могти́ + *inf.,* вмі́ти + *inf.,* **He is a. to help us.** Він мо́же допомогти́ нам.

about, *prep.* 1) про, *colloq.* за + *A.,* **She told us a. the boy.** Вона́ розпові́дала нам про (за) цьо́го хло́пця.; 2) бі́ля, бли́зько, ко́ло + *G.,* **a. ten hryvnias** бі́ля десяти́ гри́вень; ♦ **it's a. time** давно́ пора́.

above, *prep.* над, пона́д + *I.,* **a. the first floor** над пе́ршим по́верхом.

abroad, *adv.* 1) *dir.* за кордо́н, **to go a.** ї́хати за кордо́н; 2) за кордо́ном, *posn.,* **live a.** жи́ти за кордо́ном.

absolutely, *adv.* 1) цілко́м, **It's a. correct.** Це цілко́м пра́вильно.; 2) пе́вна річ (*as emphatic* 'yes').

accident, *n.* ви́падок, ♦ **by a.** випадко́во, **He learned about her decision by a.** Він дізна́вся про її́ рі́шення випадко́во.

accept, *v.* 1) прийма́ти; прийня́ти + *A.,* **Do you a. credit cards?** Чи ви прийма́єте креди́тні ка́ртки?; 2) пого́джуватися; погоди́тися з + *I.,* **I cannot a. this.** Я не мо́жу погоди́тися з цим.

accommodation, *n.* житло́, поме́шкання, **Do you have a. in Lviv?** Чи ти ма́єш де жи́ти у Льво́ві?; **hotel a.** но́мер у готе́лі.

accountant, *n.* бухга́лтер.

accustom, *v.* ♦ **to get ~ed** звика́ти до + *G.,* призвича́юватися до + *G.,* **Maria quickly got ~ed to the new place.** Марі́я шви́дко зви́кла до но́вого мі́сця.

ache, *n.* біль, **toothache** зубни́й біль, **headache** головни́й біль; **I have a toothache (headache)** Мене́ боли́ть зуб (голова́).; *v.* болі́ти.

acquaintance, *n.* 1) (act) знайо́мство; **to make an a.** познайо́митися з + *I.;* 2) (person) *m.* знайо́мий, *f.* знайо́ма.

act, *v.* 1) ді́яти, **We need to a. immediately.** Тре́ба нега́йно ді́яти.; 2) (behave) пово́дитися, **They ~ed strange.** Вони́ ди́вно пово́дилися.; 3) (in film, on stage) гра́ти, **He will a. in the role of Hamlet.** Він гра́тиме у ро́лі Га́млета.; *n.* вчи́нок, **a. of heroism** герої́чний вчи́нок, **criminal a.** криміна́льний зло́чин.

actual, *adj.* ді́йсний, реа́льний **They paid for the house much less than its a. cost.** Вони́ заплати́ли за буди́нок значно́ ме́нше, ніж його́ ді́йсна ва́ртість.; ♦ **in a. fact** напра́вді, у ді́йсності.

actually, *adv.* у ді́йсності, напра́вді, у су́тності, факти́чно, **She is a. a very gifted person.** Напра́вді вона́ ду́же обдаро́вана осо́ба.

address, *n.* адре́са; **What's your a.?** Яка́ ва́ша адре́са?; *v.* зверта́тися до + *G.*

adult, *adj.* доро́слий, **a. ticket** доро́слий квито́к; (mature) зрі́лий; *n.* доро́слий, доро́сла люди́на.

advice, *n.* пора́да, **good a.** до́бра пора́да, **He came for a.** Він прийшо́в по пора́ду.; ♦ **to give a.** дава́ти пора́ду.

advise, *v.* 1) ра́дити + *D.,* **He ~d Roman to take a day off.** Він пора́див Рома́нові взя́ти вихідни́й.; 2) рекомендува́ти.

affair, *n.* спра́ва; ♦ **love a.** рома́н, любо́вні стосу́нки.

afraid, *adj.* **to be a.** боя́тися + *G.,* **He is a. of the water.** Він бої́ться води́.

after, *prep.* пі́сля + *G.,* **a. the rain** пі́сля дощу́; че́рез, за + *A.* **a. an hour** че́рез *or* за годи́ну.

afternoon, *n.* день, **good a.!** до́брий день!; по́лудень, **in the a.** пополу́дні.; **It was a.** Було́ пополу́дні.

afterwards, *adv.* по́тім, пото́му, тоді́, **You can do it a.** Ти мо́жеш зроби́ти це по́тім.

again, *adv.* зно́ву, знов; **do it a.** ще раз; ♦ **come a.!** повторі́ть! *or Gal.* прошу́!; **What was his name a.?** Як, ви каза́ли, його́ ім'я́?

against, *prep.* 1) про́ти + *G.,* **He is a. it.** Він про́ти цьо́го.; 2) об + *A.* **a. the wall** об сті́ну.

agency, *n.* аге́нція, аге́нтство, **tourist a.** туристи́чна аге́нція, **travel a.** аге́нція подоро́жей.

ago, *adv.,* тому́, **a week a.** ти́ждень тому́, **a long time a.** давно́ тому́.

agree, *v.* пого́джуватися; погоди́тися з + *I.;* **I (don't) a. with you.** Я (не) пого́джуюся з ва́ми.

agreeable, *adj.* 1) приє́мний, симпати́чний; 2) прийня́тний, **This is an a. offer.** Це прийня́тна пропози́ція.

air, *n.* пові́тря, **fresh a.** сві́же пові́тря, **by a.** літако́м; ♦ **in the open a.** про́сто не́ба.

airplane, *n.* літа́к, **by a.** літако́м, **to take an a. to** сіда́ти на літа́к до + *G.*

airport, *n.* лето́вище, аеропо́рт, **Boryspil International A.** Міжнаро́дне лето́вище «Бори́спіль».

all, *adj.,* ввесь *m., var.* уве́сь, вся, *f., var.* уся́; (everything) все, *nt., var.* усе, (everybody) всі, *pl., var.* усі; **It's a. the same to me.** Мені́ все одно́.; ♦ **a. along** весь час, **a. but** ма́йже, **a. in a.** взагалі́, **a. kinds of** рі́зного ро́ду, усіля́кі; **a. of a sudden** ра́птом, несподі́вано; **It's a. over.** Усе скі́нчено.; **a. together** всі ра́зом, всі гурто́м; **a. the way** до кінця́.

allergic, *adj.* алергі́чний, ♦ **to be a. to** ма́ти алергі́ю на + *A.,* **He's a. to nuts.** В ньо́го алергі́я на горі́хи.

allergy, *n.* алергі́я, **a. to** алергі́я на + *A.*

all right, *adv.* (agreement) до́бре, гара́зд, (permission) без проблем, **He can come a. r.** Він мо́же прийти́ без проблем; *adj.* у поря́дку, **Your plan is quite a. r.** Ваш план цілко́м у поря́дку.; **Are you a. r.?** Ти в поря́дку?

almost, *adv.* ма́йже, **We a. finished.** Ми ма́йже закі́нчили.

alone, *adj. m.* 1) сам, *f.* сама́, *nt.* са́ме, *pl.* самі́, **home a.** сам вдо́ма; **We can do it a.** Ми мо́жемо зроби́ти це самі́.; 2) самотні́й; **all a.** цілко́м самотні́й, сам-самі́сінький; **You are not a.** Ти не сам.

along

art

along, *prep. (street, city, square)* по + *L. or n.* in *l.*, **a. the street** по вулиці *or* вулицею; **He quickly walked a. the street.** Він швидко йшов вулицею.

already, *adv.* вже, *var.* уже, **Hanna has a. returned.** Ганна вже повернулася.

also, *adv.* також, *colloq.* теж, **We a. bought some vegetables.** Ми також купили городини.; ♦ **a. known as** також відоми|ий (~а) як.

although, *conj.* 1) хоч, *var.* хоча, **A. tired, Ivan continued working.** Іван продовжував працювати, хоча й був стомлений.; 2) незважаючи на те, що **.., They played tennis a. it was cold.** Вони грали в теніс, незважаючи на те, що було холодно.

always, *adv.* завжди, *colloq.* все, *var.* усе, **He a. works.** Він усе працює.; **as a.** як завжди.

a. m. 1) ночі *(from 12:00 to 4:00 am)*, **2:00 a. m.** друга *(година)* ночі; 2) ранку *(from 4:00 am to 12:00 pm)*, **11:00 a. м.** одинадцята *(година)* ранку.

ambulance, *n.* швидка допомога, *colloq.* швидка, **to call an a.** викликати швидку.

America, *n.* Америка, **in A.** в Америці, **to A.** до Америки, **United States of A.** Сполучені Штати Америки.

American, *adj.* американський, американська; *n., m.* американець, *f.* американка.

and, *conj.* 1) і (й), та *(for notions viewed as similar)*, **all boys a. girls** усі хлопці й (та) дівчата; 2) а, тоді як *(for notions viewed as opposed)*, **Boys play and girls sing.** Хлопці грають, а дівчата співають.

animal, *n.* тварина, **wild (domestic) a.** дика (домашня) тварина; *adj.* тваринний.

another, *adj.* інший, ще один, **This is a. matter.** Це інша справа.

answer, *n.* відповідь, **in a. to** у відповідь на + *A.*; *v.* відповідати, **to a. a question** відповідати на питання.

antibiotic, *n.* антибіотик, **to take ~s** приймати антибіотики.

any, *pron.* 1) будь-який, **You can borrow a. car.** Ви можете позичити будь-яке авто.; 2) *(in questions)* який-небудь, **Can you recommend a. good hotel here?** Чи ви можете порекомендувати який-небудь добрий готель тут?; 3) *(in negated statements)* ніякий, жодний, **We didn't see a. film.** Ми не бачили ніякого (жодного) фільму.; 4) *(in conditional clauses)* щось, якийсь, **I'll give you bread if we have a. left.** Я дам вам хліба, якщо щось лишилося *(or* якийсь*)*; 5) *(in impersonal sentences)* кожен, **A. fool can do that.** Кожен дурень може це зробити.; **a. time** будь-коли; **a. place** будь-де; **not just a.** не будь-який, не який-небудь.

anybody, *pron.* 1) будь-хто, хто-небудь, всяк(ий), **A. can do that.** Це може зробити будь-хто.; 2) *(in questions)* хтось, хто-небудь, **Will a. come?** Чи хтось (хто-небудь) прийде?; 3) *(in negated statements)* ніхто, **There wasn't a. in the room.** У кімнаті нікого не було.

anyhow, *pron.* 1) якось, так чи інакше, в кожнім разі, **A. we'll talk later.** Так чи інакше, ми розмовлятимемо пізніше.; 2) *(with negligence)* як-небудь, абияк, **She did the assignment a.** Вона зробила завдання абияк.; 3) *(in negated statements) (in no way)* ніяк, жодним чином, у жоден спосіб, **We couldn't agree with this a.** Ми з цим ніяк не могли погодитися.

anyone, *pron., see* **anybody.**

anything, *pron.* 1) будь-що, що-небудь, все що, **Tell me a. you like.** Скажи мені все, що хочеш.; 2) *(in questions)* щось, що-небудь, **Did you see a. interesting?** Чи ви бачили щось цікаве?; **a. at all** хоч щось, що-небудь взагалі; 3) ніщо, **I don't know a.** Я нічого не знаю.; ♦ **a. but** ніякий не, який же з (із) + *G.?* **He is a. but a scholar.** Він ніякий не вчений. *or* Який же з нього вчений?

anyway, *see* **anyhow.**

anywhere, *pron.,* 1) *posn.* скрізь, всюди, будь-де, де-небудь, **You can find this information a.** Цю інформацію можна знайти скрізь (будь-де).; 2) *dir.* куди-небудь, будь-куди, **I'd like to go a. that's warm.** Я хочу поїхати куди-небудь, де тепло. 3) *(in questions) posn.* десь, де-небудь, **Does he study a. now?** Чи він десь учиться зараз? *dir.* кудись, **Are they in a hurry a.?** Чи вони кудись поспішають?; 4) *(in negated statements) posn.* ніде, **She hasn't worked a. for a year.** Вона вже рік ніде не працює., *dir.* нікуди, **We are not going a. for the weekend.** Ми нікуди не їдемо на вихідні.

apartment, *n.* квартира, *Gal.* помешкання, **to rent an a.** наймати (винаймати) квартиру, **a. building** багатоквартирний будинок.

appetite, *n.* апетит, **poor a.** поганий апетит; ♦ **to have an a. for** мати апетит на + *A.*

apple, *n. (fruit)* яблуко; *adj.* 1) яблучний, **a. pie** яблучний пиріг; 2) *(of apple tree)* яблуневий.

approximately, *adv.* біля + *G.*, приблизно + *N.* **He spent a. two hundred dollars on food.** Він потратив біля двохста (приблизно двісті) доларів на їжу.

April, *n.* квітень, **in A.** у квітні; **He was born on A. 5.** Він народився п'ятого квітня.

architect, *n.* архітектор, **He is a famous a.** Він славетний архітектор.

architectural, *adj.* архітектурний, **a. design** архітектурний проєкт.

architecture, *n.* архітектура, **modern (old) a.** модерна (стара) архітектура.

arm, *n.* рука, **left (right) a.** ліва (права) рука, ♦ **with open ~s** з відкритими обіймами. *Also see* **hand.**

around, *prep.* 1) навколо + *G.* **a. the house** навколо будинку; 2) *(motion)* по + *L.*, **a. the country** по країні *or I.* **We drove a. the city for half a day.** Ми їздили містом цілий день.; 3) за + *I.*, **She left the car a. the corner.** Вона лишила авто за рогом.; 4) десь + *N.*, **a. three hours** десь три години.

around-the-clock, *adj.* цілодобовий, **This is an a. gas station.** Це цілодобова автозаправка.; *adv.* цілодобово, **We work a.** Ми працюємо цілодобово.

arrange, *v.* 1) влаштовувати + *A.*, **Don't worry I'll a. everything.** Не журіться, я все влаштую.; 2) домовлятися про *(or* за*)* + *A.*, **We need to a. for a meeting.** Нам треба домовитися про зустріч.

arrive, *v.* 1) приїжджати; приїхати *(car)*; 2) прибувати; приходити *(bus, train)*; **When will he a.?** Коли він прийде?

art, *n.* мистецтво; **folk a.** народне мистецтво; **modern a.** сучасне мистецтво; *adj.* художній, мистецький, **a. gallery** художня галерея, **a. collection** колекція мистецтва.

article, *n*. 1) стаття́, **newspaper a.** газе́тна стаття́; 2) предме́т, **~s of clothing** предме́ти о́дягу.

artist, *n*. худо́жник, маля́р, **Kazymir Malevych is an a.** Казимір Мале́вич – худо́жник.

as, *adv. (manner)* як; **He lives a. he wants.** Він живе́, як хо́че.; *conj.* 1) *(while)* в той час, як; тоді, коли; поки; **She was silent a. they discussed the matter.** Вона мовча́ла, поки вони обгово́рювали спра́ву.; 2) *(in capacity of) I. of noun*, **He works a. a waiter.** Він працю́є офіція́нтом.; 3) *(because)* бо, тому́, що, **We went inside the house a. it started raining.** Ми ввійшли́ до ха́ти, бо поча́в па́дати дощ.; **a. for** щодо + *G.*, .. то, що стосу́ється + *G.*, .. то, **A. for the letter, they never got it.** Щодо листа́, то вони його́ так і не отри́мали.; **a. if** ніби, нена́че, на́че, **I am so tired a. if I worked for three days.** Я такий стомлений, нена́че працюва́в три дні.; **such ... a.** такий як, **I like such cities a. Rome, Madrid, or New York.** Я люблю такі міста́, як Рим, Мадрид чи Нью-Йорк.

ask, *v*. 1) *(to pose a question)* пита́ти, *pf.* запита́ти (спита́ти), **He ~ed if she was all right.** Він запита́в, чи вона́ в поря́дку.; 2) *(to do sth)* проси́ти + *pf. inf. / A.*; попроси́ти, **They a. us to help them.** Вони про́сять нас допомогти́.

aspirin, *n*. аспіри́на, *var*. аспіри́н, **I usually take a. for a headache.** Я звича́йно п'ю аспіри́ну від головно́го бо́лю.

assignment, *n*. завда́ння, **home a.** дома́шнє завда́ння, **do a.** роби́ти *(викону́вати)* завда́ння.

assure, *v*. 1) запевня́ти + *A.*, у + *L.*, **They ~d Mykola of their good intentions.** Вони запевни́ли Миколу у свої́х до́брих на́мірах.; ♦ **I a. you that ...** запевня́ю тебе (вас), що ...; 2) гарантува́ти, **an ~d success** гаранто́ваний успіх; 3) упе́внюватися у + *L.*, **First he ~d that everybody was asleep.** Споча́тку він упе́внився, що всі сплять.

at, *prep.* 1) в (у), на + *L.*, **a. the bank** у ба́нку; 2) бі́ля + *G.*, **a. the door** бі́ля двере́й; 3) о (об) + *L. (time by the clock)* **a. nine o'clock** о дев'я́тій годи́ні.

athlete, *n.*, *m*. спортсме́н, *f*. спортсме́нка, **She is their best a.** Вона найкра́ща ї́хня спортсме́нка.

at home, *adv*. вдо́ма (удо́ма), *colloq.* до́ма, **We decided to stay a. h.** Ми вирі́шили лиши́тися вдо́ма.

at last наре́шті, **We have met a. l.** Ми наре́шті познайо́милися.

ATM *(automatic teller machine)* банкома́т, **to draw cash from an ATM** бра́ти готі́вку з банкома́ту.

at once, *adv*. нега́йно, за́раз же, **I'll call you a. o.** Я за́раз же подзвоню́ тобі.

attend, *v*. відві́дувати; відві́дати + *A.*, **She often ~s free lectures at the museum.** Вона ча́сто відві́дує безпла́тні ле́кції в музе́ї.

attention, *n*. ува́га, **to pay a.** зверта́ти; зверну́ти ува́гу.

auburn, *adj. (of hair color)* кашта́новий, **She has a. hair.** У не́ї кашта́нове воло́сся.

August, *n*. се́рпень, **in A.** у се́рпні, **on A. 1**, пе́ршого се́рпня.

aunt, *n*. ті́тка, **Mrs. Branson is their a.** Па́ні Бра́нсон – ї́хня ті́тка.

Austria, *n*. А́встрія, **The capital of A. is Vienna.** Столи́ця А́встрії – Ві́день.

Austrian, *adj*. австрі́йський, **A. embassy** австрі́йська амбаса́да; *n.*, *m*. австрі́єць, **He is an A. by nationality.** Він австрі́єць за громадя́нством.; *f*. **австрі́йка**.

authentic, *adj*. 1) спра́вжній, пито́мий, автенти́чний, **a. document** спра́вжній докуме́нт, **a. Ukrainian cuisine** пито́ма украї́нська ку́хня; 2) достові́рний, правди́вий, **a. data** правди́ві да́ні.

autumn, *n*. о́сінь, **in a.** восени́, **last a.** мину́лої о́сени, **this a.** ціє́ї о́сени; *adj*. осі́нній.

avenue, *n*. проспе́кт, *(in U.S.)* аве́ню, **on Fifth A.** на П'я́тій аве́ню.

Azov, Sea of *(an inland sea separated from the Black Sea by the Crimea)* Азо́вське мо́ре, **to the S. of A.** на Азо́вське мо́ре, **on the S. of A.** на Азо́вському мо́рі.

B

baby, *n*. дити́на, *pl.* ді́ти; **b. brother (sister)** моло́дший брат (моло́дша сестра́).

bachelor, *n*. 1) па́рубок, **He's been a b. all his life.** Він все своє́ життя́ був па́рубком.; 2) бакала́вр, **B. A.** сту́пінь бакала́вра, **Tania has a B. A.** Та́ня ма́є сту́пінь бакала́вра., **B. A. program** бакалавра́т.

back, *n*. спина́, **behind the b.** за спино́ю; *adv*. наза́д, *im.* **go b.!** наза́д!

bad, *adj*. 1) *(of poor quality)* ке́пський, пога́ний, **b. eyesight** ке́пський зір, **b. weather** пога́на пого́да; 2) *(of pain)* си́льний, **b. pain** си́льний біль.; 3) *(causing pain)* хво́рий, **b. knee** хво́ре колі́но.; **to feel b.** пога́но почува́ти себе́.; ♦ **to come to a b. end** пога́но закі́нчитися; ♦ **too b.** шко́да, **Too b. you couldn't come.** Шко́да, що ти не міг прийти́.

balcony, *n*. балко́н, **on a b.** на балко́ні, **There are flowers on their b.** У них на балко́ні кві́ти.

ballet, *n*. бале́т; **b. dancer**, *f*. балери́на, *m*. танцівни́к бале́ту; **b. company** бале́тна тру́па.

bandura, *n. (Ukrainian musical instrument)* банду́ра, **to play the b.** гра́ти на банду́рі, **b. player** банду́рист.

bank, *n*. 1) *(financial institution)* банк, **to have money in the b.** ма́ти гро́ші у ба́нку; 2) *(of river)* бе́рег, **left (right) b.** лі́вий (пра́вий) бе́рег, **Right B. (Left B.) Ukraine** Правобере́жна (Лівобере́жна) Украї́на.

banker, *n*. банкі́р, **to be a b.** бу́ти банкі́ром, **to work as a b.** працюва́ти банкі́ром.

bar, *n*. бар, **in a b.** у ба́рі.

barbecue, *n*. 1) *(as a party)* шашлики́, **to do a b.** роби́ти шашлики́; 2) *(way of cooking)* ґриль, **~d** на ґри́лі, **~d sausages (chicken)** ковба́ски (курча́) на ґри́лі.; *v*. ґрилюва́ти, сма́жити на ґри́лі.

basketball, *n*. баскетбо́л, *Gal.* кошикі́вка.

bathe, *v*. 1) *tran.* купа́ти + *A.*, **It's time to b. the baby.** Вже час купа́ти дити́ну.; 2) *intr.* купа́тися, **He likes to b.** Він лю́бить купа́тися.

bathroom, *n*. 1) ва́нна; ва́нна кімна́та, **You can use the b. on the second floor.** Ви мо́жете користува́тися ва́нною *(кімна́тою)* на дру́гому по́версі.; 2) туале́т, **public b.** грома́дський туале́т; **Where's the b.?** Де тут туале́т?, **May I use your b.?** Чи мо́жна до туале́ту?

bazaar blood

bazaar, *n.* база́р, я́рмарок, **We like to go to the b.** Ми лю́бимо ходи́ти на база́р.

be, *v.* 1) бу́ти, *pres.* є *(for all persons, or usually omitted)*; *fut.* бу́дуть; *pa., m.* був, *f.* була́, *nt.* було́, *pl.* були́; **He wants to b. with us.** Він хо́че бу́ти з на́ми.; ♦ **to b. or not to b.?** бу́ти чи не бу́ти?; ♦ **to b. honest** якщо че́сно то .., **To b. honest ... I like his plan.** Якщо че́сно, то мені́ подо́бається його́ план.; 2) побува́ти у + *L.*, **They have just been to Kosiv.** Вони́ що́йно побува́ли у Ко́сові.; відві́дувати + *A.*, бува́ти у + *L.*, **Have you ever been to Koktebel?** Чи ви бува́ли (були́) коли́-небудь у Коктебе́лі?; ♦ **to b. about to** ма́ти от-от + *inf.*, **The film was a. to begin.** Фільм мав от-от поча́тися.; **to b. away** бу́ти у від'ї́зді, **Robert will b. away till Monday.** Ро́берт бу́де у від'ї́зді до понеді́лка.; **to b. back** поверта́тися, **He is already back from work.** Він уже́ пове́рнувся з пра́ці.; **to b. in** 1) бу́ти вдо́ма *(на мі́сці)*, **Is she in?** Вона́ вдо́ма?, **Call her office and find out if she is in.** Подзвони́ до її́ о́фісу та дізна́йся, чи вона́ на мі́сці.; 2) *(to be in fashion)* бу́ти в мо́ді, **Orange will always b. in.** Помара́нчевий ко́лір за́вжди бу́де в мо́ді.; **to b. off** 1) йти, піти́, **He can't wait to b. off.** Він не мо́же дочека́тися, щоб піти́ собі́.; 2) бу́ти ви́мкненим (зга́шеним), **All the lights are off.** Сві́тло скрізь зга́шено.; **to b. on** бу́ти уві́мкненим (запа́леним), **The computer was on.** Комп'ю́тер був уві́мкненим.; **to b. out** 1) не бу́ти вдо́ма (на мі́сці), **Ivanna is out.** Іва́нни нема́є вдо́ма (на мі́сці).; 2) *(of lights)* га́снути, **Suddenly the light was out.** Ра́птом сві́тло пога́сло.; **to b. over** закі́нчуватися, **When will this lecture b. finally over?** Коли́ ця ле́кція наре́шті закі́нчиться?; **to b. up** прокида́тися, буди́тися, встава́ти, **I am usually up at six.** Я звича́йно встаю́ о шо́стій.

beach, *n.* пляж, **on a b.** на пля́жі, **to go to a b.** ї́здити на пляж.

beautiful, *adj.* 1) га́рний, **b. landscape** га́рний краєви́д, прекра́сний, **He speaks b. Ukrainian.** Він розмовля́є прекра́сною украї́нською. 2) *(person)* вродли́вий, **b. woman** вродли́ва жі́нка.

beauty, *n.* краса́; *(human)* вро́да, **She is a person of rare b.** Вона́ люди́на рідкі́сної вро́ди.

because, *conj.* 1) тому́ що, *colloq.* бо, **I ask b. I need to know.** Я пита́ю, тому́ що мені́ тре́ба зна́ти.; 2) **b. of** че́рез + *A.*, **B. of nasty weather we did not go to the concert.** Че́рез пога́ну пого́ду ми не пішли́ на конце́рт.

become, *v.* 1) става́ти; ста́ти + *I.*, **He wants to b. a film director.** Він хо́че ста́ти кінорежисе́ром.; 2) пасува́ти + *D.*, личи́ти + *D.*, **This color ~s Tamara.** Цей ко́лір пасу́є (личи́ть) Тама́рі.

bed, *n.* лі́жко, **b. linen** пості́льна білизна́; **to go to b.** ляга́ти спа́ти; **make a b.** застеля́ти лі́жко.

bedroom, *n.* спа́льня; **b. community** спа́льна дільни́ця (райо́н).

before, *prep.* 1) пе́ред + *I.* **b. classes** пе́ред заня́ттями; 2) до + *I.*, **We need to do it b. the trip.** Нам тре́ба зроби́ти це до подоро́жі.; *conj.* перш(е), ніж, **Wash your hands b. cooking dinner.** Поми́йте ру́ки перш, ніж вари́ти вече́рю.; пе́ред тим, як, **They called b. coming here.** Вони́ подзвони́ли, пе́ред тим, як прийти́ сюди́.; *adv.* 1) рані́ше, до цьо́го (того́), **I have never done it b.** Я ніко́ли рані́ше не роби́в цьо́го., **Vasyl was a baker b.** До то́го Васи́ль був пека́рем.

begin, *v.* 1) *tran.* почина́ти; поча́ти + *impf. inf.*, **We b. classes next week.** Ми почина́ємо заня́ття насту́пного ти́жня., **Professor began explaining.** Профе́сор поча́в поя́снювати.; 2) *refl.* почина́тися; поча́тися, **The semester already began.** Семе́ст(е)р уже́ поча́вся.

beginning, *n.* поча́ток, **at the b.** на поча́тку, **from b. to end** від поча́тку до кінця́.

behind, *prep.* 1) за + *I.*, **b. the wall** за стіно́ю; 2) зза́ду + *G.*, **b. the building** зза́ду буди́нку; 3) *(in support of sb)* з + *I.*, ра́зом з + *I.* **I will b. you.** Я бу́ду (ра́зом) з тобо́ю.; 4) *(after departure or death of sb)* пі́сля + *G.* **She left b. her a wonderful book.** Вона́ лиши́ла пі́сля себе́ чудо́ву кни́жку.; *adv.* **to be b.** запі́знюватися, **They are b. with the payment again.** Вони́ зно́ву запі́знюються із опла́тою; відстава́ти на + *A.*, **We are ten days b.** Ми відстає́мо на де́сять днів; **from b.** зза́ду.

Belarus, *n.* Білору́сь, **in B.** у Білору́сі, **to B.** до Білору́си.

Belarusian, *n.* 1) *(national of Belarus) m.* білору́с, *f.* білору́ска; 2) *(language)* білору́ська мо́ва; *adj.* білору́ський.

believe, *v.* ві́рити + *D.*, **I b. you.** Я ві́рю вам.; пові́рити + *D. or* + *A.*, **I could not b. it.** Я не міг цьо́му (*or* у це) пові́рити.; ♦ **b. it or not** хоч вір, хоч ні.

beside, *prep.* 1) бі́ля + *G.*, **The chair is b. the table.** Стіле́ць стої́ть бі́ля стола́; 2) крім, *var.* окрім + *G.*, **B. Kyiv we visited Odesa.** Крім Ки́єва ми побува́ли в Оде́сі.; ♦ **to be b. oneself with anger (worry, joy)** бу́ти лю́тим (занепоко́єним, щасли́вим) до нестя́ми, **He is b. himself with anger.** Він лю́тий до нестя́ми.; ♦ **to be b. the point** не стосува́тися спра́ви, **This is completely b. the point.** Це геть не стосу́ється спра́ви.

besides, *prep.* крім, *var.* окрім + *G.*, **She has no family b. her brother.** Вона́ не ма́є ро́дичів крім бра́та.; *adv.* крім того́, до того́ ж, у дода́ток.

best, *adj.* найкра́щий, *Gal.* найлі́пший; ♦ **b. of all** найкра́щий за всіх (все); **b. film award** приз за найкра́щий фільм.

better *adj.* кра́щий, *Gal.* лі́пший, **my plan is b.** мій план кра́щий; *adv.* кра́ще, *Gal.* лі́пше, **b. not do it** кра́ще не роби́ти цьо́го.

between, *prep.* між + *I.*, **This is strictly b. us.** Це стро́го між на́ми.

bicycle, *n.* велосипе́д; **by b.** велосипе́дом.

big, *adj. (in size)* вели́кий; *(elder)* ста́рший; *(adult)* доро́слий; ♦ **b. bucks** вели́кі (*also* грубі́) гро́ші.

billion, *n.* мілья́рд + *G. pl.*, **ten b. hryvnias** де́сять мілья́рдів гри́вень.

bird, *n.* птах, пта́шка.

birth, *n.* наро́дження, **date (place) of b.** да́та (мі́сце) наро́дження.

birthday, *n.* уроди́ни *(pl.)*, день наро́дження; ♦ **Happy b.!** Многая лі́та!

bitter, *adj.* гірки́й, ♦ **b. cold** соба́чий хо́лод, **The apple tasted b.** Я́блуко було́ гірки́м на смак.

black, *adj.* чо́рний, **b. coffee** чо́рна ка́ва, **b. humor** чо́рний гу́мор, **b. mood** гане́бний на́стрій.

block, *n.* кварта́л, **Walk three ~s and turn left.** Пройді́ть три кварта́ли й поверні́ть ліво́руч.; ♦ **He has been around the b. a few times.** Він не вчо́ра народи́вся.

blood, *n.* кров, **high (low) b. pressure** висо́кий (низьки́й) тиск кро́ви.

blue

blue, *adj.* 1) синій, **sky b.** блакитний, **light b.** ясно-синій; 2) *(sad)* сумний.

boat, *n.* 1) *(with oars)* човен, **motor b.** моторний човен; **by b.** човном; 2) *(ship)* корабель, судно, **fishing b.** рибальське судно.

bon appétit, ♦ смачного!

book, *n.*, книжка, книга; *v.* замовляти, замовити, **to b. a ticket** замовити квиток.

bookstore, *n.* книгарня.

boring, *adj.* нудний, нецікавий, **What a b. book!** Що за нудна книжка!

born, *pa. pple.* народжений; ♦ **to be b.** народитися.

borshch, *n.* борщ, **red (green, meatless) b.**, червоний (зелений, пісний) борщ, **to cook (serve) b.** варити (подавати) борщ.

both, *pron., m.* 1) обидва + *N. pl.*, **b. students** обидва студенти; *f.* обидві + *N. pl*, **b. girls** обидві дівчини.; 2) і той, і інший; один з другим; **b. ... and ...** як .., так і ...; **b. my dad and mom** як тато, так і мама.

bottle, *n.* пляшка, **a b. of milk** пляшка молока.

boulevard, *n.* бульвар + *G. of name*, **Shevchenko b.** бульвар Шевченка.

box, *n.* коробка, **b. of candies** коробка цукерок.

boy, *n.* 1) хлопець, **Who is this b.?** Що це за хлопець? 2) (son) син.

boyfriend, *n.* хлопець, **Meet Yarema, my b.** Знайомтеся, це Ярема, мій хлопець.

bread, *n.* хліб, **loaf of b.** буханка хліба, **slice of b.** скибка хліба.

break, *n.* 1) перерва, **during the b.** під час перерви; 2) розрив, **b. with the past** розрив з минулим; **Christmas b.** Різдвяні вакації *(at school)*, Різдвяна відпустка *(at work)*; *v., refl.* 1) ламатися, **The car broke down.** Авто зламалося.; 2) *(of a mechanism)* псуватися, **The clock broke, can you fix it?** Годинник зіпсувався, ти можеш відремонтувати його?; 3) *(of wire, rope, relationship)* рватися, **The connection often ~s.** Зв'язок часто рветься.; *tran.* 4) ламати, **He broke his arm.** Він зламав собі руку.; 5) псувати, **I broke the washing machine.** Я зіпсував пральну машину.; 6) рвати, **We broke contact two years ago.** Ми порвали контакти два роки тому.

breakfast, *n.* сніданок, **for b.** на сніданок, **to have b.** снідати.

bring, *v.* 1) *(on foot)* приносити + *A.*, **He always ~s flowers home.** Він завжди приносить додому квіти.; 2) *(by a vehicle)* привозити + *A.*, **What did she b. from Chernivtsi?** Що вона привезла з Чернівців?

broad, *adj.* широкий, **b. plan** загальний план; ♦ **in b. daylight** серед білої днини.

bronchitis, *n.* бронхіт, **chronic (severe) b.** хронічний (гострий) бронхіт, **She has had b. for a week.** У неї вже тиждень бронхіт.

broth, *n.* юшка, бульйон, *Gal.* росіл, **She never uses concentrates to make b.** Вона ніколи не користується концентратом щоб варити юшку.

brother, *n.* брат, **elder (younger) b.** старший (молодший) брат, **Твій старший б. Олег виявляється добрим оповідачем.** Your elder brother Oleh turns out to be a good storyteller.; ♦ *excl.* **oh b.!** ой, людоньки! *or* ой, леле!

brother-in-law, *n.* швагер.

brown, *adj.* 1) брунатний, коричневий, **Він любить носити костюми ~ого кольору.** He likes to wear suits of brown color.; 2) *(eyes)* карий, **b. eyes** карі очі; **light b. hair** русе волосся; 3) *(suntanned)* засмаглий, **b. face** засмагле обличчя.

brush, *n.* 1) щітка, **tooth b.** зубна щітка; 2) **paint b.** пензель; *v.* чистити, **He ~es his teeth twice a day.** Він чистить зуби двічі на день.

buckwheat, *n.* гречка; *adj.* гречаний.

build, *v.* будувати, **They want to b. their own house.** Вони хочуть збудувати власний будинок.

building, *n.* 1) будинок, корпус *(of university)*, **This is the only old b. on the street.** Це єдиний старий будинок на вулиці.; 2) *(process of construction)* будівництво, **The b. of the bridge will end next week.** Будівництво мосту закінчиться наступного тижня.

burn, *v.,* 1) *intr.* горіти, **Stone does not b.** Камінь не горить; 2) *tran.* палити, **He ~ed all documents.** Він спалив усі документи.; 3) *refl. (burn oneself)* опікатися, отримувати опік; *n.* опік, **severe b.** сильний опік.

bus, *n.* автобус, **b. station** автостанція, *(big)* автовокзал, **b. stop** автобусна зупинка, **b. ticket** квиток на автобус; **to take a b.** сідати на автобус.

business, *n.* бізнес, справа, **I am here on b.** Я тут у справах; **do b. with sb** вести справи з + *I.*; ♦ **He means b.** Він не жартує.; ♦ **mind your own b.!** не пхай носа до чужого проса!; ♦ **none of your b.** не твоя справа; *adj.* діловий, **b. trip** відрядження, ділова поїздка.

businessman, *n.* бізнесмен.

businesswoman, *n.* бізнесменка, **Jane is a real b. now.** Тепер Джейн справжня бізнесменка.

busy, *adj.* зайнятий, **I was b. all day.** Я був зайнятий цілий день., **The line is b.** Телефон зайнятий.

but, *conj.* 1) *(however)* але, проте, **He will help, b. not today.** Він допоможе, але не сьогодні.; 2) *(in contrast)* а, **not ... b. ...** не .., а ..., **It was not my brother b. me.** Це був не брат, а я.; 3) зате, проте, **Maria is small b. Oksana is tall.** Марія низька, зате Оксана висока.; *(to express surprise, anger, etc.)* але, **b. why!** але чому!

butter, *n.* масло, **b. milk** маслянка, сколотини, **fresh b.** свіже масло, **peanut b.** арахісове масло.

buy, *v.* купувати + *A.*, **To b. a bicycle one needs money.** Щоб купити велосипед треба гроші.

buyer, *n.* покупець, **I need to find a b. for the house.** Мені треба знайти покупця на хату.

C

cabbage, *n.* капуста, **c. rolls** голубці *(Ukr. national dish)*, **c. salad** салат із капусти.

café, *n.* кав'ярня, кафе, *Gal.* кавярня, **This is our favorite c.** Це наша улюблена кав'ярня.

café

call, *v.* 1) *(cry out)* кли́кати, **He is ~ing you**. Він вас кли́че.; ♦ **be ~ed** зва́тися, назива́тися; 2) *(by phone)* дзвони́ти; **Can you c. me later?** Мо́жеш подзвони́ти мені́ пізні́ше?; 3) *(give a name)* назива́ти + *A.* + *I.*, **They ~ed their son Ivan**. Вони́ назва́ли си́на Іва́ном.; 4) *(to address)* назива́ти + *A.* + *I.*, **Please c. me Sashko.** Будь ла́ска, називайте мене́ Са́шком.; 5) *(fig. consider)* вважа́ти + *A.* + *I.*, раху́вати + *A.* + за + *A.*, **I'd like to c. him a friend.** Я хоті́в би вважа́ти його́ дру́гом.; 6) *intr. (to visit)* заходити до + *G.*, приходити, **We'll c. around tomorrow.** Ми зайде́мо за́втра.; 6) **c. for** *(on foot)* захо́дити по + *A.*, *(by vehicle)* заїжджа́ти по + *A.*, **C. for us around 7 o'clock.** Зайді́ть (заїдьте) по нас бі́ля сьо́мої годи́ни.; 7) **c. off** скасо́вувати, **We ~ed the meeting off.** Ми скасува́ли зустрі́ч.; **c. attention to** зверта́ти ува́гу на + *A.*; ♦ **c. a spade a spade** назива́ти ре́чі свої́ми імена́ми; *n.* 1) *(phone c.)* дзвіно́к; 2) *(appeal)* за́клик до + *G.*, **c. for action** за́клик до ді́ї; 3) *(vocation)* поклика́ння.

camera, *n.* *(for still pictures)* фотоапара́т; *(for movies)* кінока́мера.

can, *mod. v.* могти́, вмі́ти; **I c. do it.** Я мо́жу це зроби́ти.; **He c. read Italian.** Він вмі́є чита́ти італі́йською.; **cannot but ...** не могти́ не + *inf.*, **I cannot but think of him.** Я не мо́жу не ду́мати про ньо́го.

Canada, *n.* Кана́да, **in C.** у Кана́ді, **to C.** до Кана́ди.

Canadian, *n., m.* кана́дець, *var.* канаді́єць; *f.* кана́дка, *var.* канаді́йка; *adj.* кана́дський, *var.* канаді́йський.

cancel, *v.* відміня́ти, **I am not going to c. the party because of the weather.** Я не ду́маю відміня́ти вечі́рку че́рез пого́ду.; 2) скасо́вувати, **We need to c. our hotel reservation right away.** Тре́ба нега́йно скасува́ти на́ше замо́влення в готе́лі.; 3) анульо́вувати, **He called the bank to c. the check.** Він подзвони́в до ба́нку, щоб анулюва́ти чек.

candy, *n.* цуке́рка, **These candies are delicious.** Ці цуке́рки смачні́.

capital, *n.* 1) *(city)* столи́ця, **Kyiv is the c. of Ukraine.** Ки́їв – столи́ця Украї́ни.; 2) *(wealth)* капіта́л; 3) *(letter)* вели́ка лі́тера, **This word is written in capitals.** Це сло́во тре́ба писа́ти з вели́кої лі́тери.

car, *n.* 1) *(automobile)* автомобі́ль, а́вто, маши́на, *colloq.* авті́вка; **by c.** автомобі́лем, а́втом; **c. wash** автоми́йка; **drive a c.** ї́здити а́втом; 2) *(train)* ваго́н, **sleeping c.** спа́льний ваго́н.

card, *n.* 1) ка́ртка, листі́вка, **birthday c.** листі́вка на день наро́дження; **business c.** візи́тівка; **credit c.** креди́тна ка́ртка; 2) *(playing card)* ка́рта, **deck of ~s** коло́да карт; **play ~s** гра́ти у ка́рти.

Carpathians, the, *n., pl.* Карпа́ти, **in the C.** у Карпа́тах, **to the C.** до Карпа́т.

carpet, *n.* ки́лим; *fig.* **red c.** урочи́ста зу́стріч.

carry, *v.* *(on foot) multi.* носи́ти, **He likes to c. money in his pocket.** Він лю́бить носи́ти гро́ші в кише́ні.; *uni.* нести́, **What is it you are ~ing?** Що це ти несе́ш?; **c. on** продо́вжувати.

cash *n.* готі́вка, **pay in c.** плати́ти готі́вкою; **c. desk** ка́са; *v.* *(cash a check)* огрошевля́ти, **I'll c. the check as soon as possible.** Я огрошевлю́ чек якнайшви́дше.

cashier, *n.* каси́р.

cash-register, *n.* ка́са.

cat, *n., m.* кіт, *f.* кі́шка.

catch, *v.* 1) *(intercept)* лови́ти + *A.*, **A cat caught a mouse.** Кіт злови́в ми́шу.; 2) *(seize)* хапа́ти, **He caught her by the arm.** Він схопи́в її́ за ру́ку; 3) *(bus, train)* встига́ти на + *A.*, сіда́ти на + *A.*, **Pavlo needs to c. an evening train.** Павло́ві тре́ба встигну́ти на вечі́рній по́їзд.; 4) **c. a cold** перестуди́тися, **He caught a nasty cold.** Він ду́же перестуди́вся.

cathedral, *n.* собо́р, *Gal.* кате́дра, **St. Sophia C.** Софі́йський Собо́р.

celebrate, *v.* святкува́ти; від~ + *A.*, **to c. an anniversary (jubilee)** святкува́ти річни́цю (ювіле́й).

cell phone, *n.* мобі́льний (телефо́н), *colloq.* мобі́лка; стільнико́вий (телефо́н).

cent, *n.* цент.

center, *n.* центр, *var.* це́нтер, **in the c.** у це́нтрі, **city c.** середмі́стя.

central, *adj.* центра́льний, **c. station** центра́льний вокза́л.

certain, *adj.* 1) упе́внений, **to be c. of** sth бу́ти впе́вненим у + *L.*; 2) *(some)* пе́вний, оди́н, яки́йсь.

certainly, *adv.* звича́йно, зві́сно, пе́вна річ.

chain, *n.* 1) ланцю́г, **c. of gold** золоти́й ланцюжо́к; 2) *(of restaurants or stores)* мере́жа, **supermarket c.** мере́жа супермаркетів.

chair, *n.* 1) стіле́ць, крі́сло, **There were three ~s in the room.** В кімна́ті було́ три сті́льці.; 2) *(chair person)* голова́, **He was the committee c.** Він був голово́ю коміте́ту.; 3) *(professorship) m.* заві́дувач *or f.* заві́дувачка ка́федрою.

chance, *n.* 1) шанс, *often in pl.*, **He has a good c. to find a job here.** Він ма́є до́брі ша́нси знайти́ тут пра́цю.; 2) ви́падок, **by c.** випадко́во, ♦ **by any c.** ча́сом не .., бува́ не..., **Do you speak Ukrainian by any c.?** Ви ча́сом не розмовля́єте украї́нською.; 3) *(opportunity)* можли́вість, наго́да, **Give me a c. to explain.** Да́йте мені́ наго́ду поясни́ти.; ♦ **no c.** жо́дних ша́нсів.

change, *n.* 1) змі́на *(of weather, etc.)*; 2) зда́ча, **small c.** дрі́б'язок; *v.* 1) *tran.* міня́ти + *A.*, зміню́вати + *A.*, **Can we c. the date of departure?** Ми мо́жемо зміни́ти да́ту від'ї́зду?; 2) *tran. (trains, buses, planes)* переса́дати, **We c. in Paris.** Ми переса́даємо у Пари́жі.; 3) *refl.* міня́тися, зміню́ватися, **He hasn't ~ed at all.** Він зо́всім не зміни́вся.

cheap *adj.* 1) деше́вий, **I found a c. apartment.** Я знайшо́в деше́ву кварти́ру.; 2) *(stingy)* скупи́й, **He is too c. to buy her a present.** Він надто скупи́й, щоб купи́ти їй подару́нок.; ♦ **cheapskate** скна́ра.

check, *v.* перевіря́ти; **Did you c. the car?** Ти переві́рив а́вто?, **to c. into** *(at hotel)* поселя́тися до + *G.*; **c. out** *(of hotel)* виселя́тися з + *G.*, **You are to c. out by noon.** Ви ма́єте ви́селитися до полу́дня.; *n.* чек, **personal c.** персона́льний чек.

cheek, *n.* щока́, **rosy ~s** рожеві що́ки.

cheese, *n.* сир *or* тверди́й сир; **cottage c.** сир.

chemist, *n.* хі́мік, *var.* хе́мік, **He studies to be a c.** Він вчи́ться на хі́міка.

chemistry, *n.* хі́мія, *var.* хе́мія, **His major is c.** Він спеціалізу́ється із хі́мії.

cherry *n.* 1) *(sour)* вишня; 2) *(sweet)* черешня; 3) *(tree)* вишня, черешня; *adj. (sour)* вишневий, **c. juice** вишневий сік.

chicken, *n.* 1) курка; 2) *(young)* курча; 3) *(meat)* курятина; **c. Kyiv** котлета по-київськи; *adj.* курячий, **c. meat** куряче м'ясо, **c. soup** куряча юшка.

child, *n.* дитина, дитя, *pl.* діти, **Whose c. is it?** Чия це дитина?, **from a c.** з дитинства; ♦ **with c.** вагітна.

China, *n.* Китай, **in C.** у Китаї, **to C.** до Китаю.

Chinese, *n., m.* китаєць, *f.* китайка; *adj.* китайський.

choice, *n.* вибір, **good (wide) c.** добрий (широкий) вибір, **I have no c.** Я не маю вибору; **of one's c.** за власним вибором.

choose, *v.* 1) вибирати + *A.*, **She always ~s the wine.** Вона завжди вибирає вино.; ♦ **There's little to c. from.** Тут нема з чого вибирати.; 2) *(decide)* вирішувати, **We chose to stay home.** Ми вирішили лишитися вдома.

Christmas *n.* Різдво, **a Merry C.!** Веселого Різдва!, *relig. cliché* Христос рождається!; *colloq.* Коляди; *adj.* різдвяний, **C. break (holidays)** різдвяні вакації (свята).

church, *n.* церква; **to go to c.** ходити до церкви.

cinema, *n.* 1) *(industry)* кінематограф, **Ukrainian c.** український кінематограф; 2) *(movie theater)* кінотеатр, *var. colloq.* кіно.

citizen, *n., m.* громадянин, *f.* громадянка.

city, *n.* місто, **c. center** середмістя, цент(е)р міста, **c. hall** міська рада.

class, *n.* 1) клас, *var.* кляса, **all ~es of society** всі класи суспільства; **high c. service** обслуговування високого класу; 2) *(in school)* заняття, **We were late for c.** Ми спізнилися на заняття.; 3) *(course in discipline)* курс, **Last year she took a c. in art history.** Минулого року вона слухала курс з історії мистецтва.

clean, *v.* 1) *(house)* прибирати (tidy up), **We c. the apartment every Saturday.** Ми прибираємо квартиру щосуботи.; 2) *(teeth, clothes)* чистити, **I need to c. the suit.** Мені треба почистити костюм.; 3) *(person)* мити, **They ~ed him up for the surgery.** Його помили для операції.; *adj.* 1) чистий, **c. shirt** чиста сорочка; 2) *(of person)* охайний, **He is always so c.** Він завжди такий охайний.

clear, *adj.* 1) ясний, **It's quite c. that …** Цілком ясно, що ...; 2) *(water, glass)* прозорий, **clean and c. water** чиста і прозора вода.; ♦ **c. as day** ясно як білий день; *v.* 1) *tran. (of objects)* очищувати, **We ~ed the garden of leaves.** Ми очистили сад від листя.

climate, *n.* клімат, підсоння, **temperate c.** помірний клімат.

clock, *n.* годинник, **around the c.** цілодобово, без перерви; **by the c.** за годинником; **~wise** за годинниковою стрілкою; **counterclockwise** проти годинникової стрілки.

close, *v. tran.* закривати, зачиняти; **C. the window, please.** Закрийте вікно, будь ласка.; 2) *intr.* закриватися, зачинятися, **Watch out, the doors are ~ing!** Обережно, двері зачиняються!; *adj.* близький; **c. (friend) relative** близький (приятель) родич; *adv.* близько (від) + *G.*, неподалік (від) + *G.*, **He lives c. to the sea.** Він живе неподалік від моря.

clothes, *n.* одяг, **summer (winter) c.** літній (зимовий) одяг, **We need to buy some winter c.** Треба купити щось із зимового одягу.

coast, *n.* берег, узбережжя, **on the sea c.** на березі моря.

coat, *n.* пальто, **warm c.** тепле пальто, **fur c.** шуба.

coffee, *n.* кава, **strong (black) c.** міцна (чорна) кава; **c. with milk** кава з молоком.

cold, *adj.* холодний, **It's c. outside.** Надворі холодно.; ♦ **as c. as ice** холодний як крига; *Gal.* зимний, **c. look** зимний погляд; *n.* 1) холод, **winter c.** зимовий холод; 2) *(ailment)* перестуда, **to catch a (bad) c.** (дуже) перестудитися.

colleague, *n.* колеґа, **Mykola is my good c.** Микола – мій добрий колеґа.

collect, *v.* 1) збирати + *A.*, **Jane ~ed the students' essays.** Джейн зібрала студентські есеї.; 2) *(art, stamps, etc.)* збирати + *A.*, колекціонувати, **She ~s old postcards.** Вона збирає (колекціонує) старі поштівки.

collection, *n.* збірка, колекція, **c. of poetry (prose)** збірка поезії (прози), **art c.** збірка мистецтва, **a large Ukrainian art c.** велика збірка українського мистецтва.

collector, *n.* колекціонер, **art c.** колекціонер мистецтва.

color, *n.* 1) колір, **He likes bright ~s.** Йому подобаються яскраві кольори; 2) *(often in pl.)* барва; *adj.* кольоровий, **a c. picture** кольорова фотографія; *v.* фарбувати; **c. sth green** фарбувати у зелений колір.

come, *v.* 1) *(on foot or of a taxi, bus or train)* приходити, **He came for dinner.** Він прийшов на вечерю.; **Has the bus already c.?** Автобус уже прийшов (приїхав)?; 2) *(by vehicle)* приїжджати, **Our guests are ~ing from Paris.** Наші гості приїжджають із Парижа.; 3) *(of event, day)* наставати, **Summer has c.** Настало літо.; 4) *(be available or sold)* бувати; **Butterflies c. big and small.** Метелики бувають великі й малі.; ♦ **c. again?** як? *or* що ви сказали?; ♦ **c. what may** що би не сталося; ♦ **how c.** як це так, що …, **How c. she did it alone?** Як це так, що вона зробила це сама?; **c. across** натрапляти на + *A.*, знаходити + *A.*, **We always c. across something new in his novels.** Ми завжди натрапляємо на (*or* знаходимо) щось нове в його романах.; **c. down with** захворіти на + *A.*, **He came down with a flu.** Він захворів на грип.; **c. from** походити з + *G.*, **She ~s from an old Kyivan family.** Вона походить із старої київської родини.; ♦ **c. on!** *(encouragement)* нумо! *or* давай!; **c. out** 1) *(become known)* виявлятися, **It ~s out that she has never been to Yalta.** Виявляється, вона ніколи не бувала в Ялті.; 2) *(to result) intr.* виходити з + *G.*, **Nothing good will c. out of it.** З цього нічого доброго не вийде.; 3) *(be released)* виходити, **The magazine ~s out once a week.** Журнал виходить раз на тиждень.

comfortable *adj.* 1) *(physically)* зручний, **c. chair** зручне крісло; 2) *(mentally)* затишний, **c. room** затишна кімната.

common, *adj.* 1) спільний, загальний; **c. people** прості люди; **c. sense** здоровий глузд; 2) *(typical)* типовий, поширений, **This is a c. Ukrainian name.** Це типове українське ім'я.

company, *n.* 1) компанія, **motor c.** автомобільна компанія; 2) товариство; 3) *(theater)* трупа. **The theater has an entirely new c.** Театр має цілком нову трупу.

compartment

compartment, *n., indecl.* купе́, **car c.** купе́ ваго́ну, **cozy (comfortable) c.** зати́шне (комфо́ртне) купе́, **third-class c.** плацка́ртне купе́.

complete, *adj.* 1) по́вний, **Here's a c. list.** Ось по́вний спи́сок.; 2) цілкови́тий, **c. surprise** цілкови́та несподі́ванка. *v., tran.* закі́нчувати; **He just ~d his studies.** Він що́йно закі́нчив навча́ння.

completely, *adv.* цілко́м, **I am c. calm.** Я цілко́м споко́йний.; геть **He has c. aged.** Він геть поста́рів.

complicated, *adj.* складни́й, важки́й, **c. problem** складна́ пробле́ма.

complication, *n.* усклад́нення, **Cough is a typical c. after a flu.** Ка́шель - це типо́ве усклад́нення пі́сля гри́пу.

compliment, *n.* комплі́мент, ♦ **to pay a c.** роби́ти + *D.* комплі́мент, **He always pays his wife ~s.** Він за́вжди ро́бить жі́нці комплі́менти.; ♦ **to fish for ~s** набива́тися на комплі́менти.

computer, *n.* комп'ю́тер, **PC** персона́льний комп'ю́тер.; *adj.* комп'ю́терний, **c. network** комп'ю́терна мере́жа, **c. virus** комп'ю́терний ві́рус.

comrade, *n.* това́риш, прия́тель.

concern, *v.* **to be ~ed** жури́тися, **don't be ~ed** *sg.* не жури́ся; *pl.* не журі́ться; **as far as ... is ~ed** що стосу́ється + *G.*, то ..., **As far as the lecture is ~ed I won't be able to come.** Що стосу́ється ле́кції, то я не змо́жу прийти́.

concerning, *prep.* щодо́ + *G.*, **c. your request** щодо́ ва́шого проха́ння.

concert, *n.* конце́рт, *posn.* **at a c.** на конце́рті; *dir.* **to a c.** на конце́рт.

conference, *n.* конфере́нція, **international c.** міжнаро́дна конфере́нція, **to come for a c.** приї́хати на конфере́нцію.

congratulate, *v.* віта́ти, поздоровля́ти.

consider, *v.* 1) вважа́ти, **I c. him too young.** Я вважа́ю, що він на́дто молоди́й; 2) розгляда́ти *(an offer)*, **We'll c. your idea.** Ми розгля́немо ва́шу іде́ю.

considerable, *adj.* значни́й, помі́тний.

considerably, *adv.* значно́, помі́тно, **I feel c. better.** Мені́ значно́ кра́ще.

consist, *v.* 1) **c. of** склада́тися з + *G.*, **Our journey ~s of three parts.** На́ша по́дорож склада́ється із трьох части́н.; 2) **c. in** поляга́ти в + *L.* **Our help ~s in giving them advice.** На́ша допомо́га поляга́є в то́му, щоб ра́дити їм.

consult, *v.* 1) (seek advice) ра́дитися з + *I.*, консульту́ватися з + *I.*, **You should c. a physician.** Вам тре́ба пора́дитися (проконсульту́ватися) із лі́карем.; 2) *(a dictionary)* переві́рити + *A.* за словнико́м, **I ~ed the word in a dictionary.** Я переві́рив це сло́во за словнико́м.

contemporary, *adj.* суча́сний, **c. society** суча́сне суспі́льство; *n., m.* суча́сник, *f.* суча́сниця, **She was Shevchenko's c.** Вона́ була́ суча́сницею Шевче́нка.

continue, *v.* 1) *tran.* продо́вжувати, **He ~ed to speak for another half hour.** Він продо́вжував говори́ти ще пів годи́ни.; 2) *intr.* трива́ти, **The film ~ed for two hours.** Фільм трива́в дві годи́ни.

court

contrary, *adj.* протиле́жний, **I am of a c. opinion.** Я протиле́жної ду́мки.; **on the c.** навпаки́, **c. to** усу́переч + *D.*, **C. to our plans we were four hours late.** Усу́переч на́шим пла́нам ми спізни́лися на чоти́ри годи́ни.

convenient, *adj.* зручни́й, **We met at a mutually c. time.** Ми зустрі́лися у взає́мно зручни́й час.; **to be c.** влашто́вувати + *A.*, **I hope the place is c. for you.** Сподіва́юся, що це мі́сце вас влашто́вує.

conversation, *n.* розмо́ва, **I had an interesting c. with my colleague.** Я мав ціка́ву розмо́ву із коле́гою.

cook, *v.* 1) *tran.* вари́ти, готува́ти + *A.*, **I can teach you to c. borshch.** Я мо́жу навчи́ти вас вари́ти борщ.; 2) *intr.* вари́тися, **What's that ~ing?** Що це там ва́риться? *n., m.* ку́хар, *f.* куха́рка.

cool, *adj.* 1) прохоло́дний, **The morning was c.** Ра́нок був прохоло́дним; 2) *(reserved)* стри́маний, **He was polite and c.** Він був че́мним і стри́маним.; 3) *(hip)* кла́сний, **She is a c. girl.** Вона́ кла́сна ді́вчина.; ♦ **C.!** Чудо́во! *or* Су́пер!

copeck, *n.* копі́йка, **One hryvnia consists of a hundred ~s.** Одна́ гри́вня склада́ється зі ста копі́йок.; **one c.**, одна́ копі́йка, **two (three, four) ~s.** дві (три, чоти́ри) копі́йки, **five (and more) ~s** п'ять копі́йок.

corner, *n.* 1) *(of room)* куто́к, **in a c.** у кутку́; 2) *(of street, table)* ріг, **We are supposed to meet on this street c.** Ми ма́ємо зустрі́тися на цьо́му ро́зі ву́лиці.

correct, *v.* виправля́ти; **to c. a mistake** ви́правити поми́лку; *(adjust)* корегува́ти; *adj.* 1) пра́вильний, **c. answer** пра́вильна ві́дповідь; 2) *(proper)* коре́ктний, **He is always so c.** Він за́вжди таки́й коре́ктний.; **politically c.** полі́тично коре́ктний.

correctly *adv.* пра́вильно.

correspond, *v.* 1) *(write letters)* листува́тися, **We ~ed for two years.** Ми листува́лися два ро́ки.; 2) *(to match)* відповіда́ти + *D.*, **Ukrainian letters on the keyboard mostly c. to Latin.** Украї́нські лі́тери на кляв́іятурі здебі́льшого відповіда́ють лати́нським.

corridor, *n.* коридо́р.

Cossack, *n.* коза́к; *adj.* коза́цький.

cost, *v.* кошту́вати + *A.*, **The postcard ~s one hryvnia.** Ли́стівка кошту́є одну́ гри́вню.; **How much does it c.?** Скі́льки це кошту́є?

count, *v.* рахува́ти, **He ~ed up his money.** Він порахува́в гро́ші.; **c. to** + *G.* рахува́ти до, **C. to ten.** Порахуй до десяти́.; **c. for** кошту́вати, ва́жити, **His opinion ~s for a lot.** Його́ ду́мка бага́то ва́жить.; **c. on** покла́датися на + *A.*, розрахо́вувати на + *A.*, **You can c. on me.** Ви мо́жете покла́датися на ме́не; *n.* лік, раху́нок.

country, *n.* краї́на; ♦ **this c.** на́ша краї́на, **in this c.** у на́шій краї́ні *or* у нас в краї́ні; *(provinces)* село́, **in the c.** на селі́. **I grew up in the country.** Я ви́ріс на селі́.

couple, *n.* па́ра + *G. pl.*, **a c. of days** па́ра днів, **a married c.** подру́жжя.

course, *n.*, курс, **Ukrainian literature c.** курс з украї́нської літерату́ри; **c. of treatment** курс лікува́ння; ♦ **of c.** звича́йно, пе́вна річ.

court, *n.* 1) *(of law)* суд, **go to c.** зверта́тися до су́ду; 2) *(royal)* двір.

courtyard, *n.* двір, подвір'я, **in the c.** у дворі, на подвір'ї, **There was an old linden in our. c.** У нашому дворі росла стара липа.

cousin, *n.* двоюрідний брат, кузин; *f.* двоюрідна сестра, кузина.

cow, *n.* корова; ♦ **till the ~s come home** до третіх півнів.

Crimea, the, *n. (peninsula washed by the Black Sea)* Крим, **in the C.** у Криму, **to the C.** до Криму.

Crimean, *adj.* кримський.

cross, *v., tran.* 1) *(traverse)* пересікати; 2) *(on foot)* переходити + *A.*, **We need to c. the street.** Треба перейти (*or* пересікти) вулицю; 3) *(by car)* переїжджати, **We ~ed the whole country.** Ми переїхали (*or* пересікли) всю країну; 4) *(by boat)* перепливати, **It's impossible to c. the river here.** Тут неможливо перепливти (*or* пересікти) річку; 5) *(by plane)* перелітати; 6) *intr.* перехрещуватися, пересікатися; **All roads c. in Kyiv.** Всі дороги перехрещуються у Києві.; *n.* 1) хрест, **He wears a golden c. on his neck.** Він носить золотий хрест на шиї.; 2) *(a mark)* хрестик, **In place of signature he put a c.** Замість підпису він поставив хрестик.; *adj.* сердитий, **to be c. with sb** сердитися на + *A.*, гніватися на + *A.*, **Are you still c. with him?** Ви ще гніваєтеся на нього?

cry, *v.* 1) *(weep)* плакати, **to c. tears of joy** плакати від щастя; 2) *(shout)* кричати, **He cried for help.** Він кричав по допомогу.; *n.* крик, **c. for help** крик по допомогу.

cucumber, *n.* огірок, **c. salad** салат з огірків.

cuisine, *n.* кухня, **Ukrainian c.** українська кухня.

culture, *n.* культура, **pop-c.** поп-культура, **folk c.** народна культура.

cup, *n.* 1) чашка, філіжанка; 2) *(in sports)* кубок; **World C.** кубок світу.

cupboard, *n.* шафка, буфет, мисник, **kitchen c.** кухонна шафка.

currency, *n.* валюта, **c. exchange** обмін валюти, **c. rate** курс валюти; **Where can one change c.?** Де можна поміняти валюту?

customer, *n.* клієнт, **c. service** обслуговування клієнтів.

cut, *v.* 1) різати, **I c. my finger.** Я порізав собі пальця.; 2) *(slice)* краяти, нарізати, **He c. some bread and cheese.** Він накраяв (нарізав) хліба і сиру.; 3) **c. off** відрізати, відтинати, 4) **c. out** вирізати, витинати, **I c. this photo out of a newspaper.** Я вирізав цю світлину із газети.; 5) *(reduce)* скорочувати, зменшувати, **We need to c. the rent.** Нам треба скоротити (зменшити) плату за житло.; 6) *(stop)* зупиняти, припиняти, **The company c. the sales of its products.** Компанія зупиняє (припинила) продаж своїх продуктів.; ♦ **c. a deal** домовлятися, **They finally c. a deal.** Вони нарешті домовилися.; **c. sb/sth short** перебити, **He c. me short.** Він перебив мене.; *n.* поріз, **a bad c.** сильний поріз.

D

dad, *n.* тато, **Their d. gave them the money.** Їхній тато дав їм гроші.

daily *adj.* щоденний, **d. news** щоденні новини; **d. life** побут; *n. (newspaper)* щоденна газета, щоденник; *adv.* щодня, кожного дня.

dairy *n. (produce)* молокопродукти, молочні продукти; *adj.* молочний, **d. store** молочна крамниця, **d. department** молочний відділ.

dance, *n.* 1) танець, **My favorite d. is salsa.** Мій улюблений танець - сальса.; 2) *(social event)* only *pl.* танці, **They met at a d.** Вони познайомилися на танцях.; *v.* танцювати, **He likes to d. the tango.** Він любить танцювати танго.

dark, *adj.* 1) темний, **d. night** темна ніч; 2) *(of eyes)* чорний, **d. eyes** чорні очі, **He has d. eyes** У нього чорні очі.; 3) *(of skin)* смаглявий; 4) *(in compound colors)* темно-..., **d. blue (red)** темно-синій (темно-червоний); 5) *(evil)* чорний, **d. deeds** чорні справи; *n.* 1) темрява, **in the d.** у темряві; 2) *(nightfall)* смерк, присмерк, **We need to be back before the d.** Нам треба повернутися до смерку.

date, *n.* 1) дата, **d. of birth (death)** дата народження (смерти), **d. of arrival (departure)** дата приїзду (від'їзду); 2) число, **What d. is it today?** Яке сьогодні число?; 3) побачення, **I have a d. with him.** Я маю з ним побачення.; ♦ **to d.** до сих пір; *v.* 1) датувати, **This painting is hard to d.** Цю картину тяжко датувати.; 2) *(mark the date)* ставити дату у + *L.*, **He forgot to d. the letter.** Він забув поставити дату у листі.; 3) *(go out with)* зустрічатися з + *I.* **He have ~d her one month.** Він зустрічався з нею місяць.

daughter, *n.* дочка, *(affectionate or informal)* донька.

daughter-in-law, *n.* невістка.

day, *n.* день, **all d.** весь день, **all d. long** цілісінький день; **the d. after tomorrow** післязавтра, **the d. before yesterday** позавчора, **d. and night** цілодобово; **d. off** вихідний день; **every d.** щодня, **from d. one** із самого початку; **one (some) d.** колись, одного дня; **to this d.** до сих пір, до сьогоднішнього дня; **week d.** будній день; **working d.** робочий день; **They work a seven-hour d.** У них семигодинний робочий день.

deal, *n.*, **a great d. of** багато + *G.*; **It's a deal!** Домовилися!

dear, *adj.* 1) любий, дорогий; **d. friends!** любі друзі!; 2) *(expensive)* дорогий, **This gift is too d. I can't accept it.** Цей подарунок надто дорогий, я не можу прийняти його.

death, *n.* смерть, **natural (premature, sudden, violent) d.** природна (передчасна, нагла, насильницька смерть); ♦ **to die a natural d.** померти своєю смертю.

debt, *n.* борг, заборгованість; **to return a d.** повертати борг.

December, *n.* грудень, **in D.** у грудні, **He is supposed to arrive on D. 5.** Він має приїхати п'ятого грудня.

decide, *v.*, *tran.* *A. or inf.* вирішувати, *fam.* надумати, **He ~d to give her a call.** Він вирішив (*fam.* надумав) подзвонити їй.

deep, *adj.* 1) глибокий, **This river is d.** Ця річка глибока.; 2) *(to indicate depth)* завглибшки, **The pit is three meters d.** Яма три метри завглибшки.

delete, *v.* стирати; **I ~d the whole message.** Я стер все повідомлення.

deliberate   **door**

deliberate, *adj.* 1) (*done on purpose*) навми́сний; 2) (*careful*) рете́льний.

deliberately, *adv.* (*intentionally*) навми́сно, **He did it d.** Він зроби́в це навми́сно.

delicious, *adj.* смачни́й, до́брий.

delight, *n.* захо́пле́ння, прие́мність, **with d.** із захо́пленням; *v.* захо́плювати, викли́кати захо́плення у + *G.*; ♦ **I'd be ~ed** Із вели́кою приє́мністю.

delightful, *adj.* чудо́вий, захо́пливий, захо́плюючий.

dentist, *n.* зубни́й лі́кар, данти́ст.

depart, *v.* 1) (*of bus, train*) відхо́дити, відбува́ти; **The train ~s in five minutes.** По́їзд відхо́дить за п'ять хвили́н. 2) від'їжджа́ти, **We d. in a hour.** Ми від'їжджа́ємо за годи́ну.; 3) (*deviate*) відхо́дити від + *G.*, відхиля́тися від + *G.*, **He ~ed from the subject of the discussion.** Він відійшо́в (відхили́вся) від те́ми диску́сії.

department, *n.* 1) ві́дділ, **dairy d.** моло́чний ві́дділ, **d. store** універма́г; 2) (*at university*) факульте́т, **D. of Ukrainian Language** факульте́т украї́нської мо́ви; 3) *colloq.* (*area of expertise*) пара́фія, **Fashion is not my d.** Мо́да – не моя́ пара́фія.

departure, *n.* (*train*) від'їзд, **day of d.** день від'їзду; (*plane*) відлі́т, *Gal.* відле́т, **The d. of our flight (bus, train) was delayed.** Відлі́т на́шого ре́йсу відкла́ли.

describe, *v.* опи́сувати, **He ~d the man in detail.** Він дета́льно описа́в цього́ чолові́ка.

description, *n.* о́пис, **detailed d.** докла́дний о́пис.

desk, *n.* пи́сьмо́вий стіл, *Gal.* б'ю́рко; **a pupil's d.** па́рта.

Desna, *n.* (*left tributary of the Dnipro*) Десна́, **on the D.** на Десні́, **along the D.** Десно́ю *or* по Десні́.

dial, *v.* (*a number*) набира́ти но́мер; ♦ **You've ~ed the wrong number.** Ви набра́ли неправи́льний но́мер.; **d. sb up** набира́ти + *A.*

diarrhea, *n.* проно́с, *colloq.* швидка́ На́стя.

dictionary, *n.* словни́к, **English-Ukrainian d.** а́нгло-украї́нський словни́к.

die, *v.* умира́ти, помира́ти на + *A.*, **He ~d of cancer.** Він поме́р на рак(а).

difference, *n.* рі́зниця, відмі́нність.

different, *adj.* 1) (*unlike*) і́нший, іна́кший, **It's a d. matter.** Це і́нша спра́ва.; відмі́нний, **My plan is d. from theirs.** Мій план відмі́нний від їхнього.; 2) (*distinct*) окре́мий, **Those were two d. groups of people.** Це були́ дві окре́мі гру́пи люде́й.; **in d. ways** по-рі́зному; ♦ **to be d. from** відрізня́тися від + *G.*

differently, *adv.* іна́кше, по-і́ншому, і́ншим чи́ном, **We need to do it d.** Нам тре́ба зроби́ти це іна́кше.

difficult, *adj.* важки́й, тяжки́й, складни́й, **It's a d. matter.** Це складна́ спра́ва.

dine, *v.* вече́ряти; **d. out** вече́ряти в рестора́ні (*in restaurant*) *or* вече́ряти в гостя́х (*at sb's home*).

dining room, *n.* їда́льня, віта́льня.

dinner, *n.* вече́ря, **for d.** на вече́рю; **to have d.** вече́ряти.

direct, *adj.* прями́й, **d. train (flight, bus)** *all translated as* прями́й рейс.

director, *n.* 1) дире́ктор, керівни́к; 2) (*film*) режисе́р, кінорежисе́р.

dirt, *n.* бруд, грязь.

dirty, *adj.* брудни́й, гря́зний; ♦ **d. play** брудна́ (*нечесна*) гра.

discount, *n.* зни́жка, **at a (great) d.** за (вели́кою) зни́жкою, **to offer ~s for** пропонува́ти зни́жки на + *A.*; *v.* знижувати ці́ну; *adj.* **~ed price** зни́жена ці́на.

discuss, *v.* обгово́рювати, дискутува́ти, **We already ~ed this.** Ми вже обгово́рювали це.

discussion, *n.* диску́сія, обгово́рення.

dish, *n.* 1) *fig.* стра́ва, **first d.** пе́рша стра́ва; **for the first d.** на пе́ршу (стра́ву); 2) (*plate*) тарі́лка; **to wash the ~es** ми́ти по́суд.

distance, *n.* ві́дстань, диста́нція.

Dnipro, *n.* (*main river in Ukraine*) Дніпро́, **on the D.** на Дніпрі́, **along the D.** Дніпро́м *or* по Дніпру́.

do, *v.* 1) *tran.* роби́ти, **What are you ~ing here?** Що ти тут ро́биш? ♦ **Well done!** молоде́ць!; 2) *intr.* працюва́ти, **What does he do (for a living)?** Ким він працю́є?; ♦ **That will d.** До́сить.; 3) *intr.* **d. away with** покінчи́ти з + *I.*, **We quickly did away with the problem.** Ми шви́дко покінчи́ли із ціє́ю пробле́мою.; **d. without** обходи́тися, **I can't d. without some help.** Я не мо́жу обійти́ся без допомо́ги.; 4) (*auxiliary verb in general questions*) чи; хіба́ (*expresses incredulity*) **D. you smoke?** Чи ви па́лите?, **Did he see it?** Чи він ба́чив це?; 5) (*tags in all disjunctive questions*) чи не так? *or* пра́вда ж?, **You live in Kyiv, don't you?** Ви живете́ в Ки́єві, чи не так? (пра́вда ж?); **She told you, didn't she?** Вона́ сказа́ла вам, чи не так? 6) (*for emphasis*) справді, ді́йсно, таки́, **He ~es speak Italian.** Він справді (ді́йсно, таки́) гово́рить італі́йською.; 7) (*in positive imperative*) та … вже, ж … вже, ну́мо, **D. show me!** Та покажи́ вже мені́! *or* Покажи́ ж мені́ вже! *or* Ну́мо, покажи́ мені́!; ♦ **have … to d. with** ма́ти відно́шення до + *G.*, **We have nothing to d. with this matter.** Ми не ма́ємо нія́кого відно́шення до ціє́ї спра́ви.; ♦ **it isn't done …** не випада́є *or* не прийня́то, **It isn't done to come without a present to a birthday party.** Не випада́є (не прийня́то) прихо́дити без подару́нка на день наро́дження.; ♦ **it won't do** з цього́ нічого́ не ви́йде; ♦ **no, you don't!** на́віть не ду́май(те)!; ♦ **That ~es it.** Це вже зана́дто.

doctor, *n.* 1) (*physician*) лі́кар, **I need to see a d.** Мені́ тре́ба до лі́каря.; 2) (*title*) до́ктор, **He is not Mr. but Dr. Khanenko now.** Він тепе́р не пан, а до́ктор Ха́ненко.

dog, *n.* пес, соба́ка; ♦ **d.'s life** соба́ча до́ля; **to go to the ~s** сходи́ти на пси.

dollar, *n.* до́лар, **to exchange ~s for hryvnias** міня́ти до́лари на гри́вні.; *adj.* до́ларовий, **d. exchange rate** курс до́лара.

Donbas, *n.* Донба́с (*region of southeastern Ukraine comprising modern Donetsk and Luhansk provinces*), **to D.** на Донба́с, **in D.** у (на) Донба́сі.

door, *n.* *only pl.* две́рі, **at the d.** при вхо́ді, **Tickets will be sold at the d.** Квитки́ продава́тимуть при вхо́ді.; **out of ~s** надво́рі, на пові́трі, на ву́лиці, **The children spend much time out of ~s.** Ді́ти прово́дять бага́то ча́су надво́рі (*or* на пові́трі).

dormitory — **either**

dormitory, *n.* гуртожиток, **in a d.** у гуртожитку, **university d.** університетський гуртожиток.

doubt, *v.* сумніватися у + *L.* or що + *clause*, **They d. her honesty.** Вони сумніваються у її чесності., **I don't d. it is the case.** Я не сумніваюся, що це так.; *n.* сумнів; **beyond d.** поза сумнівом; **without a d.** без сумніву.

down, *adv., posn.* внизу, *dir.* вниз.

downtown, *n.* середмістя, центр міста, **This building is right d.** Цей будинок просто у середмісті.

draw, *v.* 1) малювати, **She ~s really well.** Вона дуже добре малює.; 2) *(technical)* креслити, **He quickly drew a plan of the room.** Він швидко накреслив план кімнати.; 3) *(pull)* тягнути, **The horses d. a wagon.** Коні тягнуть віз.

drawing, *n.* 1) малюнок; 2) *(technical)* креслення.

dream, *n.* 1) мрія, **cherished d.** заповітна мрія; 2) сон, **I had a wonderful d.** Я бачив чудовий сон. *v.* мріяти про + *A.*, **They d. of a trip to Rome.** Вони мріють про подорож до Риму.

dress, *v.* 1) *tran.* одягати, убирати + *A.* + у + *A.*, **He ~ed his son in a new suit.** Він одягнув (убрав) сина у новий костюм.; 2) *intr.* одягатися, убиратися, **He ~ed and went out.** Він одягнувся (убрався) і вийшов.; *n.* 1) сукня, плаття, **She bought a fashinable d.** Вона купила модну сукню.; 2) вбрання, одяг, **an expensive d.** дороге вбрання, **traditional d.** традиційне вбрання.

drink, *v.* 1) *tran.* пити, **I like to d. spring water.** Я люблю пити джерельну воду.; 2) *intr. (alcohol)* пити, **She doesn't d. or smoke.** Вона не п'є і не курить.; 3) *intr. (taste)* питися, **This wine ~s very well.** Це вино дуже добре п'ється.; ♦ **d. and drive** пити за кермом, **I don't d. and drive.** Я не п'ю за кермом.; ♦ **d. to sb's health** пити за чиєсь здоров'я, **We drank to the hosts' health.** Ми випили за здоров'я господарів.; *n.* 1) напій, **There were food and ~s on the table.** На столі була їжа і напої.; 2) **to have a d. of sth** напитися + *G.*, **He had a d. of tea.** Він напився чаю.

drive, *v.* 1) *tran. multi.* їздити, *uni.* їхати + *I.*, **She ~s an old car.** Вона їздить старим автом.; 2) *multi.* водити, *uni.* вести + *A.*, **I d. the car carefully.** Я воджу авто обережно.; 3) *tran. (transport sb by a vehicle) multi.* возити, *uni.* везти, **He ~s his son to school.** Він возить сина до школи.; 4) *(d. to a point)* відвозити, **I can d. you home.** Я можу відвезти вас додому.; 5) *intr. multi.* їздити, *uni.* їхати, **I learned to d. a year ago.** Я навчився їздити рік тому.; ♦ *(hint)* **to d. at** хотіти сказати, **What he is ~ing at.** Що він хоче сказати.; **to go for a d.** їздити на прогулянку.

driver, *n.* водій, шофер; **taxi d.** таксист, *f.* таксистка.

drug, *n. only pl.* ліки, медикаменти; (narcotic) наркотики; **do ~s** зловживати наркотиками.

drugstore, *n.* аптека.

dull, *adj.* 1) нудний, нецікавий, **It was a d. talk.** Це була нецікава лекція.; 2) *(blunt)* тупий, **d. knife** тупий ніж; 3) *(of weather)* похмурий; 4) *(of sound)* глухий; 5) *(stupid)* тупий.

during, *prep.*, протягом + *G.*, на протязі + *G.*; **d. the year** протягом року; під час + *G.*, **He heard a strange sound d. the conversation.** Він чув дивний звук під час розмови.

DVD, *n.* компакт-диск, компактний диск.

DVD-player, *n.* програвач ДВД.

E

each, *adj.* кожний, *var.* кожен, **E. photo was black and white.** Кожна світлина була чорно-біла.; **e. of ...** кожен з + *G.*, **E. of them knew this town.** Кожен з них знав це місто.; ♦ **e. and every** кожнісінький, **E. and every visitor took pictures of the castle.** Кожнісінький відвідувач сфотографував замок.

ear, *n.* вухо *var.* ухо; ♦ **be up to one's ~s in ...** бути по самі вуха у + *L.* ..., **I am up to my ~s in work.** Я по самі вуха у роботі.

early, *adj.* ранній, **e. strawberries** ранні полуниці; **I am an e. riser.** Я рано встаю.; **They had an e. dinner.** Вони рано пообідали.; *adv.* рано, **He comes to work e.** Він приходить на працю рано.; ♦ **An e. bird catches the worm.** Хто рано встає, тому Бог дає.

earn, *v.* заробляти, **How much does he e.?** Скільки він заробляє? **to e. a living** заробляти на життя.

earth, *n.* 1) *(soil)* земля; 2) *(planet)* **(planet) E.** (планета) Земля, 3) *(the world)* світ, земля, **on e.** на землі; ♦ **nowhere on e.** ніде на світі.

east, *n.* схід, **in the e.** на сході, **to the e. of** на схід від + *G.*, **He lives to the e. of Lviv.** Він живе на схід від Львова.; *adj.* східний; *adv.* на схід, у східному напрямку, **We drove e.** Ми поїхали на схід.

Easter, *n.* Великдень, **for E.** на Великдень. *adj.* великодній, **E. holidays** великодні свята.

eastern, *adj.* східний, **e. part of town** східна частина міста.

easy, *adj.* 1) легкий, **e. task** легке завдання, 2) *(of manners)* невимушений; **It's e. to ...** (є) легко + *inf.*, **It's e. to sit around and wait.** Легко сидіти і чекати.; ♦ **easier said than done** легше сказати, ніж зробити; *excl.* **e.!** помалу!

eat, *v., tran.* їсти, **I ate a sandwich.** Я з'їв бутерброд.; **e. in** їсти вдома, **e. out** їсти в ресторані *or* поза домом.

economist, *n.* економіст, **work as an e.** працювати економістом.

education, *n.* освіта, **secondary (higher) e.** середня (вища) освіта, **to get an e.** отримати освіту.

egg, *n.* яйце, **hard-boiled e.** круте яйце.

eight, *card.* 1) вісім + *G. pl.*, **e. months** вісім місяців; 2) *(of animate or paired nouns)* восьмеро + *G. pl.*, **e. men (doors)** восьмеро чоловіків (дверей); 3) *(of time by clock)* восьма (година), **at e. o'clock** о восьмій (годині); *n.* вісімка, **He was among the first e.** Він був у першій вісімці.

eighteen, *card.* вісімнадцять + *G. pl.*, **e. hryvnias** вісімнадцять гривень; 2) *coll.* вісімнадцятеро *(with anim. and paired nouns)* + *G. pl.*, **e. Poles** вісімнадцятеро поляків; *n.* вісімнадцятка.

eighteenth, *ord.* 1) вісімнадцятий, **e. day** вісімнадцятий день; *n.* (одна) вісімнадцята.

eighty, *card.* вісімдесят + *G. pl.*, **e. kopeks** вісімдесят копійок.

either, *adv.* також, теж, **I don't like beer e.** Я також не люблю пива.; **e. of them** хтось із них, **I'll tell you if e. of them calls.** Я скажу вам, якщо хтось із них подзвонить.; **e. way** у кожному разі; *conj.* **e. ... or**, або.., або .., **He can e. buy or rent a car.** Він може або купити, або найняти авто.

elder, *adj.* старший, **e. sister** старша сестра́.

eldest, *adj.* найста́рший.

elevator, *n.* ліфт, **There's no e. in the building.** У цьому будинку нема́є ліфта.

eleven, *card.* 1) одина́дцять + *G. pl.*, **e. sentences** одина́дцять рече́нь; 2) *(of animate or paired nouns)* одина́дцятеро + *G. pl.*, **e. horses** одина́дцятеро ко́ней; 3) *(of time by clock)* одина́дцята (годи́на), **at e. o'clock** об одина́дцятій (годи́ні); *n.* одина́дцятка **The first e. was clearly in the lead.** Перша одина́дцятка цілко́м ясно вела́ перед.

else, *adv.* ще, у дода́ток, **What e. do you need?** Що ще вам тре́ба?, **Is anyone e. coming along?** Чи ще хтось іде́ з на́ми?

e-mail, *n.* електро́нна по́шта; *slang* ми́ло; **e. address** електро́нна адре́са, **e. account** електро́нний раху́нок.

embassy, *n.* посо́льство, амбаса́да, **US Embassy in Kyiv** амбаса́да США в Ки́єві; **Peter turned to his e. for help.** Пі́тер зверну́вся до свого́ посо́льства по допомо́гу.

empty, *adj.* поро́жній, пусти́й; ♦ **e. promise** поро́жня обіця́нка; ♦ **on an e. stomach** на поро́жній шлу́нок; *v.* опоро́жняти, **He emptied the drawer.** Він опоро́жнив шухля́ду.

end, *v.* 1) *tran.* кінча́ти, закі́нчувати, **We ~ed the discussion late.** Ми (за)кі́нчили диску́сію пі́зно.; 2) *intr.* кінча́тися, **The vacation ~s sooner or later.** Вака́ції закі́нчуються ра́но чи пі́зно.; *n.* кіне́ць, **from beginning to e.** від поча́тку до кінця́; ♦ **the e. of the world** кіне́ць сві́ту; ♦ **in the e.** в ре́шті решт; ♦ **make (both) ~s meet** зво́дити кінці́ з кінця́ми; ♦ **to no e.** безме́жно, безмі́рно.

engineer, *n.* інжене́р, **He studies to become an e.** Він вчи́ться на інжене́ра.

England, *n.* А́нглія, **We spent a week in E.** Ми провели́ ти́ждень в А́нглії.

English, *adj.* англі́йський; *(language)* англі́йська мо́ва; *n., m.* англі́єць, *f.* англі́йка, **She is E.** Вона́ англі́йка.

enough, *adv.* 1) до́сить, **He is rich e.** Він до́сить бага́тий.; до́статньо, **We did more than e.** Ми зроби́ли бі́льш, ніж до́статньо.; 2) го́ді + *pf. inf.*, **e. of your complaints!** го́ді скаржи́тися!; *excl.* **e.!** до́сить! *or colloq.* го́ді вже!; 3) *(for emphasis)* як не .., але, **Strangely e., he apologized.** Як не ди́вно, але він перепроси́в.

enter, *v.* вхо́дити до + *G. or* в + *A.*, **He ~ed the room.** Він увійшо́в до кімна́ти.; захо́дити до + *G. or* в + *A.*, **He ~ed the building quietly.** Він ти́хо зайшо́в до буди́нку (*or* у буди́нок).

entire, *adj.* весь, ці́лий; **e. world** весь світ.

entirely, *adv.* 1) цілко́м, **I want to do sth e. new.** Я хо́чу зроби́ти щось цілко́м нове́.; 2) *(solely)* лише́, винятко́во, **The group was made up e. of students.** Гру́па склада́лася винятко́во із студе́нтів.; 3) зо́всім, геть, **We are of an e. different opinion.** Ми зо́всім (геть) і́ншої ду́мки.

entitle, *v.* назива́ти, дава́ти на́зву, **to be ~d** назива́тися, ма́ти на́зву, **The film is ~d Joy.** Фільм назива́ється «Ра́дість».

entrance, *n.* вхід, **We are to meet by the e.** Ми ма́ємо зустрі́тися бі́ля вхо́ду.

especially, *adv.* 1) *(in particular)* особли́во, **He likes meat, e. pork.** Він лю́бить м'я́со, особли́во свини́ну.; 2) *(specifically)* спеція́льно, **I ordered the dish e. for you.** Я замо́вив цю стра́ву спеція́льно для вас.; 3) *(very much)* ду́же, **We don't e. understand baseball.** Ми не ду́же розумі́ємо бейсбо́л.

essay, *n.* есе́й, *(school essay)* твір, **to write an e.** писа́ти есе́й (твір); **He was supposed to write an e. for his Ukrainian literature course.** Він мав написа́ти твір для ку́рсу з украї́нської літерату́ри.

Europe, *n.* Євро́па, *var.* Европа.

European, *adj.* європе́йський, *var.* европейський; *n., m.* європе́єць, *var.* европеєць, *f.* європе́йка, *var.* европейка.

even, *adv.* на́віть, **E. children know it.** На́віть ді́ти зна́ють це.; **He e. speaks Chinese.** Він на́віть говори́ть кита́йською.; **e. as ...** в той час, як...; **e. if ...** на́віть якщо...; **e. so** тим не ме́нше; **e. though** незважа́ючи на + *A.*; *adj.* 1) рі́вний, **Her teeth are all e.** Її зу́би всі рі́вні.; 2) *(of numbers)* па́рний, **Four is an e. number.** Чоти́ри – це па́рне число́.

evening, *n.* ве́чір, **good e.!** до́брий ве́чір!; **in the e.** уве́чері.

event, *n.* 1) *(occurrence)* поді́я, **international e.** міжнаро́дна поді́я; 2) за́хід, *Gal.* імпре́за, **Our e. gathered a lot of people.** На́ша імпре́за зібра́ла бага́то люде́й.; 3) *(occasion)* випа́док; ♦ **in any e.** у ко́жному ра́зі; **in that e.** в тако́му ра́зі (випа́дку).

ever, *adv.* 1) коли́-не́будь, **Did you e. work there?** Чи ти коли́-не́будь працюва́в там?; 2) *(in neg. sentence)* ніко́ли, **I don't e. do it.** Я ніко́ли не роблю́ цього́.; 3) *(always)* завжди́, **He is e. so neat.** Він завжди́ таки́й охайний., **e. since** з тих пір, як ..., **They haven't seen each other e. since he moved.** Вони́ не ба́чилися з тих пір, як він переї́хав.; **for e.** наза́вжди; 4) *(with comparative)* дедалі, щораз, **This road becomes e. more difficult.** Ця доро́га стає́ дедалі важчою.

every, *adj.* 1) ко́жний, *var.* ко́жен; *(with indications of time in G.)*, **e. hour** ко́жної годи́ни, **e. day** ко́жного дня, **e. month** ко́жного мі́сяця, **e. now and then** час від ча́су, **e. other** щодру́гий, **e. time** ко́жного ра́зу, щора́зу, **e. year** ко́жного ро́ку; 2) *(repetition)* що + *A.*, ко́жні, **e. twenty minutes** що (*or* ко́жні) два́дцять хвили́н; 3) *(all)* всі, **I have e. reason to think so.** Я ма́ю всі причи́ни так ду́мати.

everybody, *pron.* усі́, **We need to write e. about this.** Тре́ба написа́ти всім про це.

everyone, *pron.* усі́, **E. knows this fact.** Усі́ зна́ють цей факт.

everything, *pron.* усе́, **She read e. she could find.** Вона́ прочита́ла все, що могла́ знайти́.; ♦ **how's e.?** як спра́ви?

everywhere, *adv.* скрізь, **The tree grows e.** Це де́рево росте́ скрізь.; ♦ **e. else** у всіх і́нших + *L. pl.* **The style of architecture can be found e. in Europe.** Цей стиль архітекту́ри мо́жна знайти́ у всіх і́нших краї́нах Євро́пи.

exact, *adj.* то́чний, докла́дний; **e. copy** то́чна ко́пія, **e. description** докла́дний о́пис; **e. science** то́чна нау́ка.

exactly, *adv.* 1) *(of time, sum of money)* рі́вно, **It costs e. five hryvnias.** Це кошту́є рі́вно п'ять гри́вень.; 2) *(emphasis)* са́ме, **E. who did it?** Хто са́ме зроби́в це? 3) *(emph. yes)* вла́сне! *or* а са́ме!; **not e.** не зо́всім, **This is not e. true.** Це не зо́всім пра́вда.

examination, *n.* 1) *(test)* іспит, екза́мен, **to pass an e.** скла́сти іспит; **to take an e.** склада́ти іспит; 2) *(medical)* о́гляд, обсте́ження, **have a medical e.** проходити медичне обсте́ження; **He had his general medical e. at least once a year.** Він проходив загальне медичне обстеження принаймні раз на рік.

example, *n.* 1) при́клад, зразо́к, **This building is a typical e. of baroque.** Цей будинок - типовий приклад баро́ка.; **for e.** наприклад.

excellent, *adj.* відмі́нний, чудо́вий, доскона́лий, **It's an e. idea!** Це чудова ідея.

except, *prep.* крім + *G.*, **Everyone e. Ivan saw the film.** Усі крім Івана бачили цей фільм.; за винятком + *G.*, **We visited all important cities e. Lviv.** Ми побува́ли у всіх важливих містах за винятком Львова.

exchange, *n.* обмін; **currency e.** обмін валюти; **e. of ... for ...** обмін + *G.* + на + *A.*, **e. of money for services** обмін грошей на послуги; **in e. for ...** в обмін за + *A.* *v.* міняти, обмі́нювати + *A.* + на + *A.*, **to e. dollars for hryvnias** міняти долари на гривні.

excursion, *n.* екску́рсія; **e. around town** екскурсія мі́стом, **e. to** екскурсія до + *G.*

excuse, *v.* вибача́ти, **e. me** ви́бачте, дару́йте, *Gal.* перепро́шую; проба́чити; *n.* 1) *(justification)* ви́правдання, **This is no e. for rudeness.** Це не виправдання грубощі.; 2) *(reason)* причина, **What's the e. for your absence?** Яка причина вашої відсутности?; 3) *(pretext)* привід, **He needs an e. to cancel the party.** Йому потрібен привід, щоб відмінити вечірку.; **under the e. of ...** під приводом + *G.*

exercise, *n.* впра́ва, *var.* упра́ва.

exhibition, *n.* ви́ставка; **at an e.** на ви́ставці; **art e.** виставка мистецтва.

exit, *n.* 1) ви́хід, **no e.** ви́ходу нема́є; 2) *(on highway)* виї́зд, **e. 23** двадцять тре́тій виїзд.

expect, *v.* 1) споді́ватися + *A.*, **We e. the situation to improve.** Ми сподіваємося, що ситуація покращиться.; 2) *(of weather)* очі́кувати, **Nasty weather is ~ed.** Очікується погана погода.

expensive, *adj.* дороги́й, **This hotel is too e. for me.** Цей готель надто дорогий для мене.

experienced, *adj.* досві́дчений, **e. instructor (collector, lawyer, physician)** досвідчений виклада́ч (колекціонер, юрист, лікар).

expert, *n.* фахіве́ць, експе́рт, спеціялі́ст з + *G.*; **e. in physics** фахівець з фі́зики; **e. opinion** думка фахівця́.

explain, *v.* поясню́вати + *A.* + *D.*; **Can you e. this to us?** Можете пояснити це нам?

explanation, *n.* поя́снення, **His e. was clear.** Його́ пояснення було ясним.

expression, *n.* 1) *(of face)* ви́раз, **She had a happy e. on her face.** Вона мала радісний вираз на обличчі.; 2) *(verbal)* ви́слів, ви́раз, **This is a colloquial e.** Це розмовний вислів (вираз).

eye, *n.* о́ко, *pl.* о́чі, **dark (brown) ~s** чо́рні (ка́рі) о́чі; ♦ **close one's ~s to ...** заплю́щувати о́чі на + *A.*, **He closed his ~s to the truth.** Він заплющив очі на пра́вду.

F

face, *n.* 1) обли́ччя, **She has an intelligent f.** У не́ї розу́мне обли́ччя.; **to one's f. ... D.** + в о́чі, **He told it straight to her f.** Він сказав їй просто в о́чі.; 2) *(of a clock)* циферблат; *v.* *(look out to)* вихо́дити на + *A.*, **My window ~s the street.** Моє вікно виходить на вулицю.

fact, *n.* факт, **f. of life** факт життя́, **in f.** наспра́вді, **Uncle Vasyl is in f. his cousin.** Дядько Василь наспра́вді його двоюрі́дний брат.; *conj.* **the f. that ...** те, що ..., **The f. that he never called means that he didn't like the offer.** Те, що він так і не подзвонив, значить, що пропозиція йому не сподобалася.

factory, *n.* фа́брика, **at (in) a f.** на фа́бриці.

fall, *v.* па́дати, **At night the temperature ~s.** Уночі температура падає; *n.* *(autumn)* о́сінь, **in the f.** восени́, **last f.** минулої осени.

familiar, *adj.* знайо́мий, **His face seemed f.** Його́ обличчя здавалося знайомим.

familiarize, *v.,* **to f. oneself with** познайо́митися з + *I.,* **He wants to f. himself with Ukrainian art.** Він хоче познайомитися з українським мистецтвом.

family, *n.* 1) сім'я́, роди́на, **My f. is not very large.** Моя́ сім'я не дуже велика.; 2) *(relation)* *m.* ро́дич, *f.* ро́дичка, **He is close f.** Він близький родич.; ♦ **in the f. way** вагі́тна.

famous, *adj.* славе́тний, знамени́тий, **be f. for ...** славитися + *I.,* **Ukrainians are f. for their hospitality.** Українці славляться гостинністю.

far, *adj.* 1) дале́кий, **the F. East** Дале́кий Схід; 2) відда́лений, **a f. away village** віддалене село; *adv.* дале́ко; **Do you live f.?** Ви далеко живете?, **not f.** неподалі́к, недале́ко.; **as f. as ...** (аж) до ... **We got as f. as the lake.** Ми дійшли (аж) до озера.; **as f. as sb is concerned** що стосу́ється + *G.,* то ..., **As f. as the dinner is concerned, I'll cook it.** Що стосується вечері, то я її зварю́.

farther, *adj.* 1) да́льший, **The f. part of the house was rather dark.** Да́льша частина будинку була досить темною.; 2) відда́лений, **He stood in a f. part of the room.** Він стояв у віддаленій частині кімнати.; *adv.* да́лі, да́льше, **Let's go f.** Ходімо далі., **Robert lives a bit f.** Роберт живе трохи дальше.

fashion, *n.* мо́да; **to be in f.** бути в мо́ді, **to be out of f.** бути не в мо́ді, **This color is out of f. now.** Цей колір не в мо́ді зараз.; **the latest f.** остання мода.

fashionable, *adj.* мо́дний, **a f. style** мо́дний стиль.

fast, *adj.* швидки́й, би́стрий, ско́рий, **f. food restaurant** ресторан швидкого обслуговування, **f. train** скорий по́їзд; *(of clock)* **to be ... minutes f.** поспіша́ти на + *A.,* **My watch is ten minutes f.** Мій годинник поспішає на десять хвили́н.; *adv.* 1) швидко, **You're driving too f.** Ви зана́дто швидко їдете.; хутко, **Let's go, f.!** Ходімо, хутко!; 2) мі́цно, **I held his arm f.** Я міцно тримав його руку.

fat, *adj.* 1) товсти́й, гру́бий, гладки́й, **become f.** грубшати, гладшати, товщати, **He has become rather f.** Він досить погрубшав (погладшав).; 2) жирний, **f. meat** жирне м'ясо.; *n.* жир, **There's a lot of f. in this pizza.** У цій піці бага́то жиру.; **animal (vegetable) f.** тваринний (рослинний) жир.

father, *n.* ба́тько.

father-in-law, *n.* *(for wife)* све́кор, *(for husband)* тесть.

fatherland, *n.* ба́тьківщи́на, рі́дний край.

favor, *n.* по́слуга, ла́ска, **a great f.** вели́ка по́слуга; **do sb a f.** роби́ти ла́ску + *D.*

favorite, *adj.* улю́блений, **This is their f. film.** Це їхній улю́блений фільм.; *n.*, *m.* фавори́т, *f.* фавори́тка **He is an absolute f.** Він абсолю́тний фавори́т.; *m.* улю́бленець, *f.* улю́бленка, **Salomea was the f. of the public.** Соломі́я була́ улю́бленкою публі́ки.

February, *n.* лю́тий, **in F.** у лю́тому.

feel, *v.*, *tran.* відчува́ти + *A.*, **He felt a hand on his shoulder.** Він відчу́в ру́ку на плечі́.; *refl. (feel oneself)* почува́тися; **How do you feel?** Як ви почува́єтеся?; почува́тися + *I.*, **He ~s happy.** Він почува́ється щасли́вим.

festival, *n.* фестива́ль, **at f.** на фестива́лі, **film f.** кінофестива́ль, **art f.** фестива́ль мисте́цтв.

fetch, *v.* прино́сити.

fever, *n.* гаря́чка, температу́ра, **He's got a (high) f.** У ньо́го (висо́ка) температу́ра.

few, *adj.* кі́лька + *G.*, **I have a f. books for you.** Я ма́ю кі́лька книжо́к для вас.; небага́то + *G.*, **f. people responded.** Небага́то люде́й відповіло́.; *pron.* ма́ло хто, **F. came to her lecture.** Ма́ло хто прийшо́в на її ле́кцію.; **no fewer than** не ме́нш, ніж ..., щонайме́нше.

fiancé, *n.*, *m.* нарече́ний.

fiancée, *n.*, *f.* нарече́на.

field, *n.* 1) по́ле, **f. of rye** жи́тнє по́ле, **soccer f.** футбо́льне по́ле; 2) *(sphere)* га́лузь, цари́на, **f. of biology** га́лузь біоло́гії.

fifteen, *card.* 1) п'ятна́дцять + *G. pl.*, **f. cents** п'ятна́дцять це́нтів; 2) *coll.* п'ятна́дцятеро *(with anim. and paired nouns)* + *G. pl.*, **f. students** п'ятна́дцятеро студе́нтів.; *n.* п'ятна́дцятка.

fifth, *ord.* п'я́тий, **every f. person** щоп'я́та осо́ба *or* ко́жна п'я́та осо́ба; ♦ **the f. column** п'я́та коло́на; *n.* (одна́) п'я́та, **three ~s** три п'я́ті (п'я́тих).

fifty, *card.* п'ятдеся́т + *G. pl.*, **f. degrees** п'ятдеся́т гра́дусів; *n.* п'ятдеся́тка.

film, *n.* фільм, кінокарти́на, карти́на, **feature (short, documentary, full-length, animation) f.** худо́жній (короткометра́жний, документа́льний, повнометра́жний, мультипліка́ційний) фільм; *v.* зніма́ти фільм, фільмува́ти.

final, *adj.* 1) оста́нній, **Sunday is the f. day of the week.** Неді́ля – оста́нній день ти́жня.; 2) остато́чний, **This is my f. word.** Це моє́ остато́чне сло́во.

finally, *adv.* наре́шті, **He f. responded to me.** Він наре́шті відпові́в мені́.

find, *v.* 1) знахо́дити, **He found her in the library.** Він знайшо́в її в бібліоте́ці.; 2) *(discover)* виявля́ти, **They found that there were no vacancies in the restaurant.** Вони́ ви́явили, що в рестора́ні не було́ ві́льних місць.; 3) **f. out** дізнава́тися про + *A.*, **We never found out what happened.** Ми так і не дізна́лися, що ста́лося.

fine, *adj.* 1) хоро́ший, **John is a f. person.** Джон – хоро́ша люди́на.; 2) до́брий, **I like f. wines.** Я люблю́ до́брі ви́на.; 3) га́рний, **Marko is a f. friend.** Ма́рко – га́рний друг.; 4) (day, weather) чудо́вий, **What a f. day!** Що за чудо́вий день!; 5) *(of sand, etc.)* дрі́бний, **f. sand** дрі́бний пісо́к; *n. (penalty)* штраф.

finger, *n.* па́лець; ♦ **give sb the f.** пока́зувати + *D.* ду́лю.

finish, *v.* 1) *tran.* закі́нчувати + *A.*, **When will you finally f. work?** Коли́ ти наре́шті закі́нчиш робо́ту?; 2) *intr.* закі́нчуватися, **The play will soon f.** П'є́са ско́ро закі́нчиться.; *n.* кіне́ць, фі́ніш, **The game was interesting from start to f.** Гра була́ ціка́вою від поча́тку до кінця́.

fire, *n.* 1) вого́нь, *var.* ого́нь; **to be on f.** горі́ти; 2) *(of building)* поже́жа, **There was a f. in the building.** У буди́нку була́ поже́жа.

firm, *n.* фі́рма, **He works for a legal f.** Він працю́є у юриди́чній фі́рмі.; *adj.* 1) тверди́й, **f. surface** тверда́ пове́рхня; 2) *(strong)* міцни́й, **She is of f. health.** Вона́ ма́є міцне́ здоро́в'я.

first, *ord.* пе́рший, **at f. sight** на пе́рший по́гляд, **for the f. time.** упе́рше; ♦ **love at f. sight** коха́ння з пе́ршого по́гляду.; *adv.* споча́тку, **F. tell me where you obtained the document.** Споча́тку скажи́ мені́, де ти діста́в (діста́ла) цей докуме́нт.; ♦ **f. and foremost** наса́мперед; ♦ **at f.** споча́тку; ♦ **f. of all** перш за все.

fish, *n.* ри́ба, **F. is my favorite food.** Ри́ба – моя́ улю́блена ї́жа.; *v.* лови́ти ри́бу, рибали́ти; **~ing** риба́лка, **to go ~ing** ходи́ти на риба́лку, **They have not gone fishing together for two years.** Вони́ не ходи́ли ра́зом на риба́лку два ро́ки.; ♦ **to f. for compliments** напро́шуватися на комплі́менти.

fitness club, *n.* спортклу́б; *(gym)* спортза́ла.

five, *card.* 1) п'ять + *G. pl.*, **f. years** п'ять ро́ків; 2) *(of animate or paired nouns)* п'я́теро + *G. pl.*, **f. friends (pants)** п'я́теро дру́зів (штані́в); 3) *(of time by clock)* п'я́та (годи́на), **at f. o'clock** о п'я́тій (годи́ні); *n.* п'яті́рка, **Participants entered in ~s.** Уча́сники захо́дили по п'ять (п'я́теро).

five hundred, *card.* п'ятсо́т + *G. pl.*, **f. h. dollars** п'ятсо́т до́ларів.

floor, *n.* 1) підло́га, **The cup fell on the f.** Філіжа́нка впа́ла на підло́гу.; 2) *(story)* по́верх, **on the first f.** на пе́ршому по́версі; 3) *(of sea)* дно, **on the sea f.** на дні мо́ря; ♦ **to give (have) the f.** дава́ти (ма́ти) сло́во.

flower, *n.* кві́тка, *pl.* кві́ти, **She always buys ~s.** Вона́ за́вжди купу́є кві́ти.; *v.* цвісти́, квітну́ти, **Lilac ~s in May.** Бузо́к цвіте́ у тра́вні.

flu, *n.* грип, **go down with the f.** захворі́ти на грип, зля́гти з гри́пом.

fluently, *adv.* ві́льно, плинно́, **He speaks Ukrainian f.** Він ві́льно гово́рить украї́нською.

fly, *v.*, *multi.* літа́ти, **Earlier Taras often flew to Odesa for the weekend.** Рані́ше Тара́с ча́сто літа́в до Оде́си на вихідні́.; *uni.* леті́ти, **We're ~ing to London on Monday.** Ми лети́мо до Ло́ндона у понеді́лок.; *n.* (insect) му́ха.

folk, *adj.* наро́дний, **f. song** наро́дна пі́сня.

food, *n.* ї́жа, **baby f.** дитя́че харчува́ння, **cat (dog) f.** ї́жа для коті́в (соба́к).

foot, *n.* ступня́, нога́; ♦ **on f.** пішки́.

football, *n.* 1) *(a ball for playing)* футбо́льний м'яч; 2) *(American)* америка́нський футбо́л; **play f.** гра́ти в америка́нський футбо́л.

for, *prep.* 1) для + *G.*, **f. guests** для гостей, **I did it f. you.** Я зробив це для вас.; 2) *(in favor of)* за + *A.*, **Everybody was f. reforms.** Всі були за реформи.; 3) *(duration)*, *time designator in A. or* протягом + *G.*, **We worked f. one day.** Ми працювали одну добу *(or* протягом однієї доби*)*.; 4) *(destination)* до + *G.*, **I'm leaving f. Chernihiv.** Я їду до Чернігова.; 5) *(target moment in future)* на + *A.*, **assignment f. Monday** завдання на понеділок; 6) *(price)* за + *A.*, **I bought the book f. one hryvnia.** Я купив цю книжку за одну гривню.; 7) *(reason)* з + *G.*, **He was crying f. joy.** Він плакав з радости.; 8) *(object)* по + *A.*, **She sent Ihor f. milk.** Вона послала Ігоря по молоко.

foreign, *adj.* 1) чужий, чужоземний; іноземний **f. language** чужа (іноземна) мова; **f. press** міжнародна преса; 2) *(unknown)* незнайомий, **This expression seems f. to me.** Цей вислів здається мені незнайомим.

forest, *n.* ліс, **in a f.** у лісі.

forever, *adv.* 1) завжди, назавжди, **I am f. grateful for your help.** Я вам назавжди вдячний за допомогу.; 2) *(all the time)* без кінця, без перестанку, без перерви.

forget, *v.* забувати + *A.*, **Maria never ~s to call.** Марія ніколи не забуває подзвонити.

fork, *n.* 1) виделка; 2) *(in the road)* роздоріжжя, розвилка; *v. (of road)* розходитися.

former, *adj.* колишній, **She is my f. wife.** Вона моя колишня дружина.

fortunately, *adv.* на щастя, **F., he had enough money on him.** На щастя, він мав із собою достатньо грошей.

forty, *card.* 1) сорок, **There are f. names on the list.** У списку сорок імен.; 2) **the forties** сорокові роки.

four, *card.* 1) чотири, **f. seasons of the year** чотири пори року; 2) *(of animate or paired nouns)* четверо, **f. boys (spectacles)** четверо хлопців (окулярів); 3) *(of time by clock)* четверта (година), **at f. o'clock** о четвертій (годині).

four hundred, *card.* чотириста + *G. pl.*, **f. h. grams** чотириста грамів; *n.* чотири сотні.

fourteen, *card.* 1) чотирнадцять + *G. pl.*, **f. dollars** чотирнадцять доларів; 2) *coll.* чотирнадцятеро *(with anim. and paired nouns)* + *G. pl.*, **f. girls** чотирнадцятеро дівчат; *n.* чотирнадцятка.

fourth, *ord.* четвертий, **f. dimension** четвертий вимір; *n.* чверть, четвертина, четверта, **two ~s** дві чверті (четвертини, четверті).

France, *n.* Франція, **F. is known for its fine cuisine.** Франція відома своєю чудовою кухнею.

free, *adj.* вільний, **He is a f. man.** Він вільна людина.; **f. time** дозвілля, **What do you like to do in your f. time?** Що ти любиш робити на дозвіллі?; **f. of charge** безкоштовний, безоплатний, безплатний.

freedom, *n.* воля, свобода, **f. of choice** свобода вибору, **f. of expression** свобода слова.

French, *adj.* французький; *n.*, *m.* француз, *f.* француженка.

frequent, *adj.* частий, **f. visits** часті візити; *v.* часто відвідувати + *A.*, навідуватися до + *G.*, учащати до + *G.*, **Roman ~s this bar.** Роман учащає до цього бару.

frequently, *adv.* часто, **We f. see each other.** Ми часто бачимося.

fresh, *adj.* 1) *(air)* свіжий, **F. air is the best pleasure.** Чисте повітря – найкраща насолода.; 2) *(water)* прісний.

fridge, *n.* холодильник.

friend, *n.*, *m.* друг, *pl.* друзі, *f.* подруга; *m.* приятель; *f.* приятелька; **best f.** найкращий друг, найкраща подруга.

from, *prep. (origin)* з (із, зі) + *G.*, **f. Kyiv** з Києва; *(from a person)* від + *G.*, **this is f. my uncle** це від мого дядька; *(time, space limits)* **f. ... to ...** від + *G.* до + *G*, **f. Tuesday to Friday** від вівторка до п'ятниці; **She is an expert in many fields f. history to sociology.** Вона фахівець у багатьох галузях - від історії до соціології.

front, *n.* перед, *(of building)* фасад, **The f. of the museum was painted yellow.** Фасад музею був пофарбований жовтим кольором.; **in f. of** перед + *I.*, **in f. of the building** перед будинком.

frozen, *adj.* заморожений, **f. food** заморожені продукти.

fruit, *n.* фрукт, **f. and vegetables** фрукти й городина; плід; *adj.* фруктовий, **f. juice** фруктовий сік.

full, *adj.* 1) повний, **The hall was f. of people.** Зала була повна людей.; **Write your f. name.** Напишіть ваше прізвище, ім'я та по батькові.; 2) сповнений + *G.*, **The day was f. of surprises.** День був сповнений несподіванок.

fun, *n.* 1) забава, ♦ **to have f.** веселитися, приємно проводити час, гарно бавитися, **We had a lot of f. at the party.** Ми дуже весело провели час на вечірці.; 2) *(person)* дуже приємна людина, **Marta is a lot of f.** З Мартою дуже весело.; 3) *(source of pleasure)* любити, **Travelling has always been f. for us.** Ми завжди любили подорожувати.; ♦ **make f. of sb** жартувати з + *I.*, **She always makes f. of him.** Вона завжди жартує з нього.

funny, *adj.* 1) смішний, **a f. story** смішна історія; кумедний, забавний, **a f. guy** кумедний (забавний) хлопець.; 2) *(strange)* дивний, **F. he didn't call.** Дивно, що він не подзвонив.; 3) *(suspicious)* не те, **He had a feeling sth was f. here.** Він відчував, що тут щось не те.

furniture, *n. only pl.* меблі; **f. store** меблева крамниця.

further, *adv.* далі, **What happened f. was awful.** Далі сталося щось страшне.; *adj. (additional)* ще, **We spoke for a f. ten minutes.** Ми поговорили ще десять хвилин.

future, *n.* 1) майбутнє, **in the (near) f.** у (близькому) майбутньому; 2) *(success)* перспективи, **He has a f. as an economist.** Він має добрі перспективи як економіст.; *adj.* майбутній, **f. wife** майбутня жінка, **f. tense** майбутній час.

G

Galicia, *n.* Галичина *(a historical land of Western Ukraine, comprising the present-day provinces of Lviv, Ternopil, and Ivano-Frankivsk).*

Galician, *adj.* галицький, **This is a typical G. expression.** Це типовий галицький вислів.; *n. (person of Ukrainian Galician identity) m.* галичанин, *f.* галичанка, **His mother is a G., therefore he himself is half G.** Його мати галичанка, тому він сам наполовину галичанин.

gallery, *n.* галерея, *also* ґалерея, **picture g.** картинна галерея; **shooting g.** тир.

game

game, *n.* 1) гра, *pl.* ігри, **computer g.** комп'ютерна гра, **basketball (soccer, volleyball) g.** футбольна (баскетбольна, волейбольна) гра, **Olympic ~s** Олімпійські ігри; 2) *(hunted animal)* дичина.

garage, *n.* гара́ж, **to put the car in a g.** (по)ста́вити авто у гара́ж.

garden, *n.* сад, **They're somewhere in the g. now.** Вони́ зара́з десь у саду́., **botanical g.** ботані́чний сад, **vegetable g.** горо́д. **He grows cucumbers in his vegetable g.** Він виро́щує огірки́ у своє́му горо́ді.

gas, *n.* 1) газ, **I prefer to cook with g.** Я волі́ю вари́ти на га́зі.; 2) *(gasoline)* бензи́н, ♦ **to get g.** заправля́ти авто, **We need to get g.** Нам тре́ба запра́вити авто.; *adj.* га́зовий, **g. cooker** га́зова плита́.

gate, *n.* бра́ма, *(wicket gate)* хві́ртка; *only pl.* воро́та.

gay, *n.* *(a homosexual)* ґей, гомосексуалі́ст; *adj.* 1) гомосексуа́льний, **g. marriage** односта́тевий шлюб; 2) *(merry)* весе́лий.

general, *adj.* зага́льний, **g. rule** зага́льне пра́вило, **in g.** взагалі́; *n.* генера́л.

genius, *n.* ге́ній, *var.* ґе́ній, **She is a poet of g.** Вона́ ґеніа́льна пое́тка. **He is a true g.** Він спра́вжній ґе́ній.

gentleman, *n.* пан, добро́дій; *form of address* **Gentlemen!** пано́ве!

German, *adj.* німе́цький; *n., m.* німе́ць, *f.* німке́ня, *var.* ні́мка.

Germany, *n.* Німе́ччина, **in G.** у Німе́ччині, **to G.** до Німе́ччини.

get, *v.* 1) отри́мувати, дістава́ти, бра́ти, **Where did you g. this?** Де ти діста́в (взяв) це?; 2) *(to have)* ма́ти, **I g. the impression that he isn't against our offer.** Я ма́ю вра́ження, що він не про́ти на́шої пропози́ції.; 3) *(to a point)* дістава́тися, добира́тися, потрапля́ти, **How can I g. to the theater?** Як мо́жна діста́тися до музе́ю?; 4) *(on train, bus, etc.)* сіда́ти у + *L.,* **G. on the next train.** Сіда́йте на насту́пний по́тяг; 5) *(become)* става́ти, **It got dark in the room.** У кімна́ті ста́ло те́мно.; роби́тися, **The water got dirty.** Вода́ зроби́лася брудно́ю.; 6) *(understand)* розумі́ти, **I don't g. it.** Я не розумі́ю цьо́го.; ♦ **to g. acquainted with sb** познайо́митися з + *I.,* **You must g. acquainted with my boyfriend.** Ти му́сиш познайо́митися із мої́м хло́пцем.; **to g. sick** захворі́ти на + *A.,* **g. well** видужувати.

gift, *n.* 1) подару́нок, дару́нок, **I got her a nice g.** Я купи́в їй га́рний подару́нок.; 2) *(talent)* дар, тала́нт, **He has a g. for acting.** Він ма́є дар (тала́нт) акто́ра.; ♦ **To look a g. horse in the mouth.** Диви́тися в зу́би даро́ваному коне́ві.

girl, *n.* 1) ді́вчина, **This school is for ~s.** Ця шко́ла для дівча́т.; 2) *(daughter)* до́чка, до́нька, **Their little g. is three.** Їхній мали́й до́ньці три ро́ки.; 3) *(girlfriend)* ді́вчина, нарече́на, **Do you have a g.?** Ти ма́єш ді́вчину (нарече́ну)?

give, *v.* 1) дава́ти, **Can you g. me some advice?** Чи ви мо́жете да́ти мені́ пора́ду?; 2) *(pay)* дава́ти, плати́ти, **How much did he g. for the book?** Скі́льки він дав (заплати́в) за кни́жку?; 3) *(convey)* перека́зувати, **G. her my regards.** Перека́зуйте їй віта́ння від ме́не.; 4) *(as gift)* дарува́ти, **What shall we g. him?** Що ми йому́ подару́ємо?; **g. in** поступа́тися; **g. up** здава́тися.

glad, *adj.* ра́дий, задово́лений, ♦ **G. to meet you.** Ра́д|ий, *f.* ~а, познайо́митися.; **g. tidings** до́брі нови́ни.

glass, *n.* 1) *(material)* скло, *var., colloq.* шкло, **piece of g.** шмато́к скла, 2) *(vessel)* скля́нка, *var., colloq.* шкля́нка; *adj.* скля́ний, *var., colloq.* шкля́ний.

glasses, *n., only pl.* окуля́ри, **pair of g.** па́ра окуля́рів, **to wear g.** носи́ти окуля́ри.

go, *v.* 1) *(on foot)* multi. ходи́ти, uni. йти, var. іти́, **We'll g. to the river.** Ми пі́демо на рі́чку.; 2) *(by vehicle)* multi. ї́здити, uni. ї́хати, **They went to Prague last year.** Торі́к вони́ ї́здили до Пра́ги.; 3) *(leave)* іти́, піти́, **I have to go.** Я му́шу йти.; **g. away!** іди́|и ~іть геть!, **g. back** поверта́тися; **g. by** проходи́ти, мина́ти, **A year went by.** Мину́в рік.; **g. down** зме́ншуватися, па́дати, **Tomorrow the temperature will g. down.** За́втра температу́ра впаде́.; **g. on** трива́ти, **The show went on for another half hour.** Виста́ва трива́ла ще пів годи́ни.; **g. out** 1) *(exit)* вихо́дити, ви́йти, **He went out of the house.** Він ви́йшов з до́му.; 2) *(of fire)* га́снути, **The fire quickly went out.** Ого́нь шви́дко зга́с.; **g. through** 1) пережива́ти, **He went through a lot.** Він бага́то пережи́в.; 2) *(examine)* перегляда́ти, **She went through all notes.** Вона́ перегляну́ла всі нота́тки.; **g. up** зроста́ти, збі́льшуватися, **The prices g. up every year.** Ці́ни зроста́ють щоро́ку.; **be -ing to** + *inf.* збира́тися *or* ду́мати + *inf.,* **What are you -ing to do about it?** Що ти збира́єшся (ду́маєш) з цим роби́ти?; ♦ **G. figure!** Поду́мати ті́льки! ♦ **to g.** із собо́ю, на ви́ніс, **Do you offer food to g.?** Ви пропону́єте ї́жу на ви́ніс?

God, *n.* Бог, ♦ **G. forbid** боро́нь Бо́же; **Oh G.!** О Бо́же! *or* О Го́споди!; **Thank G.** дя́ку Бо́гу;

good, *adj.* 1) до́брий, **He's a g. man.** Він до́бра люди́на.; хоро́ший, **She's a g. expert.** Вона́ хоро́ший фахіве́ць.; 2) *(pretty)* **Hanna looks g. in this dress.** Га́нна вигляда́є га́рною в цій су́кні.; 3) *(tasty)* смачни́й, до́брий, **His cabbage rolls are g.** Його́ голубці́ смачні́ (до́брі).; 4) *(valid)* ді́йсний, **The tickets are g. only for today.** Квитки́ ді́йсні ті́льки на сього́дні.; ♦ **g. heavens!** лю́ди до́брі!; ♦ **to be g. for** бу́ти кори́сним для + *G.,* **Fresh air is g. for health.** Сві́же пові́тря до́бре для здоро́в'я.; **g.-for-nothing** леда́що.

goodbye, *interj.* до поба́чення.

good evening, *interj.* до́брий ве́чір.

good-looking, *adj.* га́рний, вродли́вий; *(attractive)* прива́бливий.

good morning, *interj.* до́брого ра́нку.

good night, *interj.* добра́ніч, на добра́ніч.

grade, *n.* 1) *(form)* клас, **He was in seventh g.** Він був у сьо́мому кла́сі; 2) *(mark)* оці́нка; 3) я́кість, **high-g. cotton** баво́вна висо́кої я́кості; *v. (give a grade)* ста́вити оці́нку, *(evaluate)* оці́нювати.

gram, *n.* грам, **a hundred ~s** сто гра́мів.

grammar *n.* грама́тика; *adj.* граматди́чний.

granddaughter, *n.* ону́ка.

grandfather, *n.* дід, *fam.* діду́сь, ді́до.

grandmother, *n.* ба́ба, *fam.* бабу́ся, *Gal.* ба́бця.

grandson, *n.* ону́к, *var.* внук.

gray, *adj.* сі́рий; *(hair)* сиви́й.

great, *adj.* вели́кий, чудо́вий, **That's a g. idea!** Це чудо́ва ду́мка!

great

green

green, *adj.* 1) (*color*) зеле́ний, ♦ **g. with envy** зеле́ний від заздрощів.; 2) (*unripe*) недозрі́лий; 3) (*ecologically*) зеле́ний.

greet, *v.* (*say hello*) віта́тися з + *I.*, **They always g. us.** Вони́ завжди́ віта́ються з на́ми.

greeting, *n.* віта́ння, **birthday ~s** віта́ння з уроди́нами.

groceries, *n., pl.* проду́кти, **buy g.** купува́ти проду́кти.

group, *n.* гру́па, гурт, гурто́к, **rock g.** рок-гурт, **tourist g.** туристи́чна гру́па.

grow, *v.* 1) *intr.* рости́, **An tree ~s near my house.** Бі́ля мого́ до́му росте́ де́рево.; 2) *tran.* виро́щувати, **He likes to g. flowers.** Він лю́бить виро́щувати кві́ти.

guest, *n.* 1) гість, *pl.* го́сті, **g. of honor** поче́сний гість; 2) (*visitor*) відві́дувач, клієнт; ♦ **for ~s only** ті́льки для відві́дувачів.

guide, *n.* прові́дник, **g.-book** путівни́к + *I.* **This is an excellent g.- book around Galicia.** Це - чудо́вий путівни́к Галичино́ю.; *v. multi.* води́ти, *uni.* вести́ + *I.*, (*g. through*) прово́дити, **I'll gladly g. them around the old town.** Я ра́до поводжу́ їх стари́м мі́стом.

guitar, *n.* гіта́ра, **to play the g.** гра́ти на гіта́рі (*or* на гіта́ру), **g. player** гітари́ст.

H

habit, *n.* зви́чка, зви́чай, **bad h.** пога́на зви́чка, **to get into a h.** бра́ти собі́ за зви́чку + *impf. inf.*, **Petro got into a h. of watching every new film.** Петро́ взяв собі́ за зви́чку диви́тися ко́жен нови́й фільм.

hair, *n.* 1) *coll.* воло́сся.; **have a h. cut** стри́гтися, **I need to have a h. cut.** Мені́ тре́ба постри́гтися.; 2) **a h.** воло́сина.

hair-dresser's, *n.* перука́рня.

half, *n.* полови́на, пів, **one and a h.** півтора́ + *N. pl.*, **one and a half kilometers** півтора́ кіло́метри, оди́н із полови́ною.

hall, *n.* за́ла, (*university building*) ко́рпус, **Robinson H.** ко́рпус Робінсо́на.

ham, *n.* ши́нка, **h. sandwich** бутербро́д із ши́нкою.

hand, *n.* 1) рука́, **by the h.** за ру́ку; 2) (*worker*) робітни́к; *v.* дава́ти, вруча́ти, **He ~ed me a glass of wine.** Він дав мені́ скля́нку вина́.; **h. in** здава́ти, **The students ~ed in their tests.** Студе́нти зда́ли контро́льні робо́ти.; ♦ **at h.** поблизу́; ♦ **by h.** ручни́м спо́собом; ♦ **to give a h.** допомага́ти; ♦ **h. in h.** пліч-о-пліч; ♦ **-s up!** 1) (*surrender*) ру́ки вго́ру!; 2) (*assent*) підіймі́ть ру́ку, хто ...

handkerchief, *n.* (носова́) хусти́на, хусти́нка.

handout, *n.* розда́ток, **All exercises are on the h.** Всі впра́ви на розда́тку.

handsome, *adj.* га́рний, вродли́вий, **Bohdan is young and h.** Богда́н – молоди́й і вродли́вий.

hang, *v.* 1) *tran.* ві́шати, пові́сити, **You can h. your coat here.** Мо́жете пові́сити пальто́ тут.; 2) *intr.* висі́ти, **The picture ~s on the wall.** Карти́на виси́ть на стіні́.

happen, *v.* 1) става́тися, трапля́тися, **When did it h.?** Коли́ це ста́лося?; 2) (*with inf. as polite question*) бува́ не..., ча́сом не ..., **Do you h. to know this road?** Ви бува́ (ча́сом) не зна́єте ціє́ї доро́ги?

happiness, *n.* ща́стя, **I wish you h.** Бажа́ю вам ща́стя.

happy, *adj.* 1) щасли́вий, **They're a h. family.** Вони́ - щасли́ва сім'я́.; *cliché* **H. birthday!** Многая лі́та!; 2) (*joyous*) весе́лий, **He is a h. guy.** Він весе́лий хло́пець.; 3) (*willing*) ра́дий, **We'll be h. to help.** Ми ра́до допоможе́мо.; 4) (*satisfied*) задово́лений, **I'm quite h. with the result.** Я ці́лком задово́лений результа́том.

hard, *adj.* тверди́й, **The bed is too h.** Це лі́жко зана́дто тверде́.; 2) мі́цний, **This is a really h. safe.** Це ду́же мі́цний сейф.; 3) тяжки́й, **h. work** тяжка́ пра́ця; складни́й, **h. problem** складна́ пробле́ма.; 4) (*severe*) суво́рий, **Don't be so h. with the child.** Не будь таки́м суво́рим із дити́ною.; **The climate here is h.** Підсо́ння тут суво́ре.; ♦ **h. and fast rules** непору́шні пра́вила; *adv.* бага́то, тя́жко, **He works h.** Він бага́то працю́є.

hard-working, *adj.* працьови́тий, стара́нний, **He's a h. guy.** Він працьови́тий хло́пець.

hat, *n.* капелю́х, **straw h.** бриль; **to take off a h.** зніма́ти капелю́х(а).

hate, *v.* нена́видіти, **Once Roman ~ed mobile phones.** Коли́сь Рома́н нена́видів мобі́льні телефо́ни.; *n.* не́нависть.

have, *v.* 1) (*possess*) ма́ти, володі́ти + *A.*, **Yarema has a cat.** Яре́ма ма́є кота́.; **I h. no idea.** Я не ма́ю поня́ття.; у + *G.* + бу́ти, **Yarema has a cat.** У Яре́ми є кіт.; **I had a new car.** У ме́не було́ нове́ а́вто.; 2) (*mod.*) му́сити, бу́ти пови́нним + *inf.*, **We h. to do it.** Ми му́симо (пови́нні) це зроби́ти.; ♦ **He had it coming.** Так йому́ і тре́ба.

he, *pers. pron.*, *m.* 1) він, **He sleeps a lot.** Він бага́то спить.; 2) (*in compound sentences*) той, хто (що) ... **H. who is afraid always loses.** Той, хто (що) бої́ться, завжди́ програ́є.

head, *n.* 1) голова́, **What's that on your h.?** Що це в те́бе на голові́?; 2) (*of cabbage*) кача́н, **half a h. of cabbage** пів кача́на капу́сти; 3) (*president*) голова́, **h. of government** голова́ уря́ду; прові́дник, **h. of the local community** прові́дник місце́вої грома́ди; *v.*, *tran.* (*lead*) очо́лювати + *A.*, **She sometimes ~s their meetings.** Вона́ ча́сом очо́лює їхні нара́ди.

headache, *n.* біль голови́, **I have a (bad) h.** (У) Ме́не (ду́же) боли́ть голова́.

health, *n.* здоро́в'я, **He's of sound (poor) h.** У ньо́го до́бре (ке́пське) здоро́в'я.; ♦ **to your h.!** на здоро́в'я!

healthy, *adj.* здоро́вий, **My teeth are h.** Мої́ зу́би здоро́ві.

hear, *v.* 1) чу́ти + *A.*, **I h. a train.** Я чу́ю по́тяг.; **Do you h. me?** Ви мене́ чу́єте?; 2) **h. out** вислухо́вувати, **Can we h. him out and not interrupt?** Ми мо́жемо ви́слухати його́ і не перебива́ти?

heart, *n.* 1) се́рце, **heartache** біль у се́рці; **h. attack** серце́вий напа́д; 2) *fig.* суть, **h. of the matter** суть спра́ви.; ♦ **break sb's heart** розби́ти се́рце + *D.*, **He broke her h.** Він розби́в їй се́рце.; ♦ **by h.** напа́м'ять.

heat, *n.* 1) спе́ка, жара́, **h. wave** спеко́тна пого́да; 2) (*high temperature*) тепло́, **The plant is OK both in h. and cold.** Росли́ні до́бре як в тепли́, так і в хо́лоді.; 3) (*in cooking*) вого́нь, **Reduce the h. and cook for two hours.** Зме́ншіть вого́нь і варі́ть дві годи́ни.; *v.* (*warm up*) нагріва́ти, **The sun hasn't ~ed the sea yet.** Со́нце ще не нагрі́ло мо́ре.; (*room*) опа́лювати, **Now electricity ~s our building.** Тепе́р еле́ктрика опа́лює наш буди́нок.

heavy

heavy, *adj.* 1) важки́й, **To travel with h. luggage was not easy.** Подорожувати із важким багажем було нелегко.; 2) тяжки́й, **h. work** тяжка́ робо́та.

height, *n.* 1) *(person)* зріст, **What's your h.?** Скі́льки ви на зріст? 2) *(building)* висота́, **He has a fear of ~s.** Він бої́ться висоти́.; 3) *(peak)* пік, ро́зпал, верши́на, **August is the h. of the tourist season in Yalta.** Се́рпень - це ро́зпал тури́стичного сезо́ну в Я́лті.

hello, *n.* 1) приві́т, **to say h.** віта́тися; 2) *(over phone)* альо́!, **H., who's this?** Альо́, хто це?

help, *v.* 1) (до)помага́ти + *D.*, **I can h. you if you like.** Я мо́жу (до)помогти́ вам, якщо́ хо́чете.; **How can I h. you?** Чим мо́жу (до)помогти́?; 2) **h. oneself** *(treat oneself)* частува́тися + *I.*, **They ~ed themselves to some wine.** Вони́ почастува́лися вино́м.; **Please, h. yourself.** Будь ла́ска, частуйтеся.; *interj.* **H.!** ряту́йте!; ♦ **So h. me God.** Бо́же, поможи́.; *n.* допомо́га, **to ask for h.** проси́ти допомо́ги; ♦ **There's no h. for it.** На це нема́є ра́ди.

her, *poss. pron., f.* 1) її, **H. eyes are quite blue.** Її о́чі геть си́ні; 2) *(not translated when referring to the subject's own body part)*, **Maria closed h. eyes.** Марі́я заплю́щила о́чі.; 3) *(referring to somebody or something related to the subject of sentence)* *m.* свій, *f.* своя́, *nt.* своє́, *pl.* свої́, **Maria told h. husband this story.** Марі́я розказа́ла цю істо́рію своє́му чолові́кові.; *pers. pron., f.* 1) *A.* and *G.* її, **He loves h.** Він її коха́є.; *(after prep.)* неї, **They did it without h.** Вони́ зроби́ли це без не́ї.; 2) *D.* їй, **I gave h. a pen.** Я дав їй перо́.; 3) *I.* не́ю, **I came with h.** Я прийшо́в з не́ю.; 4) *L.*, ній, **There was a new hat on h.** На ній був нови́й капелю́х.; 5) *(when used instead of she)* вона́, **That's h.** Це вона́.

here, *adv.* 1) *posn.* тут, **We are h.** Ми тут.; 2) *(dem.)* ось, це, ось це, **Here's his dad.** Ось його́ та́то.; 3) *dir.* сюди́, **Come h.!** Ході́ть сюди́!; ♦ **h. and now** за́раз же; ♦ **h. and there** тут і там; ♦ **neither h., nor there** ні в тин, ні у воро́та.

herself, *refl. pron., 3rd pers., f.* 1) себе́, **In her dreams, she sees h. young.** У свої́х мрі́ях вона́ ба́чить себе́ молодо́ю.; 2) *(for emphasis)* сама́, **She h. would like to know it.** Вона́ сама́ хоті́ла б зна́ти це.; 3) *(alone)* сама́, **She can do it h.** Вона́ мо́же зроби́ти це сама́.; 4) *(for herself)* собі́, **She baked h. a cake.** Вона́ спекла́ собі́ торт(а).

high, *adj.* 1) висо́кий, **a h. building** висо́кий буди́нок, **h. school** сере́дня шко́ла; 2) *(in measurements)* завви́шки, **The tree was two meters h.** Де́рево було́ два ме́три завви́шки.; *adv.* висо́ко, **The castle is h. up on a mountain.** За́мок стої́ть висо́ко на горі́.

him, *pron.* 1) *A.* and *G.* його́, **They like h.** Вони́ лю́блять його́.; *(after prep.)* ньо́го, **without h.** без ньо́го; 2) *D.* йому́, **I gave h. a pen.** Я дав йому́ перо́.; 3) *I.* ним, **I came with h.** Я прийшо́в з ним; 4) *L.*, ньо́му, **There was a new hat on h.** На ньо́му був нови́й капелю́х.; 5) *(when used instead of he)* він, **That's h.** Це він.

himself, *refl. pron., 3rd pers., m.* 1) себе́, **In his dreams, he sees h. young.** У свої́х мрі́ях він ба́чить себе́ молоди́м.; 2) *(for emphasis)* сам, **He h. never read the book.** Він сам ніко́ли не чита́в ціє́ї кни́жки.; 3) *(alone)* сам, **Borys can finish the assignment h.** Бори́с мо́же закі́нчити завда́ння сам.; 4) *(for himself)* собі́, **Volodia made h. an omelet.** Воло́дя зроби́в собі́ яє́шню.

his, *poss. pron., m.* 1) його́, **It's h. house.** Це його́ ха́та.; 2) *(not translated when referring to the subject's own body part)*, **Roman put h. foot on the chair.** Рома́н покла́в но́гу на стіле́ць.; 3) *(referring to somebody or something related to the subject of sentence)* *m.* свій, *f.* своя́, *nt.* своє́, *pl.* свої́, **My friend asked h. sister for help.** Мій друг попроси́в свою́ сестру́ допомогти́.

house

historian, *n.* істо́рик.

history, *n.* істо́рія, **Mr. Pavliuk is an expert in h.** Пан Павлю́к - фахі́вець з істо́рії.

hobby, *n.* захо́плення, улю́блене заня́ття, при́страсть.

hold, *v.* 1) *tran.* трима́ти, **He ~s a fork.** Він трима́є виде́лку.; трима́ти за + *A.*, **She held his hand.** Вона́ трима́ла його́ за ру́ку.; 2) *tran. (contain)* місти́ти, бу́ти на + *A.*, **The pot ~s three liters.** Кастру́ля місти́ть три лі́три.; 3) *tran. (a lecture)* прово́дити, **We'll h. a meeting next day.** Ми проведемо́ зу́стріч наступного дня.; 4) *intr.* трима́тися за + *A.* **He held on tight to the handle.** Він мі́цно трима́вся за ру́чку.; **h. on a minute!** чекай *(pl* ~те) хвили́нку!

holiday, *n.* свя́то; ~**s.** відпу́стка, кані́кули, вака́ції; **to go on ~s** (п)іти́ у відпу́стку, **Where did you spend your ~s?** Де ви прове́ли відпу́стку?; **for (on) ~s** на свя́та.

home, *n.* 1) дім, до́ма, **Where's your h.?** Де ваш дім?; **My h. is here by the Dnipro.** Моя́ до́ма тут, над Дніпро́м.; 2) *(family)* рід, **She is from a Galician h.** Вона́ із гали́цького ро́ду.; *adv.* до́ма, уд́ома, *colloq.* ха́та, **Natalia was h. all evening.** Ната́ля була́ (у)до́ма весь ве́чір.; *dir.* додо́му, домів, *colloq.* до ха́ти, **I'm going h.** Я йду додо́му.; *adj.* 1) дома́шній, **h. address** дома́шня адре́са, **h. cooking** дома́шня ку́хня; 2) націона́льний, **h. industry** націона́льна інду́стрія.

hope, *n.* наді́я на + *A.*, **h. for help** наді́я на допомо́гу, **vain h.** ма́рна наді́я; *v.* наді́ятися, **We h. you come.** Наді́ємося, що ви при́йдете.

horse, *n.* кінь, **She likes this white h.** Вона́ лю́бить цьо́го бі́лого коня́.

hospitable, *adj.* гости́нний, **The Petrenkos are always so h.** Петре́нки за́вжди такі́ гости́нні.

hospital, *n.* ліка́рня, шпита́ль, **at a h.** у ліка́рні.

hospitality, *n.* гости́нність, **Ukrainians are known for their h.** Украї́нці відо́мі своє́ю гости́нністю.

host, *n.* 1) господа́р, хазя́їн, ґа́зда, **Who is the h. here?** Хто тут хазя́їн?; 2) **a h. of** ці́лий ряд + *G.*, бага́то + *G.*, **I found a h. of photos.** Я знайшо́в ці́лий ряд світли́н.; *v.* прийма́ти, гости́ти, **Our university will be ~ing the conference.** Наш університе́т прийма́тиме конфере́нцію.

hostess, *n.* господи́ня, хазя́йка, *Gal.* ґазди́ня, **Olha is a great h.** О́льга чудо́ва господи́ня.

hot, *adj.* 1) гаря́чий, **The water was h.** Вода́ була́ гаря́ча.; 2) *(spicy)* го́стрий, **I need some h. pepper.** Мені́ тре́ба го́строго перцю́.; *adv.* гаря́че, **It's h. in here.** Тут гаря́че., **I feel h.** Мені́ гаря́че.

hotel, *n.* готе́ль, **to book (find) a h.** замовля́ти (знахо́дити) готе́ль.

hour, *n.* 1) годи́на, **We spoke for two ~s.** Ми розмовля́ли дві годи́ни.; 2) *(period)* пора́, **morning (evening) h.** ра́нкова (вечі́рня) пора́; **by the h.** погоди́нно, **He's paid by the h.** Йому́ пла́тять погоди́нно.

house, *n.* 1) *(building)* буди́нок, **This is the only old h. on the street.** Це єди́ний стари́й буди́нок на ву́лиці.; 2) *(single-family house)* ха́та, **My h. is right on the street corner.** Моя́ ха́та на самому ро́зі ву́лиці.; 3) дім, **h. of prayer** дім моли́тви, **the White H.** Бі́лий Дім; 4) *(of legislature)* пала́та, **the H. of Representatives (Lords, Commons)** Пала́та представни́ків (ло́рдів, грома́д); ♦ **h. wine** дома́шнє вино́; ♦ **on the h.** за раху́нок закла́ду, **Tonight all drinks are on the h.!** Сього́дні я частую!

how, *adv.* як, **I know h. you do it.** Я знаю, як ти це робиш.; ♦ **H. are you?** Як справи?; ♦ **H. old is she?** Скільки їй років?; ♦ **H. come?** Як (це) так?

how many, *adv.* скільки, як багато?, **H. m. books did he bring?** Скільки книжок він приніс?

how much, *adv.* скільки, як багато?, **H. m. milk do we have?** Скільки молока ми маємо?

hryvnia, *n.* (*Ukrainian currency*) гривня, **one h.** одна гривня, **two (three, four)** -s дві (три, чотири) гривні, **five (and more)** ~s п'ять гривень.

hundred, *card.* сто, **a h. and ten people (men)** сто десять чоловік (чоловіків), **over a h.** понад сто; **in the early nineteen ~s** на початку тисяча дев'ятсотих (років); ♦ **one h. percent** на сто відсотків, **He's one h. percent right.** Він на сто відсотків правий.; *n.* сотня, **many ~s of people** багато сотень людей.

hundredth *ord.* сотий.

hungry, *adj.* голодний, **I'm h.** Я хочу їсти.; **My dog is always h.** Мій пес завжди голодний.

hurry, *v.* поспішати, спішити, квапитися, **After the show they hurried home.** Після вистави вони поспішили додому.; **h. up!** поквапся! ~теся; *n.* поспіх, **In a h., I forgot my wallet.** У поспіху я забув гаманець.; **be in a h.** поспішати, **She's never in a h.** Вона ніколи не поспішає., **What's the h.?** Навіщо поспішати?

husband, *n.* чоловік, **Meet Roman Kozak, my h.** Знайомтеся - це Роман Козак, мій чоловік.

Hutsul 1) *n.* (*native of the Carpathians*) *m.* гуцул, *f.* гуцулка, **The ~s are known for their wonderful folk art.** Гуцули відомі своїм чудовим народним мистецтвом.; 2) *adj.* гуцульський, **They have a house in an old H. village.** Вони мають хату у старому гуцульському селі.

I

I, *pers. pron.* я, **I am in Kyiv now.** Я в Києві зараз.

ice cream, *n.* морозиво, **I. c. is her favorite dessert.** Морозиво - її улюблений десерт.

idea, *n.* 1) ідея, **He thinks it's a great i.** Він думає, що це чудова ідея.; 2) (*concept*) поняття; ♦ **I have no i.** Я без поняття.

ideal, *adj.* ідеальний, **i. plan** ідеальний план, **i. couple** ідеальна пара, **i. vacation** ідеальні вакації; *n.* ідеал + *G.*, **They are my i. of a happy marriage.** Вони - мій ідеал щасливого шлюбу.

i. e., *conj.* (*that is*) тобто.

if, *conj.* 1) (*for real condition*) якщо, *colloq.* як, коли, **I. you like, I'll stay home.** Якщо (як, коли) хочеш, я лишуся вдома.; ♦ **i. you don't mind** ... якщо ви не проти; 2) (*for unreal impossible condition*) якби, **We could have come i. they had asked us.** Ми прийшли б, якби вони попросили нас.; 3) (*whether*) чи, **They want to know i. it's true.** Вони хочуть знати, чи це правда.

ill, *adj.* хворий, **terminally i.** смертельно хворий; *colloq.* слабий; **to fall i.** захворіти.

illness, *n.* хвороба, **Her i. was quite common.** Її хвороба була цілком звичайною.

immediately, *adv.* негайно, тут же, одразу, **I'll call you i. upon arrival.** Я подзвоню вам одразу, як приїду.

important, *adj.* 1) важливий, **Andrukhovych is an i. writer.** Андрухович – важливий письменник.; 2) головний, **The i. thing is to find the information.** Головне знайти інформацію.; **It's not i. what you say.** Не має значення, що ви кажете.

impossible, *adj.* неможливий, **It's i. to do.** Це неможливо зробити.

in, *prep.* 1) у (в), на (*location inside a space*) + *L.*, **i. this store** у цій крамниці, **i. Cuba** на Кубі; 2) у (в) (*direction of motion*) + *A.* **He put it i. the room.** Він поставив це у кімнату.; 3) (*period of time*) за + *A.* **i. an hour** за годину; (*after a period of time*) через + *A.*, **I. one month, everything will be fine.** Через місяць все буде добре.; 4) (*at given time*) у + *L.*, **i. July** у липні, **i. 1989** у тисяча дев'ятсот вісімдесят дев'ятому році.; 5) (*in a language*) *I.* of language, **i. Ukrainian** українською (мовою), **Can you write it i. English?** Ви можете написати це англійською?; ♦ **be i.** бути в моді, **Red is i. this summer.** Червоне є в моді цього літа.

includ|e, *v.* включати + *A.*, **The program ~s short films.** Програма включає короткі фільми.; **~ing** включаючи + *A.*, **The library has various books, ~ing rare ones.** Бібліотека має різні книжки, включаючи рідкісні.

incorrect, *adj.* 1) неправильний, **This is an i. answer.** Це неправильна відповідь.; 2) некоректний, **politically i.** політично некоректний.

incredible, *adj.* неймовірний, невірогідний, **This is an i. story.** Це неймовірна історія.; ♦ (*to express disbelief*) **i.!** неймовірно!

indifferent, *adj.* байдужий до + *G.*, **I'm completely i. to him.** Я цілком байдужий до нього.

inexpensive, *adj.* недорогий, **His new car is i. but not at all cheap.** Його нове авто недороге, але зовсім не дешеве.

information, *n.* 1) інформація, **We have no i. about this event.** Ми не маємо інформації про цю подію.; 2) (*counter in a station*) довідкове (б'юро).

instead, *adv.* натомість, **Stop worrying, call him i.** Перестаньте журитися, подзвоніть йому натомість; *prep.* **i. of** ... замість + *G.*, **i. of me** замість мене.

instructor, *n.* 1) *m.* викладач, *f.* викладачка + *G.*, **She's our history i.** Вона наша викладачка історії.; 2) інструктор з + *G.*, **driving i.** інструктор з водіння авта.

intelligent, *adj.* розумний, **Myroslava is an i. woman.** Мирослава розумна жінка.

interest, *n.* 1) цікавість, **to look at sb with i.** дивитися з цікавістю.; 2) (*public*) інтерес, *also pl.* інтереси; **to take i. in sth** цікавитися + *I.*; 3) (*dividend*) процент; *v.* цікавити, **Their offer ~s us greatly.** Їхня пропозиція дуже цікавить нас.

interesting, *adj.* цікавий, **This is an i. book.** Це цікава книжка.

international, *adj.* міжнародний, **i. developments (news)** міжнародні події (новини), **i. politics** міжнародна політика.

Internet, *n.* інтернет, міжнародна мережа, *colloq.* інет; **on the I.** на інтернеті, *colloq.* в інеті; **via the I.** інтернетом.; *adj.* інтернетний, мережевий, **I. publication** інтернет-видання, мережеве видання.

interrupt, *v.* перебивати + *A.*, **He always ~s me.** Він завжди перебиває мене.; **Don't i.!** Не перебивай! ~те!

into, *prep.* 1) *dir.* у (в) + *A.* **i. the room** у кімна́ту; до + *G.* **He went i. the building.** Він увійшо́в до буди́нку.; 2) **to translate i. Ukrainian** переклада́ти + *I.* украї́нською (мо́вою); 3) *(turn into)* на + *A.,* **The snow turned i. water.** Сніг перетвори́вся на во́ду.; 4) *(math division)* на + *A.,* **Four i. two equals two.** Чоти́ри поділи́ти на два дорі́внює два.; 5) **be i.** захо́плюватися + *I.,* **She is i. our cuisine.** Вона́ захо́плюється на́шою ку́хнею.

introduce, *v.* представля́ти + *A.* + *D.* **sb to sb**, **allow me to i.** дозво́льте предста́вити; знайо́мити *A.* з + *I.* **He ~ed me to her.** Він познайо́мив мене́ з не́ю.

invitation, *n.* запро́шення, **at the i.** на запро́шення, **to extend an i. to ...** запроси́ти + *A.;* **by i. only** ті́льки на запро́шення.

invite, *v.* запро́шувати, **I want to i. you to my place.** Хочу́ запроси́ти вас до се́бе.

is, *v., pres., 3rd pers. sg.* є *(or is usually omitted in pres.),* **He i. my brother.** Він - мій брат.

it, *pron., nt.* 1) воно́ *(for all nt. nouns),* **Here's an apple. It's sweet.** Ось я́блуко. Воно́ соло́дке.; воно́ *(for all inan. f. nouns),* **This is his book, i. is interesting.** Це його́ кни́жка, вона́ ціка́ва.; він *(for all inan. m. nouns),* **This is a new film, i. is boring.** Це нови́й фільм, він нудни́й.; 2) *(demonstrative function)* це + бу́ти, **I. is a man.** Це чоло́вік., **I. will be me.** Це бу́ду я.

Italian, *adj.* італі́йський; *n., m.* італі́єць; *f.* італі́йка.

Italy, *n.* Іта́лія; **in I.** в Іта́лії, *dir.* **to I.** до Іта́лії, **Next fall they are going to I.** Наступної о́сени вони́ їдуть до Іта́лії.

its, *poss. pron., 3rd pers.* 1) *(to modify all m. and nt. nouns)* його́, **Look at this city. I. streets are so green.** Подиві́ться на це мі́сто. Його́ ву́лиці такі́ зеле́ні.; 2) її́ *(for all f. nouns),* **Pavlo has a house. I. walls are yellow.** Павло́ має ха́ту. Її́ сті́ни жо́вті.

itself, *refl. pron., 3rd pers., nt.* 1) себе́, **His horse scratched i.** Його́ кінь подря́пав себе́.; 2) *(for emphasis)* сам, сама́, саме́, **The table i. is cheap.** Сам стіл деше́вий., **The book i. was cheap.** Сама́ кни́жка була́ деше́вою.; 3) *(alone)* саме́, **The kitten i. can find the way.** Коше́ня мо́же знайти́ доро́гу саме́., **It speaks for i.** Воно́ саме́ за се́бе гово́рить.; 4) *(for himself)* собі́, **The bird built i. a little house.** Пта́шка збудува́ла собі́ ха́тку.

J

jacket, *n.* 1) *(male)* піджа́к, **He always has a j. on.** Він за́вжди у піджа́ку.; *(female)* жаке́т, **Liuda hated to wear ~s.** Лю́да ненави́діла носи́ти жаке́ти.; ку́ртка, **leather j.** шкіряна́ ку́ртка; 2) *(of book)* обкла́динка.

jam, *n.* пови́дло, джем, **Would you like some j. with your bread?** Чи ви хо́чете пови́дла (дже́му) до хлі́ба?; **apple j.** я́блучне пови́дло.

January, *n.* сі́чень, **next J.** наступного сі́чня, **in J.** у сі́чні.

Japan, *n.* Япо́нія, **Mykola always wanted to see J.** Микола за́вжди хоті́в поба́чити Япо́нію., **in J.** в Япо́нії, *dir.* **to J.** до Япо́нії.

Japanese 1) *adj.* япо́нський, **Sushi is a J. dish.** Су́ші - це япо́нська стра́ва.; 2) *n., m.* япо́нець, **This J. speaks very good Ukrainian.** Цей япо́нець ду́же до́бре гово́рить українською. *f.* япо́нка, **Her name is Yoko. She's J.** Її́ зва́ти Йо́ко. Вона́ – япо́нка.

job, *n.* 1) робо́та, **full-time (part-time) j.** робо́та на (не) по́вну ста́вку; **~less** безробі́тний; 2) *(duty)* завда́ння, обов'язок, **Her j. is to set a good example.** Її́ завда́ння – подава́ти до́брий при́клад.; 3) *(position)* робо́че мі́сце, **The company has new ~s.** Компа́нія ма́є робо́чі мсця.

joint, *adj.* спі́льний, **j. account** спі́льний раху́нок, **j. venture** СП (еспе́), спі́льне підприє́мство.

joke, *v.* жартува́ти, **Maria often ~s.** Марі́я ча́сто жарту́є.; ♦ **This isn't a j.** Це не жа́рти.; *n.* жарт, анекдо́т; ♦ **to tell a j.** розказа́ти анекдо́т.

journalist, *n., m.* журналі́ст, **Marko is a well-known j.** Марко - відо́мий журналі́ст.; *f.* журналі́стка, **Valentyna worked as a j. all her life.** Валенти́на працюва́ла журналі́сткою все життя́.

journey, *n.* по́дорож, мандрі́вка, **to go on a j.** їха́ти у по́дорож.

juice, *n.* сік, **apple (orange, tomato) j.** я́блучний (помара́нчевий, тома́тний) сік.

July, *n.* ли́пень, **in J.** у ли́пні, **on the fourth of J.** четве́ртого ли́пня.

June, *n.* че́рвень, **in J.** у че́рвні, **on the sixteenth of J.** шістна́дцятого че́рвня.

just, *adv.* 1) *(only)* лише́, ті́льки, **j. you and me** лише́ ми з тобо́ю (ва́ми); 2) *(moment ago)* щойно, **We j. arrived.** Ми щойно приї́хали.; 3) *(emph.)* про́сто, **J. do it.** Про́сто зроби́ це.; **They're j. wonderful!** Вони́ про́сто чудо́ві!; **j. about** ма́йже; **j. in case** про всяк ви́падок.

K

keep, *v.* 1) трима́ти, **He ~s three cats.** Він трима́є трьох коті́в.; 2) зберіга́ти, **Ihor ~s his money in a bank.** Ігор зберіга́ти гро́ші в ба́нку.; 3) лиша́ти собі́, **You may k. the change.** Мо́жете лиши́ти собі́ зда́чу.; 4) не перестава́ти + *impf. inf.* **Ostap kept calling her.** Оста́п не перестава́в дзвони́ти їй.; ♦ **k. one's promise** дотри́мувати(ся) сло́ва.

key, *n.* ключ, **Oles lost his ~s.** Оле́сь загуби́в ключі́.; **k. to ...** ключ від + *G.;* **spare k.** запа́сни́й ключ.

Kharkiv, *n.* Ха́рків, **in K.** у Ха́ркові, **to K.** до Ха́ркова; *adj.* ха́рківський, **K. University** Ха́рківський університе́т.

Kiev, *n., obsolescent,* see **Kyiv**.

kilogram, *n.* кілогра́м, **ten ~s** де́сять кілогра́мів.

kilometer, *n.* кіломе́тр, *var.* кіломе́тер, **how many ~s?** скільки кіломе́трів?; **He drove a hundred ~s an hour.** Він їхав сто кіломе́трів за годи́ну.

kind, *n.* тип, вид, **all ~s of apples** всі ви́ди я́блук.; **What k. of a person is he?** Що він за люди́на?; ♦ **nothing of the k.** нічо́го поді́бного; *adj.* люб'я́зний, до́брий, **That's very k. of you.** Ви ду́же люб'я́зні.

kiss, *n.* поцілу́нок, **tender k.** соло́дкий поцілу́нок; *v.* цілува́ти, **He ~ed Melanie good night.** Він поцілува́в Мала́нку на добра́ніч.

kitchen, *n.* ку́хня, **They liked to gather in the k.** Вони́ люби́ли збира́тися на ку́хні.

knee, *n.* колі́но, **My k. hurts.** Мене́ боли́ть колі́но.

knife, *n.* ніж, **a sharp (blunt) k.** го́стрий (тупи́й) ніж.

know *v.* 1) зна́ти, **Do you k. how to get there?** Чи ти зна́єш, як туди́ потра́пити?; 2) вмі́ти *(be able to)*, **I k. how to read French.** Я вмі́ю чита́ти францу́зькою.

kope(c)k, *n.*, копі́йка, **one k.** одна́ копі́йка, **two (three, four) ~s** дві (три, чоти́ри) копі́йки, **five ~s** *(and more)* п'ять копі́йок.

Kyiv 1) *n. (the capital of Ukraine)* Ки́їв, **in K.** у Ки́єві, **I often go to K.** Я ча́сто ї́жджу до Ки́єва.; 2) *adj.* ки́ївський, **K. National University** Ки́ївський націона́льний університе́т; ♦ **chicken K.** котле́та по-ки́ївськи.

L

lady, *n.* па́ні, **She is a real l.** Вона́ спра́вжня па́ні., **l. of the house** господи́ня, ґазди́ня.

lake, *n.* о́зеро, **Svitiaz is the largest l. in Ukraine.** Сві́тязь - найбі́льше о́зеро в Украї́ні.

lamp, *n.* ла́мпа, **table l.** насті́льна ла́мпа.

land, *n.* 1) земля́, **the house and the l. around** буди́нок і земля́ навко́ло; 2) край, **This is a l. of lakes and rivers.** Це край озе́р і річо́к.

lane, *n.* прову́лок, **He lives on Museum L.** Він живе́ у Музе́йному прову́лку.

language, *n.* мо́ва, **Ukrainian l.** украї́нська мо́ва, **What l. does he speak?** Яко́ю мо́вою він розмовля́є?; **speak the same l.** розмовля́ти тіє́ю ж мо́вою.

large, *adj.* вели́кий, **Their bedroom was l.** Ї́хня спа́льня була́ вели́кою.

last, *v.* трива́ти; продо́вжуватися, **The play ~ed (for) two hours.** П'є́са трива́ла дві годи́ни; *adj.* 1) *(in a line)* оста́нній, **Who is the l. in line?** Хто оста́нній у че́рзі?; ♦ **for the l. time** воста́ннє; 2) *(passed)* мину́лий, **l. week (month, year)** мину́лого ти́жня (мі́сяця, торі́к); ♦ **at l.** наре́шті; *adv.* оста́нній раз, воста́ннє, **They saw him l. a year ago.** Вони́ ба́чили його́ воста́ннє рік тому́.

late, *adj.* пі́зній, ♦ **to be (an hour) l.** запі́знюватися на + *A.*, **The train came an hour l.** По́їзд запізни́вся на годи́ну.; *adv.* пі́зно; **l. at night** пі́зно вночі́; **~r** пото́му, пі́зніше; ♦ **see you ~r!** бува́й! наразі́!

laugh, *v.* смія́тися; **l. at sb** смія́тися з (із) + *G.*, **They ~ed at Ivan loudly.** Вони́ го́лосно смія́лися з Іва́на.

laundry, *n.* 1) *(a place)* пра́льня; 2) *(washing)* пра́ння, **do the l.** пра́ти *also* пра́ти білизну (о́дяг), **He does his l. once a month.** Він пере́ раз на мі́сяць.

lawyer, *n.* адвока́т, юри́ст, правни́к; **He studies to be a l.** Він у́читься на юри́ста.

lazy, *adj.* леда́чий, лі́нивий, **He is too l. to take the job.** Він зана́дто леда́чий, щоб бра́тися за цю робо́ту.

leaf, *n.* 1) листо́к, (leaves) листя, **The leaves are falling from the trees.** Листя па́дає з дере́в; 2) *(of paper)* а́ркуш, *(page)* сторі́нка.

learn, *v.* 1) *(discipline, language)* вивча́ти, **They l. eastern languages at this university.** У цьо́му університе́ті вивча́ють схі́дні мо́ви.; 2) *(memorize)* вчи́ти, **Our assignment is to l. the new grammar.** На́ше завда́ння - ви́вчити нову́ грама́тику.; ♦ **l. by heart** *pf.* ви́вчити напам'я́ть; 3) *(find out)* дізнава́тися про + *A.*, **He ~ed about their visit yesterday.** Він дізна́вся про ї́хній візи́т учо́ра.

leather, *n.* шкі́ра, **The shoes are made of l.** Ці ту́флі зро́блені зі шкі́ри.; *adj.* шкіряни́й, **Yaryna likes her l. jacket.** Яри́на лю́бить свою́ шкіряну́ ку́ртку.

leave 1) *v.* (за)лиша́ти, **Can they l. their bags here?** Чи вони́ мо́жуть (за)лиши́ти тут свої́ су́мки?; 2) *(abandon)* (по)кида́ти, **She left her husband.** Вона́ (по)ки́нула чолові́ка.; 3) *(on foot)* піти́, **He left an hour ago.** Він пішо́в годи́ну тому́.; 4) *(by train, bus)* відхо́дити, відбува́ти, **Our train will l. in five minutes.** Наш по́тяг віді́йде за п'ять хвили́н.; 5) **l. for** від'їжджа́ти *or* поїхати до +*G.*, **Orest left for Rome.** Оре́ст від'ї́хав (поїхав) до Ри́му.; ♦ **l. sb be** дава́ти + *D.* (святий) спо́кій, **L. them be.** Да́йте їм (святий) спо́кій.; *n. (off work)* 1) (short) відгу́л, **take a two (three)-day l. …** бра́ти два (три) дні відгу́лу (відпу́стки) …, **He took a five-day l.** Він узя́в п'ять днів відгу́лу.; 2) *(longer)* відпу́стка, **be on a l.** бу́ти у відпу́стці.

lecture, *n.* ле́кція, **give a l.** чита́ти ле́кцію; **l. on** ле́кція про +*A.*, **What's today's l. on?** Про що сього́днішня ле́кція?; *v.* 1) чита́ти ле́кцію; 2) повча́ти + *A.*, **Don't l. me!** Не тре́ба мене́ повча́ти!

left, *adj.* 1) лі́вий, **l. side of the road** лі́вий бік доро́ги; 2) *(politically)* лі́вий, **l. parties** лі́ві па́ртії; *adv.* ліво́руч, **to turn l.** поверта́ти ліво́руч; *n.* **the L.** лі́виця, **the Ukrainian L.** украї́нська лі́виця.

leg, *n. (human)* 1) нога́, **Her l. hurts.** Її́ боли́ть нога́.; 2) *(of animal as food)* стегно́, **l. of lamb** бара́няче стегно́; стеге́нце, **chicken (duck) l.** куря́че (качи́не) стеге́нце.

lesson, *n.* 1) уро́к з + *G.*, **language l.** уро́к з мо́ви; заня́ття, **driving l.** заня́ття із автоїзди́; 2) *(experience)* нау́ка, **This was a l. for him.** Це бу́ло йому́ нау́кою.

let, *v.* 1) *(allow)* дозволя́ти, **l. me say…** дозво́ль (~те) сказа́ти … ; дава́ти + *pf. inf.* **l. him finish** дай (~те) йому́ закі́нчити; 2) *(exhortation)* дава́й *or* дава́йте + *inf.*, **l. us do it** дава́й (~те) зро́бимо це; 3) *(to express wish)* неха́й, хай, **L. your parents live a hundred years.** Хай ва́ші батьки́ живу́ть сто ро́ків.

letter, *n.* 1) *(written message)* лист, **I wrote them a l.** Я написа́ла їм лист (*or* листа́).; 2) *(of alphabet)* лі́тера, **capital l.** вели́ка лі́тера *or* вели́ка бу́ква; ♦ **man (woman) of ~s** письме́нник (письме́нниця).

library, *n.* бібліоте́ка, **in a l.** у бібліоте́ці, **university l.** університе́тська бібліоте́ка, **film l.** фільмоте́ка.

lie, *v.* 1) лежа́ти, **Bohdan lay quietly on his bed.** Богда́н ти́хо лежа́в на лі́жку., **Kyiv ~s on hills.** Ки́їв лежи́ть на пагорба́х.; 2) *(to tell lies)* обма́нювати + *A.*, **He is lying to you.** Він вас обма́нює.; *colloq.* бреха́ти + *D.* про + *A.*, **Vasyl ~d to his parents about his job.** Васи́ль збреха́в батька́м про свою́ робо́ту.

life, *n.* життя́, **My l. in Lviv was simply great.** Моє́ життя́ у Льво́ві було́ про́сто чудо́вим.

light, *n.* сві́тло, **bright l.** я́скра́ве сві́тло.; *adj.* 1) *(of weight)* легки́й, **l. suitcase** легка́ валі́за; 2) *(of color)* я́сний, **l. green** я́сно-зеле́ний; 3) *(opposite of dark)* сві́тлий, **l. room** сві́тла кімна́та; *v.* 1) *tran.* запа́лювати + *A.*, **He lit a cigarette.** Він запали́в сигаре́ту.; 2) *intr.* загорі́тися, запали́тися, **The lamp wouldn't l.** Ла́мпа нія́к не запа́лювалася.

like, *v.* 1) люби́ти, **I l. the way she writes.** Я люблю́, як вона́ пи́ше.; подо́батися *(logical subject in D.)*, **They l. him.** Він їм подо́бається.; 2) *(wish)* хоті́ти, **We'd l. to see the exhibit.** Ми хоті́ли б поба́чити цю ви́ставку.; ♦ **if you l.** якщо́ хо́чеш (*pl.* … хо́чете); ♦ **l. it or not** хоч-не-хоч; подо́бається це вам, чи ні; *prep.* як, **experts l. him** такі́ експе́рти, як він, **l. a novice** як нова́чок.; *conj.* на́че, нена́че, **l. you care** на́че тобі́ не одна́ково.

line　　　　　　　　　　　　　　　　　　　**mail**

line, *n.* 1) лі́нія, **phone l.** телефо́нна лі́нія; 2) *(rope)* мотузка, шнуро́к, верьо́вка; 3) *(of words)* рядок, **He read a few ~s.** Він прочита́в кілька рядків.; 4) *(queue)* черга, **stand in l.** стоя́ти в черзі.

linen, *n.* 1) по́стіль, посте́льна біли́зна; ♦ **to wash one's dirty l. in public** виноси́ти з ха́ти сміття́; 2) полотно́, льон; *adj.* полотня́ний, лляни́й.

lip, *n.* губа́, **to kiss on the ~s** цілува́ти у гу́би.

list, *n.* спи́сок, **l. of purchases** спи́сок поку́пок, **make up a l.** склада́ти спи́сок, **on the l.** у спи́ску.

listen, *v.* слу́хати + *A.*, **He ~ed but didn't hear.** Він слу́хав, але не чув.; **to l. to the radio** слу́хати ра́діо.

literature, *n.* літерату́ра, **We studied modern Ukrainian l.** Ми вивча́ли суча́сну украї́нську літерату́ру.

little, *adj.* мали́й, **l. children** малі́ діти; невели́кий, **a l. problem** невели́ка пробле́ма.; **a l. girl (boy)** дівчинка (хлопчик); *adv.* 1) ма́ло, небага́то, **I work l.** Я ма́ло працю́ю.; 2) **a l.** небага́то, трохи, **They helped me a l.** Вони трохи допомогли мені.; ♦ **l. by l.** потрохи.

live, *v. intr.* жи́ти, **My parents l. in the country.** Мої́ батьки́ живу́ть на селі́.; ♦ **long l. ..!** хай живе́ ..!; *adj.* живи́й, **Have you seen a l. lion?** Чи ви ба́чили живо́го ле́ва?.

living room, *n.* віта́льня, віта́льна кімна́та.

loaf, *n.* буха́нка, буха́нець, **a l. of bread** буха́нка хлі́ба.

lobby, *n.* 1) *(in apartment)* коридо́р, **small l.** невели́кий коридо́р; 2) *(in hotel)* фоє́, **in the l.** у фоє́.

local, *adj.* місце́вий, **The l. museum has a good art collection.** Місце́вий музе́й ма́є до́бру коле́кцію мисте́цтва.; *n.* місце́вий, **Are you a l.?** Ви місце́ві?.

located, *pa. pple.* **to be l.** *(of building, city)* розташо́вуватися, бути розташо́ваним, **Where is cathedral l.?** Де розташо́вується (розташо́ваний) собо́р?

long, *adj.* 1) до́вгий, **l. legs** до́вгі ноги; 2) *(in measurements)* завдо́вжки, **The bridge was two kilometers l.** Міст був два кіло́метри завдо́вжки.; 3) *(lasting for)* трива́ти + *A.*, **The film is eighty minutes l.** Фільм трива́є вісімдеся́т хвили́н.; **how l.?** яко́ї довжини́?, **How l. is the street?** Яко́ї довжини́ ця вули́ця?; *adv.* до́вго, трива́лий час, **I haven't seen her l.** Я до́вго не ба́чив її́.; **for a l. time** до́вго; **how l.?** скі́льки (часу)?; ♦ **l. ago** давно́.

look, *v.* 1) диви́тися (на + *A.*) **He ~ed at her with surprise.** Він подиви́вся на не́ї з по́дивом.; **L.!** Подив|и́ся! ~і́ться!; 2) **l. after** догляда́ти + *A. or* за + *I.*, **Mykola will l. after your father.** Мико́ла догляда́тиме за ва́шим ба́тьком.; 3) **l. back** огляда́тися, **She came up to the door and ~ed back.** Вона підійшла́ до двере́й і огля́нулася.; 4) **l. for** шука́ти + *A.*, **What are you ~ing for?** Що ви шука́єте?; 5) **l. forward to** з нетерпі́нням чека́ти + *A. or* коли + *clause*, **We l. forward to your arrival.** Ми з нетерпі́нням чека́ємо ва́шого прїзду (*or* коли ви прїдете).; 6) *(of windows, etc.)* **l. out** вихо́дити на + *A.*, **My room ~s out on an old park.** Моя́ кімна́та вихо́дить на стари́й парк.; 7) **l. through** передивля́тися, перегляда́ти + *A.*, **They ~ed through all his notes.** Вони передиви́лися (перегля́нули) всі його́ нота́тки.; *n.* 1) *(on face)* ви́раз, **She had a strange l. on her face.** У не́ї був дивни́й ви́раз на обли́ччі.; 2) *(appearance)* ви́гляд, **The town had a neglected l.** Мі́сто ма́ло занедба́ний ви́гляд.; **to take a l.** погля́нути, подиви́тися на + *A.*

lose, *v.* 1) *(be deprived)* втрача́ти, **They lost all their money.** Вони втра́тили всі гро́ші.; 2) *(through negligence)* губи́ти, **You lost the keys.** Ти загуби́в ключі́.; 3) *(time, opportunity)* га́яти, **We have no time to l.** Ми не мо́жемо га́яти час.; 4) *(be defeated)* програва́ти + *A.* + *D.*, **They lost the game to our team.** Вони програ́ли гру на́шій дружи́ні.; ♦ **have nothing to l.** logical subject in *D.* + нема́ що втрача́ти, **Petro has nothing to l.** Петро́ві нема́ що втрача́ти; ♦ **l. one's mind** з'ї́хати з глу́зду; ♦ **l. the way** губи́тися, **We lost our way in the old city.** Ми загуби́лися у старо́му мі́сті.; ♦ **l. weight** худну́ти, **I want to l. some weight.** Я хочу́ трохи схудну́ти.

lot, *n.* **a l. of** бага́то + *G.*, **They have a l. of friends.** Вони́ ма́ють бага́то дру́зів.; *colloq.* повно + *G.*, **There were a l. of people at the show.** На виста́ві було́ повно люде́й.

loud, *adj.* гучни́й, **l. music** гучна́ му́зика; *adv.* голо́сно, **I said it l. and clear.** Я сказа́в це голо́сно і чі́тко.

love, *n.* 1) *(romantic)* коха́ння, **confession of l.** осві́дчення в коха́нні; ♦ **fall in l. with** закоха́тися у + *A.*, покоха́ти + *A.*, **They fell in l. with each other.** Вони покоха́ли одне́ одно́го.; **l. at first sight** коха́ння з пе́ршого по́гляду; ♦ **make l. to sb** коха́тися з + *I.*; 2) *(fondness)* любо́в, **l. of music** любо́в до му́зики; ♦ **not for l. or money** ні за які́ гро́ші, **He wouldn't sell the picture, not for l. or money.** Він ні за які́ гро́ші не хо́че продава́ти карти́ну.; *v.* 1) *(romantically)* коха́ти, **I l. you** Я тебе́ коха́ю.; 2) *(love or like)* люби́ти, *(adore)* обо́жнювати, ду́же люби́ти, **All his friends l. to cook.** Усі́ його́ дру́зі ду́же лю́блять вари́ти.

low, *adj.* 1) низьки́й, **l. standard of living** низьки́й рі́вень життя́; 2) невисо́кий, **l. building.** невисо́кий буди́нок.; *adv.* 1) ни́зько, **The trees bent l. to the ground.** Дере́ва нагну́лися ни́зько до землі́; 2) *(of speaking)* ти́хо, **We talked l. not to wake up the baby.** Ми говори́ли ти́хо, щоб не розбуди́ти дити́ну.

lucky, *adj.* щасли́вий, **l. star** щасли́ва зі́рка.

luggage, *n.* бага́ж, **carry-on l.** ручни́й бага́ж, **piece of l.** мі́сце багажу́, **l. check-in** реєстра́ція багажу́, **to check in l.** здава́ти ре́чі у бага́ж, **l. cart** бага́жний візо́к.

lunch, *n.* обі́д, **for l.** на обі́д, **What are you having for l.?** Що ви їсте́ на обі́д?; **to have l.** обі́дати, **They had a late l. that day.** Того́ дня вони пі́зно обі́дали.

luxury, *n.* ро́зкіш, **This is too much of a l.** Це завели́ка ро́зкіш. **What a l. the room is!** Що за розкі́шна кімна́та!

Lviv 1) *n.* Львів, **L. is the capital of Galicia.** Львів - столи́ця Галичини́.; **to L.** до Льво́ва, **in L.** у Льво́ві; 2) *adj.* льві́вський, **L. beer** льві́вське пи́во.

M

machine, *n.* маши́на, **washing m.** пра́льна маши́на.

mad, *adj.* 1) *(crazy)* божеві́льний, **m. idea.** божеві́льна іде́я.; ♦ **be m. about** бути в захо́пленні від + *G.*, **They aren't exactly m. about the plan.** Вони не у захо́пленні від цьо́го пла́ну.; 2) *(angry)* серди́тий, лю́тий, **He's m. at me.** Він се́рдиться на ме́не.

magazine, *n.* журна́л, часо́пис, **The *Ukrainian Week* is their favorite m.** «Украї́нський ти́ждень» – їхній улю́блений часо́пис.

mail, *n.* 1) по́шта, **Can you get the m.?** Ти мо́жеш узя́ти по́шту?, **by m.** по́штою; 2) **electronic m.** електро́нна по́шта, **I need to read my e-m.** Мені́ тре́ба почита́ти електро́нну по́шту.; *v.* посила́ти по́штою, **They ~ed the books.** Вони посла́ли книжки́ по́штою.

main, *adj.* головний, основний, **m. street** центральна вулиця.

make, *v.* 1) робити, **I'll m. you some coffee.** Я зроблю вам кави. 2) *(produce)* виготовляти, **Where are these cars made?** Де роблять ці авта?; 3) *(film)* знімати, робити, **She is ~ing a film.** Вона знімає фільм.; 4) *(compel)* змушувати, примушувати, **They made us leave early.** Вони змусили нас піти рано.; ♦ **m. do** обходитися + *I.*, **I'll m. do with this money.** Я обійдуся цими грошима.; 5) *(understand)* **m. out** розбирати, **They talked softly and I didn't m. out what they said.** Вони розмовляли тихо, і я не розібрав, що вони сказали.; *n.* *(trade name)* марка, **What's the m. of his car?** Якої марки його авто?

man, *n.* 1) *(male)* чоловік, мужчина, **Roman is her type of m.** Роман - її тип мужчини.; 2) *(person)* людина, *pl.* люди, **All men are equal.** Всі люди рівні.; 3) *(husband)* чоловік, **He's my m.** Він мій чоловік.

manager, *n.* директор, адміністратор, завідувач; менеджер.

many, *adv.* багато + *G.*, **m. books** багато книжок; **how m.** скільки + *G.*, **so m.** стільки + *G.*; *pron.* багато хто, багато людей, **M. think this is impossible to do.** Багато хто думає, що це неможливо зробити.

map, *n.* мапа, карта, **on the m.** на карті, **street m.** карта міста.

March, *n.* березень, **in M.** у березні, **Mary will be here on M. 12.** Мері буде тут дванадцятого березня.

market, *n.* ринок, **on the m.** на ринку, **common m.** спільний ринок; **financial m.** фінансовий ринок; **m. square** ринкова площа.

marriage, *n.* шлюб, **happy m.** щасливий шлюб, **childless m.** бездітний шлюб; ♦ **m. of convenience** шлюб із розрахунку.

married, *pa. pple.* одружений; **m. couple** подружжя; **m. or single** одружений чи парубок (*f.* незаміжня); **get m.** одружуватися (з + *I.*), братися (з + *I.*), **When did they get m.?** Коли вони одружилися (побралися)?

marry, *v.* 1) одружуватися з + *I.*, брати шлюб з + *I.*, **Ivan will m. Maria in church.** Іван одружиться (візьме шлюб) з Марією у церкві.; *(of a female)* виходити заміж за + *A.*, **Maria married Ivan.** Марія вийшла заміж за Івана.; 2) *(to cause to marry)* одружувати + *A.* (із) + *I.*, видавати + *A.* за + *A.*, **He married his daughter to a rich man.** Він одружив дочку з багатим. *or* Він видав дочку за багатого.

matter, *n.* справа; ♦ **What's the m.?** У чім (чому) справа? ♦ **in the m. of ...** у тому, що стосується + *G.*, **They trust him in the m. of money.** Вони вірять йому у тому, що стосується грошей.;

may, *mod.* 1) *(permission)* можна + *D.*, **M. he come as well?** Можна йому теж прийти?; могти, **You m. leave now.** Тепер можете йти.; 2) *(possibility)* можливо, (що), **He m. be right.** Можливо, що він має рацію.; 3) *(wish)* хай + *pres.*, щоб + *pa.*, **M. they live a hundred years.** Хай вони живуть сто років. *or* Щоб вони жили сто років.; ♦ **be that as it m.** так чи інакше, у кожному разі.

May, *n.* травень, **in M.** у травні, **on the tenth of M.** десятого травня.

maybe, *adv.* можливо, мабуть, *colloq.* може, **M. they stayed home.** Можливо, вони лишилися вдома.

mean, *v.* 1) значити, означати, **What does it m.?** Що це значить?; 2) *(to have in mind)* мати на увазі, **to m. to say** хотіти сказати, **He really meant to say "OK, it's a deal."** Насправді він хотів сказати: «Гаразд, домовилися».; ♦ **I m.** тобто.; **What do you m.?** Що ти маєш на увазі?; *adj.* 1) *(not generous)* скупий, **Tamara is not m., simply she doesn't like to spend money.** Тамара не скупа, просто вона не любить тратити гроші.; 2) *(unkind)* лихий, злий, підлий, **He is a m. person.** Він підла людина.

meat, *n.* м'ясо, **pork m.** свиняче м'ясо; *adj.* м'ясний, **m. products** м'ясні продукти.

medicine, *n.* 1) *(science)* медицина, **Oksana always wanted to study m.** Оксана завжди хотіла вивчати медицину.; 2) *(drug)* ліки, **What m. did the doctor prescribe you?** Які ліки вам виписав лікар?; *coll.* медикаменти, **They need more food and m.** Їм потрібно ще їжі та медикаментів.

meet, *v.* 1) *tran. (encounter)* зустрічати + *A.*, **His brother met him off the train.** Його брат зустрів його з поїзда.; 2) *tran. (get acquainted)* знайомитися (з + *I.*), **We met three months ago.** Ми познайомилися три місяці тому.; ♦ **Please m. Robert, my old friend.** Будь ласка, знайомтеся. Це - Роберт, мій давній друг.; 3) *intr. (gather)* зустрічатися з + *I.*, **Lovers like to m. in this park.** У цьому парку люблять зустрічатися закохані.; збиратися, **The group ~s once a week.** Група збирається раз на тиждень.

meeting, *n.* 1) зустріч, **There can be no m.** Не може бути ніякої зустрічі.; 2) *(rendezvous)* побачення, **I'm running late for my m.** Я запізнююся на побачення.; 3) засідання, нарада, **Mr. Bondarenko isn't available now, he's in a m.** Пан Бондаренко зараз зайнятий, він на засіданні (нараді).

memory, *n.* 1) пам'ять, **m. for names** пам'ять на (+ *A.*) імена; **from m.** з пам'яті; **in m. of** у пам'ять про + *A.*; **If m. doesn't fail me.** Якщо мені не зраджує пам'ять.; 2) *(things remembered)* спомин, **This is my first m. of my hometown.** Це мій перший спомин про рідне місто.

menu, *n.* меню, **Bring us the m., please.** Принесіть нам, будь ласка, меню.; **on the m.** у меню.

message, *n.* 1) повідомлення, **There's a m. for you on the answering machine.** Для вас повідомлення на авто-відповідачеві.; **to leave a m.** лишити повідомлення; 2) *(written letter)* лист, **We exchanged ~s for three months.** Ми обмінювалися листами три місяці.; 3) *(brief written note)* записка, **I left you a m. with the administrator.** Я лишила вам записку в адміністратора.; 4) *(of text)* ідея, послання, **What is the m. of this film?** Яка ідея цього фільму?, **his m. is that ...** він хоче сказати, що ...; 5) *(on radio, TV)* оголошення, **We'll be back after these ~s.** Ми продовжимо після цих оголошень.

Mexican, *adj.* мексиканський; *n.*, *m.* мексиканець, **Jose is a M.** Хосе - мексиканець.; *f.* мексиканка.

Mexico, *n.* Мексика, **in M.** у Мексиці, **to M.** до Мексики.

middle, *n.* 1) середина, **in the m. of ...** *(space)* посеред + *G.*, по середині + *G.*, **They left the bags in the m. of the room.** Вони лишили сумки посеред кімнати.; 2) *(time)* посеред + *G.*, **in the m. of summer** посеред літа.; *adj.* середній, **the m. part** середня частина; **M. East** Близький Схід.; **M. Ages** Середні віки.

middle-aged, *adj.* середнього віку, **He was a m.-a. man.** Він був чоловіком середнього віку.

midnight, *n.* північ, **at m.** опівночі, **His flight to Rome was at m.** Його рейс до Риму був опівночі.

milk, *n.* молоко, **We need some m.** Нам треба молока.; *adj.* молочний, **m. shake** молочний коктейль.

million, *n.* мільйон.

mine, *poss. pron.*, *m.* мій, *f.* моя, *nt.* моє, *pl.* мої, **These books are m.** Ці книжки мої.

minute, *n.* 1) хвилина, **The conversation lasted for twenty ~s.** Розмова тривала двадцять хвилин.; ♦ **just a m.** одну хвилинку, *or* стривайте; 2) *(moment)* хвиля, трішки, **Stay a m. longer.** Побудь(те) ще хвилю (трішки); ♦ **any m.** ось-ось.

miss, *v.*, 1) *(train)* запізнюватися на + *A.*, **Hryhoriy ~ed the last train.** Григорій запізнився на останній потяг.; 2) *(opportunity)* втрачати, пропускати, **He ~ed a rare chance.** Він утратив (пропустив) рідкісну нагоду.; 3) *(be nostalgic)* тужити за + *I.*, скучати за + *I.*, **Lara still ~es Lviv.** Лара все ще тужить за Львовом.

Miss, *n.* 1) панна, **M. Shama will show you the building.** Панна Шама покаже вам будинок.; 2) міс, **M. Ukraine** Міс Україна.

mistake, *n.* помилка, **to make a m.** помилятися; ♦ **by m.** помилково.

misunderstanding, *n.* непорозуміння, **This happened because of an unfortunate m.** Це сталося через прикре непорозуміння.

modern, *adj.* 1) сучасний, **m. life** сучасне життя; 2) модерний, **m. technology** модерна технологія.

mom, *n.* мама, **My m. lives with my brother's family.** Моя мама живе із сім'єю мого брата.

Monday, *n.* понеділок, **on M.** у понеділок, **till M.** до понеділка.

money, *n.* гроші, **He wanted to save some m.** Він хотів заощадити гроші.; 2) *(cash)* готівка.

month, *n.* місяць; **last (this, next) m.** минулого (цього, наступного) місяця.

monument, *n.* пам'ятник + *D.*, **Dovzhenko m.** пам'ятник Довженкові.

moon, *n.* місяць, **full m.** повний місяць.

more, *adv.* 1) *(comp. of many, much)* більше, **He has m. work than I.** Він має більше роботи, ніж я.; **m. than anything** більше за все; 2) *(any longer, with negation)* більше, **They don't live here any m.** Вони тут більше не живуть.; 3) *(additional amount)* ще, *var.* іще, більше, **Can I get m. tea?** Чи можна ще чаю?, **She needs m. time.** Їй треба більше часу.; **m. and m.** все більше й більше; ♦ **the m. …, the m…** (less, etc.) чим більше …, тим більше (менше) …, **The m. I read the papers, the less I understand what's going on.** Чим більше я читаю газети, тим менше розумію, що відбувається.

morning, *n.* ранок, **in the m.** уранці, *var.* вранці, **next m.** наступного ранку, **We'll start at eight in the m.** Ми почнемо о восьмій ранку.; *adj.* ранковий, **m. newspaper** ранкова газета.

Moscow, *n.* Москва, **Thousands of Ukrainians live in M.** Тисячі українців живуть у Москві.

most, *adv.* 1) *(highest degree)* найбільше, **Of all his friends he likes Ostap the m.** З усіх друзів він любить Остапа найбільше.; 2) *(very)* дуже, надзвичайно, **It's m. generous of them.** Вони надзвичайно щедрі.; *adj.* 1) найбільший, **We had the m. trouble in mountains.** Ми мали найбільше клопоту в горах.; 2) *(majority)* більшість + *G.*, **M. Ukrainians speak at least two languages.** Більшість українців говорять принаймні двома мовами.; 3) *in superlative adj.* a) найбільш + *adj.* **the m. favorite** найбільш улюблений, *or* b) най~ + *comp. adj.*, **the m. interesting** найцікавіший; ♦ **for the m. part** головно, переважно, здебільшого.

mostly, *adv.* 1) головно, переважно, **They traveled m. in the south.** Вони подорожували переважно півднем.; 2) *(usually)* звичайно.

mother, *n.* мати; ♦ **m. tongue** рідна мова.

mother-in-law, *n.* *(for wife)* свекруха, *(for man)* теща.

motorcycle, *n.* мотоцикл, **by m.** мотоциклом.

mountain, *n.* гора, **in the ~s** у горах, **to the ~s** у гори, **They're soon going to the ~s.** Вони скоро їдуть у гори.

mouse, *n.* 1) миша; 2) *(computer)* мишка.

mouth, *n.* рот, **open (close) one's m.** відкривати (закривати) рота; ♦ **shut your m.!** заткнися!

move, *v.* *(to another place)* переселятися, *pf.* переселитися; переїжджати, *pf.* переїхати.

movie, *n.* фільм, *colloq.* кіно, **go to the s** ходити в кіно; **m. theater** кінотеатр.

Mr., *n.* пан, **Mr. Novak** п. Новак.

Mrs., *n.* пані, **Mrs. Novak** пані Новак.

much, *adv.* 1) багато, + *G.*, **m. coffee** багато кави; **how m.** скільки + *G.*; **so m.** стільки + *G.*, так багато + *G.*; 2) *(as intensifier)* набагато, **m. better (worse)** набагато краще (гірше); 3) дуже, **I miss you m.** Я дуже тужу за тобою.; 4) часто, **Do you see them m.?** Ви часто їх бачите?; *pron.* багато, багато чого, **M. was written on the subject.** Багато було написано на цю тему.

multistory, *adj.* багатоповерховий, **a m. building** багатоповерховий будинок.

museum, *n.* музей, **in a m.** у музеї, **to m.** до музею.

music, *n.* музика, **He composes m.** Він пише музику.

musical, *adj.* музичний, **m. education** музична освіта.

musician, *n.* музикант, музика, **He is a fine m.** Він – добрий музикант (музика).

must, *mod. v.* 1) бути повинним (or повинен), **We m. do it.** Ми повинні зробити це.; 2) *(despite one's will)* мусити, **You m. stay.** Ви мусите лишитися.; 3) *(supposition)* здається, **Something m. be wrong.** Здається, тут щось не те.

my, *poss. pron.*, *m.* 1) мій, *f.* моя, *nt.* моє, *pl.* мої, **M. sister will come soon.** Моя сестра скоро прийде.; 2) *(not translated when referring to the subject's own body part)* **I closed m. eyes.** Я заплющила очі.; 3) *(referring to somebody or something related to the subject of sentence)* *m.* свій, *f.* своя, *nt.* своє, *pl.* свої, **I told m. wife about it.** Я розповів про це своїй жінці.

myself, *refl. pron.*, 1ˢᵗ *pers. sg.* 1) себе, **In my dreams, I see m. young.** У своїх мріях я бачу себе молодим.; 2) *(for emphasis)* сам, **I m. love to cook.** Я сам дуже люблю варити.; 3) *(alone)* сам, **I can do it m.** Я можу зробити це сам.; 4) *(for myself)* собі, **I bought m. a puppy.** Я купив собі цуценя.

N

nail, *n.* 1) *(finger)* ніготь, *pl.* нігті, **to clip -s** стригти нігті; 2) *(iron)* цвях.

name, *n.* 1) *(of person)* ім'я, **by the n. of** на ім'я + *N.*, **What's your n.?** Як твоє (ваше) ім'я? *or* Як тебе (вас) звати? **first n.** ім'я, **last n.** прізвище; 2) *(of institution)* назва, **The n. of this street is familiar to me.** Назва цієї вулиці мені знайома.; **What's the n. of this hotel?** Як називається цей готель?; *v.* називати + *I.*, **They ~d their son Vasyl.** Вони назвали сина Василем.

narrow, *adj.* вузький; **n.-minded** обмежений, недалекий, **n.-minded person.** Він недалека людина.

national, *adj.* 1) національний, **n. culture** національна культура; 2) *(institution)* державний, **n. library** державна бібліотека; **n. (citizen)** *m.* громадянин, *f.* громадянка, **Maria is a Ukrainian n.** Марія - громадянка України.

native, *adj.* рідний, **n. country** рідна країна, **n. town** рідне місто; *n., m.* уродженець, *f.* уродженка, **Maria Lomakivska is a n. of the city of Poltava.** Марія Ломаківська - уродженка міста Полтави.

nature, *n.* 1) природа, **laws of n.** закони природи, **Mother N.** мати-природа; 2) *(character)* натура, характер, **He is an optimist by n.** За натурою він оптиміст.

near, *adj.* близький, **in the n. future** у недалекому майбутньому; *prep.* біля, поруч, неподалік + *G.*, **the store n. my house** крамниця близько мого дому; *adv.* поблизу, неподалік, **The park is situated right n.** Парк розташований зовсім неподалік.

nearly, *adv.* майже, **It was n. midnight.** Була майже північ.; трохи не + *inf.*, **We n. missed the train.** Ми трохи не запізнилися на потяг.

necessary, *adj.* 1) необхідний, **all things n. for the trip** всі речі, необхідні для подорожі.; **it's n.** треба, необхідно + *pf. inf.*; 2) потрібний, **The passport isn't n.** Паспорт не потрібний.

neck, *n.* шия, **She has a beautiful long n.** Вона має гарну довгу шию.

necktie, *n.* краватка, **He hates wearing a n.** Він ненавидить носити краватку.

need, *n.* потреба, **there's no n.** нема потреби + *impf. inf.*; *v.* потребувати, **What do we n. for the road?** Що ми потребуємо у дорогу?; *D.* + треба, **I n. to buy some bread.** Мені треба купити хліба.

neighbor, *n., m.* сусід, *f.* сусідка, **Oksana is our n.** Оксана - наша сусідка.

neither, *adj.* 1) жодний, *var.* жоден, **N. of the guides suited us.** Жодний (жоден) із провідників не підходив нам.; **He selected two postcards and bought n.** Він вибрав дві листівки і не купив жодної.; 2) *(with negative statements)* теж, також, **She didn't see the play, n. did I.** Вона не бачила п'єси, і він також.; *conj.* **n. ... nor** ні ..., ні…, **Mykola speaks n. Russian nor German.** Микола не розмовляє ні російською, ні німецькою.

nephew, *n., m.* племінник, небіж, **Yurko and Serhiy are his ~s.** Юрко та Сергій - його племінники (небожі).

never, *adv.* 1) ніколи, **I have n. seen Athens.** Я ніколи не бачив Атен.; 2) *(with past simple)* так і не ..., **He n. got anything from them.** Він так нічого і не отримав від них.; ♦ **n. mind** менше з тим.

nevertheless, *adv.* проте, однак, тим не менше, **It's hard to find a car there, n. we'll try.** Там важко знайти авто, проте ми спробуємо.

new, *adj.* новий, **What's new?** Що нового?, **N. Year** Новий Рік.

news, *n.* новини, вісті, **latest n.** останні новини, **a piece of n.** новина, **This is no n. to me.** Для мене це не новина.

newspaper, *n.* газета, **morning (evening, daily) n.** ранкова (вечірня, щоденна) газета.

New York, *n.* Нью-Йорк, **in N.Y.** у Нью-Йорку, **N.Y. State** штат Нью-Йорк, **in N.Y. State** у штаті Нью-Йорк.

next, *adj.* наступний, **n. day (time, week) things will be different.** Наступного дня (разу, тижня) все буде інакше. **Who's n.?** Хто наступний?; *adv.* 1) далі, потім, після того, **N. we called the police.** Потім ми подзвонили до міліції.; 2) *(almost)* майже, **He ate n. to nothing.** Він майже нічого не їв.

nice, *adj.* гарний, приємний, **They're such n. people.** Вони такі приємні люди.; **It's very n. of you.** Це дуже гарно з вашого боку.

niece, *n.* племінниця, небога, **His n. always takes him to the station.** Його племінниця завжди завозить його на вокзал.

night, *n.* 1) ніч, **at n.** уночі; **spend a n.** (за)ночувати; 2) *(at hotel)* доба, **a hundred hryvnias per n.** сто гривень за добу; *adj.* нічний, **n. train** нічний поїзд.

nine, *card.* 1) дев'ять, **n. apples** дев'ять яблук; 2) *(of animate or paired nouns)* дев'ятеро, **n. men (pants)** дев'ятеро хлопців (штанів); 3) *(of time by clock)* дев'ята (година), **at n. o'clock** о дев'ятій (годині); *n.* дев'ятка, **He was among the first n.** Він був у першій дев'ятці.

nineteen, *card.* дев'ятнадцять, **n. minutes** дев'ятнадцять хвилин; 2) *coll.* дев'ятнадцятеро *(with anim. and paired nouns)*, **n. Canadian women** дев'ятнадцятеро канадок; *n.* дев'ятнадцятка.

ninety, *card.* дев'яносто, *Gal.* дев'ятдесят, **n. meters** дев'яносто (дев'ятдесят) метрів.

ninth, *ord.* дев'ятий, **n. time** дев'ятий поверх; *n.* (одна) дев'ята, **seven ~s** чотири дев'яті (дев'ятих).

no, *neg. part.* 1) ні, **I asked and they said, "N."** Я запитала, і вони відповіли: «Ні».; 2) *(in signs)* не, **n. smoking** не палити; *adj.* ніякий, жодний, **I know no Ivan.** Я не знаю ніякого (жодного) Івана.; ♦ **n. way** нізащо *or* ні за які гроші.

nobody, *neg. pron.* ніхто, **N. came.** Ніхто не прийшов., **N. knows.** Ніхто не знає.

nonalcoholic, *adj.* безалкогольний, **n. drink** безалкогольний напій.

noon, *n.* південь, полудень, **at n.** о півдні, о полудні.

nor, *neg. part.* ні, ані, **The room is neither cheap, n. cozy.** Кімната ні дешева, ні затишна.

north

north, *n.* північ, **in the n.** на півночі, **to the n. of** на північ від + *G.*, **to the n. of Kyiv.** на північ від Києва.; *adv.* на північ, у північному напрямку, **He drove an hour n.** Він проїхав годину на північ.; *adj.* північний, **n. shore** північний берег; *(in compounds)* північно-, **n.-eastern (-western)** північно-східний (-західний).

northern, *adj.* північний, **n. wind** північний вітер.

nose, *n.* 1) ніс, **He has a straight n.** Він має прямий ніс.; 2) *(intuition)* нюх, чуття на + *A.*, **Olha had a n. for money.** Ольга мала нюх на гроші.

not, *neg. part.* 1) *(when negating a word)* не, **I do n. know.** Я не знаю.; **n. a shirt, but a sweater** не сорочка, а светер; **n. so fast** не так швидко; 2) *(when representing a negative statement)* ні, **He said he'd come. I hope n.** Він сказав, що прийде. Я сподіваюсь, що ні.

note, *n.* 1) *(in a diary)* запис, нотатка; 2) *(written message)* записка, **He left a n. for you.** Він залишив для вас записку.; 3) *(music)* нота.

notebook, *n.* 1) *(school)* зошит, **The exercises are to be written in the n.** Вправи треба написати у зошиті.; 2) записник, **reporter's n.** записник репортера.; 3) *(computer)* новтбук, портативний комп'ютер.

nothing, *pron.* 1) нічого, **The book says n. about it.** У книжці про це нічого не пишеться.; 2) *(zero)* нуль.; **for n.** 1) *(for free)* безоплатно, безплатно, *colloq.* задарма; 2) *(in vain)* марно, намарно, *var.* намарне; **n. but** лише, тільки, **He's n. but trouble.** З ним сам тільки клопіт.

novel, *n.* роман, **This is a new n. by Valeriy Shevchuk.** Це новий роман Валерія Шевчука.

November, *n.* листопад, **in N.** у листопаді, **on the first of N.** першого листопада.

now, *adv.* зараз, тепер, **He lives in Warsaw n.** Зараз він живе у Варшаві.; **for n.** поки що, **That's all we have for n.** Це поки що все, що ми маємо.; ♦ **n. and again** час від часу.

nowhere, *adv.* ніде, **This rare book is n. to be found.** Цю рідкісну книжку ніде не можна знайти.; **out of n.** нізвідки; **n. near** і близько ... не, **The city is n. near as green as it once was.** Це місто і близько не таке зелене, як колись.

number, *n.* 1) число, **even (odd) n.** парне (непарне) число; 2) номер, **The n. of my house is 21.** Номер мого будинку 21.; **What's your phone n.?** Який в тебе номер телефону?; ♦ **wrong n.** неправильний номер (телефону); 3) кількість, **a great n. of people** велика кількість людей; 4) *(of a magazine)* число, номер.

O

occupation, *n.* фах, **by o.** за фахом; професія, **His o. is a lawyer.** Його професія - юрист.

occupied, *adj. (of room)* зайнятий, **Is this seat o.?** Це місце зайняте?. *Also see* **occupy**.

occupy, *v. tran.* займати + *A.* **Ivan has occupied the position for a year.** Іван займає цю посаду рік.

ocean, *n.* океан, **the Atlantic (Pacific) O.** Атлантичний (Тихий) океан.

o'clock, *adv. (in time indications)* година, **It's 5 o. now.** Зараз п'ята година; **at an hour** о (об) + *L. sg. of card. of hour* + *N. of minute*, **at 5:25 o.** о п'ятій (годині) двадцять п'ять (хвилин).

once

October, *n.* жовтень, **in O.** у жовтні.

Odesa, *n.* Одеса, **in O.** в Одесі, **to O.** до Одеси; *adj.* одеський, **O. humor** одеський гумор.

odd, *adj.* 1) дивний, **He was a rather o. fellow.** Він був досить дивний гість.; 2) *(of numbers)* непарний.

of, *prep.* 1) *(made of material)* з (*var.* із, зі) + *G.* **of glass** зі скла, **wall o. stone and wood** стіна із каменю і дерева.; 2) *(possession, relationship)* N. + *G.*, **picture o. my brother** фото мого брата, **administration o. a plant** адміністрація заводу, **minister of culture** міністр культури; 3) *(part of a whole)* N. + *G.*, **window o. a house** вікно будинку, **day o. the week** день тижня; 4) *(about)* про + *A.*, *colloq.* за + *A.*, **I think o. them.** Я думаю про (за) них.; 5) **to be o.** представляти + *A.*, **The proposal is o. great interest to the company.** Ця пропозиція представляє великий інтерес для компанії.

off, *prep. (away, from)* з (із) + *G.*, **He went o. the road.** Він зійшов з дороги.; **He fell o. the chair.** Він упав із крісла.; *adv.* **to be o.** 1) мати вихідний (відгул), бути вихідним, **He's o. on Mondays.** Він має вихідний по понеділках.; 2) *(be cancelled)* бути скасованим (відміненим), **The birthday celebration is o. for an unknown reason.** Святкування уродин відмінено з невідомої причини.; ♦ **day o.** вихідний, відгул; ♦ **o. and on** з перервами, час від часу.

offer, *v.* пропонувати + *A.* + *D.*, **He ~ed help to all travelers.** Він запропонував допомогу всім мандрівникам.; *n.* пропозиція, *Gal.* оферта, **He accepted the o.** Він прийняв пропозицію.

office, *n.* 1) офіс, **My o. is five minutes from home.** Мій офіс п'ять хвилин від дому.; 2) *(position)* посада, **the o. of the minister** посада міністра.

often, *adv.* часто, **How o. do you go to Ukraine?** Як часто ви їздите до України?

oil, *n.* олія, **olive o.** оливкова олія, **sunflower o.** соняшникова олія.

OK, *adv.* гаразд, добре, гарно; *adj.* в порядку, *(acceptable)* може бути, непоганий, **The car is OK.** Авто може бути.; ♦ **everything's OK** все в порядку.

old, *adj.* 1) старий, **This o. gentleman is our teacher.** Цей старий пан - наш учитель.; **o. age** похилий (літній) вік; **o. friend** давній друг; 2) *(indication of age)* **to be two (three, four, five) years o.** D. + *num.* + рік (2, 3, *or* 4 роки, 5 *and more* років), **Mykhailo is ten years o.** Михайлові десять років.

on, *prep.* 1) *posn.* на + *L.*, **The book is o. the table.** Книжка на столі.; 2) *dir.* на + *A.* **to put o. the table** покласти на стіл; 3) *(about)* з + *G. or* про + *A.*, **lecture o. history** лекція з історії, **book o. Italian architecture** книжка про італійську архітектуру; 4) *(indication of time) (with days of week)* у + *A.*, **o. Sunday** у неділю; *(with dates) no preposition, date and month in G.*, **o. August 1**, першого серпня; **o. that day** того дня; 5) *(possession)* при + *L.*, **I have no money o. me.** Я не маю грошей при собі.; 6) *(about films)* **be o.** іти, *(in impersonal sentence)* показувати, **There's a new film o. tonight.** Сьогодні йде (показують) новий фільм.

once, *adv.* 1) раз, один раз, **It's enough to do it o.** Досить зробити це (один) раз.; 2) *(on one occasion)* одного разу, якось, **O. he decided to make a paella.** Одного разу він вирішив зробити паею.; 3) *(repetition)* на + *A.*, **o. a day (week, month, year)** раз на день (тиждень, місяць, рік).; ♦ **at o.** негайно; ♦ **o. again** знову, ще раз; ♦ **o. in a while** час від часу.

one, *card.* 1) один, **I have o. brother.** У мене є один брат.; **o. after another** один за одним; **o. another** *m.* один одного, *f.* одна одну, *m. and f.* одне одного, **Petro and Olha love o. another.** Петро й Ольга кохають одне одного.; 2) *(time by clock)* перша (година), **at o. o'clock** о першій (годині).

oneself, *refl. pron.* 1) себе, **It's easy to imagine o. in this situation.** Легко уявити себе у цій ситуації.; *or refl. part.* ~ся added to *v.* **to wash o.** умиватися; 2) *(alone)* **One can do it o.** Можна зробити це самому (*f.* самій).

onion, *n. coll.* цибуля, **o. soup** цибулевий суп.

only, *adv.* тільки, лише, **There are o. sleeping cars in this train.** У цьому поїзді є лише спальні вагони.; *adj.* єдиний, **He was an o. child.** Він був єдиною дитиною.

open, *v. tran.* 1) відкривати *(both literally and metaphorically)*, **He ~ed the door.** Він відкрив двері.; 2) відчиняти *(usu sth locked)*, **Halyna ~ed the safe.** Галина відчинила сейф.; *intr.* 1) відкриватися *(both literally and metaphorically)* **A new exhibit ~s tomorrow.** Нова виставка відкривається завтра.; 2) відчинятися *(usu sth locked)*, **The ticket-office ~s early.** Квиткова каса відчиняється рано.; *adj.* відкритий, **o. question (society)** відкрите питання (суспільство).

opera, *n.* опера, **o. house** оперний театр, *var.* оперовий театр; *colloq.* опера, **We are meeting near the O.** Ми зустрічаємося біля опери.; **National O. House** Національна Опера; **go to the o.** ходити на оперу; **listen to the o.** слухати оперу.

opposite, *adj.* протилежний, **on the o. side** на протилежному боці; *n.* протилежність.

or, *conj.* 1) чи *(in mutually exclusive alternatives)*, **Is Ivan Ukrainian o. Belarusian?** Іван українець чи білорус?; 2) або *(in inclusive alternatives)*, **I'd like to do it today o. tomorrow at the latest.** Я хотів би зробити це сьогодні, або завтра, найпізніше.

order, *n.* 1) *(system)* порядок, лад, **Everything's in o.** Все у порядку; **to keep o.** тримати порядок; 2) *(commission)* замовлення, **Is my o. ready?** Чи моє замовлення готове?; 3) *(command)* наказ, **the o. to leave the building** наказ покинути будинок; 4) *(social)* лад, **social o. in Ukraine** суспільний лад в Україні; **in o. to** (для того), щоб… , **I called in o. to tell you …** Я подзвонив (для того), щоб сказати вам …; **be out of o.** бути зіпсованим, не працювати, **The answering machine is out of o.** Автовідповідач зіпсований (не працює).; *v.* замовляти, робити замовлення; ♦ **Are you ready to o.?** Ви готові замовляти?

original *adj.* 1) *(unlike others)* своєрідний, **Arkhypenko is a truly o. artist.** Архипенко - справді своєрідний мистець.; 2) оригінальний, **These are o. Maksymovyches.** Це оригінальні роботи Максимовича.; 3) *(initial)* первинний, **According to our o. plan, we visited Ternopil first.** За нашим первинним планом ми спочатку відвідали Тернопіль.

other, *adj.* 1) інший, **Have you seen o. Ukrainian films?** Чи ви бачили інші українські фільми?; ♦ **on the o. hand** з іншого боку; 2) *(the rest)* решта, **He finished five exercises and the o. three he'll do later.** Він закінчив п'ять вправ, а решту три він зробить пізніше.; 3) *(additional)* ще, **one o. matter we need to discuss** ще одна справа, яку нам треба обговорити; 4) *(opposite side)* зворотний, **o. side** зворотний бік; ♦ **each o.** *both m.* один одного, *both f.* одна одну, *m. and f.* одне одного, **They** (he and she) **love each o.** Вони люблять одне одного, (he and he) … один одного, (she and she) … одна одну.

otherwise, *adv.* інакше, **We need to hurry, o. we'll miss the train.** Треба поспішати, інакше ми запізнимося на потяг.

ought, *v. D.* + слід, **Mykola o. to do it.** Миколі слід зробити це.

our, *poss. pron., m.* 1) наш, *f.* наша, *nt.* наше, *pl.* наші, **Olena knows o. city.** Олена знає наше місто.; 2) *(not translated when referring to the subject's own body part)* **We all closed o. eyes.** Ми заплющили очі.; 3) *(referring to somebody or something related to the subject of sentence)* *m.* свій, *f.* своя, *nt.* своє, *pl.* свої, or not translated, **We wrote o. parents a long letter.** Ми написали (своїм) батькам довгого листа.

ourselves, *refl. pron., 1st pers. pl.* 1) себе, **In our dreams, we see o. young.** У своїх мріях ми бачимо себе молодими.; 2) *(for emphasis)* самі, **We o. never called them.** Ми самі так і не подзвонили їм.; 3) *(alone)* сам, **We can finish the assignment o.** Ми можемо закінчити завдання самі.; 4) *(for ourselves)* собі, **We made o. a dinner.** Ми зробили собі вечерю.

out, *prep.* 1) з (із, зі) + *G.*, **o. of the room** з кімнати; **o. of here** звідси, **Ivan is o.** Івана нема(є).; **to run o. of sth** закінчуватися, **We ran o. of milk.** У нас закінчилося молоко.; 2) *(cause)* від + *G.* **o. of fear** від страху.

outdoors, *adv.* надворі, на вулиці, **In the summer, we like to eat o.** Улітку ми любимо їсти надворі.

outside, *adv. prep.* 1) зовні / назовні + *G.*, **o. the house** зовні будинку; 2) поза + *I.* **o. my home** поза моїм домом.; 3) від + *G.*, **They live twenty km o. of Lviv.** Вони живуть двадцять кілометрів від Львова.; *adv.* надворі, **It was warm o.** Надворі було тепло.

over, *prep.* 1) *(above)* над + *I.*, **The sky is blue o. Kherson.** Небо синє над Херсоном.; 2) *(beyond)* за + *I.*, **o. the river** за рікою, **all o. the place** скрізь; 3) *(more than)* понад + *A.* **o. two million** понад два мільйони; 4) *(duration)* протягом, на протязі + *G.*, **The beer has been made o. many centuries.** Це пиво робиться протягом багатьох століть.; 5) *(through, via)* по + *L.*, **o. the phone (TV)** по телефону (телебаченню).

own, *v.* володіти + *I.*, бути власником, **Who ~s this hotel?** Хто власник цього готелю?; *adj.* власний, **our o. car** наше власне авто.

P

pack, *v.* 1) *tran.* пакувати + *A.*, **Have you ~ed the suitcases?** Ви вже спакували валізи?; 2) *intr.* пакуватися, **to p. for the road** пакуватися у дорогу.; *n.* пачка, **p. of cigarettes** пачка сигарет.

package, *n.* пакунок, пакет, **There's a p. for you here.** Для вас тут пакет.

page, *n.* сторінка, **on the p.** на сторінці.

pain, *n.* біль, **He has severe ~s in his back.** Він має сильний біль у спині.

paint, *n.* фарба, **She has too much p. on her face.** У неї забагато фарби на обличчі.; *v.* фарбувати, *Gal.* малювати, у + *A.* **We want to p. the house yellow.** Ми хочемо пофарбувати хату у жовтий колір.

painter, *n.* художник, *Gal.* маляр.

painting, *n.* картина, **Her ~s sell very well.** Її картини дуже добре продаються.

pair, *n.* па́ра + *G.*, **p. of shoes** па́ра ту́флів.

palm, *n.* 1) *(of hand)* доло́ня; 2) *(tree)* па́льма.

pancake, *n.* млине́ць; **potato p.** деру́н, картопля́ник.

pants, *n. only pl.* штани́, **loose (tight) p.** ві́льні (тісні́) штани́.

papa, *n.* та́то.

paper, *n.* 1) папі́р, **sheet of p.** а́ркуш папе́ру; 2) *(ID)* докуме́нт; 3) *(course paper)* курсова́ (робо́та); *adj.* папе́ровий, **p. money** папе́рові гро́ші.

parcel, *n.* паке́т, *(postal)* бандеро́ль, поси́лка.

pardon, *n.* ви́бачення, **I beg your p.** Прошу́ проба́чення; *v. tran.* вибача́ти, проба́чати + *A.*, **p. me** ви́бачте мене́ (*or* мені́); *Gal.* перепро́шую.

parents, *n.* батьки́, **Please meet my p.** Будь ла́ска знайо́мтеся, це мої́ батьки́.

Paris, *n.* Пари́ж, **in P.** у Пари́жі, **to P.** до Пари́жа.

park, *n.* парк, **in the p.** у па́рку, **to walk in the p.** гуля́ти па́рком; *v.* 1) *tran.* паркува́ти + *A.*, **Where did you p. your car?** Де ви запаркува́ли а́вто?; 2) *refl.* паркува́тися, **Have you already -ed?** Ви вже запаркува́лися?

part, *n.* 1) части́на, **greater (smaller) p.** бі́льша (ме́нша) части́на; 2) *(role)* роль, **play a p.** гра́ти роль + *G.*; 3) у́часть, **take part in** бра́ти у́часть у + *L.*; *v. intr.* *(take leave)* розстава́тися, розлуча́тися, **It was hard to p. with him.** Було́ тя́жко розстава́тися з ним.

particular, *adj.* 1) особли́вий, **p. case** особли́вий ви́падок.; 2) конкре́тний, **p. example** конкре́тний приклад; ♦ **in p.** конкре́тно, зокрема́, са́ме, **Who do you mean in p.?** Кого́ са́ме ви ма́єте на ду́мці?

party, *n.* 1) па́ртія, **political p.** політи́чна па́ртія; 2) *(fun)* вечі́рка, **birthday p.** уро́дини, день наро́дження,

pass, *v.*, 1) *intr.* *(to end)* прохо́дити, мина́ти; **Another day ~ed.** Мину́в (*or* пройшо́в) ще оди́н день.; 2) *tran.* to pass sth, pass by sth *(on foot)* прохо́дити (повз) + *A.*, **Will we be ~ing a bank?** Чи ми бу́демо прохо́дити (повз) банк?; *(by vehicle)* проїжджа́ти + *A.*, **They ~ed the village at night.** Вони́ проїхали село́ вночі́.; 3) *(to spend time)* проводити, **We ~ed the evening outside.** Ми прове́ли ве́чір надво́рі.; 4) *(test)* скла́сти + *A.*, **p. an exam** скла́сти і́спит; *n.* *(permit)* перепу́стка.

passenger, *n.* пасажи́р, **Three ~s can travel in the compartment.** У купе́ мо́жуть ї́хати три паса́жири.

passport, *n.* па́спорт, **foreign (internal) p.** закордо́нний (вну́трішній) па́спорт.

past, *n.* мину́ле, **in the p.** у мину́лому; *adj.* 1) мину́лий, **p. tense** мину́лий час; 2) коли́шній, **p. chairman** коли́шній голова́.; *prep.* повз + *A.*, **We drove p. the university.** Ми проїхали повз університе́т.

patient, *n.* хво́рий, паціє́нт, **The doctor examined a p.** Лі́кар огля́нув хво́рого (паціє́нта).; *adj.* терпля́чий, **p. teacher** терпля́чий вчи́тель.

patronymic, *n.* по ба́тькові, **What's his (her, your) p.?** Як його́ (її́, тебе́/вас) по ба́тькові?

pay, *v. tran.* плати́ти + *A.* за + *A.*, **He paid for the book.** Він заплати́в за кни́жку.; **p. attention** зверта́ти ува́гу на + *A.*, **P. attention to the new rules.** Зверні́ть ува́гу на нові́ пра́вила.; **p. back** відплати́ти + *A.*

peace, *n.* мир, **world p.** мир у сві́ті.

pear, *n.* гру́ша, гру́шка, **ripe (sweet) p.** сти́гла (соло́дка) гру́ша.

peasant, *n., m.* селяни́н, *f.* селя́нка; *adj.* селя́нський, **He comes from a p. family.** Він (похо́дить) із селя́нської роди́ни.

pen, *n.* перо́, ру́чка, **fountain p.** авторучка, **write with a p.** писа́ти перо́м (ру́чкою).

pencil, *n.* олі́вець, **draw with a p.** малюва́ти олівце́м.

people, *n.* 1) лю́ди, **Who are these p.?** Що це за лю́ди?; **many p. think that …** бага́то хто ду́має, що … ; 2) наро́д, **the Ukrainian p.** украї́нський наро́д.

pepper, *n.* пе́рець, **hot (sweet) p.** го́стрий (соло́дкий) пе́рець, **with p.** з пе́рцем, **without p.** без пе́рцю; *v.* перчи́ти + *A.*,

per, *prep.* на / за + *A.*, **p. minute** за хвили́ну, **a hundred p. person** сто на осо́бу.

performance, *n.* виста́ва, **watch a p.** диви́тися виста́ву.

perhaps, *adv.* можли́во, мабу́ть, *colloq.* мо́же, мо', **p. you know** мо́же, ви зна́єте.

person, *n.* осо́ба, люди́на, **unknown p.** незнайо́ма осо́ба; ♦ **What kind of p. is he?** Що він за люди́на?

personal, *adj.* 1) особи́стий, **p. life** особи́сте життя́, **I am here on p. business.** Я тут в особи́стій спра́ві.; 2) персона́льний, **p. check** персона́льний чек.

photo, *n.* see **photograph**; **p. album** фотоальбо́м.

photograph, *n.* світли́на, фотогра́фія, фо́то, зні́мок; **black and white (color)** чо́рно-бі́ла (кольоро́ва) світли́на; **in the p.** на світли́ні, на фотогра́фії, на фо́ті.

physician, *n., m.* лі́кар, *f.* лі́карка, **She is an experienced p.** Вона́ досві́дчена лі́карка.

physicist, *n.* фі́зик, **He was trained as a p.** Він фі́зик за осві́тою.

physics, *n.* фі́зика, **nuclear p.** я́дерна фі́зика, **study (teach) p.** вивча́ти (виклада́ти) фі́зику.

piano, *n.* фортеп'я́но, *colloq.* піані́но; **p. player** піані́ст, *f.* піані́стка; **to play the p.** гра́ти на + *L.* фортеп'я́ні, *var.* на + *A.* фортеп'я́но.

picture, *n.* 1) карти́на, **in the p.** на карти́ні, **draw a p.** малюва́ти карти́ну; 2) світли́на, фо́то, фотогра́фія, зні́мок, **take a p.** фотографува́ти, зніма́ти фо́то, роби́ти зні́мок.

piece, *n.* шмато́к, ку́сень, **p. of cheese** шмато́к си́ру; **p. of advice** пора́да, **p. of news** нови́на, **p. of luggage** мі́сце багажу́; **tear to ~s** рва́ти на шматки́.

pill, *n.* пігу́лка, табле́тка, **take a p.** пи́ти пігу́лку.

pity, *n.* жаль, **What a p.!** Шкода́!

place, *n.* мі́сце, ♦ **at somebody's p.** у ко́гось до́ма, **at my (his, her) p.** у ме́не (ньо́го, не́ї) вдо́ма; **take p.** відбува́тися, става́тися, **The concert will take p. tomorrow.** Конце́рт відбу́деться за́втра.

plan, *n.* план, **make ~s** роби́ти пла́ни, **pension p.** пенсі́йний план, **street p.** ка́рта мі́ста; *v.* планува́ти + *A.*, **p. a trip** планува́ти подоро́ж.

plant   **propose**

plant, *n.* 1) *(factory)* заво́д, фа́брика, **at a p.** на заво́ді (фа́бриці); 2) *(vegetation)* росли́на, **to water ~s** полива́ти росли́ни; **room p.** вазо́н.

plate, *n.* 1) тарі́лка, **on a p.** на тарі́лці; 2) *(loaded with food)* ми́ска, **p. of soup** ми́ска су́пу.

play, *n.* 1) гра, **children's p.** дитя́ча гра; 2) п'є́са, **put on a p.** ста́вити п'є́су; *v.* гра́ти у + *A.*, **p. football** гра́ти у + *A.* футбо́л; **p. the piano** гра́ти на + *L. or* + *A.* фортеп'я́ні; ♦ **p. by the rules** гра́ти за пра́вилами.

pleasant, *adj.* 1) приє́мний, **What a p. surprise!** Що за приє́мна несподі́ванка!; 2) *(of person)* симпати́чний, **p. person** симпати́чна люди́на.

please, *adv.* будь ла́ска, **tell me p.** скажі́ть, будь ла́ска; *v.* роби́ти приє́мність; ♦ **if you p.** як ва́ша ла́ска; ♦ **~ed to meet you** приє́мно познайо́митися.

pleasure, *n.* 1) приє́мність, **with a great p.** з вели́кою приє́мністю; **It's a p. meeting you.** Приє́мно познайо́митися.; 2) насоло́да, **This car is a sheer p.** Це а́вто - сама́ насоло́да.; **for p.** для насоло́ди.

p.m. *in fam. use* 1) дня *(from 12:00 p.m. till 5:00 p.m.)*, **at 4:00 p.m.** о четве́ртій (годи́ні) дня; 2) ве́чора *(after 6:00 p.m.)*, **at 7:00 p.m.** о сьо́мій (годи́ні) ве́чора; *(in form. use 24-hour frame is used)* **at 4:00 p.m.** о шістна́дцятій (годи́ні), **at 7:00 p.m.** о дев'ятна́дцятій.

pocket, *n.* кише́ня, **deep p.** глибо́ка кише́ня; *adj.* кишенько́вий, **p. dictionary** кишенько́вий словни́к.

poem, *n.* поезія, вірш, **write ~s** писа́ти ві́рші.

poet, *n., m.* пое́т, *f.* пое́тка, *var.* поете́са; **national p.** націона́льний пое́т.

poison, *n.* отру́та, отра́ва, **deadly (strong) p.** смерте́льна (си́льна) отру́та; *v.* отру́ювати + *A.*

poisoning, *n.* отру́єння, **food-p.** (харчо́ве) отру́єння, **to have a food-p.** отру́юватися, **he's got a food-p.** він чи́мось отру́ївся.

Poland, *n.* По́льща, **to P.** до По́льщі.

Pole, *n., m.* поля́к, *f.* по́лька.

Polish, *adj.* по́льський; *n.* (language) по́льська (мо́ва), **speak P.** розмовля́ти по́льською.

politics, *n.* полі́тика, **be engaged in p.** займа́тися полі́тикою.

poor, *adj.* 1) *(not rich)* бі́дний; 2) *(bad)* пога́ний, **p. grades** пога́ні оці́нки; 3) слабки́й, ке́пський, **p. health** слабке́ (ке́пське) здоро́в'я.

popular, *adj.* популя́рний, **to be p.** бу́ти популя́рним, **This song is rather p.** Ця пі́сня до́сить популя́рна.; **by p. demand** на вимо́гу публі́ки.

pork, *n.* свини́на, свиня́че м'я́со; **p. chop** свиня́чий биток, **p. stew** тушко́вана свини́на.

Portugal, *n.* Португа́лія, **to P.** до Португа́лії.

Portuguese, *adj.* португа́льський; *n., m.* португа́лець; *f.* португа́лка.

possible, *adj.* 1) можли́вий, **p. solution** можли́ве рі́шення, **It's quite p. that ...** Цілко́м можли́во, що ...; 2) *(potential)* потенці́йний, **Taras Marchenko is our p. doctoral student.** Тара́с Ма́рченко – наш потенці́йний аспіра́нт.

post, *n.* *(mail)* по́шта.

postal, *adj.* пошто́вий, **p. services** пошто́ві по́слуги, **p. stamp** пошто́ва ма́рка.

postcard, *n.* полтíвка, листíвка, пошто́ва листíвка, **send sb a p.** посла́ти + *D.* листíвку.

post office, *n.* по́шта, **at the p.** на по́шті, **main p.** головпошта́мт.

potato, *n.* карто́пля, **p. pancakes** картопля́ники, деруни́, *Gal.* тертю́хи; **mashed ~es** товкани́ця, картопля́не п'ю́ре.

prefer, *v.* віддава́ти перева́гу + *D.* пе́ред + *I.*, **I p. chicken to pork.** Я віддаю́ перева́гу куря́тині пе́ред свини́ною.; волі́ти + *inf.*, **We p. to discuss this now.** Ми волі́ємо обговори́ти це за́раз.

prepare, *v.* 1) *tran.* готува́ти + *A.*, **He ~d delicious sandwiches.** Він приготува́в смачні́ кана́пки.; 2) *refl. (oneself)* готува́тися до + *G.*, **We p. for exams.** Ми готу́ємося до іспи́тів.

prescription, *n.* реце́пт, **p. for medicine** реце́пт на лі́ки, **to write out a p.** виписувати реце́пт.

present, *n.* подару́нок, **birthday p.** подару́нок на уроди́ни; **give sb a p.** (по)дарува́ти + *A.* + *D.*; *adj.* 1) тепері́шній, **p. tense** тепері́шній час, **at p.** за́раз, тепе́р; 2) (in attendance) прису́тній, **all those p.** усі́ прису́тні; *v.* представля́ти, **Pavlo ~ed all options.** Павло́ предста́вив усі́ варія́нти.

president, *n.* 1) президе́нт, **P. of Ukraine** Президе́нт Украї́ни; 2) голова́, **committee p.** голова́ коміте́ту.

pretty, *adj.* гарне́нький, **p. little girl** гарне́нька дівчинка; *adv.* до́сить, *colloq.* до́ста, **p. expensive** до́сить дороги́й.

price, *n.* ціна́, **at any p.** за вся́ку ціну́, *colloq.* за вся́кі гро́ші, **exorbitant (moderate) p.** надмі́рна (помірко́вана) ціна́.

principal, *adj.* головни́й, **p. city** головне́ мі́сто; основни́й, **p. part of** основна́ части́на + *G.*; *n. (of school)* дире́ктор шко́ли.

private, *adj.* прива́тний.

probably, *adv.* можли́во, мабу́ть, ймові́рно, *colloq.* мо́же., **We'll p. be staying at a hotel.** Ми, можли́во, зупиня́тимемося у готе́лі.

problem, *n.* пробле́ма, ♦ **no p.** нема́ пробле́м, **What's the p.?** У (чім) чому́ пробле́ма?

profession, *n.* фах, профе́сія, **by p.** за профе́сією (фа́хом), **What's your p.?** Хто ви за фа́хом?

professor, *n.* профе́сор, **full p.** профе́сор, **assistant p.** доце́нт.

program *n.* 1) програ́ма, **weekly (monthly) p.** програ́ма на ти́ждень (мі́сяць); 2) *(theater)* програ́мка; 3) *(TV)* програ́ма, переда́ча, **TV p.** програ́ма переда́ч, **on the p.** у програ́мі.

promise, *n.* обіця́нка, **p. of help** обіця́нка допомо́ги; **promises! promises!** обіця́нка-цяця́нка!; *v.* обіця́ти + *A.* + *D.*, **He ~d her some money.** Він пообіця́в їй гро́ші.

propose, *v.* пропонува́ти + *A.* + *D., or* + *inf.* **Mykola will p. to them a new program.** Мико́ла запропону́є їм нову́ програ́му.

proposition, *n.* пропозиція, **attractive p.** приваблива пропозиція.

Prypiat, the, *n. (right tributary of the Dnipro)* Прип'ять, **on the P.** на Прип'яті, **along the P.** Прип'яттю *or* по Прип'яті, **They sailed down the P.** Вони плавали вниз Прип'яттю.

pupil, *n.* 1) учень; 2) *(of eye)* зіниця.

puppy, *n.* щеня, *pl.* щенята, цуценя, *pl.* цуценята.

purchase, *n.* покупка; *v.* купувати, *only in pf.* придбати + *A.*

purpose, *n.* мета, ціль, **with what p.?,** з якою метою?, **on p.** навмисно.

put, *v.* 1) *(put sth in a prone position only)* класти, **He p. the paper on the table.** Він поклав газету на стіл., *(also of part of one's body)* **He p. his head on the pillow.** Він поклав голову на подушку.; 2) *(put sth in an upright position)* ставити, **He p. the book on the shelf.** Він поставив книжку на полицю.; 3) *(of signature, name)* ставити, **P. your signature here.** Поставте підпис тут.; 4) **p. off** відкладати + *A.*, **They p. off the meeting.** Вони відклали зустріч.; 5) **p. on** вдягати, одягати, вбирати + *A.*, **She p. on her red dress.** Вона одягнула червону сукню.; 6) **p. up at** *(hotel)* зупинятися у + *L.*

Q

quarter, *n.* 1) чверть + *G.* **in a q. of an hour** за чверть години; 2) *(three months)* квартал; 3) *(part of town)* квартал, дільниця.

question, *n.* 1) питання, *var.* запитання; **answer a q.** відповідати на питання, **pose a q.** ставити питання; 2) *(matter)* справа; **be a q. of** бути справою + *G.* **This is a q. of taste.** Це - справа смаку.; **beyond q.** поза сумнівом, **without q.** без сумніву; ♦ **This is out of the q.** Про це не може бути й мови.; *v.* 1) *(doubt)* ставити під сумнів, **He ~s her account of events.** Він ставить під сумнів її версію подій.; 2) *(interrogate)* допитувати + *A.*

quick, *adj.* швидкий, **q. change** швидка зміна; ♦ **the q. and the dead** живі і мертві.

quickly, *adv.* швидко, скоро, хутко, **He q. agreed.** Він швидко погодився.

quiet, *adj.* тихий, спокійний, **q. (person) room** тиха (людина) кімната, **q. night** тиха ніч.

quite, *adv.* 1) цілком, *colloq.* геть, **He is q. certain about it.** Він у цьому цілком впевнений.; *(in neg.)* зовсім, **I don't q. understand.** Я не зовсім розумію.; 2) *(sufficiently)* достатньо, **q. good** достатньо добрий.

R

radio, *n.* радіо, **on the r.** по радіо, **listen to the r.** слухати радіо, **turn on (off) the r.** вімкнути (вимкнути) радіо.

railroad, *n.* залізниця, **to travel by r.** подорожувати залізницею (потягом, поїздом); *adj.* залізничний, **r. station** залізнична станція.

rain, *n.* дощ; *v.* **It's ~ing.** Йде (падає) дощ; **if it doesn't r.** якщо не буде дощу; ♦ **r. cats and dogs** лити як із цебра, **It ~ed cats and dogs yesterday.** Вчора лило як із цебра.

raincoat, *n.* плащ.

rare, *adj.* 1) *(of cooking)* недосмажений, **r. steak** біфштекс з кров'ю; 2) рідкісний, **r. book** рідкісна книжка, **r. specimen** рідкісний вид, **He is a person of r. beauty.** Він людина рідкісної краси.

rarely, *adv.* рідко, **He r. watches films.** Він рідко дивиться фільми.

rather, *adv.* 1) досить, достатньо, **r. strong** досить сильний; 2) *(in indication of preference)* **should / would r.** краще, радше, **I'd r. do it now.** Краще (радше) я зроблю це зараз.

read, *v.* 1) *tran.* читати + *A.*, **She likes to r. detective stories.** Вона любить читати детективні історії.; 2) *intr.* читатися, **His report ~s like a novel.** Його доповідь читається як роман.

reader, *n., m.* читач, *f.* читачка.

reading, *n.* читання, **literary r.** літературне читання.

ready, *adj.* готовий, **I am all r.** Я цілком готовий.; *intr.* **to get r. for …** готуватися до + *G.*,

real, *adj.* 1) справжній, **His r. name is Ivan.** Його справжнє ім'я – Іван.; 2) реальний, **Plato was a r. person.** Платон був реальною особою.; 3) *(utter)* цілковитий, повний, **r. disaster** цілковита катастрофа; 4) *(genuine)* справжній, щирий, **r. gold** щире золото.

really, *adv.* 1) дійсно, справді, **He r. loves her.** Він дійсно її любить.; 2) насправді, **What did he r. say?** Що він насправді сказав?; 3) *(intensifier)* дуже, справді, **r. good** дуже добрий; ♦ **r.!?** невже!?

receive, *v.* 1) *(things)* отримувати, одержувати, *Gal.* діставати, **r. a letter** отримувати лист; 2) *(guests, patients)* приймати, **Visitors are ~d on Mondays.** Відвідувачів приймають по понеділках.

recent, *adj.* недавній, нещодавній, **r. meeting** недавня зустріч.

recently, *adv.* 1) *(with pa.)* недавно, нещодавно, **I saw him r.** Я бачив його недавно.; 2) *(with pres. pf.)* останнім часом, **I have seen many new films r.** Останнім часом я бачив багато нових фільмів.

reception, *n.* 1) прийняття, **invite to a r.** запрошувати на прийняття; 2) *(hotel)* реєстратура.

receptionist, *n.* 1) *(in hotel)* (черговий) адміністратор; 2) *(in hospital)* реєстратор.

recipe, *n.* перепис, рецепт, **r. for French onion soup** перепис французького цибулевого супу.

recognize, *v.* 1) *(person)* упізнавати, **He didn't r. his friend.** Він не впізнав свого друга.; 2) *(fact)* визнавати, **r. a state** визнавати країну. **Malevych is ~d around the world.** Малевич визнаний у всьому світі.

recover, *v.* 1) *(from illness)* одужувати, видужувати від + *G.*, **He quickly ~ed from the flu.** Він швидко одужав від грипу.; 2) *(from shock)* оговтуватися, **r. from a surprise** оговтатися від несподіванки.

red, *adj.* червоний; *(of hair)* рудий, **r.-haired** рудоволосий.

refrigerator, *n.* холодильник, **Our r. is already empty.** Наш холодильник уже порожній.

region, *n.* 1) реґіон, **southern r.** південний реґіон; 2) *(administrative province in Ukraine)* область, **Kyiv R.** Київська область.

relative

relative, *n., m.* ро́дич; *f.* ро́дичка, **close (distant) r.** близьки́й (дале́кий) ро́дич.

relax, *v., intr.* 1) відпочива́ти, **We like to r. after work.** Ми лю́бимо відпочи́ти пі́сля робо́ти.; 2) розслабля́тися, **I can't r.** Я не мо́жу розсла́битися.

remember, *v.* пам'ята́ти + *A.*, **She doesn't r. the film title.** Вона́ не пам'ята́є на́зви фі́льму.

rent, *v.* 1) *(a room)* найма́ти, винайма́ти, орендува́ти + *A.*; 2) *(a car)* винайма́ти, бра́ти напрока́т, **to r. a car** винайня́ти а́вто.; *n.* пла́та за кварти́ру, **to pay the r.** плати́ти за кварти́ру.

repeat, *v.* 1) *tran.* повто́рювати + *A.*, **r. a question** повто́рювати пита́ння.; 2) *intr. (oneself)* повто́рюватися, **He often ~s himself.** Він ча́сто повто́рюється.

repetition, *n.* повто́рення, **There are some ~s in the text.** У те́ксті є де́які повто́рення.

reply, *v.* відповіда́ти на + *A.*, **r. to a letter** відповіда́ти на лист; *n.* ві́дповідь на + *A.*

report, *n.* 1) *(at conference)* до́повідь, **make a r.** роби́ти до́повідь; 2) *(press)* повідо́млення; 3) звіт, **quarterly r.** кварта́льний звіт; 4) *(military)* ра́порт; *v.* 1) повідомля́ти, *The Weekly* **~s that ...** «Ти́жневик» повідомля́є, що ...; 2) допові́дати, **She ~ed the results of the tests.** Вона́ доповіла́ результа́ти іспи́тів.

reporter, *n.* репорте́р, **Once he worked as a radio r.** Коли́сь він працюва́в ра́діо-репорте́ром.

request, *n.* проха́ння, **information r.** інформаці́йний запи́т; *v.* проси́ти, проха́ти.

residence, *n.* поме́шкання, кварти́ра; **at my (your, his, her, their) r.** у ме́не (те́бе, ньо́го, не́ї, них) до́ма; **place of r.** мі́сце прожива́ння.

rest, *n.* 1) *(leisure)* відпочи́нок, **I need a r.** Мені́ тре́ба відпочи́ти.; 2) *(remainder)* ре́шта + *G.*, **the r. of the tourists** ре́шта тури́стів; ♦ **the r. of it** все і́нше; *v.* відпочива́ти.

restaurant, *n.* рестора́н, **to a r.** до рестора́ну.

return, *n.* пове́рнення, **r. home** пове́рнення додо́му, **r. flight** зворо́тній рейс; *v.* 1) *tran.* поверта́ти + *A.*, **r. a book** поверта́ти кни́жку; 2) *intr.* поверта́тися, **When will she r.?** Коли́ вона́ пове́рнеться?

rice, *n.* рис, риж.; **boiled r.** ва́рений рис; *adj.* рисови́й.

rich, *adj.* бага́тий, **r. person** бага́ч, багаті́й, бага́та люди́на; **r. in** бага́тий + *I.* or на + *A*, **Spinach is r. in vitamins.** Шпина́т бага́тий вітамі́нами (*or* на вітамі́ни).

ride, *v., uni.* ї́хати + *I.*, *multi.* ї́здити + *I.*, *tran.* **r. a bicycle (car, bus)** ї́здити велосипе́дом (а́втом, авто́бусом).; *n.* пої́здка, **r. to town** пої́здка до мі́ста, **give sb a r. to ...** підво́зити + *A.* до + *G.*, **He gave Olha a r. to the store.** Він підві́з О́льгу до крамни́ці.

right, *adj.* 1) *(correct)* пра́вильний, **the r. answer** пра́вильна ві́дповідь; **to be r.** ма́ти ра́цію, **You're quite r.** Ви ма́єте цілкови́ту ра́цію.; 2) *(side)* пра́вий, **r. hand** пра́ва рука́, **r. party** пра́ва па́ртія; *adv.* 1) право́руч, **to turn r.** поверта́ти право́руч; 2) *(exactly)* якра́з, **r. in the middle** якра́з посереди́ні; 3) *(yes)* так, вла́сне; ♦ **yeah, r.!** якра́з!; *n.* пра́во на + *A.*, **r. to education** пра́во на осві́ту.

ring, *v.* 1) *tran.* дзвони́ти + *D.*, **He rang me up early.** Він подзвони́в мені́ ра́но.; 2) *intr.* дзвони́ти, **The phone is ~ing.** Дзво́нить телефо́н.

river, *n.* рі́чка, ріка́, **by the r.** бі́ля рі́чки, **down the r.** вниз рі́чкою, **swim in a r.** пла́вати у рі́чці.

road, *n.* доро́га, шлях; **to be on the r.** подорожува́ти; **the r. home** доро́га додо́му.

room, *n.* 1) кімна́та, **hotel r.** но́мер; ♦ **r. and board** харчі́ і прожива́ння; 2) *(space)* мі́сце; **there's little r. here** тут ма́ло мі́сця.

route, *n.* маршру́т, **bus r.** маршру́т авто́буса.

rule, *n.* пра́вило, **r. of grammar** пра́вило грама́тики, **as a r.** як пра́вило, **to break the ~s** пору́шувати пра́вила, **play by the ~s** гра́ти за пра́вилами.

run, *v.* 1) *uni.* бі́гти, *multi.* бі́гати, **He ~s every morning.** Він бі́гає щора́нку.; 2) *(manage)* керува́ти + *I.*, **Who ~s this company?** Хто керу́є ціє́ю компа́нією?; **r. out of sth** закі́нчуватися, **They ran out of gas.** У них закі́нчився бензи́н.

Russia, *n.* Росі́я, **in R.** у Росі́ї, **to R.** до Росі́ї.

Russian, *adj.* росі́йський, **R. influence** росі́йський вплив, **R. salad** сала́т-олів'є́ *or* м'ясни́й сала́т; *n., m.* росія́нин, *f.* росія́нка.

S

sad, *adj.* сумни́й, засму́чений, **s. face** сумне́ обли́ччя, **s. news** сумна́ нови́на; ♦ **s. to say** на жаль.

sail, *v. uni.* пливти́ (*var.* плисти́) + *I.*, **This time we plan to s. north.** Цьо́го ра́зу ми ду́маємо пливти́ на пі́вніч.; *multi.* пла́вати + *I.*, **He likes to s. his new boat.** Він лю́бить пла́вати свої́м нови́м чо́вном.

salad, *n.* сала́т, **fruit (Caesar, vegetable) s.** фрукто́вий (ці́сарський, овоче́вий) сала́т, **tuna s.** сала́т із тунця́.

sale, *n.* 1) про́даж, **to be on s.** бу́ти у про́дажі; 2) ро́зпродаж, **season s.** сезо́нний ро́зпродаж.

salesman, *n.* продаве́ць.

saleswoman, *n.* продавчи́ня.

salt, *n.* сіль; ♦ **take things with a grain of s.** не бра́ти все на ві́ру; *v.* соли́ти + *A.*

salty, *adj.* соло́ний, **s. water** соло́на вода́.

same, *adj.* одна́ковий, **s. views** одна́кові по́гляди; той са́мий, **We made the s. mistake.** Ми зроби́ли ту са́му помилку.; оди́н і той же, **We live in the s. city.** Ми живемо́ в одно́му й то́му мі́сті.; ♦ **It's all the s. to me.** Мені́ байду́же (*or* одна́ково).; ♦ **one and the s.** оди́н і той же; ♦ **the s. to you!** взає́мно!; *pron.* те ж са́ме, **He left and we decided to do the s.** Він пішо́в, і ми ви́рішили зроби́ти те ж са́ме.

sandwich, *n.* бутербро́д, *Gal.* кана́пка, **cheese (ham) s.** бутербро́д із си́ром (ши́нкою).

Saturday, *n.* субо́та, **on S.** у субо́ту, **I'll see you next S.** Поба́чимося насту́пної субо́ти.

sausage, *n.* ковбаса́, **homemade (smoked) s.** дома́шня (ву́джена) ковбаса́.

save, *v., tran.* 1) *(life)* рятува́ти + *A.*, **s. a person** рятува́ти люди́ну; 2) *(money, etc.)* (за)оща́джувати + *A.*, **We stay at this hotel to s. money.** Ми зупиня́ємося в цьо́му готе́лі, щоб (за)оща́дити гро́ші.

say

say, *v.* 1) *(with reported speech)* каза́ти, **They s. that this tree is very old.** Ка́жуть, що це де́рево ду́же старе́.; **"Fine," he said.** «До́бре,» – сказа́в він.; 2) *(about a text)* писа́тися, **The rules s. that** У пра́вилах пи́шеться, що; ♦ **let's say that** скажі́мо, що; ♦ **it goes without ~ing that** само́ собо́ю зрозумі́ло, що; ♦ **that is to s.** то́бто; ♦ **to s. nothing of** вже не ка́жучи про.

schedule, *n.* 1) гра́фік, **busy s.** напру́жений гра́фік; 2) ро́зклад, **train s.** ро́зклад поїзді́в.; *v.* планува́ти + *A.*, **The show was ~d for Saturday.** Виста́ва заплано́вана на субо́ту.

scholar, *n., m.* уче́ний, *f.* уче́на; науко́вець, **well-known s.** відо́мий науко́вець.

school, *n.* 1) *(high school)* шко́ла, **high s.** сере́дня шко́ла; 2) *(university)* виш (ви́щий навча́льний за́клад); 3) *(department)* факульте́т, **Law S.** юриди́чний факульте́т; **finish s.** закі́нчити шко́лу; **go to s.** ходи́ти до шко́ли, **leave s.** кида́ти навча́ння.

schoolboy, *n.* школя́р.

schoolgirl, *n.* школя́рка.

science, *n.* нау́ка, **applied s.** прикладна́ нау́ка, **exact (natural, social) ~s** то́чні (приро́дничі, суспі́льні) нау́ки, **s. and technology** нау́ка і те́хніка.

scientist, *n., m.* уче́ний, *var.* вче́ний; *f.* уче́на, *var.* вче́на.

sea, *n.* мо́ре, **the Black S.** Чо́рне мо́ре, **the S. of Azov** Азо́вське мо́ре; **by the s.** на мо́рі, **We vacationed by the s.** Ми відпочива́ли на мо́рі.; *(by ship)* мо́рем, **to the s.** на мо́ре.

season, *n.* 1) пора́ ро́ку, **What's your favorite s.?** Яка́ ва́ша улю́блена пора́ (ро́ку)?; 2) сезо́н, **rainy s.** сезо́н дощі́в, **soccer s.** футбо́льний сезо́н.

seat, *n.* мі́сце, сиді́ння, **take a s.!** сіда́й; **~те!**, **Is this s. taken?** Чи тут хтось сиди́ть?, **aisle (window) s.** мі́сце у прохо́ді (бі́ля вікна́); *v. tran.* сади́ти + *A.*, **They ~ed us near the window.** Нас посади́ли бі́ля вікна́.

second, *ord.* дру́гий, ♦ **s. to none** найкра́щий, неперевершений.; ♦ **for the s. time** удру́ге *or* дру́гий раз; *n. (in a minute)* секу́нда; ♦ **just a s.** одну́ хвили́ну;

secret, *n.* таємни́ця, **keep a s.** зберіга́ти таємни́цю; секре́т, **s. of success** секре́т успі́ху; *adj.* таємни́й, **s. place** таємне́ мі́сце; секре́тний.

secretary, *n., m.* 1) секрета́р, *f.* секрета́рка; 2) міні́стер, **S. of Commerce** мініст(е)р торгі́влі; **S. of State** держа́вний секрета́р.

see, *v.* 1) *tran.* ба́чити + *A.*, **He looks and ~s nothing.** Він ди́виться і нічо́го не ба́чить.; 2) *tran. (watch a film, etc.)* диви́тися + *A.*, **He saw the play last week.** Він подиви́вся цю п'є́су мину́лого ти́жня.; **s. off** проводи́ти; ♦ **... has seen better days** ... зна́в (-ла) кра́щі часи́.

seem, *v.* здава́тися + *D.*, **It ~s to me that ...** (мені́) здає́ться, що …

seldom, *adv.* рі́дко, **He s. sings.** Він рі́дко співа́є.

self, *refl. pron.* себе́, **He loves himself so much.** Він так себе́ лю́бить.

sell, *v.* 1) *tran.* продава́ти + *A.*, **Oleh sold his bicycle.** Оле́г прода́в свій велосипе́д.; 2) *intr.* продава́тися, **Her book ~s very well.** Її кни́жка ду́же до́бре продає́ться.

shopping

seminar, *n.* семіна́р, **at a s.** на семіна́рі, **Ukrainian history s.** семіна́р з украї́нської істо́рії.

send, *v.* посила́ти + *A.* + *D.*, **We sent Petro a postcard.** Ми посла́ли Петро́ві пошті́вку., **to s. a letter** посила́ти лист(а́) + *D.* (to sb).

separate, *adj.* окре́мий, **s. room** окре́ма кімна́та.

September, *n.* ве́ресень, **in S.** у ве́ресні.

serious, *adj.* серйо́зний, пова́жний, **It's a s. matter.** Це пова́жна спра́ва., **I am quite s. about it.** Я це ці́лком серйо́зно.

serve, *v.* 1) *intr.* служи́ти, **Did he s. in the army?** Чи він служи́в в армі́ї?; 2) *tran. (clients)* обслуго́вувати + *A.*; 3) *(food)* подава́ти + *A.*, **They s. great food here.** Тут подаю́ть чудо́ву ї́жу.

service, *n.* 1) слу́жба, **information s.** інформаці́йна слу́жба; 2) се́рвіс, **excellent (poor) s.** чудо́вий (пога́ний) се́рвіс; 3) по́слуга, **What ~s do you offer?** Які́ по́слуги ви пропону́єте?; **self-s.** самообслуго́вування.

set, *n.* 1) *(for tea, coffee)* серві́з, набі́р, **tea (coffee) s.** ча́йний (ка́вовий) набі́р; **s. of rules** набі́р пра́вил; 2) **TV s.** телеві́зор; 3) компле́кт, **a s. of bed linen** компле́кт пості́льної біли́зни.

seven, *card.* 1) сім, **s. dollars** сім до́ларів; **at s. o'clock** о сьо́мій годи́ні; 2) *coll.* се́меро, **They have s. children.** У них се́меро діте́й.; *n.* сі́мка.

seven hundred, *card.* сімсо́т + *G. pl.*, **s. h. seconds** сімсо́т секу́нд; *n.* сім со́тень.

seventeen, *card.* сімна́дцять, **s. dollars** сімна́дцять до́ларів; 2) *coll.* сімна́дцятеро, **There were s. children in the family.** У сім'ї́ було́ сімна́дцятеро діте́й.; *n.* сімна́дцятка.

seventh, *ord.* сьо́мий, **s. day** сьо́мий день; *n.* (одна́) сьо́ма, **five ~s** п'ять сьо́мих.

seventy, *card.* сімдеся́т., **s. kilograms** сімдеся́т кілогра́мів; *n.* сімдеся́тка.

several, *adj.* де́кілька, кі́лька, **s. museums** кі́лька музе́їв.

sharp, *adj.* го́стрий, **s. as a knife** го́стрий як ніж; ♦ **s.-tongued** гостроязи́кий, го́стрий на язи́к.

she, *pers. pron., f.* вона́, **S. lives here.** Вона́ тут живе́.

sheet, *n.* 1) *(of paper)* а́ркуш, листо́к, **blank s.** чи́стий а́ркуш; 2) *(for bed)* простира́дло.

shelf, *n.* поли́ця, **book-s.** книжко́ва поли́ця, **I put the vase on a s.** Я поста́вив ва́зу на поли́цю.

ship, *n.* 1) корабе́ль; 2) *(passenger)* паропла́в; *v. tran. (deliver)* перевози́ти, перепра́вляти, **The furniture was ~ped by train.** Ме́блі перевезли́ по́їздом.

shirt, *n.* соро́чка, **nice ~s** га́рні соро́чки.

shoe, *n.* ту́фля, череви́к, **~s** ту́флі, взуття́, череви́ки, **s. department** відді́л взуття́.

shop, *n.* 1) крамни́ця, магази́н; 2) майсте́рня, **(auto) repair s.** (авто)ремо́нтна майсте́рня; *v., intr.* купува́ти

shopping, *n.* поку́пки, **to do s.** роби́ти поку́пки (заку́пи), **to go s.** іти́ до крамни́ці (магази́ну), іти́ по поку́пки, іти́ на заку́пи.

short

short, *adj.* коро́ткий, **s. day** коро́ткий день, **s. hands** коро́ткі руки; **in s.** сло́вом, коро́тко ка́жучи.

should, *mod. v.* 1) *(obligation, duty, advice)* слід *(with subject in D.),* **You s. rest.** Вам слід відпочи́ти.; 2) *(correctness) (with subject in D.)* годи́тися, *Gal.* випада́ти, **I s. bring flowers for the hostess.** Мені́ годи́ться (випада́є) принести́ кві́ти для господи́ні.; 3) *(probability)* ма́ти + *inf.,* **Ten hryvnias s. help him.** Де́сять гри́вень ма́є (мало́ б) допомогти́ йому́.

shoulder, *n.* 1) плече́, **broad -s** широ́кі пле́чі; 2) *(of animal)* лопа́тка, **lamb s.** баня́ча лопа́тка.

show, *v.* 1) пока́зувати, **to s. the way** пока́зувати доро́гу, прово́дити; 2) *(film)* пока́зувати, **They s. a new film tonight.** Сього́дні пока́зують нови́й фільм.; *n.* 1) *(performance)* виста́ва, **theater s.** театра́льна виста́ва; 2) *(exhibition)* виста́вка; 3) *(radio)* переда́ча, програ́ма, **radio s.** радіопрогра́ма (радіопереда́ча), **TV s.** телепрогра́ма (телепереда́ча).

shower, *n.* 1) душ, **to take a s.** прийма́ти душ; 2) *(rain)* зли́ва, **warm summer s.** те́пла лі́тня зли́ва; ♦ **s. of greetings** зли́ва привіта́нь.

shut, *v.* 1) *tran.* закрива́ти + *A.,* **s. a window** закрива́ти вікно́; 2) *intr.* закрива́тися, **The door quietly s.** Две́рі ти́хо закри́лися.; ♦ **s. up!** заткни́ся! ~і́ться.

sick, *adj.* хво́рий, слаби́й; **be s.** хворі́ти, **Has he been s. for long?** Він уже́ до́вго хворі́є?; **to get s.** захворі́ти; **feel s.** *(nauseous) (with logical subject in A.)* нуди́ти, **I feel s.** *(nauseous).* Мене́ нуди́ть.

side, *n.* 1) бік, око́лиця, сторона́; **on the opposite s.** на протиле́жному (і́ншому) бо́ці, **southern s. of town** півде́нна око́лиця мі́ста; 2) **s. of the road** узбі́ччя.

sight, *n.* 1) *(vision)* зір, **lose s.** втрача́ти зір; ♦ на пе́рший по́гляд; 2) *(spectacle)* видо́вище; 3) *(place of interest)* пам'я́тка, **a tourist s.** (туристи́чна) пам'я́тка; **to show (do) sights** пока́зувати (диви́тися) пам'я́тки.

sign, *n.* знак, **s. of consent** знак зго́ди; **give a s.** дава́ти знак; *v.* 1) *tran. (put signature)* розпи́суватися, **S. please.** Будь ла́ска, розпиши́ться.; ста́вити пі́дпис 2) *tran. (agreement)* підпи́сувати + *A.,* **They finally ~ed the agreement.** Вони́ наре́шті підписа́ли уго́ду.

signature, *n.* пі́дпис, **illegible s.** нерозбі́рливий пі́дпис, **The letter has no s.** Цей лист без пі́дпису.

simple, *adj.* про́стий, **s. plan** про́стий план, **s. to operate** про́стий у використа́нні.

simply, *adv.* про́сто, **s. interesting** про́сто ціка́во.

since, *prep.* 1) *(beginning with)* з + *G.,* **s. last year** з мину́лого ро́ку; 2) *(after)* з тих пір як, з того́ ча́су, як + *clause,* **s. he left** з тих пір, як він пої́хав; *adv.* пі́сля того́; *conj. (because)* тому́ що, оскі́льки, **s. this is her son** оскі́льки це її́ син.

sing, *v.,* 1) *intr.* співа́ти, **He can't s.** Він не вмі́є співа́ти.; 2) *tran.* співа́ти + *A.,* **s. a song** співа́ти пі́сню.

sister, *n.* сестра́, **elder (younger) s.** ста́рша (моло́дша) сестра́.

sister-in-law, *n.* брато́ва, **She is my s.** Вона́ - моя́ брато́ва.

sit, *v.* 1) *intr. (be sitting)* сиді́ти, **He ~s here.** Він тут сиди́ть.; 2) *intr. (take a seat)* сіда́ти, **They sat down.** Вони́ сі́ли.; 3) *tran. (cause to sit)* сади́ти, **Maria sat the guests on the floor.** Марі́я посади́ла госте́й на підло́гу.

soap

situate, *v.* **be ~d** *(of city, village)* лежа́ти, **Kyiv is s. on hills.** Ки́їв лежи́ть на па́горбах.; бу́ти розташо́ваним, розташо́вуватися, **Where is the bank ~d?** Де розташо́ваний цей банк?

situation, *n.* ситуа́ція, стано́вище, **difficult s.** складне́ стано́вище.

six, *card.* 1) шість, **s. weeks** шість ти́жнів; 2) *(of anim. or paired nouns)* ше́стеро, **s. Englishmen (pants)** ше́стеро англі́йців (штані́в); 3) *(of time by clock)* шо́ста (годи́на), **at s. o'clock** о шо́стій (годи́ні).

six hundred, *card.* шістсо́т, **s. h. grams** шістсо́т гра́мів.

sixteen, *card.* шістна́дцять, **s. hryvnias** шістна́дцять гри́вень; 2) *coll.* шістна́дцятеро *(with anim. and paired nouns),* **s. Spaniards** шістна́дцятеро іспа́нців.

sixth, *ord.* шо́стий, **s. time** шо́стий раз; *n.* (одна́) шо́ста, **four ~s** чоти́ри шо́сті (шо́стих).

sixty, *card.* шістдеся́т, **s. meters** шістдеся́т ме́трів.

size, *n.* ро́змір, **What's your s.?** Яки́й ваш ро́змір?; **s. six** шо́стий ро́змір; ♦ **s. matters** ро́змір ва́жить.

skin, *n.* шкі́ра, **dark (light, soft) s.** те́мна (сві́тла, м'яка́) шкі́ра; ♦ **s. and bones** сама́ шкі́ра і ко́сті.

skirt, *n.* спідни́ця, **wear a s.** носи́ти спідни́цю.

sky, *n.* не́бо, **clear (cloudy) s.** чи́сте (хма́рне) не́бо.

sleep, *n.* сон, **deep s.** глибо́кий сон, **in a s.** уві́ сні; *v.* спа́ти, **to s. well (poorly)** до́бре (ке́псько) спа́ти.

sleepy, *adj.* со́нний; ♦ **to be s.** хоті́ти спа́ти.

slow, *adj.* пові́льний, **s. movement** пові́льний рух; **be ... minutes s.** відстава́ти на + *A.,* ... **My watch is a minute s.** Мій годи́нник відстає́ на одну́ хвили́ну.

slowly, *adv.* пові́льно, поволі́, **drive s.** пові́льно їхати, **think s.** ду́мати поволі́.

small, *adj.* мали́й, мале́нький, **s. favor** мала́ по́слуга, **s. boy** хло́пчик; невели́кий, **s. sum of money** невели́ка су́ма гро́шей; ♦ **s. wonder (that)** не ди́вно, що.

smoke, *n.* дим; *v.* пали́ти, кури́ти, **to s. a lot** бага́то пали́ти; ♦ **no ~ing** не пали́ти.

snack, *n.* переку́ска, заку́ска; **to have a s.** перекуша́ти.

snow, *n.* сніг; **s. drift** сніго́ви́й за́ме́т, кучугу́ра; **s.-white** бі́лий як сніг; **wet s.** мо́крий сніг; *v.* **It's snowing.** Па́дає сніг.

so, *adv.* 1) так, **I want to see him s.** Я так хо́чу поба́чити його́.; 2) ду́же, *collog.* стра́шенно, **He works s. much.** Він ду́же бага́то працю́є; **I liked the film s. much.** Фільм стра́шенно сподо́бався мені́.; ♦ **s. long!** бува́й(те)!; ♦ **and s. on (and s. forth)** і так да́лі, (і тому́ поді́бне); *conj.* тому́, **It was cold s.** I put on a warm coat. Було́ хо́лодно, тому́ я одягну́в те́пле пальто́; **s. as** щоб, для того́ щоб + *pf. inf.,* **He called s. as to order the tickets.** Він подзвони́в, щоб замо́вити квитки́.; **s. that** щоб, для того́ щоб + *pa. clause,* **I bought a sandwich s. that you could have a snack.** Я купи́в бутербро́д (для того́), щоб ти міг перекуси́ти.; ♦ **s. to say** як то ка́жуть, так би мо́вити; **not s. much ... as** не так .., як ; **I feel not s. much sad as bored.** Мені́ не так су́мно, як ну́дно.; **s. what if ...?** То й що (з того́), як ...?, **S. what if the weather is bad?** То й що, як бу́де пога́на пого́да?

soap, *n.* ми́ло; *v.* ми́лити.

soccer, *n.* футбо́л, **play s.** гра́ти у футбо́л.

soft, *adj.* 1) м'яки́й, **s. pillow** м'яка́ поду́шка; 2) (*voice*) ти́хий, **s. voice** ти́хий го́лос; 3) легки́й, **s. wind** легки́й ві́тер.

some, *pron.* 1) де́які, з (із) + *G. pl.*), **s. guests** де́які го́сті, **s. of the books** де́які з книжо́к; 2) (*anim.*) дехто з + *G. pl.*, **s. of us** дехто з нас; 3) (*several*) кілька + *G.*, **s. apples** кілька я́блук; 4) (*unspecified*) яки́йсь, **He met s. strange guy.** Він познайо́мився з яки́мось ди́вним хло́пцем.; ♦ **s. day** коли́сь, коли-не́будь; 5) (*with uncountable nouns*) *G. sg.* **We had s. coffee.** Ми ви́пили ка́ви.; 5) (*approximation*) десь + *N.*, бі́ля + *G.*, **s. six kilos** десь шість кілогра́мів *or* бі́ля шести́ кілогра́мів.

someone, *pron.* хтось, **S. has left you a message.** Хтось лиши́в вам повідо́млення.

something, *pron.* щось, **S. is not right here.** Тут щось не те.

sometimes, *adv.* де́коли, ча́сом, і́нколи, іно́ді, **We meet only s.** Ми ба́чимося лише́ де́коли.

somewhere, *pron.* 1) *posn.* десь, **The passport is s. in the suitcase.** Па́спорт десь у валі́зі.; 2) *dir.* куди́сь, **They went s. far.** Вони́ пішли́ куди́сь дале́ко.

son, *n.* син, **elder (younger) s.** ста́рший (моло́дший) син; ♦ *vulg.* **s. of a bitch** су́чий син, *Gal.* з ку́рви син.

song, *n.* пі́сня, **folk s.** наро́дна пі́сня; ♦ **for a s.** за безці́нь, утри́дешева, **He bought the painting for a s.** Він купи́в цю карти́ну за безці́нь.

son-in-law, *n.* зять.

soon, *adv.* 1) ско́ро, незаба́ром, **I'll be back s.** Я ско́ро поверну́ся., **S. everybody will find out about it.** Незаба́ром всі дізна́ються про це.; 2) (*early*) ра́но, **They finished too s.** Вони́ на́дто ра́но закі́нчили.; ♦ **~er or later** ра́но чи пі́зно.

sorry, *adj.* 1) (*with logical subject in D.*) жаль, су́мно, **He is s. to hear about it.** Йому́ жаль чу́ти про це.; ♦ **I'm s.** ви́бач, ~те, *Gal.* перепро́шую.

soup, *n.* суп, **chicken s.** куря́ча ю́шка.

sour, *adj.* 1) ки́слий, квасни́й, **s. face** ки́сле обли́ччя, **The wine tastes s.** Це вино́ ки́сле (ква́сне) на смак.; 2) (*of food that went sour*) ски́слий, **s. milk.** ски́сле (ква́сне) молоко́.

south, *n.* пі́вдень, **in the s.** на пі́вдні, **to the s. of** на пі́вдень від + *G.*; *adj.* півде́нний, **s. Kyiv** півде́нний Ки́їв; *adv., dir.* на пі́вдень, у півде́нному на́прямку, **They went s.** Вони́ пішли́ на пі́вдень.

southern, *adj.* півде́нний, **s. climate (wind)** півде́нний клі́мат (ві́тер).

souvenir, *n.* сувені́р, **nice s.** га́рний сувені́р, **buy ~s** купува́ти сувені́ри.

Spain, *n.* Іспа́нія, *var.* Еспа́нія, **in S.** в Іспа́нії, **to S.** до Іспа́нії.

Spaniard, *n., m.* іспа́нець, *var.* еспа́нець, *f.* іспа́нка, *var.* еспа́нка.

Spanish, *adj.* іспа́нський, *var.* еспа́нський.

speak, *v.* 1) говори́ти, **s. slowly** говори́ти пові́льно; розмовля́ти; 2) (*language*) розмовля́ти, говори́ти + *I.*, **Do you s. Ukrainian?** Ви говори́те (розмовля́єте) украї́нською?; ♦ **so to s.** так би мо́вити.

special, *adj.* особли́вий, спеція́льний, **s. person** особли́ва люди́на, **s. city** особли́ве мі́сто.

specialist, *n.* спеція́ліст, фахіве́ць, **s. in history** спеція́ліст з + *G.*

specific, *adj.* 1) конкре́тний, **s. example** конкре́тний прикла́д; 2) окре́мий, **in each s. case** у ко́жному окре́мому ви́падку; 3) пито́мий, **The custom is s. to our region.** Цей звича́й є пито́мим для на́шого регіо́ну.

specifically, *adv.* 1) конкре́тно, са́ме, **What s. do you propose?** Що конкре́тно (са́ме) ви пропону́єте?; 2) окре́мо, **He s. mentioned this article.** Він окре́мо згада́в цю статтю́.; 3) пито́мо, специфі́чно, **s. Ukrainian expression** пито́мо украї́нський ви́раз.

speed, *n.* шви́дкість; **at a high (low) s.** на вели́кій (малі́й) шви́дкості.

spell, *v.* продиктува́ти; сказа́ти по літера́х; ♦ **s. your name** скажі́ть своє́ ім'я́.

spend, *v.* 1) (*time*) проводи́ти, **How many days did you s. in Paris?** Скі́льки днів ви провели́ у Пари́жі?; 2) (*money*) тра́тити, **I spent all my money.** Я ви́тратив усі́ гро́ші.

spite, *prep.* **in s. of** незважа́ючи на, по́при + *A.*, усу́переч + *D.*, **In s. of nasty weather we went for a walk.** Незважа́ючи на пога́ну пого́ду ми пішли́ гуля́ти.

spoon, *n.* ло́жка, **s. of ...** ло́жка + *G.*, **two ~s of sugar** дві ло́жки цу́кру.

sport, *n.* спорт; **to play ~s** займа́тися спо́ртом; *adj.* спорти́вний, **s. competition** спорти́вні змага́ння.

sportsman, *n., m.* спортсме́н, *f.* спортсме́нка.

spring, *n.* весна́, **in s.** весно́ю *or* навесні́.

square, *n.* пло́ща, майда́н, **on a s.** на пло́щі (майда́ні).

stamp, *n.* (пошто́ва) ма́рка.

stand, *v.* 1) стоя́ти; **to s. in line for ...** стоя́ти в че́рзі по + *A.* ...; 2) (*tolerate*) зно́сити, терпі́ти, **He can't s. this man.** Він не мо́же зно́сити ціє́ї люди́ни.; **s. out** виділя́тися з + *G.*; **s. up** встава́ти, підво́дитися.

standard, *adj.* станда́ртний; *n.* станда́рт.

start, *v.* 1) *tran.* почина́ти + *A.*, **s. a class** почина́ти заня́ття; + *impf. inf.* **s. planning a trip** поча́ти планува́ти по́дорож; 2) *tran.* (*car*) заво́дити + *A.*, **I can't s. the car.** Я не мо́жу завести́ а́вта.; 3) *intr.* почина́тися, **The season ~ed last month.** Сезо́н поча́вся мину́лого мі́сяця.; **s. over** почина́ти з поча́тку; *n.* поча́ток, **from s. to finish** від поча́тку до кінця́.

station, *n.* ста́нція, **subway s.** ста́нція метра́, **train (bus) s.** залізни́чна (авто́бусна) ста́нція.

stay, *v.* 1) (за)лиша́тися, **I'm ~ing** Я (за)лиша́юся; **to s. home** (за)лиша́тися (в)до́ма; 2) (*at hotel*) зупиня́тися, **What hotel can I s. at?** У яко́му готе́лі я мо́жу зупини́тися?; *n.* перебува́ння; ♦ **I wish you a pleasant s.** Бажа́ю вам приє́мно провести́ час.

still, *adj.* (*quiet*) ти́хий, **s. weather** ти́ха пого́да; *adv.* 1) (*yet*) все ще, **I s. live here.** Я все ще живу́ тут; 2) (*even*) наві́ть, **s. more interesting** наві́ть ціка́віший; 3) (*nevertheless*) все одно́, одна́к, **It's hard but we'll s. do it.** Це тяжко́, але́ ми все одно́ це зро́бимо.

stomach, *n.* 1) (*digestive organ*) шлу́нок; 2) (*abdomen*) живі́т.

stop, *n.* зупи́нка, **bus (train, metro) s.** зупи́нка автобуса (потяга, метра); *v.* 1) *tran.* зупиня́ти, **He'll s. the car at the intersection.** Він зупи́нить а́вто на перехре́сті.; 2) *intr.* зупиня́тися, **We need to s. and rest.** Нам тре́ба зупини́тися і відпочи́ти.; **s. doing sth** переста́ти + *impf. inf.*, **I ~ped seeing him long ago.** Я давно́ переста́в ба́читися з ним.

store, *n.* крамни́ця, магази́н, **grocery s.** продукто́ва крамни́ця, гастроно́м.

story, *n.* 1) *(narrative)* істо́рія, **tell a s.** розка́зувати істо́рію; ♦ **It's a long s.** Це до́вга істо́рія. 2) *(literary genre)* оповіда́ння; 3) *(tale)* о́повідь; 4) *(floor)* по́верх, **multi-storied** багатоповерхо́вий.

straight, *adj.* 1) прями́й, **s. street** пряма́ ву́лиця; 2) *(frank)* відве́ртий, **s. answer** відве́рта відпо́відь; *adv.* 1) пря́мо, про́сто, **go s.** іді́ть про́сто.

strange, *adj.* 1) ди́вний, **s. person** ди́вна люди́на; **It's s. you know her.** Ди́вно, що ви її зна́єте.; 2) *(foreign)* чужи́й, **s. country** чужа́ краї́на.

street, *n.* ву́лиця, **on the s.** на ву́лиці.

strong, *adj.* 1) си́льний, **s. impression** си́льне вра́ження, **s. woman** си́льна жі́нка; 2) *(hard to break)* мі́цний **s. ties** мі́цні зв'язки́.

student, *n.*, *m.* студе́нт; *f.* студе́нтка; *adj.* студе́нтський, **s. dormitory** студе́нтський гурто́житок.

study, *v.* 1) *tran.* вивча́ти + *A.*, **What do you s.?** Що ти вивча́єш?; 2) *tran. (learn)* вчи́ти + *A.*, **s. grammar** вчи́ти грама́тику; 3) *intr. only impf.* вчи́тися, навча́тися, **Where do you s.?** Де ти вчи́шся?; *n.* вивча́ння, **climate s.** вивча́ння клі́мату; дослі́дження з + *G.*, **chemistry s.** дослі́дження з хі́мії.

stupid, *adj.* дурни́й, **s. remark** ду́рне заува́ження; *colloq.* дурнува́тий.

subject, *n.* 1) *(of studies)* предме́т, дисциплі́на, **What ~s do they teach (study) here?** Які́ предме́ти тут виклада́ють (вивча́ють)?; 2) *(part of sentence)* пі́дмет.

subway, *n.* метро́, метрополіте́н, **by s.** метро́м, **to take the s.** сіда́ти в метро́.

such, *adj.* таки́й; **s. ... as** таки́й ... як + *N.*, **We need to buy s. groceries as bread, coffee, and apples.** Тре́ба купи́ти такі́ проду́кти, як хліб, ка́ва та я́блука.

sudden, *adj.* рапто́вий, несподі́ваний.

suddenly, *adv.* ра́птом, несподі́вано, **He s. stood up.** Він ра́птом встав.

sugar, *n.* цу́кор, **with s.** із цу́кром, **no s.** без цу́кру.

suggest, *v.* пропонува́ти + *inf.*, **I s. that we do it now.** Пропону́ю зроби́ти це за́раз., **What do you s. that we do?** Що ви пропону́єте роби́ти?

suit, *v.* підхо́дити + *D.*, **This plan ~s Vasyl.** Цей план підхо́дить Васи́леві; влашто́вувати + *A.*, **Does that s. you?** Вас це влашто́вує?; *n. (set of clothes)* костю́м, **business s.** ділови́й костю́м.

suitcase, *n.* валі́за; **to pack the ~s** пакува́ти валі́зи.

summer, *n.* лі́то, **in the s.** влі́тку, *var.* улі́тку; **this (last, next) s.** цього́ (мину́лого, насту́пного) лі́та; *adj.* лі́тній; **s. time** лі́тній час.

sun, *n.* со́нце, **in the s.** на со́нці.

Sunday, *n.* неді́ля, **on S.** у неді́лю.

supermarket, *n.* суперма́ркет, **to go to a s.** ходи́ти до суперма́ркету.

supper, *n.* вече́ря, **for s.** на вече́рю, **to have s.** вече́ряти.

sure, *adj.* впе́внений, **to be s.** бу́ти впе́вненим, **I'm not quite s.** Я не зовсі́м упе́внений.; *adv.* пе́вна річ, звича́йно.

surely, *adv.* пе́вна річ, звича́йно, я́сно.

surprise, *n.* 1) несподі́ванка, сюрпри́з, **pleasant s.** приє́мна несподі́ванка; **What a s.!** Оце́ так несподі́ванка!; 2) по́див, **Andriy looked at her with s.** Андрі́й подиви́вся на не́ї із по́дивом.; ♦ **take by s.** заско́чити + *A.*, злови́ти (застава́ти) + *A.* знена́цька, **Her criticism took me by s.** Її кри́тика злови́ла мене́ знена́цька (заско́чила мене́).; *v. tran.* дивува́ти + *A.* + *I.*, **Halyna ~d her boyfriend by such words.** Гали́на здивува́ла свого́ хло́пця таки́ми слова́ми.

sushi, *n.* су́ші, **We ordered some s.** Ми замо́вили собі́ су́ші.

sweet, *adj.* соло́дкий, **s. pear** соло́дка гру́ша.

swim, *v.*, *intr.*, *uni.* пливти́, *var.* пли́сти; *multi.* пла́вати, **He likes to s.** Він лю́бить пла́вати.

swimming pool, *n.* басе́йн, **to go to a s.** ходи́ти до басе́йну.

switch, *v.*, *tran.* перемика́ти + *A.*; **s. channels** перемика́ти кана́ли; **to s. on** вмика́ти + *A.*, **I wanted to s. on the TV.** Я хоті́в вімкну́ти телеві́зор.; *(of light)* запа́лювати, **He ~ed on the lamp.** Він запали́в ла́мпу.; **to s. off** вимика́ти + *A.*, *(of light)* (з)гаси́ти, **Yaryna ~ed off the light.** Яри́на згаси́ла сві́тло.

symptom, *n.* *(of disease)* симпто́м, **s. of a disease** симпто́м хворо́би.

T

table, *n.* 1) стіл, **The vase is on the t.** Ва́за на столі́., **I put the vase on the t.** Я поста́вив ва́зу на стіл.; 2) *(chart)* табли́ця, **t. of contents** зміст.

tablespoon, *n.* столо́ва ло́жка.

take, *v.* 1) *tran.* бра́ти + *A.*, **t. a pen** бра́ти перо́; 2) *tran. (take out)* вийма́ти + *A.*, **She took the money from his wallet.** Вона́ ви́йняла гро́ші у ньо́го з гама́нця.; 3) *tran. (on foot)* відво́дити, **T. me to his room.** Відведи́ мене́ до його́ кімна́ти.; *(by vehicle)* відво́зити + *A.*, **Oleh took him to the station.** Оле́г відві́з його́ на вокза́л.; 4) *(accept) intr.* прийма́ти + *A.*, **He took the offer right away.** Він одра́зу прийня́в пропози́цію.; 5) *(medicine)* пи́ти, прийма́ти + *A.*, **T. something for fever.** Ви́пийте *(приймі́ть)* щось від температу́ри.; 6) *tran. (to measure)* мі́ряти + *A.*, **t. blood pressure** мі́ряти + *D.* тиск (кро́ви); 7) *tran. (tolerate)* терпі́ти + *A.*, **I can't t. it any more.** Я не мо́жу цьо́го бі́льше терпі́ти.; 8) *(require) (logical subject in D.)* потрі́бно, тре́ба + щоб + *clause*, **It ~s Mykola an hour to make dinner.** Мико́лі тре́ба годи́на, щоб звари́ти вече́рю.; **t. off** зніма́ти + *A.*, **He took off his shirt.** Він зняв соро́чку.; **t. part in** бра́ти у́часть у + *L.*; **t. place** відбува́тися, ма́ти мі́сце.

talented, *adj.* талано́витий, **t. photographer** талано́витий фото́граф.

talk, *n.* розмо́ва; *v.* говори́ти про + *A.*, **He always ~ed about movies.** Він за́вжди говори́в про кіно́.; ♦ **What are you ~ing about?** Про що ти (говори́ш)?

tall, *adj.* 1) високий, **t. woman** висо́ка жі́нка; 2) *(in measurement of height)* заввишки, **He is two meters t.** Він два ме́три заввишки.

taste, *n.* смак, **poor (refined) t.** кепський (ви́шуканий) смак; **be to sb's t.** бу́ти *D.* до смаку, **Her jokes were not to Bohdan's t.** Її жа́рти не були́ Богда́нові до смаку.; *v.* 1) *tran.* куштува́ти + *A.*, **Would you like to t. the cake?** Хо́чете скуштува́ти торт?; 2) *intr.* бу́ти + *adj.* на смак, **These apples t. sour.** Ці я́блука кислі́ на смак.

tasty, *adj.* смачни́й, до́брий, **t. dinner** смачна́ вече́ря.

taxi, *n.* таксі́вка, *var.* таксі́; **go by t.** їхати таксі́вкою, **hail a t.** лови́ти таксі́, **order a t.** замовля́ти таксі́вку.

taxi-driver, *n.* таксист.

taxi stand, *n.* стоя́нка таксі́вок (таксі́).

tea, *n.* чай; **black (green, fruit) t.** чо́рний (зеле́ний, фрукто́вий) чай, **ice t.** чай з кри́гою.

teach, *v.* 1) *intr.* виклада́ти, *colloq.* вчи́ти, **They t. every day.** Вони́ виклада́ють щодня.; 2) *tran.* виклада́ти, *colloq.* вчи́ти + *A.*, **What do you t. there?** Що ви там виклада́єте?; 3) *tran. (show how to)* навча́ти, вчи́ти + *A.* + *inf.* or + *G.*, **Father taught Olia to ride a bicycle.** Ба́тько навчи́в О́лю їздити велосипе́дом., **He ~es me Italian.** Він вчить мене́ італі́йської.

teacher, *n.* 1) *(at high school)* вчи́тель, **brilliant (poor) t.** чудо́вий (кепський) вчи́тель; 2) *(at university)* виклада́ч.

teaspoon, *n.* ча́йна ло́жка.

telephone, *n.* телефо́н, **over the t.** по телефо́ну; *v.* дзвони́ти, телефонува́ти + *D.*, **Somebody ~d you just now.** Хтось що́йно вам дзвони́в.

television, *n.* телеві́зор, **on t.** по телеві́зору, **What's on t. today?** Що сього́дні по телеві́зору?, **watch t.** диви́тися телеві́зор (телеба́чення); *adj.* телевізі́йний, **t. program** телепрогра́ма.

tell, *v.* 1) *intr. (in reported speech)* каза́ти + *D.*, **He told me that the meeting was interesting.** Він сказа́в мені́, що зу́стріч була́ ціка́вою.; 2) *tran.* каза́ти + *A.* + *D.*, **He told Oksana the truth.** Він сказа́в Окса́ні пра́вду.; **t. me**, **~ ~іть**; 3) *tran.* розка́зувати, розповіда́ти + *A.* + *D.*, **T. me the whole story.** Розкажі́ть мені́ всю цю істо́рію.; 4) *(distinguish)* відрізня́ти + *A.* від + *G.*, **Can you t. an original from a replica?** Ви мо́жете відрізни́ти оригіна́л від ко́пії?

temperature, *n.* температу́ра, **high (low) t.** висо́ка (низька́) температу́ра.

ten, *card.* де́сять, **t. books** де́сять книжо́к; 2) *(of anim. or paired nouns)* де́сятеро, **t. drivers (pants)** де́сятеро воді́їв (штані́в); 3) *(of time by clock)* деся́та (годи́на), **at t. o'clock** о деся́тій (годи́ні); *n.* деся́тка, **the first t.** пе́рша деся́тка.

tenant, *n.* квартира́нт.

tennis, *n.* те́ніс, **play t.** гра́ти у те́ніс; **t. player** тенісист.

tenth, *ord.* деся́тий, **t. seat** деся́те мі́сце; *n.* (одна́) деся́та, **seven ~s** чоти́ри деся́ті (деся́тих).

terrible, *adj.* страшни́й, жахли́вий.

text, *n.* текст; *v.* 1) *tran.* тексту́вати + *D.* + *A.*, **He ~s us all his news.** Він тексту́є нам всі свої́ нови́ни.

textbook, *n.* підру́чник, **a Ukrainian t.** підру́чник (з) украї́нської мо́ви.

thank, *v.* дя́кувати; ♦ **t. you very much** ду́же дя́кую.

thanks to, *prep.* завдяки́ + *D.*, **t. to you** завдяки́ тобі́.

that, *dem. pron. (referring to sth previously mentioned)* це, **T. was a horse.** Це був кінь., **T. is a good idea.** Це слу́шна ду́мка.; *adj.* (**that** *as opposed to* **this**) той, *f.* та, *nt.* те, **t. building and not this** той буди́нок, а не цей, **t. street and not this** та ву́лиця, а не ця, **t. city and not this** те мі́сто, а не це; *conj.* 1) *(introducing object clause)* що; **I know t. he's sick.** Я зна́ю, що він хворі́є.; ♦ **t. is** тобто; 2) *(introducing attribute clause)* що, *m.* яки́й (*f.* яка́, *nt.* яке́, *pl.* які́), **the ticket t. I have** квито́к, яки́й (*or* що) я ма́ю; **the assignment t. he gave us** завда́ння, яке́ (*or* що) він нам дав; **the medicine that they have taken** лі́ки, які́ (*or* що) вони́ прийма́ють; 3) *(with clause of purpose, intention, etc.)* щоб + *pa.*, **I wrote her t. she be ready for the trip.** Я написа́в їй, щоб вона́ була́ гото́ва до подоро́жі.; *adv. (so)* так, **t. close** так бли́зько; ♦ **and all t.** і таке і́нше; ♦ **like t.**, **things like t.** такі́ ре́чі; ♦ **t. said** і все ж, одна́к; ♦ **t. will do** (цьо́го) до́сить.

the, *article* 1) either not translated or corresponds to the *dem. pron.* цей, ця, це, ці this, *or* той, та, те, ті that, **I am t. man who called you.** Це я дзвони́в вам.; 2) *(indicating family)* сім'я́, подру́жжя + *G. pl.*, **the Petrenkos** *(family)* сім'я́ Петре́нків *or (married couple)* подру́жжя Петре́нків *or surname in pl.* Петре́нки; 3) *(emphasis) m.* той са́мий, *f.* та са́ма, *nt.* те са́ме, *pl.* ті са́мі, **There she was, t. impossibly beautiful woman.** Вона́ була́ там, та са́ма немо́жливо га́рна жі́нка.

theater, *n.* теа́тр, **We were in the t.** Ми були́ у теа́трі., **We went to the t.** Ми ходи́ли до теа́тру.

their, *poss. pron.*, *m.* 1) їхній, *f.* їхня, *nt.* їхнє, *pl.* їхні; **t. friend** їхній друг, **t. sister** їхня сестра́, **t. puppy** їхнє цуценя́, **t. words** їхні слова́; 2) *(not translated when referring to the subject's own body part)* **They finally opened t. eyes to the world.** Вони́ наре́шті відкри́ли о́чі на світ.; 2) *(referring to somebody or something related to the subject of sentence) m.* свій, *f.* своя́, *nt.* своє́, *pl.* свої́, **They love t. country.** Вони́ лю́блять свою́ краї́ну., **The Johnsons have t. own problems.** Джо́нсони ма́ють свої́ вла́сні пробле́ми.

themselves, *refl. pron.*, 3rd *pers. pl.* 1) себе́, **In their dreams, they see t. rich.** У свої́х мрі́ях вони́ ба́чать себе́ бага́тими.; 2) *(for emphasis)* са́мі, **They t. would like to know it.** Вони́ са́мі хоті́ли б зна́ти це.; 3) *(alone)* са́мі, **They can do it t.** Вони́ мо́жуть зроби́ти це са́мі.; 4) *(for themselves)* собі́, **They baked t. a cake.** Вони́ спекли́ собі́ торт(а).

then, *adv.* 1) *(at that time)* тоді́, **Borys worked hard t.** Тоді́ Бори́с бага́то працюва́в.; 2) *(after)* по́тім, тоді́, **Svitlana finished the translation and t. sent it away.** Світла́на закінчи́ла пере́клад і по́тім відісла́ла його́.; **if … then …** якщо́ … то … **If you have time, t. you must help these people.** Якщо́ ти ма́єш час, то ти пови́нен допомогти́ цим лю́дям.

there, *adv.* 1) *posn.* там, **There is a tree t.** Там стої́ть де́рево.; 2) *dir.* туди́, *Gal.* там, **We need to go t.** Нам тре́ба піти́ туди́ (*Gal.* там).; **t. and back** туди́ й наза́д; 3) *as introductory subject in **There is/are** corresponds to construction with verbs бу́ти to be, стоя́ти to stand, рости́ to grow, висі́ти to hang, лежа́ти to lie, etc. Ukrainian sentence starts with the adverbial modifier of place that is at the end of the English sentence.; **T. is a student in the room.** У кімна́ті (є) студе́нт., **T. is a chair in the corner.** У кутку́ стої́ть стіле́ць., **T. was a picture on the wall.** На стіні́ висі́ла карти́на., **T. will be a carpet on the floor.** На підло́зі лежа́тиме ки́лим.

therefore

therefore, *adv.* тому́, відта́к, **They speak Ukrainian, t. we do not need a translator.** Вони́ розмовля́ють украї́нською, тому́ нам не тре́ба переклада́ч.

they, *pers. pron.* 1) вони́, **What did t. say?** Що вони́ сказа́ли?; 2) *(omitted in impersonal sentence; no subject is used in Ukrainian sentence which starts with the adverbial modifier of place of the English sentence)*, **T. sell milk in this store.** В цій крамни́ці продаю́ть молоко́.

thick, *adj.* 1) товсти́й, грубий, **t. book** груба кни́жка; 2) густи́й, **t. forest** густи́й ліс, **t. hair** густе́ воло́сся, **t. soup** густи́й суп; 3) (in measurements) завтовшки, **The computer is three centimeters t.** Комп'ю́тер три сантиме́три завтовшки.; 4) *(dumb)* тупи́й, **He's a bit t.** Він трохи тупи́й.

thin, *adj.* 1) тонки́й, **t. line** тонка́ лі́нія; 2) *(skinny)* худи́й, **t. woman** худа́ жі́нка; 3) рідки́й, **t. beard** рідка́ борода́, **t. grass** рідка́ трава́.

thing, *n.* 1) річ, **interesting t.** ціка́ва річ; 2) *(sth)* що, **He told me many ~s.** Він бага́то чого сказа́в мені́.; 3) *(in neg. sentences)* нішо́, **I can't do a t.** Я не мо́жу нічого зроби́ти.; 4) *(all, in pl.)* все, **We love all ~s Spanish.** Ми лю́бимо все іспа́нське. ♦ **How are ~s?** Як спра́ви?; ♦ **The t. is that** Річ у тім, що; ♦ **for one t.** по-перше *or* до́сить сказа́ти, що.

think, *v.* 1) *intr.* ду́мати, **I think he knows Olena.** Ду́маю, що він зна́є Оле́ну.; *intr.* ду́мати про + *A.*, **He often ~s about Natalia.** Він ча́сто ду́має про Ната́лю.; **What do you t.?** Як ви ду́маєте?; 3) *(be of opinion)* вважа́ти, **I t.** я вважа́ю (*or* гада́ю, *or* раху́ю).

third, *ord.* тре́тій, **t. place** тре́тє мі́сце; *n.* (одна́) трети́на, тре́тя, **two ~s** дві трети́ни (тре́ті, тре́тіх).

thirteen, *card.* 1) трина́дцять, **t. pages** трина́дцять сторі́нок; 2) *(of anim. or paired nouns)* трина́дцятеро, **t. individuals** трина́дцятеро осіб; *n.* трина́дцятка.

thirty, *card.* 1) три́дцять, **t. seconds** три́дцять секу́нд; 2) *coll.* тридця́теро *(with anim. and paired nouns)*, **t. guests** тридця́теро госте́й; *n.* тридця́тка.

this, *dem. pron., m.* 1) цей, *f.* ця, *nt.* це, **t. magazine and not that one** цей журна́л, а не той, **t. cup and not that one** ця філіжа́нка, а не та, **t. window and not that one** це вікно́, а не те; 2) *(to point to sth)* це, **T. is my flat.** Це моя́ кварти́ра., **T. is him.** Це він., **T. was her.** Це була́ вона́.

though, *conj.* 1) *(despite)* хоч, **He continued to work t. he was tired.** Він продо́вжував працюва́ти, хоч і був стомлений.; 2) *(however)* одна́к, проте́, **She is talented t. nobody knows it.** Вона́ талано́вита, одна́к (проте́) цього́ ніхто́ не зна́є.

thousand, *n.* ти́сяча, **It was a t. years ago.** Це було́ ти́сячу ро́ків тому́.; **several t. people** кілька ти́сяч чолові́к.

three, *card.*, 1) *m.* три, **t. days** три дні; 2) *coll. (of anim. or paired nouns)* тро́є, **t. boys** тро́є хло́пців; 3) *(of time by clock)* тре́тя (годи́на), **at t. o'clock** о тре́тій (годи́ні); *n.* трі́йка.

three hundred, *card.* три́ста, **t. h. hryvnias** три́ста гри́вень; *n.* три со́тні.

three hundredth, *ord.* трьохсо́тий.

throat, *n.* го́рло, **I have a sore t.** Мене́ боли́ть го́рло.

Thursday, *n.* четве́р, **on T.** у четве́р, **till next T.** до насту́пного четверга́.

toward

ticket, *n.* квито́к, **train (bus, airplane) t.** квито́к на по́їзд (авто́бус, літа́к), **theater (movie) t.** квито́к до теа́тру (кіна́).

till, *prep.* 1) до + *G.*, **t. Monday** до понеді́лка; 2) по́ки ... не, доки ... не, **He did not come t. I asked him to.** Він не прихо́див, по́ки я не попроси́в його́.

time, *n.* 1) *(duration)* час, **all this t.** весь цей час, **for a long t.** до́вгий час, **on t.** вча́сно, **What's the t. now?** Котра́ за́раз годи́на?; 2) *(instance)* раз; **for the first t.** упе́рше; **for the last t.** воста́ннє; **how many ~s?** скі́льки раз(ів)?; **last (next) t.** мину́лого (насту́пного) ра́зу, **this t.** цього́ ра́зу; **all the t.** весь час; **at the same t.** водно́час; **to have no t. for** не ма́ти ча́су на ...; **lose no t.** не гая́ти ча́су.

timetable, *n.* розкла́д, гра́фік, **according to the t.** за розкла́дом.

tired, *adj.* сто́млений, **to get t. of** втоми́тися від + *G.*, **He got t. of work.** Він втоми́вся від робо́ти.

title, *n.* на́зва, заголо́вок, **under the t. of** під на́звою; **What's the t. of the book?** Як назива́ється кни́жка?

to, *prep.* 1) *(motion)* до + *G.*, **a trip t. Kyiv** подоро́ж до Ки́єва; 2) *(destination) D.*, **letter to my brother** лист моє́му брато́ві; 3) *(towards)* на + *A.*, **t. the south** на пі́вдень; 4) *(time by clock)* за + *A.*, *or* без + *G.*, **It's ten minutes t. one.** За́раз за де́сять (без десяти́) хвили́на пе́рша.; *part.* щоб, для того́ щоб, **Robert came t. speak to you.** Ро́берт прийшо́в (для того́), щоб поговори́ти з ва́ми.

today, *adv.* сього́дні, **The excursion will be t.** Екску́рсія бу́де сього́дні.; **'s** сього́днішній, **today's newspaper** сього́днішня газе́та.

toe, *n.* па́лець, *pl.* па́льці.

together, *adv.* 1) ра́зом (з + *I.*), *colloq.* гурто́м (з + *I.*), **They sat t. with their children.** Вони́ сиді́ли ра́зом зі свої́ми ді́тьми.; 2) *(at the same time)* одноча́сно, водно́час.

tomato, *n.* помідо́р, **t. juice** тома́тний сік.

tomorrow, *adv.* за́втра, **till t.** до за́втра, **I'll call you t.** Я подзвоню́ тобі́ за́втра.; **t. morning (afternoon, evening)** за́втра вра́нці (пополу́дні, увече́рі); ♦ **As if there was no t.** Як перед лихи́м кінце́м.

tongue, *n.* язи́к; **mother t.** рі́дна мо́ва.

tonight, *adv.* сього́дні вве́чері, **What's on t.?** Що сього́дні в кіні́?

too, *adv.* 1) *(also)* тако́ж, теж, **I read it t.** Я теж чита́в це; 2) *(excessively)* (за)на́дто, **We live here t. long.** Ми живемо́ тут на́дто до́вго.; за~ *added to any adj. or adv. to express excessive quality or quantity*, **t. much** забага́то, **t. red** зачерво́ний.

tooth, *n.* зуб, **I have a toothache.** Мене́ боли́ть зуб.; **wisdom t.** зуб му́дрости.

tour, *n.* 1) *(trip)* подоро́ж, **to go on a t. to** пої́хати у подоро́ж до + *G.*; 2) *(short)* екску́рсія, **t. of Kyiv (museum)** екску́рсія Ки́євом (музе́єм); **package t.** тур.

tourist, *n.* тури́ст, **international t.** міжнаро́дний тури́ст; *adj.* туристи́чний, **t. agency** туристи́чна аге́нція.

toward, *prep.* до + *G.*, **t. a metro station** до ста́нції метра́; у на́прямі до + *G.*, **We walked t. the bank.** Ми йшли у на́прямі до ба́нку.

towel

umbrella

towel, *n.* рушни́к, **embroidered t.** виши́ваний рушни́к.

town, *n.* 1) мі́сто, **He's in t.** Він у мі́сті., **She won't be in t. then.** Її тоді не бу́де в мі́сті.; 2) *(small town)* місте́чко, **home t.** рі́дне мі́сто.

traffic, *n.* рух, **heavy t.** си́льний рух; **t. jam** ко́рок, **get into a t. jam** потра́пити у ко́рок, **t. light** світлофо́р.

train, *n.* по́тяг, по́їзд; **by t.** по́тягом, по́їздом, **I often travel by t.** Я ча́сто їжджу по́тягом.; **fast (commuter, freight) t.** швидки́й (примі́ський, това́рний) по́тяг; **t. station** залізни́чна ста́нція; *v.* 1) *tran.* тренува́ти + *A.*, **He ~ed many good athletes.** Він тренува́в бага́тьох до́брих спортсме́нів.; 2) *tran. (educate)* готува́ти, навча́ти + *A.*, **They t. accountants in this school.** У цій шко́лі навча́ють бухга́лтерів.; 3) *intr.* тренува́тися, **They t. a lot for the next competition.** Вони́ бага́то трену́ються до насту́пних змага́нь.; 4) *intr.* вчи́тися на + *A.*, **Taras ~ed as a film director.** Тара́с вчи́вся на кінорежисе́ра.

tram, *n.* 1) *(cablecar)* фунікуле́р; 2) *(streetcar)* трамва́й, **take a t.** сіда́ти на трамва́й; **Where does this t. go?** Куди́ йде цей трамва́й?

translate, *v.*, 1) *tran.* переклада́ти + *A.* з *G.* + *I.*, **t. from English into Ukrainian** переклада́ти з англі́йської украї́нською; 2) *intr.* переклада́тися (як + *N.*), **This expression ~s as "Welcome!"** Цей ви́раз переклада́ється: «Віта́ємо вас!».

translation, *n.* пере́клад, **consecutive (descriptive, literal, simultaneous) t.** послідо́вний (описо́вий, досло́вний, синхро́нний) пере́клад.

transportation, *n.* 1) тра́нспорт, **public t.** грома́дський тра́нспорт; 2) перевезе́ння, **t. of goods** перевезе́ння това́рів.

travel, *n.* по́дорож, **~s around the world** подоро́жі сві́том; *v.* подорожува́ти + *I. or* по + *L.*, **He likes to t. around Africa.** Він лю́бить подорожува́ти А́фрикою (по А́фриці).

traveler, *n.* мандрівни́к, мандрівни́ця, **inveterate t.** затя́тий мандрівни́к.

tree, *n.* де́рево, **in a t.** на де́реві, **under a t.** під де́ревом; ♦ **family t.** родові́д.

trip, *n.* по́дорож; **business t.** відря́дження, ділова́ по́дорож; **Mykhailo goes on a business t. to Odesa next Monday.** Миха́йло ї́де у відря́дження до Оде́си насту́пного понеді́лка.

true, *adj.* 1) спра́вжній, **t. love** спра́вжнє коха́ння; 2) правди́вий, **t. story** правди́ва (реа́льна) істо́рія; 3) *(faithful)* ві́рний, **a t. friend** ві́рний друг; ♦ **a t. Ukrainian** щи́рий украї́нець; **It's (not) t.** Це (не) пра́вда.

trust, *v.* ві́рити, довіря́ти + *D.*, **He cannot be ~ed.** Йому́ не мо́жна ві́рити.; **~ed friend** наді́йний (*or* ві́рний) друг; *n.* дові́ра; **take sth on t.** прийма́ти на ві́ру, **Robert never takes anything on t.** Ро́берт ніко́ли нічо́го не прийма́є на ві́ру.

truth, *n.* 1) пра́вда; ♦ **to tell the t.** каза́ти пра́вду; 2) і́стина, **This is a scientific t.** Це - науко́ва і́стина.

try, *v.* 1) намага́тися, стара́тися, **I t. to convince her.** Я намага́юся перекона́ти її́.; 2) пробува́ти, **Bohdan tried to calm down.** Богда́н спро́бував заспоко́їтися.; **t. on** примі́ряти, **I'd like to t. on these pants.** Я хоті́в би примі́ряти ці штани́.; *n.* спро́ба, **on the first t.** з пе́ршої спро́би.

Tuesday, *n.* вівто́рок, **on T.** у вівто́рок, **till T.** до вівто́рка (*var.* вівті́рка).

Turk, *n.*, *m.* ту́рок; *f.* турке́ня, *var.* турча́нка, **Kemal is a T. who speaks good Ukrainian.** Кема́ль - ту́рок, що до́бре гово́рить украї́нською.

Turkish, *adj.* туре́цький; *n.* туре́цька мо́ва, **speak T.** розмовля́ти туре́цькою (мо́вою).

turn, *v.* 1) *tran.* поверта́ти + *A.*, **t. the steering wheel** поверта́ти кермо́; 2) *intr.* поверта́тися, **He ~ed and looked at her.** Він поверну́вся і погля́нув на не́ї.; 3) *(change direction of motion)* зверта́ти, поверта́ти, **t. right (left)** поверта́ти право́руч (ліво́руч); 4) *(page)* перегорта́ти + *A.*, **They ~ed a new page.** Вони́ перегорну́ли но́ву сторі́нку.; 5) *(light, radio, etc.)* **t. on** вмика́ти + *A.*, **t. off** вимика́ти + *A.*, **If you ~ed on the TV, please t. it off.** Якщо́ ти вві́мкнув телеві́зор, будь ла́ска, ви́мкни його́.; 6) **t. out** *intr.* виявля́тися, **It ~s out that they know each other.** Виявля́ється, що вони́ знайо́мі.; 7) *intr.* **t. to** зверта́тися до + *G.* **You should t. to a lawyer for advice.** Вам тре́ба зверну́тися до юри́ста по пора́ду.; *n.* 1) поворо́т, **left (right) t.** лі́вий (пра́вий) поворо́т; 2) черга́, **It's your t. to pose a question.** Тепе́р ва́ша черга́ ста́вити пита́ння.

TV, *see* **television**.

twelve, *card.* 1) двана́дцять + *G. pl.*, **t. people** двана́дцять осі́б; **at t. o'clock** о двана́дцятій годи́ні; 2) *coll.* двана́дцятеро *(with anim. and paired nouns)*, **t. women** двана́дцятеро жіно́к; 3) *(of time by clock)* двана́дцята (годи́на), **at t. o'clock** о двана́дцятій (годи́ні) *n.* двана́дцятка.

twentieth, *ord.* двадця́тий.

twenty, *card.* 1) два́дцять, **t. hryvnias** два́дцять гри́вень; 2) *coll.* двадця́теро *(with anim. and paired nouns)*, **t. participants** двадця́теро уча́сників.

twice, *adv.* 1) дві́чі, два ра́зи, **He said it t.** Він сказа́в це дві́чі.; 2) *(in comparison)* удві́чі, у два ра́зи, **This hotel is t. as cheap as that one.** Цей готе́ль удві́чі деше́вший за той.

two, *card.*, 1) *m.* два, **t. days** два дні, *f.* дві, **t. nights** дві но́чі; 2) *(of anim. or paired nouns)* дво́є, **t. puppies (doors)** дво́є щеня́т (двере́й); 3) *(of time by clock)* дру́га (годи́на), **at t. o'clock** о дру́гій (годи́ні); *n.* дві́йка.

two hundred, *card.* дві́сті + *G. pl.*; *n.* дві со́тні.

two hundredth, *ord.* двохсо́тий.

type, *n.* тип, **What t. of person is he?** Що він за люди́на?; *v.* друкува́ти + *A.*

typical, *adj.* типо́вий, **t. name** типо́ве ім'я́, **be t. of sb/ sth** бу́ти типо́вим для + *G.*

U

ugly, *adj.*, нега́рний, потво́рний, *(disgusting)* оги́дний, *colloq.* паску́дний.

Ukraine, *n.* Украї́на, **in U.** в Украї́ні, **to U.** до Украї́ни.

Ukrainian, *adj.* украї́нський; *n.* 1) *m.* украї́нець, *f.* украї́нка, *pl.* украї́нці, **They are U.** Вони́ украї́нці.; 2) украї́нська мо́ва, **He speaks fluent U.** Він ві́льно розмовля́є украї́нською.

umbrella, *n.* парасо́ля, парасо́лька, **folding u.** складна́ парасо́ля.

unbelievable, *adj.* неймовірний, невірогідний, **It's u. they did it.** Неймовірно, що вони це зробили.

unbelievably, *adv.* неймовірно, неправдоподібно.

uncle, *n.* дядько, **my u.** мій дядько.

under, *prep.* 1) *posn.* під + *I.*, **u. the table** під столом; 2) *dir.* під + *A.*, **Put it u. the table.** Поклади це під стіл.; 3) *(during the period)* за + *G.* **u. the the Soviet rule** за совітської влади.

understand, *v.*, *tran.* розуміти + *A.*, **Do you u. me?** Ви мене розумієте?, **I don't u. anything.** Я нічого не розумію.

undoubtedly, *adv.* безперечно, без сумніву, безсумнівно.

undress, *v.*, *intr.* роздягатися, **He ~ed and went to bed.** Він роздягнувся і ліг спати.

unfortunately, *adv.* на жаль, **The store is already closed u.** Крамниця, на жаль, уже зачинена.

university, *n.* університет, **at u.** в університеті; *adj.* університетський, **a u. library** університетська бібліотека, **u. campus** кампус, університетське містечко.

unknown, *adj.* незнайомий, **an u. person** незнайомець, незнайома людина.

up, *adv.* 1) *dir.* угору, догори, **cruise up the Dnipro** круїз угору Дніпром; **this side up** цим боком вгору (догори); 2) *posn.* угорі, нагорі, **up there** там нагорі.; **u. to** аж до + *G.*, **water u. to the knees** вода аж до колін.

urban, *adj.* міський, **u. culture** міська культура, **u. population** міське населення.

use, *v.*, 1) *tran.* використовувати + *A.*, **to u. a book** використовувати книжку; користуватися + *I.*, **We u. our own car.** Ми користуємося своїм власним автом.; 2) *(exploit) tran.* використовувати + *A.*, **He never hesitates to u. others.** Він ніколи не вагається використовувати інших.; 3) ~**d to** колись *or* було + *impr. inf.*, **He ~d to like Arkhypenko.** Йому колись подобався Архипенко.; **Roman ~d to see her often.** Роман було часто її бачив. *n.* використання, застосування, **This method has a number of ~s.** Цей метод має низку застосувань.; ♦ **what's the u. of ...** марно + бути + *impf. inf.*, **What's the u. of crying?** Марно плакати. **It was no u. persuading them.** Марно було переконувати їх.

used, *adj.* 1) використаний, **He discarded all u. paper.** Він викинув весь використаний папір.; 2) вживаний, **u. car** вживане авто; 3) *(accustomed)* призвичаєний, звиклий, ♦ **to be (get) u. to** звикати до + *G.*, **He got u. to my jokes.** Він звик до моїх жартів. *See also* **use.**

useful, *adj.* 1) корисний, **u. piece of advice** корисна порада; 2) потрібний, **This pot is always u. in the kitchen.** Ця каструля завжди потрібна на кухні.

usually, *adv.* звичайно, як правило, **Ivan u. shaves for work.** Іван звичайно голиться на роботу.

V

vacant, *adj.* 1) *(a hotel room, seat)* вільний, **v. room** вільна кімната; 2) *(of look)* відсутній, **She gave me a v. look.** Вона подивилася на мене відсутнім поглядом.

vacation, *n.* 1) *(at work)* відпустка, **be on v.** бути у відпустці, **take a v.** брати відпустку; 2) *(at school)* канікули, *Gal.* вакації, *both only pl.*, **to go on v.** їхати (їздити) на канікули (вакації).

various, *adj.* різний, *var.* ріжний, **v. colors** різні кольори.

vegetable, *n.* овоч; *coll.* ~**s** городина; **fresh ~s** свіжа городина; **fruit and ~s** фрукти й городина (*or* овочі). *adj.* овочевий, **v. garden** город, **v. soup** суп з городини.

very, *adv.* дуже, **v. far** дуже далеко, **v. well** дуже добре; *adj.* самий, **at the v. beginning** на самому початку, **this v. moment** у цей самий момент, **the v. thought of you** сама думка про тебе.

victory, *n.* перемога, **v. over** перемога над + *I.*

view, *n.* 1) вид, **a room with a v. of the sea** кімната із видом на море; 2) *(convictions)* погляд, **political ~s** політичні погляди; **in v. of ...** з огляду на + *A.*, **In v. of the change of plans I decided to stay home.** З огляду на зміну планів я вирішив залишитися удома.; *v., tran.* оглядати + *A.*, **We can v. the exhibit next week.** Ми можемо оглянути виставку наступного тижня.

village, *n.* село, **This guy is from our v.** Цей хлопець із нашого села.; *adj.* сільський, провінційний, **v. council** сільська управа, **v. life** сільське життя.

violet, *n.* фіялка. *adj.* фіялковий, фіолетовий, **v. color** фіялковий колір.

violin, *n.* скрипка; **play the v.** грати на скрипці.

violinist, *n.* скрипаль.

visit, *n.* відвідини, візит; *v.* 1) відвідувати + *A.*, **Oleksa ~s his doctor once a year.** Олекса відвідує лікаря раз на рік.; 2) *(places)* бувати у + *L.*, **We often v. this part of town.** Ми часто буваємо у цій частині міста.; *(people's homes)* бувати у + *G.*, **Next year Petro is going to v. his sister in Paris.** Наступного року Петро думає побувати у сестри в Парижі.

vocabulary, *n.* 1) словник, **Ihor keeps a v. of new words.** Ігор веде словник нових слів.; 2) вокабуляр, **This word is from the v. of theoretical mathematics.** Це слово із вокабуляру теоретичної математики.; 3) словниковий запас, **With such small v. of Italian Oksana can discuss almost any subject.** Із таким малим словниковим запасом з італійської Оксана може обговорювати будь-яку тему.

vodka, *n.* горілка, **straight v.** чиста горілка, **v. on the rocks** горілка з кригою, **v. with pepper** горілка з перцем.

vogue, *n.* мода, **in v.** у моді. *See* **fashion.**

voice, *n.* голос, **in a loud (soft) v.** голосно (тихо), **lose v.** втратити голос.; *v.* висловлювати + *A.*, **He did not get the chance to v. his opinion.** Він не мав нагоди висловити свою думку.

Volhynia, *n.*, *also* **Volyn** Волинь *(historical region in north-western Ukraine comprising modern provinces of Lutsk, Rivne and, in part, Zhytomyr and Ternopil)*, **in V.** на Волині, **He was born and grew up in V.** Він народився і виріс на Волині.; *dir.* **to V.** на Волинь.

W

wait, *v.*, 1) *tran.* чекати + *A.*, **Can you w. for me?** Ви можете почекати мене?; *or* на + *A.*, **Who are you ~ing for?** На кого ви чекаєте?, *or* + *G.* **The travelers are ~ing for warm and sunny weather.** Мандрівники чекають теплої і сонячної погоди.; *or* щоб + *pf. inf.*, **Stepan ~ed to tell what had happened.** Степан чекав щоб розказати, що сталося.; 2) *tran. (serve table)* обслуговувати + *A.*, **He ~ed three tables in the restaurant.** Він обслуговував три столи в ресторані.

waiter   **when**

waiter, *n.* офіціянт, *Gal.* кельнер, **to call a w.** покликати офіціянта; **to work as a w.** працювати офіціянтом.

waitress, *n.* офіціянтка, *Gal.* кельнерка.

wake, *v.* 1) *tran.* будити + *A.*, **The rain woke him.** Дощ розбудив його.; 2) *refl.* будитися, прокидатися, вставати, **When do you w. up?** Коли ти будишся (прокидаєшся, встаєш)?, **Time to w. up!** Час вставати!

walk, *n.* прогулянка, **to go for a w.** ходити на прогулянку; *v.* 1) *intr.* йти; 2) *intr.* гуляти, прогулюватися, **Every morning Natalia ~s in the park.** Щоранку Наталя гуляє парком.; 3) *tran. (accompany)* проводити + *A.*, **Roman ~ed Ivan to the station.** Роман провів Івана до станції.

wall, *n.* стіна, **brick (stone) w.** цегляна (кам'яна) стіна; *posn.* **on a w.** на стіні, *dir.* **on the w.** на стіну, **He hung the picture on the w.** Він повісив фото на стіну.

wallet, *n.* гаманець; **put the money into a w.** класти гроші до гаманця; **take the money out of the w.** виймати гроші з гаманця.

want, *v. tran.* 1) хотіти + *A.*, **I w. a pear.** Я хочу грушу.; *or (with substances)* + *G.*, **Do you w. coffee or tea?** Ви хочете кави чи чаю?; **What do they w.?** Чого вони хочуть?; *or + inf.*, **Vira always ~ed to learn Belarusian.** Віра завжди хотіла вивчити білоруську.; 2) *tran. (desire)* жадати, прагнути, **I w. him.** Я жадаю (прагну) його.; **for w. of ...**, через брак, через відсутність + *G.*, **They did it for w. of common sense.** Вони зробили це через брак здорового глузду.

wardrobe, *n.* 1) *(in theater)* роздягалка, гардероб; 2) *(piece of furniture)* шафа.

warm, *adj.* 1) теплий, **w. day** теплий день; 2) *(cordial)* сердечний; *v., tran.* **to w. up** гріти, зігрівати + *A.*

warn, *v.* попереджати + *A.*, **Our guide ~ed us that there could be snow in the mountains.** Наш провідник попередив нас, що в горах може бути сніг.

was, *v.*, ра., *m.* був, *f.* була, *nt.* було, **The day w. cold.** День був холодний.; **The room w. warm.** Кімната була тепла.; **The window was open.** Вікно було відкрите.

wash, *v.* 1) *tran.* мити + *A.*, **w. the dishes** мити посуд; 2) *tran. (clothes)* прати, **I need to w. my towel.** Мені треба випрати рушник.; 3) *intr. (oneself)* митися, **They quickly ~ed and dressed.** Вони швидко помилися й одягнулися.; *(face and hands)* умиватися.; 4) *intr.* змиватися, відпиратися, **The stain easily ~ed out.** Пляма легко змилася (відіпралася).; 5) *tran. (of sea)* омивати + *A.*, *only impf.*, **In the south, Ukraine is ~ed by the Black Sea.** На півдні Україну омиває Чорне море.

watch, *v.* 1) дивитися + *A.*, **to w. TV** дивитися телебачення, *or* на + *A.*, **They came out to w. the parade.** Вони вийшли подивитися (на) парад.; 2) *(observe)* спостерігати за + *I.*, **I like to w. people.** Мені подобається спостерігати за людьми.; 3) *(secretly follow)* стежити за + *I.*, **Somebody was ~ing him.** За ним хтось стежив.; ♦ **W. out!** Обережно!; **W. your language!** Прикуси язика!; *n.* годинник, **wrist w.** наручний годинник.

water, *n.* вода, **mineral (spring, soda) w.** мінеральна (джерельна, содова) вода; **fresh (sea) w.** прісна (морська) вода.; *v., tran.* поливати, підливати + *A.*, **He ~s his plants every week.** Він підливає вазони щотижня.

watermelon, *n.* кавун, **Kherson is famous for it ~s.** Херсон славиться своїми кавунами.

way, *n.* 1) *(road)* дорога, шлях, **This w. leads to the castle.** Ця дорога веде до замку.; ♦ **be in the w.** заважати, **You are in the w.** Ви заважаєте.; 2) *(direction)* напрям, напрямок, **Which w. is downtown?** У якому напрямку середмістя?; 3) *(method)* спосіб, **the easiest (quickest) w.** найлегший (найшвидший) спосіб, **to do it this w.** робити це у такий спосіб; 4) *(aspect)* відношення, смисл, **in every w.** у всіх відношеннях; ♦ **by the w.** до речі; ♦ **lose one's w.** губитися.

we, *pron.* ми, **W. will come to the exhibit.** Ми прийдемо на виставку.

weak, *adj.* 1) слабкий, **w. light** тьмяне світло, **w. tea** слабкий чай; 2) *(exhausted)* ослаблений, кволий, **He feels w. after the flu.** Він почувається ослабленим (кволим) після грипу.

wear, *v.* 1) *tran.* носити + *A.*, **He likes to w. jeans.** Він любить носити джинси.; 2) *intr.* носитися, **This suit ~s very well.** Цей костюм дуже добре носиться.

weather, *n.* погода, **w. forecast** прогноз погоди, **What's the w. like there?** Яка там погода?; **nasty w.** негода.

Wednesday, *n.* середа, **on W.** у середу, **till W.** до середи.

week, *n.* тиждень, **next w.** наступного тижня, **last w.** минулого тижня, **in a w.** за тиждень, **every w.** щотижня.; *adj.* **weekday** будній день.

weekend, *n.* вихідні, **for the w.** на вихідні, **every w.** у кожні вихідні; **What are you doing this (next) w.?** Що ти робиш у (на) ці (наступні) вихідні?

welcome, *v.* вітати, ♦ **W. to Kyiv!** Вітаємо до Києва! *or* ... у Києві!; ♦ **you are w.** дуже прошу!

well, *adv.* добре, **Maksym plays the violin w.** Максим добре грає на скрипці.; **as w.** також; ♦ **to get w.** одужати, **Get w. soon!** Бажаю (тобі / вам) швидко одужати!; *adj.* 1) добрий, **all is w.** все добре; ♦ **All's w. that ends w.** Добре те, що добре закінчується.; 2) *(healthy)* здоровий, **He is quite w.** Він цілком здоровий.

well-known, *adj.* відомий, знаний, **w. writer** знаний письменник, **w. artist** відомий художник.

were, *v.*, ра, *pl.* були, **Where w. you?** Де ви були?; ♦ **if I w. you, I'd ...** на твоєму (вашому) місці, я б + ра., **If I w. you I'd visit Kyiv first.** На вашому місці я спочатку побував би у Києві.

west, *n.* захід, **in the w.** на заході, **to the w. of** на захід від + *G.*; *adj.* західний, **w. part of city** західна частина міста; *adv.* на захід, у західному напрямку, **He drove w.** Він поїхав на захід.

western, *adj.* західний, **w. Ukraine** західна Україна.

wet, *adj.* 1) мокрий, **w. floor** мокра підлога; 2) *(of paint)* свіжий, ♦ **w. paint!** свіжа фарба!

what, *pron.* 1) *(when stands for noun)* що, **w. is it?** що це (таке)?; 2) *(when stands for adjective)* який, *colloq. (for all genders)* що за, **W. a great idea!** Яка (що за) чудова ідея!, **W. kind of film is it?** Що це за фільм?; *conj.* те, що, **I brought you w. I promised.** Я приніс тобі те, що обіцяв.; ♦ **w. about ..?** як стосовно ..? *or* а як же ..? **W. about your promise to help?** А як же ваша обіцянка допомогти?

when, *pron.* 1) коли, **W. is her birthday?** Коли в неї уродини?; 2) *(after)* коли, *colloq.* як, **I will tell you w. I finish working.** Я скажу вам, як закінчу працювати.

where, *pron.* 1) *posn.* де, **W. do you live?** Де ти живе́ш?; 2) там, де, **He hung the picture w. everyone could see it.** Він повісив картину там, де всі могли її ба́чити.; 3) *dir. (where to)* куди; *Gal.* де, **W. are you going?** Куди ти йдеш? **w. from** зві́дки, **W. do you come from?** Зві́дки ти?

whether, *pron.* чи, **He is asking w. you can talk.** Він пита́є, чи ви мо́жете говори́ти.

which, *pron.* яки́й, котри́й, **W. one of them is Petro?** Котри́й із них Петро́?

while, *conj.* 1) в той час як, по́ки, **She slept w. he was reading.** Вона́ спала́ в той час, як він чита́в *or* ... по́ки він чита́в.; *n.* трохи, яки́йсь час, хвиля, хвили́на. **They talked for a w.,** Вони́ трохи поговори́ли.

white, *adj.* бі́лий, **w. snow** бі́лий сніг, **w. wine** бі́ле вино́.; *n.* *(in egg or eye)* біло́к.

who, *inter. pron.* хто, **W. is he?** Хто він (таки́й)?; ♦ **w. is w.** хто є хто.; *relative pron.* яки́й (яка́, яке́, які́), що, **the actor w. plays Hamlet** ... актор, яки́й (що) гра́є Га́млета ...; **the person w. called you ...** люди́на, яка́ (що) дзвони́ла вам ...; **the Americans w. came to the reception ...** америка́нці, які́ (що) прийшли́ на прийняття́ ...

whole, *adj.* уве́сь, *var.,* весь, ці́лий, **the w. world** уве́сь світ, **the w. truth** уся́ пра́вда.

whose, *pron., m.* 1) чий, *f.* чия́, *nt.* чиє́, *pl.* чиї́, **W. passport is it?** Чий це па́спорт?; 2) яки́й + *clause*, etc., **She is the woman w. daughter is an architect.** Це жі́нка, дочка́ яко́ї - архіте́ктор.

why, *pron.* 1) чому́, **W. do you ask?** Чому́ ви пита́єте?; 2) *(what for)* наві́що, *colloq.* на́що, **W. did she do it?** Наві́що вона́ зроби́ла це?; **that is w.** ось чому́.

wide, *adj.* 1) широ́кий, **w. street** широ́ка ву́лиця; 2) *(in measuring)* завши́ршки, **sidewalk a meter w.** хідни́к ме́тер завши́ршки; *adv.* широ́ко, **eyes opened w.** широ́ко відкри́ті о́чі.

wife, *n.* жі́нка, *form.* дружи́на, ♦ **old wives' tales** побрехе́ньки.

Wi-Fi, *adj.* бездро́товий інтерне́т, бездро́това мере́жа; **W.-F. connection** бездро́товий зв'язо́к.

wind, *n.* ві́тер, **high w.** си́льний ві́тер, **gust of w.** пори́в ві́тру, **Which way is the w. blowing?** Куди́ дме ві́тер?

window, *n.* 1) вікно́, **He looked in the w.** Він диви́вся у вікно́.; 2) *(in a store)* вітри́на.

wine, *n.* вино́, **dry (dessert, red) w.** сухе́ (десе́ртне, черво́не) вино́, **w. list** ви́нне меню́.

winter, *n.* зима́; **in w.** узи́мку; *adj.* зимо́вий, **w. clothes** зимо́вий одяг.

wish, *n.* 1) *(desire)* бажа́ння; 2) *(holiday)* побажа́ння, **holiday ~es** побажа́ння на свято́; *v.* бажа́ти + *D.*, **I w. you happiness, health, and success.** Бажа́ю вам щастя, здоро́в'я й успі́хів., **He ~ed her a Happy Birthday.** Він побажа́в їй «Многая лі́та».

with, *prep.* 1) з, *var.* із, зі + *I.*, **together w.** ра́зом із + *I.*, **He came w. friends.** Він прийшо́в із дру́зями; 2) *(signifying tool or instrument)* *n.* in *I.*, *and no preposition*, **I paid w. a check.** Я заплати́в че́ком.; 3) *(relation)* на + *A.*, **He is angry w. his brother.** Він серди́тий на свого́ бра́та.; 4) *(cause)* від + *G.*, **a voice trembling w. fear** го́лос, що тремти́ть від страху́.

without, *prep.* 1) без + *G.*, **w. a doubt** без су́мніву; 2) *(parallel action)* і не, **They sat together w. speaking.** Вони́ сиді́ли ра́зом і не розмовля́ли.

woman, *n.* жі́нка, **old (young) w.** стара́ (молода́) жі́нка, **Olena is an independent w.** Оле́на - незале́жна жі́нка.

women's, *adj.* жіно́чий, **w. department** жіно́чий ві́дділ.

wonder, *v.* ціка́витися, **I w. what this means.** (Мені́) Ціка́во, що це значить.; *n.* диво, дивина́, чу́до; **seven ~s of the world** сім див сві́ту; ♦ **no w. ...** не дивно, що ...

wonderful, *adj.* чудо́вий, дивови́жний, **We had a w. time by the sea.** Ми чудо́во провели́ час на мо́рі.

wood, *n.* 1) *(material)* де́рево, **table made of w.** стіл, зро́блений з де́рева; ♦ **knock on w.** стука́ти по де́реву; 2) *(forest)* ліс, **in the w.** у лі́сі.

word, *n.* сло́во; ~ **w. of honor** сло́во че́сти, **to give (keep) one's w.** дава́ти (стри́мувати) сло́во; ♦ **in a w.** сло́вом; **in other ~s** іна́кше ка́жучи; **in w. and deed** сло́вом і ді́лом; **man (woman) of his (her) w.** люди́на сло́ва; **to put sth into ~s** висло́влювати + *A.*; **w. for w.** сло́во в сло́во.

work, *v., intr.* 1) працюва́ти, **to w. as** працюва́ти + *I.*, **He ~s as a physician.** Він працю́є лі́карем.; **to w. full (part) time** працюва́ти на (не)по́вну ста́вку; **to w. hard** бага́то працюва́ти; **w. on sth** працюва́ти над + *I.*, **Maryna is ~ing on her presentation.** Мари́на працю́є над свое́ю презента́цією.; 2) *intr. (of equipment)* працюва́ти, ді́яти, **My computer does not w.** Мій комп'ю́тер не працю́є (ді́є).; 3) *tran. (operate)* користува́тися + *I.*, **Do you know how to w. a projector?** Чи ви зна́єте, як користува́тися проє́ктором?; *n.* 1) пра́ця, робо́та, **at w.** на пра́ці, на робо́ті, **hard w.** тяжка́ пра́ця, **He is looking for w.** Він шука́є пра́цю.; **out of w.** безробі́тний; 2) твір, ви́твір, **literary w.** літерату́рний твір, **w. of fiction** ви́твір фанта́зії.

worker, *n.* 1) *(member of working class)* *m.* робі́тник, *f.* робі́тниця; 2) *(sb who works)* праці́вник, праці́вниця; **He is a hard w.** Він бага́то працю́є.

working, *adj.* робо́чий, **w. day** робо́чий день.

world, *n.* світ, **all over the w.** у всьо́му сві́ті.; *adj.* 1) світови́й, **w. war** світова́ війна́, **w. championship** чемпіона́т сві́ту; 2) всесві́тній, **w. revolution** всесві́тня револю́ція.

worry, *v., intr.* жури́тися, *Gal.* прийма́тися + *I.*, **There's nothing to w. about.** Нема́ чого́ жури́тися.; **Don't w.!** *sg.* Не журися!, *pl.* Не журі́ться!; **I don't want to w. about the future.** Я не хочу́ жури́тися (прийма́тися) майбу́тнім.

worse, *adj.* гі́рший, **even w.** ще гі́рший.; *adv.* гі́рше, **She swims w. than I.** Вона́ пла́ває гі́рше, як я.; **He feels w.** Він почува́ється гі́рше.; ♦ **so much the w. for ...** тим гі́рше для + *G.*

worst, *adj.* найгі́рший, **This is the w. car he's ever had.** Це найгі́рше авто, яке́ він коли́-не́будь мав.; ♦ **if worse comes to w.** у найгі́ршому ви́падку.; *adv.* найгі́рше, **This is w. of all.** Це найгі́рше за все.

write, *v.* 1) *tran.* писа́ти + *A.*, **w. a letter** писа́ти лист(а́); **w. in** *(a language)* писа́ти + *I.*, **I can speak but not write in French.** Я мо́жу говори́ти, але́ не писа́ти францу́зькою.; 2) *tran. (a check)* випи́сувати, **Maria wrote a check for a hundred hryvnias.** Марі́я ви́писала чек на сто гри́вень.; **w. down** запи́сувати, **Vira wrote down everything they said.** Ві́ра записа́ла все, що вони́ сказа́ли; **w. off** спи́сувати, скасо́вувати, **The bank wrote off his debt.** Банк списа́в його́ борг.

writer, *n.* письме́нник, *f.* письме́нниця, **Mykola Hohol is a Ukrainian w. who wrote in Russian.** Мико́ла Го́голь - украї́нський письме́нник, яки́й писа́в росі́йською.

wrong, *adj.* 1) непра́вильний, **w. answer** непра́вильна ві́дповідь, **w. number** непра́вильний но́мер; **Something was w.** Щось було́ не так., **What's w.?** В чо́му спра́ва? 2) не той, **He is the w. man.** Він не та люди́на.; *n.* кри́вда, **do sb w.** роби́ти кри́вду + *D.*, кри́вдити, **They did us a great w.** Вони́ зроби́ли нам вели́ку кри́вду.

X

Xerox, *n.* ксе́рокс, **to make a x. copy** роби́ти ксерокопі́ю.

Y

year, *n.* рік, **calendar y.** календа́рний рік, **in two ~s** через два ро́ки, **last y.** то́рік, мину́лого ро́ку, **leap y.** висо́косний рік, **next y.** насту́пного ро́ку, **this y.** цьо́го ро́ку *or* у цьо́му ро́ці; **Happy New Y.!** Щасли́вого Ново́го Ро́ку!

yellow, *adj.* жо́втий, **y. sunflower** жо́втий со́няшник; *fig.* **y. press** жо́вта пре́са.

yes, *adv.* *(affirmative)* так; *colloq.* ага́, еге́, еге́ ж.

yesterday, *adv.* учо́ра, *var.* вчо́ра; **Marko was not at work y.** Ма́рко не був на пра́ці вчо́ра.; **the day before y.** позавчо́ра.; **y. morning (afternoon, evening)** вчо́ра вра́нці (пополу́дні, вве́чері); *adj.* вчора́шній, **This is y.'s news.** Це вчора́шні нови́ни.

yet, *adv.* 1) *(in questions)* вже, *var.* уже́, **Has he come y.?** Він вже прийшо́в?; 2) *(with neg.)* ще, **He has not finished y.** Він ще не закі́нчив.; 3) *(still)* все ж, **He knew Tamara, yet he hoped to convince her.** Він знав Тама́ру, все ж він сподіва́вся переконати її́.

yogurt, *n.* йо́ґурт.

you, *pers. pron.*, 1) *fam. sg.* ти, **Pavlo, do y. know when the guests will come?** Па́вле, ти зна́єш, коли́ приї́дуть го́сті?; 2) *form. and pl.* ви, **Mr. Petrenko, can y. call later?** Па́не Петре́нко, ви мо́жете подзвони́ти пізні́ше?

young, *adj.* молоди́й, **y. generation** молоде́ поколі́ння, **y. man** молоди́й чолові́к, **y. woman** молода́ жі́нка; **the y.** мо́лодь.

younger, *adj.* моло́дший, **y. brother** моло́дший брат.

your, *poss. pron.* 1) *sg., m.* твій, *f.* твоя́, *nt.* твоє́, *pl.* твої́, **Is this y. car, Vasyl?** Це твоє́ а́вто, Васи́лю?; 2) *pl., m.* ваш, *f.* ва́ша, *nt.* ва́ше, *pl.* ва́ші, **How are y. parents, Mrs. Shevchenko?** Як ва́ші батьки́, па́ні Шевче́нко?

yourself, *refl. pron.* 1) себе́, **In your dreams, you see y. rich.** У своїх мрі́ях ти ба́чиш (*pl.* ви ба́чите) себе́ багати́м(и).; **look at y.** подиви́ся на се́бе.; 2) *(for emphasis) sg., m.* сам, *f.* сама́, *nt.* саме́, *pl.* самі́, **Did you do it y.?** Ти зроби́в (*f.* зроби́ла, *nt.* зроби́ло) це сам (*f.* сама́, *nt.* саме́)?; *pl.* Ви зроби́ли це самі́?; **You y. would like to know it.** Ви самі́ хоті́ли б зна́ти це.; 3) *(alone)* самі́, **You can do it y.** Ви мо́жете зроби́ти це самі́.; 4) *(for yourself)* собі́, **You baked y. a cake.** Ви спекли́ собі́ торт(а).

youth, *n.* 1) *(young people)* мо́лодь; 2) *(young age)* мо́лодість, **in one's y.** у мо́лодості.

Z

zero, *n.* нуль, **above z.** ви́ще нуля́, **below z.** ни́жче нуля́, **to z.** до нуля́, **The temperature dropped to z.** Температу́ра впа́ла до нуля́.; *adj.* нульови́й, **z. temperature** нульова́ температу́ра.

zoo, *n.* зоопа́рк, **in a z.** у зоопа́рку, **to a z.** до зоопа́рку, **walk around a z.** гуля́ти зоопа́рком.

MORE UKRAINIAN TITLES FROM HIPPOCRENE BOOKS

LANGUAGE GUIDES

LANGUAGE & TRAVEL GUIDE TO UKRAINE, *5th Edition*
Linda Hodges and George Chumak
This one-of-a-kind guide not only provides visitors to Ukraine with all the information needed to navigate this age-old civilization, but also gives them the ability to explore Ukraine's most important resource: its people. With an in-depth introduction to the Ukrainian language that covers everything from ordering vodka to proposing marriage, this fifth edition provides up-to-date information on what to see and do in all parts of Ukraine. Features include a 16-page color photo insert, numerous English maps, and links to a companion website filled with updates and other information.

ISBN 978-0-7818-1201-6 • $24.95 pb

UKRAINIAN-ENGLISH/ENGLISH-UKRAINIAN PRACTICAL DICTIONARY
REVISED EDITION WITH MENU TERMS
ISBN 0-7818-0306-3 • $19.95 pb

UKRAINIAN-ENGLISH/ENGLISH-UKRAINIAN PHRASEBOOK & DICTIONARY
ISBN 0-7818-0188-5 • $12.95 pb

COOKBOOKS

THE NEW UKRAINIAN COOKBOOK
Annette Ogrodnik Corona

The New Ukrainian Cookbook introduces readers to the fresh foods, exquisite tastes, hospitality and generous spirit of the Ukrainian table. Scattered amongst the recipes are quotes, poems, historical facts, folklore, and illustrations, making this cookbook not only a culinary adventure but a unique cultural exploration as well.

Included are more than 200 easy-to-follow recipes; an introduction to Ukraine's history, culture, and cuisine; helpful tips and notes with many recipes; and charming illustrations by renowned Ukrainian-American artist Laurette Kovary.

ISBN 978-0-7818-1287-0 · $29.95 hc

ALSO AVAILABLE FROM HIPPOCRENE

LANGUAGE GUIDES

Byelorussian-English/English-Byelorussian Concise Dictionary
ISBN 0-87052-114-4 • $9.95 pb

Chechen-English/English-Chechen Dictionary & Phrasebook
ISBN 0-7818-0446-9 • $11.95 pb

Croatian-English/English Croatian Dictionary & Phrasebook
ISBN 0-7818-0810-3 • $11.95 pb

Beginner's Croatian with 2 Audio CDs
ISBN 978-0-7818-1232-0 • $32.00 pb

Czech-English/English-Czech Concise Dictionary
ISBN 0-87052-981-1 • $14.95 pb

Czech-English/English-Czech Dictionary & Phrasebook
ISBN 0-7818-0942-8 • $13.95 pb

Beginner's Czech with 2 Audio CDs
ISBN 0-7818-1156-2 • $26.95 pb

Estonian-English/English-Estonian Concise Dictionary
ISBN 0-87052-081-4 • $11.95 pb

Estonian-English/English-Estonian Dictionary & Phrasebook
ISBN 0-7818-0931-2 • $11.95 pb

Beginner's Georgian with 2 Audio CDs
ISBN 978-0-7818-1230-6 • $29.95 pb

Beginner's Hungarian with 2 Audio CDs
ISBN 978-0-7818-1192-7 • $26.95 pb

Hungarian-English/English-Hungarian Dictionary & Phrasebook
ISBN 0-7818-0919-3 · $14.95 pb

Hungarian-English/English-Hungarian Practical Dictionary
ISBN 0-7818-1068-X • $27.95 pb

Latvian-English/English-Latvian Dictionary & Phrasebook
3,000 entries · 0-7818-1008-6 · $14.95 pb

Lithuanian-English/English-Lithuanian Concise Dictionary
ISBN 0-7818-0151-6 • $14.95 pb

Lithuanian-English/English-Lithuanian Dictionary & Phrasebook
ISBN 0-7818-1009-4 • $14.95 pb

Polish-English/English-Polish Practical Dictionary
ISBN 0-7818-0085-4 • $19.95 pb

Beginner's Polish (*book only*)
ISBN 0-7818-0299-7 • $9.95 pb

Mastering Polish with 2 Audio CDs
ISBN 0-7818-1065-5 • $29.95 pb

Romanian-English/English-Romanian Practical Dictionary
ISBN 978-0-7818-1224-5 • $24.95 pb

Russian-English/English-Russian Concise Dictionary
ISBN 0-7818-0132-X • $12.95 pb

Russian-English/English-Russian Dictionary & Phrasebook
ISBN 0-7818-1003-5• $14.95 pb

Russian-English/English-Russian Pocket Legal Dictionary
ISBN 978-0-7818-1222-1 • $19.95 pb

Beginner's Serbian with 2 Audio CDs
ISBN 978-0-7818-1231-3 • $29.95 pb

Serbian-English/English-Serbian Dictionary & Phrasebook, *Romanized*
ISBN 0-7818-1049-3 • $13.95 pb

Slovak-English/English-Slovak Concise Dictionary
ISBN 0-87052-115-2 • $14.95 pb

Slovak-English/English-Slovak Dictionary & Phrasebook
ISBN 0-7818-0663-1 • $13.95 pb

Slovene-English/English-Slovene Dictionary & Phrasebook
ISBN 0-7818-1047-7 · $14.95 pb

Slovene-English/English-Slovene Modern Dictionary
ISBN 0-7818-0252-0 • $24.95 pb

COOKBOOKS

THE ART OF LITHUANIAN COOKING
Maria Gieysztor de Gorgey

Here is a wonderful collection of classic Lithuanian recipes that will be welcome on any table! The author provides easy, step-by-step instructions for creating authentic and delicious Lithuanian fare. With over 150 recipes, this cookbook includes traditional hearty favorites like Fresh Cucumber Soup, Lithuanian Meat Pockets, Hunter's Stew, and Potato Zeppelins, as well as delicacies like Homemade Honey Liqueur and Easter Gypsy Cake. Among the chapters included are Appetizers, Aspics, Soups, Meat Dishes, Fowl, Fish, Vegetables, Noodle Dishes, Beverages, and Desserts.

ISBN 978-0-7818-0899-6 • $12.95 pb

THE BEST OF RUSSIAN COOKING
Alexandra Kropotkin

Originally published in 1947, *The Best of Russian Cooking* is a treasured classic that combines authentic Russian recipes with culinary tips and invaluable cultural insights. This expanded edition features a concise list of menu terms, sections on Russian table traditions and mealtimes, and a guide to special cooking utensils. A survey of the tastiest Russian cuisine, this book includes 300 recipes for popular dishes such as *beef stroganoff* and *borscht,* as well as many lesser-known dishes which are daily fare in Russia—*kotleti* (meatballs), *piroshki* (dumplings with meat or vegetables) and *tvorojniki* (cottage cheese cakes).

ISBN 978-0-7818-0131-7 • $16.95 pb

Prices subject to change without prior notice. **To purchase Hippocrene Books** contact your local bookstore, visit www.hippocrenebooks.com, call (212) 685-4373, or write to: HIPPOCRENE BOOKS, 171 Madison Avenue, New York, NY 10016.